High-Speed Internet Connection Types and Typical Costs

Type	Download Speeds	Upload Speeds	Setup Cost	Monthly Cost
Cable	4 Mbps to 15 Mbps	384 Kbps to 1.5 Mbps	$0 to $100	$40 to $80
DSL	768 Kbps to 6 Mbps	128 Kbps to 768 Kbps	$0 to $100	$15 to $45
Wireless ISP (WISP)	Varies	Varies	$0 to $300	$40 to $60
Satellite	512 Kbps to 1.5 Mbps	128 Kbps to 256 Kbps	$300 to $800	$50 to $120
Mobile (Cellular) Broadband	400 Kbps to 1.4 Mbps	Up to 800 Kbps	$0 to $200	$20 to $60

Hardware Requirements for Home Networks

Need	Purpose
Modem	To connect you to your high-speed Internet service
Wired or wireless router	To regulate the data traffic and hook your computers together; for a traditional wired or wireless network
Wired or wireless Network adapters	Gives your computer an Ethernet port (for a wired connection) or an antenna/radio (for wireless connectivity)
Ethernet cabling	To connect your computers directly to your wired or wireless router, if you prefer

Wireless Networking Standards

	802.11a	802.11b	802.11g	802.11n
Frequency	5 GHz	2.4 GHz	2.4 GHz	2.4 GHz
Speed (Data Rate)	54 Mbps	11 Mbps	54 Mbps	248 Mbps
Range	115 feet	125 feet	125 feet	230 feet
Cost	High	Low	Moderate	High
Compatibility	None	802.11g/n	802.11b/n	802.11b/g

For Dummies: Bestselling Book Series for Beginners

Home Networking All-in-One Desk Reference For Dummies®

Cheat Sheet

Networking Lingo at a Glance

Wi-Fi: The term or buzzword coined by the Wi-Fi Alliance to help identify wireless networking products in order to promote them to you (the consumer).

LAN (Local Area Network): Multiple computers connected together in the same general area.

WLAN (Wireless LAN): Multiple computers connected together wirelessly in the same general area.

ISP (Internet Service Provider): A company that offers Internet access.

802.11: The "code name" given for the wireless networking standards developed by the Institute of Electrical and Electronics Engineers (IEEE). These standards specify how the wireless devices should operate and are intended to help manufacturers develop products that will work with products from other manufacturers. In this book, I refer to the standards usually as wireless A or wireless G rather than use the formal names 802.11a and 802.11g.

RJ-45: The technical name for the connectors at the end of Ethernet cables. They look similar to telephone connectors but are slightly wider.

CAT5/6 (Category 5/6) cable: The technical name for a certain type of Ethernet cable used in networks to connect computers to the network (router), to connect computers directly together, and for other purposes. You may see CAT5, CAT5e, and CAT6 cabling. Each type looks the same but offers slight performance enhancements.

IP address: The address used on the Internet and networks to identify servers and computers.

Mbps (Megabits per second): The measurement of the speed at which data can travel; in this case, one million bits per second.

NIC (Network Interface Card): The piece of equipment that installs in your computer to give you the ability to connect to a network, either by wire or wirelessly.

For Dummies: Bestselling Book Series for Beginners

Home Networking
ALL-IN-ONE DESK REFERENCE
FOR
DUMMIES®

by Eric Geier

WILEY

Wiley Publishing, Inc.

Home Networking All-in-One Desk Reference For Dummies®

Published by
Wiley Publishing, Inc.
111 River Street
Hoboken, NJ 07030-5774
www.wiley.com

Copyright © 2008 by Wiley Publishing, Inc., Indianapolis, Indiana

Published by Wiley Publishing, Inc., Indianapolis, Indiana

Published simultaneously in Canada

For general information on our other products and services, please contact our Customer Care Department within the U.S. at 800-762-2974, outside the U.S. at 317-572-3993, or fax 317-572-4002.

For technical support, please visit www.wiley.com/techsupport.

Wiley also publishes its books in a variety of electronic formats. Some content that appears in print may not be available in electronic books.

Library of Congress Control Number: 2008930525

ISBN: 978-0-470-27519-1

Manufactured in the United States of America

10 9 8 7 6 5 4 3 2 1

WILEY

About the Author

Through spending countless days and nights in front of the computer since he could type and working in the Information Technology (IT) field, **Eric Geier** has gained expertise in computers and networking. To help others understand this digital world better (and save numerous computers and networking gear from being thrown out the window), he writes books that go on the shelves and articles that are published on the Web.

In the IT field, Eric's done a little bit of everything, from fixing and upgrading computers, building Web applications, and administrating small networks to performing radio frequency (RF) site surveys and testing large-scale municipal (city-wide) Wi-Fi networks. In his work, he's achieved the Certified Wireless Network Administrator (CWNA) and Tropos Certified Associate (TCA) certifications.

For more information about Eric Geier and his writings, visit his Web site at www.egeier.com.

Dedication

To my beautiful wife, Sierra, and my daughter, Madison.

Author's Acknowledgments

First, I would like to thank my family for their cooperation when I went into hiding day and night to try to meet deadlines. This is my biggest book yet. It was a challenge.

I would also like to thank everyone who has worked on this book. It takes many more people than just the writer to make a book.

Special thanks to my mom, Aylsie Geier, for letting me borrow her Mac Mini (it's really mini) during the writing so that I could include Mac OS X coverage in the book.

Publisher's Acknowledgments

We're proud of this book; please send us your comments through our online registration form located at www.dummies.com/register/.

Some of the people who helped bring this book to market include the following:

Acquisitions, Editorial, and Media Development

Project Editor: Susan Christophersen

Acquisitions Editor: Amy Fandrei

Copy Editor: Susan Christophersen, Linda Morris

Technical Editor: Dan DiNicolo

Editorial Manager: Jodi Jensen

Editorial Assistant: Amanda Foxworth

Sr. Editorial Assistant: Cherie Case

Cartoons: Rich Tennant (www.the5thwave.com)

Composition Services

Project Coordinator: Patrick Redmond

Layout and Graphics: Claudia Bell, Ronald Terry, Christine Williams

Proofreaders: John Greenough, Jessica Kramer, Penny L. Stuart,

Indexer: Becky Hornyak

Publishing and Editorial for Technology Dummies

    Richard Swadley, Vice President and Executive Group Publisher

    Andy Cummings, Vice President and Publisher

    Mary Bednarek, Executive Acquisitions Director

    Mary C. Corder, Editorial Director

Publishing for Consumer Dummies

    Diane Graves Steele, Vice President and Publisher

    Joyce Pepple, Acquisitions Director

Composition Services

    Gerry Fahey, Vice President of Production Services

    Debbie Stailey, Director of Composition Services

Contents at a Glance

Table of Contents

Introduction

Welcome to *Home Networking All-in-One Desk Reference For Dummies*!

Although the use of home networking has exploded in the past several years, networks have been used in business for more than 20 years. Many things have fueled the growth of networks in homes. Lower prices for computers and networking gear, growth in the number of computers in homes, and the rise of high-speed Internet have all played major roles. Standardized networking technologies have made a huge difference as well.

Whether you have a family with several computers in the home or you're a single person with just one desktop and a notebook computer, having a home network is beneficial for you if you have more than one computer under the roof. It's beneficial even if your chief reason to have a network is to distribute your high-speed Internet connection among your multiple computers. But as you'll soon discover, connecting your computers together offers much more than a shared Internet connection. Sharing files between computers, sending pages to a printer from all your computers, and enhanced entertainment are just a few more of the rewards of home networking.

You also have a variety of ways to connect your computers together. Although going wireless in many homes makes sense to support laptops, hand-held game consoles, and Personal Digital Assistants (PDAs) with Wi-Fi capability, running cables to your computers to create a wired network still offers some advantages. Or you can consider plugging into and using your home's electrical or phone lines to connect your digital toys together. This book gives you the know-how to take whatever approach suits you best.

About This Book

This book gives you the tools to understand, purchase, set up, and use a home network. Even if you are a self-proclaimed computer illiterate and have barely a clue about what a network is, this book will take all the mystery out of it for you. As long as you can turn a computer on and know how to click around the screen, you'll be a whiz at networking in no time. On the other hand, if you're computer literate and are even your family's or friends' "computer geek," you'll find plenty of tips and strategies in this book that you can apply to networks made up of computers of all persuasions — various versions of Windows and Mac, and even Ubuntu.

This book isn't strictly a networking guide; it includes other relevant topics as well, such as adding user accounts to your computers, protecting yourself against infections and hackers on the Internet, and keeping children safe from Internet dangers. This book also covers using Wi-Fi hotspots, the public networks offering wireless Internet access in airports, hotels, restaurants, and other public areas. As a bonus, this book even helps you set up your very own Wi-Fi hotspot, which can be useful if you or someone you know owns a small business.

Here are the main topics I cover in this book:

+ Discovering what a network can do for you and understanding how to make it work

+ Choosing a network type that works best for your needs and planning what equipment you'll need

+ Installing and configuring your computers and networking gear

+ Upgrading your networking gear with the manufacturers' updates

+ Using particular versions of operating systems — Windows, Mac, and Linux — with your network

+ Connecting to networks, sharing files and printers, checking connection status, and much more

+ Discovering networking accessories to get the most out of your network

+ Finding and using Wi-Fi hotspots, plus setting up your own

How This Book Is Organized

This book, as an *All-in-One Desk Reference For Dummies,* is divided into "minibooks" instead of the usual parts. Each minibook contains its own set of chapters, with their own numbering. For example, Book I starts with Chapter 1 and ends in Chapter 3; Book II starts with Chapter 1, and so on.

The minibooks are organized by topic and progress in a sequential fashion, starting with a basic understanding of networking and progressing on to planning, setting up, and using your network. However, you can feel free to skip around to suit your needs.

Book 1: Intro to Networking

+ This minibook introduces you to home networking, providing you with an overview of what's involved before you jump into buying equipment and setting up your network:

+ **Chapter 1: Grasping the Main Concepts behind Networking:** In this chapter, you discover the types of home networks, and their advantages and requirements. I help you figure out whether your computers are already network ready (they might be) and what to do if they're not. I introduce you to the wireless networking technologies, or standards (A, B, G, and N).

✦ **Chapter 2: Operating Systems and Networks:** Here you see how the operating system you use — Windows, Mac, or a flavor of Linux known as Ubuntu — affects your networking experience, and you'll become acquainted with the networking interfaces of each of these operating systems.

✦ **Chapter 3: Networking Hardware:** And finally, this chapter tells you about the common home networking gear, including what each piece of equipment does and its contribution to the network, along with a tour of what's on the outside (ports, plugs, and buttons).

Book II: Setting Up Networks

✦ This minibook includes all the information you need to install and configure your network:

✦ **Chapter 1: Setting Up User Accounts on Computers:** Here you can follow the steps to create separate computer accounts for each person in the home who uses the computers. You'll benefit from this later when you're setting up shared folders and any parental controls you might want to enact if you have children in the household.

✦ **Chapter 2: Planning for Your Network:** This chapter is where your real work begins as you find out about picking a high-speed Internet connection and creating a shopping list for your network. I provide sample network plans for each network type to help you understand what you need and how you can customize your network to your situation.

✦ **Chapter 3: Installing Network Adapters:** This chapter walks you through the first half of your network installation, connecting the network adapters to your computers (or installing them inside) so that each computer can connect to your home network.

✦ **Chapter 4: Setting Up and Configuring the Network:** In this chapter, I show you how to find a good spot to install the equipment and figure out both the physical installation and configuration of the equipment. I give you tips on running and connecting cables and describe how to set the Workgroup and Computer Names for all your computers.

✦ **Chapter 5: Working with the Brains of Your Equipment:** Use this chapter to find out about what makes your networking gear tick — drivers and firmware. You can check to see whether your gear has updates, and upload or replace them so that you have the latest features and technologies. You can also safeguard your configuration settings by backing them up. You can even get techy by loading your wireless router with aftermarket or replacement firmware. Finally, you can update your operating system to patch up any known security holes.

✦ **Chapter 6: Taking the Wire Farther:** This chapter helps you extend your wired network, by using your home's electrical outlets instead of Ethernet cabling, adding wireless access, or using wireless to connect cables instead of Ethernet cabling.

✦ **Chapter 7: Getting a Better Reach with Wireless:** This chapter shows you how to extend or increase your wireless router's coverage. From simply changing out your antennas to adding more wireless access points, you can find a way to get better coverage and performance from your Wi-Fi network.

Book III: Network Security

This minibook discusses how to keep your computers free of infections and hacking while using your network on the Internet, securing your wireless network so that people can't connect and access your files, and protecting children from the dangers of the World Wide Web:

✦ **Chapter 1: Addressing Internet Security:** In this chapter, you discover how a firewall can stop hackers and how to set up your firewall software. I show you how to outfit your computers for the battle against Internet viruses and infections and how you can fight back against spam, phishing, and junk e-mails. Plus you can discover what to do about those annoying Internet pop-ups.

✦ **Chapter 2: Securing the Airwaves: It's Possible:** This chapter shows you what someone with the right tools can see from your wireless network when you leave it unencrypted. Then you can follow the steps to make sure your Wi-Fi is secure.

✦ **Chapter 3: Protecting Youngsters:** If you have kids, you need to be aware of the dangers your children can face when they're on the Internet. This chapter tells you what to look for in parental control and Internet filtering software, in addition to guiding you through the simple actions you can take to keep kids safe.

Book IV: Connecting and Sharing

This minibook gets you going on some the best and most rewarding aspects of home networking:

✦ **Chapter 1: Dealing with Your Network Connections:** Starting with the basics, this chapter shows you how to turn your network adapters on and off. I step you through connecting to your wireless network and managing your wireless connections. This chapter also shows you exactly where to look for the status information of your network connections and how to set your network adapter's address.

✦ **Chapter 2: Remote Connections:** Here you can discover how to configure your computer for remote connections so that you can log in from the Internet to use your computer. You also find out how to set up your own Virtual Private Network (VPN) connections so that you can securely access your network and files from the Internet. To make sure that these features will work, I step you through configuring your network and firewall for these types of remote connections. Last, you see how you can log into your router's Web-based configuration utility while you're away from home.

✦ **Chapter 3: Allowing Sharing of Files and More:** This chapter covers enabling overall sharing for your operating system, whether it's Windows, Mac, or Linux Ubuntu, and how to configure your firewall software so that it will let you share. The sharing covered here applies to both file and printer sharing.

✦ **Chapter 4: Sharing Files: Hosting a Folder Party:** After overall sharing is enabled for your operating system, you can use this chapter to find out how to make folders (and their subfolders and files) on your computers available to everyone connected to the network. Additionally, this chapter helps you find out what folders are currently shared.

✦ **Chapter 5: Sharing a Printer: Spreading the Ink:** Again, when you have overall sharing enabled for your operating system, you can add printers to the network, whether they're attached to a computer or directly hooked to the network by a print server, and this chapter shows you how. Then, when you have a printer set up to be shared on the network, you can make it available to other computers on your network as well.

✦ **Chapter 6: Other Sharing Options:** This chapter covers other ways you can share your files on your network, including sharing your entire hard drive and purchasing and using a network storage drive or server. Plus you can manipulate how you access your shared resources. For example, you can map shared folders or drives for quick and easy access, creating hidden shares that people can't easily access, and setting up access to shared folders when you're disconnected from your network.

✦ **Chapter 7: Accessing Shared Files and Folders:** This chapter shows you how you can access folders you've set up to be shared on your network. I also discuss how you can manually access shares in case they don't appear in the network browser.

✦ **Chapter 8: Serving Files over the Internet:** Here you can see how to set up your very own Web server for a Web site, and how you can use an FTP server to offer files for you or others to download and to accept file uploads.

Book V: Network Troubleshooting

This minibook is where you can go if you run into problems when using your network:

+ **Chapter 1: Dealing with Connection and Performance Problems:** This chapter helps you know what to check for if you're having problems with your wired or wireless connections, or with the Internet. It also helps you diagnose and combat interference with your wireless network.

+ **Chapter 2: Fixing Sharing Issues:** In case you can't access shared resources at all on your network, or from certain computers, come here to see how to verify whether everything is configured correctly.

+ **Chapter 3: Troubleshooting Methods and Tools:** You might find this chapter useful for troubleshooting and configuring special networking features and equipment; including finding IP and MAC addresses of equipment and the computer names and Workgroup assignments you've given your computers. Additionally, I cover miscellaneous troubleshooting techniques, such as resetting your router to factory default settings and pinging computers or servers.

+ **Chapter 4: Getting More Help:** If you're still having problems with your network even after trying the troubleshooting techniques offered in the previous chapters of this minibook, or if you simply have some networking questions that go beyond the scope of this book, this chapter shows you where you can go to find more help and information.

Book VI: Networking Gadgets

This minibook covers many networking accessories, gadgets, and add-ons that you can use with your network:

+ **Chapter 1: Voice and Video:** Here you discover the cost savings and benefits of digital phone solutions, figure out what you need, and find out how to set your gadgets up to work with your computers. This chapter also helps you shop for and install network video cameras for surveillance and Web cam purposes, and describes Internet video conferencing packages that you can use with your network.

+ **Chapter 2: Family Entertainment:** This chapter covers networking accessories and gadgets, including wireless capabilities of digital cameras, media players, and digital picture frames. Plus you discover what's so great about hooking your TiVo DVR or game consoles to the network.

+ **Chapter 3: Traveling Gadgets:** This chapter reveals the conveniences of taking a travel router along on the trip. You see how you can take your home entertainment center anywhere with Sling Media. Plus you discover a nifty little gadget that can help you find Wi-Fi hotspots.

✦ **Chapter 4: Bluetooth Devices:** This chapter shows how the Bluetooth wireless technology can make your day-to-day life better. You can review what gadgets have Bluetooth and figure out how to equip your devices with Bluetooth. Then I show you how to synchronize your cellphone or PDA with your PC using Bluetooth.

✦ **Chapter 5: Network Magic: Ways to Manage Your Home Network:** This chapter introduces you to Network Magic, a software package that you can install on all your computers to help you manage and use your network. After stepping through the installation, you can take a grand tour of screens and features. You can even install add-ons for more functionality.

Book VII: Wi-Fi Hotspots

This minibook covers offering and using public wireless Internet:

✦ **Chapter 1: Wi-Fi Hotspots, Hot Zones, and Cities:** Here you discover the types of public Wi-Fi — Wi-Fi hotspots, hot zones, and municipal wireless networks. I show you how to find these public Internet locations and guide you through using them, including securing your communications and getting past the common e-mail block.

✦ **Chapter 2: Making Your Location a Wi-Fi Hotspot:** This chapter helps you understand what it takes to be a Wi-Fi hotspot owner. I help you figure out whether you should charge for access and how to pick a Wi-Fi hotspot solution. I provide a bundle of configuration and promotion tips in case you do decide to set up a hotspot.

✦ **Chapter 3: Using FON to Share or Get Wireless Internet Access:** This chapter discusses the ever-growing wireless sharing community called FON. Read this chapter to find out how you might benefit from offering your wireless Internet to FON users around the world, and how to set up the whole system.

Conventions Used in This Book

Here are a few conventions I use in this book:

✦ To tell you to choose a sequence of menu commands, I write something like "Choose File⇨Open."

✦ Text that you're supposed to type appears in bold type, **like this**.

✦ Sometimes an entire a sentence is in boldface, as you see when I present a numbered list of steps. In those cases, I leave the bold off what you're supposed to type.

✦ Web addresses and messages that appear on-screen are shown in a special monofont typeface, `like this`.

Icons Used in This Book

As do all *For Dummies* books, this book uses icons to point out special information:

I use this icon when I tell you something special that may provide some extra help with what you're trying to do (and maybe save you time or money.

Beware! I use this icon when I want you to be sure to proceed carefully to avoid messing up your computer.

You see this icon when I provide technical details that you may (or may not) want to know. It's up to you!

When I tell you something that you should really try to remember, I use this icon.

Where to Go from Here

Where you go from here depends upon where you are in the process of learning about networks, planning, setting up and configuring, and using your network.

If you haven't set up any networking gear yet, or purchased any, you should start from the beginning for best results. On the other hand, if you already have a network up and running but need assistance in using your network, you can skim through to see what interests you. Plus you could review the steps, recommendations, and tips I give in the setting up and configuring chapters (all of Book II) to see whether you can make your network even better. Or if you are having problems and are about to throw your gear out the window, you can go straight away to the using and troubleshooting chapters.

Get ready, set, network!

Book I

Introduction to Networking

The 5th Wave   By Rich Tennant

"That's it! We're getting a wireless network for the house."

Contents at a Glance

Chapter 1: Grasping the Main Concepts behind Networking

In This Chapter

✔ Discovering what a network is and how it can benefit you

✔ Finding out about the ways you can network your computers

✔ Figuring out whether your computers are network ready

✔ Exploring the wireless flavors — A, B, G, and N

The first mission in creating your home network is to familiarize yourself with networking — how it will benefit you and your family, types of home networks you can create, and what technologies and products you should use. You should do this before you go out and buy what the salesperson at the electronics store is told to sell.

I'm not talking about days of research, but instead maybe an hour or two spent reading through this first minibook and the first two chapters of the next minibook, and reviewing your wants and needs for your particular situation.

In this chapter, you discover the benefits of having a home network and find out how to go about creating one. You are also introduced to the technologies that are available, and figure out whether your computers are network ready.

Welcome to the World of Networking

First things first: What's a network? A network is a collection of computers interconnected through some means with the aim of sharing resources and transferring information. The technical term for the type of computer network used in homes and businesses is LAN *(Local Area Network)*. Businesses have used LANs for a long time — more than 20 years.

If you're not familiar with the term LAN, you might be wondering why you haven't heard about LANs before now? The answer comes down to lower computer prices, growth in the number of computers in people's homes, and the rise of the Internet, particularly high-speed Internet. You have to have at least two computers to make a network. Families probably didn't have two computers (at least, ones that work) until at least the late 1990s, so creating a network wasn't possible before then. With the increase of high-speed Internet connections in homes around the turn of the century, home networks have become more practical, beneficial, and desirable for more individuals and families.

The benefits you can enjoy from connecting your computers together at home, and creating a home network, include the following:

+ **Share high-speed Internet:** Instead of just plugging one computer into your high-speed (DSL, cable, ISDN, or whatever you use) Internet connection, you can use your home network to distribute access to all your computers. No more fighting over the "Internet computer"; everyone can be connected to the digital world at the same time. The key is to have "high speed." Though sharing dial-up Internet connections is possible, sharing on dial-up is not very realistic because the speed is very low.

+ **Share files:** On your home network, you won't have to use that old 3.5-inch floppy disk — or, these days, burn a CD or use a flash drive — to get a file from one computer to another. Instead, you can view and access all files of all computers from each computer. Transferring files between your networked PCs just takes a quick click or two, a drag and drop, or a copy and paste, and it's done.

+ **Share printers:** Your home network can also help you share your printers among all your computers. This is great if you have more computers than printers. No more people getting kicked off the "printer computer" so that a school or work report can be printed. You can print to the printer from any computer.

+ **Play multiplayer games:** You can play multiplayer games against or with others on your home network. One player could be on the family room PC, and the other could be posted out on the deck with the wireless laptop. A home network will also make it much easier for you to put your video game consoles online, so you can battle it out with people all over the world.

+ **Share multimedia:** If you're going the wireless way, you can transfer and share photos with your Wi-Fi–enabled digital camera or digital picture frame.

+ **Enhance entertainment:** A home network can also open new entertainment avenues. Network media players and TiVo boxes can provide access to online music and services from your TV. Sling Media lets you access your cable programming and other audio/video sources from the Internet anywhere in the world.

Understanding the Multiple Ways to Network

You have many ways you can connect your computers together to create your home network using the two main connecting methods of either wires or the air waves (wireless). Each networking method has its advantages and disadvantages.

The next subsections cover the following different network types that you can set up in your home:

✦ **Wired (Ethernet):** All computers are connected to a router by cable, which makes it harder to quickly set up your network. However, wired networks provide faster network speeds than do wireless networks, and are simpler than wireless in the sense that you don't have to learn as many technical terms.

✦ **Wireless (Wi-Fi):** Computers connect wirelessly to a wireless router, which eliminates the need for cables and lets you move around your home with your laptop. Wireless networks, however, are prone to inter-ference and are initially less secure than wired connections because the data travels through the air. (Keep in mind, however, that you can make your wireless network very secure; also, you can usually fix interference problems that arise.)

✦ **Computer to Computer:** This type of network doesn't require a router, which can save money but also means that you lose out on some fea-tures. You can set up either a wired or wireless computer-to-computer network. You can incorporate computer-to-computer connections into a traditional wired or wireless network, in addition to creating a strictly computer-to-computer network.

✦ **Power or phone lines:** This type of network also doesn't require a router. Again, this saves you money but makes you lose out on some fea-tures and functionality. Setting up a power- or phone-line network is great if you don't want to go wireless, and you don't want to run cables throughout your home. As with computer-to-computer networks, you can also incorporate power- or phone-line network connections into a traditional wired or wireless network.

Keeping it simple with wired (Ethernet) networks

Wired networks use a device called a *router* that you hook to your Internet connection. You connect all your computers directly to the router with spe-cial cable called *Ethernet* cable. The router distributes the Internet access among the connected computers. Additionally, the router serves as the han-dler for the communications between the computers. Figure 1-1 shows a basic, Ethernet-based wired network.

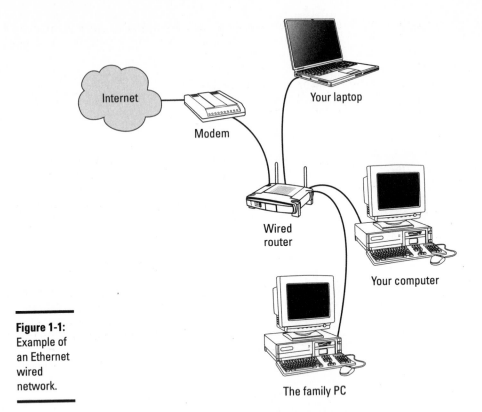

Figure 1-1:
Example of
an Ethernet
wired
network.

The family PC

As with everything, you'll find both advantages and disadvantages of going the totally wired route. The pros are that it involves a simple concept and requires you to understand little in the way of technical jargon. All you have to do is connect a cable between your computers and the router. Another advantage to having a wired network is that your network speeds can be much higher than what wireless networks can provide. You can get up to 1,000 Mbps (megabits per second) for wired connections, but only around 100 Mbps for wireless connections.

Megabits per second (Mbps) is a common unit of measure for the speed at which data or information is transferred on a network. For example, think of this as the miles per hour (MPH) unit of measure when you're on the road. Your car would be the data traffic, and MPH would be the speed at which the data is being transferred. If you are going 10 MPH (or you are using 10 Mbps networking equipment), your car (or the data traffic on your network) would be going one-tenth the speed of cars traveling 100 MPH (or networking equipment supporting 100 Mbps).

On the other hand (or other end of the wire, so to speak), are cons of using a wired connection rather than going wireless. The first, of course, is that you have to run wires. This means that for every computer you want on your network, you have to run a cable from the router to it. If all the computers are in the same room, you don't have much to worry about. But you likely have computers located throughout your home. Hiding these cables takes some planning and time — including some time in your basement, crawl space, or attic.

Another disadvantage going the totally wired route is a lack of mobility. If you don't have a laptop and don't expect to have one in the near future, being without wireless access might not be an issue for you. However, you should keep in mind that even desktop computers come with wireless capabilities, which can be useful if you decide to move your computer from one room to another.

When setting up a wired Ethernet network, you need the following:

✦ **Wired router:** This type of router is the heart of your network. You use one router that's centrally located in your home (or in relation to the computers you want to connect to the network), so you conserve the amount of cables and lengths needed to connect the computers to it. Figure 1-2 shows an example of a wired router.

Figure 1-2: An Ethernet wired router to which all your computers are connected.

Courtesy of Linksys.

✦ **Network cards:** These cards give your computer an Ethernet port, which allows you to connect an Ethernet cable between your computer and the router. You need one for each computer that you want to wire to the network. Computers built in the last several years typically come with an integrated (or built-in) Ethernet port or include a network card like the one shown in Figure 1-3.

Figure 1-3:
An Ethernet wired network adapter that goes inside your desktop computer.

Courtesy of Linksys.

✦ **Ethernet cable:** This is the wire you run between your computers and the router. You can use one of the two popular categories of Ethernet cable: Cat5e (enhanced) or Cat6. The connecters on these cables are called RJ-45. See Figure 1-4 for an example of Ethernet cabling.

Figure 1-4:
Ethernet cabling used in wired networks.

Going mobile: Wireless (Wi-Fi) networks

As the name implies, computers that use wireless networks aren't connected to the network using wires or cables. Instead, these computers communicate through a device called a *wireless router,* as Figure 1-5 depicts. As does a wired router, the wireless router provides Internet access and handles the computer traffic.

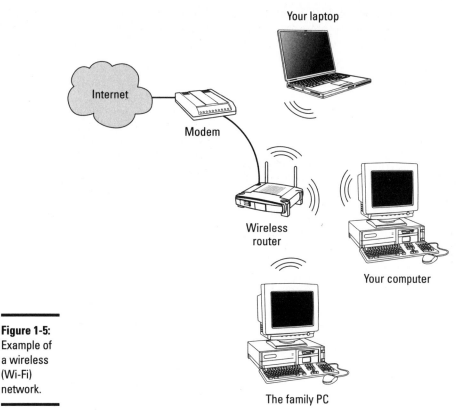

Figure 1-5:
Example of
a wireless
(Wi-Fi)
network.

Your laptop

Internet

Modem

Wireless
router

Your computer

The family PC

TECHNICAL STUFF

Technically, computers in a wireless network communicate through an
access point (AP) radio, which a wireless router contains. See the "What's an
access point?" sidebar for more information.

An AP simply connects wireless devices together, enabling file and resource
sharing between them. A wireless router includes the AP to connect the
wireless devices as well; however, the router component enables all the
devices to access the Internet. Stand-alone APs are used on wireless networks (connected to a wired router or wireless router) to add more wireless
coverage. This is because only one device on the network has to have the
routing capabilities. The best aspect of connecting your network wirelessly
is that you aren't tied down by cables. If you have a laptop, you can sit on
the front porch, the back deck, in bed — anywhere within range — and be
connected to the World Wide Web. Having a wireless connection also gives
you better options when moving your wireless-enabled desktop PCs around
the home.

What's an access point?

During your home networking journey, you'll probably see the words access point (AP) and wireless router used interchangeably, which isn't technically accurate; these are two different pieces of networking gear.

An *access point* (AP) is the name of a piece of wireless networking equipment that is essentially a radio that receives and transmits wireless networking data traffic or information to and from computers and devices that are wireless enabled. An AP can be a stand-alone device, in which case it is technically referred to simply as an AP. However, an AP can be included in other devices, such as a network router that lets you share an Internet connection, in which case it is technically a *wireless router*.

Wireless networks don't have to just be 100 percent wireless — that is, you can throw some wires into the mix. Wireless routers have four ports that you can plug your computers into, just as wired routers do. This is useful if you have a computer that has a wired (Ethernet) port but isn't wireless enabled. Additionally, wired connections can be much faster than wireless.

Another great thing about having a wireless connection is that you can use it for all your Wi-Fi devices. Anything Wi-Fi will work on a wireless network. In addition to your laptop, you can use, for example, Wi-Fi–enabled Personal Digital Assistants (PDAs), mobile phones, and digital picture frames.

On the flip side, going wireless does have a few minor drawbacks. You certainly don't need a computer degree or networking background to put a wireless network in your home (not by a very long shot), but setting up your wireless connection properly involves just a bit more understanding of some technical jargon than setting up wired networks does. Because the network data travels through the air, you need to *encrypt,* or scramble, that data, so you need to know just enough about encryption to keep your data secure. Plus, wireless connections aren't as reliable as direct wired connections. This is because wireless networks communicate through the air waves along with your (and your neighbors') other wireless doohickeys, and the signals can occasionally collide and interfere with each other. This can slow down your Internet browsing as well as file transfers between your computers, and can even make it impossible to connect to the wireless network. (But you can usually fix the problem with some troubleshooting and setting changes, as discussed in Book V, Chapter 1.)

Another potential drawback of going wireless is that wireless networks have coverage boundaries. Wireless signals don't just go on and on; instead, their signal range is similar to that of your cordless phone. This means that you may not get 100 percent coverage in all the nooks and crannies of your home with a typical wireless home setup. However, expanding coverage as much as you want is possible if you're willing to invest some extra time and money. But you probably don't have to worry about this unless you have a home larger than about 3,000 square feet.

For a wireless network, you just need the following two items:

✦ **Wireless router:** This provides your computers with the wireless connections, plus wired connections if desired. As is a wired router, this is the heart of the network and should be centrally located in your home. Figure 1-6 shows an example of a wireless router.

Figure 1-6:
A wireless router gives you both Wi-Fi and wired connectivity.

Courtesy of Linksys.

✦ **Wireless network adapter cards:** These cards, which go inside your computer, have an antenna that enables your computer to receive the wireless signals. Each computer you want to join to the wireless network must have a wireless card. If you bought a desktop computer in the past few years, chances are that a wireless card is built in. Newer laptops also have integrated (or built-in) wireless cards. Figure 1-7 shows an example of a wireless card.

Figure 1-7:
A (Wi-Fi) wireless network adapter that goes inside your desktop computer.

Courtesy of Linksys.

Doing without a router: Computer-to-computer networks

The previous two sections tell you about wired and wireless network connections, both of which require a router to enable the connectivity. In contrast to those, computer-to-computer networks don't use any "middle man" or central device; instead, any computers on this type of network are hooked directly to each other. Internet access can be hooked to one of the computers in the network and shared among the others. The computers basically self-manage the distribution of the Internet and network communications. These types of networks are also commonly called *peer-to-peer* networks, or more technically, *ad hoc* networks.

Despite having no router, computer-to-computer networks can also come in wired and wireless flavors. Figure 1-8 shows an example of a wired computer-to-computer network with just two computers, which is typical of this flavor of network. (More than two computers can be in a wired computer-to-computer network; however, such a setup requires that most of the computers have two Ethernet network cards.) The wireless computer-to-computer flavor can easily handle more than two computers, though, as you can see in Figure 1-9, which shows an example of this type of network.

Figure 1-8:
Example of
a wired
computer-
to-computer
network.

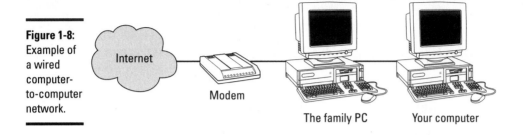

Modem

The family PC   Your computer

Your laptop

Figure 1-9:
Example of
a wireless
computer-
to-computer
network.

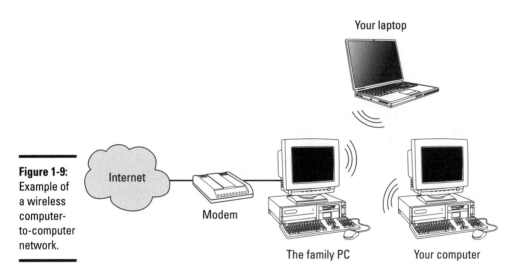

Modem

The family PC   Your computer

Computer-to-computer networks offer the benefits of being cheap (no router required) and providing mobility (when you go with a wireless setup).

Keep in mind, though, that computer-to-computer networks aren't perfect by any means. One drawback of going with this type of network is that you'll miss out on the features and functionalities that a router in a regular wired or wireless network provides. You don't get the built-in protection against Internet hackers that's provided by a router's firewall feature. In addition, some of the extra things you can do with a router to help protect your wireless connections (such as disabling network name or SSID broadcasting) aren't available. Without a router, it's also harder to set up access to remote connections to your network and run virtual servers, which I discuss in Book IV, Chapters 2 and 9.

If you are looking to use a computer-to-computer connection within a traditional wired or wireless network (rather than create a strictly computer-to-computer network), a router would be included on the network. This type of setup is discussed in Book II, Chapter 6.

Another consideration when you're setting up a wireless computer-to-computer network is that you usually won't have a centrally located access point for your wireless computers and gadgets. (See the "What's an access point?" sidebar in this chapter to find out more about access points.) This means that you might not have as much coverage as you would if you went with a regular wireless network.

When setting up a computer-to-computer network, here's what you need:

✦ **For a wired network:** Both computers on the wired network need to have an Ethernet port (which looks like a wide telephone connector would fit into it). Computers built in recent years typically come with a built-in Ethernet port or network card.

   You also need an Ethernet cable that runs between the computers. You can use one of the two popular categories of Ethernet cable: Cat5e (enhanced) or Cat6. The connecters on these cables are called RJ-45.

✦ **For a wireless network:** Each computer on a computer-to-computer wireless network needs a wireless card. Desktop computers purchased in the past few years typically come with a wireless card, and newer laptops have built-in wireless cards.

Networking across power or phone lines

Yet another type of network is one that is connected through power or phone lines. In this type of network, your computers are connected to your home's electrical or phone-line system, which provides the means for your computers to communicate with one another. In this respect, they are similar to computer-to-computer networks (discussed in the previous section). You can hook your Internet connection up to just one computer on the network (which can provide Internet for the others), or you can hook the Internet connection directly to the power or phone lines to give all the computers on the network access to the Internet. Figure 1-10 shows an example of a power-line network.

Networking across your power or phone lines is a good way to extend a traditional wired or wireless network. Say, for example, that you set up a wireless router, but you aren't getting full coverage throughout your home. You can use your power or phone lines to put another wireless access point (AP) in your home. Without using these existing wires, you would have to run an Ethernet cable all the way to the new AP from your wireless router.

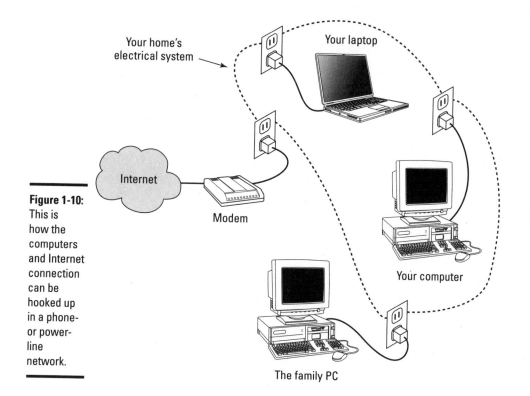

Figure 1-10:
This is
how the
computers
and Internet
connection
can be
hooked up
in a phone-
or power-
line
network.

You can set up a network that consists solely of power- or phone-line networking equipment — that is, you don't use a router — but without a router,
you don't have some of the features and functionalities that you typically
find in other types of networks. (See the preceding section, "Doing without a
router: Computer-to-computer networks," for more about the drawbacks of
having a routerless setup.) However, if you are looking to use your power or
phone lines to just extend your wired or wireless network (rather than
create a strictly power- or phone-line network), a router would be included
on the network. This type of setup is discussed in Book II, Chapters 6 and 7.

A power-line or phone-line network requires two pieces of hardware (in addition to your computers, of course):

✦ **Power-Phone-line adapters:** You must have a special adapter (for an
example of an adapter, see Figure 1-11) for each computer that you want
to hook up to your home's electrical or phone system. You also need
another adapter if you connect your Internet connection directly to the
electrical or phone system.

Figure 1-11:
A pair of power-line adapters that plug your computer and Internet into your home's electrical or phone system.

Courtesy of D-Link.

You can save yourself some money if you can hook the Internet connection to a computer that's already going to be connected to the system with an adapter. Whether you do so depends upon the connector types of the adapters you buy and the types of adapters on your Internet modem. For example, if both components require you to use an Ethernet cable, and you have only one port on your computer, you won't be able to hook up both. But both could be connected to your computer if the power-line adapter uses a USB cable, and the modem uses an Ethernet cable.

✦ **Network card/USB:** Power- and phone-line adapters require either an Ethernet or USB connection to your computers and Internet modem.

Mixing and matching network types

Up to now, I've presented each type of network as basically an either/or choice, but you can, in fact, mix and match network types. Rather than go with a wired only network, for example, you can have combined wireless/wired network. With this setup, your mobile computers and devices can use a wireless connection, but you can also still connect computers via cable to the ports on a wireless router. What's the advantage of doing so? You get to take advantage of the extremely fast network speeds that you can get by connecting through cables while also enjoying the freedom of mobility for your wireless computers.

Another mixed network type that you can create is one that uses your power or phone lines to extend either your wired or wireless network. Rather than run a long cable between computers, you can tap into your home's existing wires to serve as a bridge. You might benefit from doing this if, for example, one of your computers is on the other side of the house, away from the others that you have on a wired network. Instead of having to map a way to get the cable from your wired network to the renegade computer, you can just plug a power- or phone-line adapter into your wired router and another into the distant computer. This is discussed further in Book II, Chapter 6.

Figure 1-12 shows an example of these types of mixed networks, that is, a combined wired, wireless, and power-line network.

Don't forget about computer-to-computer networks, which you can also throw into the mix. Say that you're setting up a wireless network, but you have one computer that doesn't have a wireless card. Sure, you can go out and buy one for $30 or $40, but you can get a computer on the network for just $10 if it has an Ethernet port. Simply connecting the computer to a port on your wireless router could work, but what if that computer is far enough away from the router to be out of range of the signal? You'd have to run a cable to it, which is a hassle. However, if the computer is close to another one that does have wireless connectivity (and also has an Ethernet port), you can simply connect these two computers together (thereby creating a computer-to-computer network within your wireless network. Figure 1-13 shows an example of this situation.

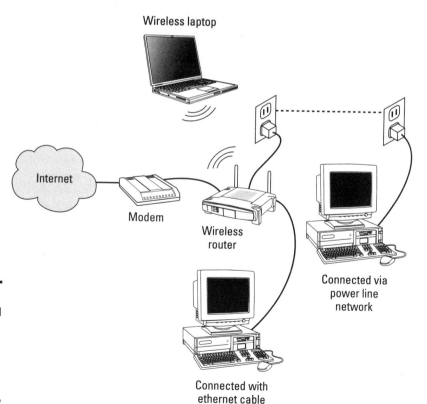

Wireless laptop

Internet

Modem

Wireless router

Connected via power line network

Connected with ethernet cable

Figure 1-12:
A converged wireless, wired, and power- or phone-line network.

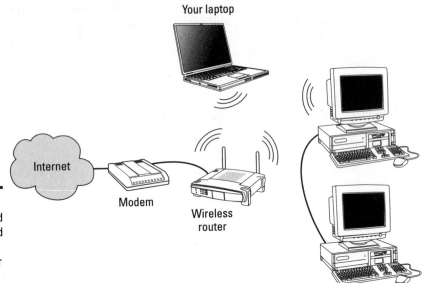

Figure 1-13:
A converged
wireless and
computer-
to-computer
network.

Summing up and comparing the network types

I've covered a lot of ground and discussed many network types in the preceding subsections. For a quick comparison of these network types, see
Table 1-1, which sums up their characteristics in comparison with one
another, with one X standing for Low and four Xs indicating Very High.

Table 1-1: Comparing the Home Network Types You Can Use

	Wired (Ethernet)	*Wireless* (Wi-Fi)	*Computer-to-* Computer	*Power or* Phone Lines
Costs	xx	xxxx	X	Xxx
Time	xxx	xxx	X	Xx
Difficulty	xx	xxx	X	X
Performance	xxx	xx	XXX	X

When it comes to the speeds of different types of networks, be aware that a
faster network speed doesn't mean faster Internet speeds. The speeds of
Internet connections are much lower than the lowest typical speed a network will operate on. For example, a good cable Internet connection may
provide up to 5 Mbps (megabits per second), but a wired network will usually run at least at a range of 100 Mbps, and wireless connections run at
around 54 Mbps. The point is that if you spend more money on faster networking gear (say, at a speed of 1,000 Mbps for wired connections and 100

Mbps or more for wireless connections), your Internet speed won't increase (and for this example, it stays at the 5 Mbps speed). A faster network does provide faster file transfers between your computers, however, making the extra cost of higher-speed networking gear worth it if you think you'll be regularly sharing files between your computers.

Checking to See Whether Your Computers Are Network Ready

If your computer was built in the past several years, it's highly likely it has an Ethernet port so that you can connect to wired networks, and also a wireless card for Wi-Fi networks. If you aren't sure of your computer's network readiness, don't worry — you have a few ways to find out.

Take a look at the PC tower

You can usually take a quick peek behind your computer to see whether it has a wireless or Ethernet card (or adapter) installed. To do so, follow these steps:

✦ **On the back of your computer, check for what appears to be an enlarged telephone port.** Obviously, you may have to move your computer tower to be able to see the back. When you try to move it, be careful not to pull any wires loose. If the wires are too tight and you can't pull the computer out far enough, shut down the computer and then unplug the wires.

   If your computer has a wired (Ethernet) card, you'll see a port that looks like a bigger-than-normal telephone jack.

✦ **Check for a card-mounted antenna.** If a wireless card is installed in your computer, you'll most likely see an antenna (or several of them) extending from a card that's plugged inside the computer. Most antennas are black and about five to seven inches long.

✦ **Check for a desktop antenna.** Some wireless cards may use a desktop antenna that sits near your computer and connects to the wireless card with its antenna wire. If you have such an antenna, then you have wireless.

Check your laptop

Although you can't see an internal wireless card in your laptop because it's, well, internal and therefore hidden, you might be able to find a Wi-Fi sticker or decal. You can, however, see whether you have an internal wired card, and external wired or wireless cards, by checking for the following:

✦ **A port that looks like a bigger-than-normal telephone port.** Look on the back or side of your laptop where all the other connectors and ports are located. If you have an internal wired (Ethernet) card, you'll see a port that looks like a large telephone jack.

✦ **Protruding cards.** If you have an external wired or wireless card, you'll see a noticeable card sticking out of a slot (called a PCMCIA slot) on the side of your laptop. Figure 1-14 shows an example of an external wireless card. An external wired card would look similar in size and form but would have an Ethernet port.

Figure 1-14: This is what an external wireless card looks like when out of the slot.

Courtesy of Linksys.

Check your computer for a USB port

Both your desktop and laptop computers might be able to use a USB wired or wireless adapter (see Figure 1-15 for an example of this type of adapter). Instead of having an internal card, a card that slides into a slot, or one that you insert inside a computer's case, you can have a USB adapter that plugs into a USB port on the back of a desktop or laptop computer. Of course, your computer must have a USB port to make use of USB components.

Find out what devices are listed in your computer Device Manager

Another way to determine whether an internal wireless device exists in your laptop (or, for that matter, any other devices, including network cards), you can check the Device Manager utility in Windows to see what's listed there. To do so, follow these steps:

Figure 1-15:
With a wireless USB adapter, you can turn your computer into a wireless device.

Courtesy of Linksys.

1. **Click the Start button and then click Control Panel.**

If you're using Window's Classic Start menu, hover your mouse cursor over Settings and then click Control Panel when you see it in the pop-up menu that appears.

2. **Choose the Performance and Maintenance category (in Windows XP) or System and Maintenance category (in Windows Vista).**

If you're using the Classic Control Panel view in Windows XP or Vista, however, ignore this step.

3. **Click System.**

The System Properties window appears.

4. **In Windows XP, click the Hardware tab, and then click the Device Manager button. In Windows Vista, click the Device Manager link under the Tasks list on the left (click Continue on the prompt if UAC is active).**

The Device Manager window appears.

5. **Click the plus sign for Network Adapters to expand the category.**

If you have any type of network card or adapter installed on your computer, you should see it listed here.

If you have an Ethernet card/port, its device name may include something like "10/100" or "Ethernet," as shown in Figure 1-16.

If you see a device name with the word *wireless,* you have a wireless adapter.

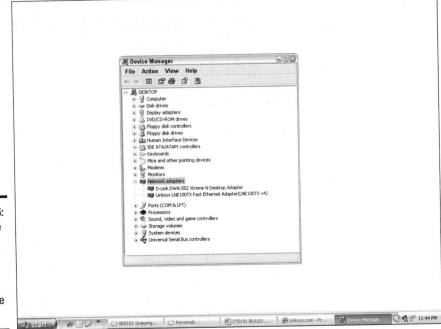

Figure 1-16:
The Device Manager lists the network adapters it finds on the computer.

Some device names may not indicate whether it's a wireless or wired adapter; however, it would probably include the model number, as does the D-Link wireless adapter shown in Figure 1-16. If you have only a model number, you can Google it (use the Google search engine online) for more information.

Understanding the Wireless Flavors: A, B, G, or N

When you set up a wireless network, you have a choice of which wireless technology or standard you want to use. Each wireless standard has varying characteristics, such as speed and range. The way these technologies work is regulated by the *Institute of Electrical and Electronics Engineers* (IEEE), and the code name for the wireless networking standards is 802.11. The standards are basically documents written by the IEEE that describe how wireless devices should operate. These documents help manufacturers develop wireless products that will work with products from other manufacturers.

Understanding the wireless "alphabet"

From the earliest to the still-evolving, here are the wireless standards that have been created by the IEEE for the wireless networking industry:

✓ **802.11a:** This is the least used standard, especially in the consumer market, but some computers come with dual-band wireless (802.11a/g). Though this standard is as old as 802.11b (described next), it has the same (or better) maximum speeds as 802.11g, a later standard. The 802.11a is the only standard that uses a different frequency range (5 GHz instead of 2.4 GHz), so using this standard means that you aren't likely to have a problem with interference from other networks — it isn't nearly as popular or widespread. However, because of the high frequencies, the signals from 802.11a products generally don't go as far as do the signals from devices using the other standards.

✓ **802.11b:** This is the first wireless networking standard widely used in homes and businesses. This standard has basically been replaced by 802.11g. If you purchased a computer with integrated (built-in) wireless or bought wireless products before the first half of 2003, its wireless components likely use 802.11b.

✓ **802.11g:** This is the most widely used standard today. It's similar to 802.11b but is an improved version with much greater speeds (data transmission rates) — up to 54 Mbps. The 802.11g standard products are backward-compatible with 802.11b, so you can mix the two devices within the same wireless network. The earlier 802.11a standard, though, is not compatible with these two standards and does not even use the same frequencies.

If you purchased a computer with integrated wireless or bought wireless products after the first half of 2003, its wireless components are likely based on the 802.11g standard.

✓ **802.11n:** An evolving standard that's backward-compatible with 802.11b and g products. When the standard is finalized, you may be able to get data rates up to 540 Mbps, which is ten times faster than existing standards. Additionally, these products will have a much longer range by using a powerful smart-antenna technology, called *Multiple Input Multiple Output* (MIMO), which is already available in some wireless networking products.

You can already buy products based on this technology, which is referred to as pre-n or 802.11n draft products. But both your wireless router and your computers must be 802.11n to achieve all the benefits.

As wireless networking has progressed, the IEEE has come up with a few different wireless standards. If you're interested in knowing the details, check out the sidebar "Understanding the wireless "alphabet"." Otherwise, all you really need to know is that the code 802.11 with a *g* appended to it is the most common current standard. Code 802.11 with an *n* appended to it is the newest standard, and computers are beginning to appear on the market with this standard built in to the wireless components.

Another wireless term you'll come by is *Wi-Fi,* created by the Wi-Fi Alliance. The *Wi-Fi Alliance* is a nonprofit industry trade association devoted to promoting wireless networking that coined this catchy new term to describe the technology. The term *Wi-Fi* stands for wireless fidelity — which means freedom from wires.

Table 1-2 provides a comparison of the wireless standards/technologies.

Table 1-2: A Brief Comparison of the Wireless "Alphabet"

	802.11a	*802.11b*	*802.11g*	*802.11n*
Frequency	5 GHz	2.4 GHz	2.4 GHz	2.4 GHz
Speed (Data Rate)	54 Mbps	11 Mbps	54 Mbps	248 Mbps
Range	115 feet	125 feet	125 feet	230 feet
Cost	High	Low	Moderate	High
Compatibility	None	802.11g/n	802.11b/n	802.11b/g

The range that your wireless network reaches can vary greatly. The ranges shown in Table 1-2 are just an estimate of what you may see in your home. It all depends upon the amount of walls, type of building materials, and furniture in your home.

Though the official names for the different wireless standards begin with 802.11, in this book I refer only to the standard letter and drop the 802.11; for instance, wireless G or wireless N.

Chapter 2: Operating Systems and Networks

In This Chapter

✔ How the operating system affects networking

✔ Discovering the network interfaces in Windows and Mac

✔ Checking out Windows Vista's new Network and Sharing Center

*O*ne important ingredient in networks is the operating system (OS) of your computer — which could be any of various versions of Windows, Mac, or Linux Ubuntu. The OS changes certain essential features of how you experience networking. The types of networking interfaces included in operating systems, and their user friendliness, play a role in your networking experience.

The older OS versions lack user friendliness for some networking features, or don't include them at all. Examples of features that can vary from one OS version to another, or be nonexistent, are an interface for configuring network connections, a utility to manage wireless connections, and a built-in firewall for protection against hackers and infections. As home networking, and networks in general, have become more popular, operating systems have been developed to better support networks and engineered so that average (that is, nontechnical) consumers can reap the benefits of home networking.

If you're still using an earlier version of an OS — such as Windows 98, ME, or 2000 — it's time to upgrade to a better version, or a whole new computer system altogether.

In this chapter, you discover the networking features of Windows, Mac OS X, and Linux Ubuntu.

Knowing What to Expect from Newer Operating Systems

Though different operating systems can vary greatly in how they look and operate, as is the case with Windows, Mac, and Ubuntu, they all include some similar features when it comes to networking. For example, all operating systems typically include a network icon on the main taskbar or toolbar, built-in configuration for wireless connections, and firewall software.

Network icon

Operating systems typically feature some type of an icon on their main taskbar or toolbar for networking. For example, in Windows XP, you'll see an icon for each network adapter you have installed on your computer. When you hover your mouse cursor over this icon (see Figure 2-1), you can quickly see the status of your network connection, such as its speed, and if it's for a wireless connection, the signal strength.

Figure 2-1:
Hovering
over a
network
icon in
Windows XP.

Windows Vista features only one network icon, the one for the Network and Sharing Center. When you hover over this icon, you see the status of all your network connections. Hovering over the network icons in Mac OS X and Ubuntu doesn't show the connection status but shows the wireless networks that are nearby (plus indicates the one you are connected to). Shortcuts to places to configure your network connections are also listed.

Built-in wireless network utility

Newer versions of operating systems also include an integrated wireless network utility for use if you have wireless capability. This utility shows you the wireless networks in your area. (See Figure 2-2 for an example.)

Built-in wireless utilities also let you manage the wireless networks you connect to. (Ubuntu, however, is an exception. It doesn't come with this functionality automatically; you must install it, which Book IV, Chapter 1 discusses.) For example, you can prioritize them and create a preferred list (see Figure 2-3) and save encryption keys so that you don't have to enter them each time you connect.

These management utilities also let you configure wireless preferences. For instance, Windows lets you specify whether your computer should automatically connect to any wireless network it picks up or connect only to those in your preferred list.

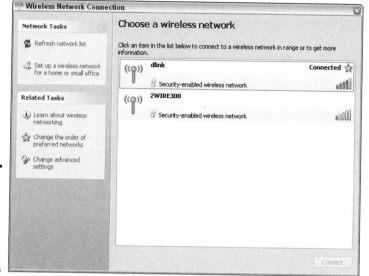

Figure 2-2:
Available
wireless
networks as
displayed in
Windows XP.

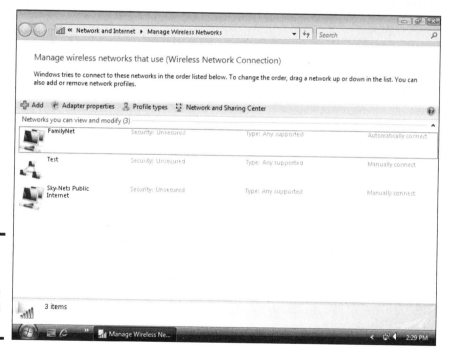

Figure 2-3:
Preferred
wireless
network list
in Windows
Vista.

Networking manufacturers also develop their own wireless utilities. For operating systems that don't include a built-in wireless utility, you must use the wireless utility that came with the network adapter.

Built-in firewall

Another feature common among newer versions of operating systems is a built-in firewall, which helps protect against hackers and unauthorized access to the Internet from your computer. (Again, as with the wireless management feature, Ubuntu doesn't automatically come with a firewall installed. See Book III, Chapter 1 on how to install and configure a firewall for Ubuntu.) A firewall works by blocking most ports to and from the Internet and network, except those you authorize. You can buy third-party firewall software that provides similar protection; however, the built-in firewall works with the OS and configures itself to authorize ports when you turn on features in the OS that have to communicate with the Internet or network.

Getting Acquainted with Windows XP's Networking Interfaces

If you have wireless capability on your computer in Windows XP, you have a wireless network status icon (shown here in the margin) in the system tray in the lower-right corner of the screen. If you aren't connected, the icon appears with a red *X* on it. When you want to connect to a wireless network, or just check out what networks are around, all you have to do is double-click the icon. When you do so, the Choose a Wireless Network window pops up. At that point, if you are already connected to a network, you must right-click the icon and select View Available Wireless Networks.

The integrated wireless network utility in Windows XP is sometimes referred to as Wireless Zero Configuration.

The Choose a Wireless Network window

The Choose a Wireless Network window shows you all the wireless networks (and their signals) that your computer can pick up. Networks using encryption require you to input the encryption key before you can connect. These networks are identified by a yellow padlock icon that appears under the network name.

From the Choose a Wireless Network window, you can access the window to manage your preferred wireless networks. This window is also where you can change your connectivity preferences. To access this window, click the

Change the Order of Preferred Networks link under the Related Tasks section on the left.

Network connection status

Another spot you'll access in Windows XP when networking either wirelessly or through a wired connection is the Network Connection Status dialog box. You can easily access this window when you're connected to a network by double-clicking the network icon in the system tray. This dialog box gives you detailed status information on your network connection, such as how long you've been connected, as well as activity information in addition to the info you can see (network name, speed, and signal strength information) when hovering over the network.

Network connection properties

You can bring up the Network Connection Properties window by double-clicking the network icon in the system tray and clicking the Properties button. The Network Connection Properties dialog box then opens to show the protocols and services enabled for the connection. Clicking the Wireless Networks tab (when viewing the properties for a wireless adapter) takes you to where you can set up your preferred wireless networks. Finally, the Advanced tab provides a button (called Settings) to access the firewall utility and may contain the settings to share your Internet connection.

Using Windows Vista's Network and Sharing Center

Windows Vista includes increased security and a much more user-friendly interface for networking. The networking configuration items in Windows XP are spread between many different dialog boxes and windows. Vista, however, offers the Network and Sharing Center (see Figure 2-4), which provides a one-stop shop for all your networking and Internet configuration needs.

Accessing the Network and Sharing Center

You have several ways to get to the Network and Sharing Center, as follows:

✦ Right-click or double-click the network icon in the system tray and then select the Network and Sharing Center link.

✦ Double-click the Network and Sharing Center icon in the Control Panel.

✦ When viewing the Network window (showing all the computers in your network), click the Network and Sharing Center button on the toolbar of the window.

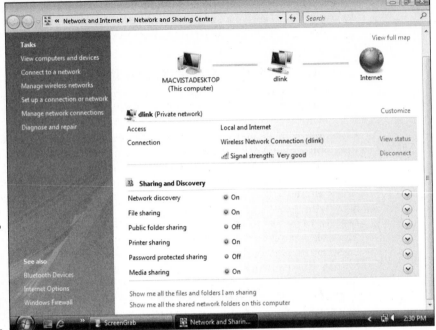

Figure 2-4:
Windows
Vista's
Network
and Sharing
Center.

The Network and Sharing Center provides you with a simple diagram of your network on the main window and a full map of your network by clicking the View Full Map link. The full map provides you with an easy way to access shared resources and the configuration utilities of devices (such as your router) on your network. Just click the icon of the computer or device you want to access, and its shared files and printers (for computers) or configuration screen (for devices) will pop up.

Just below the network map on the Network and Sharing Center, you can view your basic connection information, and access detailed information by clicking the View Status link. The Customize link allows you to change the name of the network connection, the type (private or public), and the icon given to the network connection.

Under the connection information, you're provided with the status of all the main sharing and discovery settings and the ability to make quick changes, which is a big enhancement over Windows XP.

Another exceptional improvement is the set of links on the bottom of the window. These links show you all the files and folders your account and computer are sharing on the network.

As a final point, the task pane on the left side of the window provides access to common connectivity settings and tasks you need, as well as a shortcut to the Internet Options and Wireless Firewall settings.

The network classification scheme

In Windows Vista, the first time you connect to a network, you must classify its location or type as Home, Work, or Public.

This new scheme is extremely useful because it automatically modifies the appropriate network settings based upon the location type you choose. For example, say that you connect to the Wi-Fi hotspot at your local café. In that case, you choose Public as the location type. Vista then automatically disables all network discovery and sharing to protect your documents and privacy while on the unsecured network. When you return home and connect to your home network, which you've classified as a Home location, Windows Vista allows network discovery and sharing because you trust the other users on the network.

Support for nonbroadcasting wireless networks

Windows Vista makes it easier to use wireless networks that do not broadcast their SSID (also known as the network name.) In Windows XP, these types of networks don't appear on the list of available wireless networks, whereas in Vista, they appear as unnamed networks.

Rather to manually adding a nonbroadcasting wireless network to the preferred network list in order to connect, in Vista, select the Unnamed Network, click Connect, and when prompted, enter the SSID.

You may think that this degrades the security that hidden networks offer; however, anyone attempting to connect to the network still needs the SSID. Additionally, not broadcasting your SSID doesn't offer a whole lot of security, anyway.

The Mac OS X Networking Interfaces

 If you have wireless capability on your Mac, you have a network icon on the toolbar, shown here in the left margin. When you click the icon, a menu drops down showing you the available wireless networks in your area. If you are connected to a wireless network, a check mark appears next to that one. Networks that have encryption enabled require you to input the encryption key before you can connect. Encrypted networks are identified by a padlock icon that appears to the right of the network name.

Shortcuts from the network icon

When you click the network icon, a drop-down menu appears with a list of options. If you click the Join Other Network option, you can manually enter the connection information for wireless networks that don't broadcast their network name. Clicking the Create Network option opens a window in which you can create a wireless computer-to-computer network. This feature lets you network with other wireless-enabled computers without having a wireless router or access point (AP).

If you click the Open Network Preferences options, the Network window (which is also accessible from System Preferences) opens.

The network window

The Network window is where you can turn network adapters on and off, view a network's connection status, and configure all the networking settings. You can choose the network adapter (or connection) you want to configure from the list on the left. On each adapter's screen you see an Advanced button, which drops down another window, where you can configure the settings such as the IP address (the unique number assigned to the network adapter to identify itself on the network, which is discussed further in Book I, Chapter 3) and AppleTalk (Apple's old networking suite of protocols). If you have wireless capability, clicking its Advanced button also takes you where you can manage your preferred wireless networks and set connectivity settings.

The Sharing window

Another key area for networkers in Mac OS X to be familiar with is the Sharing window. You can't access this window from the network icon's drop-down menu, though. You have to get to it by going through the main System Preferences menu.

In the Sharing window, you can modify the Computer Name, which is how you identify your computer on the network when sharing. But the main thing you can do here is enable, disable, and edit the settings for many different types of sharing. The basic File Sharing feature lets you add folders you want to share with others on the network. (You can find out exactly how to share in Book IV, Chapter 3 and 4.)

This Sharing window also contains settings for other types of sharing, such as the sharing of the screen, printer, Internet, and Bluetooth. — it's the one-stop shop for sharing!

Networking with Ubuntu

The overall networking tasks in Ubuntu aren't as streamlined as they are in Windows. (However, putting Ubuntu computers on your network is certainly possible.) For example, enabling Windows sharing in Ubuntu may not just take selecting a checkbox; you may have to install a feature and activate it manually, as discussed in Book IV, Chapter 3. And Ubuntu doesn't automatically come loaded with a wireless management feature for prioritizing the networks you connect to. (Book IV, Chapter 1 shows how to install and configure this type of feature.) Additionally, Ubuntu doesn't automatically come with a firewall installed. (Book III, Chapter 1 shows how to install and configure a firewall for Ubuntu.)

Network icon

Just as with Windows and Mac OS X, you have a wireless icon on the menu bar in Ubuntu (shown here in the margin). Its menu, which drops down when you click the icon, almost mimics that of the Mac OS X's network icon. You see the wireless networks in your area (with it indicating the one you're connected to). You also see shortcuts to windows that let you connect to hidden (nonbroadcasted) networks and create a computer-to-computer network, and connect you to the network settings. Ubuntu, however, also includes a submenu (of the network icon's menu) that has shortcuts to VPN (Virtual Private Network) connections you've created to remotely connect to your home or office network, as discussed in Book IV, Chapter 2.

When connected to a wireless network, the network icon itself shows the signal strength of the connection, out of four signal indicator bars. When you hover over the icon, you also see the network name (SSID) that you're connected to and the signal strength. Right-clicking the network gives you options to enable/disable wired and wireless networking, plus a shortcut to the Connection Information window, which is discussed in the next subsection.

Connection Information window

When you want to see the details of your network connection, you can bring up the Connection Information window by right-clicking the network icon and selecting the Connection Information shortcut. This window gives you the data rate (or speed) at which you're connected to the network. It also gives you the IP and MAC (labeled as Hardware Address) address assigned to your network adapter to identify itself on the network, and the router's IP address (labeled as Default Route).

Network settings

The Network settings are accessible by clicking the network icon and selecting the Manual Configuration option or by clicking System from the Ubuntu toolbar, choosing Administration, and selecting Network.

The Network Settings window consists of four tabs: Connections, General, DNS, and Hosts. (You'll probably use only the first two.) On the Connections tab, you can edit the properties of each network adapter to manually configure the network information, which is useful when you need to assign a static IP address, discussed in Book IV, Chapter 1. The General tab lets you specify your Host Name, which is the equivalent to the Computer Name setting for Windows computers, which identifies the computer on the network when accessing shared files. The other two tabs (DNS and Hosts) let you configure advanced settings.

Shared Folders window

Another spot you'll use in Ubuntu when networking is the Shared Folders window, accessible by clicking System from the Ubuntu toolbar, choosing Administration, and selecting Shared Folders. The main purpose of this window is to allow you to add and remove the folders on your computer that you want to share (or not share) with others on the network. The General tab lets you specify the Domain/Workgroup (same as Workgroup in Windows) that your computer is assigned to (which should be the same as your other computers) and the WINS Server information, usually used only on advanced corporate networks.

Chapter 3: Networking Hardware

Discovering What Connects You to the Internet: Modems

Although not solely used for networking, a modem is typically one of the most important components of a network if your network is intended to share an Internet connection. Your modem, highlighted in Figure 3-1, connects to your Internet-active line (that is, a cable or a phone line from your wall) and is responsible for communicating with your *Internet service provider* (ISP).

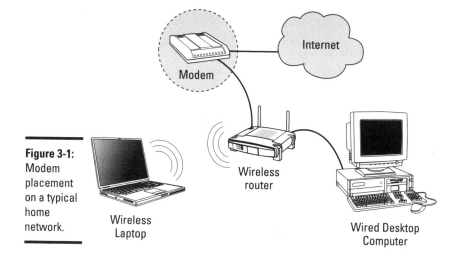

Figure 3-1:
Modem placement on a typical home network.

Internet

Modem

Wireless router

Wireless Laptop

Wired Desktop Computer

Although the exact processes and inner workings of modems differ depending upon the connection type (DSL, cable, dial-up, or other), a modem basically interprets what would sound like digital gibberish to you to something your computer (or router) can understand.

(If you've been using computers for many years, you might remember the awful screeching and static noises from the old dial-up modems. Well, you can think of broadband or high-speed modems converting those sounds into a language your computer understands (and vice versa.)

Your router (or computer) sends data to your modem, which converts or encodes it into information best fit for your particular Internet connection. After the information travels through the Internet to your ISP's location, the ISP's modem then converts or decodes it back into data that its computers understand.

The technical terms used to describe the general functions of a modem are modulation and demodulation. *Modulation* occurs when the modem converts the digital information (your computer's language of ones and zeros) into an analog carrier signal, and *demodulation* occurs when the modem decodes the analog carrier signal and converts it to digital information.

Getting a modem from your Internet provider

When you sign up for high-speed Internet (which is different from dial-up) service, your ISP should install an external modem. However, in cases in which you are shipped a self-installation package (common for DSL connections), you should be given a modem to install yourself.

Getting your own

If your ISP doesn't provide a modem for your high-speed Internet service, or you've damaged it, you can purchase and use your own. You just need to make sure that you get the right type for your service — that is, for either DSL or cable. You can even think about getting a router with a built-in modem, discussed in a later section of this chapter.

When you're browsing the shelves or surfing the online stores, you may see a modem referred to as a *broadband modem* or *USB/Ethernet modem*. These terms mean the same thing.

Checking out your modem

Enough of the theory; it's time to check out your modem! Take a few minutes to become one with your modem, because it will work day and night for your surfing needs.

As you'll begin to know very well, the front of most of your networking gear is full of status (LED) lights to inform you of what's working and what's not, whether data is traveling or not, and so on. DSL and cable modems differ some from one another; however, they are very similar.

The back of a cable modem includes a cable input jack (similar to a wall jack) to hook up the Internet connection. You can see this port in Figure 3-2. DSL modems include a telephone input port instead of a cable port.

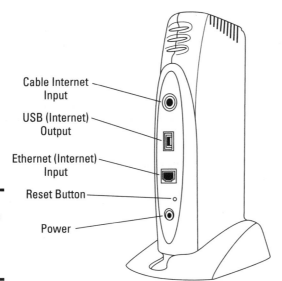

Cable Internet Input

USB (Internet) Output

Ethernet (Internet) Input

Reset Button

Power

Figure 3-2: The back of a cable Internet modem.

The router or computer plugs into one of the modem's output ports, as follows:

✦ **USB:** This is not likely to be the only output port on a modem. A USB port is sometimes included on modems so that you can connect it to your computer's USB port, if your computer doesn't have an Ethernet port.

✦ **Ethernet:** This port is usually included on modems so that you can connect it to your computer (if it has an Ethernet port) or connect it to a router when setting up a traditional wired or wireless network.

Some modems have a reset button so that you can restore the device's factory default settings, which may be useful if the modem "locks up." You may be able to easily see the button and press it with a finger, or you may find only a small hole and have to use a paper clip or something similar to push the button.

One last obvious but critical spot on the modem is its power connector. Don't forget to plug it in!

Distributing Internet with Routers

The first piece of real networking hardware I discuss in this chapter is the *router*. No, I'm not talking about that old dusty tool in the garage that you used to carve your family name in a wooden plaque. I mean a network router, although these two very different items do have a couple of similar traits: They can be wired or wireless, and they both use bits. Nevertheless, anyway you cut it, a network router is much different.

Now get the creative and woodworking thoughts out so that you can get back to networking!

Routers are typically used in home or small-office networks (unless you're going the computer-to-computer way, as I discuss in Book I, Chapter 1) and serve as the centerpiece of most types of networks.

When you're browsing the shelves or surfing the online stores, you may see a router referred to as a *broadband router* or *cable/DSL router*.

The router: Your network's courier

The overall purpose of a router on your network is to direct all the data traffic to the right locations, whether it's to and from the Internet for data originating from a computer on your network (see Figure 3-3 for an example) or for data that just travels between your computers for file sharing (see Figure 3-4).

You can think of this function of the router as a courier service that works like this:

1. The router (courier) receives information.

2. The router looks for the specified destination(s) for that information.

3. The router passes the information to the right place (a computer or the Internet).

In contrast to a human courier, your router doesn't take scheduled lunch breaks or vacations; it can, however, become sick. This is when you experience weird hardware quirks (which this book can help you deal with).

You have some control over the router's direction of traffic through firewall settings, filters, and port redirection. Refer to Book III, Chapter 1 for more information.

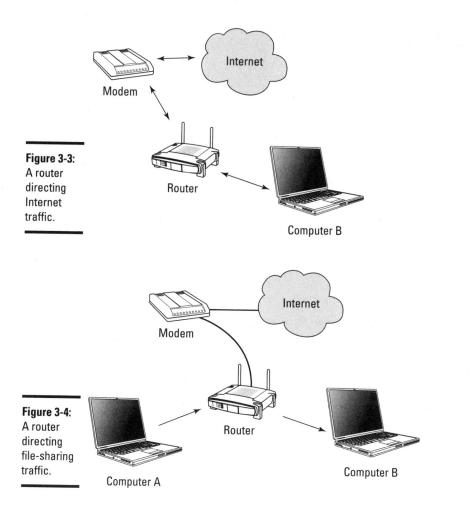

Figure 3-3:
A router
directing
Internet
traffic.

Figure 3-4:
A router
directing
file-sharing
traffic.

Your router enables sharing of your Internet connection

In addition to acting as a courier (see the preceding section), your router also provides another vital function for your small network: It connects your multiple computers to one larger (or the largest in the world) network. I refer, of course, to the Internet.

But to be technically correct, I should say that your router doesn't actually connect you to the original Internet connection. (Remember, that's the job of your modem!) However, your router does extend your Internet connection to all your computers and essentially makes all the computers on your small network seem to be one computer as far as your Internet connection is concerned. Why? Well, you have only one main connection to the Internet because you receive only one IP address (a unique number that identifies you on the Internet and networks) for a single, standard Internet connection. You need an IP address for each of your computers (or devices) in order for them to use the Internet.

Basically, if you don't have a router, you have to order separate Internet connections for each computer. That costs money that you surely prefer to spend on other techy things, such as DVR or HD TV service, or even a 42-inch plasma screen (which you can stream media to from your network.).

I'm glad to inform you that even as your router grabs and uses the only (public) IP address that comes with your single Internet connection, your router in return can create a network that gives you many more (private) IP addresses for your Web surfing needs. How nice, huh? No, this isn't illegal — it's smart! Make sure that you give your router special thanks — and go spend all that money you save on something fun!

Your router provides your (DHCP) IP addresses

As touched on in the previous section, all your computer and devices typically require their own, unique IP addresses (for example, 192.168.1.101) for Internet, sharing, and other network communication purposes. Instead of manually assigning and configuring the addresses, your router can provide all your computers and other network devices with IP addresses. This service is brought to you by your router's DHCP *(Dynamic Host Configuration Protocol)* server, depicted in Figure 3-5.

Figure 3-5 shows the single IP address (for example, 555.555.555.555) provided by your Internet service provider (ISP) being converted into multiple addresses (192.168.1.100, and so on) by your router's DHCP server. The addresses are then distributed as needed to the computers and devices on your network.

After a computer or device connects to your router (and when the adapter and router are set to use DHCP, which is set by default using the factory settings), an IP address is automatically requested by the network adapter (computer or device) and assigned by your router.

Routers can be wired or wireless

As mentioned previously, a network router comes in two different flavors: wired and wireless.

Both types of routers include Ethernet ports (typically four) for wired connections, but a wireless router also includes an access point (AP) for wireless (Wi-Fi) connections.

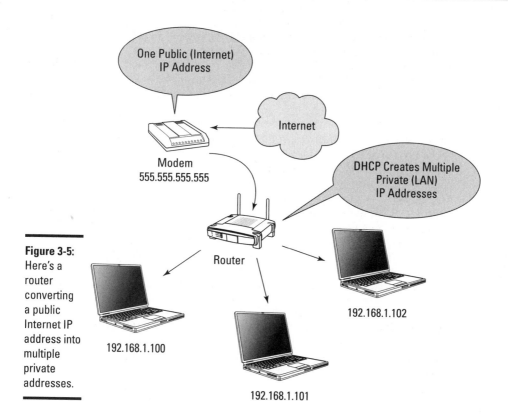

Figure 3-5:
Here's a router converting a public Internet IP address into multiple private addresses.

Typically, the only noticeable difference you see between a wired and wireless router is that the wireless router has one, two, or three antennas emerging from the back of the box. A wired router, however, doesn't have antennas, because it doesn't support wireless (Wi-Fi) connections. Figure 3-6 shows a wireless network router.

Figure 3-6:
A wireless network router, shown here, has at least one antenna; a wired router has none.

A router can (but doesn't have to) include an Internet modem

Computer networking manufacturers also produce wired and wireless routers with built-in Internet (cable or DSL) modems.

When you're browsing the shelves or surfing the online stores, you may see a router referred to as a *cable modem with built-in wireless router, ADSL modem router,* or something similar.

Although a router with a built-in modem can free you from some clutter around your wireless networking gear in your home or office, you should be careful not to make a decision that you'll regret later. Keep in mind these combo devices may not use the latest and greatest technologies. Manufacturers typically don't release the built-in modem feature for each router version or type. This fact is true not only of technologies currently available when making your purchase but also new technologies that will emerge in the future. For example, you might find a built-in wireless router/modem that comes with the latest Wi-Fi standard and technologies for today. However, say that three years pass by without any updates from the manufacturer (which are downloadable from its Web site, usually to fix known bugs or issues but sometimes new features) to the combo device, passing by the new technologies. If this is the case and you want to have the latest and greatest (those three years later), you probably have to abandon the combo idea and purchase the two devices (modem and router) separately.

Your router's basic physical features

This section gets you up close and personal with your router and takes you on a physical tour. I start off with the simplest angle (the front of your router.

The front of your router shouldn't differ from other networking gear in the sense that it should be filled with status (LED) lights. Lights are usually included for each port or jack on the back of the router to show whether the device or computer is connected.

You may find some *wireless* routers that have a (proprietary) button that can be used to help secure your wireless network. Instead of having to access the router's configuration pages to set up encryption, you can just press the button on the router and (after a certain amount of time, such as a minute) click a button on the manufacturer's software on your computers. Then your router and computers are configured with the same encryption settings and key, just by performing a few pushes and clicks of buttons, without your having to understand all the technical jargon and settings.

Now, to see where all the action takes place, check out the back of your router (or see the example in Figure 3-7).

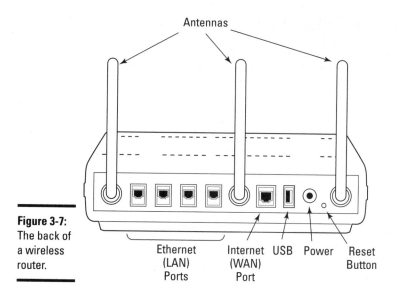

Antennas

Figure 3-7:
The back of
a wireless
router.

Ethernet   Internet USB   Power   Reset
(LAN)   (WAN)   Button
Ports   Port

Figure 3-7 shows antennas because it's an example of a wireless router. (As noted previously, wired routers don't need antennas.) The router shown in actually has three antennas, which is typical in wireless N products; however, the number of antennas varies, depending upon the type of router you're using.

As mentioned earlier in this chapter, your router, whether it's wired or wireless, typically includes four Ethernet ports (refer to Figure 3-7) for wired connections to computers or other network devices. These ports may or may not be labeled on the router; however, you can usually easily identify them because they are typically set right next to each other, away from other ports.

The router includes another Ethernet port usually labeled *WAN* (for Wide Area Network) or *Internet*. This is the port where you plug in the Internet connection. You can easily identify this port because it's usually a loner that's set apart from the regular (usually four) Ethernet ports.

Your router may also have a USB port (depending upon the supported features) that may give you another way to connect your Internet connection or to plug in a flash drive loaded with an encryption key (which can make securing your network easier). Even though you can check whether your router has a USB port (either by looking on the back of it or reading the specifications online or on the box before you buy), you need to check the product documentation for a definite answer on the functionality of the USB port.

Your router needs electrical power, so of course it has a power plug to connect the power adapter.

Last but not least, most routers include a reset button so that you can restore the device's factory settings if need be. This may be a button that you can easily see and press or may be inside a small hole that requires you to push a paper clip through to be able to press the button.

Untangling the Cables Used in Networking

The previous sections of this chapter tell you about your main networking components. This section tells you about the cables and wires that provide the connections between all those components. Though you won't be a certified electrician at the end of this section, you will understand enough to purchase your own cables for small runs, or even enough to figure out the specification requirements to wire your entire home or small office.

The long-beloved Ethernet cable (Cat5)

No matter what type of network you plan to set up, you're highly likely to use Ethernet cables of some sort. Ethernet cables are even used in wireless scenarios in which you may not think that wires need to be used.

The many uses of Ethernet cable

You may find yourself using Ethernet cables to interconnect the following devices:

+ Modem to computer or to router

+ Router to computer

+ Computer to computer

There are many types and categories of Ethernet cable (which I discuss in a bit); however, you'll probably use Cat6 or Cat5e, short for Category 6 and Category 5 Enhanced, respectively. You'll most likely use the unshielded twisted-pair (UTP) version of cable, as well.

The look and feel of an Ethernet cable

Despite the technical names, Ethernet cable is quite simple. Although cable makers produce this cabling in many colors, blue has been the most common until recently. The cable is circular and about one-quarter of an inch wide. The connectors (technically named RJ-45 connectors) on each end look like enlarged, or widened, telephone connectors.

These days, cable makers are getting fancy, so you may see different Ethernet cable designs, such as a variety of colors (maybe gray, white, or yellow) or a flat, tape-like cable. (Who says geeks can't be creative?) Nevertheless, all Ethernet cables should have the enlarged, phone-like connectors.

Unless you're setting up a wired network and your computers sit more than several feet apart, you'll probably use short Ethernet cables (between two to three feet. This is typically long enough to connect your modem and router or a PC to your router (again, as long as the computers are close together). These cables should come with your devices, and you don't want to throw them out. Unless you misplace a cable (or your dog decides to exercise its jaws), you won't have to go out and purchase your own.

If you're setting up a wired network with long runs between your computers, your router, or both, you'll probably have to purchase your own Ethernet cable(s). This is usually when you'll need to study up a bit on the specifications and flavors (covered in the remaining sections; otherwise, you may want to save your brain power and skip over the next sections.

Standards for Ethernet networking products

Similarly to wireless, there are standards that Ethernet cables and Ethernet hardware follow so that products and cables from all manufacturers work together. Products that support Ethernet connections are labeled with the supported standards, which can be one or more of the following:

+ **10BASE-T:** Supports Ethernet speeds of 10 Mbps. Its formal IEEE standard is named 802.3i.

+ **100BASE-TX:** Supports Ethernet speeds of 100 Mbps. Its IEEE standard is named 802.3u. Just about all networking products that support this standard also support 10BASE-T.

+ **1000BASE-T (Gigabit):** As you can probably assume, this type supports Ethernet speeds of 1,000 Mbps, or 1 Gbps (gigabit) — which is ten times faster than products that support 100 Mbps. Its IEEE standard is 802.3ab. Products that support this standard may also support the two other standards.

You find the supported Ethernet standards listed on product boxes, descriptions, and on data sheets of networking hardware that supports Ethernet connections (has Ethernet ports). Additionally, the product name or labeling for Ethernet products, as with wired routers and adapters, may include the speed. For instance, you may see 10/100 Ethernet, 10/100 network card, or gigabit router.

Ethernet cabling categories: Cat5, 5e, and 6

In addition to Ethernet standards, there are categories of Ethernet cable, a set of standards to define the specifications and requirements of just the cabling used for Ethernet connections. The varying cabling categories support certain Ethernet standards. The common Ethernet cable categories used today in homes and small businesses are as follows:

✦ **Cat5:** An older cable design that supports data rates (speed) at 10 or 100 Mbps, with a maximum cable length of 328 feet (100 meters).

✦ **Cat5e:** An enhanced version of Cat5, which supports an increased data rate up to 1,000 Mbps (equivalent to a gigabit) while maintaining the same maximum-length specification.

✦ **Cat6:** This is the most likely category you see today on the shelves or when browsing online stores. Although this category of Ethernet cable doesn't offer an additional increase of data rates and actually has more stringent length requirements (295 feet, or 90 meters), it does offer other performance enhancements.

Each category of Ethernet cable has two versions, as follows:

✦ **Stranded (or braided) cable** has several small-gauge wires in each insulation sleeve, making it more flexible and more suitable for shorter distances, such as 30 feet or less.

✦ **Solid cable** has one larger-gauge wire in each sleeve, thus providing better electrical performance than stranded cable does. This cabling is traditionally used for permanent installations, such as inside walls and through ceilings. This is also the recommended cabling to use when running additional access points (APs) to expand a wireless network.

Straight and crossover cable types

For the stranded versions of all the categories of Ethernet cables, two additional types (or technical terms!) exist (straight (also called patch) and crossover. The differences between these two are in the wiring of the pins in the connectors, which you can see only by cutting open the cable.

You use the straight type Ethernet cabling in most cases, such as when you're connecting the following:

✦ Modem to computer

✦ Modem to router

✦ Router to computer

You usually use crossover Ethernet cables only when directly connecting two network components that you would normally connect through a router. For example, you can use the crossover cable type when directly connecting computers together to create a computer-to-computer network.

You should keep in mind that newer technologies have eliminated the need for crossover cables in some situations. For example, most network adapters now contain some type of automatic crossover feature, which allows you to use a "regular" (straight type) Ethernet cable for a computer-to-computer connection.

The cable of choice in stores and businesses

Ethernet is also a common choice (or must) among professionals and network administrators when installing networks and computers within office buildings and stores. Now you find out that Ethernet surrounds us all!

The next time you're at the check-out counter of your favorite store, grocery, or mall, you can impress your loved one by pointing out any Ethernet cables emerging from the back of the cash register. You might even make a bigger impression by taking a stab at its technical specs, such as by mentioning "100-Base-T."

Telephone-line cable

Telephone wire isn't traditionally a networking cable, so I don't get into the details about it here. However, you should know that you may come across it somewhere on your network, such as when using the following:

✦ DSL Internet connections

✦ Digital (VoIP) phones

✦ The Phone-Line networking method

USB cables

USB cabling is also not a traditional networking cable, so I don't go into detail about it in this book; however, you may come across it during your home networking (and computing) journey, such as when connecting the following:

✦ Modem to computer

✦ Print server to computer

Going Wireless with Access Points (APs)

Access points (APs for short) can give you the freedom to move about your home or office while staying connected to your network and Internet service. The networking industry and media often use the term *Wi-Fi*, sometimes defined as "wireless fidelity" or "freedom from wires," to describe these types of connections and the equipment that enables them.

Wireless routers and APs

As touched on in an earlier section, wireless routers contain an AP. This built-in capability is what distinguishes a wireless router from a wired router. A wireless router is the closest most home networkers will come to an access point. Independent APs are usually needed only in larger networks within enterprises, and sometimes in small offices.

Independent APs

In addition to their being integrated within wireless routers, APs are produced as independent or stand-alone network devices, one of which is shown in Figure 3-8.

Figure 3-8:
A stand-alone access point (AP).

Courtesy of D-Link Systems, Inc.

The omission of routing features (or the "courier" service performed by routers discussed earlier) from these traditional APs is what sets them apart from a typical wireless router.

Network expansion with APs

Traditional independent APs are often used within large businesses, and possibly small offices, to extend the coverage of an existing wired network, provide another access method (wireless) for the network users, or both. In some cases, you may also choose to install access points within your home for similar reasons.

Figure 3-9 shows an example of where APs may be placed on a home network. In the figure, two APs are connected to a wireless router, which is connected to the modem for Internet service in a home. You should keep in mind that the wireless router can be a wired router instead. In that case, the only Wi-Fi access is from the two APs.

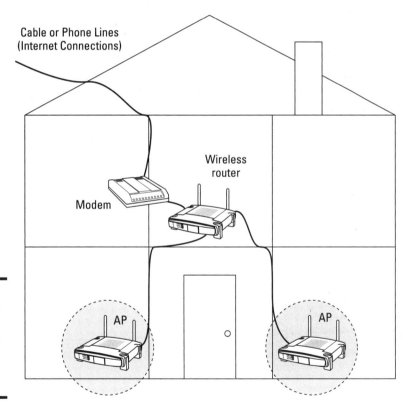

Figure 3-9: Placement of access points on a typical home network.

APs and wires

Even though access points are supposed to offer "freedom from wires," the use of APs still requires you to run cables. The connections from the AP to the users are wireless, but for you to use the network and Internet, the APs must be wired directly to the network (or router.) You can see an example of this in Figure 3-9, shown in the previous section.

A, B, G, N standardization

As with many other electronic products and goods, standards are followed for computer networking gear. When manufacturers develop their networking products, they follow certain defined and published requirements so that their networking products will also work with those from other manufacturers, achieving interoperability.

In some cases, you may not need to take the time to learn about the standards of a particular product or technology; however, with wireless networking you should do so, or at least be aware of their existence. This is a good idea in part because of the complexities of wireless networking and because multiple standards (A, B, G, and N (exist. You can't just pick any access point off the shelf and expect it to work with a randomly selected wireless network card. Instead, you need to make sure that you pick a common standard, or multiple standards that you know are interoperable.

If you haven't already, you can read up on these different standards in Book I, Chapter 1.

The look of an AP

This section examines the outer surfaces of this piece of equipment, an access point (AP).

As do modems and routers, the fronts of APs contain status (LED) lights to let you know what's happening. An access point typically only includes three such lights, indicating the following:

✦ Power

✦ LAN (router or hub) connection

✦ Wireless LAN or WLAN (Wi-Fi) activity

The backs of network devices are full of places to which you connect wires and cables, and the back of a typical AP (see Figure 3-10) has four such connection points:

✦ Antennas

✦ Ethernet (LAN) port

✦ Power

✦ Reset button

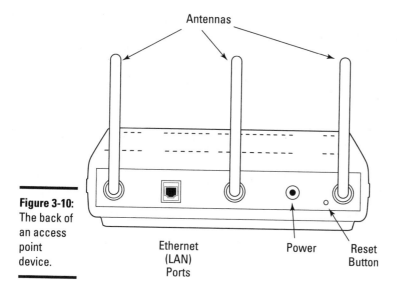

Antennas

Ethernet
(LAN)
Ports

Power

Reset
Button

Figure 3-10:
The back of
an access
point
device.

Connecting with Adapters (or NICs)

In order for computers and devices to connect and communicate with a network, they must have their own network adapter, also called a network interface card (NIC). Without help, computers don't have the ability to understand the language used by networks and don't have the resources (that is, an Ethernet port or antennas) to make the connections. A network adapter has these capabilities and physical attributes, thus making it a vital requirement for your network.

Wired and wireless adapters

For traditional home networks, such as when using a router or using the computer-to-computer method, you can use two different types of network adapters (wired and/or wireless adapters. A wired adapter enables you to physically connect to a network using an Ethernet cable; a wireless adapter allows you to connect to a network with wireless (Wi-Fi) capability.

An adapter's "form factor"

Although there are only two main types (wired and wireless) of network adapters, there's a wider variety of interfaces that you can use to "plug in" a network adapter. This type of characteristic is commonly known as an adapter's form factor. The types of form factors fall under a few categories, as follows:

✦ **Desktop cards:** Installed in your computer by way of a PCI, PCI express, or SCSI slot

✦ **Laptop (or notebook) cards:** Either an external card that slides into a computer's PCMCIA slot or integrated within the laptop

✦ **USB adapters:** Plugged into any computer or device with a USB port

✦ **Mobile device adapters:** Used for PDAs, cameras, and game consoles; installed into a CF or a unique proprietary slot

Not dependent on routers

Adapters aren't dependent on routers, meaning that network adapters can communicate with each other directly. Wired adapters can be connected to each other with an Ethernet cable, and wireless adapters can connect through the airwaves.

Having adapters communicate directly with each other is called *ad hoc,* *computer-to-computer,* or *peer-to-peer networking* — all of which refer to the same thing.

The look of adapters

Because there's a wide assortment of network adapter types and form factors, this section takes a look at just a few particular configurations, which should be enough to give you an idea of what network adapters generally look like.

To begin with, the desktop adapter shown in Figure 3-11 is an Ethernet adapter for wired network connections. (A wireless adapter looks very similar but has an antenna, or multiple antennas, instead of an Ethernet port.) Additionally, a desktop adapter's bus connector differs from others, depending upon the type of slot it goes into — PCI, PCI express, or SSCI.

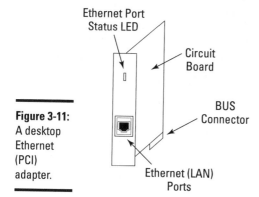

Figure 3-11: A desktop Ethernet (PCI) adapter.

A desktop network card slides into an open slot within your computer and plugs into its particular connector. The circuit board part of the adapter remains inside the computer case but the back is exposed, so you can access the Ethernet port or antenna(s) and the see the status lights.

Another type of notebook card, which is shown in Figure 3-12, is a wireless adapter. (A wired adapter, in contrast, includes an Ethernet port instead of an antenna.) Both types of notebook cards, wireless and wired, often feature a raised or enlarged surface and a status LED light at one end, as depicted in the figure. The end of the notebook card that slides into the computer has little holes that accept the PCMCIA pins when the card is fully inserted.

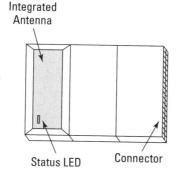

Figure 3-12: A wireless notebook (PCMCIA) adapter.

The antennas for notebook wireless adapters can be integrated into the card, as shown in Figure 3-12, or have a plug that connects to an external antenna.

Yet another type of adapter is an Ethernet USB adapter (for wired connections), which has an Ethernet port instead of an integrated antenna. Some USB adapters may be designed as one component (such as the one shown in Figure 3-13); others may include a short cable with the adapter on the end.

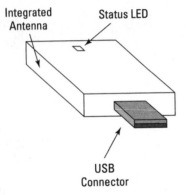

Integrated
Antenna

Status LED

USB
Connector

Figure 3-13:
A USB
adapter.

Book II

Setting Up Networks

The 5th Wave   By Rich Tennant

"Good news! I found a place where the router works with the PC upstairs and the one in the basement."

Contents at a Glance

Chapter 1: Setting Up User Accounts on Computers

In This Chapter

✔ Discovering the world of user accounts and privileges

✔ Adding, removing, and editing accounts

✔ Setting login preferences

✔ Creating a password reset disk

*B*efore you set up your network, you should get your computers situated with user accounts for each member of the family. When you do so, all the household members have their own Desktops to fill with icons, and their own backgrounds to showcase their favorite photos, and so on, to personalize their computing experience.

Setting up separate user accounts on computers also gives those of you who are parents the ability to enable parental controls and properly implement network sharing preferences.

In this chapter, you discover the types of user accounts you can create and how to add, remove, and edit them. You also see how to set login preferences and create a password reset disk that you can use if a user forgets his or her password.

Understanding User Account Types and Privileges

To make computers easy to share on a network, operating systems (Windows, Mac, and Ubuntu) let you create multiple user accounts — one (or more) for each person in your home if you want. This way, each user can customize his or her own computer. Examples of items that can be unique to an account include the following:

✦ Look and feel of the desktop, windows, and more

✦ Desktop and Start menu icons

✦ Background color/image

✦ Document folders

+ Favorite Web sites

+ Web browsing history

+ Account password

 Having separate user accounts even allows programs to be installed so that only one user account can access them. Look for this type of option in the installation or setup program of an application, which is usually called Install This Application For. On the part where you fill in your personal information, you usually have two options: Anyone Who Uses This Computer (All Users) or Only For Me (Your Account Name).

To make your computer more secure and to keep children safer, operating systems have multiple account types. These account types have various privileges. This way, the little ones of a household can't install software, change system settings, and do other important things without parental guidance. Additionally, newer operating systems (Mac OS X Leopard and Windows Vista) let parents impose parental controls for accounts they select.

The exact names for the account types and their privileges vary among operating systems and even among the different versions of the same operating system (such as Windows 2000, XP, and Vista). The next sections review each operating system's account types.

Windows account types

Windows XP and Vista have three different user account types, as follows:

+ **Computer Administrator (in Windows XP); Administrator (in Vista):** People with this account can do everything and anything on the computer. Because no restrictions are enabled, this type of account usually isn't suitable for children. This account also lets you modify the accounts on your computer.

+ **Limited (in Windows XP); Standard (in Vista):** This account type restricts many important privileges, such as adding and removing software and hardware and making system settings changes. This type is great for children and any other people you don't want messing with any settings.

+ **Guest:** This account doesn't appear by default and must be enabled. It also restricts important privileges as the Limited (or Standard) account does; however, it can't be password protected. This is great if you want to have an account ready for people — such as your friends and extended family — when they want to hop on the computer.

Windows 2000 includes similar account types using different names. Because this Windows version was built more for enterprise networks, you'll see many more account types when adding or editing users.

For an even a better idea of the differences between the account types of Windows XP and Vista, see Table 1-1.

Table 1-1:	Comparing Account Types of Windows XP and Vista		
	(Computer) **Administrator**	*Limited* **(or Standard)**	*Guest* **Account**
Install and uninstall programs and hardware	X		
Make system-wide changes	X		
Access and read all (non-private) files	X		
Create, edit, and delete user accounts	X		
Change your own account name or type	X		
Run and use programs already installed	X	X	X
Can be password protected	X	X	
Change your own account picture	X	X	
Create, change, or remove your own password	X	X	

Even though people with Limited accounts can, by default, create, change, or remove their own passwords, you can disable this privilege. I cover this feature in more detail in the "Changing Advanced Account Settings" section later in this chapter.

Windows Vista User Account Control (UAC) feature — for extra security

Windows Vista includes a feature that's new to the Windows operating system. This feature is called *User Account Control* (UAC), and it provides additional security to help protect you from viruses and spyware. It provides this protection by putting Windows in the Standard account state (even for Administrator accounts) until a task that requires Administrator-level access is performed, such as when system settings are accessed in the Control Panel. A dialog box (see Figure 1-1) then appears, showing the program trying to be accessed and asking you whether you started it.

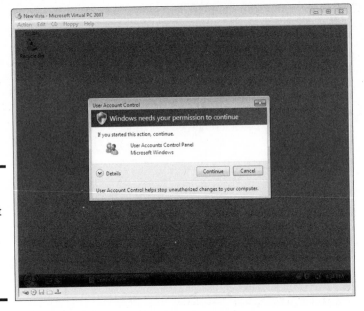

Figure 1-1:
The UAC
prompt that
appears
in an
Admini-
strator
account.

This way, you're notified if a virus or spyware infection or some other unauthorized process is trying to modify your system settings. If this is the case, click Cancel on the UAC verification prompt to stop the harmful action.

Links and shortcuts to programs or tasks that require Administrator-level access are marked with the Windows shield. For an example of the Windows shield I'm talking about, click Start, open Control Panel, and look for the two links under the User Accounts and Family Safety category, and the one under the Security category, that have this shield.

When people on Standard accounts try to access or perform Administrator-level programs or tasks, they get a similar prompt.

However, a password for an Administrator account must be entered before the program is opened or the action is performed. If you have a child who's trying to do something on the computer, this is when you'll hear him or her calling for you. Then you can enter your password, if you choose to do so, and monitor what the little one is doing. When you close down the restricted program, authorization for it will be required again.

These UAC pop-up alerts can, however, be annoying, especially if you access these restricted areas regularly and don't have anyone around to worry about restricting access from. The good news is that you can easily disable the UAC feature and get rid of the alerts. You have two ways to go about doing this: disabling the UAC altogether, or disabling it only for administrators.

Completely disabling the UAC

Disabling the UAC will make your system a bit less secure and more prone to malware, as discussed earlier. Also, the UAC pop-ups will be disabled for Standard accounts. Rather than be able to input an Administrator's password to access restricted programs or actions, Standard account users are simply told that they don't have privileges. In that case, you'll have to log in to your Administrator account, perform the action, and then return to the Standard account. If you still want to disable UAC, here's how to do it:

1. **Click Start.**

2. **Click Control Panel.**

If using the Classic Start menu, click Settings first.

3. **Click the User Accounts and Family Safety category.**

If in the Classic view, skip this step.

4. **Click User Accounts.**

5. **Click the Turn User Account Control On Or Off link.**

6. **Deselect the option and click OK.**

A pop-up menu appears, stating that a restart is required in order to apply the changes. Specify whether to restart now or later (either is fine).

You may notice that people in Standard user accounts can view some restricted settings, but any changes they make won't be saved.

Disabling the UAC only for Administrator accounts

Disabling the UAC this way makes your system less secure only for Administrator accounts. Standard accounts continue to receive the UAC pop-up verification alerts. This is probably the way to go if Standard accounts are regularly used on your computer. This, however, requires editing the Windows Registry.

Be *very* careful when editing your Windows Registry. Mistakes can cause major problems for your computer. It's also a good idea to make a backup copy prior to making any changes.

To disable the UAC for the Administrator account, follow these steps:

1. **Click Start.**

2. **In the Search field (just under All Programs), type regedit and press Enter.**

If you're using the classic Start menu, click Run, enter regedit, and click OK.

HKEY_LOCAL_MACHINE\SOFTWARE\Microsoft\Windows\

CurrentVersion\Policies\System

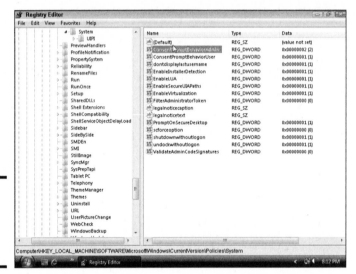

Figure 1-2:
Navigating
to the
correct
folder.

3. **In the pane on the right, double-click the following item:**

ConsentPromptBehaviorAdmin

4. **In the Value data field, enter the number zero and then press OK.**

5. **Close the Registry Editor by clicking the X button in the upper-right corner of the window to apply the changes.**

Account types in Mac OS X and Leopard

In Mac OS X Tiger, you have the choice between two account types:

✦ **Administrator:** Just as in Windows, Administrator accounts have full privileges and access to the computer, so this type of account should be given only to trusted people.

✦ **Standard:** This account type restricts the user from editing or configuring other account settings. Software can still be installed and settings belonging to the account can be changed.

Mac OS X Leopard introduces three more account types (in addition to Administrator and Standard):

✦ **Managed with Parental Controls:** Lets you manage the account privileges through parental controls. You can, for example, filter Internet content and limit access and usage of applications, e-mail, iChat, and the computer itself.

✦ **Sharing Only:** This is a dummy account into which no one can log in on the computer; however, the account can be used when trying to remotely access shared files on the computer from other Apple computers. When a Sharing Only account is used to access shared files, no personal account folders are accessible. So if you have other Apple computers that you want to be able to access shared folders, but you don't want to give access to anyone's personal files, creating this account type is useful.

✦ **Group:** This allows you to assign multiple user accounts to a group, which can simplify editing sharing privileges for folders you share on the network. This is particularly useful when you have lots of different user accounts on the computer.

Book II
Chapter 1

Account types in Ubuntu

The Linux distribution Ubuntu uses the word *Profile* to describe the privilege classes, which are the following:

✦ **Administrator:** As do the accounts in Windows and Mac OS X, the accounts set to the Administrator Profile have full privileges and access to the computer. So this type of account should be given only to trusted people such as you.

✦ **Desktop user:** This is similar to the Limited and Standard account types of Windows XP and Vista. Access is given to just about everything except making system changes.

✦ **Unprivileged:** Accounts set to this profile don't have any of the listed privileges, including access to external, CD-ROM, and floppy drives, and the use of hardware such as modems, scanners, and audio devices. These accounts can still use programs and configure account settings and preferences, though.

Adding, Removing, and Editing Accounts

When you're creating or modifying your user accounts, keep the following things in mind:

✦ **Create the same accounts on each computer:** If you or other people in your home use multiple computers, you may find it useful to use the same exact name and password for the accounts on all the computers. So, for example, if Billy's account name is Wild Billy on his own computer, it should be Wild Billy on the family PC he uses, and Wild Billy on anyone else's laptop he likes to get on once in a while. This not only helps you remember your login information but also can help out when you need to configure sharing permissions for your shared folders and computers.

✦ **Create secure passwords:** Because your password is the key to unlocking the computer to change settings, disabling parental controls, installing software, and much more, make sure that you create a good password. Do *not* use or include easy, guessable, information such as the following:

- Family or pet names
- Street name or number
- Phone number
- The word *password* or *pass*
- The word *administrator* or *admin*
- Common words or names

To have a secure password, *do* include the following:

- Seven or more characters
- A variety of characters, including letters, numbers, and symbols
- Upper- and lowercase letters

✦ **You can create a password reset disk:** This is a feature of Windows that was created in case you forget your password. You can pop in the password reset disk to create a new password. This ability can be very useful, especially for people who don't use the computer regularly or who easily forget passwords. First, though, you must create the disk, which I tell you how to do in the "Creating and Using a Password Reset Disk (for Windows XP and Vista Only)" section, later in this chapter.

Accessing user account settings

To add, remove, or edit accounts in Windows 2000 or XP and in Mac OS X, you should make sure you are logged into your Administrator account so that you have full access to the settings. If you are in Windows Vista or Ubuntu, you can actually be logged into a Standard account and still have full access. Just enter your password when you receive the prompt.

Accessing user account settings in Windows 2000

Here's how to access the user account settings in Windows 2000:

1. **Click Start.**
2. **Click Settings.**

3. **Click Control Panel.**

4. **Double-click Users and Passwords.**

The User and Password window appears, listing the accounts on the computer and containing buttons for you to add, remove, and edit the accounts.

Accessing user account settings in Windows XP or Vista

To access the user account settings in Windows XP or Vista, follow these steps:

1. **Click Start.**

2. **Click Control Panel.**

If using the Classic Start menu, click Settings and then click Control Panel.

3. **Click the User Accounts (in XP) or User Accounts and Family Safety (in Vista) category.**

If you're using the Classic view, skip this step.

4. **Click User Accounts.**

Figure 1-3 shows the User Accounts window that appears in Windows XP.

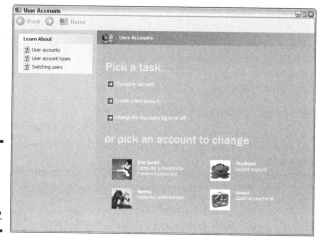

Figure 1-3:
The User Accounts window in Windows XP.

Accessing user account settings in Mac OS X Tiger and Leopard

Here's how to access the user account settings in Mac OS X Tiger and Leopard:

1. **Click the Apple icon on the taskbar.**

2. **Click System Preferences.**

3. **Click Accounts.**

The Accounts window appears, listing the accounts on the computer and containing buttons for you to add, remove, and edit the accounts.

Accessing user account settings in Ubuntu (Linux)

If you're using Ubuntu, here's how to do it:

1. **Click System from the Ubuntu toolbar.**

2. **Choose Administration.**

3. **Click Users and Groups.**

4. **Enter your Administration password and click OK.**

The User Settings window appears, listing the accounts on the computer and containing buttons for you to add, remove, and edit the accounts.

Adding user accounts

As mentioned earlier, in the "Understanding User Account Types and Privileges" section, for each of your computers, you should create a separate user account for each person who uses a particular computer. This way, all users can change their Desktops and have their own document folders, and you can properly set parental controls if you have children.

Adding user accounts in Windows 2000

In Windows 2000, here's how to create another user account:

1. **Choose Start⇨Settings⇨Control Panel.**

2. **Double-click Users and Passwords.**

The Users and Passwords window appears, listing the accounts on the computer and containing buttons for you to add, remove, and edit the accounts.

3. **Click the Add button.**

The Add a New User wizard appears.

4. **Enter desired account information.**

5. **Click Next.**

6. **Enter a password (twice) and click Next.**

If you don't want the account to be password protected, click Next without entering a password.

7. Select an account level and click Finish.

You see the Users and Password window again, with the new account added to the list.

Adding user accounts in Windows XP

If you are using Windows XP, here's how to create a user account:

1. Click Start and then choose Control Panel.

If using the Classic Start menu, click Start and then choose Settings⇨ Control Panel.

2. Click the User Accounts category.

If you're using the Classic control panel view, skip this step.

3. Click User Accounts.

You should see the main User Accounts window, listing the accounts on the computer and containing buttons for you to add, remove, and edit the accounts.

4. Under the Pick a Task title, click the Create a New Account link.

You should see a window such as that in Figure 1-4.

Figure 1-4:
Creating a
new user
account in
Windows XP.

5. Enter a name for the account and click Next.

You continue on to Pick an Account Type page.

6. Pick an account type.

You can refer to the "Understanding User Account Types and Privileges" section, earlier in this chapter, for details on the differences between the two types.

To create a password for the account, you must edit the account (discussed later) and apply the password after it's created. If you prefer, you can force the user to create a password when he or she logs in. You can force this by using the advanced settings, discussed later in this chapter in the "Changing Advanced Account Settings" section.

7. Click Create Account.

You see the Users Accounts window again, with the new account added to the list.

In Windows XP and Vista, you can force your computer to return to the Welcome screen after resuming from the screen saver. This way, if you walk away from the computer and the screen saver comes on, to get back into your account, someone must enter your password. You can enable this in your screen saver settings.

Adding user accounts in Windows Vista

Here's how to create users in Windows Vista:

1. Choose Start⇨Control Panel.

If using the Classic Start menu, choose Start⇨Settings⇨Control Panel.

2. Click the User Accounts and Family Safety category.

If you're using the Classic view, skip this step.

3. Click User Accounts.

You should see the main User Accounts window, listing the accounts on the computer and containing buttons for you to add, remove, and edit the accounts.

4. Click the Manage Another Account link.

5. Just under the box that contains the user account pictures, click the Create a New Account link.

6. Enter a name for the account into the New Account Name box.

7. Click a radio button to select an account type.

You can refer to the "Understanding User Account Types and Privileges" section, earlier in this chapter, for details on the differences between the two types.

To create a password for the account, you must edit the account (discussed later) and apply the password after it's created. If you prefer, you can force the user to create a password when he or she logs in. You can do so by using the advanced settings, discussed later in the "Changing Advanced Account Settings" section.

8. Click Create Account.

You return to the Manage Accounts window, where you see the account you just created added to the list.

Shortcuts to the Manage Accounts window are displayed in the Control Panel when in Category view. These shortcuts are labeled Add or Remove User Accounts.

Adding user accounts in Mac OS X Tiger and Leopard

Here's how to add users in Mac OS X Tiger and Leopard:

1. Click the Apple icon and then click System Preferences.

2. Click Accounts.

The Accounts window appears, listing the accounts on the computer and containing buttons for you to add, remove, and edit the accounts.

3. Click the padlock icon in the lower-left corner (if it's locked), enter your administer account name and password into the fields, and click OK.

4. Below the list of accounts on the left side of the window, click the plus sign.

A drop-down menu appears, containing the settings to create a new account.

5. Select an account type in Leopard by choosing New Account. If using Tiger, either select the Allow User To Administer This Computer option at the bottom to create an Administrator account, or leave it unselected to create a Standard account.

Refer to the "Understanding User Account Types and Privileges" section, earlier in this chapter, for details on the differences between these types of accounts.

6. Enter a Name and Short Name into their respective fields.

The Name is what you'll see on the login window, and the Short Name is the name of the Home directory that will be created in the Users folder for the account.

After the account is created, you cannot easily change its Short Name.

7. Enter a password into the Password and Verify fields and click Next.

If you don't want the account to be password protected, leave the password fields blank.

8. Enter something that will remind you of the password into the Password Hint field.

Book II
Chapter 1

Setting Up
User Accounts
on Computers

This is optional to help you remember your password. Just bear in mind that everyone can see this hint from the login screen, so don't hint too much.

 9. **In Leopard, select or deselect the Turn On FileVault Protection option.**

When enabled, this feature encrypts the contents of the account's home directory, providing protection of your data if your computer gets into the wrong hands.

10. **Click Create Account.**

You are returned to the Manage Accounts window, where you see the account you just created added to the list.

Adding user accounts in Ubuntu

If you're using Ubuntu, here's how to add a user account:

 1. **From the Ubuntu toolbar, choose System➪Administration➪Users and Groups.**

 2. **Enter your Administration password and click OK.**

The User Settings window appears, listing the accounts on the computer and containing buttons for you to add, remove, and edit the accounts.

 3. **Click the Add User button.**

You see a window similar to Figure 1-5.

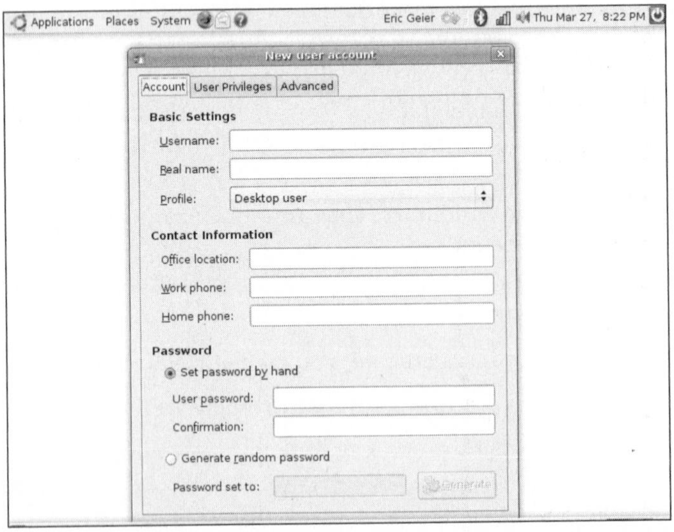

Figure 1-5:
Creating a new user account in Ubuntu.

4. **Enter a username and real name into their respective fields.**

   Your personal folders are named after the username you specify here. The Username must be all lowercase.

5. **Select an account type from the drop-down list labeled Profile.**

   Refer to the "Understanding User Account Types and Privileges" section, earlier in this chapter, for details on the differences between these types of accounts.

6. **Enter your contact information, if you want, into the Office Location, Work Phone, and Home Phone fields.**

7. **Either select the Set Password By Hand option and enter a password into the User Password and Confirmation fields, or select the Generate Random Password option to have Ubuntu create a secure password for you, shown in the Password Set To field.**

8. **Click the User Privileges tab.**

   Here you can see exactly what privileges the account will have.

9. **Click OK to create the account.**

   You are taken back to the User Settings window, where you see the account you just created added to the list.

Book II
Chapter 1

Setting Up
User Accounts
on Computers

Removing user accounts

Because user accounts can have their own look and feel, settings, folders, and favorites, something must be done to this information and these files when you delete an account. What happens exactly depends upon what operating system you're using and what you tell it when you delete the account. Following is a list of the items and folders that can be automatically saved if you choose to do so during the account deletion:

✦ Windows 2000:

  • Desktop

  • My Documents

  • Favorites

✦ Windows XP:

  • Desktop

  • My Documents

✦ Windows Vista:

  • Desktop

  • Documents

- Favorites

- Music

- Pictures

- Video folders

✦ Mac OS X Tiger/Leopard and Ubuntu:

- Home folder

 Usually not covered in any automatic saving are e-mails, account settings and preferences, and Web history. If you need these items, save or move them to another (nonuser) location on the hard drive.

Removing user accounts in Windows 2000

In Windows 2000, here's how you can remove user accounts from your computer:

1. **Choose Start➪Settings➪Control Panel.**

2. **Double-click Users and Passwords.**

The User and Password window appears, listing the accounts on the computer and containing buttons for you to add, remove, and edit the accounts.

3. **Choose the account you want to remove.**

4. **Click the Remove button.**

5. **Verify that you are deleting the correct account and then click Yes.**

Removing user accounts in Windows XP

If you are using Windows XP, remove user accounts by following these steps:

1. **Choose Start➪Control Panel.**

If using the Classic Start menu, choose Start➪Settings➪Control Panel.

2. **Click the User Accounts category.**

If you're using the Classic Control Panel view, skip this step.

3. **Click User Accounts.**

You see the main User Accounts window, listing the accounts on the computer and containing buttons for you to add, remove, and edit the accounts.

TIP

4. **Click the account you want to remove.**

You can't delete the account you're currently logged into. Also, the account you want to delete must be logged off.

5. **Click the Delete the Account link.**

This should be the last link of the list.

6. **Specify whether you want to keep the files on the account's Desktop and My Documents.**

7. **Verify that you are deleting the right account and understand that you may be deleting files that you can't recover; then click Delete Account.**

You should be returned to the main User Accounts window.

Removing user accounts in Windows Vista

Here's how to remove a user account in Windows Vista:

1. **Choose Start⇔Control Panel.**

If using the Classic Start menu, choose Start⇔Settings⇔Control Panel.

2. **Click the User Accounts and Family Safety category.**

If you're using the Classic view, skip this step.

3. **Click User Accounts.**

You see the main User Accounts window, listing the accounts on the computer and containing buttons for you to add, remove, and edit the accounts.

4. **Click the Manage Another Account link.**

5. **On the UAC prompt that appears, click Continue.**

You see icons for all your accounts.

6. **Click the account you want to remove.**

7. **Near the bottom of the Account task list, click the Delete the Account link.**

The Account isn't deleted just yet; first, you're asked what you want to do with the Account files.

8. **Click the Keep Files button to keep the files on the account's Desktop and My Documents or click the Delete Files button to delete the files contained in the Account folders.**

9. **Verify that you are deleting the right account and understand that you may be deleting files that you can't recover and then click Delete Account.**

You return to the main Manage Accounts window.

Removing user accounts in Mac OS X Tiger

Here's how to remove a user account in Mac OS X Tiger:

1. **Click the Apple icon and then choose System Preferences.**

2. **Click Accounts.**

The Accounts window appears, listing the accounts on the computer and containing buttons for you to add, remove, and edit the accounts.

3. **Click the padlock icon in the lower-left corner (if it's locked), enter your administrator account name and password into the fields, and click OK.**

4. **Select the account you want to delete and click the minus sign.**

The minus sign is under the list of accounts on the left side of the window.

5. **Look at the user account specified in the dialog box that's on the screen to confirm that you're deleting the right account.**

6. **Click OK to save the contents of the account's home folder, or click Delete Immediately to delete the home folder.**

Removing user accounts in Mac OS X Leopard

Here's how to remove a user account in Mac OS X Leopard:

1. **Click the Apple icon and then choose System Preferences.**

2. **Click Accounts.**

The Accounts window appears, listing the accounts on the computer and containing buttons for you to add, remove, and edit the accounts.

3. **Click the padlock in the lower-left corner (if it's locked), enter your administrator account name and password into the fields, and click OK.**

4. **Select the account you want to delete and click the minus sign.**

The minus sign is under the list of accounts on the left side of the window.

5. **Look at the user account specified in the dialog box that's on the screen to confirm that you are deleting the right account.**

6. **Specify what you want to do with the account's home folder by selecting one of the radio buttons.**

You're asked to choose one of these buttons when you're deleting a real user account, which is any type except Shared Only.

7. **Click OK to delete the account.**

Removing user accounts in Ubuntu (Linux)

If you're using Ubuntu, here's how to remove an account:

1. **From the Ubuntu toolbar choose System⇨Administration⇨Users and Groups.**

2. **Enter your Administration password and click OK.**

   The User Settings window appears, listing the accounts on the computer and containing buttons for you to add, remove, and edit the accounts.

3. **Choose the account and click the Delete button.**

4. **Confirm that you are deleting the right account.**

   Look at the user account specified in the dialog box that's on the screen.

5. **To delete the account, click the Delete button.**

Editing user accounts

You can easily go back and modify the account name, password, and type for the accounts on your computer. To get these privileges, make sure you're logged into an Administrator account.

Editing user accounts in Windows 2000

Here's how to edit user accounts in Windows 2000:

1. **Choose Start⇨Settings⇨Control Panel.**

2. **Double-click Users and Passwords.**

   The Users and Passwords window appears, listing the accounts on the computer and containing buttons for you to add, remove, and edit the accounts.

3. **Select an account to modify and click Properties.**

4. **Edit the general account information by entering your desired values into the text fields.**

5. **Click the Group Membership tab.**

6. **Change the account type as you wish by selecting a radio button.**

7. **Click OK to save and apply the changes.**

Editing user accounts in Windows XP

If you are using Windows XP, here's how to modify account properties:

1. **Choose Start⇨Control Panel.**

   If using the Classic Start menu, choose Start⇨Settings⇨Control Panel.

2. Click the User Accounts category.

If you're using the Classic Control Panel view, skip this step.

3. Click User Accounts.

You should see the main User Accounts window, listing the accounts on the computer and containing buttons for you to add, remove, and edit the accounts.

4. Click the account you want to edit.

5. Click the links in the main part of the window as needed to make your desired changes.

The only setting you can't access on the other accounts is the .NET Passport setting. Signing up for a .NET Passport account and associating it with your Windows account can help streamline access to numerous services and Web sites.

Editing user accounts in Windows Vista

Here's how to edit user account settings in Windows Vista:

1. Choose Start➪Control Panel.

If using the Classic Start menu, choose Start➪ Settings➪ Control Panel.

2. Click the User Accounts and Family Safety category.

If you're using the Classic view, skip this step.

3. Click User Accounts.

You should see the main User Accounts window, listing the accounts on the computer and containing buttons for you to add, remove, and edit the accounts.

4. Click the Manage Another Account link.

5. Click the account you want to edit.

6. Click the links as needed to make your desired changes.

Though the links for settings aren't arranged the same for other accounts, you can still edit any account setting. Just keep in mind that you can only access (or even enable) the Parental Controls settings for accounts labeled as Limited.

Editing user accounts in Mac OS X Tiger and Leopard

If you're using Mac OS X Tiger or Leopard, here's how to edit accounts:

1. Click the Apple icon and then choose System Preferences.

2. **Click Accounts.**

   The Accounts window appears, listing the accounts on the computer and containing buttons for you to add, remove, and edit the accounts.

3. **Click the padlock icon in the lower-left corner (if it's locked), enter your administrator account name and password into the fields, and click OK.**

4. **Select an account to edit.**

5. **Make your desired changes.**

   Here you can change the account's name, password, and (in Leopard) .Mac User Name. You can quickly enable or disable administrative privileges and Parental Controls for the account.

6. **If you want, click the padlock icon to lock the settings when you're done.**

Editing user accounts in Ubuntu (Linux)

If you're using Ubuntu, here's how to edit user accounts:

1. **From the Ubuntu toolbar, choose System⇨Administration⇨ Users and Groups.**

2. **Enter your Administration password and click OK.**

   The User Settings window appears, listing the accounts on the computer and containing buttons for you to add, remove, and edit the accounts.

3. **Choose the account you want and then click the Properties button.**

4. **Change the login and contact information as you want.**

5. **Click the User Privileges tab to edit the account's specific privileges.**

   You can make it an Administrator account by selecting all items, a Desktop user account by selecting all but the Administer the System item, and an Unprivileged account by checking no items.

Changing the global login preferences

You have a few login options or preferences you can set that apply to all accounts. The following sections show you how.

Ubuntu doesn't have login preferences that are easy to change, as do Windows and Mac OS X.

Changing the login options for Windows 2000

Here's how to change the login options for Windows 2000:

1. **Choose Start⇨ Settings⇨ Control Panel.**

2. **Double-click Users and Passwords.**

The Users and Passwords window appears, listing the accounts on the computer and containing buttons for you to add, remove, and edit the accounts.

3. **You can disable password protection for all accounts by deselecting the Users Must Enter a User name and Password To Use This Computer option at the top.**

4. **Click the Advanced tab.**

5. **Specify whether you want to use Secure Boot.**

Enabling this option means you'll have to press Ctrl+Alt+Del before you can log in to an account. This can help ensure that you don't have a key logger or other hacker or spyware infection on your computer recording your login credentials. The window that appears before you can log in reminds you that you must click these keys in order to log in. Also, a Help link is provided to show you exactly what keys these are on your keyboard.

6. **Click OK to save and apply the changes.**

In Windows XP and Vista, you can press the Windows key and the letter *L* on your keyboard to lock your computer. If you have to walk away from your computer, you can do this quickly. Then to access your account again, you have to enter your password.

Changing the login options for Windows XP

If you're using Windows XP, here's how to change the login preferences:

1. **Choose Start⇨Control Panel.**

If using the Classic Start menu, choose Start⇨Settings⇨Control Panel.

2. **Click the User Accounts category.**

If you're using the Classic Control Panel view, skip this step.

3. **Click User Accounts.**

You should see the main User Accounts window, listing the accounts on the computer and containing buttons for you to add, remove, and edit the accounts.

4. **Click the Change the Way Users Log On or Off link.**

The Select Logon and Logoff Options window appears.

5. **Select the Use the Welcome Screen option if you want to use the Welcome screen.**

   Using the Welcome screen is best because it lists all the accounts, and all you have to do is click one to log in. When the Welcome screen is disabled, you must manually enter the username of the account you want to connect to. The classic prompt (a simple dialog box into which you can enter a username and password to log in) will be automatically filled, however, with the username of the last account that had been logged into. To log in to another account, you have to erase what's already there and type the username of the account you want. On the other hand, the advantage of not showing all the usernames is that it provides somewhat more security.

   If you disable this feature, you can't use the Fast User Switching feature.

Book II
Chapter 1

6. **Click the Use Fast User Switching option if you want to use Fast User Switching.**

   The Fast User Switching feature lets you switch between accounts without having to close applications and documents. This feature can be very useful if you have multiple people using one computer. For instance, say another member of your household needs to get on the computer for a few minutes. You are logged into an Administrator account, but the other person's account is classified as Limited. If you have Fast User Switching on, you just click Start, Log Off, and Switch User to get to the Welcome screen. If you don't have the feature on, you have to close the applications you are working with and completely log out of your account. With the feature on, when the other person is done with the computer, you can just click Switch User again, click your account, and enter your password.

   Before switching accounts, you should still save any open files or documents. This is because the other user can shut down the computer, which forces any other open accounts to close, without saving files. The user, however, is prompted that other users are connected.

7. **Click Apply Options.**

Changing the login options for Windows Vista

In Windows Vista, it's much harder to configure the type of user account preferences included in previous versions of Windows. You actually don't find any global settings while browsing through the preferences in the Control Panel. However, I cover a few tasks you may want to perform.

Enabling the Secure Boot feature forces a user to press Ctrl+Alt+Del before logging in to an account. This feature can help ensure that you don't have a key logger or other hacker or spyware infection on your computer recording your login credentials. The window that appears before you can log in reminds you that you must click these keys in order to log in. Also, a Help link is provided to show you exactly what keys these are on your keyboard.

To enable the Secure Boot feature, follow these steps:

1. **Click Start.**

2. **In the Search field, type** netplwiz **(see Figure 1-6) and press Enter.**

Figure 1-6: Bringing up the Advanced User Accounts control panel.

If using the classic Start menu, click Run, enter **netplwiz**, and click OK.

3. **At the UAC prompt that appears, click Continue.**

The Advanced User Account Control Panel window appears.

4. **Click the Advanced tab.**

5. **In the Secure Logon section, select the Require User to Press Ctrl+Alt+ Delete checkbox.**

6. **Click OK.**

If you want similar functionality as the classic login prompt (a simple dialog box into which you can enter a username and password to log in), follow these steps to achieve this in Windows Vista:

Be very careful when editing these settings. Mistakes can cause major problems!

1. **Click Start.**

2. **In the Search field, type** secpol.msc **to open the Microsoft Management Console (shown in Figure 1-7) and press Enter.**

Figure 1-7:
Bringing
up the
Microsoft
Manage-
ment
Console.

If using the classic Start menu, click Run, enter **secpol.msc**, and click OK.

3. **At the UAC prompt that appears, click Continue.**

The Microsoft Management Console appears, showing the Local Security Policy settings.

4. **Double-click the Local Policies folder.**

5. **Double-click the Security Options folder.**

6. **Find and double-click the Interactive Logon: Do Not Display Last User Name item.**

A window appears for the security option.

7. **Select Enabled (see Figure 1-8).**

Enabling this item removes the accounts from the Welcome screen. You don't see the classic logon window as you do in earlier Windows versions; however, you see blank Username and Password fields. You can manually input your username rather than pick it from a list of accounts. Doing so makes your computer more secure.

8. **Click OK and close the Local Security Policy window.**

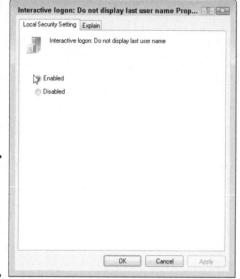

Figure 1-8:
Choose the
Enabled
option in the
Security
Options
window.

Changing the login options for Mac OS X Tiger and Leopard

Here's how you can change the global login settings of Mac OS X Tiger and
Leopard:

1. **Click the Apple icon and then choose System Preferences.**

2. **Click Accounts.**

The Accounts window appears, listing the accounts on the computer
and containing buttons for you to add, remove, and edit the accounts.

3. **Click the padlock icon in the lower-left corner (if it's locked), enter
your administrator account name and password into the fields, and
click OK.**

4. **On the bottom of the account list, click the Login Options button.**

5. **Select an Account from the Automatic Login (in Leopard) or
Automatically Log In As (in Tiger) drop-down list that you want the
computer to automatically log into when it boots up, or choose
Disabled (in Leopard) or deselect the Automatically Log In As option
to have the login window displayed when the computer boots up.**

Keep in mind that you won't be prompted for a password when an
account is automatically logged into, even if the account you set for
automatic login is password protected.

6. **For the Display Login Window As option, select either the List of Users
radio button, which is the default (and easier) way to log in, or select**

the Name and Password radio button, which requires you to manually enter the account name rather than select one from the list.

7. Select the Show the Restart, Sleep, and Shut Down Buttons option if want these buttons to appear on the login window.

8. Select the Show Input Menu in Login Window option if you want the menu that lets you choose the type and language of the keyboard you are using to be accessible from the login window.

This usually isn't necessary and might actually cause a problem if included on the login window.

9. Select the Show Password Hints option if you want the password hints created for each account shown on the login window.

If you think that a user of the computer may forget his or her password, you may want to enable this. That way, if the user specified a hint when the account was created, it will be shown. However, keep in mind that everyone can see these hints. It's not "Charades" — you don't want other people guessing your password!

10. Select the Use VoiceOver at Login Window if you want a computer voice to tell you what you're selecting on the login window.

This can be very useful for people with impaired vision.

11. Select the Enable Fast User Switching option if you want Fast User Switching enabled, and then select the way you want the accounts displayed from the drop-down list labeled View As.

When enabled, the name of the account is displayed in the upper-right corner of the screen. You can click the name to bring down a list of the other accounts, and click to login or switch accounts.

In contrast to how this work in Windows, if a user tries to shut down the computer when other accounts are still opened, it takes an Administrator password to power down the computer. This helps prevent people from losing unsaved files.

Enabling and disabling the Guest account

Some operating systems have a Guest account feature. It restricts important privileges, similar to the Limited (or Standard) account in Windows; however, it can't be password protected. This is great if you want to have an account ready for people — such as your friends and extended family — when they want to hop on the computer.

There is no official Guest account you can create in Mac OS X Tiger and Ubuntu. You can, however, create an account in the normal way (discussed in the "Adding user accounts" section) and name it Guest without applying a password, enabling Parental Controls (in Mac OS Tiger), or restricting the User Privileges (in Ubuntu). In this way, you simulate a Guest account.

The Guest account in Windows 2000

Windows 2000 by default includes a Guest account that's configured to the Guests group or privilege level. However, if you don't see it listed with your user accounts, or if you want to add another Guest account, here's how to create one:

1. **Choose Start⇨Settings⇨Control Panel.**

2. **Double-click Users and Passwords.**

   The Users and Passwords window appears, listing the accounts on the computer and containing buttons for you to add, remove, and edit the accounts.

3. **Click the Add button.**

4. **Enter the desired account information.**

   To distinguish this account from others, you may want to include the word Guest in the username.

5. **Click Next.**

6. **Enter a password (twice) and click Next.**

   If you don't want the account to be password protected, simply click Next without entering a password.

7. **Select the Other option and choose Guests from the list.**

8. **Click Finish.**

The Guest account in Windows XP and Vista

Windows XP and Vista come loaded with a single Guest account; however, it's turned off by default. You should also know that you can't password protect a Guest account. If you want to set up an account with password protection and restrictions, think about creating a Limited account.

If you're using Windows XP, here's how to enable or disable the Guest account:

1. **Choose Start⇨Control Panel.**

   If using the Classic Start menu, choose Start⇨Settings⇨Control Panel.

2. **Click the User Accounts (in XP) or User Accounts and Family Safety (in Vista) category.**

   If you're using the Classic Control Panel view, skip this step.

3. Click User Accounts.

You should see the main User Accounts window, listing the accounts on the computer and containing buttons for you to add, remove, and edit the accounts.

Under the Guest account's name, you can see whether it's on or off.

4. Click the Guest account.

5. To enable the account, click the Turn On the Guest Account button.

You can click the Guest account again to change the default picture or to turn it off.

6. To disable the account, click the Turn Off The Guest Account link.

Here's how to turn the Guest account on and off in Windows Vista:

1. Choose Start⇨Control Panel.

If using the Classic Start menu, choose Start⇨Settings⇨Control Panel.

2. Click the User Accounts and Family Safety category.

If you're using the Classic view, skip this step.

3. Click User Accounts.

You should see the main User Accounts window, listing the accounts on the computer and containing buttons for you to add, remove, and edit the accounts.

4. Go to the main Manage Accounts window.

If the Guest account is off, you see this stated under the Guest account's name. If it's enabled, you see "Guest Account" under the account name.

5. Click the Guest account.

6. To enable the account, click the Turn On button.

You can click the Guest account again to change the default picture or to turn it off.

7. To disable the account, click the Turn Off The Guest Account link.

The Guest account in Mac OS X Leopard

Mac OS X Leopard also has a Guest account. Follow these steps to enable and disable it:

1. Click the Apple icon and then choose System Preferences.

2. Click Accounts.

The Accounts window appears, listing the accounts on the computer and containing buttons for you to add, remove, and edit the accounts.

3. **Click the padlock in the lower-left corner (if it's locked), enter your administrator account name and password into the fields, and click OK.**

4. **Select the Guest Account from the list of accounts on the left.**

5. **Select or deselect the Allow Guests to Log Into This Computer option to enable or disable the Guest account.**

6. **Select the Enable Parental Controls option if you want to control exactly what guests can do on the computer.**

   After you're done configuring the main Guest Account settings on this window, click the Open Parental Controls button to configure the Parental Controls.

7. **Select the Allow Guests to Connect to Shared Folders option if you want to let the Guest account be used when connecting to the computer's shared folders from another computer on your network.**

Creating and Using a Password Reset Disk (for Windows XP and Vista Only)

For Windows XP and Vista, you can create a disk to keep in a safe place in case someone forgets his or her password. This way, you can easily create a new password for an account rather than lose files, documents, and personalized settings if the account is accidentally deleted. Here are a few things you should understand, however, before you think about using the reset disk:

✦ **One disk works for one account:** You must create a different disk for each account you want to make a reset disk for.

✦ **The disk is the key for the account:** Keep in mind that anyone who can get his or her paws on a reset disk can log into the account associated with the disk. So keep the disk out of sight and don't tell anyone about your little reset disk trick.

✦ **You can keep changing the password:** You don't have to create a reset disk every time the account's password is changed; one time is enough.

✦ **You need a 3½-inch floppy disk or a USB drive:** If you don't have one of those archaic floppy disks still sitting around or a USB flash drive, you are out of luck. You'll just have to make sure everyone remembers his or her password or write them all down and put them in a safe spot.

✦ **You can use the disk as you normally would:** Though it's recommended to place the disk in a safe spot so that you won't lose it, you can still use the disk as you normally would, meaning that you can still read and write files to the disk. Additionally, creating the reset disk won't delete any files on the disk.

✦ **Previous reset disks won't work:** After you create a reset disk, any other reset disks for the account won't work anymore. So if you create multiple disks over time, you should discard all but the most current one. You don't literally have to throw it in the trash — especially if you are using a USB drive — but do make sure that you aren't confused about which one is the most current.

✦ **You must log in to the account:** You must log in to the account you want to create the password reset disk for — Administrator accounts can't even create disks for other accounts.

Creating a reset disk

To create a reset disk in Windows XP and Vista, follow these steps:

1. **Choose Start⇨Control Panel.**

   If using the Classic Start menu, choose Start⇨Settings⇨Control Panel.

2. **Click the User Accounts (in XP) or User Accounts and Family Safety (in Vista) category.**

   If you're using the Classic Control Panel view, skip this step.

3. **Click User Accounts.**

   You should see the main User Accounts window, listing the accounts on the computer and containing buttons for you to add, remove, and edit the accounts.

4. **In Windows XP, click the Account for which you want to create a Password Reset Disk for. (In Windows Vista, just stay on the main User Accounts window).**

5. **Click the Prevent a Forgotten Password (in XP) or Create a Password Reset Disk (in Vista) link.**

   You can find the option under the Related Tasks section (in Windows XP) or Tasks section (in Vista), in the upper-left corner of the window. Clicking this link starts the Forgotten Password Wizard.

6. **Click Next.**

7. **Insert a blank, formatted disk into your drive or plug in a USB drive.**

8. **Choose the disk or USB drive and click Next.**

9. **Enter the account password and click Next.**

10. **When the Progress value shows 100% Complete, click Next.**

The file created by the wizard is `userkey.psw`, and its description appears as "password backup," which you can see when you view the contents of your disk or flash drive.

Using the password reset disk

When the time comes to use the password reset disk, you can use it at the Welcome screen:

1. **Verify that you've inserted the reset disk or flash drive.**

2. **Click the account you want to reset and try to enter a password.**

   You want to enter something (or nothing) and click the button to log in. Now you can access the link to the reset password wizard.

3. **Click the link.**

   In Windows XP, click the Use Your Password Reset Disk link in the Did You Forget Your Password? pop-up bubble that appears. In Windows Vista, click the Reset Password link that appears under where you type in the password.

   The Password Reset Wizard starts.

4. **Click Next.**

5. **Choose the disk or USB drive and click Next.**

6. **Enter a new password twice.**

   Don't forget this one!

7. **(Optional) Enter a password hint.**

   Entering a hint can help you remember your password. Just remember that everyone can see this hint from the Welcome screen, so don't hint too much.

8. **Click Next.**

9. **Click Finish.**

Changing Advanced Account Settings

Windows includes some additional user account settings that deal particularly with passwords, and these settings are located where most average home users won't find them. You may find these settings useful, so read on to see where to find these settings depending on your operating system.

Here's how to find these settings in Windows 2000:

1. **Choose Start⇨Settings⇨Control Panel.**

2. **Double-click Administrative Tools.**

3. **Double-click Computer Management.**

I show you what to browse to after the following set of directions that show how to get to this point in Windows XP and Vista.

If you are using Windows XP or Vista:

1. **Choose Start⇨Control Panel.**

If you're using the Classic view, choose Start⇨Settings⇨Control Panel instead.

2. **If in Classic view, click the Performance and Maintenance category (in Windows XP) or the System and Maintenance category (in Vista); otherwise, skip this step.**

3. **Click Administrative Tools.**

4. **Double-click Computer Management.**

If you're in Windows Vista, click Continue if you get a UAC prompt.

Here's what you should do after you have the Computer Management program open:

1. **In the System Tools folder, open the Local Users and Groups folder.**

2. **Click the Users folder to open it.**

The right half of the window fills with the user accounts you have on your computer. See Figure 1-9 for an example.

3. **Double-click the user account you want to edit.**

4. **Configure the following properties, as desired:**

- **User Must Change Password At Next Logon:** This does exactly what it says. This is great to enable just after creating accounts for other people. Because you don't set the password when you actually create the account (for Windows XP and Vista), this option is a good idea to enable if you want to make sure that everyone has a password. For this option to appear, the following two options must not be selected.

- **User Cannot Change The Password:** Enable this option if you have Limited or Standard accounts in Windows XP or Vista (that by default allow password changes), and you don't want users to disable or change their passwords.

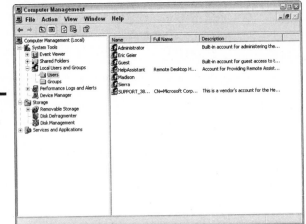

Figure 1-9:
List of user
accounts
in the
Computer
Manage-
ment
program.

- **Password Never Expires:** This option must not be selected for the first option in this list to appear.

- **Account Is Disabled:** This option, of course, disables the account so that it can't be logged back into. If someone tries, he or she will see a message on-screen saying that the account has been disabled. This is good to use when any little ones in a household get their computer time revoked.

5. **Click OK when you're done configuring all your options.**

Chapter 2: Planning for Your Network

In This Chapter

✓ **Exploring your high-speed Internet options**

✓ **Figuring out what you need for your network**

✓ **Checking out sample network plans**

*T*aking the time to plan your network can save you time and money in the long run — by reducing the number of trips to the store for equipment and by knowing exactly what you need. This chapter helps you through this planning phase. First, I provide a review of the different high-speed Internet connections and help you discover the features that various Internet service providers (ISPs) may offer you so that you can choose one that works with your budget and meets your needs. Then I help you figure out what things you need to buy at the store to get your network up and running. Finally, you can review sample network plans for each network type to help you understand what's involved and required to set up a home network.

To better understand home networking and the hardware involved, I encourage you to look over Book I as well as the previous chapters in this minibook before you try to make total sense of this one. Also, planning your network involves knowing which type of network — wired, wireless, computer-to-computer, or power- or phone-line network — you want to set up, and you can get help with making those decisions in Book I, Chapter 1.

Choosing Your Internet Connection

Before setting up your home network, you should order high-speed Internet access — also referred to as *broadband Internet* — through an Internet service provider (ISP). Though sharing dial-up Internet access (the older and slower connection type) is possible, it's not very practical. Also, I bet you want to surf at much faster speeds.

You've likely heard of the many high-speed Internet types — maybe DSL, cable, or broadband over cellular — from seeing commercials and talking to friends and family. But you should look over your options and see what's best for you. Table 2-1 gives you a quick comparison, and the following sections discuss each of these high-speed Internet types in more detail.

Table 2-1	Comparing High-Speed Internet Connection Types			
Type	*Download Speeds*	*Upload Speeds*	*Setup Cost*	*Monthly Cost*
Cable	4 Mbps –15 Mbps	384 Kbps – 1.5 Mbps	$0 – $100	$40 – $80
DSL	768 Kbps – 6 Mbps	128 Kbps – 768 Kbps	$0 – $100	$15 – $45
Wireless ISP (WISP)	Varies	Varies	$0 – $300	$40 – $60
Satellite	512 Kbps – 1.5 Mbps	128 Kbps – 256 Kbps	$300 – $800	$50 – $120
Mobile (Cellular) Broadband	400 Kbps – 1.4 Mbps	Up to 800 Kbps	$0 – $200	$20 – $60

It can be confusing to understand the download and upload speeds, especially when compared in two different formats. However, keep in mind that 1,000 Kbps (kilobits per second) equals 1 Mbps (megabit per second). So 768 Kbps is about 76 percent of 1 Mbps, and 1.5 Mbps is 1,500 Kbps. This comparison is similar to the ratio between types of hard disk space, measured in MB (megabytes) and GB (gigabytes). For example, 1,000MB equals 1GB.

Dial-up Internet connections offer up to 56 Kbps and usually cost about $10 a month. As you can see by looking at Table 2-1, shown previously, going with cable Internet can give you more than 71 times the speed of a dial-up connection. But the cost doesn't multiply quite as much: Cable costs about five times the price of dial-up. (And trust me: The high-speed connection is worth it!)

Connecting with lightning speed through cable

Cable Internet and DSL are two of the most popular Internet services used in homes. You'll probably find that your local Internet cable provider offers high-speed connections at a reasonable price. In contrast to other Internet services, cable connections are "shared" among other subscribers in your area. Therefore, the speeds you experience vary depending upon the overall usage in your area at any given moment. Still, cable Internet is good if you want fast download speeds, and it's great for online gaming.

As you can probably guess, the Internet service is delivered through your cable by your local TV cable company. When you order this service, the cable company usually comes out and fiddles with your cable box outside, maybe wires a new cable outlet, and plugs the cable into a modem that stays in your home.

Saving money with DSL

As noted previously, *Digital Subscriber Line* (DSL) service is also very popular in homes. Along with a few national providers (for example, AT&T Yahoo!

and EarthLink) and local providers, your local phone company should offer DSL Internet service. DSL Internet connections are delivered over phone lines. However, in contrast to dial-up Internet access, DSL doesn't prevent you from using the phone when you're connected to the Internet.

You'll probably find DSL service at a lower price than cable service, but typically offering slightly lower speeds than cable connections. However, DSL providers these days usually offer multiple service levels with some options at the same speeds, or higher, than cable. Plus, you'll have a dedicated connection to your home that isn't shared among other subscribers in your area.

When you sign up for DSL service, you may be offered professional installation, but self-installation is common. With self-installation, you'll receive a package consisting of a DSL modem, modem/line filter, several line filters, and, of course, instructions. You just have to plug the modem/line filter into a phone line outlet and then plug the DSL modem into the filter. If you want, you can also plug a phone into the filter. Then you just have to place the other line filters between phone line outlets and any other phones in your home.

Connecting through Wireless ISP (WiMAX or Wi-Fi)

Wireless ISPs (Wireless Internet service providers, or WISPs), also called wireless broadband providers, deliver Internet connections to homes and businesses via radio waves (using WiMAX or Wi-Fi wireless technology) instead of physical lines. Additionally, some WISPs may offer or support mobile access to their Internet service when you are out and about in their coverage area, rather than just from a single location. WISP Internet service is usually located in rural areas where no DSL or cable Internet service is available. You may also find this Internet access offered in and around major cities by WISPs such as Clearwire and Sprint.

Many cities (or third-party companies) around the United States have set up *city-wide networks,* also called *municipal (or muni) wireless networks.* These types of networks can also be considered wireless ISPs. Some of these networks, though, may be available only to businesses or city and public service departments. However, some cities offer free or paid residential wireless Internet plans.

When you sign up for Internet service through a WISP, you'll probably get a piece of hardware, usually called a wireless modem or CPE *(customer premise equipment),* by the provider. This is essentially a signal booster or repeater. The wireless modem unit is usually placed near a wall, window, or outside so that it can pick up the best possible signal from the WISP. Then you can plug in your computers or wireless router into the wireless modem, just as you would when using DSL, cable, or any other Internet service.

Here are two Web sites you can visit to find WISPs:

✦ www.wispdirectory.com

✦ www.bbwexchange.com/wisps

Going with satellite: Internet in the boondocks

If you're in "digital darkness," where no cable, DSL, or any other Internet service is available, you may want to check into satellite Internet service. Keep in mind, though, that this service isn't cheap and usually requires a setup cost and a one- or two-year contract. So check, and double-check, for any other Internet providers in your area, including WISPs and mobile broadband service, before settling with satellite service.

Because of the delay of the satellite signals transmitting over such long distances, certain applications such as *voice-over IP* (VoIP) — Skype or Vonage, for example — or *virtual private network* (VPN) connections may not work well on networks using this type of Internet connection.

Here are the URLs for the Web sites of several satellite Internet providers you may want to check into:

✦ www.wildblue.com

✦ www.hughesnet.com

✦ www.skywayusa.com

✦ www.mybluedish.com

Going mobile with cellular broadband

Another way to get connected to the Internet is through a cellular phone carrier that provides the service, such as Verizon, Sprint, or AT&T. Newer technologies now make it possible to get high-speed Internet connections (some offering up to 1.4 Mbps download speed) in some of the cellular coverage areas. This puts the Internet at your fingertips — on your phone or laptop — when you are out and about. Though you won't have as much Internet power as you do when using Wi-Fi hotspots (set up in many hotels and public areas; see Book VII, Chapter 1 for more details about these hotspots), you can get just about anywhere in the coverage area.

There is a "catch" with mobile broadband Internet, however. The catch is the limit on the amount of data you can access on the Internet. The problem is that the typical maximum amounts in plans today are much too low for typical family use. Cellular broadband Internet is best for occasional use of light-data applications, such as those for checking e-mail. Browsing Web sites with lots of images and photos, downloading files, and even downloading or sending e-mail attachments quickly racks up your data usage — and your cellular broadband bill!

Similarly to other data plans offered on your mobile phone, the Internet usage is measured in the amount of data you download and upload, in megabytes (MB) or gigabytes (GB). You can pick an Internet plan with a certain amount of data, for instance 5MB to 5,000MB (or 5GB). Of course, as with voice plans, you can expect a hefty overage fee, typically 50 cents to a $1 per megabyte used that is in excess of your limit.

This type of Internet connection can still be very useful, particularly in the following cases:

✦ To check e-mail and use the Web when traveling in the car, for personal or work related reasons

✦ To get online when staying with your friends or family, when the home has no Internet access

✦ For use with small businesses, such as home repair service companies, to charge credit cards, check schedules, and get information about equipment and parts

✦ For quick "emergency" or back-up Internet access when you're at home or around town

Examples of mobile broadband networks include:

✦ Verizon Wireless's Data Optimized (EV-DO) network

✦ AT&T's BroadbandConnect 3G and EDGE network

✦ Sprint's Power-Vision (EV-DO) network

If you're thinking about getting mobile broadband Internet, keep the following in mind:

✦ **Device compatibility:** Whatever you plan to use to connect to the mobile broadband Internet should be compatible with the latest technologies. For instance, if you purchase a used mobile broadband laptop card, be aware that it may not support the higher data rates.

✦ **Coverage areas:** Make sure that you check whether the areas in which you plan to use the service have sufficient coverage. Remember, mobile broadband Internet won't work as well in all areas that receive regular cell phone coverage. You must be in a supported area.

✦ **Data allowances:** As mentioned previously, you should keep an eye out for the data allowances for these Internet plans.

✦ **Indoor coverage:** The signal and speeds you experience may not be as good when you use the service in your home, especially in the basement.

**Book II
Chapter 2**

Planning for Your Network

✦ **Connectivity method:** When browsing mobile broadband Internet products, you can find a variety of devices that connect to the service, including the following:

- **Laptop card:** This is a radio card, similar to a Wi-Fi PC card, which slips into your laptop's PCMCIA slot. This is for people who want Internet service available on their computers.

- **Wireless router:** You may also find mobile wireless routers that support mobile broadband Internet service. This type of router lets you quickly set up access for multiple computers.

- **Built-in phone/PDA:** Some phones and PDAs may support the service, giving you high-speed Internet in the palm of your hand.

- **Phone modem:** Some cellular phones may allow you to pump Internet access to your computer, with a USB cable, thereby making your phone function as a modem.

- **Built-in to the computer:** Some newer laptops have built-in broadband Internet capability, just as nearly all laptops have built-in Wi-Fi.

Discovering the popular features that ISPs offer

Here are several features typically offered by ISPs that you should be aware of when shopping for a high-speed Internet service provider:

✦ **Package/bundle discounts:** You'll probably find that your local telecom providers (such as telephone, cellular, and cable companies) offer package discounts when you sign up for multiple services. Keep this in mind when looking for your Internet service.

✦ **DHCP or Static IP:** One major difference between residential and business-class Internet service is the type of IP address you receive. Just about all residential services use only DHCP, which gives your Internet connection an IP address automatically. However, your IP address will change once in a while, making it a bit more difficult if you access servers or your network from outside your home. Because businesses usually use servers, and so on, it's better to have the same address all the time. But even if you have service with DHCP, you can get around this issue. You can sign up for a service that gives you a domain name you can use that will always point to your home's Internet IP address; for instance, you may use the Dynamic DNS service at www.dyndns.com.

✦ **Service contract:** Be careful: Some ISPs (generally for satellite or mobile Internet providers) may require you to sign a one- or two-year contract when signing up for Internet service. If this is the way you have to go, look into any money-back guarantees they may offer before you sign the contract.

✦ **Free dial-up Internet access:** Some ISPs offer complimentary dial-up Internet access to you when you sign up for high-speed Internet. This way, you can have an Internet connection while away from your home Internet service. This can come in handy while traveling, if your hotel doesn't offer free Internet, or as a backup Internet connection at home.

✦ **E-mail addresses:** Most ISPs provide you with some type of e-mail service, whether a Web-based or POP3 account that you can set up with an e-mail application such as Microsoft Outlook or Mozilla Thunderbird. This can be very useful if you don't have a good e-mail account already; it can get you away from having to use free accounts that inject advertisements in the messages.

POP3 e-mail accounts are different from other e-mail systems used by some ISPs, such as America Online (AOL). When you get a POP3 account, you receive mail server addresses, username, password, and other information. You can then input this information into an e-mail client program, such as Microsoft Outlook. When you have your e-mail account set up, you typically press a button to synchronize, or send and receive, your e-mail. The addressing methods, though, are the same as other e-mail services. For instance, you still get an e-mail address like *yourname@domain.com* when using a POP3 e-mail account.

✦ **Web site space:** Some ISPs may offer Web site space for your very own Web site. This can be very useful if you want to create a personal or business presence on the Web. Some ISPs may give you a virtual domain name, such as *yourname.yourisp.com*. On the other hand, some may even pay for a domain name registration so that you can get your own domain, such as *yourname.com*.

✦ **Internet security suite:** Some ISPs may also offer spam and pop-up ad protection, and sometimes even full Internet Security Suites. As you may know, these ISPs hope to entice and win you over from other ISPs. Going with them can, however, save you money, so they're worth checking out.

**Book II
Chapter 2**

**Planning for
Your Network**

Determining Your Hardware Needs

Before you go out and start buying everything, you need to do some thinking and planning. When you get to the store, you should know exactly what hardware you need or want. The following sections discuss the main pieces of hardware you'll need for your home network.

A modem for your Internet connection

In order to connect to your Internet service, you have to have a modem. This is almost always given to you by your ISP. You can, however, buy routers with built-in DSL or cable modems to help conserve space and simplify your setup.

Modem/router combo devices may not include the newest wireless standards and networking technology; separate routers are more likely to do so.

Adapters to connect to the network

You'll need a network adapter — also referred to as a Network Interface Card (NIC) — for every computer that you want on your home network. However, you may not need to buy adapters for all your computers. Some of your computers may already be loaded with network adapters. The types of network adapters — Ethernet, wireless, or power- or phone-line — you need depend upon the network type you are setting up.

Check out Book I, Chapter 1 for some guidance in deciding on the best network type for your needs and to review its required adapters. You can also look over Book I, Chapter 3 to find lots of information on adapters.

Network adapters are built in a variety of form factors, such as PCI cards for desktop computers, PC cards for laptops, and USB adapters for any computer with a USB port. You need to make sure that the network adapters you purchase are compatible with your computers.

Another thing to consider when picking out your network adapters is the maximum supported data rate, or speed at which the data is transmitted and received. The data rates are matched among the different wireless and wired networking standards, which I discuss more in the previous subsections.

If you're setting up a power-line network (explained in Book I, Chapter 1), here are a few things to take into account when searching for power-line adapters:

✦ **HomePlug Certification:** As do wireless devices, power-line devices have a certification program (called HomePlug) to ensure that the devices meet certain common standards, so products from different vendors are compatible.

You should make sure that the power-line devices you buy are certified with one of the two HomePlug certifications:

- *HomePlug 1.0 certified:* This is the first certification designed to allow networking communications via in-home power lines. The basic criteria include a 10 Mbps data rate, whole-house coverage, and 56-bit DES *(Data Encryption Standard)* encryption.

Because wireless and wired networking products have greatly surpassed the maximum speeds of HomePlug 1.0, this certification is not practical for use with most of today's home networking solutions.

- *HomePlug AV Standard:* This is an enhanced version of HomePlug 1.0 that's designed to support high-performance traffic such as digital (VoIP) phone traffic and high-definition (HD) video, in addition to regular networking traffic. It offers data rates of up to 200 Mbps and increased security at 128-bit AES *(Advanced Encryption Standard)*, and it is much more practical and much faster.

✦ **Supported data rate:** You'll discover a variety of data rates (or speed) supported by power-line bridges/adapters, such as 14, 85, or 200 Mbps. Though not required, it's usually best to stick with a similar data rate for all your networking equipment (meaning your network adapters in your computers).

✦ **Built-in AP:** Some manufacturers produce power-line wireless access points, so you don't have to purchase a separate wireless access point (AP). These access points can provide wireless access to the power-line network for your laptops and other Wi-Fi devices.

✦ **Connection type:** Some power-line devices use a USB cable for the connection to the computers, so you don't have to have an Ethernet adapter on the computer.

✦ **Kits:** Most manufacturers have come out with power-line kits that provide enough products and instruction for at least one AP. If you require more APs, you can buy more bridges or adapters separately.

Book II
Chapter 2

Planning for
Your Network

A router to create the network

If you're setting up a traditional home network, you need a router. If you're going with a wired-only network, you need a wired router, and if you're going wireless (in combination with wired, if you choose to add wired connections), you need a wireless router. Your router will be the heart of your network, connecting your computers together and controlling the data traffic.

When searching for a router, the biggest differentiator is the supported data rate. Just as with network adapters, wireless and wired routers are marked with different standards concerning data rate among other characteristics. These topics are discussed in the previous two subsections.

To find out more about routers, check out Book I, Chapter 3.

Ethernet cabling for wiring needs

If you're setting up a wired-only network with a router, a wired computer-to-computer network, or are wiring computers directly to a wireless router, you need Ethernet cables. You should measure the distance for all the cable runs and buy the appropriate lengths.

When shopping for Ethernet cabling, you should understand the three main types, which are all interoperable and support data rates of up to 1,000 Mbps (or 1 Gbps):

+ **Category 5 (Cat5):** An older cable type typically used for networks/connection running at 10 or 100 Mbps. Though you won't find this type sold in all stores, it's the cheapest and should work fine in most home networks.

+ **Category 5 enhanced (Cat5e):** An improved version of the Cat5 cabling, but with the same data transfer rate of up to 100 MHz. Minor changes in the cable specifications make this one better for gigabit networks, or networks operating at 1 Gbps (or 1,000 Mbps). This cabling should be sold right along with the newer Cat6 cabling, described next.

+ **Category 6 (Cat6):** Data rates of up to 1,000 Mbps (1 Gbps) with enhanced performance make this cabling even better, especially for 1 Gbps networks. If you're especially concerned with speed or quality, you can go with this type; however, it's not needed in most home networks.

You may run into strained and solid flavors of Ethernet cabling (which are the two types of conductors cased inside the cable); if you do, go with strained because it's easier to work with and cheaper than solid cabling, which is stiff and fragile. You should also stick with "patch" or prefabricated cabling that is already loaded with connectors, as opposed to buying Ethernet cabling and wiring on your own connectors.

Before hitting the stores, you need to be sure to measure the required lengths of your cabling runs. But before you can do this, you must figure out how you plan to run the cabling through your home. Here are several ideas of where you can run it:

+ **Attic:** You can drill a small hole through your ceiling, run the cable up into the attic and over to the desired spot, and drill again to bring the cable down into wherever you need it in your home.

  To conceal the cabling, you can drill the holes in the ceilings of closets. Otherwise, you might try making it a "professional" installation by bringing the end of the cable down between interior walls. To do that, you drill into a wall beam from the attic and then drill a hole into the wall where you want it to come out; you then fish the cable down the wall and out the hole. You can top off your Ethernet cabling installation by using an Ethernet faceplate/jack, or just run the cable directly to the computer or device.

+ **Basement or crawl space:** This is similar to the attic route described previously, but instead, you go through your basement or crawl space to run the cable. You can drill holes through the flooring of your main ground level to run the cable along the exposed beams of your unfinished basement or crawl space.

For the cable end running to your computer, you can either drill the hole through the flooring near a wall or try to drill the hole through the wall beams so that you can fish the cable up and out of a hole in your wall. You may also use an Ethernet faceplate/jack to terminate the cable, or just run the cable directly to the computer or device.

✦ **Along and through interior walls:** You can run the cables along the trim or baseboard of walls (or tuck them between the carpet and trim) and drill small holes to pass the cable through the walls or baseboards.

✦ **Along and through exterior walls:** You can drill holes through your exterior walls to run the cable outside, in a similar (out and in) fashion as the other methods. You will, however, need to place exposed Ethernet in conduit (a metal or plastic tub to protect cabling from the outside elements).

When thinking about running the cables, think about where the best place is to place the router. Basically, you want to place the router in a spot that's central in relation to all the computers to minimize the amount of Ethernet cable you need. Also, keep in mind that the router needs to be close to the Internet modem.

In addition to the cabling, you may need to buy some accessories and cable-mounting devices:

✦ **Cable mounts:** Simple cable mounts can be very useful to tack the cabling in place along walls or beams.

✦ **Conduit:** Simple or heavy-duty conduit may be useful to hide the Ethernet cabling or to provide protection when the cable is run outside and exposed to the elements.

✦ **Caulking:** Use caulk to seal holes in exterior walls.

✦ **PVC pipe:** This can be useful if you plan on drilling holes through interior walls. Use this pipe to pass the cabling through rooms. You can slip a small piece of PVC pipe into the hole, flush with the opening, to seal the hole from the inside of the wall (so that you can't see the inside of the wall when looking through the hole you just drilled).

✦ **Ethernet faceplate/jack:** This is nice if you plan to terminate the cabling ends with a professional look. Keep in mind that you don't have to run the cabling down walls to take advantage of these jacks; you can do this easily when going through interior or exterior walls.

You can probably find these items at your local hardware or electronics store. Refer to Book I, Chapter 3 for more information and tips on shopping for networking hardware.

**Book II
Chapter 2**

**Planning for
Your Network**

Making Choices Based on Wireless and Wired Networking Standards

If you're going wireless, remember that there are a few different wireless standards — A, B, G, and N — that have varying speeds and ranges. You don't necessarily have to use the same standard for all your adapters and your wireless router, but you want to keep in mind the existence of these standards. If you need help comparing and picking a wireless standard, see Book I, Chapter 1.

For wired networks, you have the choice between the following three popular standards:

✦ **10BASE-T:** Supports Ethernet speeds of 10 Mbps. Its formal IEEE standard is named 802.3i.

✦ **100BASE-TX:** Supports Ethernet speeds of 100 Mbps. Its IEEE standard is named 802.3u. Just about all networking products that support this standard also support 10BASE-T.

✦ **1000BASE-T:** As you can probably assume, this type supports Ethernet speeds of 1,000 Mbps, or 1 Gbps (gigabit) — which is ten times faster than most products today that support 100 Mbps. Its IEEE standard is 802.3ab. Products that support this standard may also support the other two standards.

You'll find the supported Ethernet standards listed on product boxes, descriptions, and data sheets. Additionally, the product name or labeling for Ethernet products, as for wired routers and adapters, may include the speed, such as 10/100 Ethernet, 10/100 network card, or gigabit (meaning 1,000 Mbps) router.

Putting It All Together: Sample Network Plans

To better help you understand how to plan for your home network, I show you sample plans for each type of network. Your plans are primarily based upon the amount and type (desktop or laptop) of computers you have in your household and their locations. Therefore, I start off by setting up an example scenario consisting of the following computers:

✦ **Parent desktop:** Located in the parent's room with an Ethernet and wireless g adapter.

✦ **Parent laptop:** Moves from room to room with an integrated wireless g and Ethernet adapter.

✦ **Office desktop:** Is set up in a room that serves as an office; the computer here has an Ethernet adapter installed.

- ✦ **Kid #1 desktop:** In a child's room with an Ethernet adapter installed.

- ✦ **Kid #2 desktop:** In another child's room with no adapter installed.

- ✦ **Kid laptop:** Roams around the house with an integrated Ethernet adapter.

Because this scenario contains two laptops that move around the home, a wireless setup is likely the best, but the following sections discuss setups for each network type — wired and wireless.

Laying out the wired network

For a wired network based on the example scenario described previously, you need the following equipment:

- ✦ **Wired (Ethernet) network adapters:** You need one for each computer so that every computer can be on the network. Evaluating the network adapters already in all the computers tells you that you need to purchase and install only one Ethernet adapter, for the desktop for Kid #2. All the other computers already have Ethernet adapters.

- ✦ **Wired (Ethernet) router:** This serves as the heart of the network. It connects all the computers together and to the Internet to create the network. Because the wired adapters in the computers don't support the fastest Ethernet type (gigabit), you should get a router that supports 10/100 Mbps. Having six computers means that you need to purchase a router with enough ports. However, most stores carry only four-port routers. You can go online and buy an eight-port router, or you might purchase the four-port router and a switch (hub) to have more ports.

- ✦ **Ethernet cabling:** Each computer needs to be directly connected back to the router. You need to measure the distance between the router and the computers on the path through which you want to run the cables. Then, when shopping, you want to buy appropriate cable lengths. Because you aren't using a gigabit router, and to save money, you can just buy the Cat5 or Cat5e Ethernet cabling instead of the better Cat6.

Figure 2-1 shows the layout of this wired network.

Figure 2-1 shows an example of a wired router with eight Ethernet ports (instead of the usual four ports) set up in the office closet and connected to the Internet modem.

 Running the cables this way can be done, for example, by putting the cables up a hole drilled into the ceiling of the office closet, running the cables through the attic, and then running the cables down a hole drilled into each of the bedroom closets.

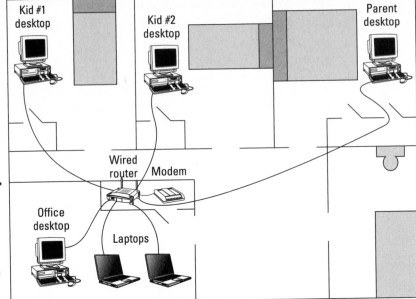

Figure 2-1:
Layout for
a wired
network
based on
the example
scenario.

Instead of tying the laptops down by a wired connection to the network, you can use a wireless access point (AP) to create a wireless connection to your wired network. However, it's usually better to swap out the wired router with a wireless router that has enough Ethernet ports to support all the computers you want to wire to the router.

Going the wireless route

For a wireless network based on the example scenario, you need the following equipment:

✦ **Wireless (Wi-Fi) network adapters:** To make it so that every computer can be on the network, you need a wireless (or Ethernet) adapter for each computer. After examining each computer, you find that four computers lack wireless adapters. However, one of these computers, the office desktop, can be hooked up using Ethernet cable because the router will be in the same room. This way, you don't have to spend money purchasing a wireless adapter. Now you have all three of the kids' computers to worry about — two with only Ethernet adapters and one with no adapter at all. To solve that problem, you can buy PCI wireless adapters to slip into the PCI slots of the two kids' desktops. For the laptop, you can buy a notebook wireless card that slides into the PCMCIA slot on the side of the computer.

Before you can pick the exact adapters to buy, you must first decide on the wireless standard — A, B, G, or N — that you want to use. (Refer to Book I, Chapter 1 for help with this decision.) In the example scenario, you decide to go with wireless N. This is because it offers much more speed (for transferring files between your computers) and range. You need to understand, however, that the older wireless G adapters in the other computers won't be able to take full advantage of the increased performance of wireless N. Therefore, with this scenario, you want to consider swapping out the two preexisting wireless G adapters for wireless N adapters.

✦ **Wireless (Wi-Fi) router:** This is what all the computers will connect to in order to communicate with each other and to get Internet access. This router creates the network. For this example, the network adapter is wireless N, so you need to buy a wireless N router. Although the official wireless N standard still isn't finalized, and you actually have to buy "draft" N products, you should make sure that all these products (adapters and the router) are from the same manufacturer.

✦ **Ethernet cabling:** When you're wiring the office desktop directly to the wireless router, you need to buy only one Ethernet cable. You should measure the distance between the router and the computer so that you can buy an appropriate cable length. You don't need a router that supports gigabit Ethernet in this example, so to save money, you can buy the Cat5 or Cat5e Ethernet cabling instead of the better Cat6.

Figure 2-2 shows the layout of a wireless network based upon the example scenario.

The wireless router is set up in the office closet and connected to the Internet modem. The solid line running to the office desktop represents the Ethernet cable. The set of three curved lines next to the wireless router and computers depicts the radio waves or signals being transmitted.

Computer-to-computer network

For a wireless computer-to-computer network based on the example scenario, the only types of equipment you need are wireless (Wi-Fi) network adapters. To enable every computer to be on the network, you need one for each computer. After examining each computer, you find that four computers lack wireless adapters. The office desktop and all three of the kids' computers need wireless adapters; three have only Ethernet adapters, and one has no adapter at all. So you need to buy PCI wireless adapters to slip into the PCI slots of the two kids' desktops and the office desktop. For the kid's laptop, you need to buy a notebook wireless card that slides into the PCMCIA slot on the side of the computer.

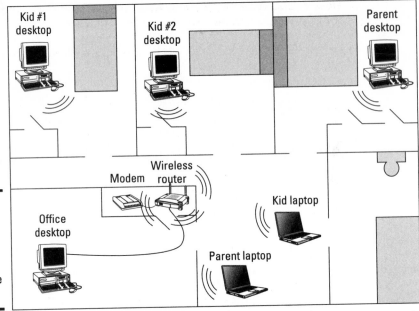

Figure 2-2:
Layout for
a wireless
network
based on
the example
scenario.

Wired computer-to-computer networks are also possible. However, this is generally realistic only for connecting two computers together; otherwise, most computers would need two Ethernet adapters in order to chain the computers together. Another possible situation for wired computer-to-computer connections is to connect computers without the desired adapter type to the network. For example, imagine that both of the kids' desktops have Ethernet adapters but no wireless adapters. Rather than buy two wireless adapters, you can just install a wireless adapter in one of them. You can connect the kid's desktop with that has the wireless adapter to the wireless computer-to-computer network and run an Ethernet cable from the computer with both adapters to the one that has only the wired adapter. In Windows, you create a virtual bridge that "connects" the network connections of the wireless and wired adapters, and does so in the computer that has both adapters. Then if you enable Internet access sharing, the kid's desktop with only the wired adapter is essentially connected to the wireless computer-to-computer network.

As with the wireless network setup, you have to pick the wireless standard — A, B, G, Or N — that you want to use for your network. A good choice is to go with wireless N because you plan to do a lot of file transferring between computers; also, if you have laptops that you want to be able to use in the basement, wireless N is best because it provides higher data rates and more range than other standards. However, the older wireless G adapters in the other computers can't take full advantage of the increased performance of wireless N. Consequently, you may want to eventually swap out the two pre-existing wireless G adapters with wireless n adapters.

Figure 2-3 shows the layout of a wireless computer-to-computer network based upon the example scenario.

Book II
Chapter 2

Planning for Your Network

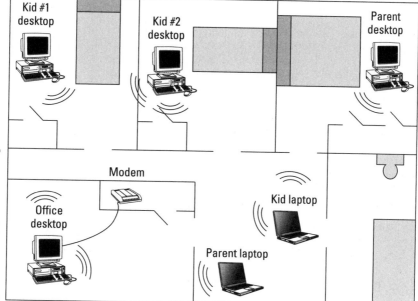

Figure 2-3: Layout for a wireless computer-to-computer network based on the example scenario.

Kid #1 desktop

Kid #2 desktop

Parent desktop

Modem

Office desktop

Kid laptop

Parent laptop

The Internet modem is set up in the office closet. The office desktop is connected to the modem by a short piece of Ethernet cabling provided with the modem (represented by solid line in the figure) and is configured to share the Internet access among computers that are connected to the computer-to-computer network. The set of three curved lines next to the computers depicts the radio waves or signals being transmitted to and from all the computers.

Power- or phone-line network

You may want to go with a power-line network if you have many more electrical outlets than telephone jacks in the house. Also, if you have two laptops that you want to move around with, you want wireless access for them. For a power-line network, here's the equipment you need:

✦ **Power-line adapters for computers:** For each desktop computer, you need to buy a power-line adapter. If not all the computers have an Ethernet adapter, you need to try to find adapters that use USB cables to plug into the computers rather than use Ethernet cables. To save even more money, you don't have to buy power-line adapters for the desktops that have wireless adapters already installed, because you can set up wireless access for the laptops anyway.

✦ **Power-line adapter for the modem:** To inject the Internet connection into the power-line network, you need one adapter for the modem.

✦ **Power-line wireless access point:** To create the wireless access for the laptops, you need to buy a power-line wireless access point or adapter.

✦ **Wireless (Wi-Fi) network adapter:** To enable the kid's laptop in this scenario to use the wireless access, you need to buy a notebook wireless card that slides into the PCMCIA slot on the side of the computer.

Figure 2-4 shows the layout of a power-line (and wireless) network based upon the example scenario.

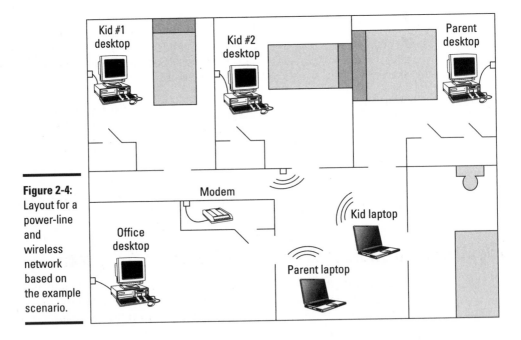

Figure 2-4: Layout for a power-line and wireless network based on the example scenario.

The Internet modem is set up in the office closet and connected to a power-line adapter to pump the Internet into the power-line network. The small boxes and lines connecting to all the desktop computers represent the connection to the power-line adapters. The larger box in the hallway is the power-line wireless access point (AP). The sets of three curved lines next to the laptops and power-line wireless AP depict the radio waves or signals being transmitted.

Chapter 3: Installing Network Adapters

In This Chapter

✔ Getting installation guides and documentation for your network adapter

✔ Installing your adapter's driver and software

✔ Plugging in or installing your adapter

✔ Setting up power-line and phone-line adapters

*W*hen you're setting up your network for the first time, you need to make sure that you've planned your entire network (see Chapter 2 in this minibook for help on that), figured out what computers need network adapters, and what types of adapters they need.

Next, you need to install and set up those adapters so that your computers can access your network. Installing the various types of network adapters that your network requires can seem intimidating, but all you have to do is follow the instructions carefully. It's no big deal, really. This chapter shows you how!

In this chapter, you find out how to prepare for and install each type of network adapter.

Preparing to Install Wired and Wireless Adapters

Your network adapter should come with instructions on how to install and configure it, usually called the Quick Installation Guide. In addition to that, the upcoming sections of this chapter provide you with the information you need.

If you're installing a wireless adapter, you may want to refer to the product manual for specifics on using that adapter's configuration utility. However, if you prefer to use the Windows or Mac OS X configuration utility for the wireless adapter, you can disable the manufacturer's utility. Refer to Book IV, Chapter 1 to see how to switch between the manufacturer's and Windows utilities, and how to use the Windows and Mac OS X utility.

If you're using the manufacturer's utility, or if you need the product manual for any other reason, you can obtain your product's documentation in two ways:

✦ **On the CD:** If your networking product came with a CD, pop it in and browse the contents. This is particularly useful if you can't access the Internet at the time.

✦ **On the Web:** Go to the manufacturer's Web site (most of the popular ones are listed in Book V, Chapter 4) and find the Downloads or Support section to download the product manual or installation guide. You may find this in the same area of the site where you download drivers and firmware.

If you haven't done so already, you should double-check to see whether your computer already has network connections before you install adapters. For help on checking this, refer to the Book I, Chapter 1.

Installing the Software and Drivers

Network adapters come with *drivers,* which are files that tell the network what to do and act as its brain. The drivers must be installed in order for the network adapter to work at all. These are on a CD that should be included with your network adapter. The adapters may also come with a configuration utility, which is software that lets you configure the network adapter's settings and management the networks you connect to.

If you have the disc, pop it in your CD drive. The installation program for the driver and software may come up automatically and help you. If not, browse the contents of the disc using My Computer or Computer for an installation file, such as `setup.exe`. Then run the install file and follow the directions that appear on your screen.

If you don't have the disc that came with the network adapter, don't worry. You can download the drivers and software from the manufacturer's Web site. Of course, you have to be able to get on the Internet to do so. If you need help figuring out the Web site address, check Book V, Chapter 4 for a list. Then go to the appropriate site and find the Downloads or Support section.

If you're installing the drivers from the disc, you may just want to quickly check the manufacturer's Web site to see whether a newer version is available. Even if you just bought your network adapter from the store, you may find a newer driver. (The product you bought could have been sitting in stock rooms for a while.) Book II, Chapter 5 discusses how to upgrade drivers.

Inserting the Adapter

After you have installed the drivers and software, you need to do the physical installation. The following sections tell you how to do just that, and you can go to the section that corresponds to the type of network adapter you're installing (and skip the rest).

A PCI adapter goes inside your computer

If you have a PCI or PCI Express adapter, you need to get it in place inside your computer. As you might infer, installing PCI adapters takes the most time and is the most complicated part. But even if you have never looked inside a PC before, you can still do it. Most of the time, the hardest part is just figuring out how to remove the computer cover.

Before starting the project, you should gather a few things:

✦ **Philips screw driver:** You'll need one of these to do some unscrewing and screwing. Yes, this is the screwdriver with the star-shaped end that comes to a point, not one with a flat head — thanks to Henry F. Phillips.

✦ **Workstation:** To keep from losing any screws, you should clear off an area on a flat, solid surface. A kitchen table will do just fine.

✦ **PCI adapter:** Obviously, you need your PCI network adapter. It should look something like Figure 3-1.

**Book II
Chapter 3**

**Installing Network
Adapters**

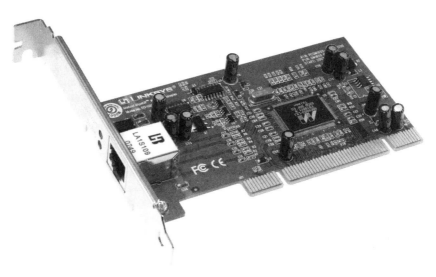

Figure 3-1:
Example of
a PCI
network
adapter,
particularly
a wired
(Ethernet)
adapter.

Courtesy of Linksys.

Carefully take it out of its packaging and set it to the side of your workstation.

When you're ready to give it a go, the following steps can take you through the entire project:

1. **Shut down and unplug your computer.**

   Carefully disconnect all the cables from your computer after you have your computer completely shut down. Then you can move your computer to your workstation.

2. **Remove the PC cover.**

   Some computer cases are held together by screws; others may have sliding covers (that may take some time to figure out).

   When you open the computer, you should touch the metal frame of the computer before touching any of the innards. You do this to release any static electricity that's in your fingers.

3. **Find an open PCI slot.**

   Your PCI and/or PCI Express slots should be easily identifiable. You should see a row of cards (and open slots), about five in total. The card's brackets are seen from the back of the computer, so you can plug in whatever goes with the card. Figure 3-2 shows an example of an open slot among the collection of PCI cards.

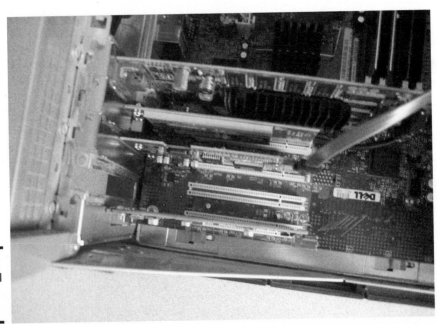

Figure 3-2:
An open PCI slot in a computer.

4. Remove the slot cover.

Open slots should have a cover on them to prevent dust and debris from entering from the back of your computer. You need to remove a slot cover so that you can put in your network adapter. Older computers probably have single screws for each slot cover or PCI bracket. Newer computers may just have movable mounts that come down and cover all the PCI cards to hold them in place.

5. Insert the network adapter.

It's best to line up the card with the slot, press gently to see whether you have it in the right place, and then push — firmly but gently — down until it snaps into place, which may take some good pressure.

6. Replace the PCI card screw or mount.

7. Replace the PC cover and plug in the cables.

You can reassemble your computer, move it back to its regular place, and plug all your cables back into the right spots. If you just installed a wireless adapter, screw on the antenna(s) that came with the network adapter onto the antenna connectors.

You did it! Congratulations!

USB adapter plugs right in

Installing a USB network adapter is probably going to be the easiest task of setting up your home network. It's as easy as one, two — there's not even a three. Here's how to connect your USB network adapter:

1. Find a USB port.

If you have an older computer, you may find only USB ports on the back (no other ports). If you have a newer computer, you should have at least two USB ports on the front of your PC. Your PC may have compartment doors to hide these along with other ports.

If you aren't familiar with USB ports, take a look at your network adapter to see what you're looking for. USB ports are rectangular and small, about ¾ inch long by 2mm wide.

2. Plug it in.

Simply plug the network adapter into one of your open USB ports.

You're done! See how simple that was?

For a wireless USB adapter, you may get a bit better wireless signal by plugging it into a port that leaves it more exposed. For instance, rather than plug it into the back of your computer where it will be against your wall, plug it into the front.

Laptop adapters insert into the slot

As with the USB adapter, installing a laptop adapter takes only two very simple steps:

1. Find the PC Card or ExpressCard slot.

Find the slot that you can slide PC Cards or ExpressCards into, usually on the side of your laptop. Older notebook computers should include a PC Card slot, which is just over two inches long. Newer notebooks probably have a smaller slot for ExpressCards.

2. Insert it into the slot.

Simply slip your PC Card or ExpressCard into the slot (see Figure 3-3 for an example). Be careful to make sure it goes in right. Push the card firmly to make sure it's all the way in.

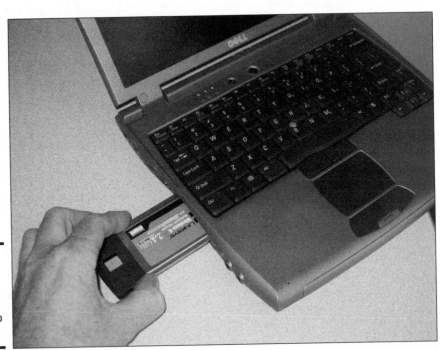

Figure 3-3: Inserting a PC Card network adapter into a laptop.

To save your laptop's battery life, you can disable your network card if you aren't using the network or Internet. See Book IV, Chapter 1 if you don't know how to turn your adapters on and off.

Using Power-Line and Phone-Line Adapters

If you are setting up a power-line or phone-line network, each computer (and possibly your Internet connection) must be connected to your home's power or phone lines, and it is connected through the use of an adapter. Installation and setup are usually easy and straightforward. As with regular network adapters, you can use the directions that came with your equipment or follow the steps in this book.

If you need to obtain the product installation guide or manual, refer to "Preparing to Install Wired and Wireless Adapters," earlier in this chapter. The suggestions there also apply here.

If you want to follow the steps in this book to install and set up your power-line or phone-line network, you need to have a power-line or phone-line adapter for each of your computers you want to be on the power-line or phone-line network. You also need one for your Internet connection, unless you're sharing the Internet in some other way, such as that discussed in the Book II, Chapter 2.

Then, follow these steps for each adapter you're setting up:

1. **Plug the adapter into an electrical outlet.**

When using power-line adapters, don't plug them into power strips, extension cords, or surge protectors. Adding these extra components between your adapters can prevent them from working correctly, keep them from working at all, or make them work below their highest potential. Power-line equipment often has its own surge protectors.

Also, you may not want to plug in power-line devices to outlets controlled by wall switches. Someone may unintentionally turn your network connection off.

2. **If you have any phone-line adapters, plug them into a phone jack.**

3. **Connect the adapter to a computer or your router.**

If you're connecting a computer to the network, connect one end of an Ethernet cable (probably included with the adapter) to the adapter and the other end to the computer.

**Book II
Chapter 3**

**Installing Network
Adapters**

If connecting your Internet connection to the network, run the Ethernet cable between the adapter and one of the Ethernet ports (usually four in a row) on the back of your router. Also, make sure your wireless router is plugged in and ready to go.

4. Insert the CD-ROM to install the software.

On the computer(s) you just hooked up to the power-line or phone-line adapter, insert the CD included with your adapter and proceed with the software installation. If an installation wizard appears and asks you to hook up the devices, just ignore it and proceed with the software installation, because you have already hooked up the devices.

5. Configure Encryption.

After the software has been installed, open the configuration utility for the adapter, which is usually accessible by the new entry to your Start menu. You should enable encryption for all your power-line or phone-line adapters.

Now your power-line or phone-line network is up and running. If further setup is necessary, the next chapter, which discusses setting up the entire network, should help you out.

Chapter 4: Setting Up and Configuring the Network

In This Chapter

✔ **Finding spots and installing the equipment**

✔ **Running and connecting cables**

✔ **Configuring routers and Internet connections**

✔ **Creating wireless computer-to-computer networks**

✔ **Setting Workgroups and Computer Names**

*T*o make use of this chapter, you should have all the required hardware for your network bought and gathered together. Also, if you haven't done so already, you need to read the preceding chapter of this minibook to get the network adapters installed in the computers you want to be on the network. Additionally, you should have your high-speed Internet activated and the modem hooked up to the Internet line. With all those preparations made, you're ready to set up and configure the rest of the network.

If you're setting up a wired or wireless network (using a router) or setting up a power- or phone-line network, you can follow the instructions given by the manufacturer, if you prefer. These directions are usually given on a quick install sheet, with more details and information in the product manual that's usually loaded on a disc and included in the box with your products. However, you can alternatively follow the steps and advice given in this chapter to set up and configure your network. These two sets of information may differ in some details, but either should get you up and networking.

If you're setting up a computer-to-computer network, you'll have to follow this chapter's directions — product documentation usually doesn't include information on how to create this type of network.

In this chapter, you find out how to physically install your networking equipment and cables and configure your network equipment and computers.

Get ready, your network is almost complete!

Getting Physical with the Installation

First, you need to do the physical part of the installation — install the router, run wires, plug things in, and so on. The following sections step you through these tasks. After that, I take you through the process of configuring all your settings.

Installing the router

If you're setting up a wired or wireless network with a router, you first have to figure out where to place the router. Usually, the bigger the square footage and floors your home has and the more computers you have, the harder it is to find the sweet spot (or the location that gives you the maximum range for wireless and lets you use the least amount of cable for wired connections). If you have just a few computers and a home on the smaller side — fewer than 1,500 square feet — with only two levels or less, placement won't be as crucial.

Thinking about your modem

For either a wired or wireless router, keep in mind that it will need to be close to the Internet modem. You can usually move your modem around, though you're limited, of course, by the number and placement of outlets for the connection type, such as phone jacks for DSL and TV outlets for cable Internet. If needed, call your Internet service provider for more information on moving your modem.

If you can't seem to get the modem close to the optimum spot for your router, consider purchasing and using a longer Ethernet cable between the two devices. In that case, you obviously would need to figure out how to hide the cable. I provide some ideas about that later in this chapter.

Finding a spot for your wired router

See Book II, Chapter 2 for help in finding your wired router's sweet spot if you haven't already done that and measured your Ethernet cabling paths. Also, you need to establish the location of your Internet modem, as discussed in the previous section.

Finding a spot for your wireless router

Because wireless routers use the airwaves to communicate with your computers, you have many things to consider when picking a good location, as follows:

✦ **Place it in a central location.** You probably want the best connection possible for all your computers, so the wireless router will probably work best if placed in the middle of your home or desired coverage area.

This location helps ensure that you have relatively equal coverage in all directions. Book V, Chapter 1 helps you troubleshoot possible problems and shows you the differences between good and bad placements.

✦ **Think about attenuators.** The fact that wireless routers send and receive signals with your computers brings up another issue: The signals can be blocked or degraded by objects in your home. When finding a place for the router, try to stay away from big solid objects that may attenuate the signals. For example, rather than place the router against a wall that has a big, solid, wood entertainment center behind the wall, move the router down several feet or find a different location altogether. Additionally, you don't want to put the router inside anything. You want the router to be exposed as much as possible.

✦ **Keep away from interfering devices.** Don't place the wireless router next to devices that may interfere with the Wi-Fi signals. This includes electrical and radio devices that use — or bleed onto — the same frequency band (2.4GHz) of your wireless network. A few of the devices that can interfere with your wireless network are

- **Neighboring wireless networks**
- **Cordless phones**
- **Baby monitors**
- **Wireless speakers and headphones**
- **Kitchen microwaves**

If you're using the less popular wireless A equipment, you're using the 5GHz frequency band instead. You may experience interference from other, similar 5GHz devices.

Plugging in the router

When you have found the place for your wired or wireless router, go ahead and plug it in, as follows:

✦ **Connect your modem to the Internet.** If you haven't already, make sure that your Internet modem is set up and connected to the Internet, which you can verify by looking at the status lights on the modem.

✦ **Connect your router and modem:** Your router (and maybe your modem) should have come with an Ethernet cable — with similar but a bit wider connectors than telephone cords. You want to connect one end to the Internet modem's Ethernet port. You plug the other end into the router's port for the Internet connection, usually labeled "Internet" or "WAN."

✦ **Plug in the power.** Simply plug the power cord into the back of the router and the other end into an electrical outlet.

Book II
Chapter 4

Setting Up and Configuring the Network

Laying and connecting the cables

Now's the time to run your Ethernet cable if you're creating a wired-only network or wiring computers directly to a wireless router. If you haven't already figured out the paths for your Ethernet cables to be run between your router and computers, see Chapter 2 of this minibook.

After you have run the cables, hook them up to the router and/or computers as follows:

+ **For cables going to a router:** You can connect the cables coming from computers to the regular Ethernet ports on your router — usually you can use any of the other (4 or 8) ports except for the Internet or WAN port.

+ **For cables going to computers:** Plug the cable into the Ethernet port of the network adapter.

+ **If setting up a computer-to-computer network:** You need to hook one computer up to the Internet modem. Simply connect one end of an Ethernet or USB cable (probably provided with the modem) to the modem's port and the other end to the appropriate port of the computer. Later, you'll set up this computer to share its Internet connection among the others on the computer-to-computer network.

Make sure that all the cable connectors are pushed in and snapped into place. A gentle tug on the cable can help make sure you have them in right.

Plugging into power lines

If you're setting up a power-line network, you should have already installed and configured the power-line adapters for your computers and Internet modem. If you haven't done so yet, flip back to the previous chapter.

If you want to save money, you can connect your Internet modem to one of the computers on the power- or phone-line network rather than dedicate a power- or phone-line adapter to your modem. Then you can configure your computer to share its Internet connection with others on the network. I discuss this approach in the "Configuring Internet for nonrouter networks" section, later in this chapter.

Before you complete your network installation, though, here are a few things to consider:

+ **Plug directly into an outlet.** You shouldn't connect power-line equipment into power strips, extension cords, or surge protectors. Adding these extra components between your adapters can prevent the connection from working right, or at its best potential, or can even cause it to not work at all. Power-line equipment often has its own surge protectors.

✦ **Avoid wall-switch outlets.** If you plug in power-line devices in outlets controlled by wall-switches, you run the risk that someone might unintentionally turn your network connection off.

✦ **Enable power-line encryption:** You should enable encryption for all your power-line devices. You might do this during installation as recommended by the manufacturer's installation guide, or you can usually do it by accessing a configuration utility on your computer after you've already installed the device.

Setting Up and Configuring the Network

When you have all your networking equipment installed, you can configure your network. The following sections help you through the process.

**Book II
Chapter 4**

Setting Up and Configuring the Network

Setting up your wired or wireless router

To configure the settings, you must first connect at least one computer to the router. For wired connections, you probably need to just plug in the Ethernet cable on both ends, which you may have already done if you followed along in the previous section. To connect wirelessly, find and choose the default network name (usually stated in the product documentation) of the wireless router and click the button to connect.

For step-by-step directions on how to connect (and how to check whether you're connected), see Book IV, Chapter 1. If you can't seem to connect your computers to the router, you can refer to the troubleshooting steps in Book V, Chapter 1.

Accessing the Web-based configuration utility

After you are successfully connected to the router, you need to bring up its Web-based configuration utility to configure all the settings for your router. To access the utility, open your Web browser, such as Internet Explorer, Netscape, or Firefox, enter the IP address of your router into the browser's address bar, and press Enter.

Keep in mind that some manufacturers may use a domain name, instead of an IP address, that looks like a Web site address.

If you don't know the IP address, refer to Book V, Chapter 3 for help.

When the configuration utility opens, you receive a prompt, such as that shown in Figure 4-1, to enter the default username and password for the router. The default username and password are given in the product documentation. You can also refer to Book V, Chapter 3 for a list of default usernames and passwords for many popular brands.

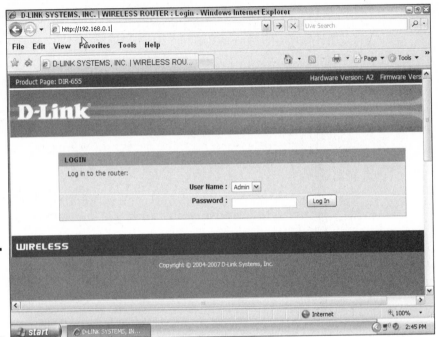

Figure 4-1:
Logging into
a router
using its IP
address.

Using setup wizards

After you log in to the router's configuration utility, you may see links or
buttons to take you to setup wizards. Some routers may have only one
wizard to configure all the initial settings; others may have separate wizards
for the Internet connection, wireless, and network settings. You can either go
through these wizards or follow the steps in the next two subsections, which
also cover the initial settings you need to configure. But even if you go the
wizard route, you can refer to the tips given here.

Configuring the Internet connection

First you need to find the Internet connection settings in the Web-based configuration utility, such as Figure 4-2 shows.

You may find these settings in a Setup, WAN, or Internet section. When you
locate them, select the connectivity type for your particular Internet connection and enter any required information. Following are the typical choices:

✦ **DHCP (Automatic Configuration):** Choose this if your Internet connection automatically provides you with an IP Address and doesn't require
you to enter any login or address information. Most cable modems use
this type of connection.

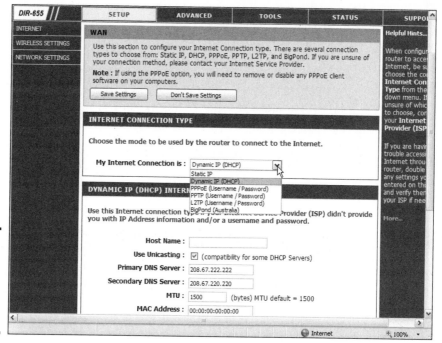

Figure 4-2:
An example
of a router's
Internet
connection
settings.

✦ **Static IP:** Choose this option if your ISP provided you with IP Address information that has to be manually configured, which usually includes the following pieces of information: Internet IP address; subnet mask; gateway; and static DNS addresses.

✦ **PPPoE:** Point-to-Point Protocol over Ethernet (PPPoE) is commonly used by DSL modems and typically requires a username and password to get online.

✦ **PPTP:** Point-to-Point Tunneling Protocol (PPTP) uses a virtual private network to connect to your ISP. This method of connection is primarily used by DSL modems, typically just in Europe. This type of connection typically requires a username and password to get online.

✦ **L2TP:** Layer Two Tunneling Protocol (L2TP) also uses a virtual private network to connect to your ISP. This type of connection is used by some DSL modems and typically requires a username and password to get online.

This information should have been provided to you from your Internet Service Provider (ISP) when you signed up. If needed, contact your ISP for the information. However, if you didn't receive any connection or login information, you're probably supposed to use DHCP (Automatic Configuration).

Some ISPs may require a few more pieces of information, including the following:

+ **Host Name:** They may check your router's Host Name against the Host Name that is registered with your account. This helps the ISP ensure that your router and the service are legitimate.

+ **MTU:** The Maximum Transmission Unit (MTU) is the largest packet size (in bytes) that the router will send through your Internet connection. Typical values are 1,500 bytes for an Ethernet connection and 1,492 bytes for a PPPoE connection. The default value set in your router is usually fine; however, sometimes you may have to make a slight change.

+ **MAC address (cloning):** In some cases, your ISP may require the MAC (physical) address of the router be equal to the MAC address that is registered with your ISP account. This address registered with your ISP account may be set by the computer or router first used to initially connect to the ISP's service. Therefore, Internet access is granted only when the device you have hooked to the modem has the MAC address of that initial device. However, most routers have a MAC address cloning feature that lets you change the address seen by your ISP — essentially tricking your ISP.

Don't forget to save any changes you've made. You can usually do this by clicking a Save button on the top or bottom of the page. The wireless router may reboot and you may be disconnected for a minute.

Setting your router's password

Because the default password for your router is publicly known, you need to change it. To do so, follow these steps:

1. **Click the Admin, Management, Tools, or Administration tab (or other tab containing the password settings, as shown in see Figure 4-3).**

2. **Type in your desired password into the Password and Verify fields.**

Some wireless routers may allow you to specify a user account (which can't make any changes) in addition to the necessary administration account (which has full privileges).

Because you could forget your username and password, you may want to write it on a small piece of paper and tape it on the bottom of your router. You may also want to include the IP address of the router so that you don't forget how to access the utility.

3. **Click the Save or Apply button, on the top or bottom of the page, if you made any setting changes.**

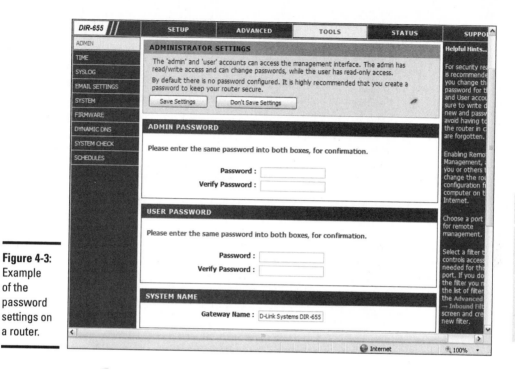

**Book II
Chapter 4**

Setting Up and
Configuring the
Network

Figure 4-3:
Example
of the
password
settings on
a router.

The wireless router may reboot and you may be disconnected for a minute. When you're connected to the network again, you can access the Web-based utility again (discussed in an earlier section) with your new (username and) password.

Configuring wireless-specific settings on the router

If you are using a wireless router, you have a few more settings to configure before you're done. To complete the configuration, follow these steps:

1. **Click the Wireless tab (or other, similarly named tab containing the basic wireless settings. (See Figure 4-4 for an example.)**

2. **Enter your own name in the Network Name (or SSID) field. (Figure 4-3 shows an example.)**

Keep the following in mind when creating a network name:

- It is case sensitive and must not exceed 32 characters.

- You can use any of the characters on your keyboard.

- Don't include information that might give away your location, such as a street number or last name.

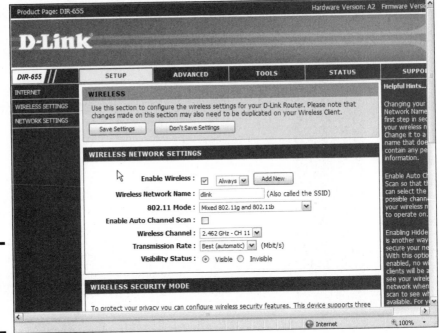

Figure 4-4:
Wireless
settings on
a wireless
router.

3. **Set your channel, usually by selecting one from a drop-down list.**

   Setting your channel isn't necessarily required (because it's set by default) but may help in the long run.

   If your router supports automatic channel selection, use that option. If it doesn't, you should pick a channel other than channel 6 — such as channel 1 or 11. Channel 6 is the default used by nearly all wireless routers. Selecting another channel reduces the chances of being interfered with by (or causing interference with) a neighboring network. But you should always try to stick with the nonoverlapping channels of 1, 6, or 11.

4. **If the encryption settings aren't located with the basic wireless settings, click the Wireless Security tab (or another tab containing the encryption settings).**

   See Figure 4-5 for an example of these settings.

   To prevent others from connecting to your wireless network and also from seeing what you are doing on your network, you need to enable encryption.

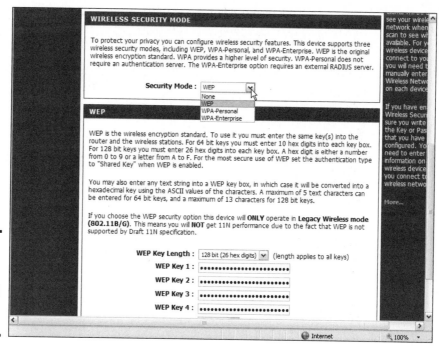

Book II
Chapter 4

Setting Up and
Configuring the
Network

Figure 4-5:
A wireless
router's
security and
encryption
settings.

For the best protection, use WPA2-PSK (Personal) or WPA-PSK (Personal) encryption. You may, however, be limited to using the less secure type (WEP) when you have older wireless adapters on your network that don't support these newer types.

For help on setting up encryption, refer to Book IV, Chapter 1.

To remember the network key for your wireless network, you may want to save it in a text document and put it in a safe place. (I save mine to the My Documents folder of all my computers.) This way, when you have to reconfigure your adapters down the road, add new computers, set up a networking accessory, or whatever, you always have the key where you can get it. This is especially useful when using WEP keys, which aren't easy to remember and are much easier to copy and paste than to type in. But for any type of key, you can always write it on that piece of paper under your router, as mentioned previously.

5. (Optional) Enable additional security features.

Limiting network access by using MAC address filtering and "hiding" your wireless network by disabling network name broadcasting are two ways you can better secure your wireless network. However, using these optional techniques requires additional setup and configuration time and can sometimes cause issues and inconveniences when using your network. It's up to you whether you want to spend a bit more time to get your network even more secure.

For help on setting up these features, refer to Book III, Chapter 2.

6. **Click the Save or Apply button, on the top or bottom of the page, if you made any changes to settings.**

The wireless router will reboot and you will be disconnected for a minute. If you were connected wirelessly (rather than by an Ethernet cable), you have to reconnect with the new network name. You can probably just choose the new network name from your available wireless network list. However, if you have broadcasting disabled (from Step 5), you need to manually set up a connection by adding a network to your preferred list. Refer to Book IV, Chapter 1 for more information.

If you have enabled encryption on your wireless router, you must enter the same key on your computers. You can do so when connecting to the network the next time (from your available wireless network list) or you can (manually) set this network up as a preferred network.

When you're reconnected to the network, you can access the Web-based utility again, as discussed previously.

Configuring your Internet connection for nonrouter networks

If you are creating a computer-to-computer without a router, one computer must be connected to your Internet modem. However, you still may have to configure your computer with the proper connection information in order for the Internet connection to work. The following sections describe how to do this based on the type of connectivity method specified by your ISP.

You may also have to configure your computer with your Internet connection information if you're setting up a power- or phone-line network and hooking your Internet modem to a computer, which saves money by not requiring you to dedicate an adapter to your modem. You can just set up your modem and a power- or phone-line adapter with your computer. Then you can configure your computer to share its Internet connection with others on the network.

If you're creating a computer-to-computer or power- phone-line network but have a wired or wireless network with a router, you don't have to configure a computer with your Internet connection. You can skip down to the "Bridging network connections" section.

The type of connectivity method and any necessary information should have been provided to you from your Internet Service Provider (ISP) when you signed up. If needed, contact your ISP for the information. However, if you didn't receive any connection or login information, you're probably supposed to use DHCP (Automatic Configuration), which means that you don't have to continue with configuring your Internet connection.

For information about the various types of connections, including DHCP, see the "Configuring the Internet connection" section under "Configuring your wired and wireless routers," earlier in this chapter. Meanwhile, the following sections take you step-by-step through configuring your modem (for the various operating systems covered in this book) for Point to Point Protocol over Ethernet (PPPoE) connectivity, which is typical for DSL modems and requires a username and password to get online.

If your Internet connection uses a static IP address, you can refer to Book IV, Chapter 1 to configure the static IP address information given to you by your ISP. If your Internet connection uses any other method than DHCP, PPPoE, or static, refer to the directions given to you by your ISP.

Configuring PPPoE in Windows XP

You can set up your Windows XP computer for a PPPoE connection by following these steps:

1. **Click Start.**

2. **Click Control Panel.**

   If using the Classic Start menu, click Settings, and then click Control Panel.

3. **In the Control Panel window, click the Network and Internet Connections category.**

   If in Classic Control Panel view, skip this step.

4. **Click the Network Connections icon.**

5. **In the Network Tasks pane, click the Create a New Connection link.**

6. **On the New Connection Wizard that appears, click Next.**

7. **On the Network Connection Type page, select the Connect to the Internet radio button and click Next.**

8. **On the Getting Ready page, select the Set Up My Connection Manually radio button and click Next.**

9. **On the Internet Connection page, select the Connect Using a Broadband Connection that Requires a User Name and Password radio button and click Next.**

Book II
Chapter 4

Setting Up and
Configuring the
Network

10. **On the Connection Name page, enter a name for your connection into the ISP Name text box and click Next.**

    This can be anything you wish to help you identify the connection in your Network Connections window.

11. **On the Internet Account Information page, enter your account credentials into the User Name, Password, and Confirm Password fields, and click Next.**

    Your ISP should have provided you with this information when you signed up for service.

12. **On the Completing the New Connection Wizard page, review your settings, select the Add a Shortcut to this Connection to My Desktop checkbox, if you prefer, and then click Finish.**

    The connection window should appear. You can connect to the Internet by clicking Connect.

 You can bring up this connection window again by choosing Start⇨Connect To and then the name of your Internet connection. If you're using the Classic Start menu, you choose Start⇨Settings⇨Network Connections and then the name of your Internet connection. The connection is also listed in your Network Connections window, which is accessible from the Control Panel.

Configuring PPPoE in Windows Vista

If you're using Windows Vista, here's how to set up a PPPoE Internet connection:

1. **Click the network icon in the system tray.**

2. **Click Network and Sharing Center.**

3. **Under Tasks in the left pane, click Set Up a Connection or Network.**

4. **In the Set Up a Connection or Network Wizard that appears, select Connect to the Internet and click Next.**

    If Windows detects an Internet connection, it asks whether you want to browse the Internet now or set up a new connection anyway. You should select the Set Up a New Connection Anyway option.

5. **On the How Do You Want to Connect page, click Broadband (PPPoE).**

6. **On the Type the Information from Your Internet Service Provider (ISP) page, enter your account credentials into the User Name and Password fields.**

    Your ISP should have provided you with this information when you signed up for service.

7. Enter a name into the Connection Name field.

This can be anything you wish to help you identify the connection in your Network Connections window.

8. Select the Allow Other People to Use This Connection checkbox.

9. Click Connect.

You can access the connection by clicking the network icon in the system tray, selecting Network and Sharing Center, and clicking the Manage Network Connections link in the left task pane. You'll see the connection listed in your Network Connections window.

Configuring PPPoE in Mac OS X Leopard

Here's how to set up a PPPoE connection in Mac OS X Leopard:

1. Click the Apple icon and then click System Preferences.

2. In the System Preferences window, click the Network icon.

3. On the Network window, click the plus sign under the list of network connections and adapters.

4. On the pop-up window that appears, select PPPoE from the For Interface drop-down list, select Ethernet from the Ethernet drop-down list, type a name into the Service Name text box, and click the Create button.

The Service Name distinguishes this connection from the other connections and adapters in the Network window.

Your connection is added to the list and its settings are displayed.

5. On the Network window with the newly created PPPoE connection selected, enter your PPPoE Service Name if required by your ISP.

Enter this only if your ISP specifies a service name.

6. Enter your account credentials into the Account Name and Password fields and then select the Remember this Password checkbox if you don't want to enter the account credentials each time you connect.

Your ISP should have provided you with this information when you signed up for service.

7. To save your changes, click the Apply button.

When you want to connect, click the Connect button.

To be able to quickly access your DSL connection status and settings, you can select the Show PPPoE Status in Menu Bar option. You can also bring up this information whenever you want by choosing System Preferences⇨Network.

Configuring PPPoE in Mac OS X Tiger

To configure a PPPoE connection in Mac OS X Tiger, follow these steps:

1. **Click the Apple icon and then click System Preferences.**

2. **In the System Preferences window, click the Network icon.**

3. **In the Network window, select the Ethernet adapter that's connected to your modem from the Show drop-down list.**

4. **From the adapter page that appears, click the PPPoE tab.**

5. **Check the Connect Using PPPoE checkbox.**

6. **If required by your ISP, enter your ISP's name into the Service Provider text box.**

   Enter this only if your ISP specifies that you do so.

7. **Enter your account information into the Account Name and Password fields.**

   These are the credentials that your ISP should have provided you with when you signed up for service.

8. **If required by your ISP, enter your PPPoE Service Name into the text box.**

   Enter this only if your ISP specifies a service name.

9. **To set your PPPoE advanced and dialing settings, click the PPPoE Options button, select or deselect the checkboxes as you desire, and click OK to return to the adapter's page.**

10. **To save your changes, click the Apply button.**

    When you want to connect, click the Connect button.

To be able to quickly access your DSL connection status and settings, select the Show PPPoE Status in Menu Bar option. You can also find this information whenever you want by choosing System Preferences⇨Network.

Configuring PPPoE in Ubuntu

Here's how to configure a PPPoE connection in Ubuntu:

1. **From the Ubuntu toolbar, choose Applications⇨Accessories⇨Terminal.**

   A DOS-type window appears.

2. **Type** sudo pppoeconf, **as Figure 4-6 shows.**

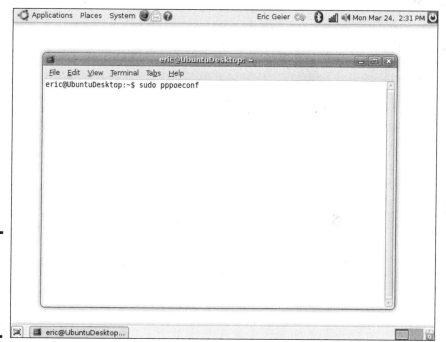

Book II
Chapter 4

Setting Up and
Configuring the
Network

Figure 4-6:
Starting the
PPPoE
connection
configu-
ration utility.

3. **If requested, type your Ubuntu account password into the Terminal**
   and press Enter.

4. **Complete the setup wizard by reading and responding to the prompts.**

Sharing the Internet for nonrouter networks

If you are creating a computer-to-computer or power- or phone-line network
(without a router), you need to set up the computer that's hooked to the
modem to share the Internet connection. Doing so gives the other computers on the computer-to-computer network access to the Internet.

If you can't enable Internet Connection Sharing, you can try bridging the two
network adapters in Windows, as discussed in the "Bridging network connections" section, later in this chapter.

Sharing the Internet connection in Windows XP

Here's how to enable Internet Connection Sharing (ICS) in Windows XP:

1. **Click Start.**

2. Click Control Panel.

If using the Classic Start menu, click Settings, and then click Control Panel.

3. In the Control Panel window, click the Network and Internet Connections category.

If in Classic view, skip this step.

4. Click (or double-click) the Network Connections icon.

5. In the Network Connections window, right-click the network adapter and select Properties.

You want to right-click the network adapter (or network bridge) that connects to the computer-to-computer or power- or phone-line network.

6. In the Network Connection Properties window, click the Advanced tab.

7. On the Advanced tab, check the Allow Other Network Users To Connect Through This Computer's Internet Connection checkbox (see Figure 4-7).

Figure 4-7:
Letting other computers use your Internet connection in Windows XP.

8. Click OK.

Sharing the Internet connection in Windows Vista

Here's how to enable Internet Connection Sharing (ICS) in Windows Vista:

1. Click the network icon in the system tray.

2. Click Network and Sharing Center.

3. Under Tasks in the left pane, click Manage Network Connections.

4. In the Manage Network Connections window, right-click the network adapter and select Properties.

    You want to right-click the network adapter (or network bridge) that connects to the computer-to-computer or power- or phone-line network.

    If User Account Control is active, click Continue on the prompt.

5. In the Network Connection Properties window, click the Sharing tab.

6. On the Sharing tab, check the Allow Other Network Users To Connect Through This Computer's Internet Connection checkbox.

7. Click OK.

Sharing the Internet connection in Mac OS X Leopard

Follow these steps to share an Internet connection in Mac OS X Leopard:

1. Click the Apple icon and then click System Preferences.

2. In the System Preferences window, click the Sharing icon.

3. In the Sharing window, click the Internet Sharing checkbox in the Service list on the left, and when prompted to confirm that you want to turn on Internet sharing, click the Start button.

4. If more than one adapter is active, choose the connection that has the Internet connection from the Share Your Connection From drop-down list, and in the To Computers Using list box, select the checkboxes for the connections you want to share your Internet connection on.

    If only one network adapter or connection is active, these settings are grayed out and you can't select them.

Sharing the Internet connection in Mac OS X Tiger

To share an Internet connection in Mac OS X Tiger, follow these steps:

1. Click the Apple icon and then click System Preferences.

2. Click the Sharing icon.

3. In the Sharing window, click the Services tab.

4. Select the Personal Web Sharing checkbox in the Service list box.

5. Click the Internet tab.

6. Choose the connection that has the Internet connection from the Share Your Connection From drop-down list, and in the To Computers Using list box, select the checkboxes for the connections you want to share your Internet connection on.

If only one network adapter or connection is active, these settings are grayed out and you can't select them.

7. **Click the Start button.**

Creating a wireless computer-to-computer network

If you are setting up a wired computer-to-computer network, you should have already plugged in the Ethernet cables to your computer, which usually completes the connection process. If you're going with a wireless computer-to-computer network, though, you have to create the network from one of your computers and then join the other wireless computers to the network name you create.

When creating a network name for your computer-to-computer network, keep the following in mind:

✦ It is case sensitive and must not exceed 32 characters.

✦ You can use any of the characters on your keyboard.

✦ Don't include information that might give away your location, such as a street number or last name.

Just as when using wireless routers, you need to enable encryption for your computer-to-computer network to prevent others from connecting to your wireless network. Encryption also prevents people from seeing what you are doing on your network.

For the best protection, use WPA2-PSK or WPA-PSK encryption. You may be limited, however, to using the less secure type (WEP) when you have older wireless adapters on your network that don't support these newer types.

WPA-PSK and WPA2-PSK keys can consist of from 8 to 63 characters in a combination of letters, numbers, and symbols. The key is case sensitive. These types of keys are comparable to a regular password, in contrast to the keys entered for WEP encryption, which requires an exact number of limited types of characters. WEP keys require you to use Hex digits, which are numbers from 0 to 9 and letters from A to F. For instance, 01234aBcde constitutes a 64-bit encryption key.

The following sections describe how to create a wireless computer-to-computer network in the various operating systems covered in this book.

Creating a computer-to-computer network in Windows XP

Here's how to create a computer-to-computer network using Windows XP's built-in configuration utility:

1. **Double-click your wireless adapter icon in the system tray.**

2. **In the Network Connection Status window, click the Properties button.**

3. **In the Network Connection Properties window, click the Wireless Networks tab.**

4. **On the Wireless Networks tab, click the Add button.**

You should see the window shown in Figure 4-8.

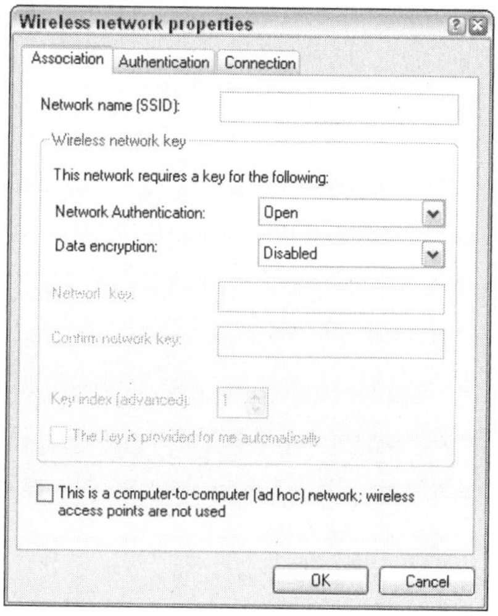

**Book II
Chapter 4**

Setting Up and
Configuring the
Network

Figure 4-8:
Adding a
Network
window in
Windows XP.

Wireless network properties

Association | Authentication | Connection

Network name (SSID):

Wireless network key

This network requires a key for the following:

Network Authentication: Open

Data encryption: Disabled

Network key:

Confirm network key:

Key index (advanced): 1

☐ The key is provided for me automatically

☐ This is a computer-to-computer (ad hoc) network; wireless access points are not used

OK | Cancel

5. **In the Wireless Network Properties window that appears, enter something for the name of your computer-to-computer network that you're creating in the Network Name (SSID) field.**

Tips for choosing a Network Name are given earlier in this section.

6. **Set up encryption for the computer-to-computer network.** If you don't want to enable encryption for your computer-to-computer network, set Network Authentication to Open and Data Encryption to Disabled. To enable WPA-PSK or WPA2-PSK, set Network Authentication to one of the types and set Data Encryption to AES because it provides stronger encryption. Then enter your desired Network Key into both boxes. To enable WEP, set Network Authentication to Open and set Data Encryption to WEP. Then enter your desired Network Key into both boxes, using the valid type and amount of characters. To enter a 128-bit key (which is recommended), you must enter 26 hexadecimal (hex) digits. For 64-bit keys, you must enter 10 hex digits.

Network key requirements are discussed earlier in this section.

7. **Select the This Is a Computer-to-Computer (Ad Hoc) Network; Wireless Access Points Are Not Used checkbox (found at the bottom of the window).**

8. **Click the Authentication tab to specify the authentication settings.**

   You can deselect the Enable IEEE 802.1x Authentication for This Network option since 802.1x is primarily used in enterprises. You don't have to worry about, or change, the other settings.

9. **Click the Connection tab and select the Connect When This Network is in Range option if you want Windows to automatically connect to the wireless network when it is available.**

10. **Click OK.**

Creating a computer-to-computer network in Windows Vista

If you're using Windows Vista, here's how to create the network with Vista's configuration utility:

1. **Right-click the network icon in the system tray and select Network and Sharing Center.**

2. **In the Tasks pane, click the Set Up a Connection or Network link.**

3. **In the Set Up a Connection or Network Wizard that appears, select Set Up a Wireless Ad Hoc (Computer-To-Computer) Network and click the Next button.**

4. **On the Set Up a Wireless Ad Hoc Network page, click the Next button.**

   You should see a window like the one shown in Figure 4-9.

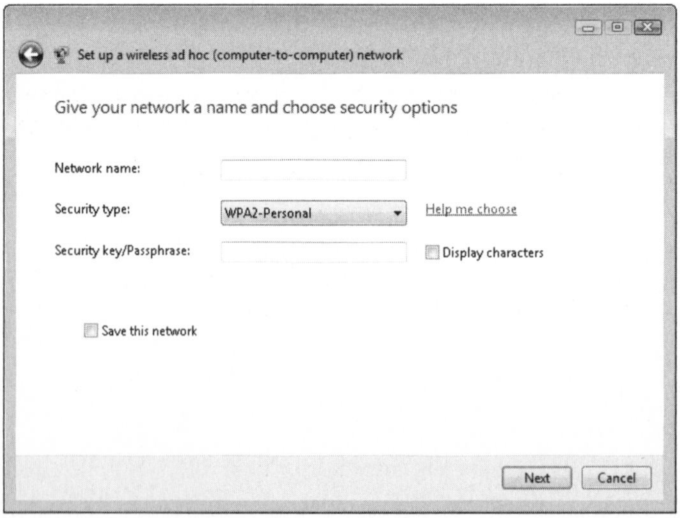

Figure 4-9: Creating a wireless ad hoc network in Windows Vista.

5. **Enter a name for your computer-to-computer network into the Network Name field.**

   Tips for choosing a network name (SSID) are given earlier in this section.

6. **Set up encryption for the computer-to-computer network.**

   If you don't want to enable encryption for your computer-to-computer network, set Security Type to No Authentication (Open). To enable WPA-Personal (PSK) or WPA2-Personal (PSK), set Security Type to one of the types. Then enter your desired Security Key into both boxes. To enable WEP, set Security Type to WEP. Then enter your desired Security Key into both boxes using the valid type and number of characters. To enter a 128-bit key (which is recommended), you must enter 26 hexadecimal (hex) digits. For 64-bit keys, you must enter 10 hex digits.

   Security Key requirements are discussed earlier in this section.

7. **If you want to save this network, which is probably the case, select the Save This Network option.**

8. **Click the Next button.**

   The program sets up the network and lets you know when it's done.

9. **On the Network is Ready to Use window, click the Close button.**

Creating a computer-to-computer network in Mac OS X Tiger and Leopard

Here's how to create a computer-to-computer network in Mac OS X Tiger and Leopard:

1. **Click the Airport icon in the upper-right corner of the desktop and click Create Network.**

   You should see a window like the one shown in Figure 4-10.

2. **In the Create a Computer-To-Computer Network window that opens, enter the network name (SSID) for your network into the Name field.**

   Tips for choosing a network name are given earlier in this section.

3. **Choose a channel for your network from the Channel drop-down list.**

   You should pick a channel other than channel 6 — such as channel 1 or 11. Channel 6 is the default used by nearly all wireless routers. Selecting another channel reduces the chances of being interfered with by (or causing interference with) a neighboring network. But you should always try to stick with the nonoverlapping channels of 1, 6, or 11.

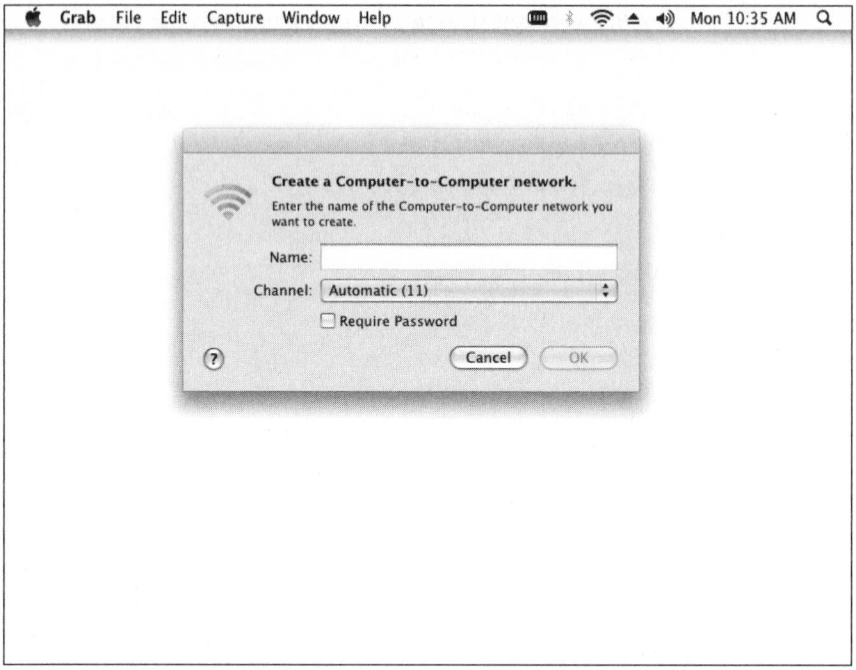

Figure 4-10:
Creating a
wireless ad
hoc network
in Mac OS X.

4. **To enable encryption for your network in Tiger, click the Show Options button and select the Enable Encryption (using WEP) option and then select an encryption type (128-bit key is best) from the WEP Key drop-down menu list; in Leopard, select the Require Password checkbox and select an encryption type (128-bit key is best) from the Security drop-down list.**

Then, for both Tiger and Leopard, type in the network key you want to set for your network into the Password and Verify (or Confirm) fields, using the valid type and amount of characters.

Enabling encryption helps prevent others from connecting to your computer-to-computer network and also from seeing what you are doing on your network.

Security Key requirements are discussed earlier in this section.

5. **Click OK.**

Creating a computer-to-computer network in Ubuntu

Here's how to create a computer-to-computer network in Ubuntu:

1. **Click the network icon from the Ubuntu toolbar and select Create New Wireless Network.**

   You should see a window like the one shown in Figure 4-11.

**Book II
Chapter 4**

**Setting Up and
Configuring the
Network**

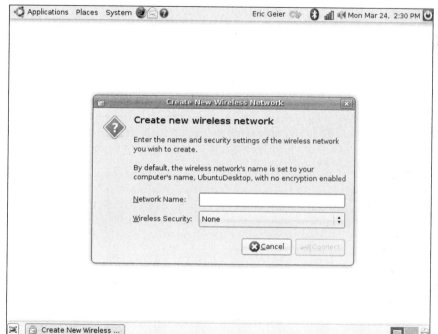

Figure 4-11:
Creating a
wireless ad
hoc network
in Ubuntu.

2. **In the Network Name field, enter a network name (SSID) for your computer-to-computer network.**

   Tips for choosing a Network Name are given earlier in this section.

3. **Set up encryption for the computer-to-computer network.** If you don't want to enable encryption for your computer-to-computer network, leave Wireless Security set to None. To enable WPA-Personal (PSK), set Wireless Security to WPA Personal, and enter your desired WPA password/key into the Password field. To enable WEP, set Wireless Security to WEP 64/128-bit Hex and enter your desired key, using the

valid type and number of characters, into the Key field. To enter a 128-bit key (which is recommended), you must enter 26 hexadecimal (hex) digits. For 64-bit keys, you must enter 10 hex digits.

Security Key requirements are discussed earlier in this section.

4. Click the Connect button.

After you've created the computer-to-computer network, you should see the Network Name (SSID) in your list of available wireless networks, as with any other wireless network. To join your computers in the computer-to-computer network, connect to your Network Name. If you need help on connecting to wireless networks, see Book IV, Chapter 1.

Bridging network connections

If you have two network adapters on a computer, connected to two different networks, you can bridge them together, thereby letting you share resources between the computers on both networks. This is useful when, for example, you are creating a computer-to-computer network but have a wired or wireless network with a router.

Say that PC A is connected to your wireless (router) network, but PC B has only an Ethernet adapter (no wireless). Rather than run a cable all the way from the wireless router, you can run a cable from PC A or PC B, which is much shorter distance. Then, on PC A, you can bridge the wireless and wired network adapters.

In Windows, you can create only one Network Bridge on a computer, but the bridge can accommodate numerous network connections. You can't create a Network Bridge using network adapters that have Internet Connection Sharing (ICS) enabled. (ICS is discussed in the "Sharing the Internet for non-router networks" section, earlier in this chapter.) You must first disable the ICS feature before adding the network adapter to a Network Bridge. Also keep in mind that you can't create a Network Bridge on a computer running Windows 2000 or earlier.

Creating bridges in Mac OS X isn't possible. Ubuntu offers the feature; however, it requires advanced configuration, which is discussed at http://help.ubuntu.com/community/NetworkConnectionBridge.

To bridge network connections in Windows XP and Vista, you must first open the Network Connections window. To do so in Windows XP, follow these steps:

1. Click Start.

2. Click Control Panel.

If using the Classic Start menu, click Settings, and then click Control Panel.

3. In the Control Panel window, click the Network and Internet Connections category.

If in Classic Control Panel view, skip this step.

4. Click (or double-click) the Network Connections icon.

Here's how to open Network Connections in Windows Vista:

1. Click the network icon in the system tray.

2. Click Network and Sharing Center.

3. In the Network and Sharing Center, under Tasks on the left pane, click the Manage Network Connections link.

When you have the Network Connections window open, select the network connections you want to bridge (either by clicking and dragging your cursor or clicking the icons while holding the Ctrl key), right-click one of them, and select Bridge Connections (see Figure 4-12).

Book II
Chapter 4

Setting Up and
Configuring the
Network

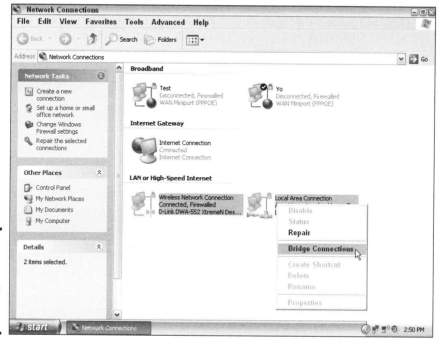

Figure 4-12:
Bridging
network
connections
in Windows
XP.

Next, you set up the network bridge to share the Internet connection, by following the steps in the previous "Sharing the Internet for nonrouter networks" section.

If you ever want to delete the Network Bridge, just right-click the icon in the Network Connections window and click Delete. If you want to remove certain network adapters from the Network Bridge, right-click the adapter and click Remove from Bridge.

Organizing into a Workgroup and Naming PCs

When you have all the networking gear set up, you have one more group of settings to configure — network identification — for each of your computers. For Windows-based networks, you have a Workgroup (and Domain) setting that helps group your computers. In most cases, particularly for sharing purposes, having all your computers in the same Workgroup is best.

For each computer, you have to choose to classify it in a Workgroup or a Domain. There are some differences between the two. You should use Workgroup, though. Domains are primarily used in corporate networks.

Then you have another (unique) setting for each computer, called the Computer Name, which helps you identify your computers when sharing and configuring network settings on your router.

The following sections will show you how to configure your network identification values for your computers.

Setting the Workgroup and Computer Name in Windows 2000 and XP

Here's how to set the Workgroup and Computer Name in Windows 2000 and XP:

1. **Click Start, right-click My Computer, and select Properties.**

2. **In the System Properties window that appears, click the Computer Name (in XP) or Network Identification (in 2000) tab.**

   Figure 4-13 shows the Computer Name tab in Windows XP.

3. **Click the Change (in XP) or Properties (in 2000) button.**

4. **On the Computer Name (or Identification) Changes window, enter a name for your computer into the Computer Name field.**

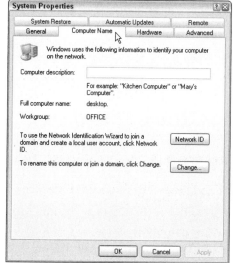

Figure 4-13:
The network
identifi-
cation
info in
Windows XP.

5. **Select the Workgroup radio button and enter the same value that you use for all your computers into the text box.**

   Domains are primarily used in large corporate or enterprise networks, so you probably don't need a domain.

6. **Click OK.**

All your computers should reside in the same Workgroup, and the Computer Names need to be unique.

Setting the Workgroup and Computer Name in Windows Vista

Here's how to configure the Workgroup and Computer Name in Windows Vista:

1. **Click Start, right-click My Computer, and select Properties.**

2. **In the System window, under the Computer Name, Domain, and Workgroup Settings section, click the Change Settings link.**

   If UAC is active, click Continue on the prompt.

3. **In the System Properties window that opens, click the Change button.**

4. **In the Computer Name/Domain Changes window, enter a name for your computer into the Computer Name field.**

5. **Select the Workgroup radio button and enter the same value that you use for all your computers into the text box.**

   Domains are primarily used in large corporate or enterprise networks, so you probably don't need a domain.

6. **Click OK.**

Setting the Workgroup and Computer Name in Mac OS X

Here's how to configure the Computer Name in Mac OS X Leopard and Tiger:

1. **Click the Apple icon and then click System Preferences.**

2. **In the System Preferences window, click the Sharing icon.**

3. **At the top of the Sharing window that appears, change the name in the Computer Name text box to whatever you want.**

Here's how to configure the Workgroup name in Mac OS X Leopard:

1. **Click the Apple icon and then click System Preferences.**

2. **In the System Preferences window, click the Network icon.**

3. **In the Network window, click the desired network adapter from the list on the left.**

4. **Click the Advanced button in the lower-right corner of the window.**

5. **In the pop-up window, click the WINS tab.**

6. **Change the Workgroup field to contain whatever name you want.**

Here's how to configure the Workgroup name in Mac OS X Tiger:

1. **Choose Go⇨Utilities.**

2. **In the Utilities window that opens, double-click the Directory Access icon.**

3. **On the Directory Access window that appears, select the SMB/CIFS checkbox and click the Configure button.**

4. **In the pop-up window that appears, change the name in the Workgroup field to whatever name you want.**

Setting the Workgroup and Computer Name in Ubuntu

Here's how to set the Computer Name and Workgroup in Ubuntu:

1. **Click the network icon on the Ubuntu toolbar.**

2. **Choose Manual Configuration and enter a password in the prompt.**

3. **In the Network Settings window, click the General tab.**

4. **Enter a name for your computer into the Host Name field, which is equivalent to the Computer Name in other applications.**

5. **Enter the same value you use for all your computers into the Domain Name field, which is equivalent to the Workgroup in other applications.**

Chapter 5: Working with the "Brains" of Your Equipment

In This Chapter

✔ Discovering the world of firmware and how to update it on routers, APs, repeaters

✔ Understanding and updating the drivers of your network adapters

✔ Figuring out how to safeguard your configuration settings

✔ Getting techy with aftermarket or replacement firmware for wireless routers

✔ Updating your Windows or Mac to keep your operating system free of known security holes

As you will soon discover, firmware and device drivers — which are part of what comprises the "brains" of your equipment — play an important role in your home network. Though you can "control" your network through the settings you choose, the firmware and device driver files contain the intelligence that powers all the features and functions of your devices. The fact that your firmware and device drivers can be swapped with others gives you some neat opportunities. For example, you can update your devices with fixes and new features, or with a whole new "brain," thereby transforming your original device into something much greater. This chapter tells you how to check the firmware and driver files currently on your networking equipment and how to upgrade them if needed.

Also part of the brains of your equipment is your computer's operating system (Windows, Mac, or other), and keeping your operating system updated is discussed in this chapter as well. As do device updates, operating system updates include fixes, security patches, and new features. Some of these updates may be related to networking and the Internet, which means that they can be important to achieving and maintaining the smooth functioning of your home network.

Upgrading Firmware: Keep Your Network Components Up-to-Date

As you perhaps know, you work with two *wares* just about every day — *hardware and software*. Hardware is pretty much any physical computer part or component, such as a network adapter, network router, and video card (just to name a few). Software is the computer programs you use, basically made up by computer code, or in other words, specific instructions that tell your computer what to do and how to do it.

But did you know that you have another ware — *firmware* — at your fingertips? It's true; firmware is loaded on some of the devices you use from day to day and is

✦ **The middle ground between hardware and software.** This is because firmware is computer code similar to software; however, it's essentially the only computer code on a particular device and is embedded into permanent memory.

✦ **A device's brain.** Firmware has a more vital role than regular software and could be comparable to some of a human brain's functions. For example, a human body (your hardware) won't function without a brain (your firmware).

✦ **Loaded (and updateable) on just about all your networking infrastructure components.** Examples of firmware-powered components include:

- Wired or wireless routers

- Range extenders or repeaters

- Access points (APs)

- Media players

The key point to all this "ware" talk is that most of your networking infrastructure gear supports firmware upgrades. Manufacturers occasionally release updates to their products' firmware (in the form of a file that you download from their Web site and upload to your device), offering you free new features, such as the latest and greatest security methods and features, and to address known errors and issues with the product.

 Your network adapters don't use firmware but do use a somewhat similar concept. They use (updateable) drivers, loaded on the operating system (such as Windows) of the computer or device that the adapter is installed on. I discuss more about this topic later in this chapter.

Don't you wish it were that easy to swap out your brain for one that works better, faster, and gives you more talents and abilities? And that when updating your own "firmware," you wouldn't have to fork over boatloads of money to a brain surgeon (or an insurance company!). When it comes to your computer devices' firmware, you can be the doc; it just takes about a half-hour for the studying, preparation, and surgical procedure.

You should check for updates of all your networking gear periodically, at least every six months. Additionally, you should check for firmware updates in the following cases:

+ **Right after you buy a networking product:** Before setting your device up, you should check for firmware updates. An update may have been released while the product has been sitting in the stock room or on the shelf.

+ **Before replacing a piece of networking equipment:** If you can get a product's new features just by updating the one you have, why fork out money for a new one with the same features? You might be able to stay with the product you already have and come out with the same benefits as a new one would provide.

+ **After adding any other gear or new computers:** This is to ensure that the existing equipment is running at its full potential and with features that may be included with your new networking gear or computers.

+ **When you have networking issues:** An issue you're experiencing may be fixed by updating your firmware.

  As mentioned earlier, other electronics you have around your home or office also use firmware, including CD and DVD writers, cellphones, digital cameras, and your iPod, to name a few.

You might want to check into updating the firmware on these other devices for similar advantages. Taking a look at the product's manual or browsing the support section of the manufacturer's Web site can usually point you in the right direction. Soon you could have all your geeky toys running with the latest updates!

 Some newer models of network infrastructure products have an automatic firmware update e-mail notification feature to alert you of new releases. You should be able to find these settings in the same spot as the firmware update and status section.

Updating the firmware of your network infrastructure devices consists of the following main steps:

1. Verify the model number of your hardware.

2. Check the firmware version you're currently using for your hardware.

3. Discover the current firmware release, and if a newer release exists, download it.

4. Prepare for the firmware update.

5. Upload the new firmware file to your hardware.

The next sections guide you through all these steps.

Verifying the model number of your hardware

The first thing to do in this firmware updating endeavor is to get the model number and, if applicable, the version number, of the piece of networking hardware you're trying to update. This is very important to get right!

Remember that you're the "surgeon," and making any mistakes with your firmware can ruin (or kill) your hardware, which is sort of similar to making a false identification of a person (or body parts) in the operating room. Just be careful throughout the entire process!

Here are a few places you can check that ought to reveal your model information:

✦ **On the product:** Finding out the model information of hardware is usually as easy as examining the product. The model number might be printed on the front of the equipment (see Figure 5-1 for an example) or on a label stuck somewhere.

Figure 5-1:
Finding the model number on the front of a wireless router.

Model number

Courtesy of D-Link Systems, Inc.

✦ **On the product box:** Check the box that it all came packed in — that is, of course, if it isn't already in your local landfill.

✦ **Sales or shipping receipts:** If you still have your receipts, they should help out. If purchased online, check your old or deleted e-mail messages for the order confirmation.

Most models of routers have multiple versions that have been released over time (for example, WTR54GS v1.0, v2.0, and v2.1). Make sure to check whether your router has a particular version number, which is usually identified only on the product itself. Using an incorrect revision can easily "brick" a router (lock up the router and make it very hard to revive).

When you've properly identified your patient (network device), you're on schedule for the brain transplant (or firmware update).

Checking the firmware version of your hardware

The next step is to identify what firmware version is loaded in your hardware so that you can compare it to the current version the manufacturer is offering. Solving this part of the puzzle, though, takes a bit more than just glancing at your equipment.

The firmware version can be discovered only by bringing up the configuration or setup screen of your router, AP, or other piece of networking gear. But even if this is your first time accessing the configuration screens, I'm happy to tell you it isn't that difficult. Now to get started:

1. **Bring up your Web browser (Internet Explorer, Netscape, Firefox, or other).**

For media players and other network components that don't have a Web-based setup utility, getting to the configuration screen involves bringing up the normal interface and accessing its settings menu. For example, for a media player, you turn it on as usual and then view the interface via your TV.

2. **Type in the IP address of your router, range extender/repeater, or access point (AP) and press Enter.**

Keep in mind that some manufacturers may use a domain name (http://www.routerlogin.net) that looks like a Web site address instead of an IP address (192.168.1.1).

If you don't know the IP address or the username or password, refer to Book V, Chapter 3 for help.

3. **When prompted (see Figure 5-2) enter the username and password.**

If you don't know the default username and password, refer to Book V, Chapter 3.

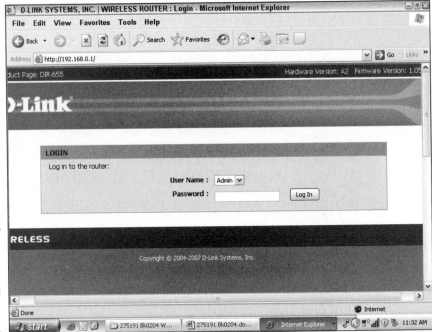

Figure 5-2:
Logging into
a network
device using
its IP
address.

4. **Find the firmware version and (preferably) the release date by clicking the Status or Firmware tab (or other tab containing the firmware details).**

   On routers, range extenders/repeaters, and APs, the version number may also be found on a border of every page. See Figure 5-3 for an example.

   For devices with a non-Web–based utility, you should search for a firmware or system page. For example, for a media player, use your remote to scroll or page through the menus.

5. **Make a note of the firmware version and, if available, the release date.**

When you've properly identified the brains of your "patient," you can move on to the next step, which lets you know whether you need to perform a transplant.

Version number

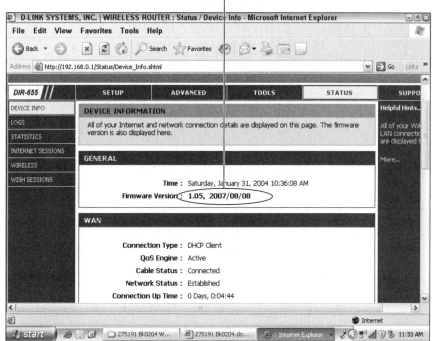

Figure 5-3:
Firmware
information
found on the
firmware
page in a
router's
Web-based
utility.

Discovering (and getting) the current firmware release

You should check the manufacturer's Web site to see the version number of the latest firmware release, and if you have an older release, you can update it; otherwise, you can just forget the whole mess if you already have the most current release. To find out the version number of the latest release, follow these steps:

1. **Open your Web browser and type in the Web site address of the device manufacturer into the address bar and press Enter.**

The Web site is usually the same as the manufacturer's name (for example, dlink.com, linksys.com, netgear.com). If you need help identifying the Web site, refer to Book V, Chapter 4.

2. **Find and go to a Support or Downloads section.**

This section may mention something about firmware or driver downloads. Figure 5-4 shows an example.

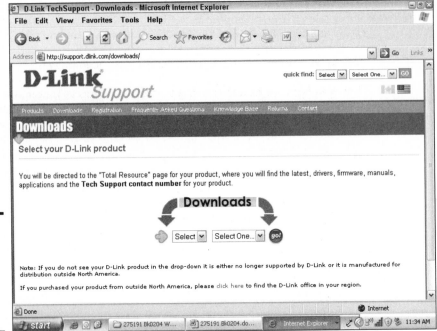

Figure 5-4:
The
Downloads
section of
a manu-
facturer's
Web site.

3. **Select the model (and possibly version) of your device.**

   Using the manufacturer's particular method, identify the piece of equipment you have.

4. **Find the most current firmware version.**

   If the latest firmware version number is greater than your current one (that you noted earlier), you should download the new firmware file. Make sure that you remember where you put the file!

You may want to check out the main improvements or changes for the new firmware release compared to the previous release. This information (or a link to the information) is usually provided when you're downloading the firmware.

If you've verified that your patient will benefit from a brain transplant, you can start making the final preparations for the surgery by following the directions in the next section.

Preparing for a firmware update

As is recommended by most network device manufacturers, you should update your firmware only through a direct, wired (Ethernet) connection to a device rather than by a wireless connection when you're working with Wi-Fi devices. Wireless isn't always reliable, and firmware updates can't be interrupted or the device may be "bricked" (become unusable).

Before you update, you should make sure of the following:

✦ **You have an Ethernet cable to connect your computer and the device.** If you don't have a spare, you could temporarily use one that's currently being used, such as the one for your Internet connection. If you can't find an Ethernet cable, you can purchase one from most consumer electronic stores.

✦ **The computer you're using is wired to the device you want to update.** If your device and computer are already located closely (and connected) to one another, you're good to go. If not, you can temporarily move your device next to the computer you're using to update the firmware. You could just unplug any cables that are currently connected (such as your Internet or other computers) to the device. You'll have to hook it all back up after you're done with the firmware update, so remember where the cables are supposed to go.

To connect your computer and the device, plug one end of an Ethernet cable into a LAN port of the device, and plug the other end of the Ethernet cable into your computer's Ethernet port. Make sure that the device is plugged into an electrical outlet and then verify that your computer (Ethernet adapter) is successfully connected to the device.

✦ **The new firmware file is on the computer you are using.**

✦ **Your device settings are backed up before updating the firmware.** You want to have a backup because your device's settings may be reset to the factory defaults when you update the firmware. The device and firmware documentation, and notes in the configuration screens, should give you a clue as to whether the settings will be reset. If they are reset, you can just restore your saved settings from the backup file you create. To create these backup files, refer to the "Backing up Configuration Settings" section, later in this chapter.

When you're ready, you can begin the "surgery" on updating your device's brain by following the directions given in the next section.

Updating your hardware's firmware

To perform the update of your firmware, you need to upload the file to your network device. To do so, follow these steps:

1. **Bring up your Web browser (Internet Explorer, Netscape, Firefox, or other).**

Refer to Figure 5-2, shown previously, for an example of where to enter your login info.

For media players and other network components that don't have a Web-based setup utility, getting to the configuration screen involves bringing up the normal interface and accessing its settings menu. For example, for a media player, you turn it on as usual and then view the interface via your TV.

2. **Type in the IP address of your router, range extender/repeater, or access point (AP) and press Enter.**

   Keep in mind that some manufacturers may use a domain name (`http://www.routerlogin.net`) that looks like a Web site address instead of an IP address (192.168.1.1).

   If you don't know the IP address or the username or password, refer to Book V, Chapter 3 for help.

3. **When prompted (refer to Figure 5-2), enter the username and password.**

   If you don't know the default username and password, refer to Book V, Chapter 3.

4. **Click the Firmware, System, or Management tab (or other tab that contains the firmware upgrade settings).**

   Figure 5-5 points out an example of a router's firmware settings.

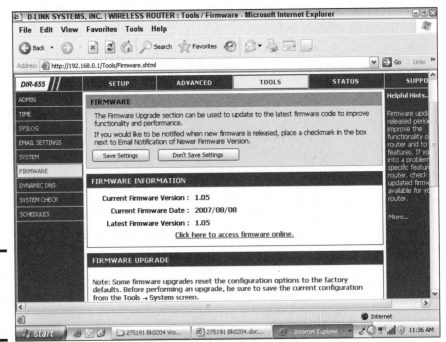

Figure 5-5:
Example of a firmware upgrade page.

As discussed previously, make sure that your device is connected via an Ethernet cable to your computer. Additionally, make sure that you've backed up your device settings because firmware updates usually wipe out your settings. For help, refer to the "Backing up Configuration Settings" section, later in this chapter.

5. Find and select the new firmware file located on your computer.

When the firmware upgrade process starts, do not disturb it! Stop using your computer and sit tight. A disruption to this process could ruin your device forever.

6. Click OK and follow any further instructions.

Congratulations! With luck, you've successfully completed a device's brain transplant (firmware update). Pat yourself on the back and take advantage of those new features and fixes!

Upgrading Drivers: Ensuring That Your Network Adapters Are Current

You may have heard of device drivers during your computing experiences, especially when hooking up a printer, camera, scanner, or other device to your computer. You'll also work with drivers during your networking journey, so you should familiarize yourself with some driver know-how:

✦ **Drivers are required for many computer devices.** Most devices require that you load a specific driver on your computer to communicate with your operating system. Network adapters aren't excluded from this requirement.

✦ **Device drivers drive the devices.** As is true of firmware, a driver is basically a device's brain. The driver contains computer code that enables and handles the communication of the device with the operating system and other software and hardware on your system. Also similarly to firmware, a device driver is simply a file but is installed on your computer rather than the device.

✦ **Network adapters are driven.** The only type of device (in the networking realm) that you'll probably have that uses device drivers are your network adapters, such as the following:

- Desktop Ethernet or wireless cards

- Notebook PCMCIA Ethernet or wireless cards

- USB Ethernet or wireless adapters

Just as with network infrastructure components (routers, APs, and so on), the networking product makers release driver updates for their network adapters, which can include, at no cost, new features such as support for new security methods and can contain bug fixes to address known issues. However, updating drivers is generally easier and less time consuming than updating firmware.

Driver updates are usually in the form of an installation program (a `setup.exe` file) that contains the actual driver files. You download them from the manufacturer's Web site and install them on your computer. Drivers are hardware dependent and operating-system specific, so you must acquire separate drivers for each of your devices, as well as acquire the appropriate version for your operating system.

You should check for updates to all your networking gear periodically, at least every six months. Additionally, you should check for driver updates to your network adapters for all the same reasons I give for updating firmware in the previous section of this chapter.

To ensure that your network adapter(s) is up-to-date, you need to find the model and version numbers, determine what driver version you're using now, check whether a new driver is available, and if so, update it. The following sections describe how to do each of these tasks.

Verifying the model number of your adapter

Before you can do anything, you must figure out the model number and, if applicable, the version of the network adapter you plan to update. Here are some tips:

✦ **For external adapters, such as USB or notebook PCMCIA adapters:** You can usually find this information (both the model and any version number) easily on the product.

✦ **For desktop (PCI) cards:** You can refer to the product's original box or documentation for the model number, if it's still around. You can find the version number, however, only on the product itself, located in your PC. You can refer to the final bullet in this list for information on looking inside your PC.

✦ **For all adapters:** If you have trouble finding the model number, you may also be able to find it in the list of device properties, such as when checking the driver version of your adapter. So see the "Checking the driver version of your adapter" section of this chapter.

✦ **Peeking inside your desktop PC:** If your desktop (PCI) adapter has multiple versions, you have to temporarily remove it to figure out the hardware version number, because this is the only place that you'll find this info.

Before going through the trouble, though, don't do this unless you know your particular adapter has multiple versions, which you figure out when downloading the driver. So for now, you can move on to the next section, but if needed, you can return to this section later.

If you know that your network adapter model has multiple versions, you can follow these steps to remove your desktop adapter:

1. **Carefully disconnect all the cables from your computer after you shut down your computer.**

2. **Prepare your workstation by moving the computer to a flat solid surface so that you can work without losing any screws.**

3. **Remove the PC cover by removing screws or sliding covers off (that may take some time to figure out!).**

   When you open the computer, you should touch the metal frame of the computer before touching the parts to release any static electricity.

4. **Find the network adapter.**

   It should be sitting in one of the PCI slots. You can look behind the PC at the Ethernet port or antenna to make sure that you've identified the correct card.

5. **Unplug the Ethernet cable or antenna.**

   Do this so that you can freely remove the network adapter to find the version number on the card.

6. **Remove the PCI card holder/mount by removing a single screw or a movable mount that comes down and covers all the PCI cards to hold them in place.**

7. **Remove the network adapter by firmly — but gently — pulling the network adapter up and out of the PCI slot.**

8. **Look for the version number.**

   This may be easy to identify; however, you may have to refer to the guidelines given while downloading the driver, which I discuss in the "Finding the current driver release" section, later in this chapter.

9. **After you're done, replace the network adapter (similar to how you removed the PCI card) by firmly — but gently — inserting the network adapter back into the PCI slot.**

   It's best to line up the card with the slot, press gently to see whether you have it in the right place, and then push firmly down until it snaps into place, which may take some good pressure.

10. **Replace the PCI card holder/mount by replacing the screw or mount that securely holds your PCI card(s) in place.**

11. **Replace the PC cover and plug in the cables.**

    You can move your computer back into the regular place and plug or screw in the Ethernet cable or antenna, and all your other cables.

Checking the driver version of your adapter

You should check which driver version your adapter is currently using so that you can compare it to the releases listed on the manufacturer's Web site. To do so, refer to one of the following sections for the operating system you are using.

For Windows Vista

Follow these steps to check the driver version for your adapter in Windows Vista:

1. **Click the network icon in the system tray.**

2. **Click Network and Sharing Center.**

3. **Under Tasks in the left pane, click Manage Network Connections.**

4. **In the Manage Network Connections window, right-click your desired adapter icon and select Properties.**

   If User Account Control (UAC) is active, click Continue on the prompt.

5. **In the Network Connection Properties window, click the Configure button.**

6. **In the Network Adapter Properties window, click the Driver tab.**

7. **Note the driver version number and release date, which are shown in Figure 5-6.**

Figure 5-6:
Device
driver
information
of a network
adapter in
Windows
Vista.

For Windows XP

To check your driver in Windows XP, follow these steps:

1. **Click Start⇨Connect To⇨Show All Connections.**

   If using the Classic Start menu, click Start, click Settings, right-click Network Connections, and click Open.

   The Network Connections window appears.

2. **Right-click the desired network adapter and select Properties.**

3. **In the Network Connection Properties window, click the Configure button.**

4. **In the Network Adapter Properties window, click the Driver tab.**

5. **Note the driver version number and release date, which are shown in Figure 5-7.**

Figure 5-7:
Device driver information of a network adapter in Windows XP.

Finding the current driver release

You can navigate through the network adapter's manufacturer's Web site to discover the latest driver release and compare it to the current version loaded on your computer. To do so, do an Internet search to bring up the Web site, find a Support or Downloads section, select the model or version of your device, and find the most current driver version.

You may want to check out the main improvements or changes for the new driver release, compared to the previous release. This information or a link to the information is usually provided when downloading the driver.

If the latest driver version number is greater than your current one (that you noted earlier), you should download the new driver file and continue with the next section to make the final preparations. Make sure you remember where you put the file!

Preparing for a driver update

Before performing the driver update, make sure that you

✦ **Get the driver:** You need to have the new driver file on the computer you are updating.

✦ **Unzip the driver:** If the driver download is in the form of a compressed zip file (that is, has a `.zip` extension), unzip (extract) the contents.

✦ **Note adapter settings:** For wireless adapters, note any encryption keys and nonbroadcasted network names you may use, because this information may be deleted when updating your driver.

Now you can begin with the actual update process.

Updating your adapter's driver

You can choose between two different methods to update your adapter's device driver:

✦ **Automatic updates:** Uses the manufacturer's setup or installation program.

✦ **Manual updates:** Uses the Windows driver update feature.

The method you use is limited to the file(s) offered by your adapter's manufacturer. If the only option is to download a single setup or installation file, you have to stick with the automatic method. If only the actual driver files are available, you have to go with the manual method. In some cases, the setup and raw driver files are both included in the driver download, in which case you choose either method.

The main difference between these two methods is that many manufacturers include a software utility for their network adapters in the setup or installation program for the driver.

To update your driver using a setup or installation program, simply run the program and follow the instructions; otherwise, you can perform a manual update by referring to one of the following sets of step-by-step directions for the operating system you are using:

Updating an adapter's driver in Windows Vista

To update an adapter's driver in Windows Vista, follow these steps:

1. **Click the network icon in the system tray.**

2. **Click Network and Sharing Center.**

3. **Under Tasks in the left pane, click Manage Network Connections.**

4. **In the Manage Network Connections window, right-click your desired adapter icon and select Properties.**

If User Account Control (UAC) is active, click Continue on the prompt.

5. **On the Network Connection Properties window, click the Configure button.**

6. **On the Network Adapter Properties window, click the Driver tab.**

7. **Click the Update Driver button (shown in Figure 5-8).**

Book II
Chapter 5

Working with the "Brains" of Your Equipment

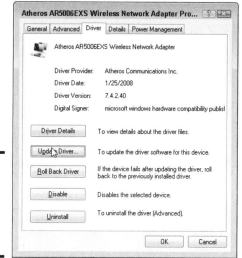

Figure 5-8:
The Update Driver Wizard in Windows Vista.

8. **On the Update Driver Software wizard that opens, click the Browse My Computer for Driver Software option and follow the directions given by the wizard to find and update the new driver.**

Updating an adapter's driver in Windows XP

You can update an adapter's driver in Windows XP by doing the following:

1. **Choose Start⇨ Connect To⇨ Show All Connections.**

If using the Classic Start menu, click Start, click Settings, right-click Network Connections, and click Open.

The Network Connections windows should appear.

2. **Right-click the desired network adapter and select Properties.**

3. **In the Network Connection Properties window, click the Configure button.**

4. **In the Network Adapter Properties window, click the Driver tab.**

5. **Click the Update Driver button.**

6. **In the Hardware Update Wizard that appears, select the Install From a List or Specific Location (Advanced) option and click Next, as shown in Figure 5-9.**

Figure 5-9:
Selecting an advanced method of updating a driver in Windows XP.

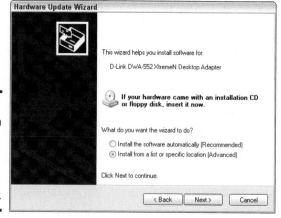

7. **On the Please Choose Your Search and Installation Options page, select the Don't Search. I Will Choose the Driver to Install option and click Next (see Figure 5-10).**

8. **On the Select Network Adapter page, click the Have Disk button.**

9. **In the Install From Disk dialog box that appears, click the Browse, button, locate and select the new driver, and click Open.**

10. **Click OK and follow the remaining directions given by the wizard.**

Congratulations! With luck, you've successfully completed a driver update.

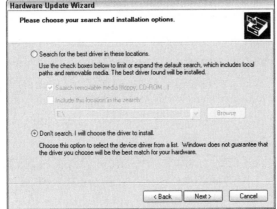

Figure 5-10:
Specifying
the driver
search and
installation
options in
Windows XP.

Backing Up Configuration Settings

Every so often, you should save or back up the settings of your infrastructure components (routers, range extenders/repeaters, APs,), especially in the following cases:

✦ Before performing firmware upgrades

✦ After the initial setup of your infrastructure component(s)

✦ Before and after making configuration changes

Here's how to do it:

1. **Bring up your Web browser (Internet Explorer, Netscape, Firefox, or other).**

Refer to Figure 5-2, shown previously, for an example of where to enter your login info.

For media players and other network components that don't have a Web-based setup utility, getting to the configuration screen involves bringing up the normal interface and accessing its settings menu. For example, for a media player, you turn it on as usual and then view the interface via your TV.

2. **Type in the IP address of your router, range extender/repeater, or access point (AP) and press Enter.**

Keep in mind that some manufacturers may use a domain name (http://www.routerlogin.net) that looks like a Web site address instead of an IP address (192.168.1.1).

If you don't know the IP address or the username or password, refer to Book V, Chapter 3 for help.

3. **When prompted (see Figure 5-2), enter the username and password.**

If you don't know the default username and password, refer to Book V, Chapter 3.

4. **Click the System, Backup, Tools, or Management tab (or other tab) to find the Backup or Save Settings feature.**

Figure 5-11 shows an example.

5. **Click the button to save the backup to a file, select where to save the file, and click OK.**

When it's time to restore your settings, just go back to the same place in the configuration utility where you made the backup; it should have a restore function close by.

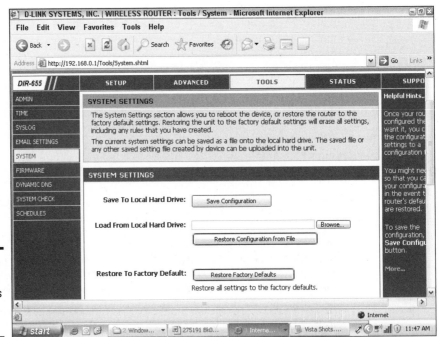

Figure 5-11:
An example
of a settings
backup
page.

Getting More Features (for free) with Aftermarket Firmware

If you have some geeky tendencies, spare time, the willing to take a slight risk, and would like to pack your wireless router with some useful and expensive enterprise (and sometimes just cool) features (then aftermarket firmware might be for you!

The built-in computer systems of some networking gear (for example, wireless routers) use the Linux operating system. Linux is an *open source* operating system, which means that its source code or computer language is freely distributed to the public, in contrast to that of Microsoft Windows or the Mac. Network hardware manufacturers who base their products on the Linux operating system must also make the source code of the hardware's firmware — the computer code that essentially acts like the device's brain and controls all the functions — available to the public. This allows individuals and groups to easily modify a piece of networking gear's firmware and thereby make some neat feature additions and changes.

This modified or nonmanufacturer-developed firmware is known as *aftermarket firmware*. In the tech world, this also called *open-source firmware* or simply *firmware replacement*. In the networking arena, aftermarket firmware is usually developed only for simple wireless routers such as what you use in your home or small office.

Discovering features of aftermarket firmware

Although the features and their attributes vary depending upon the particular aftermarket firmware used, most offer the following:

✦ **Multiple or virtual SSIDs:** You can create multiple network names or service set identifiers (SSIDs) and customize their individual security and broadcast settings, allowing you to securely segregate access to the Internet or your network. For example, you could use encryption on the main SSID and create a virtual SSID without encryption but with AP isolation on and unbridged. This would allow your friends to easily access your wireless Internet but protects your shared files and services.

✦ **Virtual LANs:** Similar to virtual SSIDs but applies to the wired connections. You can assign the Ethernet ports to different VLANs in order to segregate the network traffic. For example, you could secure your wireless connection with encryption but have an Ethernet port on the back of your router on a separate VLAN so that people could plug in and use the Internet but not have access to your shared files and services.

✦ **Auto channel:** When enabled, this feature automatically chooses the best channel, factoring in channels already being used and radio interference.

✦ **Site survey features:** This would display any nearby wireless networks and their signal information, which is useful when choosing your channel(s).

✦ **Static DHCP:** This feature allows you to still use DHCP, which automatically and randomly hands out IP addresses (which is required to use the Internet) to each computer or device on your network, but enables you to make sure that a certain device gets the same IP address each time. This is useful if you run (Web, FTP, and so on) servers on your computers or play multiplayer games among computers on your network.

✦ **QoS (Quality of Service):** This feature gives you a set of settings to control and regulate the amount and type of traffic allowed through your router. You could, for example, apply a maximum amount of Internet speed for certain wireless and wired connections. You could also set priorities based upon certain computers, services, and ports.

✦ **Wireless repeating:** You could set up your aftermarket firmware-enabled router to repeat the Wi-Fi signal of another wireless network (or router). This is useful when you want to expand the wireless coverage of a network belonging to you or a neighbor.

✦ **Wireless bridging:** This would give you the ability to wirelessly connect two wired Ethernet networks together. For example, say that you already have a wired router with several computers connected to it. Now say that you want to set up more computers in another room or area but don't want to run Ethernet cable. You could enable the wireless bridging feature on a wireless router in the existing room and in the new room, bridging the Ethernet connections of both routers together, thus creating a network between all the (existing and new) computers.

✦ **Hotspot (captive portal) features:** These features would allow you to set up your inexpensive wireless router as a Wi-Fi hotspot, which usually requires expensive equipment. Hotspot solutions included in aftermarket firmware typically enable you to set up a captive portal screen that users see when they connect and must agree to terms or payment before Internet access is given.

✦ **RADIUS support:** This lets you configure your router to use a RADIUS server to provide user or account authentication, useful in security or hotspot solutions.

✦ **SSH management:** This gives you secure (command-line) remote access to your router to get status information or to make setting changes.

Table 1-1 lists some popular aftermarket (open-source) firmware projects you might want to look into.

Table 1-1	Popular Aftermarket Firmware Projects
Firmware	*Description*
DD-WRT (www.dd-wrt.com)	One of the most feature-packed and supported aftermarket firmware projects, which offers many versions to support many different routers.
Sveasoft (www.sveasoft.com)	Another popular aftermarket firmware with multiple firmware versions; however, it restricts access to more advanced versions to members, which requires a small monetary contribution.
Tomato (www.polarcloud.com)	A bit smaller, leaner, and simpler replacement firmware with only one version.
OpenWRT (www.openwrt.org)	Unlike most other firmware replacements, this firmware lacks a graphical interface (without the use of add-ons) and for the most part requires advanced knowledge.

The next section takes you through setting up and using the DD-WRT firmware.

Using the DD-WRT firmware

I've chosen to cover setting up DD-WRT (see Figure 5-12 for a sneak peek) because it's a well-rounded, feature-rich firmware replacement.

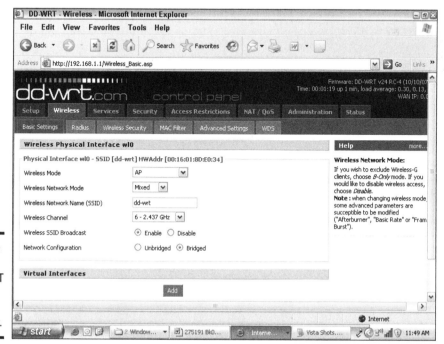

Figure 5-12:
Example of the DD-WRT Web-based configuration utility.

The following sections walk you through the process of installing and setting up this firmware replacement.

Getting a supported router

The first step toward using the DD-WRT firmware is to round up a supported wireless router, such as the following:

✦ Linksys WRT54G/GL/GS

✦ Buffalo WHR-G125 and WHR-HP-G54

✦ Asus WL-500G and WL-300G

Along with a great comparison chart and list of the top routers, you can also view the full list of supported devices on the DD-WRT Web site at the following address:

```
www.dd-wrt.com/wiki/index.php/Supported_Devices
```

Try to avoid devices with only 2MB of flash memory (such as WRT54G/GS v5.0/6.0) because they'll let you run only the micro version of DD-WRT. You should also note that the Asus WL-500G premium is supported only by v23 SP3 and better releases.

Getting the DD-WRT firmware

Next you need to download the firmware file, based on the particular router you're using and your desired features, from the download section of the DD-WRT Web site:

```
http://www.dd-wrt.com/dd-wrtv3/dd-wrt/downloads.html
```

Before you start browsing the download section, though, you should familiarize yourself with the firmware naming and organization schemes. You'll see the firmware organized into three different sections:

✦ **Stable:** These releases are your best bet, providing thoroughly tested firmware releases.

✦ **Beta:** These releases can be unstable and aren't recommended for public use. These releases are used to test the firmware during the development.

✦ **Release candidates:** These are a bit more stable releases compared to beta versions. These releases are in the final testing stages before being released as stable. Use these at your own risk.

Each firmware release offers a common set of versions, which gives you more control over the features included in the firmware to conserve router resources and to support low-end memory routers. In most cases, the

Standard version is the best choice because it embraces all the features except the special VoIP and VPN components.

Then you have various firmware types to navigate through:

✦ **ASUS:** Specific firmware versions for the WL-300/500G models

✦ **Generic:** For routers that don't require their own version and for special cases

✦ **Linksys specific:** Specific firmware versions for the particular models, beginning with wrt

✦ **Motorola specific:** For micro and mini file versions only, and identified by moto

Book II
Chapter 5

Working with the
"Brains" of Your
Equipment

When flashing from original Linksys firmware, you must first use the mini version and then you can upgrade/flash to another version. When using the Web interface method, you must use the generic firmware types.

When browsing through the firmware collections, you'll see filenames in the following format: dd-wrt.v*XX_set_type*.bin. The *XX* identifies the firmware version, *set* defines the firmware collection (such as micro or VoIP — displayed for only nonstandard sets), and *type* identifies the hardware type (such as ASUS or Generic).

Flashing your Router with the DD-WRT firmware

The two basic methods to flash your router are as follows:

✦ **Trivial File Transfer Protocol (TFTP):** A simple file transfer method that uses a command-line interface.

✦ **Web-based utility:** This method uses the router's Web interface and the firmware upgrade feature.

Flashing via the Web interface is easier and supported by most routers, except Buffalo devices, for which you must use TFTP.

As with any open source firmware, it's very important to follow all the directions and precautions, because one mistake could ruin (brick) your router.

Because the exact flashing procedure can vary depending on the router vendor and model, you need to reference the flashing directions on the DD-WRT Web site:

http://www.dd-wrt.com/wiki/index.php/Installation#Flashing.

Configuring the DD-WRT firmware

After successfully flashing your router with the DD-WRT firmware, you need log in to the Web-based configuration screen. Do so by following these steps:

1. **Bring up your Web browser.**

2. **Type in the default IP address of 192.168.1.1.**

3. **When prompted, as shown in Figure 5-13 (after you click any tab), enter the default login credentials, which are root (for the username) and admin (for the password).**

Figure 5-13 shows an example of the login prompt.

Now you can configure your router for your particular needs. Changing the Internet connection, wireless, and other generic settings should be similar to what you did with your original router.

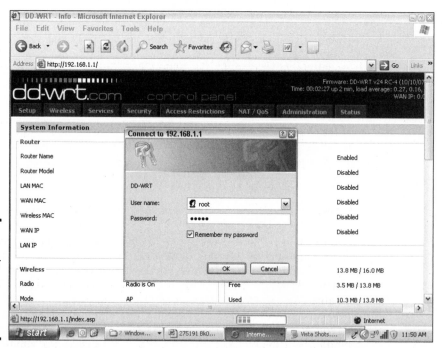

Figure 5-13: Accessing the DD-WRT Web-based configuration screen.

For help on configuring your DD-WRT-enabled router, you can make use of the following:

✦ **DD-WRT Wiki** (www.dd-wrt.com/wiki/): Contains information and help on installing and setting up DD-WRT and its features through frequently asked questions (FAQ) and tutorials.

✦ **Discussion Forum** (www.dd-wrt.com/phpBB2): You can review previous discussions and/or post questions or start conversations with the developers and other users worldwide.

✦ **Bugtracker** (www.dd-wrt.com/dd-wrtv2/bugtracker): This allows you to review the list of known bugs of the firmware and submit additional bugs.

✦ **IRC** (www.dd-wrt.com/wiki/index.php/Support:IRC): You can chat with DD-WRT users and developers using an Internet Relay Chat (IRC) client.

Updating the Operating System to Patch Security Holes

Thought you'd read the last of updating and upgrading? No, you haven't! In addition to keeping up with new driver and firmware releases for your network equipment, you should also regularly update your operating systems (Windows, Mac, and so on) because updates can

✦ Contain enhanced or new networking features or interfaces.

✦ Fix known bugs or errors with the operating system relating to networking connections or settings.

✦ Address known security holes that may compromise your computer or network to Internet or local hackers.

To find out how to update your operating system, refer to Book III, Chapter 1.

If you're using an ancient version of an operating system (such as 95, 98, or ME for Windows), you should think about upgrading to a better version (such as Windows Vista, the latest and greatest Windows version, or at least Windows XP). But if you're using such an old operating system (OS), it's probably also time to get a better computer system.

The countless enhancements and new features of newer operating systems, including redesigned networking interfaces, will make your home or small office networking experience much easier. Plus, these newer operating systems inherently contain better security mechanisms. The monetary and time investment in upgrading your OS or your entire computer system will be worth it!

Chapter 6: Taking the Wire Farther

In This Chapter

✔ **Using your home's electrical outlets instead of Ethernet cabling**

✔ **Adding wireless to your wired network**

✔ **Using wireless bridges instead of Ethernet cabling to connect cables**

*T*his chapter helps you extend your wired network. However, rather than concentrate on running longer cables or adding more wires to your network, this chapter tells you how to use your home's existing wiring. (For tips on running Ethernet cables through your home, see Book II, Chapter 2.) Plus this chapter discusses adding wireless access to your strictly wired network and extending a wired computer or device.

In this chapter, I discuss using power-line technology to extend your wired network, adding wireless capability with access points (APs) or by swapping out your router with a wireless one, and using wireless bridges to connect computers or devices back to your wired router without having to lay down more cables.

Using Your Electrical System to Connect Distant Devices

If you want to connect a wired computer or device to your wired network but don't want to run Ethernet cables, creating a small power-line network may be the answer. It's a pretty simple setup. You connect your existing network to your home's electrical system, and then plug in computers or devices into the electrical system.

If you want to use this method of connecting wired devices or computers to your network, you can refer to Book II, Chapters 2 – 4 (keeping your eye out for the material covering power-line networking) for help on planning what you need and on installing and setting up power-line adapters.

While going through the chapters, keep in mind that you don't want to set up a strictly power-line network. You want to connect one power-line adapter from your wired router to your electrical system and then connect a power-line adapter from each computer or device to your electrical system.

Adding Wireless Access to Your Wired Network

Adding wireless access to your existing wired network can free you of additional wires. You'll be able to use your Wi-Fi devices — such as laptops, PDAs, and handheld gaming consoles — around your home without being restricted to a cable. You'll be able to surf the Web on the couch, the patio, or while in bed. Also, you can easily move computers around within your home without having to rerun cable. You have a few ways you can go about adding the wireless access to your wired network, as follows:

✦ **Add a wireless access point (AP).** This is a device similar to a wireless router but doesn't include the routing features that control the network. Your wired router would continue to control the network — for instance, offering IP addresses to wired and wireless computers and handling port forwarding if you access servers or your computers remotely from the Internet. The AP would simply offer wireless access to your existing network.

✦ **Replace your wired router with a wireless router.** This would replace your wired router with one that includes an access point, which is called a wireless router.

To save money, you can hook a wireless router to your existing wired router. Disabling the DHCP feature of the wireless router basically makes it an AP, and your wired router continues to handle the network. By doing this, however, you sacrifice special features usually included in APs, as discussed in the next set of bullets.

Adding access points (APs)

Besides factoring in the fact that APs cost a bit more than wireless routers, you'll probably find it hard to figure out which way to go. To help you decide, here are a few benefits of going with an AP:

✦ **You don't have to move your wired router.** When setting up wireless access, you should have the access point or wireless router located in the middle of your desired coverage area for best results. This becomes a problem if your wired router isn't already located in this "sweet spot." However, you can run a cable to the AP and place it anywhere. Doing so lets you set up the wireless access properly and without rewiring all your computers and moving your router.

✦ **You don't have to lose your settings.** Keeping your wired router will save you the time that you'd spend configuring another router with your Internet connection information. This makes a bigger difference if you've set special features and settings, such as static IP addresses, port forwarding, virtual servers, and dynamic DNS service.

✦ **Includes Power over Ethernet (PoE).** You'll find that many APs support PoE, which lets you run power to the device through the Ethernet cable instead of having a separate power cord. This makes placing the AP away from the wired router easier. It gives you more choices as to where to place the AP because you don't have to worry about putting it close to an outlet. This is a "trick" used in the enterprise networking arena.

✦ **Includes multiple SSIDs.** Some APs even let you create virtual network names that are all broadcasted from your single AP. This is used regularly in businesses to separate internal wireless network access, separate their private and public (hotspot) network, and support multiple wireless encryption methods. You may also find this feature useful, or just plain neat.

✦ **Supports more wireless modes.** Because APs are used often in business and complex networking environments, they usually include a few different wireless modes in addition to the regular AP mode:

  • **Wireless bridging:** As discussed in the previous section, wireless bridging gives a wired computer or network device (plugged into the AP in bridge mode) access to the network through the wireless access.

  • **Wireless repeater:** This lets you extend wireless coverage. You place the AP (in repeater mode) on the fringe of the coverage area, and it repeats the traffic to and from the original wireless router (or AP) and the computers it reaches in its range, which is farther than the original area. This method of extending wireless coverage is discussed more in the next chapter.

If you want to go the route of adding wireless to your wired router, you can refer to the next chapter of this minibook (Book II, Chapter 7) to find out how to add access points (APs).

Replacing your wired router with a wireless one

Replacing your router with a wireless router provides the following benefits:

✦ **You can upgrade to gigabit Ethernet.** If your wired router doesn't already support gigabit Ethernet (1,000 Mbps), you can replace your router with a gigabit wireless router to increase the speed of your wired computers tenfold. You probably won't even have to replace your Ethernet cabling to your computers. Although the newest Ethernet cabling (Cat6) provides better performance, Cat5e works with gigabit networks. The regular Cat5 should also work.

✦ **You can get new network features.** Getting a new router may offer you more features to control your network. One example is Quality of Service (QoS) features, which let you prioritize your traffic for better performance when using applications such as VoIP or Wi-Fi phones and on-line gaming.

✦ **You have more Ethernet ports.** You won't have to throw out your wired router; you can use it in conjunction with a wireless router. This lets you increase the number of Ethernet ports you have for your network. You just need to disable the DHCP feature on one of the routers.

If you want to add wireless to your wired network by replacing your wired router with a wireless router, you can just treat the whole project as though you're setting up a network for the first time. Therefore, you can start the process by checking out Book II, Chapter 2.

Using a Wireless Bridge to Link Wires Together

If you have wireless access to your network, either through a wireless router or access point (AP), you can use a wireless bridge instead of Ethernet cabling to provide connectivity to wired computers or devices. This would basically convert any Ethernet port on a computer or other network device (such as a gaming console or TIVO) to a wireless device. The wireless bridge will act as the wireless adapter for the computer or device. You have two ways to obtain this wireless bridging feature:

✦ **Use an AP with a Wireless Bridging Modes:** Many APs include different modes you can use, including wireless bridging. Going this route provides the following benefits:

- **Less expense:** Because APs are used more, they tend to be a bit cheaper.

- **Supports more wireless modes:** You may be able to use the AP for a different mode, such as wireless repeating, in the future when upgrading and expanding again.

- **Includes multiple SSIDs:** Some APs even let you create virtual network names that are all broadcasted from your single AP. This approach is used regularly in businesses to separate internal wireless network access, separate their private and public (hotspot) networks, and support multiple wireless encryption methods. You may also find this feature useful and neat.

✦ **Use a real Ethernet Wireless Bridge:** This consists of a device that is specifically designed for wireless bridging. You don't actually want to set up a "real" wireless bridge network (which requires two bridges); however, wireless bridges usually include a wireless client mode. Wireless bridging products aren't as popular as APs, so you won't find many to compare with, and you'll pay a little more than for an AP. However, going with a wireless bridge has some benefits over using an AP:

- **More Ethernet ports:** Some wireless ridges have multiple Ethernet ports (APs only have one), so you can plug in multiple computers or devices.

- **Easier to set up:** Because the product is built specifically for wireless bridging, you may find it easier to configure and follow the documentation than you would using an AP.

- **Supports more bridging type modes:** You may be able to use the wireless bridge for a different mode, such as to connect to a wireless ISP in the future when upgrading and expanding again.

Shopping for your wireless bridge or AP

Reading through the bullets in the previous section and looking at the specs for wireless bridges and APs can give you a good start in picking the right one for you. For either device, remember that there are a few different wireless standards — A, B, G, and N — with varying performance, speeds, and ranges. However, you don't necessarily have to use the same standard for your wireless bridge or AP as your existing wireless network.

If you need help comparing and picking a wireless standard, see Book I, Chapter 1.

Making the bridge or AP work with your network

In order for your wireless bridge (or AP) to work with your existing network, you must verify that its IP address is set within the same range (subnet) as your existing network. You should also verify that the IP addresses for the two devices don't match exactly, which is more likely if you have an existing AP and are setting up another AP for bridging, and they are the same brand. You can't have devices on the same network with the same exact IP address assigned. IP addresses need to be unique values.

This verification is necessary because wireless bridges and APs come already set up with a static IP address, rather than have a dynamic setting that automatically retrieves a correct address. If you're using the same brand for your wireless bridge as for your wireless router, you'll probably be fine because the manufacturer usually sets a static IP address within range of the default settings of its routers. However, you still should double-check before doing the install. But if you're using an AP for the wireless bridge and you already have an AP of the same brand, you probably have a problem, because manufacturers typically set their APs with the same IP addresses.

To see how to figure this out, refer to the next chapter of this minibook (Book II, Chapter 7), which contains information about adding access points to your network.

Book II
Chapter 6

Taking the
Wire Farther

Doing the physical installation

The physical installation for a wireless bridge is quick and simple:

1. **Connect an Ethernet cable(s) to the wireless bridge (or AP).**

If you're using a real wireless bridge, you may have multiple ports. However, you'll have only one if you're using an AP.

Make sure that you place the wireless bridge within the wireless range. Because the wireless bridge will be connected wirelessly to your existing wireless signal, it must be within good range. Also refer to Book II, Chapter 4 for information on attenuators and interfering devices that may affect wireless routers and wireless bridges.

2. **Connect the other end of the Ethernet cable(s) to the computers or devices you are bridging.**

3. **Plug in the power.**

Simply connect the power cord to your AP wireless bridge (or AP) and plug the other end into a wall outlet.

Configuring the wireless bridge (or AP)

To configure the settings, get on the computer that you connected to your wireless bridge (or AP). If you connected something other than a computer (like a gaming adapter) to your wireless bridge, you need to connect a computer up to it. Then after you configure everything you can plug the other device back in.

Here are the steps to follow to configure your wireless bridge:

1. **Connect to the wireless bridge by finding and choosing the default network name (usually stated in the product documentation) of the wireless bridge on your wireless network utility and press the button to connect.**

For step-by-step directions on how to connect (and how to check whether you're connected), see Book IV, Chapter 1. If you can't seem to connect your computers to the AP, refer to the troubleshooting steps in Book V, Chapter 1.

2. **Access the Web-based configuration utility of the wireless bridge by opening a Web browser (such as Internet Explorer, Netscape, or Firefox), typing in the IP address of your wireless bridge into the address bar, and, when prompted, entering the username and password of your AP.**

3. Click the Wireless or Mode tab (or other tab containing the wireless mode settings, such as those shown in Figure 6-1).

Don't get these settings mixed up with the wireless modes such as 802.11b or 802.11g. You want the wireless mode settings that list the modes, such as Bridging, AP, and Repeater.

If you see multiple bridging modes, you probably want to use the Wireless Client mode. Then you probably have to enter the MAC address of the wireless route or AP of your existing network. If you need help figuring out the MAC address, refer to Book V, Chapter 3.

4. Click the Save or Apply button, on the top or bottom of the page if you made any setting changes.

The AP will reboot and you will be disconnected for a minute. Now you can move on with configuring the rest of the settings.

Book II
Chapter 6

Taking the
Wire Farther

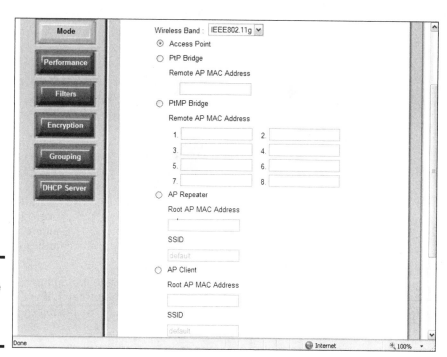

Figure 6-1:
An example
of an AP's
mode
settings.

Chapter 7: Getting a Better Reach with Wireless

In This Chapter

✔ Comparing ways to extend or increase your Wi-Fi router's coverage

✔ Discovering the simplicity of replacing your antennas for better reception

✔ Upgrading to wireless N gear for superior performance

✔ Expanding coverage using wireless extenders to repeat your Wi-Fi signal

✔ Finding out how to add more wireless access points

Do you want to expand the range or coverage of your Wi-Fi network? Do you want to fill in the dead spots throughout your home or office? This chapter covers just that — several ways to build upon your existing wireless router to keep yourself connected in all those nooks and crannies.

Say goodbye to the frustration of constant disconnects and low (or no!) signal. Renovate your wireless network — and welcome more coverage and better performance.

Going Cheap with Aftermarket Antennas

The antennas included with most wireless G (and the old wireless B) products are low-gain cheap antennas, also known as "stock" antennas. If you are using wireless G or B, replacing one or more of your original or factory antennas with some higher gain "aftermarket" antennas (see Figure 7-1) can help increase the range of your wireless network.

This method of extending your range isn't practical for any wireless N (or MIMO) products, for example, those with three antennas. If you're not sure what wireless technology or standard you're using (or what the heck I'm talking about), refer to Book I, Chapter 1 for information on the wireless standards.

Figure 7-1:
Example
of an
aftermarket
antenna.

*Courtesy of Linksys, a division
of Cisco Systems, Inc.*

Figure 7-2 depicts this concept. Replacement antennas can aid in situations in which you have low signal levels, and experience dropped and intermittent connections on one or more of your computers (your problem computer(s), as I refer to them in this section.

As depicted in Figure 7-2, higher-gain antennas can slightly increase the range of a wireless product. Although the range increase is minimal compared to other methods, this can be a very economical solution.

For example, instead of putting in a range extender (discussed later in this chapter) that costs $70 to $90, you could replace an antenna or two, at $20 to $30 apiece. Plus, unscrewing your original antenna and screwing in the replacement takes only 10 seconds, whereas setting up a range extender can take an hour or more.

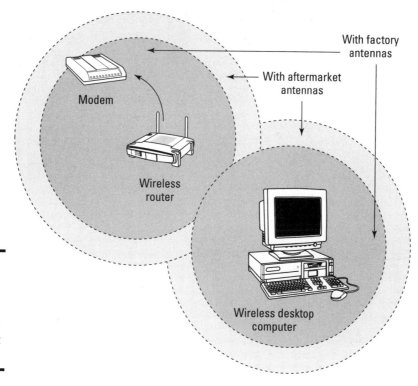

With factory
antennas

With aftermarket
antennas

Modem

Wireless
router

Wireless desktop
computer

Figure 7-2:
Coverage
examples
when using
factory and
aftermarket
antennas.

Before proceeding, you should understand that any products with wireless A
capability (including dual-band or tri-band equipment) usually don't support
replacement antennas (the factory antennas usually can't be removed.

Aftermarket antennas may look a bit different, and be larger. Some aftermarket antennas may not attach directly to the wireless adapter in your computer but may be attached to a base with a wire running to the adapter, such
as Figure 7-3 shows.

Your "replace antenna" dilemma

You should do some thinking before going out and buying a whole bunch of
antennas. You have a few decisions to make. You need to figure out what
wireless products in your network need a better antenna and what type of
replacement antenna provides the best fit.

Figure 7-3:
Example of
aftermarket
antenna
with base.

*Courtesy of D-Link, a division
of Cisco Systems, Inc.*

The two antenna types you can choose from are the following:

✦ **Omni-directional:** Wi-Fi signals from this type of antenna are sent (almost) equally in all directions. Additionally, omni-directional antennas are also tuned to receive signals from all directions.

✦ **Directional:** Wi-Fi signals sent or propagated from these types of antennas are aimed in a certain direction. Imagine that, instead of sending the signals in all directions, a directional antenna concentrates the signals in one direction, thus making the signal travel farther. Furthermore, these antennas are tuned to receive signals from one direction.

You can replace all your antennas (your Wi-Fi router and adapters) or pick and choose those that will provide just enough increased range to fix your problem. To help with these predicaments, take a look at these common "replacement scenarios" and pick the one that best fits:

✦ **Replace just the wireless router antenna:** Doing this with an omni-directional antenna is beneficial when all your computers are scattered around your home. In the less common situation in which you have all your wireless computers closely located in the same area, a directional antenna would be feasible.

✦ **Replace antennas on only your "problem computer(s)":** If you have only one or two problem computers with low signals and connectivity issues, this may be the best solution. In this case, using a directional antenna would make sense, at least for desktop computers, because you probably won't need to ever send signals in any other direction than to your wireless router. It's a different story for laptops, which you move around your home and use with other networks away from home. When away from home, you might not know where the signals should be sent or received. So for your laptop, you should only use omni-directional antennas. But keep in mind that only a handful of wireless cards for laptops include a connector for external or replacement antennas. Thus you'll have to probably get a new wireless card as well.

✦ **Replace the wireless router and "problem computer(s)"antennas:** As with the first scenario, this solution is best if all (or most) of your computers are having connectivity issues. However, replacing the computer antennas in addition to the wireless router provides a better chance of fixing your low-signal problem. Plus it provides better performance, which is particularly useful when transferring files over your network. As discussed in the first bullet, you probably need to use an omni-directional antenna for your router. For your desktop computers, you could use directional antennas for best results and stick with omni-directional for laptops, as I discuss in the second bullet.

Choosing your aftermarket antennas

When you know how many antennas you want to replace and have chosen the types for the replacements, you can continue by finding and acquiring them. Here are some tips to help you along:

✦ **Try your brands:** First, check the brands of your existing equipment, because networking manufacturers usually produce replacement antennas that fit all or most of their wireless gear.

✦ **Check online first:** Before hitting up your local electronic stores, do some research online. You can go to the Web sites of your equipment manufacturers and search for a compatible antenna, usually listed on the same page as all the wireless products. You can also do some price matching; you'll probably find the best deals online.

✦ **Get the right connector type:** If you aren't sticking with the same brands, make sure that the antenna supports the connector type (such as SMA or TNC) of your router or adapter.

✦ **For laptops:** You have two options to get a better antenna for your laptop. The first option is to use an enhanced USB wireless adapter (such as the one shown in Figure 7-4), with an included high-gain antenna or one that supports wireless N.

Courtesy of Linksys, a division of Cisco Systems, Inc.

Figure 7-4:
An enhanced USB wireless adapter.

The next option is to use a wireless card with antenna jacks — the card (model #G54A) produced by Buffalo (www.buffalotech.com), for instance — and use a separate, high-gain antenna.

Replacing your antennas

Not much explanation is needed about replacing antennas, except that you should turn off the device before removing the antenna: Disable your wireless adapter, shut down your computer, or unplug your wireless router. Then you can simply remove the existing antenna by unscrewing or pulling it, depending on the connector type. When you have it off, screw or push on the connector of the new replacement antenna.

You've done it! Now turn that adapter or router back on and see whether you have better luck.

Renovating Your Network with Wireless N

For those of you with existing wireless B or G networks, one way to significantly increase the range of your wireless network is to use wireless N products. As a bonus, you'll get faster transfer speeds (or data rates) when sharing files on the network, many times over what you would get from wireless G equipment. This is the newest of the Wi-Fi technologies (or standards), making use of multiple transmitter and receiver antennas. This method is termed MIMO (multiple input multiple output) and it provides the greatly improved range and performance over the wireless G products.

As you can see in Figure 7-5, these products usually use three antennas rather than the usual one or two antennas on wireless B and G equipment.

Figure 7-5: A wireless N (MIMO) Wi-Fi router and network adapter.

Courtesy of D-Link Systems, Inc.

Upgrading to wireless N can help bring your computers with low (or zero) signals (and dropped and intermittent connections) to better levels, and most likely get rid of all the problems. Even better news for you is that it should enable you to surf the Web from places originally marked as dead-zones and out-of-the-coverage area.

Although the wireless N technology is still being developed and isn't slated for finalization until at least 2008 or 2009, manufacturers already have products out based upon the draft versions of the technology. You may see these products identified as pre-N, draft n, or MIMO-based.

Here are some tips to put into memory:

✦ **Think about replacing all your products:** If you want to take full advantage of this new technology, you need to replace your wireless router, plus the wireless adapters in the computers you want to have the extended range and increased performance.

✦ **Can work with B and G:** Although using wireless B and G wireless adapters on a wireless N router doesn't provide significant increase in range and performance, some increase is possible. So if you don't use a certain computer much, you could just keep that old adapter and save money and time by only upgrading adapters on computers that you use regularly. Having these old adapters connected to your wireless network won't hurt the performance of the wireless N adapters.

✦ **Stay with one brand:** Because this technology isn't fully standardized yet, you should stick with a single brand for all your wireless N gear. This is to be on the safe side, because the coding and methodology behind the products may differ between manufacturers.

✦ **Keep it updated:** Because the development of the wireless N standard is still ongoing and the MIMO technology is new, stay current with firmware and driver updates. These hardware updates are released periodically by the manufacturers. If you need help, check out Book II, Chapter 5.

Wireless Extenders: Extending Range Inexpensively

If the methods discussed so far don't seem to fit with your lacking range problem, you should look into using wireless extenders/repeaters (see Figure 7-6 for an example) before settling on the last resort of actually adding more wireless access points.

Here are a few things to consider about using range extenders:

✦ **Coverage increase of 50 percent per extender:** Adding a wireless extender increases your coverage by about 50 percent, rather than the 100-percent increase provided by access points.

Book II
Chapter 7

Getting a Better
Reach with
Wireless

Figure 7-6:
A wireless
extender.

Courtesy of Linksys, a division of Cisco Systems, Inc.

✦ **Easier than adding APs:** Because you don't have to run wires throughout your home or buy and set up power-line devices to provide a network connection to the extender, it's usually much easier and cost
   effective to add an extender or two, compared to wiring new access
   points.

✦ **Repeats your Wi-Fi signals:** Wireless extenders increase your Wi-Fi
   coverage by repeating the signal from your existing wireless router or
   access point.

✦ **Access points (APs) have repeating capabilities:** Many access points
   have a variety of other wireless modes, including Repeater mode, which
   makes the AP just like an extender.

✦ **Performance is degraded:** The data rates (or speeds) experienced on
   wireless extenders can be as much as half the normal amount. Keep in
   mind that this shouldn't affect Web browsing and Internet downloading
   but will affect file transferring from computers on the extender to computers on your original wireless router or access points.

✦ **New technologies may not be supported:** Networking manufacturers
   usually don't reproduce their entire stock of networking gear in every
   new wireless standard and technology that comes along. Therefore,
   some extenders or repeating-capable APs may not have (at least at first)

all the new encryption and security methods, or even support the new wireless standards.

✦ **Supported wireless routers may be limited:** Some extenders work only with certain wireless routers and APs. Carefully check the product description and requirements for wireless extenders.

Along with the usual determining factor — the price — keep in mind the following when shopping for a wireless extender (or repeater-capable AP):

✦ **Multiple names exist:** Networking manufacturers come up with their own trade names to describe their products, including range "extender" and range "expander."

✦ **Look for antenna gain:** The more gain an antenna has, the farther the signal will go, so you might want to compare the antenna gain of extenders.

✦ **Think about going with an AP:** Most high-grade access points include a repeater mode, in addition to a variety of other wireless modes. You might spend a bit more on an AP with repeating functionality; however, if you want even more coverage later, you can just use the AP mode.

Although the manufacturer's installation guide for your extender gives you exact directions for your model, the following steps should help you set up just about any wireless extender or repeater-capable AP — with a bit more hand-holding.

Just as with any other wireless networking product, before you set it up, you should check for any available firmware/driver updates. See Book II, Chapter 5 for more information.

1. **Connect your extender to a computer.**

If you're using an AP (with automatic or dynamic IP addressing with DHCP) with a repeater feature rather than an exclusive extender, you can connect to the Web-based utility normally. Just make sure that you're wirelessly connected to the AP and skip down to Step 2.

However, if you're using an actual extender (not an AP), you must first physically connect the extender to a computer, as follows:

a. Make sure that your computer has a wired (Ethernet) network adapter installed and enabled.

b. Plug the extender into an electrical outlet to power it up.

c. Plug one end of an Ethernet cable (probably included with the product) into the port of the extender, and plug the other end into the Ethernet port of your computer.

d. Most extenders are set by default with a static IP address; you can check your product documentation. In order to properly connect to the extender and access the Web-based configuration utility, you must assign your computer a static IP address within the same range as the extender.

You'll need to look in the installation guide or manual of your extender to figure out the default IP address and subnet mask (most likely 255.255.255.0), the two pieces of information you need to configure your computer with a correct static IP address.

When you know the default IP settings, configure your computer with an address in the same range; Figure 7-7 shows an example.

For instance, if the IP address is 192.168.0.210, you could use 192.168.0.211 or 192.168.0.212; or if the default is 192.168.0.30, you could use 192.168.0.31 or even 192.168.0.166.

If you need help with configuring static addresses, refer to Book IV, Chapter 1.

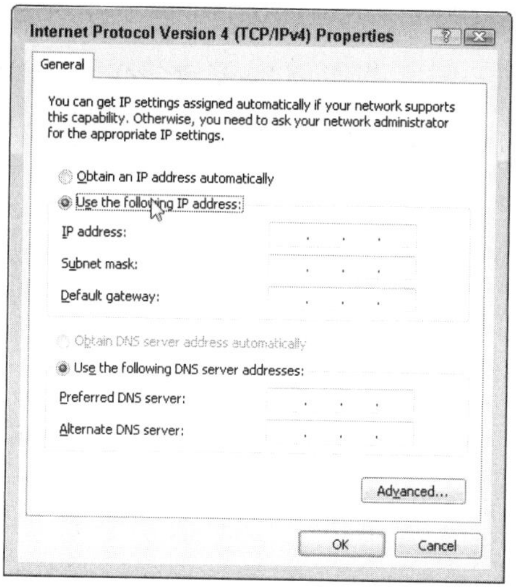

Figure 7-7:
Configuring
a static IP
address in
Windows
Vista.

2. **Access the Web-based configuration utility of the extender or AP by opening a Web browser (for example, Internet Explorer, Netscape, or Firefox), typing in the IP address of your extender or AP into the address bar, and, when prompted, entering the username and password of your AP.**

3. **If you're using an AP, you must enable the Repeater mode by clicking the Wireless or Advanced wireless tab (Figure 7-8 shows an example), selecting Repeater for the Mode option, and then clicking Save or Apply.**

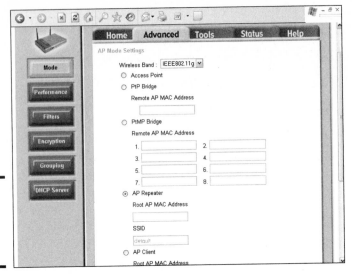

Figure 7-8:
Wireless
mode
settings of
an AP.

The device may reboot, and you may be disconnected for a minute.

4. **If you're using a extender, select the signal source (your wireless router) that you would like to extend or repeat, either by selecting the wireless router (identified by network name) from a list populated with all the nearby wireless networks (see Figure 7-9), or manually entering the MAC address of the wireless router.**

To find out the MAC or IP address of a device you can refer to Book V, Chapter 3. When you've identified the source, click Save or Apply.

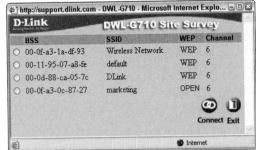

Figure 7-9:
Signal
source
settings of
an extender.

5. **Click the Wireless tab (or other similarly named tab containing the basic wireless settings, as shown in Figure 7-10).**

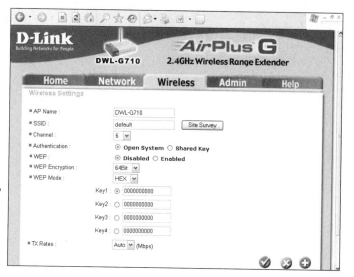

Figure 7-10: Wireless settings of an extender.

6. **Enter your own name in the Network Name (or SSID) field and then click Save or Apply.**

   The network name (or SSID) for all your extenders, APs, and wireless routers should be the same. This is so that your mobile devices (such as a laptop) can roam seamlessly without being officially disconnected from the network and disrupting your network or Internet connection.

7. **Click the Advanced tab as shown in Figure 7-11 (or Wireless Security or other tab, depending on your utility), and configure the extender or AP with the same encryption settings as your wireless router; then click Save or Apply.**

   If you need assistance in configuring the settings, refer to Book III, Chapter 2.

8. **Disconnect the extender from your computer.**

   If you're using an actual extender (not an AP), you can now disconnect the Ethernet cable from your computer and unplug the extender from the wall. Additionally you can reenable automatic IP addressing (DHCP) on your computer; refer to Book IV, Chapter 1 if you need help.

9. **Place the extender.**

   Now that you have configured your extender or AP, you just need to find a good spot in which to put it — around the edge of the source signal's coverage.

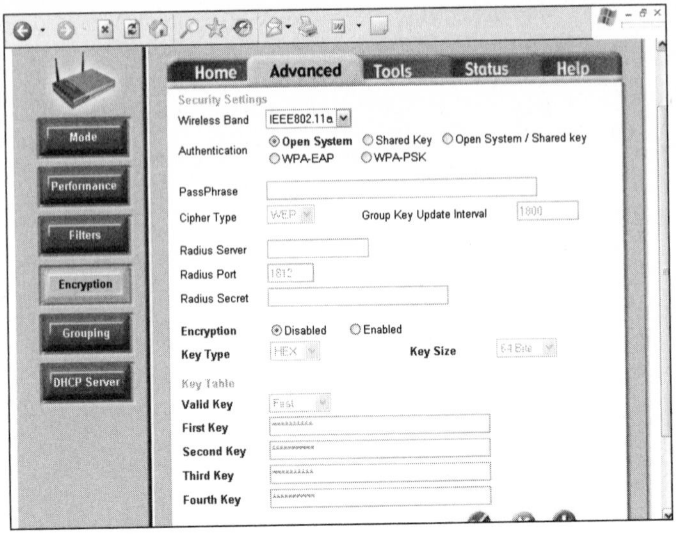

Figure 7-11:
Encryption
settings on
an AP.

You can discover your coverage boundaries by walking and checking
signal levels with a laptop:

a. Open your laptop and connect to the AP or wireless router you indicated as the source signal.

b. Bring up your wireless status information, either a utility provided by
your wireless adapter or the one built in to Windows (see Figure 7-12),
which shows signal strength and data rate. See Book IV, Chapter 1 for
steps on accessing these utilities.

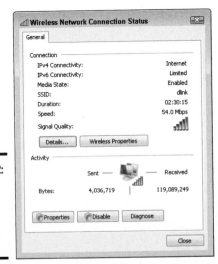

Figure 7-12:
Wireless
network
stats in
Windows
Vista.

c. Starting close to the source, walk out (slowly) toward one direction while monitoring the signal levels on the laptop. When you see the signal level drop very low, stop and change direction. Try to walk in a circle around the router, again while monitoring the signal levels — and remember where you are walking.

Figure 7-13 offers a depiction of this process.

Your objective is to stay connected to the source but to keep signal levels down. This is defining your coverage boundaries. Keep walking the circle around the wireless router while making adjustments (going closer or farther from the router) to stay at the poor levels. When you reach the starting point, you can quit.

If you're working with multiple floors, you should do a similar walk-around on each floor to see what the vertical coverage is like. Try to start above or below the wireless router.

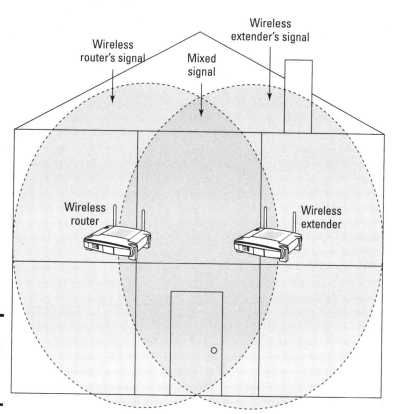

Figure 7-13: Discovering your coverage boundaries.

d. Now think of the area your wireless router filled. You can expect an extender or AP to provide similar coverage. But keep in mind that the coverage will overlap with the source. Your entire wireless coverage won't double, but you will get about 50 percent more coverage per extender.

Additionally, obstructions reduce the signal, and the reduction differs depending on the obstruction. For example, brick or concrete walls reduce radio signals much more than drywall does.

e. Determine exact extender/AP placement by thinking where you want the coverage extended and keeping in mind that the device must be placed around the coverage boundary of the source router or AP.

Also, don't forget that the final resting place should have an electrical outlet nearby.

Adding Access Points (APs): True Coverage Increase

The amount of coverage increased by adding access points (APs) — see Figure 7-14 for an example — is essentially endless: Adding one AP doubles the coverage, two APs triple it, three provide quadruple coverage, and so on. The range or coverage increase just depends on how many APs you add to your network and how much time and money you want to spend.

Figure 7-14:
Example of
an access
point.

Courtesy of D-Link Systems, Inc.

This network extending method basically consists of placing more wireless routers around your home. The APs provide another wireless connection point for your Wi-Fi computers and devices, hence the name access point. It's important to understand that wireless computer users can still move around; their wireless adapters will automatically roam to the best available access point or wireless router.

Adding more than one AP to your wireless router usually isn't necessary unless you want full coverage in a building of more than 4,000 square feet, constructed of drywall.

Deciding whether to run Ethernet cables or use your existing power lines

Each AP you place throughout your home must be connected back to your central network, most likely your wireless router. So much for a "wireless" (freedom of wires (network, huh? Well, just keep in mind that you'll have a great time later when you're roaming about your home while staying connected. The APs must be connected to your router so that the computers on the new APs can communicate with your computers connected to your router, and so that the new APs have an Internet connection.

You have two choices for this "backend" connection:

✦ **Run Ethernet cables:** This method requires you to run a wire out to each of your APs from the ports on the back of your router. This traditional technique requires much more work than the other method but offers a significant cost savings.

✦ **Use power-line technology:** Instead of running more wires throughout your home, this method uses your home's electrical lines.

For this method, you buy special power-line bridges or adapters. One plugs into an electrical outlet near your router, with a cable running off it and connecting to a port on the back of your router, supplying your electrical lines with the network and Internet connections. Then wherever you want an AP, you plug another power-line bridge or adapter into an electrical outlet and connect it to your AP.

This can be a great way to add additional APs if you don't want to run new wires.

Properly setting up a power-line network requires you to have at least one computer with a wired network adapter, or Ethernet port.

To help you decide between these two methods, take a look at Table 2-1 which points out the differences.

Table 2-1	Comparing Backend AP Connection Techniques			
Method	*Setup Time*	*Price*	*Data Rate*	*Max Distance*
Running Ethernet cables	Much more involved	$10–$50 for 50- to 100-foot cable	Up to 1,000 Mbps (gigabit)	328–492 feet (100 to 150 meters)
Using Power-line technology	Less involved	$40–$60 per bridge	Up to 200 Mbps	656–984 feet (200–300 meters)

A faster data rate doesn't help on the Internet side but does on your private network. That is, you won't get faster Web browsing and downloading by going with the higher data rate backend connection, but you could receive much faster file transfers between your computers. However, this also depends on the data rates supported by your wireless router and access points.

Planning and preparing

Adding access points (APs) to your network requires a good amount of planning and preparing, which this section discusses.

Determine layout: Do a walk-around

First you need to figure out how many APs you need or want to add to your existing wireless router, plus where they should be placed. In the enterprise world, this is called a site survey. *Your* site survey, though, will be a slimmed-down version. Here's how to do it:

1. **Open your laptop, connect to your wireless router, and bring up your wireless status information, either through a utility provided by your wireless adapter or using the one built in to Windows (see Figure 7-15), which shows signal strength and data rate.**

If you don't have a laptop, you're pretty much out of luck unless you want to move your desktop computers from room to room. But you can take the easy way out and just guess where your coverage boundaries are compared to the signal levels on your desktop computer(s).

2. **Discover existing coverage boundaries by walking and checking signal levels.**

This is the same process as described previously for placing a wireless extender, which you can find in Step 9 of the "Wireless Extenders: Extending Range Inexpensively" section, earlier in this chapter.

3. **Find rough AP placements, using your imagination.**

Figure 7-15:
Wireless
network
stats in
Windows
Vista.

Now think of the area your wireless router filled. You can expect an AP
to provide similar coverage. But keep in mind that obstructions reduce
the signal, and the reduction differs upon the obstruction. For example,
brick or concrete walls reduce radio signals much more than drywall
does. The point is that the coverage, without a doubt, won't be the exact
same, but the comparison is okay for your purposes.

You want the coverage from the additional AP(s) to slightly overlap the
coverage from adjacent APs or wireless routers, so you still have a good
Wi-Fi signal if later located in between coverage zones. If you're working
with multiple floors, you also need to imagine the vertical coverage,
based upon testing from your wireless router's coverage.

4. **Pick exact AP placements by finding outlets or cabling paths.**

   When you have a rough idea where the AP(s) should be located, you
   need to figure out the exact placement by doing some searching and
   more thinking:

   If you're going the power-line way:

   - Simply find an outlet nearby to plug in the power-line bridge/adapter.

   - Find a second outlet for the AP if you don't plan on purchasing the
     power-line/AP combo device.

   If you're going with Ethernet cabling, you should figure out exactly how
   and where the cable is going to be run. You can refer to Book II, Chapter 2
   for more information and tips on running Ethernet cabling.

Next you need to:

- **Determine lengths:** Figure out exactly how many cable sections you need and measure the lengths.

- **Find electrical outlets:** Remember that you should place the end of the cable(s) near an electrical outlet so that you can power your AP. However, you can use APs with power-over-Ethernet (PoE) capabilities with a power injector at your wireless router; doing so can power your AP instead of your having to plug it into an outlet.

Choosing and buying your APs

Access points (APs) in general are pretty generic and don't have many differences or special features, but here are a few pointers when selecting your AP(s):

- ✦ **Pick the right wireless technology:** The main thing to look for in an AP is the supported wireless standards or technologies, for example A, G, or N (or multiband APs). Although doing so is not required, you should stick with the same standard used by your wireless router.

- ✦ **Power-over-Ethernet (PoE) capability:** Some APs have this feature, which allows you to power the AP through the Ethernet cable rather than have to plug the AP into an electrical outlet. But keep in mind that you must have a PoE-supported router or a separate PoE adapter/injector on the other end of the cable.

- ✦ **Multiple-mode APs exist:** Some access points support other modes in addition to AP, such as: Point-to-Point Bridge, Point-to-Multipoint Bridge, Repeater, and Wireless Client. This can be useful if you want to experiment with other range-extending techniques.

 If you prefer, you can use a wireless router instead of an access point, which is especially useful if you have a spare router lying around. With a few settings changes, you can basically turn a wireless router into an AP, as discussed later in the "Setting up the AP" section.

Buying your power-line adapters

If you're using power-line bridges/adapters (see Figure 7-16 for an example) for your backend AP connections, make sure that you take into account the HomePlug standards and other varying characteristics, discussed in Book II, Chapter 2.

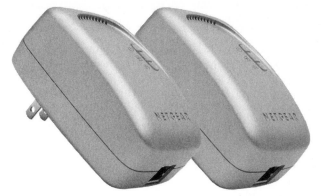

Courtesy of NETGEAR®, Inc.

Figure 7-16:
An example
of power-
line
adapters.

Getting the Ethernet cables

When shopping for Ethernet cabling (see Figure 7-17), you should understand the three main types, Cat5, Cat5e, and Cat6, which are all interoperable and support data rates of up to 1,000 Mbps (gigabit). These cable types and other information pertaining to Ethernet cabling are discussed in Book II, Chapter 2.

Figure 7-17:
Example of
Ethernet
cabling.

Setting up your backend connection

First you should install and set up your backend connection — Ethernet cables or power-line devices. For installation instructions for power-line adapters, you can refer to Book II, Chapters 2 through 4 (keeping your eye out for the material covering power-line networking) for help on planning what you need, installing, and setting up power-line adapters. While going through the chapters, keep in mind that you don't want to set up a strictly power-line network. You want to connect one power-line adapter from your router to your electrical system and then connect a power-line adapter from each AP to your electrical system.

If you're using Ethernet cabling for the backend connection of your AP(s), here are the steps to follow:

1. **Plug one end of the Ethernet cable into your wireless router.**

2. **Install the Ethernet cable.**

Take the other end of the cable and run with it! It's time to do the actual physical installation of your Ethernet cable. Information and tips on undertaking running Ethernet cabling appear in Book II, Chapter 2 and the "Determine layout: Do a walk-around" section of this chapter. Good luck!

3. **Connect the AP.**

When you have your Ethernet run to your desired spot, connect the AP to the cable or the jack, if installed.

Making the AP work with your network

In order for your AP to work with your existing network, you must verify that its IP address is set within the same range (subnet) as your existing network. This verification is necessary because APs come set with a static IP address, rather than a dynamic setting that automatically retrieves a correct address. If you're using the same brand for your AP as your wireless router, you'll probably be fine because the manufacturer usually sets a static IP address within range of the default settings of its routers. However, you still should double-check before doing the install.

1. **Get the IP information for your existing wireless router.**

First you need to figure out the IP address subnet of your current network. You can do this by bringing up the network connection status information on a computer currently connected to your wireless router. You need to find and write down the IP address of the default gateway and subnet mask. If you need help, refer to Book V, Chapter 3.

2. **Get the IP information for your AP.**

Now you need to get the AP's default subnet, listed in the Install Guide and manual for the product. You won't find a value for the subnet; instead, you should look for the IP address and subnet mask.

3. **Compare the values.**

If all but the last numbers of the IP addresses (of the wireless router and AP) match, you're good to go. For instance, if your current network (wireless router) is set to 192.168.1.1 and your AP is set to 192.168.1.151 (or anything from 192.168.1.2 to 192.168.254), you're in the same subnet. In this case, both subnet masks would be 255.255.255.0.

But if the second-to-last number doesn't match, you're probably in different subnets, and you need to change one device's IP address. For instance, if your current network (wireless router) is set to 192.168.0.1, and your AP is set to 192.168.2.151, you're not in the same subnet. In this case, both subnet masks would be 255.255.255.0.

If you need to change the subnet of your AP, you must connect the AP to your computer and bring up its Web-based configuration utility:

1. **Connect an Ethernet cable to the AP and the other end of the cable to your computer.**

2. **Set a static IP address, within range of the AP, for your computer's network adapter.**

If you need help configuring your network adapter (that's connected to your AP) with a static IP address, refer to Book IV, Chapter 1.

3. **Connect the power cord to your AP and plug the other end into a wall outlet.**

4. **Access the Web-based configuration utility of the AP by opening a Web browser (such as Internet Explorer, Netscape, and Firefox), typing in the IP address of your AP into the address bar, and, when prompted, entering the username and password of your AP.**

5. **Click the Basic or LAN tab (or other tab that contains the IP address setting for the AP).**

6. **Either change the IP address to one within range of your current network (starting with the same three sets of numbers) or enable DHCP (which is slightly easier to do) so that the AP will automatically retrieve a correct IP address from your current network.**

7. **Click the Save or Apply button.**

The AP will reboot and you will be disconnected for a minute. Now you can disconnect the AP from the computer and move on with the installation.

Book II
Chapter 7

Getting a Better
Reach with
Wireless

 Because you've changed the default IP address, you should mark it next to the values given in the product documentation so that you can find it if you forget it. You may also want to tape a piece of paper under the AP with the new value.

Setting up the AP

To set up your AP, you can follow the installation and setup directions included with your AP or power-line/AP combo device, or you can use the steps provided here. These cover the main settings that you should change or set for each of your APs.

Converting a Wireless Router into an AP

You can use a wireless router instead of an access point. The main difference between the two devices is that an AP doesn't include the routing and IP features that enable features such as Internet sharing and dynamic (or automatic) IP addressing. An AP doesn't need these features because they're provided by other components, such as routers.

To turn a wireless router into the equivalent of an AP, you can just disable these special features by following these steps:

1. **Power-on the wireless router you want to convert and then plug an Ethernet cable into an Ethernet port (one out of the usual four) of your wireless router and the other end into your Ethernet port of your computer.**

2. **Access the Web-based configuration utility of the wireless router by opening a Web browser (such as Internet Explorer, Netscape, or Firefox), typing the IP address of your wireless router into the address bar, and, when prompted, entering the username and password of your wireless router.**

3. **Click the Basic, Setup, or LAN tab (or other tab containing the IP address setting) and change the IP address so that it's in the same range (but has a different address) as your main router. Then click Save or Apply.**

   For instance, if the IP address of your main router is 192.168.0.1, you can use 192.168.0.2 or 192.168.0.3; or, if it's 192.168.1.1, you can use 192.168.1.2 or even 192.168.1.66.

4. **Click the Basic, Setup, or LAN tab (or other tab containing the IP address settings) and disable DHCP. Then click Save or Apply.**

   You want to disable DHCP because you want only your main router to handle the IP addresses for the network users.

5. **You can disconnect the wireless router from your computer and treat it as an AP. When you're ready to connect your make-shift AP to your main router, connect one end of an Ethernet cable to one of the four Ethernet ports on the back (not the WAN port). Then connect the other end of the cable to one of the four ports on the back of your main router, as you normally would.**

 As with other wireless networking products, before you set up your AP, you should check for any available firmware/driver updates. See Book II, Chapter 5 for more information.

Here's how to set up the AP(s):

1. Access the Web-based configuration utility of the AP by opening a Web browser (such as Internet Explorer, Netscape, and Firefox), typing in the IP address of your AP into the address bar, and, when prompted, entering the username and password of your AP.

2. Click the Wireless tab (or other, similarly named tab containing the basic wireless settings, as shown in Figure 7-18), enter the same network name as that used by your wireless router into the Network Name (SSID) field, and click Apply or Save.

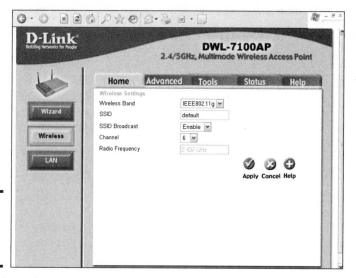

Figure 7-18: Wireless settings on an AP.

The network name (or SSID) for all your APs and wireless routers should be the same. This is so that your mobile devices (such as a laptop) can roam seamlessly between your router and AP(s) without being officially disconnected from the network and disrupting your network or Internet connection.

3. **Click the Wireless tab (or other, similarly named tab containing the basic wireless settings, as shown in Figure 7-18), choose a channel using the recommendations in the following paragraphs, and click Apply or Save.**

In contrast to the network name, your wireless router and your AP(s) should not be on the same (or even close) channels. You should set each AP and wireless router to a different and nonoverlapping channel — channels 1, 6, or 11.

So if you have a wireless router and two additional APs, you can set (or leave) the wireless router to channel 6, set one of the APs to channel 1, and set the other AP to channel 11. Doing so would prevent the APs from interfering with each other but also still allow roaming between them.

4. **Click the Advanced tab, such as that shown in Figure 7-19, and configure the AP with the same encryption settings as your wireless router. Then click Save or Apply.**

As is true of the network name, the encryption keys/settings of all your wireless routers and AP should be the same. This allows for seamless roaming.

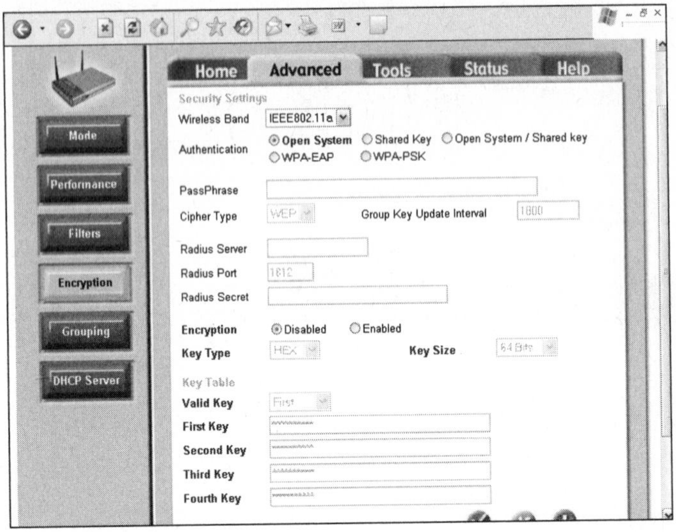

Figure 7-19:
Encryption
settings on
an AP.

If you need assistance in configuring the settings, refer to Book III, Chapter 2.

5. Verify and configure any additional security settings.

If you've configured any other security settings (such as disabling SSID broadcasting or MAC address filtering), you might want to make similar changes to your AP(s). Refer to Book III, Chapter 2 for information on configuring these items.

Additionally, if you find that you're having problems getting your AP(s) to work, you should verify that these additional security techniques aren't what are holding you up. For example, if you aren't using dynamic IP addresses (DHCP) on your router, you must manually configure the IP address of your AP(s), with an address within the acceptable range, or you could just reenable DHCP on the router.

Book III

Network Security

The 5th Wave   By Rich Tennant

"Amy surfs the Web a lot, so for protection we installed several filtering programs that allow only approved sites through. Which of those nine sites are you looking at now, Amy?"

Contents at a Glance

Chapter 1: Addressing Internet Security

In This Chapter

✔ **Stopping hackers with a firewall**

✔ **Getting outfitted for the battle against Internet viruses and infections**

✔ **Fighting back against spam and junk e-mails**

✔ **Realizing the dangers of the virtual fishing game — phishing**

✔ **Putting your foot down on pop-ups and staying safe when surfing**

As you may know, the Internet opens your computer up to infections — those nasty little programs like viruses and spyware — and to hackers. But did you know you can protect yourself against these infections and threats? It isn't hard and you don't have to have a computer degree: just at most some money and an hour of your time.

In addition to viruses, you have to worry about other online threats and annoyances, like spam and phishing e-mails. You can protect yourself, but first you need to know how. This chapter shows you how.

Blocking Internet Hackers Using Firewalls

The Internet is in effect just a big network, similar to your home network, but with billions of computers interconnected from around the world. Some of the people behind these computers are trustworthy, but others are not. Connecting your computer to the Internet without proper protection gives hackers the opportunity to connect to your computer to do nefarious things like

✦ Getting your files and sensitive information

✦ Monitoring your Internet traffic

✦ Taking over your computer to change settings and cause havoc

You can, however, use a firewall to protect yourself from these hackers.

The big picture behind what firewalls do

A *firewall* is a filter that monitors data traffic to either let it through or block it, depending on the settings you've created when you set up your firewall. You could compare this process to a DUI checkpoint set up by the authorities:

1. Cars (data traffic) on both sides of the road (incoming and outgoing) must stop at the road-block (firewall) to be inspected.

2. Safe drivers (authorized data traffic) are let through to the other side of the roadblock (firewall).

3. Impaired drivers (unauthorized data traffic) are blocked and aren't allowed through the roadblock (firewall).

Figure 1-1 gives you a visual of this type of filter provided by computer firewalls.

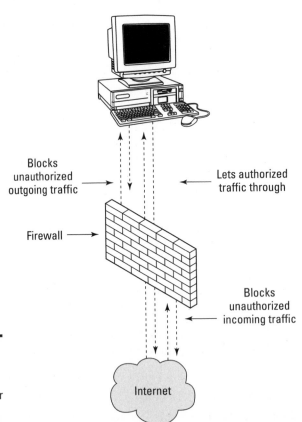

Blocks
unauthorized
outgoing traffic

Lets authorized
traffic through

Firewall

Blocks
unauthorized
incoming traffic

Internet

Figure 1-1:
A depiction
of a firewall
filtering your
data traffic.

A firewall doesn't come with authorities to do the inspection, nor does it automatically prosecute violators; however, a firewall helps keep your computers from being hacked.

What a firewall actually blocks: Ports

The previous section helps paint a good picture in your mind to understand the basic concept behind firewalls, but to better understand firewalls, you should know that they work by blocking ports. A firewall doesn't just magically know what data is good or bad for your computer out of thin air, or from some type of inspection of the data itself.

On a network and the Internet, there are different ports (thousands of them) that data can travel through. For instance, think of a CB radio: You have 40 channels you can talk on, but all the talk is done through one medium, the airwaves. Likewise, all the data on a network and the Internet travels through the same mediums, but on a variety of ports.

Half of the protection provided by firewalls is blocking all ports except those specified as authorized ports. The other half of the protection is provided by blocking all programs on your computer (no matter what port is used) from using the network or Internet, again, except for those you have specifically authorized.

Getting a firewall to protect yourself

A firewall can be a software program loaded on your computers or a piece of hardware that sits between your Internet connection and your computers (or router). Newer operating systems such as the following come with built-in firewall software:

✦ Windows Vista

✦ Windows XP

✦ Mac OS X

Ubuntu doesn't automatically come with a firewall installed and active. However, you can set it up, which is discussed shortly.

You can also find firewall software available as a standalone product or as a part of an entire Internet security suite, for purchase (or for free) from companies such as

✦ **McAfee:** www.mcafee.com

✦ **CA (Computer Associates):** shop.ca.com

✦ **Norton (Symantec):** www.symantec.com/norton

✦ **ZoneAlarm (basic firewall software is free):** www.zonealarm.com

✦ **Comodo Firewall Pro (free):** www.personalfirewall.comodo.com

Because your operating system (Windows, Mac, and so on) probably includes a firewall, using a third-party firewall isn't necessary. However, if you are purchasing an Internet security suite for viral and spyware protection, and it includes a firewall, you may want to disable the built-in firewall for your operating system. You'll probably find it easier to use the third-party firewall because it will be from the same vendor, providing you with streamlined access and configuration of all your Internet security products.

Hardware firewall solutions are covered later in this chapter, in the "Using Internet Security Hardware Solutions for Your Entire Network" section.

Configuring the Windows Firewall

Windows XP and Vista come with a firewall (called Windows Firewall) installed and enabled by default. Because common programs and services are authorized by default, you don't have to configure the Windows Firewall that much. Additionally, when a program on your computer tries to access the Internet or network for the first time, you're prompted to authorize or block the access. Then, depending upon your response to whether to authorize or block, the firewall utility is automatically updated.

The firewall settings are saved, so when you restart your computer nothing needs configured again. You basically need to configure your firewall settings only when you want to disable or enable the feature or manually add or remove an application or software.

Using Windows XP

You can access the firewall settings in Windows XP from the Control Panel. To do so, choose Start⇨Control Panel⇨Network and Internet Connections⇨ Windows Firewall.

Figure 1-2 shows the main window of Windows Firewall, where you can easily turn it on or off.

Clicking the Exceptions tab shows you all the programs/ports that are authorized to pass by the firewall, such as those shown in Figure 1-3. These exceptions apply to all your network adapters.

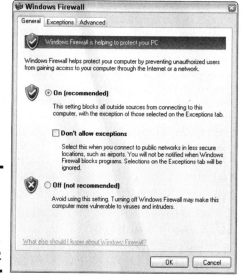

Figure 1-2:
The main window of the firewall utility in Windows XP.

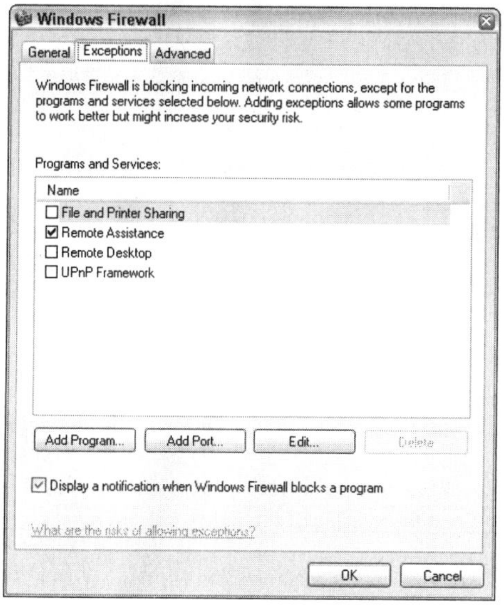

Figure 1-3:
The Exceptions tab of the firewall utility in Windows XP.

Clicking the Advanced tab (see Figure 1-4) gives you access to more complex settings:

✦ Enable/disable firewall protection for certain network adapters

✦ Configure the logging settings of the Windows Firewall

✦ Configure the Internet Control Message Protocol (ICMP) settings

✦ Restore Windows Firewall to its defaults, which is useful if you think you've caused problems by changing its settings

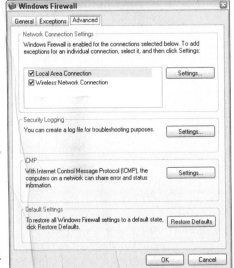

Figure 1-4:
The Advanced tab of the firewall utility in Windows XP.

Using Windows Vista

You can access the firewall settings in Windows Vista from your Control Panel by choosing Start⇨Control Panel⇨Security⇨Windows Firewall. If UAC is active and you received an alert, click OK to continue.

Figure 1-5 shows the main window of Windows Firewall. On the left are the main tasks, such as turning the firewall off and on or allowing a program through the firewall.

You can click the Change Settings link to bring up the Windows Firewall Settings dialog box, which enables you to review or change other settings:

✦ **General tab:** This is where you can easily turn the firewall on or off, or block all incoming connections for maximum protection.

✦ **Exceptions tab:** Shows you all the programs/ports that are authorized to pass by the firewall. These exceptions apply to all your network adapters.

✦ **Advanced tab:** Lets you enable/disable firewall protection for certain network adapters. From here, you can also restore Windows Firewall to its defaults, which is useful if you think you've caused problems by changing its settings.

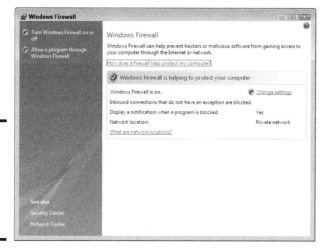

Configuring Mac OS X's firewall

The firewall feature in Mac OS X Tiger and Leopard is also installed and enabled by default. Just as with the Windows Firewall, you don't have to do much configuring of the firewall in Mac OS X. Common programs and services are authorized by default, and the firewall is updated when you turn on and off most other features that communicate with the Internet or your network, such as Personal File Sharing or Personal Web Sharing. You basically need to configure your firewall settings only when you want to disable or enable the feature or manually add or remove an application or software.

Accessing the firewall feature in Tiger

Here's how to access the firewall feature in Mac OS X Tiger:

1. **Click the Apple icon on the menu bar.**

2. **Click System Preferences.**

3. **Click Sharing.**

4. **Click the Firewall tab.**

The status of the firewall (shown as Firewall On or Firewall Off) is displayed in the upper-left of the Firewall tab window. Just below the status is the button (labeled Stop or Start, depending upon the current status) to disable or enable the firewall.

**Book III
Chapter 1**

**Addressing Internet
Security**

Many common features and programs are listed in the scrolling list box. Only the items that are checked are authorized to pass through the firewall. Many items can't be selected or deselected; in that case, the feature can be turned on or off in the Services pane (by clicking the Services tab button in the Sharing window). You can, however, choose an item and click the Edit button to see exactly what ports the item uses. If the item is editable (meaning that you can select or deselect it), you can edit the ports for the item.

You can add new features and applications to the firewall to allow their traffic to and from the Internet or your network from the particular Mac computer you're currently using. To do this, click the New button. On the drop-down menu, select the appropriate feature or application from the Port Name drop-down list. Click OK to add the new entry to the firewall.

If you want to block a service or application (remove it from the firewall), select the desired item from the scrolling list box and click Delete.

Clicking the Advanced button brings up the following three advanced firewall settings:

✦ **Block UDP Traffic:** Selecting this can help secure your computer.

✦ **Enabled Firewall Logging:** Enabling this feature logs the activity of the firewall (such as the IP addresses and ports that are blocked by the firewall), which is useful if you want to see whether someone is trying to hack into your computer, or when trying to troubleshoot an application or feature that isn't communicating over the Internet or network.

✦ **Enable Stealth Mode:** When this option is enabled, your computer won't respond to unrequested data traffic, thereby making your computer virtually invisible on the Internet. One benefit of this is that it can prevent you from being detected by a hacker using a popular method of detection called a *ping*. Hackers can send pings to random IP addresses (what identifies you on the Internet) and when a response is sent back, they know that a computer or network is there and may try to hack into it. Stealth mode keeps your computer from responding to pings.

Accessing the firewall feature in Leopard

Here's how to access the firewall feature in Mac OS X Leopard:

1. **Click the Apple icon on the menu bar.**

2. **Click System Preferences.**

3. **Click Security.**

4. **Click the Firewall tab.**

When you have the Firewall tab opened on the Security window, you can select one of the following radio button options:

✦ **Allow All Incoming Connections:** This option provides the least amount of protection and essentially turns the firewall feature off.

✦ **Allow Only Essential Services:** This option provides a great amount of protection; however, it blocks ports and services that you may want to use while on your home network, such as file and printer sharing. Only a few system-essential ports (for example, those that support networking services, such as DHCP, Bonjour, and IPSec) are opened by default when this option is selected.

This option is best when you are connected to other networks, such as Wi-Fi hotspots or other public connections to the Internet.

✦ **Set Access for Specific Services and Applications:** This is typically the best option to use when connected to your home network because it lets you control the firewall while also being flexible. This option is comparable to using the Windows Firewall feature in Windows. Ports and services typically used in home networks (such as file and printer sharing) are automatically authorized, letting you add other (non-Mac) applications or services as you want.

If you select either Allow Only Essential Services or Set Access for Specific Services and Applications, you can click the Advanced button and choose the Enable Firewall Logging and Enable Steal Mode options, if you want. See the "Accessing the firewall feature in Tiger" section for a description of these two options.

Additionally when you have Allow Only Essential Services or Set Access for Specific Services and Applications selected, you can add and remove applications (that you want to either block or allow through the firewall) from the list. Click the plus sign near the bottom-left corner of the window, select the application from dialog box, and click Add. Then select whether you want to allow or block the application.

Installing and setting up Ubuntu's firewall

Ubuntu doesn't come with a firewall feature automatically installed and active. You must install the firewall feature (called Firestarter). Here's how to do it:

1. **Click System from the Ubuntu toolbar.**

2. **Choose Administration.**

3. **Open Synaptic Package Manager.**

4. **If prompted, enter your account password and click OK.**

5. **Click Settings from toolbar.**

6. Choose Repositories.

7. Make sure that the Community-Maintained Open Source Software (universe) option is selected.

8. Click Close.

9. If prompted, click Close again.

10. Click the Reload button on the Synaptic Package Manager window.

11. Click the Search button, type firestarter, and hit Enter.

12. Click the checkbox next to the Firestarter item and choose Mark for Installation.

13. Click Apply, review changes, and click Apply.

14. Close Synaptic Package Manager.

Now you can configure Firestarter:

1. Click System from the Ubuntu toolbar.

2. Choose Administration.

3. Select Firestarter.

4. If prompted, enter your account password and click OK.

   The Firewall Wizard should run. If it doesn't, you can bring it up manually by clicking Firewall, and then clicking Run Wizard.

5. Click Forward.

   You should be taken to the Network Device Setup page.

6. From the Detected Device(s) drop-down list, select the network adapter that's connected to the Internet.

   Viewing the Connection Information window when you're connected to your network or Internet connection can give you a hint as to the device/adapter to select. Right-click the Ubuntu's network icon in the upper-right side of the screen and click Connection Information. If the window is filled with your network connection information, you'll most likely want to select the same device/adapter from the Firestarter Wizard as the value for the Interface field, which is at the top of the window.

7. Select the Start the Firewall on Dial-Out option if your computer is hooked directly to a dial-up Internet connection device, such as a DSL modem, or you connect to VPN (Virtual Private Network) connections.

   Most likely, this won't apply to you and you can leave the option unselected.

8. Select the IP Address Is Assigned via DHCP option if your computer is hooked directly to an Internet connection and it uses DHCP to obtain

its IP address (which is the case for just about all home Internet connections), or if the computer is connected to a network using DHCP (which is set by default on all home networking products).

This option applies to most people and usually needs to be selected.

9. **Click Forward to go to the Internet Connection Sharing Setup page.**

10. **If you plan to use your computer in a computer-to-computer network, or otherwise want to share your computer's Internet connection among other computers connected to your computer, select the Enable Internet Connection Sharing option.**

If you also want to provide other computers with an IP address, select the Enable DHCP for Local Network option. However, you probably don't need to worry about either of these options if you are connecting all your computers to a router, either wirelessly or via an Ethernet cable.

11. **Click Forward.**

12. **Make sure that the Start Firewall Now option is selected and then click Save.**

To make changes to Firestarter or add/remove applications from the firewall, you can bring up the Firestarter application:

1. **Click System from the Ubuntu toolbar.**

2. **Choose Administration.**

3. **Select Firestarter.**

4. **If prompted, enter your account password and click OK.**

When you have Firestarter open, you can easily disable and enable the firewall by clicking the Stop Firewall or Start Firewall button (depending upon the current status), which is on the top-right side of the window.

You can find documentation and further help on installing and using Firestarter at www.fs-security.com/docs.

Blocking Viruses, Spyware, and Adware with Software

Using the Internet makes you more susceptible to three major computer infections:

✦ Viruses

✦ Spyware

✦ Adware

In the following sections, I detail a little more about these major threats and how to protect your computer and data from them.

The wrath of computer infections

Whether downloaded automatically without your knowledge or disguised as a real program or file that you voluntarily downloaded, viral and spyware infections can cause problems, such as the following:

✦ Altering your computer settings to cause chaos

✦ Deleting your personal or system files

✦ Monitoring your Internet activity

✦ Displaying pop-up advertisements

✦ Spreading the infection to other computers on your network or on the Internet

Protecting your computers against infections

Even though newer operating systems (Windows XP and Vista, Mac OS X Tiger and Leopard) include a firewall (to protect your computer from hackers), you need to protect your computer from viral and spyware infections. You can use a software program loaded on all your computers, or install a piece of hardware between your Internet connection and your computers (or router). These anti-infection solutions usually work by

✦ Constantly scanning commonly infected areas for infections so that they are found quickly and the damage they do is minimal, if any.

✦ Performing routine, full-system scans of all files for infections to make sure your computer is completely free of infections.

✦ Alerting you to any infections that are found and automatically fixing them or asking you what you want to do.

You can find antivirus, antispyware, and antiadware software as standalone products or as a part of an entire Internet security suite for purchase from companies such as

✦ **McAfee:** www.mcafee.com

✦ **CA (Computer Associates):** shop.ca.com

✦ **Norton (Symantec):** www.symantec.com/norton

You can also find free software products that provide similar protection, such as

✦ **AVG Anti-Virus Free Edition:** `free.grisoft.com`

✦ **avast! 4 Home Edition:** `www.avast.com`

✦ **PC Tools AntiVirus:** `www.pctools.com/free-antivirus`

✦ **AVG Anti-Spyware Free Edition:** `www.grisoft.com`

✦ **Ad-Aware:** `www.lavasoftusa.com`

✦ **Avira AntiVir:** `www.free-av.com`

Windows Vista includes Windows Defender, an antispyware program. However, as is true of Windows Firewall, you may find it easier to use a security suite with all protections rather than have a separate application for each item.

Hardware solutions for combating infections are covered later in this chapter, in the "Using Internet Security Hardware Solutions for Your Entire Network" section.

Controlling Your Spam or Junk E-Mail

Spam is any unsolicited e-mail message that arrives at your inbox that doesn't provide proper contact information, contains illegal content, or doesn't give you a way to stop further e-mails from that source. E-mails that meet all of those criteria and are legitimate — for instance, advertisements and announcements — can still be considered junk mail if they are unwanted.

You can find out more about spam laws and regulations at the Federal Trade Commission's Web site:

`http://www.ftc.gov/bcp/conline/edcams/spam/`

You can probably relate these types of e-mails to the snail-mail junk mail — credit card offers, product advertisements, and occasional scams — that you receive in your mailbox at home. Snail-mail junk mail, however, costs companies and illegal enterprises money in paper, envelopes, and stamps. E-mail communication is virtually free and allows scammers and spammers to send messages to thousands or millions of people with just a touch of a button — just the right ingredients to support illegal, fraudulent, and fake operations, originating from anywhere in the world.

Problems behind spam and junk e-mail

Besides the fact that spam and junk e-mails are annoying, they can also cause real problems:

✦ **Can contain illegal, adult, and false content:** First off, this type of material often isn't appropriate for youngsters — think about your children's e-mail accounts — and you may find it offensive as well. Second, scams are extremely prevalent in spam and junk e-mails. These scams can range from selling frivolous products to sending you to fake Web sites that can con you out of money and your identity. The "Protecting Yourself Against Phishing Scams" section, later in this chapter, gives you more information on this practice.

✦ **Just pressing Delete doesn't help:** You can do nothing to prevent spam/junk messages and just keep deleting them as they arrive, but they'll just keep coming.

✦ **Causes extra traffic for all:** In addition to the time you'll spend deleting your junk messages (if you don't help prevent them), the messages are still being sent and delivered to your inbox, which wastes the resources of our entire e-mail/Internet system.

Preventative measures against spam and junk e-mail

Besides using spam and junk mail filtering solutions provided by your e-mail account provider or e-mail software, you can do a few simple things yourself to help prevent spam altogether:

✦ **Don't publish your e-mail address:** If people don't know your e-mail address exists, you won't receive much, or any, spam or junk mail.

Spammers often get e-mail addresses right from Web sites. Similarly to how Google and other search engines compile their enormous databases of sites, spammers use automated systems that scan the Web and extract e-mail addresses. So try not to post your e-mail addresses on public Web pages, such as discussion forums or social networking sites. But if you do, you can help prevent spammers from extracting your address by putting it in a different format to foil programs that search the Web for e-mail addresses. For example, if your e-mail address is `youraccount@domain.com`, you may want to use one of the following formats (note the use of spaces in the last two):

- `youraccountATdomainDOTcom`
- `youraccount (AT) domain . com`
- `youraccount AT domain DOT com`

Another source of your spam or junk e-mails could be from organizations selling your address. Large or respected businesses that obtain your address typically do not sell it, but free Web sites or services that you've signed up for certainly might.

✦ **Remove yourself from the lists:** Unsolicited e-mail is supposed to include a way for you to remove yourself from further mailings. Some spam/junk messages follow this rule; others don't. Those that have a removal method usually describe it at the bottom of the message, which usually involves just clicking a link and maybe entering your e-mail address. Removing yourself from mailings may help your problem (when you are dealing with a legitimate company); however, in some cases it may worsen your problem because spammers may use this opting out to verify that their messages are going to legitimate addresses, and you'll end up with more spam messages

✦ **Create a secondary account:** You may find it necessary to create a secondary e-mail account that you can make public to post on Web sites and use for free services. Then you can use another account for corresponding with family, friends, colleagues, and Web sites or places that you can trust.

Stopping spam when you've had enough

If spam and junk e-mails are still an issue after you follow the preventative measures I cover in previous sections, you may want to use a spam or junk mail solution. The main types are as follows:

✦ **Address filtering:** This is the least effective spam solution. When an e-mail arrives, the filter checks the sender against your blacklist. If the sender is on the list of blocked senders, the filter sends the e-mail to the spam/junk folder; otherwise, it's delivered to your regular inbox.

To help the filter do its job, you mark unwanted messages that arrive in your inbox as spam or junk. These messages are then moved to the spam/junk folders and the senders are put on your blacklist. The problem is that spammers usually change their e-mail addresses regularly, so you may be doing a lot of work for nothing.

✦ **Content filtering:** Content filters scan your e-mails for words or attributes that you typically find in spam/junk e-mails. Flagged messages go to a spam/junk folder instead of your normal inbox. Although content filtering isn't the best solution, it usually helps. You just have to remember to regularly check the junk folder for real messages that may have been flagged for some reason.

✦ **Verification:** Verification is generally the best solution because your messages are manually verified by the senders before the messages reach your inbox.

People who send you e-mail get an automated response right back after their first e-mail to you (if you haven't sent them an e-mail in the past), which tells them that they must verify the message. They usually have to click a link in the automated message that takes them to a Web page where they must enter a string of letters or numbers that's displayed in an image. This process helps ensure that the e-mail is from a real person rather than an automated mailer.

Most spammers don't spend time responding to verifications. Unverified messages are put into a different folder that you may want to check periodically for messages that you may want to read.

Some legitimate senders don't verify their messages because they're sent automatically, such as newsletters, notifications for online accounts, or other mass mailings. But when you go through your unverified e-mails, you can authorize those senders' e-mails from that point on.

When using any spam filter, you should periodically check your spam or junk folder for e-mails and carefully monitor the situation when you're expecting important e-mails.

You can find spam and junk e-mail solutions from a variety of places:

✦ **E-mail (Internet) service provider:** Your e-mail provider may offer some sort of spam or junk mail filter.

✦ **E-mail client software:** You may want to check whether your e-mail client — for example, Outlook, Thunderbird, or Windows Mail — offers built-in filtering.

✦ **Internet security software:** Most Internet security suites include a spam feature.

✦ **Third-party applications or services:** A search of Google will probably give you plenty of results, but here are a few good leads of other applications or services that help combat spam:

   • Spam Arrest: www.Spamarrest.com

   • SPAMfighter: www.spamfighter.com

   • MailWasher: www.mailwasher.net

   • Spamihilator: www.spamihilator.com

Protecting Yourself Against Phishing Scams

Phishing — pronounced like *fishing* — is the attempt to criminally and fraudulently extract sensitive information from you. You can receive phishing attempts from e-mail messages, instant messages, and Web pages that you stumble across on the Web. The people behind these attempts use these items as their bait, and you are the fish that they hope to catch. In other words, they hope that you fall for the trick and are fooled into handing them sensitive information such as

+ **Account info:** Usernames and passwords for e-mail accounts, social networking sites, online auction sites, or, more important, financial Web sites

+ **Credit card info:** Your credit card number, verification number, and billing address

+ **Your identity:** Your full personal details, such as your full name, address, and Social Security number

Additionally, some phishers or scammers may even con you out of some cash. For example, you may receive an e-mail telling you that you have won a prize or have inherited money but that you must send a fee of some amount before your money is turned over to you.

Watch out for imposters

The most popular way phishers catch their prey is to impersonate legitimate companies. They do this by crafting and sending out e-mail messages that are formatted just like the ones the real company sends, asking you to update information and pointing to a Web site that's also crafted to look just like the company's real site. Then the fake or dummy site captures your personal or login information.

A list of the types of companies prone to being impersonated and some examples of them follows:

+ **Internet service providers:** AOL

+ **Auction and payment companies:** eBay and PayPal

+ **Financial institutions:** National banks and mortgage companies

+ **Government organizations:** The Internal Revenue Service

+ **Non-profit organizations:** The Red Cross

+ **Social networking sites:** MySpace and Facebook

Stories that reel you in

Popular scenarios that phishers use to get you to hand over information include

+ **Requesting that you update or verify information:** They may imitate a company you have services through and tell you that you need to update your credit card information.

+ **Selling (legal) drugs:** They may say they sell prescription drugs for pennies on the dollar.

✦ **Informing you of an inheritance of money:** Someone may say you've inherited a large sum of money and that you need to hand over personal information or money to start the collection process.

✦ **Announcing that you're a lottery winner:** You may be told you've won a prize or the lottery and be asked for personal information or money.

✦ **Requesting donations:** You may be asked for donations to some good cause or another, although your money will actually go to a con artist.

Phishers try to copy a real company's look and feel in their e-mails and Web sites, including a company's logo and sayings.

Spotting the bait of phishers

To help spot phishing scams before you're reeled in, you can

✦ **Examine the Web site address:** When imitating a real company, a phisher usually tries to use a Web site address that won't look fake at first glance. They do this using subdomains. For example, say you own the Web site www.yoursite.com. Scammers can easily create a subdomain of paypal.yoursite.com, making it look as though the address is related to the real www.paypal.com, the Web site for the popular online payment processing company.

✦ **Inspect the Web site:** Review the Web site for anything that looks odd. Or if you suspect the site to be an imitation, look for elements on it that are different from what you can remember from the real Web site of the company.

You may also be able to get a clue from links on the Web site. Compare the links against the Web site address of the Web page you're on; just hover over the links to see the address that should appear on the bottom of your browser. Phishers usually create only a few fake Web pages, not an entire Web site, so they usually include links on their Web site that go back to the real Web site of the company. Using these links may help them fool you into the idea that the site is authentic; however, these links may also help you recognize the imposture. For instance, say they told you to go to their fake Web site at paypal.1947395.com (remember, a subdomain — see the first bullet in this list), but some links on the Web site point to just paypal.com. This is a red flag.

✦ **Look for misspellings:** Some phishing e-mails may contain intentional spelling and grammatical errors to get by spam filters that look for typical words or phrases of junk messages. Some e-mails may also just have errors due to poor review.

✦ **If it sounds too good to be true:** It's probably fake, period.

✦ **Research the company:** If you are suspicious of something with a company you aren't familiar with, you should do some research. Do some searching on Google or your favorite search engine. Consider checking the BBB (Better Business Bureau) at `www.bbb.org`.

✦ **Contact the company directly:** If you think an e-mail or Web site is an imitation of a real company, contact the company through means other than those described in the suspicious e-mail or Web page. For instance, check your bills or statements for the company's Web site address or phone number.

Reporting the catch

If you do determine that you've received a phishing e-mail, you can report it to a variety of places:

✦ **Company Web site:** Go to the real Web site of the company that's being mimicked and find where you can report phishing or scam e-mails; these areas are often called *security centers*.

✦ **Government:** You can also report suspicious e-mails to the United States Computer Emergency Readiness Team (US-CERT) at `www.us-cert.gov/nav/report_phishing.html`.

✦ **Anti-phishing organizations:** Independent organizations also track phishing e-mails, including the Anti-Phishing Working Group:

   `www.antiphishing.org/report_phishing.html`

✦ **Friends:** Don't forget about your friends! Forwarding them your phishing e-mail and letting them know about it can help raise awareness of the issue.

If you think you've already been reeled in by a phisher or scammer, you can report ID theft and fraud to these two government organizations, which can investigate the crime:

✦ **Federal Trade Commission:**

   `www.consumer.gov/idtheft`

✦ **FBI's Internet Fraud Complaint Center:**

   `www.ifccfbi.gov/index.asp`

Checking for phishing licenses

In addition to watching out for the signs of phishing scams, you can use phishing detectors. These tools maintain a list of known phishing sites and alert you if you go to a site on the list. Here are a few places you may be able to find this feature:

**Book III
Chapter 1**

Addressing Internet Security

✦ **Built into Web browsers:** Most of the latest versions of the popular Web browsers (for example, Microsoft Internet Explorer 7 and Mozilla Firefox 2.0) contain this type of anti-phishing feature.

✦ **Internet security software:** Many Internet security suites also include an anti-phishing feature.

The Safari 3 Web browser (at the time of this writing) doesn't include a phishing filter feature.

Using Internet Explorer's phishing filter

If you're using Internet Explorer 7 for your Web browser, here's how you can access the settings for the anti-phishing feature:

1. **Open Internet Explorer 7.**

2. **Choose Tools⇨Internet Options.**

3. **Click the Advanced tab.**

4. **Find the Phishing Filter setting, shown in Figure 1-6.**

Scroll near the bottom of the list, under the Settings section.

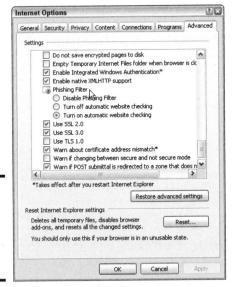

Figure 1-6:
The phishing settings for Internet Explorer 7.

5. **Choose one of the following options:**

- **Disable Phishing Filter:** Just as it sounds, selecting this option disables the filter. Internet Explorer won't alert you of suspicious or known phishing scam Web sites.

- **Turn off automatic Web site checking:** You still have some protection, but Web sites you visit are checked only against a list of known phishing Web sites that resides on your computer.

- **Turn on automatic Web site checking:** Selecting this option offers better protection because Web sites you visit are also checked against Microsoft's list on the Web. To do this check, Internet Explorer sends your information (Web site address, your computer's IP address, and so on) to Microsoft. Microsoft has privacy and security policies, but if you are a privacy-head, you can disable automatic Web site checking.

Configuring the phishing filter in Firefox 2.0

The phishing filter in Firefox 2.0 is enabled by default; however, you may want to check to make sure that someone hasn't disabled it, and verify that you are using the filter method you desire. Here's how to configure the phishing settings:

1. **Open Firefox.**

2. **On Windows and Linux, choose Tools⇨Options⇨Security. On Mac OS X, choose Firefox⇨Preferences⇨Options⇨Security.**

3. **Select the Tell Me If the Site I'm Visiting Is a Suspected Forgery option.**

4. **Choose Check Using a Downloaded List of Suspected Sites for basic protection, or Check By Asking (Google or Another Service) About Each Site I Visit for the greatest protection.**

The downloaded list of suspected sites is automatically updated regularly. Checking the sites on Google or another search engine, however, provides the greatest protection because each site you visit would be checked in real time from a list that's updated all the time.

5. **Click OK to save your changes and exit the Options window.**

You can test the phishing filter in Firefox by visiting the following Web page in Firefox:

```
http://www.mozilla.com/firefox/its-a-trap.html
```

Using Internet Security Software Suites: On Each Computer

One popular option you have to combat Internet threats is to buy and install Internet security software suites or bundles on all your computers. These software packages typically run from $50 to $80, and support up to three computers.

Common protection provided by software suites

Features and components commonly included in Internet security software suites protect you from the main Internet threats:

✦ **Viruses:** Viruses are blocked with antivirus software that continuously scans commonly infected areas of your computer plus your full system periodically. Depending upon the particular antivirus software, it should instantly detect viruses from your e-mails, downloads, and Web browsing before the virus can do harm.

✦ **Spyware:** Spyware is blocked with antispyware software that performs scanning similar to the antiviral software.

✦ **Hackers:** Hackers are stopped by firewall software that only lets data pass in and out through safe ports and by authorized programs.

✦ **Spam:** Spam is prevented by antispam software, usually by using content filtering.

Bonus protections and features

Some extras you may find in various Internet security packages or suites include

✦ **Parental controls:** This may consist of Internet filtering that protects your children from inappropriate Web sites and monitoring features to see what they're doing on the computer. There's more on this in the next chapter of this minibook.

✦ **Anti-phishing:** To help detect phishing scams you may run across on the Web or in an e-mail, some Internet security solutions may include an anti-phishing feature.

✦ **Backup capabilities:** Some software suites incorporate backup features to protect your sensitive files and documents against loss from viruses or computer crashes. You may even find some offering online storage.

✦ **PC performance tune-ups:** You could possibly even find solutions with tools to increase your computer's performance.

Getting and using an Internet security suite

Here are some companies that develop popular Internet security suites:

+ **McAfee:** www.mcafee.com

+ **CA (Computer Associates):** shop.ca.com

+ **Norton (Symantec):** www.symantec.com/norton

When using Internet security software, make sure you

+ **Keep it updated:** To get full protection, make sure you keep your Internet security products updated. Vendors may name updates for anti-infection software as signature files or threat updates.

+ **Keep it enabled:** Make sure you're always protected. If you need to disable protection, such as for a software or hardware installation, make sure you enable it again as soon as possible.

+ **Install only what you need:** If you already have protection against a certain threat, you probably don't want another program for the same thing. For instance, if you already use a spam solution, you may want to forgo any spam features provided by the Internet security suite.

Using Internet Security Hardware Solutions for Your Entire Network

A newer method to protect your computers from all the infections and threats is to use a hardware solution. You may see these products named Internet Security Adapters, selling for around $100 and offering support for several computers. Figure 1-7 shows an example of one.

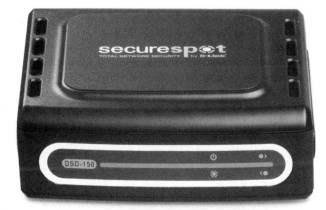

Figure 1-7: An example of an Internet security adapter.

Courtesy of D-Link Systems, Inc.

These products offer similar features and components as the software suites, plus they have some additional benefits, such as

✦ **Protects your entire network:** Instead of protecting just one computer, like with software, hardware solutions can provide protection for your entire network.

✦ **Is easier on your PC:** Because the protection is hardware-based, these won't bog down your computers as much. Constantly running software takes much more computing power.

You should keep in mind most hardware solutions are only firewalls that don't include any protection for the other threats such as spam and viruses.

When choosing a hardware solution for your Internet security needs, consider the following:

✦ **Features and components:** Make sure it provides protection against all the threats, like software suites do.

✦ **Protection when away from home:** Because hardware solutions are supposed to reside on your home network, make sure you have protection for your laptops when you're away. Hardware manufacturers usually have solutions for this situation.

✦ **Number of supported computers:** Although theoretically hardware solutions can provide protection for your entire network, there may be a limit on the number of computers that can be protected.

Keeping Your OS Free of Security Holes

In addition to installing and using an Internet security solution, you should regularly update your operating systems (Windows, Mac, Ubuntu and so on), as updates can

✦ Address known security holes that may compromise your computer or network to Internet or local hackers

✦ Contain enhanced or new networking features or interfaces

✦ Fix known bugs or errors with the operating system relating to networking connections or settings

Upgrading to a newer OS version

If you are using an ancient version of an operating system (such as 95, 98, or ME for Windows), you should think about upgrading to a better version (like Windows Vista or Windows XP). Then again, if you are using such an old operating system (OS), it's probably also time for you to get an entirely new computer.

The countless enhancements and new features of newer operating systems (like Windows XP and Vista) include better security mechanisms. Plus, these newer operating systems make your home or small office networking experience much easier. The monetary and time investment in upgrading your OS or your computer system is well worth it!

Manually updating Windows

If you have Internet Explorer, it's very easy to get to the Windows Update site to manually download and install updates:

1. **Open Internet Explorer.**

2. **Click the Tools menu on the toolbar and click Windows Update.**

You should be taken to the Windows Update Web site, shown in Figure 1-8.

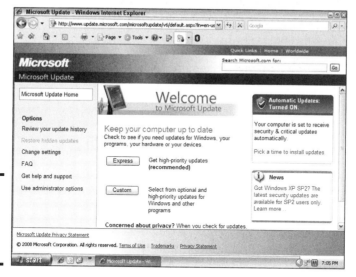

Figure 1-8:
The Windows Update Web site.

Book III Chapter 1

Addressing Internet Security

3. **Follow the directions.**

Follow the directions and any alerts from the Windows Update site. If you're asked if it's okay to download plug-ins or other software, go ahead and download and install them as instructed.

Alternatively, you can type the following address into Internet Explorer:

```
http://windowsupdate.microsoft.com
```

The Windows Update site isn't supported in other browsers (such as Mozilla Firefox); however, you can obtain updates directly from the Microsoft Download Center (www.microsoft.com/downloads) or use WindizUpdate (www.windizupdate.com).

Setting up automatic updates for Windows

The Automatic Updates feature in Windows can automatically download and install updates as they become available, checking every day at the time you specify. This works well if you have an always-on Internet connection (DSL, cable, and so on), which you probably have if you use a computer network. Here's how to set up automatic updates in Windows XP and Vista:

1. **Choose Start⇨Control Panel.**

2. **Click the Security Center (in XP) or Security (in Vista) category.**

If in the Classic control panel view, double-click Automatic Updates (in XP) or Windows Updates (in Vista) and skip to Step 4.

3. **Click Automatic Updates (in XP) or Windows Update (in Vista).**

4. **In Vista, click the Change Settings link on the left task pane.**

5. **Choose your desired settings and click OK to apply the changes.**

Updating Mac OS X

Mac OS X Tiger and Leopard automatically download updates for the operating system and your applications that are supported by the Software Update feature. After the updates have downloaded, you're notified by an icon appearing on the Mac toolbar that they're ready to be installed. As with Windows, you can specify how often your computer should check for updates, or whether or not you want it done automatically.

Here's how to configure the Software Update feature in Mac OS Leopard:

1. **Click the Apple icon on the menu bar.**

2. **Click System Preferences.**

3. **In the System category, click Software Update.**

4. **Select or the Check For Updates option to enable your computer to automatically check for available updates.**

I certainly recommend selecting this option, but you can deselect this option if you don't want automatic updates to occur.

5. **If the Check For Updates option is enabled, select how often (Daily, Weekly, or Monthly) you want your computer to check for updates, using the combo list box to the right of the Check For Updates option.**

It's best to check for and update your computer weekly.

6. **If the Check For Updates option is enabled, select the Download Important Updates Automatically (in Leopard) or Download Important Updates in the Background (in Tiger) option if you want to enable system and security updates to be automatically downloaded.**

   Typically, it's best to enable or select this option so that all you have to do later, when updates are downloaded, is to agree to install them by using the icon that appears in the Mac toolbar. You can, however, deselect this option to disable it.

You can also manually check for updates by clicking the Check Now button. You can view what updates have been installed by clicking the Installed Updates tab.

Keeping Ubuntu up-to-date

Follow these steps to check for updates for Ubuntu:

1. **Click System from the Ubuntu toolbar.**

2. **Choose Administration.**

3. **Open Software Sources.**

4. **If prompted, enter your account password and click OK.**

5. **Click the Updates tab.**

6. **In the Ubuntu Updates section, select which type of updates you prefer.**

   Important Security Updates and Recommended Updates are well advised.

7. **Select the Check For Updates option to enable your computer to automatically check for available updates.**

   I certainly recommend checking (or enabling) this option. You can, however, disable it by deselecting this option.

8. **If the Check For Updates option is enabled, select how often (Daily, Every two days, Weekly, or Every two weeks) you want your computer to check for updates, using the combo list box to the right of the Check For Updates option.**

   It's best to check for and update your computer weekly.

9. **If the Check For Updates option is enabled, select what you want your computer to do when new updates are available.**

   Select Install Security Updates Without Confirmation if you want updates downloaded and installed automatically. Select Download All Updates in the Background to have your computer download but not install them automatically. Select Only Notify About Available Updates if you don't want them even downloaded automatically.

Typically, it's best to select the first option (Install Security Updates Without Confirmation), to make sure that your computer is kept up-to-date.

In addition to the icon that will appear on the Ubuntu toolbar when updates are available, you can use the Update Manager to specify exactly which updates you want installed (if they aren't automatically being installed), check for updates manually, and start installing downloaded updates. Open the Update Manager by following these steps:

1. **Click System from the Ubuntu toolbar.**

2. **Choose Administration.**

3. **Click Update Manager.**

Blocking Those Annoying Pop-Ups

Pop-ups are those usually small toolbar-less windows that come up on your computer screen with some sort of advertisement. Most pop-ups display a Web page or image from the Internet; however, they can originate from a variety of places and at varying times:

✦ When you enter or leave a Web site or Web page.

✦ When you open or close your Web browser.

✦ Anytime you're connected to the Internet, if your computer is infected with adware or spyware.

Stopping them with pop-up blockers

To stop pop-ups from coming up, you can use a pop-up blocker, which you can acquire from a few different places:

✦ **Built into Web browsers:** Microsoft's Internet Explorer 7 browser, Mozilla Firefox 2.0, and Opera include a pop-up blocker feature.

✦ **Web browser toolbars:** Yahoo! or Google

✦ **Internet security software:** Some Internet security suites include a pop-up blocker.

When you're running pop-up blockers, any pop-up windows that try to open are blocked. You are usually notified when this happens. Figure 1-9 shows an example of Internet Explorer's pop-up blocker alert.

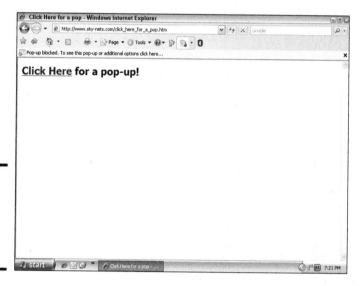

Figure 1-9:
Internet Explorer's pop-up blocker alert.

Because not all pop-ups are bad, you can usually temporaly disable a blocker by holding down a key — usually Ctrl or Ctrl+Alt — on your keyboard. For instance, if you're clicking on a link that is suppose to open another window but the pop-up blocker prevents it from working, you can just click the link while holding down Ctrl.

Most pop-up blockers give you the ability to allow pop-ups from certain Web sites, which can be manually inputted (flip ahead to Figure 1-11 for an example) or selected from individual pop-up alerts.

Using Internet Explorer's pop-up blocker

You can access the settings for Internet Explorer's pop-up blocker from Internet Options:

1. **Open Internet Explorer 7.**

2. **Click Tools from the menu bar.**

3. **Click Internet Options.**

4. **Click the Privacy tab.**

5. **Turn it on or off.**

You can turn the blocker on or off by selecting or deselecting the checkbox in the Pop-up Blocker section.

6. **Configure blocker settings.**

You can click the Settings button in the Pop-up Blocker section to set the protection level, add sites to the allow list, and more.

Figure 1-10 shows the Pop-Up Blocker Settings dialog box.

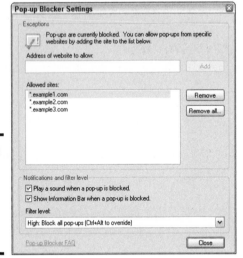

Figure 1-10:
Internet
Explorer's
Pop-Up
Blocker
Settings
dialog box.

You can configure the following settings in the Pop-Up Blocker Settings dialog box:

✦ **Allowed Sites:** This is the list of sites that the pop-up blocker ignores. You can input sites here by typing an address in and pressing Add. You can also add sites from the information bar that's displayed when a pop-up is blocked.

✦ **Play a Sound When a Pop-Up Is Blocked:** If you select this option, you receive an audible alert when a pop-up is blocked. If you tend to receive a lot of pop-ups, you might want to pass on this feature as it can get annoying.

✦ **Show Information Bar When a Pop-Up Is Blocked:** This is the bar that appears in Figure 1-10. I recommend that you keep this notification on so that you know when pop-ups are being blocked because some pop-ups may be desirable.

✦ **Filter Level:** You can pick one of these three levels of protection:

 • *High:* Blocks all pop-ups, at least those originating from Internet Explorer. If you still receive pop-ups at this level, you probably have a spyware or adware infection.

 • *Medium:* Stops most pop-ups from Web sites you visit, except those listed in the Local Intranet or Trusted Sites content zones.

- *Low:* Won't stop pop-ups from secured Web sites using SSL, indicated by the yellow padlock — like when logging onto bank Web sites. This is a good level to start at. If you receive too many undesirable pop-ups, you can later move to the next level up, and so on.

Blocking pop-ups in Safari 3

In Safari 3, you simply enable or disable the pop-up blocker feature, as follows:

1. **Open Safari 3.**

2. **Click Edit.**

3. **Click Block Pop-Up Windows to enable or disable the feature.**

When the feature is enabled, a check mark appears just to the left of the option.

You can also turn this feature on and off in the Security section of the browser Preferences window.

Using Firefox 2.0's pop-up blocker

Firefox 2.0 lets you enable a pop-up blocker, plus specify sites that you trust or that have pop-up windows that you need to see. Here's how to set up the feature:

1. **Open Firefox.**

2. **On Windows and Linux, choose Tools⊏>Options⊏>Content. On Mac OS X, choose Firefox⊏>Preferences⊏>Options⊏>Content.**

3. **Select or deselect the Block Pop-Up Windows option (on the top of the Options window).**

4. **When the Block Pop-Up Windows option is enabled, you can click the Exceptions button to add the addresses of Web sites to the list of sites that you don't want the feature to be active for.**

It's not very practical to sit there and think up all the sites you want to add to the list, but you can easily add one when you encounter a site that you don't want the pop-ups blocked on.

Preventing Security Issues When Web Browsing

Your Web browser's settings and the sites you visit play a major role in whether your computer gets infections. If your security or privacy settings are set to a low threshold, your computer is much more likely to get viruses, spyware, and adware. This is also the case if you visit typically infected Web sites, which I discuss shortly.

Verify the security settings of your Web browser

You should review the security settings of your Web browser to ensure they are set to a reasonable level. You can usually access a browser's preferences or options from the File, Edit, or Tools menu on the toolbar. The methodology behind the security and privacy settings of browser's is similar, so in this step list, I just cover configuring the most popular one, Internet Explorer 7:

1. **Open Internet Explorer 7.**

2. **Click Tools on the menu bar.**

3. **Click Internet Options.**

4. **Click the Security tab.**

Figure 1-11 shows the dialog box that you should see.

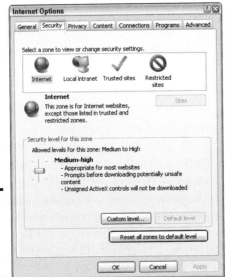

Figure 1-11:
Internet
Explorer's
security
settings.

The security settings of Internet Explorer can be set based upon different zones. This is because you probably want to be more lenient on the security of sites that you can trust and stricter on sites you don't trust. The zone you should be most worried about is the Internet zone; this makes up all Web sites, except those you list as Trusted or Restricted.

After clicking on a zone, you can edit its predefined security level using the up and down slider, or you can click the Custom level button to edit details. You shouldn't mess around with customization unless you know what you're doing. You can add sites to your Trusted and Restricted zones by clicking the Sites button that appears.

The default levels for all the zones should be fine — clicking the Reset All Zones to Default Level button on the bottom of the dialog box restores the defaults if you've made changes that you later want to undo.

If you are having problems viewing or using a site correctly, it might be due to your security settings. In this case, you might want to add the Web site to your Trusted zone. Because these settings are by default more relaxed, the site might work — don't forget to refresh the page before trying again. If the site still doesn't work, you can try lowering the security level; try it again, and so on. Using the Trusted zone feature lets you keep your security settings at a good level for all other sites.

Check your Web browser's privacy settings

You should also review your browser's privacy settings. These should be located on a different tab of the same window as your security settings of your preferences or options. Again, privacy settings are similar between browsers, so I cover just configuring Internet Explorer 7:

1. **Open Internet Explorer 7.**

2. **Click Tools on the menu bar.**

3. **Click Internet Options.**

4. **Click the Privacy tab.**

Figure 1-12 shows the dialog box that you should see.

You can use the up and down slider to change the privacy level. The default setting of Medium is usually fine.

If you are having problems logging in to a site correctly, it might be due to your privacy settings. In this case, you might want to add the Web site as a site that should be always allowed. Click the Sites button, enter the address of the problem site, click Allow, and click OK. This way, you don't have to modify (lower) your privacy settings that apply to all the sites you visit.

Figure 1-12:
Internet
Explorer's
privacy
settings.

Discovering the "bad" sites that can cause havoc

For the most part, your computer won't fill with viruses and other bugs just because you visit Web sites. If you are using antivirus software and actively protecting against the other major infections, these viruses and bugs should be detected and removed before they become a problem. However, you may run a much higher risk of infection when you visit certain Web sites, such as those that contain

✦ Illegal content, including pirated software or music downloads

✦ Pornographic material

✦ Free downloads and stuff: for example, layouts and code for social net-working Web sites

It's best to stay away from these types of sites — you should especially avoid downloading files from them.

Deleting your Web browsing history and temporary Internet files

Your Web browsing history is not necessarily a security issue, but it does pertain to your personal privacy. Your Web browser by default keeps a history of all the sites you visit. But did you know you can erase it? Sometimes you may not want others to see what you've been looking at on the Web. I'm not just talking about adult material: Maybe you're shopping for a diamond ring for your loved one or researching on pregnancy.

In addition to the sites you visit, the cookies, passwords, and other temporary files downloaded from Web sites can leave traces of your Internet activity.

All Web browsers let you erase your browsing history along with cookies, which are usually called your temporary Internet files. You can probably find a way to do this from the Internet options or preferences menu of your Web browser.

Here's how to do it in Internet Explorer 7:

1. **Open Internet Explorer 7.**

2. **Click Tools on the menu bar.**

3. **Click Delete Browsing History.**

Figure 1-13 shows the Delete Browsing History dialog box that appears.

Figure 1-13: Internet Explorer's browsing history.

4. **Choose to delete particular types of files or just click the Delete All button to get rid of all of the Internet files.**

In Safari 3, you must delete your temporary Internet files separately to remove the three main types: Web browsing history, cookies, and cache. To remove your Web browsing history, open Safari 3 and choose History➪Clear History.

And to remove your cookies in Safari 3, follow these steps:

1. **Open Safari 3 and choose Edit⇨Preferences.**

2. **Click the Security tab.**

3. **Click the Show Cookies button and then click the Remove All button.**

4. **On the confirmation prompt that appears, click Remove All.**

5. **Click Done and then close the window.**

And finally, remove your cache in Safari 3:

1. **Open Safari 3 and choose Edit.**

2. **Click Empty Cache and then click Empty on the confirmation prompt that appears.**

In Firefox 2.0, you can delete your temporary Internet files this way:

1. **Open Firefox.**

2. **Choose Tools (in Windows and Linux) or Firefox (in Mac OS X).**

3. **Click Clear Private Data and in the menu that appears, select the options for the types of information you want to delete and then click Clear Private Data Now.**

Chapter 2: Securing the Airwaves: It's Possible

In This Chapter

✔ Understanding the risks of leaving your network unsecured

✔ Discovering exactly what a Wi-Fi eavesdropper or hacker can see

✔ Finding ways to secure your wireless network

✔ Encrypting, hiding, and filtering your Wi-Fi communications

*B*ecause a Wi-Fi network communicates through the air, it's inherently not secure and is open for others to capture and listen in on — that is, if you aren't encrypting your Wi-Fi communications. When Wi-Fi communications are encrypted, others (without the key) can still capture your Wi-Fi network's traffic; however, they can't decipher what it says. In this case, it's a secured network. In this chapter, I discuss the risks of leaving a network unsecured. I also show you how to encrypt, hide, and filter your Wi-Fi communications.

Discovering Wi-Fi Security Concerns

If you leave your wireless network unsecured (without encryption), you have two major concerns to worry about:

✦ **Your real-time traffic is compromised.**

- People can see what Web sites you're visiting.

- Your login information and content of unsecured Web sites that you visit are compromised.

- Login information and content from services such as POP3 e-mail accounts and File Transfer Protocol (FTP) connections are compromised.

✦ **Your wireless network is open for others to connect to.**

- Your Internet connection may be used for sending or receiving illegal information, such as spam e-mail and pirated software and media.

- Others can access any shared files on PCs or servers connected to the network.

Looking at What an Eavesdropper Sees

If your wireless network is unsecured, the worst-case scenario is a neighbor or someone sitting in his or her car outside your house eavesdropping — or scanning the airwaves with the right software programs loaded on a laptop or PC — with a mission to deliberately capture or access your sensitive information or files.

To get a better idea of how this all works, in this section, I show you exactly what an eavesdropper can see when your Wi-Fi network is *unsecured,* meaning that you don't use an encryption method like WEP or WPA.

For this example, imagine that you have a nosy neighbor with a little too much time on his hands. He likes to sit in his house and monitor your Wi-Fi communications. He has some sort of packet analyzer software running on his computer, showing him the raw packets of information (which I discuss more later in this chapter) being sent and received from all the nearby wireless routers and computers. He could filter the results, showing the communications from just a specific wireless network or computer (your network and computers, in this case).

Ethereal, TamoSoft, AirMagnet, and WildPackets are a few companies that produce packet analyzer software programs that can display the raw data of Wi-Fi communications. The first two companies offer free or trial versions of their software (which shows you how obtainable this type of software is); however, the last two companies cater to the enterprise field and charge thousands of dollars.

Now imagine you send an e-mail message (Figure 2-1 shows an example) from your computer while connected to your unsecured wireless router. In this case, say you sent the e-mail with Microsoft Outlook using a POP3 account.

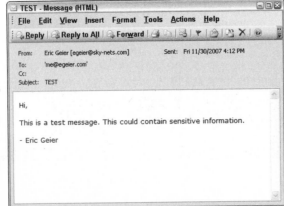

Figure 2-1:
A test e-mail message sent on an unencrypted wireless network.

While you were sending your e-mail, your neighbor was capturing your traffic, and, unfortunately, the few data packets that contain your message and e-mail account information. As shown in Figure 2-2, he was able to see exactly what was in the message.

If that isn't bad enough, see what else he captured, shown in Figure 2-3 (with my username and password blurred). When you synchronized your e-mail, your account credentials were sent over the airwaves also.

As shown in Figure 2-3, your neighbor now has your server, username, and password for your account — enough to start sending and receiving e-mails from your account.

You could have followed many security measures, like changing the default network name (or SSID), disabling network name broadcasting, and enabling MAC and IP address filtering; however, the only thing that would have prevented your neighbor from clearly seeing all that information is if your network was using encryption, such as WEP or WPA. In that case, he would have only seen a bunch of gibberish, and must know (or break) your encryption key to see the real information.

**Book III
Chapter 2**

**Securing the
Airwaves:
It's Possible**

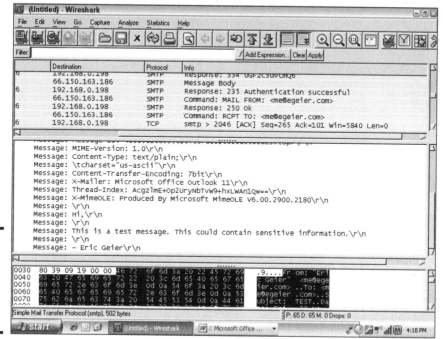

Figure 2-2:
The contents of a captured test e-mail message.

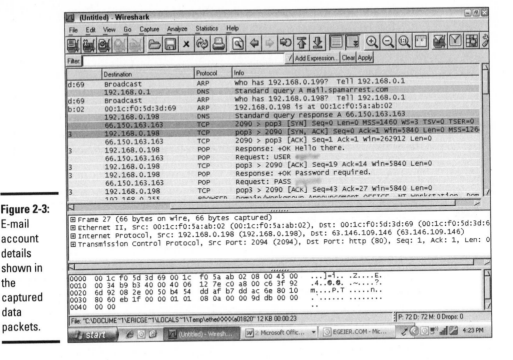

In addition to getting your e-mail account info, he could have also browsed through the shared files of all your computers — that is, he could do it if you weren't using other security measures like MAC and IP address filtering in addition to not using encryption. Furthermore, if you had configured shared folders to allow network users to make changes, he could have just copied your files to his PC and deleted your originals. Of course, depending upon the particular files, this could cause major problems if the files were a school or work assignment, or a document that contains your financial information or Social Security number.

Securing Your Wireless Network

To ensure that you don't fall victim to a Wi-Fi eavesdropper or hacker, make sure that you

+ Secure your real-time traffic and prevent others from connecting.

+ Use encryption, such as WPA (Wi-Fi Protected Access) or WPA2.

+ Perform necessary initial changes:

  • Change your router's password.

  • Change your router's default network name.

✦ Implement other (optional) safeguards to provide further prevention against others from connecting:

- Disable network name (SSID) broadcasting.
- Use MAC address filtering.

Using the latest encryption (WPA or WP2) alone usually provides adequate protection against Wi-Fi eavesdroppers and hackers. On the other hand, you should ideally address network security in layers, meaning that you should use other methods in addition to encryption. But in the long run, it's all up to you.

Using these optional techniques to prevent unauthorized access to your wireless network requires more setup and configuration time and can sometimes cause issues and inconveniences when using your network.

For example, you must manually enter your network name on your computer if your SSID broadcasting is disabled. Although your computer usually saves this information so you don't have to keep entering it, new computers introduced to your network (such as your friend's laptop or your new computer) must also do this. It's even worse for the MAC address technique: To set it up, you have to enter each computer's MAC address into your wireless router.

Which wireless security methods you should implement boils down to whether you are willing to spend more time, do some more reading (of this book), and be okay with some extra clicks of the mouse. If you consider yourself computer illiterate, you should probably forget the extra security techniques, but remember, *everyone* should at least use encryption.

Make your decision(s) now on which security measures you're going to use; the next sections show how to apply these techniques.

Encrypting Your Wi-Fi

Most wireless routers prompt you to configure security and encryption settings during their initial setup, whether it's through a software program loaded from a CD or on the router's Web-based configuration utility. Setting up encryption during that time is fine; however, the directions in this section are geared toward those who have already set up their routers without encryption.

Using newer encryption methods (such as WPA) may require you to update your operating system with the current updates and patches. For example, to use WPA with Windows XP, you must have a certain update installed that is included with Service Pack 2 and is also individually available on the Windows Update Web site at `http://update.microsoft.com`.

If you haven't done the initial setup of your router, you can either choose to use the recommendations and terminology given to help you set up encryption during the initial setup, or you can just skip those settings (don't enable any encryption) and use the directions that follow to enable encryption after you have your router and network set up.

Either way, you have two basic steps to set up encryption:

✦ Configure encryption settings and keys on your wireless router.

✦ Configure or enter the encryption keys on your computers.

Using security buttons

To make Wi-Fi security easier (and possibly more appealing) for consumers like you, some networking manufacturers have developed their own encryption-enabling methods using buttons. Buttons on the hardware itself or in a software application allow you to set up encryption with just a few presses or clicks.

To find out whether your equipment has this capability, take a look at your Wi-Fi router and wireless adapter utilities to see if there are any buttons labeled with terms such as Security, Encryption, or Secure. Figure 2-4 shows an example of a wireless router with this feature.

Figure 2-4:
An example
of wireless
router with
a security
button.

Security button

Keep in mind that manufacturers usually come up with their own trade-marked names for this type of feature.

If you do find that your router has this type of feature, you should refer to your product's documentation for information on exactly how to use it. However, you generally press a button on your Wi-Fi router and, within a certain amount of time, press a button on all your wireless adapter utilities.

Manually setting up a wireless router: Choosing an encryption method

To encrypt your wireless network, you must first choose the settings and keys on it. Here's how:

1. **Open your Web browser (Internet Explorer, Netscape, Firefox, or other), type in the IP address of your router, and press Enter.**

If you don't know the IP address or the username or password, you can refer to Book V, Chapter 3 for help. Keep in mind that some manufacturers may use a domain name, which looks like a Web site address, instead of an IP address.

2. **When prompted, enter your login credentials, as shown in Figure 2-5.**

3. **Find the encryption settings (Figure 2-6 shows an example), usually on a tab labeled Wireless Security, in the Security subsection of the Wireless section.**

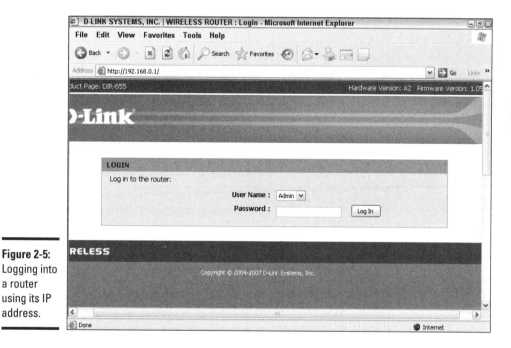

Figure 2-5: Logging into a router using its IP address.

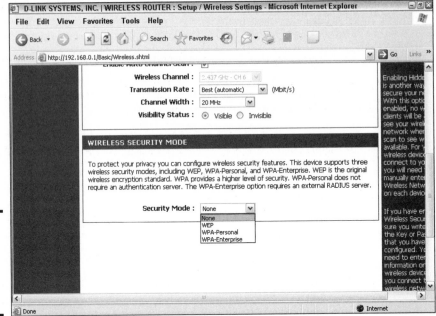

Figure 2-6:
The
encryption
settings on
a wireless
router.

Some newer wireless routers may offer wizards to help with security configuration; however, you still may be able to manually configure wireless security settings, which is preferred for your purposes.

4. Determine what encryption methods are supported by your router, such as by clicking a drop-down menu list.

If you are using wireless N components and you use the older and less secure WEP encryption, you'll probably lose the performance enhancements that wireless N provides and will be operating the same as you would if you were using wireless b/g equipment. Check your product documentation or configuration utilities for more information.

5. Select the best encryption method that's supported by all your computers (or wireless adapters).

In order of best to worst, choose one of the following methods:

• WPA2-PSK (Personal)

• WPA-PSK (Personal)

• WEP

You can see the encryption methods supported by your computers (wireless adapters) as you manually set up a connection (adding a network to your preferred list). Refer to Book IV, Chapter 1 for more information.

Continue with the next section to complete the manual setup of your wireless router's encryption.

Configuring the encryption method's settings

After selecting an encryption method, you must configure its settings. The following subsections tell you the procedure to follow depending on the type of encryption method you're using.

Configuring for WPA or WPA2 Pre-Shared Key (PSK) or Personal

To encrypt for either of these two settings, follow these steps:

1. **Enter your desired key/passphrase.**

   This can be 8 to 63 characters long, made of letters, numbers, or symbols, and it is case sensitive. This could be comparable to a regular password, in contrast to the keys entered for WEP encryption, which require limited types of characters.

2. **If you find an option for choosing the encryption technique (also called "cipher type" or "WPA algorithm"), choose one of the following: TKIP (Temporal Key Integrity Protocol); AES (Advanced Encryption Standard); TKIP+AES; or Auto.**

   If available, use AES because it provides stronger encryption; otherwise, use Auto or TKIP+AES.

3. **If you see a Key Renewal Interval option, leave it at the default value.**

Configuring for WEP

To configure a WEP encryption method, follow these steps:

1. **Select the authentication method, Open or Shared Key, if the option exists.**

   Shared Key is recommended because it provides the greatest security.

2. **Select 64-bit or 128-bit encryption.**

   Going with 128-bit encryption is recommended because it provides the greatest security.

3. **Create your encryption keys using one of two methods:**

   • **Use passphrase feature:** Some routers include a passphrase box, which can save a lot of time and brain power. You can just enter a passphrase made up of any letters or numbers and click a button to automatically create four valid encryption keys.

   • **Manually create keys:** The traditional way requires you to come up with your own encryption keys. For 64-bit keys, you must enter 10 hexadecimal (hex) digits; for 128-bit keys, you must enter 26 hex digits. Hex digits are numbers 0 to 9 and letters from A to F. For instance, 01234aBcde would constitute a 64-bit encryption key.

Some routers allow you to choose between hexadecimal and ASCII (pronounced ASK-E) formats for both 64-bit and 128-bit encryption keys. If you choose ASCII, your keys can consist of any letters, numbers, or symbols, with 5 characters in length for 64-bit keys and 13 characters for 128-bit keys.

4. **Select the WEP key you would like to use now, by selecting the number of the WEP key from the Default WEP or Transmit Key drop-down list (if it exists) or select a radio button next to where you input the keys.**

Only one encryption key is really needed. Wireless routers usually allow you to input four different keys for your convenience. It's best to change your active encryption key once in awhile, so instead of inputting a new key each time in your router, you can just select a different key from the list.

Furthermore, some wireless adapter utilities can save all four of your keys, again allowing you to just select a different one instead of manually inputting a new key. You input the four encryption keys in the same order on both your router and adapter utilities.

For example, if you want to change your WEP key, log in to your router, change the default or transmit key to number three, and then go to your adapter utility and change to the number three key (if the option is available) or input it manually.

Completing your configuration

When you've finished working through the settings for your encryption method, write down the encryption keys and settings you have chosen and keep them handy. You'll need to reference them when setting up your computers.

Sometimes encryption keys can wind up getting cleared out of your computers or a friend may want to get on your network (in which case, your friend needs your encryption key), so you should keep this information in a safe and memorable spot. Taping it on the bottom of your wireless router or back of your computer, putting it with your software collection, or writing it in the box the router came in are a few ideas.

Be sure to save and apply the changes, such as by clicking a Save button on the top or bottom of the page.

Now you can set up your computer (that is, its wireless adapters) with the encryption keys.

Setting up the adapters

Now that you have enabled encryption on your wireless router, you must enter the same key on your computers. You can do this either when you connect to the network the next time (from your available wireless network list), or you can manually set up it up as a preferred network.

If you need help connecting or setting up preferred networks or profiles, refer to Book IV, Chapter 1.

Performing the Necessary Initial Changes to Your Wireless Network

If you haven't already done so during the initial setup of your wireless router, you need to change your router's default password (for the Web-based utility) and the default network name (or SSID). These settings are publicly known and their default values pose the following issues:

✦ Wi-Fi eavesdroppers and hackers can easily log in to your wireless router if you are using the default password and your network is left unsecured, or if they manage to break your encryption key.

✦ If you decide to disable network name (SSID) broadcasting (which I discuss in the next subsection) and you leave the default network name intact, someone could easily guess the hidden network name, virtually making the feature useless.

✦ Additionally, it's a good idea to change your network name to better distinguish your network from others nearby who might use the same equipment with the same network name.

The following subsections take you through these steps. But first you must connect and log in to your router:

1. **Bring up your Web browser (Internet Explorer, Netscape, Firefox, and so on).**

2. **Type in the IP address of your router and press Enter.**

Keep in mind that some manufacturers may use a domain name (http://www.routerlogin.net) that looks like a Web site address instead of an IP address (192.168.1.1).

If you don't know the IP address or the username or password, refer to Book V, Chapter 3 for help.

3. **When prompted to do so, enter the username and password.**

If you don't know the default username and password, refer to Book V, Chapter 3.

Specifying your own network name

When you're logged into the router, here's how to configure the network name:

1. **Click the Wireless tab (Figure 2-7 shows an example), or other tab containing the basic wireless settings (network name or SSID and channel).**

   Some newer wireless routers may offer wizards to help with wireless configuration; however, you still may be able to manually configure the wireless settings, which is preferred for our purposes.

2. **Enter your own name into the Network Name (or SSID) field.**

   Keep in mind that the network name is case sensitive and must not exceed 32 characters. You can use any of the characters on your keyboard. Be sure not to include information that might give away your location, such as a street number or last name.

3. **Click the Save or Apply button, on the top or bottom of the page, to save your new network name.**

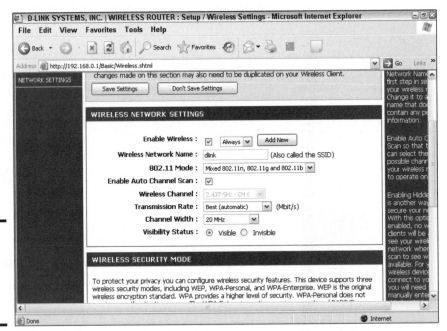

Figure 2-7: Example wireless settings on a wireless router.

The wireless router may reboot and you may be disconnected for a minute. If you were connected wirelessly (rather than by an Ethernet cable), you'll have to reconnect with the new network name. You can probably just choose the new network name from your available wireless network list. However, if you have broadcasting disabled, you need to manually set up a connection (add a network to your preferred list). Refer to Book IV, Chapter 1 for more information.

After you're connected to the network again, the Web-based utility may return to the page that you left off on in your router's configuration screens. Sometimes, however, the Web browser errors out and goes to a Not Found page. If this is the case, after you know you're reconnected, follow the directions in Step 1 again to log back on.

Changing the default password

When you're logged into the router, here's how to create a new password:

1. **Click the Admin or Management tab (Figure 2-8 shows an example) or other tab containing the password settings.**

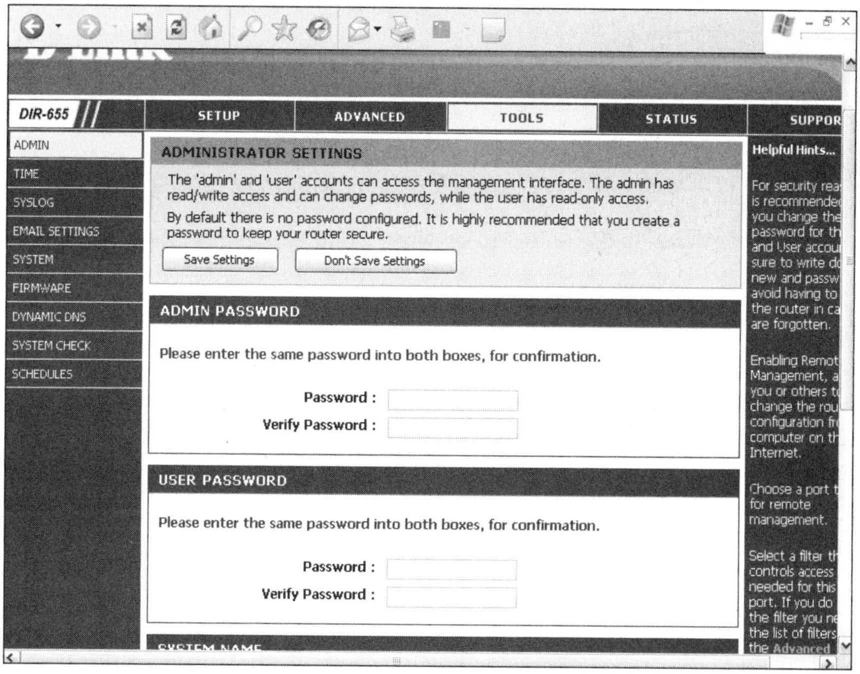

Figure 2-8: Entering password settings on a wireless router.

2. **Enter a new password (and if available, a new username as well) into the appropriate fields.**

   Some wireless routers may allow you to specify a user account, which can't make any changes, in addition to the necessary administration account, which has full privileges.

3. **Click the Save or Apply button, on the top or bottom of the page, to save your new password.**

   Again, the wireless router may reboot and you may be disconnected for a minute. After you're reconnected with the router, just close the Web browser — you're done!

Hiding Your Network: Disabling Broadcasting

By default, your wireless router constantly broadcasts its network name, technically called the Service Set Identifier (SSID). This makes the network name appear in your (and other people's) available wireless network list. Although this makes connecting to your network a bit easier, it also gives out your network name to others in the area.

Turning network name broadcasting off — or, in other words, creating a "hidden network" — makes it a bit harder for others to hack onto your network. Along with any encryption keys that are enabled (which could possibly be cracked), someone must also know your network name in order to connect. This feature allows you to add another layer of protection around your wireless network.

If you do disable your network name broadcasting, you have to manually connect to your network by adding the network to your preferred network list. You can refer to Book IV, Chapter 1 for more information on connecting.

If you prefer to disable network name (SSID) broadcasting, follow these steps:

1. **Bring up your Web browser (Internet Explorer, Netscape, Firefox, and so on).**

2. **Type in the IP address of your router and press Enter.**

   Keep in mind that some manufacturers may use a domain name (`http://www.routerlogin.net`) that looks like a Web site address instead of an IP address (192.168.1.1).

   If you don't know the IP address or the username or password, refer to Book V, Chapter 3 for help.

3. **When prompted to do so, enter the username and password.**

If you don't know the default username and password, refer to Book V, Chapter 3.

4. **Click the Wireless, or sometimes Advanced Wireless, tab, whichever contains the broadcasting settings (which may be named Visibility Status or Broadcast SSID); see Figure 2-9.**

   Some newer wireless routers may offer wizards to help with wireless configuration; however, you still may be able to manually configure the wireless settings, which is preferred for your purposes.

5. **Using radio buttons or a drop-down menu, select the option from the Broadcast (or Hidden Wireless or Visibility Status) field to make your network name not visible or broadcasted.**

6. **Click the Save or Apply button, on the top or bottom of the page, to save your changes.**

   The wireless router may reboot and you may be disconnected for a minute. Remember, from now on, you must manually connect to your wireless router. Your network won't appear on your available network list, at least until you set it up as a preferred network. You can refer to Book IV, Chapter 1 for information on manually connecting.

   When you're reconnected with the router, just close the Web browser.

Book III
Chapter 2

Securing the
Airwaves:
It's Possible

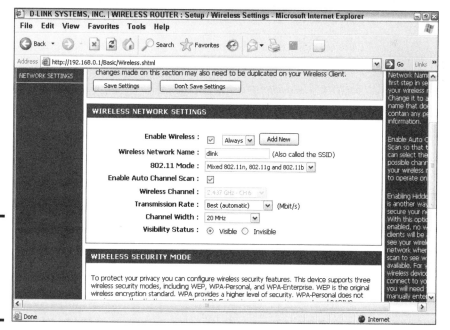

Figure 2-9:
SSID broadcast settings on a wireless router.

Using MAC Address Filtering

Every one of your networking devices (routers, adapters, and so on) has its own unique *media access control* (MAC) address, sometimes also referred as the *physical* address. The MAC address is used to help identify and differentiate the communication and traffic of the devices on your network.

Because your Wi-Fi router already looks at the MAC addresses of connected computers (or network adapters), it's easy to set up filtering based upon this unique identifier. Wireless routers usually have two different filtering lists or methods that allow you to either

✦ Block only certain computers (or network adapters) that you put on a list from connecting to the wireless router

✦ Specify the only computers (or network adapters) allowed to connect to the wireless router, by adding each of them to a list

For security purposes, you should use the second technique. This allows you to input the MAC addresses of all your devices while blocking network access to any other devices.

First you must figure out the MAC addresses of all the devices you want to add to this authorized list. In addition to the network adapters in your computers, don't forget about any other devices that use your network, such as

✦ Print servers

✦ Media players

✦ Wi-Fi and VoIP phones

✦ Range extenders or repeaters

Generally, you have three methods to find out the MAC addresses of your network devices:

✦ **When setting up the filtering:** This is the most convenient method; you don't have to look up the addresses before setting up the filtering. Many routers have some type of method to display the MAC addresses of current and previous network users.

✦ **By checking in the logs of your router:** Some wireless routers may have connection logs that display the MAC addresses of your network users.

✦ **By checking on the device itself:** As a last resort, you can manually check each device; refer to Book V, Chapter 3 for more information.

When you're ready to configure the MAC filtering, follow these steps:

1. **Bring up your Web browser (Internet Explorer, Netscape, Firefox, and so on).**

2. **Type in the IP address of your router and press Enter.**

   Keep in mind that some manufacturers may use a domain name (`http://www.routerlogin.net`) that looks like a Web site address instead of an IP address (192.168.1.1).

   If you don't know the IP address or the username or password, refer to Book V, Chapter 3 for help.

3. **When prompted to do so, enter the username and password.**

   If you don't know the default username and password, refer to Book V, Chapter 3.

4. **Click the Network Filtering or Access Control tab (or other tab containing the MAC address filtering settings, such as that shown in Figure 2-10).**

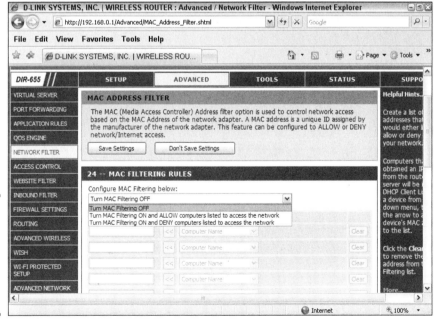

Figure 2-10: MAC address filtering settings of a wireless router.

5. **Enable MAC address filtering with your desired method of filtering by selecting a radio button or an option from a drop-down list.**

6. **Add the MAC addresses by inputting them into boxes or selecting the computers/devices from drop-down list boxes.**

7. **Click the Save or Apply button, on the top or bottom of the page, to save your changes.**

Any new computers you introduce to your network have to be added to the MAC authorization list before they can connect.

Chapter 3: Protecting Youngsters

In This Chapter

- Realizing the potential dangers of a child's Internet usage
- Discovering the simple things you can do to protect your children
- Getting a second pair of eyes with parental controls and filtering
- Using Windows Vista's built-in Parental Controls
- Setting up and using a free Internet filter

Computers and the Internet can provide your children with never-ending entertainment and educational resources. However, on the flip side, they can also be a source of problems and dangers — from porn and online predators to Internet addiction and explicit communications. Thinking about these issues, implementing safeguards, and talking with your children can help provide a better experience for everyone. This chapter helps get you and your children on the right track.

Dangers Kids May Face on the Computer

The following are some of the types of content your children may come upon when using the computer:

+ **Adult material:** Probably the most common thing most people want to prevent their children from seeing on the Internet — pornographic Web sites. The Internet is basically uncontrolled and the amount and type of adult material on the Internet is endless. This material can be found quickly by using a search engine, such as Google, or even easily stumbled upon from links and images on other non-adult Web sites. Spyware, adware, and viruses also provide additional ways your children can be inadvertently exposed.

+ **Inappropriate material:** You shouldn't think pornographic Web sites are the only bad thing on the Internet. The Internet is filled with information and material on any and every topic under the sun. Some things you just might not want your children researching, for example, include bomb-making, illegal drugs, and hacking.

+ **Explicit communications:** The Internet has become a place for youngsters to communicate freely. This can be good, but can also be bad if your children are having inappropriate conversations or posting unsuitable content or photos online. Social networking sites, such as MySpace, Friendster, and Facebook, are examples of sites where these types of communication can incur. Additionally, the Internet is filled with chat rooms, discussion forums, and instant messaging services.

✦ **Online predators:** The Internet has also become a way for pedophiles to meet youngsters — talk explicitly, exchange photos, or to try to meet in person. If you've seen the *To Catch a Predator* series by Dateline NBC, you know what I'm talking about. (The show routinely catches adults in the act of trying to arrange sexual encounters with decoys whom they believe are kids they've been communicating with online.) Communicating over the Internet also allows people to lie about their age, among other things. It's much easier for your children to fall victim of online predators when Internet access isn't controlled or monitored.

✦ **Inappropriate games:** Some computer games may not be suitable for your children; for instance, those that contain

- Blood, gore, and intense violence

- Strong language and crude humor

- Sexual themes and nudity

- Drug and alcohol references

✦ Games that contain these types of content may negatively influence your children. You should select your child's games depending upon your child's age and maturity. You can use the rating system developed by the Entertainment Software Rating Board to help you analyze the content of computer and video games. I cover these ratings further in the next section.

Twelve percent of all Web sites are pornographic Web sites. There are 4.2 million pornographic Web sites, 420 million pornographic Web pages, and 68 million daily pornographic search engine requests (or 25% of total search engine requests), according to Internet Filter Review, 2006.

Although this information may be scary, you can do many things to help protect your children and ensure that everyone has a positive computing and Internet experience.

Using Common Sense

Protecting your children on the computer doesn't just consist of installing an Internet filter or setting some parental controls and walking away. Using some common sense and being involved in your children's Internet and computing lives can also work wonders. The following bullets discuss some things you can do to provide some basic protection and filtering:

✦ **Talk to them:** You should talk to your children about the Internet dangers they may face, and what they can do to stay safe, for instance:

- Don't post or give out personal info, such as their address, phone number, or school.

- Take precautions when meeting Internet friends and require that a parent be present.

- Tell a parent or adult if someone is harassing them.

✦ **Put computers in public places:** Putting your children's computers in a public or open place in your home lets you keep an eye on them a bit better and reduces the chance that they'll try to view inappropriate content.

✦ **Set time limits:** You may think about setting time limits on when and for how long your children can use the computer and Internet, which reduces the chance of them getting addicted and lets you better monitor usage.

✦ **Monitor activity and be involved:** Try to keep an eye out for what your children do on the computer and Internet, for instance, whom they talk to, what Web sites they like, and which games they enjoy.

✦ **Be age-appropriate:** Instead of just creating one set of rules and limits for computer and Internet usage for all your children, be age-specific. Your 15-year-old may be mature and ready enough to use social networking sites — with some parental monitoring — but your 12-year-old might not be.

Teens readily post personal info online. Sixty-four percent post photos or videos of themselves, whereas more than half (58 percent) post info about where they live. Females are far more likely than male teens to post personal photos or videos of themselves (70 percent of females versus 58 percent of males). (These stats come from the *National Teen Internet Survey* funded by Cox Communications, in partnership with NCMEC and John Walsh, March 2007.)

Teens whose parents have talked to them a lot about Internet safety are more concerned about the risks of sharing personal info online than teens whose parents are less involved. For instance, 65 percent of those whose parents have not talked to them about online safety post info about where they live, compared to 48 percent of teens with more involved parents (*National Teen Internet Survey*).

Deciphering Internet lingo and talk

Try to decipher the following example of a chat room or instant message conversation — without cheating:

Book III
Chapter 3

Protecting Youngsters

Eric: A/S/L/P

Sierra: 15/f/oh/y

Eric: 17/m/oh/n

Eric: LMIRL

Sierra: PIR BRB

Eric: WYCM

Sierra 2: y

You can probably figure out the first three lines, but the rest is very tough for those who don't hang out in chat rooms or use instant messaging with other Internet lingo talkers. This is an example of how the Internet is changing the language of our younger generation. To converse more quickly and under the radar of parents, children have come up with hundreds of acronyms and symbols for words, phrases, questions, and emotions. You can probably also see these terms used in text messaging conversations, which also has become popular.

Teens are willing to meet with strangers: 16 percent of teens considered meeting someone they've only talked to online and 8 percent have actually met someone they only knew online (Online Victimization of Youth: Five Years Later, 2006).

As you can probably guess, this language barrier causes problems for parents. Even though you might monitor your children's Internet activity, it's often hard to figure out what they are exactly saying. But if you're aware of some of the shorthand and know where to look up ones you don't know, you're much better off:

Here's what that confusing conversation said in real words:

Eric: What's your age, sex, and location? And do you have a picture of yourself?

Sierra: I'm a 15-year-old female from Ohio. Yes, I have a picture.

Eric: I'm a 17-year-old male from Ohio. No, I don't have a picture.

Eric: Let's meet in real life.

Sierra: My parents are in the room; I'll be right back.

Eric: Will you call me?

Sierra: Yes.

Now you know why acronyms are used: They save a lot of time typing — in this case, 148 characters or keystrokes. You should also notice how open teens can be in exchanging personal information, how they can keep parents in the dark, and how easily they may meet their online friends in the real world.

Netlingo (www.netlingo.com) compiles an enormous database of acronyms and symbols used in online business, technology, and text lingo.

To help decipher your children's Internet lingo, you can refer to the following sections that show you commonly used acronyms and symbols.

Miscellaneous acronyms

Some miscellaneous acronyms are listed in Table 3-1.

Table 3-1	Miscellaneous Acronyms
Acronym	*Meaning*
A/S/L/P	Age/Sex/Location/Picture
BRB	Be Right Back
J/K	Just Kidding
THX	Thanks
TTYL	Talk to You Later

Acronyms to alert that parents are watching

Table 3-2 gives you an idea of the acronyms that your children can use to alert their online friends that you're by the computer.

Table 3-2	Acronyms to Alert People of Parents
Acronym	*Meaning*
MOS	Mom Over Shoulder
P911	Parent Alert
PAW	Parents Are Watching
PIR	Parent in Room
POS	Parent Over Shoulder

Off-line communication-related acronyms

Table 3-3 lists some acronyms that may indicate your children plan to meet or talk with their online friends.

Book III
Chapter 3

Protecting Youngsters

Table 3-3	Off-line Communication-Related Acronyms
Acronym	*Meaning*
ADR or addy	Address
LMIRL	Let's Meet in Real Life
WYCM	Will You Call Me
WYWH	Wish You Were Here

Sexually related acronyms

Table 3-4 contains some sexually related acronyms you may want to watch out for.

Table 3-4	Sexually Related Acronyms
Acronym	*Meaning*
GYPO	Get Your Pants Off
IWSN	I Want Sex Now
KFY	Kiss for You
KOTL	Kiss on the Lips
NIFOC	Nude in Front of Computer
SorG	Straight or Gay
TDTM	Talk Dirty to Me

Symbols and acronyms to show emotions or expressions

Table 3-5 lists some symbols and acronyms that can be used to show emotions or expressions.

Table 3-5	Symbols and Acronyms to Show Emotions or Expressions
Acronym	*Meaning*
%\	Hangover
:-!	Bored
:-(	Sad
:-)	Basic
:*(	Crying
:-{	Angry
;-)	Winking
ILY	I Love You
LMAO	Laughing My A** Off

Acronym	Meaning
LOL	Laugh out loud

Discover the gaming ratings

For help in choosing the right games for your children, you can use the rating system developed by the Entertainment Software Rating Board (ESRB). In addition to you using this rating to manually monitor the games brought into your household, most parental control software packages can also control games based upon this rating system. The ESRB ratings are conveyed using two items:

✦ **Rating symbols:** This suggests the recommend age group for the game. This consists of a logo on the front of the box of just about every computer and video game sold in the United States and Canada. You can see an example of this logo in the bottom-left corner of the game box pictured in Figure 3-1. This game is rated E for Everyone.

✦ **Content descriptors:** These try to express the types of content of interest or concern in the game. These appear on the back of games, next to the rating symbol.

Figure 3-1:
An example
of an ESRB
rating
symbol.

Courtesy of Microsoft.

Here is a list of the ESRB ratings and what they mean:

✦ **Early childhood:** Titles rated EC (Early Childhood) have content that may be suitable for those 3 and older. Contains no material that parents would find inappropriate.

✦ **Everyone:** Titles rated E (Everyone) have content that may be suitable for ages 6 and older. Titles in this category may contain minimal cartoon, fantasy, or mild violence or infrequent use of mild language.

✦ **Everyone 10+:** Titles rated E10+ (Everyone 10 and older) have content that may be suitable for ages 10 and older. Titles in this category may contain more cartoon, fantasy or mild violence, mild language or minimal suggestive themes.

✦ **Teen:** Titles rated T (Teen) have content that may be suitable for ages 13 and older. Titles in this category may contain violence, suggestive themes, crude humor, minimal blood, simulated gambling, or infrequent use of strong language.

✦ **Mature:** Titles rated M (Mature) have content that may be suitable for persons ages 17 and older. Titles in this category may contain intense violence, blood and gore, sexual content, or strong language.

✦ **Adults only:** Titles rated AO (Adults Only) have content that should only be played by persons 18 years and older. Titles in this category may include prolonged scenes of intense violence or graphic sexual content and nudity.

✦ **Rating pending:** Titles listed as RP (Rating Pending) have been submitted to the ESRB and are awaiting final rating. (This symbol appears only in advertising prior to a game's release.)

The ESRB also has definitions for all its content descriptors, which is available on its Web site (www.esrb.org) along with plenty of other information and resources.

You can get even better insight into computer and video games by reviewing screen shots and reviews, and maybe even demos. Here are some Web sites that may help:

✦ CVG (www.computerandvideogames.com)

✦ GameRankings.com (www.gamerankings.com)

✦ GameSpot (www.gamespot.com)

✦ IGN.com (www.ign.com)

Other steps to take

Here are even more things you should consider or keep in mind when addressing the safety of your children's computing experience:

✦ **Talk to other parents:** Start up a discussion with other parents about Internet and computer safety. You can see what they do about the problem and possibly recommend the solution you use. You may also discuss computer usage when your children are at another adult's home.

✦ **Think about loopholes:** Even if you follow all the right steps, you can never guarantee 100 percent protection. Your Internet filter or parental control software may let something through or your children may find a way around it. Also think about other computers your children may be able to access that don't have proper protection, like yours or their friends and relatives.

✦ **Prevent viral and spyware infections:** You shouldn't forget about protecting your children's computers from infections. In addition to altering settings and messing with files, infections may lead to inappropriate material being displayed.

✦ **Don't stop at the computer:** You can lock down your computer as much as you want, but your children probably have other items that you may want to control and monitor, such as mobile phones and video game consoles.

One in ten young people (10 percent) reports having a handheld device that connects to the Internet, according to the Henry J. Kaiser Family Foundation Study, March 2005.

Advanced Protection: Parental Controls

Because you might not always be right beside your children when they're on the computer, you can use parental controls to be your second pair of eyes and ears. In addition, parental controls can even do more than you can do because they block inappropriate content. On the Internet, you don't always know what's around the corner without taking a peek — parental controls and Internet filters can take the peek for you.

It's important to understand parental controls can do much more than just filter Web sites. Solutions today are able to control and monitor just about every aspect of the computer, including the following items:

✦ **Web sites:** An Internet filter blocks access to Web sites based upon ratings and content categories you specify.

✦ **E-mails and instant messaging:** You can block or monitor the use of e-mail or instant messaging.

✦ **Games and programs:** You can specify exactly the type of games or programs that can be opened on the computer.

✦ **Time limits:** You can impose time limits to develop a schedule for computer usage of your children's accounts.

✦ **Video and music:** You may be able to block or monitor the media played on your children's accounts.

Internet rating systems

Unlike with computer and video games, the Internet doesn't have a single rating system — there are many. Some parental control systems and Internet filtering programs may base their products off of publicly established rating platforms, like PICS (Platform for Internet Content Selection), and some create their own methods. Additionally, the intelligence behind these rating systems (and their effectiveness) and products can vary.

Here are the different types of methods that can be used to filter Web sites:

✦ **Keywords:** Examines keywords on a particular Web page to make a decision about its rating category. Keywords were often used in earlier Internet filtering products.

✦ **Human examination:** Involves manual examination and rating of Web sites by the filter's staff and recommendations by users.

✦ **Server:** Bases the rating and content of a Web site off of what the Web site owner has specified in the code of its Web pages or a file that resides on the Web server.

✦ **Dynamic:** Takes into account all the methods and other statistical analysis and artificial intelligence to automatically determine a rating for new and previously unrated Web sites.

Finding a parental control system

You can find Internet filtering and parental control systems from various sources:

✦ **Windows Vista:** If your children's computers use Windows Vista, you might not have to go any further. Windows Vista includes a full-feature parental control system, which the next section discusses.

✦ **Mac OS X Leopard:** For you Macintosh lovers, the new Mac OS X 10.5 operating system also sports a new parental control system.

✦ **Your ISP:** Your Internet Service Provider might also provide parental controls and an Internet filtering solution, especially community or portal-based services like AOL.

✦ **Your network router:** You may want to check your router's documentation and Web-based configuration utility for any parental controls. Keep in mind that most routers don't have this feature, and if yours does, it's probably just Internet filtering.

If you're interested in filtering your entire network, you should look into routers designed specifically for the purpose, such as ZyXEL's (`www.zyxel.com`) HomeSafe product line.

✦ **Internet Explorer:** No matter what Windows version you're running, you can always use Internet Explorer's Content Advisor feature, accessible from Internet Options, for Internet filtering.

✦ **Internet security suites:** You may also be able to set up Internet filtering through your Internet security software.

✦ **Third-party solutions:** You can also find many third-party applications, such as the following products:

- **K9 Web Protection:** `www.k9webprotection.com` (I discuss it more later in this chapter in the section called "Using K9 Web Protection").

- **KidsWatch:** `www.kidswatch.com`

- **Chronager:** `www.chronager.com`

- **Webroot:** `www.webroot.com`

When comparing parental control solutions, you may want to keep an eye out for features beyond the Internet filter, such as

✦ **Computer usage controlling:** Instead of just Internet usage limits, some systems offer control over the usage of Windows user accounts. This way, you can set limits on the entire computer usage rather than just Internet use.

✦ **Settings control:** You can even find parental control solutions that can lock down account and system settings and preferences. This helps prevent problems if your children get bored and try to mess around with things or try to disable the parental controls.

✦ **Safe searching:** Most search engines can be put into some sort of safe mode that filters the types of results that are shown. Some parental control solutions let you enable and lock this feature in for the popular search engines.

Even though you use an Internet filter, you can still see the results of searches on inappropriate keywords, if you're not using safe searching features. Pornographic and inappropriate photos can also be shown when searching image engines like `www.images.google.com`. But if you have the search engine's safe searching feature on, text and image results are filtered.

✦ **Remote administration:** Instead of having to log into your children's computers to make changes to parental controls, some solutions may offer remote administration. This way, you can change settings and view the activity logs from your computer at home, or even from the Internet anywhere in the world.

**Book III
Chapter 3**

**Protecting
Youngsters**

Using Windows Vista's Parental Controls

One of Windows Vista's great new features is Parental Controls. Windows XP and previous versions of Windows only offered the Internet filtering feature, Content Advisor, of Internet Explorer. Windows Vista, though, includes a full-featured Parental control system that you can enable for individual Windows accounts.

In addition to Internet filtering, Vista offers control over applications and games that are run on protected accounts and monitors e-mail and instant messaging. Plus, just like with other Parental Control solutions you can purchase, it offers reporting to show you what your children are doing on the computer.

If your child's computer is loaded with Windows Vista, you may want to just use these free Parental Controls. If her computer is still running an older version of Windows, you may want to think about upgrading.

Your controlling capabilities with Vista

Windows Vista's Parental Controls offers the following features to help keep your children safe:

✦ **Web filter:** Gives you control over the Web sites your children can surf to with the following features:

- *Levels of protection:* You can either pick between the predefined levels of high or medium protection, or customize your own level. Customization lets you choose exactly the types of things to be filtered: for example, categories such as drugs, tobacco, pornography, or bomb-making.

- *Block/Allow list:* You can build a list of specific sites to block. This option is great if you're having a problem with certain places, such as social networking sites. Alternatively, you could list allowed sites, blocking access to any other site.

- *Override capability:* You would have the power to override the filter. If your children come upon a site that's blocked, but you don't see any problem with the site, you can enter your password to open access to the site.

- *Download control:* You can block your children from downloading files or applications.

  When your children visit a restricted Web site, a page such as Figure 3-2 is shown.

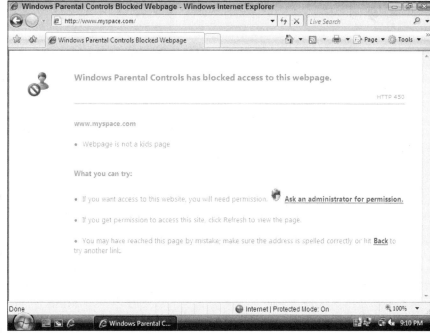

Book III
Chapter 3

Protecting
Youngsters

Figure 3-2: Visiting a Web site restricted by Windows Vista Parental Controls.

✦ **Gaming filter:** You can filter computer games based upon the following:

- *Block all games:* If desired, you can prevent your children from playing games altogether — keep this in mind when a punishment is needed for little Johnny.

- *Levels of protection:* Because the content of games can vary greatly, Vista lets you authorize the games that are played (or blocked) by ratings (such as Everyone, Teen, and Mature) and content types (such as Crude Humor, Blood, Language, and Online games).

- *Game specific:* You can also choose to just manually authorize games yourself. You can pick exactly what games to allow and block.

✦ **Program filter:** In addition to games, you have control over the applications used. You can allow the use of all programs on the computer, or only those you put on the allow list.

✦ **Time limits:** This lets you specify exactly when your children can use their user accounts. If they're logged in at the cut-off time, they'll be notified (see Figure 3-3 for an example) and Windows automatically logs them off their account.

Figure 3-3:
An example of the time limit reminder of Windows Vista Parental Controls.

Your monitoring capabilities in Vista

Not only can you filter and block content with Windows Vista's Parental Controls, but you can also monitor all your children's computer activity. See what sites they're visiting, how much time they're on the computer, the music they've listened to, and much more. Checking out the reports (Figure 3-4 gives you an example) can give you an idea if you need to tighten their restrictions, or have a talk.

The activity report contains the following categories and items:

✦ **Web browsing:** Their entire Web browsing activity, including

  • Visited Web sites

  • Web sites blocked by the filter

  • Instances where a restricted Web site was visited, and the administrator who performed the override — so you are aware if they've figured out your password, or if Daddy is paying attention to what he's unblocking

  • Downloaded files and application, including their filenames and locations

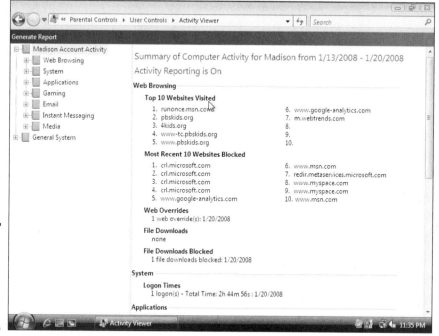

**Book III
Chapter 3**

**Protecting
Youngsters**

Figure 3-4:
An example
of a
Computer
Activity
Summary.

✦ **System:** When the account was used, including the dates, times, and durations.

✦ **Applications:** Applications and software used, including

  • Opened applications.

  • Applications blocked by the filter.

  • Instances where a restricted application was run, and the administrator who performed the override.

✦ **Gaming:** The games that were played along with their ratings and how long they were played.

✦ **E-mail:** Details of the following e-mail actions:

  • Received e-mail

  • Sent e-mail

  • Contact list changes

✦ **Instant Messaging:** Details of a variety of instant messaging communications:

  • General instant messaging, such as AOL, AIM, or Yahoo Messenger

  • Video/audio messaging

- Gaming messaging

- Any files or links exchanged

- SMS messages sent to mobile phones

- Contact list changes

✦ **Media:** List of media (music, movies, and so on) played, including details such as song and album titles, and their ratings.

✦ **General System:** The following items are also included to track system changes:

  - Details of any system or Windows setting changes, including the affected accounts.

  - System clock changes, which may indicate they're trying to bypass your time limits.

  - Failed login attempts — shows if they're trying to get into your account.

Getting started with the parental controls in Vista

You can access the Windows Vista Parental Controls via the Control Panel:

1. **Open the Start menu.**

2. **Click Control Panel.**

3. **Click Users Accounts and Family Safety.**

   If your system is in Classic Control Panel view, skip this step.

4. **Click Parental Controls.**

5. **Enter an Administrator password, if required, and click Continue.**

When you first bring up Parental Controls (see Figure 3-5), you see a listing of your Windows accounts, along with a few global tasks on the left and a link to create additional users.

To properly implement Parental Controls, everyone should have his or her own Windows accounts. Parent accounts should have Administrator accounts with password protection, and child accounts should be set to Limited accounts with their own Parental Control limits in force. If you have more than one child, your children's accounts should also be password-protected. For instance, say 12-year-old Sammy wants to get on myspace. com that's blocked on his account, but 15-year-old Sierra is allowed to get on the site with her account. If Sierra's account isn't protected (or if Sammy knows the password), Sammy can just log into her account and get on the site that's restricted on his.

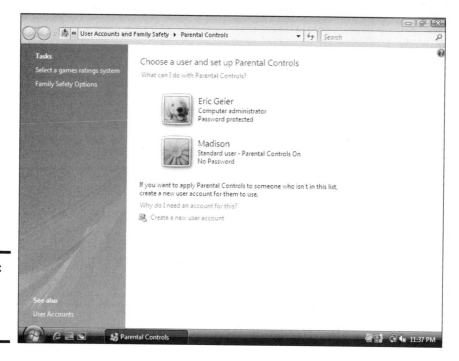

**Book III
Chapter 3**

Protecting
Youngsters

Figure 3-5:
Windows
Vista's
Parental
Controls.

You can click an account to open its individual parental control settings, as Figure 3-6 shows.

Enforcing limits and changing settings

The following sections take you through changing the main settings of Windows Vista's Parental Controls.

Turning Parental Controls on

Follow these steps to quickly enable Parental Controls:

1. **Open Parental Controls.**

   You can get to Parental Controls from the Control Panel, accessible on your Start menu.

2. **Click the desired Windows account.**

3. **Select the On, Enforce Current Settings radio button, as shown in Figure 3-7.**

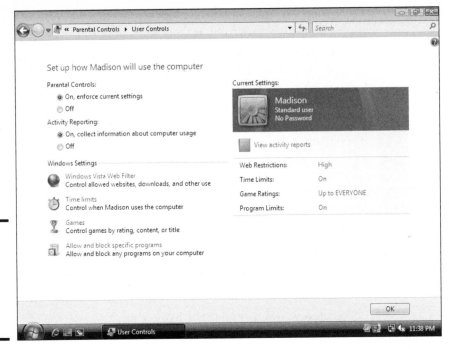

Figure 3-6:
A screen
showing a
user's
parental
control
settings.

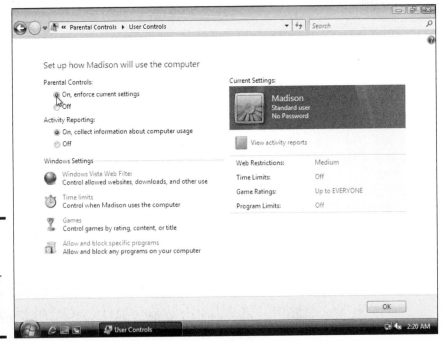

Figure 3-7:
Turning on
Parental
Controls for
a Windows
Vista
account.

4. **Specify whether you want activity reporting turned on by selecting a radio button under the Activity Reporting heading.**

The previous section, "Your monitoring capabilities in Vista," shows exactly what activity is logged when you have this feature on. To view the logs, refer to the "Viewing a user's activity reports" section.

Changing the Web filter level and settings

These steps take you through the settings of Web or Internet filter:

1. **Open Parental Controls.**

You can get to Parental Controls from the Control Panel, accessible on your Start menu.

2. **Click the desired Windows account.**

3. **Click Windows Vista Web Filter.**

Figure 3-8 shows an example of the screen you should see now.

You can turn Web filtering on and off using the options on the very top.

4. **Review allowed and blocked Web sites.**

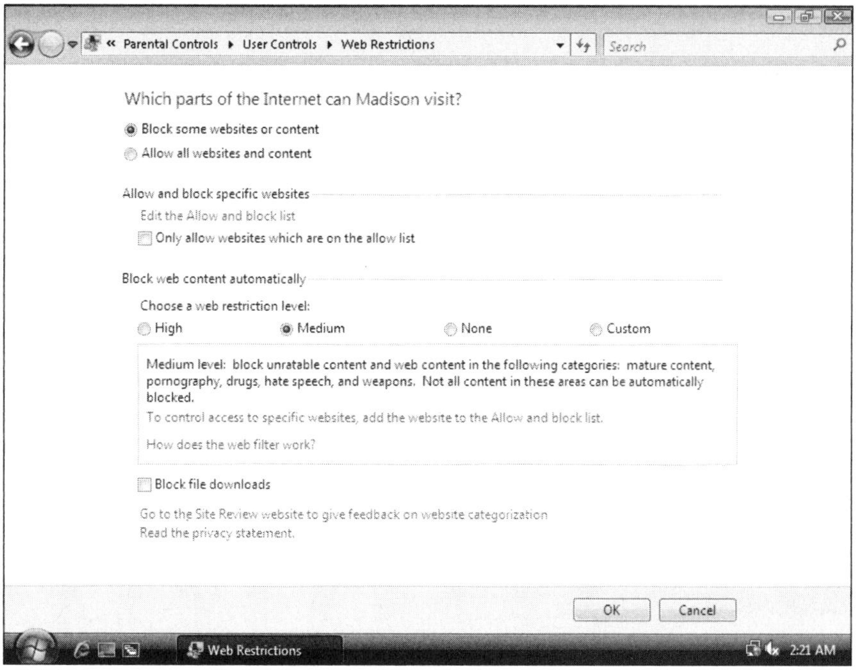

Figure 3-8:
Windows
Vista Web
Filter
screen.

You can specify Web sites that you want to block and allow, regardless of the filtering. You can also block all Web sites besides the ones you allow by checking the Only Allow Web Sites Which Are on the Allowed List option.

To add Web sites to the allowed or blocked list, click the Edit the Allow and Block List link. Figure 3-9 shows an example of the screen you should see.

Simply enter the Web site address and click either Allow or Block. If you want to remove a Web site from either list, just select the address and click Remove.

If you have more than one child, you may find the import/export feature of the Web filters Allow/Block list very useful. If you develop a list of many sites that you want to explicitly block or allow, you don't have to type them all in for each child's account. When you're viewing the Allow/Block list, simply click the Export button and find a good spot to save the file. Then you can go to another account's Allow/Block list, click Import and select the file, and save yourself a lot of time.

5. **When you're done specifying Web sites to allow or block, click OK to return to the Web Restrictions page.**

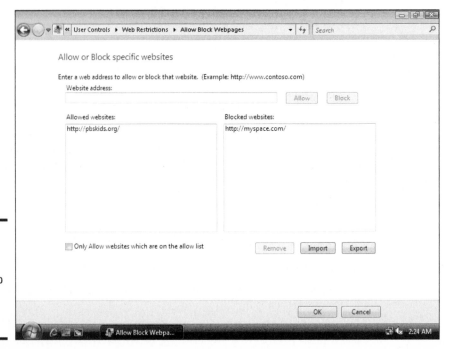

Figure 3-9:
Editing the
Web sites
you want to
explicitly
allow or
block.

6. **Review the restriction level.**

You can click the High and Medium levels to read what type of content is automatically blocked. You can also click Custom to define exactly what type of content you want filtered.

7. **Review the file downloads block.**

You can specify whether you want to block your child from downloading anything from the Internet by using the Block File Downloads option on the bottom of the screen.

8. **When you're done with the Web Restrictions, click OK to return to the main User Controls page.**

Enforcing account time limits

You can limit how much time your children spend on the computer. Here's how:

1. **Open Parental Controls.**

You can get to Parental Controls from the Control Panel, accessible on your Start menu.

2. **Click the desired Windows account.**

3. **Click Time Limits.**

4. **Click or drag the blocks of time.**

Figure 3-10 shows an example of only allowing computer access on weekend mornings and weeknights between 7 and 9 p.m.

5. **Click OK to return to the main User Controls page.**

If you are going to block access much more than allow it, like the example shown in Figure 3-10, you may want to just start off by blocking all times and then going through and specifying periods of time to allow access. This saves you a little bit of time.

Blocking games and defining gaming rules

You can specify which types of games your children play:

1. **Open Parental Controls.**

You can get to Parental Controls from the Control Panel, accessible on your Start menu.

2. **Click the desired Windows account.**

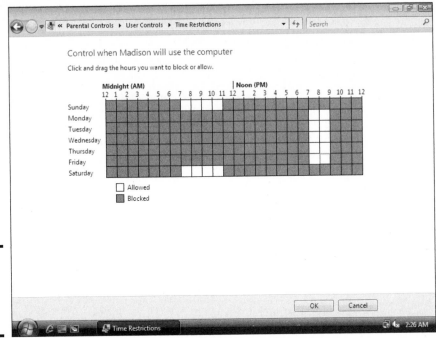

Figure 3-10:
Example of
a child's
computer
schedule.

3. **Click Games.**

   If you want to block all games from being played, click the No option for the Can [Child's Name] Play Games? question, on the top of the screen.

4. **Review gaming limiting by rating/content.**

   Click the Set Game Ratings link to bring up the Game Restrictions screen, as Figure 3-11 shows.

   First, specify whether your child is allowed to play games without a rating. Then you can choose the rating category you think is best for your child. Plus, you can also specify games to explicitly block based upon content types like violence, gore, or foul language.

5. **When you're done setting the game ratings, click OK to return to the main Games Controls page.**

6. **Review the allow/block list.**

   Click the Block or Allow Specific Game link to open the Game Overrides screen, such as Figure 3-12 shows.

7. **When you're done setting the game overrides, click OK to return to the main Game Controls page.**

Figure 3-11:
The Game
Restrictions
screen.

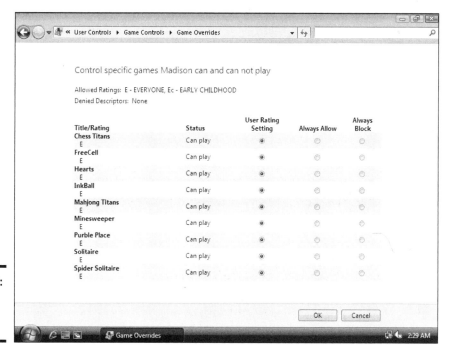

Figure 3-12:
The Game
Overrides
screen.

You can find out more about the gaming rating system in the "Discover the gaming ratings" section earlier in this chapter.

Limiting access to programs

You can specify exactly which software programs your child is allowed to use:

1. **Open Parental Controls.**

You can get to Parental Controls from the Control Panel, accessible on your Start menu.

2. **Click the desired Windows account.**

3. **Click Allow and Block Specific Programs.**

Figure 3-13 shows the screen you should now see.

4. **Choose an option on the top of the screen.**

If you choose not to allow access to all programs, you can select the ones you approve of from the list of detected programs. If a program isn't on the list, you can click the Browse button to add it.

Figure 3-13:
The
Applications
Restrictions
screen.

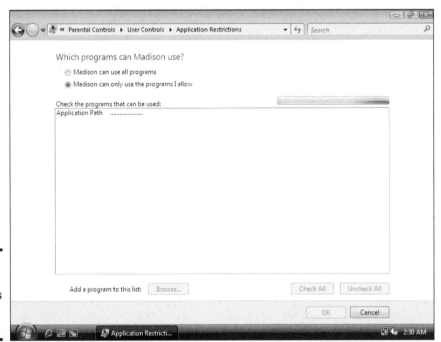

Internet Explorer is always allowed — you can't block it. But you can limit access to the Internet.

5. **When you're done, click OK to return to the main User Controls page.**

Setting an alert to remind you to review activity logs

So that you remember to check up on your children's Internet and computer activity reports, you can set an alert:

1. **Open Parental Controls.**

   You can get to Parental Controls from the Control Panel, accessible on your Start menu.

2. **Click Family Safety Options.**

   It's under the tasks on the left side of the screen.

3. **Select how often you want to be alerted.**

4. **Click OK to return to the main Parental Controls page.**

Viewing a user's activity reports

When you want to check the activity reports, you can access them through each user's parental controls page:

1. **Open Parental Controls.**

   You can get to Parental Controls from the Control Panel, accessible on your Start menu.

2. **Click the desired Windows account.**

3. **Click the View Activity Reports link, under the Current Settings column on the right of the page.**

   You can refer to the previous section, "Your monitoring capabilities in Vista," for exactly what activity is recorded and reported.

Using Parental Controls in Mac OS X Leopard

The Parental Controls in Leopard offers about the same protection as in Tiger, with some enhancements. The addition of an automatic content filter for Safari helps ensure that adult Web sites aren't accessed. Also, time limit features are added to control the amount of time an account can be used and during what times of the day. Another neat new feature is the ability to remotely manage the Parental Controls and monitor user activity from other Macs on your network. Children won't even know when their parents make changes to their Parental Control settings or check the logs of their activities.

Enabling Parental Controls for Accounts

One way to enable Parental Controls for a Mac OS X Leopard account is through the main Accounts window; however, because you'll want to configure the restrictions and settings, too, a good way to turn this feature on is through the Parental Controls window, as follows:

1. **Click the Apple icon on the menu bar.**

2. **Click System Preferences.**

3. **In the System category, click Parental Controls.**

4. **Click the padlock icon in the lower-left corner of the window (if it's locked), enter your administrator account name and password into the fields, and click OK.**

5. **Choose the account you want to enable Parental Controls for and click the Enable Parental Controls button that appears in the middle of the window.**

   If Parental Controls are already enabled, you won't see this button; instead, you'll see the settings for the Parental Controls.

   Only non-Administrator accounts appear in the list because you can't give an account Administrator privileges and have Parental Controls enabled. If you want to remove the Administrator privileges, click the Show All button on the top of the Parental Controls window, click Accounts, select the account, deselect the Allow User to Administer This Computer option, click Show All, and click Parental Controls to return.

Now you can click the tabs (System, Content, Mail & iChat, Time Limits, and Logs) to set up the Parental Controls. The following subsections summarize the settings and options found on each tab.

Controlling what applications and settings users can access

The System tab gives you the ability to control access to system settings and applications using the following options:

+ **Use Simple Finder:** This option greatly limits the files and settings that can be viewed or modified, thus simplifying the desktop, dock, and menu bar. This helps protect files and settings from being messed with and unclutters the desktop to make the Mac easier to use — which is great for children and new Mac users.

+ **Only Allow Selected Applications:** This option lets you specify exactly what applications and features can be run from the account. Selecting to limit access to the Utilities, for example, prevents the user from changing settings and getting into things that aren't necessary for non-Administrators. Parents might also find this a useful means of enforcing discipline. For example, if a child refuses to clean up his or her room, the parent can deselect this option and disable the child's favorite games.

✦ **Can Administer Printers:** This option prevents the user from changing any printer preferences and settings (which can be a pain if someone changes them!) but still lets the user print.

✦ **Can Burn CDs and DVDs:** When this option is disabled, the user can't create any type of CDs or DVDs.

✦ **Can Change Password:** Simply indicates whether users can change their own password without an Administrator's authorization. This is good if you always want to make sure you know a user's password. Enabling this option when you know the user's password prevents the user from changing it to another one.

Filtering dictionary and Web content

The Content tab lets you set what type of content the account can access with only two basic settings:

✦ **Hide Profanity in Dictionary:** This option prevents some inappropriate words from appearing in the Dictionary application and in other applications that use the Dictionary. Just do some searching in the Dictionary for yourself to see why I recommend enabling this option for children; it can contain some quite explicit words, to say the least.

✦ **Website Restrictions:** Enabling this option allows you to choose your Web browsing filtering method, with an option to disable it altogether, another to enable filtering for adult Web sites, and an option to allow only the sites you add to the list.

Deciding whom the user can communicate with in Mail and iChat

On the Mail & iChat tab, you can control which people are allowed to be communicated with via e-mail and instant messages in iChat:

✦ **Limit Mail:** Enabling this option allows the account to send e-mail to only the people who are on the list you create.

✦ **Limit iChat:** When selected, this option allows the user to communicate on iChat only with people you add to the list, which is a great way to keep children safe on the Internet.

✦ **Send Permission Requests To:** You can enter your e-mail address so that if an e-mail is sent from the account to a recipient whose address isn't on the list, you receive an e-mail that asks you whether the message is allowed to be sent.

Imposing time limits on computer usage

The Time Limits tab lets you set how much time a user has on the computer and gives you the ability to set a bedtime limit, using the following options:

✦ **Weekday Time Limits:** When this option is enabled, you can choose how much accumulated time the account can be used Monday through Friday.

✦ **Weekend Time Limits:** This option lets you limit the accumulated time the account be used on Saturday and Sunday.

✦ **Bedtime limits:** Here you can enter exactly when you don't want the account to be available, both for school nights (Sunday – Thursday) and the weekend (Friday and Saturday).

When the time is coming close to the user's limit, an alert pops up and notifies him or her of how much time is left. Also, more time can be added if an Administrator's username and password are typed in, which is useful because you don't have to go back to the settings just to let the user on for a bit longer.

Seeing the activity of the account

The Logs tab shows you what the user has been doing on the computer, giving you the following information:

✦ **Websites Visited:** All the sites and Web pages that have been visited will be shown.

✦ **Websites Blocked:** Each time a Web site is blocked by the automatic adult content filter or from those sites you've manually blocked, it's logged here.

✦ **Applications:** This shows what applications have been used by the account.

✦ **iChat:** All instant messaging communications in iChat are recorded and saved here so that parents see what their children and their friends are up to. Just so you know, the user is reminded of this monitoring by the message "This chat will be viewable by your computer's administrator," which appears in each instant message box.

Using K9 Web Protection

One third-party Internet filtering solution that may interest you is Blue Coat K9 Web Protection. Although it doesn't control and monitor anything other than Web browsing and Internet usage, it's a very effective Internet filter — plus it's totally free! This is great if your computer doesn't have Windows Vista.

The following sums up the features of K9 Web Protection:

✦ **60 content categories:** Includes plenty of categories you can block — from pornography to jokes.

✦ **Time restrictions:** Lets you select exactly when you want to allow or block Internet access.

✦ **Web site exceptions:** You can add sites to always allow or to block.

✦ **Blocking sound effects:** Includes blocking preferences such as an audible alert (a bark) when a Web page is blocked, so you know if someone is trying to view restricted content, even from the other room.

✦ **Keyword blocking:** Lets you specify keywords to block in Web site addresses.

✦ **Web search options:** You can enable Google's SafeSearch, which tries to block Web pages (and other media like images) that are explicitly sexual from appearing in search results.

Beware that Google's SafeSearch feature may not block all questionable (or explicit) content from its search results.

✦ **Internet activity reports:** Lets you see exactly what Web sites have been accessed (and blocked), sorted by categories.

If you prefer just a Web site filter, this solution should work fine.

When your children come upon a restricted site, the block page (shown in Figure 3-14) appears and the Web site address is logged for your reference.

At this point, your child can click the Back button, exit the browser, or go to another Web site. They can also call you over to unblock the Web site with your password, using one of the administrator override options:

✦ Allow access to all pages on the Web site that's trying to be accessed, for the next 15 minutes or permanently.

✦ Allow access to all Web sites classified with the same category or content type, for the next 15 minutes or permanently.

✦ Allow access to all categories and content types, disabling all filtering for the next 15 minutes.

Figure 3-14:
This page is displayed when accessing a restricted Web site.

Downloading and installing K9

If you would like to give Blue Coat K9 Web Protection a try, here's how to get started:

1. **Go to their Web site:**

   www.k9webprotection.com

2. **Click the Get K9 Now link.**

3. **Request a license.**

   Fill out the form and click Request License.

4. **Check your e-mail.**

   Follow the instructions in the e-mail you receive.

Use a secure e-mail account that your children can't access. Reset passwords are sent to you via e-mail when requested.

Opening Blue Coat K9 Web Protection Administration

To change your parental controls and settings, and to view Internet activity, you use the Blue Coat K9 Web Protection Administration portal, which is accessible from a few places on your computer:

✦ **Start menu:** You can browse to the following path on your start menu: Programs (or All Programs) ➪ Blue Coat K9 Web Protection ➪ Blue Coat K9 Web Protection Admin.

✦ **Desktop icon:** If you choose to install a desktop icon for Blue Coat K9 Web Protection during the installation, you can simply double-click the icon.

✦ **Quick launch:** If you choose to install an icon in quick launch for Blue Coat K9 Web Protection during the installation, you can simply click the icon.

After opening Blue Coat K9 Web Protection Administration, you see a page similar to Figure 3-15.

Book III
Chapter 3

Protecting
Youngsters

Figure 3-15:
K9 Web
Protection
Admini-
stration.

You have three things you can do: View Internet activity, set up and configure the parental controls, or get help. You must enter the administrator password you created during the installation process to access everything besides help — this way, little Billy can't just go in and change the settings.

Configuring the Internet filter settings

The first thing you should do is review the default parental control settings and make desired changes based upon your particular situation. You can do this from the Setup section of K9 Web Protection Administration:

1. **Open K9 Web Protection Administration.**

2. **Click the Setup button.**

3. **Enter your administrator password and click Login.**

You should see a page similar to the example in Figure 3-16. You can access all the settings from the menu on the left side of the main page.

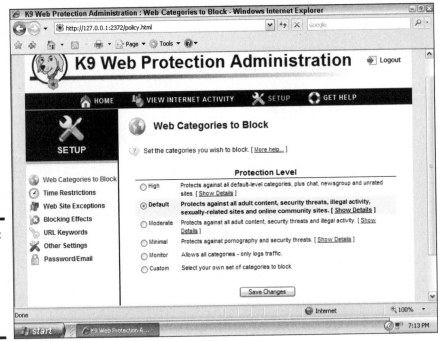

Figure 3-16:
The Setup section of K9 Web Protection Administration.

If you ever forget your administrator password, you can click the Forgot Your Password? link on the login page. You receive a confirmation explaining that an e-mail will be sent to you with a new password. For this reason, you should also keep your e-mail secure from your children. You might also want to just permanently delete this e-mail after you get the new password.

K9 Web Protection Administration automatically logs out after five minutes without activity. This helps prevent your children from changing settings while you go check on the little one.

Web Categories to Block: Overall protection level

This is the first page that comes up when you log into Setup. It allows you to choose one of the following protection levels:

✦ **High:** Provides the most protection by blocking chat, newsgroup, and unrated sites, in addition to the most commonly blocked categories. This is usually ideal for children under 10 years of age.

✦ **Default:** Provides protection against commonly chosen categories, such as adult and illegal content and social networking sites, but allows unrated sites. This is usually sufficient protection for children 10 to 13 years of age.

✦ **Moderate:** Protects your children from adult content, security threats, and illegal activity. This is ideal for children from 14 to 18 years old.

✦ **Minimal:** Recommended for children over 18 years of age because it blocks only pornography and security threats.

✦ **Monitor:** Doesn't block any content, but logs Internet activity. This can be useful to let you check out what Web sites your children are visiting before you start filtering content.

✦ **Custom:** Lets you pick exactly what type of content you want to block or filter. As Figure 3-17 shows, you can pick from a variety of categories.

Time Restrictions: Internet access schedule

Here you can specify exactly when the Internet can or can't be used. This is very helpful when you want to limit the amount of time and when your children use the Internet. Being able to specify usage for half-hour blocks throughout the entire week lets you merge Internet usage into any schedules you already have set up for your children.

Simply click a single block of time, or select multiple blocks using your cursor, and click whether you want to allow or block access during that time.

Figure 3-18 shows an example of allowing Internet access only on weekend mornings and weeknights between 7 and 8 p.m.

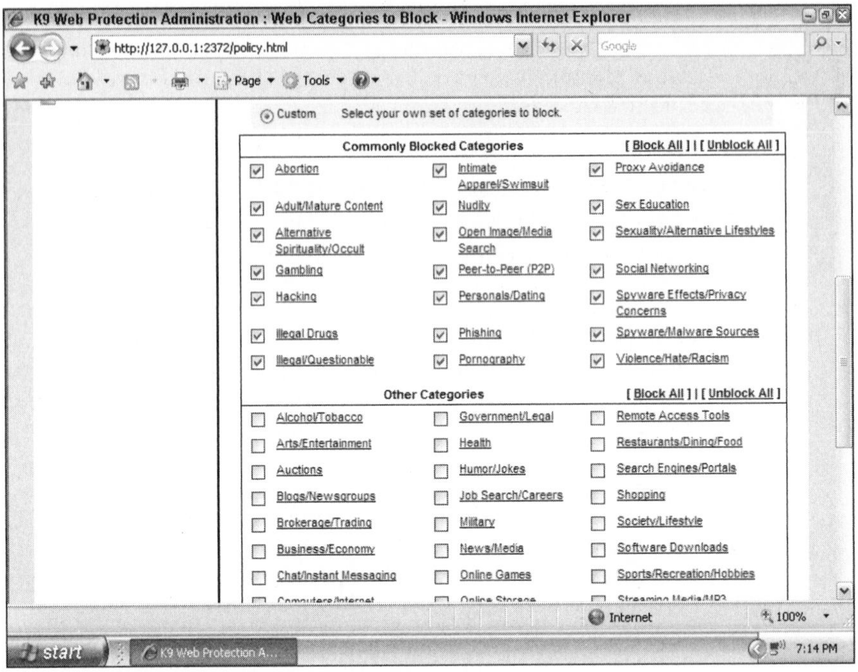

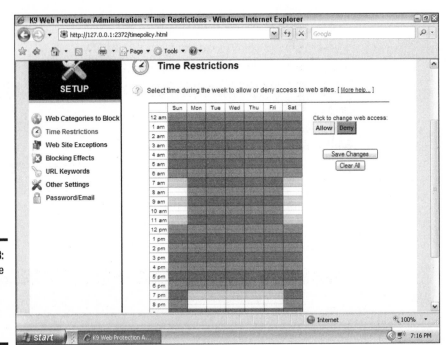

Figure 3-17:
Content
categories
you can
choose to
customize
your own
protection
level.

Figure 3-18:
An example
of an
Internet
access
schedule.

If you are going to block access much more than allow it, like the example shown in Figure 3-18, you may want to just start off by blocking all times and then go through and specify periods of time to allow access. This saves you a little bit of time.

Web Site Exceptions: Allow or block specific sites

On this page (see Figure 3-19), you can specify Web sites that you want to block and allow, regardless of the filtering.

This is great if you have a problem with a site your children visit that the filter lets through. Simply enter the Web site address into the Sites to Always Block section and click Add. On the other hand, you can specify sites you always want to allow, which comes in handy when your children stumble upon a site that's blocked, but that you approve of.

Blocking Effects: Setting what happens when blocked

From this page, you can specify what happens when a page is blocked, such as playing an audible alert that can help you keep track of anyone trying to view restricted Web sites.

Figure 3-19: Overriding the filter's decisions by adding sites to explicitly allow or block.

Book III Chapter 3

Protecting Youngsters

URL Keywords: Blocking problem words

The URL Keywords page, as Figure 3-20 shows, allows you to block access to Web pages based on keywords in the Web page URL. You can, for example, block any Web page that has the word "sex" in the URL.

Other settings

The Web Search Options Page lets you specify whether to enforce the use of Google SafeSearch, which diminishes the amount of adult material that might be returned as a result of a Google Internet search, when using the Google search engine.

Password/E-mail

This page allows you to change your administration password.

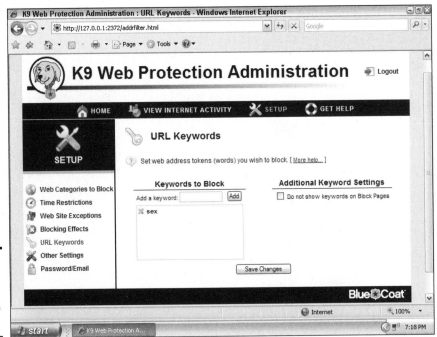

Figure 3-20: Specifying URL keywords to block.

Viewing your children's Internet activity

When you want to check on the Web sites that your children have been visiting, or trying to visit, go to the View Internet Activity section. This is accessible from the main page of K9 Web Protection Administration.

When you log in, you see a page similar to the example shown in Figure 3-21. You can page between the two sections (Internet Activity Summary and View Activity Detail) using the menu on the left.

View Activity Summary

The View Activity Summary section provides you with an overall view of the logged Internet activity, including

✦ **Category Summary:** Lists all content categories K9 Web Protection uses, with allowed categories shown in green and those you've restricted in red; orange is used for those that have changed statuses during the reporting period. Next to each category is the number of Web site requests for the given type of Web site.

You can click the categories to see the Web site requests in that category, as Figure 3-22 shows.

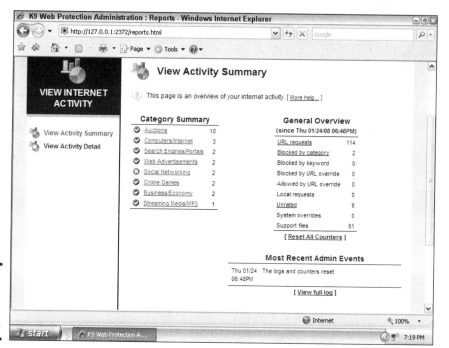

Figure 3-21:
Viewing the
Internet
activity logs.

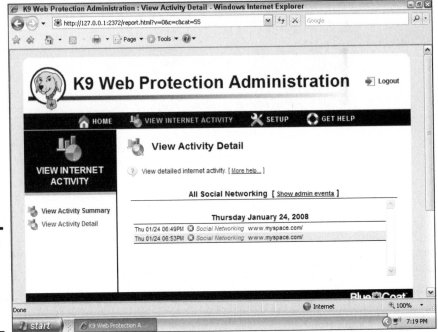

Figure 3-22:
Viewing a
detailed
report for a
specific
category.

+ **General Overview:** Gives you a breakdown of the Internet activity based upon the types of Web site requests and their results. Clicking on an entry shows its detailed view, as Figure 3-23 shows.

+ **Most Recent Admin Events:** Shows you the most recent setting changes and failed login attempts, so you can find out whether anyone else is making changes, or trying to do so.

So you can better track the Internet activity, you may want to periodically reset the logs of the Internet activity. Simply click the Reset All Counters link below the General Overview section.

View Activity Detail

Accessible from the menu on the left, this section shows a detailed view of all the Internet activity. It shows an uncategorized list of all the requests made to the Internet. Figure 3-23, shown previously, presents an example of this page.

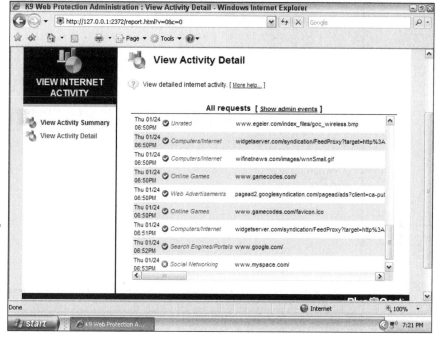

Figure 3-23:
Viewing a detailed report for general activity logs.

Book IV

Connecting and Sharing

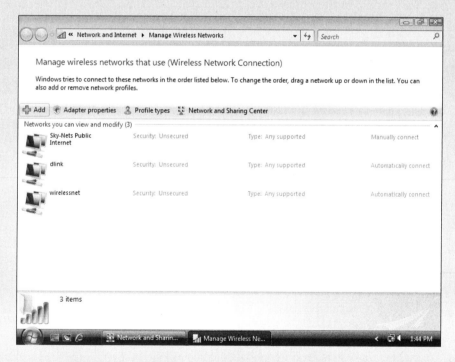

If you use Windows Vista, you'll get to know the Network and Sharing Center very well! This part covers sharing with other operating systems as well.

Contents at a Glance

Chapter 1: Dealing with Your Network Connections

In This Chapter

✔ Turning your network adapters on and off

✔ Connecting wirelessly to Wi-Fi networks

✔ Managing your wireless network connections

✔ Checking the status of your network connections

✔ Dealing with your adapter's IP address

*A*fter you've set up your home network, you need to connect! Wired connections require just connecting the cables; however, connecting to wireless networks requires a few clicks of the mouse. Also, both types of connections have a variety of tasks that you might need to know how to perform, such as checking whether you're connected and changing network settings and preferences.

In this chapter, you see how to turn your network adapters on and off, connect to and manage wireless networks, check the status of your connections, and change your network adapter's IP address.

Using Network Icons to Gain Quick Access to Network Settings and Options

Windows 2000, XP, and Vista feature icons for your network adapters in the system tray (notification area), which is at the lower-right corner of Windows. Windows 2000 and XP have icons for each network adapter that's enabled (see Figure 1-1), whereas Windows Vista has a single icon (see Figure 1-2) for all your network adapters. These icons let you access the networking utilities and shortcuts of common tasks. You'll probably find these icons quite helpful to your networking experience.

Figure 1-1:
Network
adapter
icons in
Windows
XP.

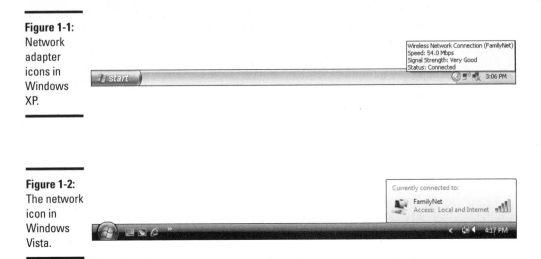

Figure 1-2:
The network
icon in
Windows
Vista.

You can't disable the network icon in Windows Vista, but you can do so in Windows 2000 and XP. If you can't find the icons for your adapters in Windows 2000 or XP, the icon might not be set to appear — or the adapter might just be disabled.

Here's how you can enable or disable the icon in Windows XP for a particular network adapter:

1. **Choose Start⇨Connect To⇨Show All Connections.**

If using the Classic Start menu, click Start, click Settings, right-click Network Connections, and click Open; and then skip to Step 2.

2. **In the Network Connections window that opens, right-click the desired network adapter and select Properties.**

3. **In the Network Connection Properties window, select or deselect the Show Icon in Notification Area When Connected option, which is near the bottom of the window.**

If you are using Windows 2000, here's how you can enable or disable your network adapter icons:

1. **Click the Start button.**

2. **Click Settings.**

3. **Click Network and Dial-up Connections.**

4. **In the Network and Dial-up Connections window, right-click the desired network adapter and select Properties.**

5. **In the Network Connection Properties window, select or deselect the Show icon in taskbar when connected option, which is near the bottom of the window.**

Mac OS X Tiger and Leopard also feature an icon on the menu bar for your AirPort wireless adapter, if you have one. This icon is set by default to appear on the menu bar, but it can be hidden. If you can't find the AirPort icon, here's how you can make it appear:

1. **Click the Apple icon on the menu bar.**

2. **Click System Preferences.**

3. **In the System Preferences window, click the Network icon.**

4. **Choose the AirPort adapter in Leopard by choosing the adapter from the list on the left and in Tiger by selecting the adapter from the Show list on the top of the window.**

5. **Select or deselect the Show AirPort Status in Menu Bar option.**

What do you know — the Linux distribution, Ubuntu, also features a network icon, as Figure 1-3 shows. It's enabled by default and can't be hidden.

Network icon

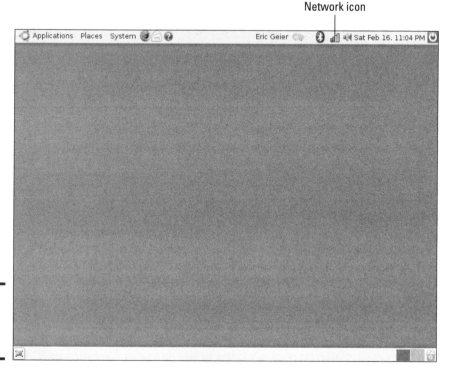

Figure 1-3:
Network
icon in
Ubuntu.

**Book IV
Chapter 1**

Dealing with
Your Network
Connections

Flipping the Switch on Adapters

You can turn your network adapters on and off. You might ask, "Why would I want to?" Well, you might want to turn your network adapters off on your laptop when not using the Internet or network to help save battery life. On either a laptop or desktop computer, you may want to turn off a wired or wireless adapter if you don't ever use it. Turning your adapters off and on can also help if you're having problems with a connection. The following sections show you exactly how to enable and disable your network adapters.

Enabling/disabling an adapter in Windows 2000

If you're using Windows 2000, here's how you can flip the switch on your network adapters:

1. **Click the Start button.**

2. **Click Settings.**

3. **Click Network and Dial-up Connections.**

4. **In the Network and Dial-up Connections window, right-click the desired network adapter and select Disable or Enable.**

Enabling/disabling an adapter in Windows XP

In Windows XP, the quickest way to turn a network adapter off (called *disabling* it) is by the adapter icon in the system tray. Simply right-click the icon and select Disable.

You can also enable or disable a network adapter using Network Connections, as follows:

1. **Choose Start⇨Connect To⇨Show All Connections.**

If using the Classic Start menu, click Start, click Settings, right-click Network Connections, and click Open; and then skip to step 2.

The Network Connections windows should appear. You should see an icon for each of your network adapters that tells you its status (Disabled, Connected, or Not Connected).

2. **In the Network Connection Properties window, right-click the desired network adapter and select Disable or Enable.**

Enabling/disabling an adapter in Windows Vista

In contrast to Windows XP, you can't turn a network adapter off (called disabling it) using the icon in the system tray. Microsoft decided to make it a bit harder: You have to go through the new Network and Sharing Center.

Here's how you can enable or disable a network adapter in Windows Vista:

1. **Click the network icon in the system tray.**

2. **Click Network and Sharing Center.**

3. **Under Tasks in the left pane, click Manage Network Connections.**

4. **In the Manage Network Connections window, right-click your desired adapter icon and select Disable or Enable.**

If User Account Control (UAC) is active, click Continue on the prompt.

Enabling/disabling an adapter in Mac OS X Tiger and Leopard

Turning the AirPort wireless adapter on and off takes two quick clicks of the mouse. Simply click the AirPort icon on your menu bar and click Turn AirPort Off or Turn AirPort On.

Turning a wired (Ethernet) adapter on or off takes a few more clicks:

1. **Click the Apple icon on the menu bar.**

2. **Click System Preferences.**

3. **In the System Preferences window, click the Network icon.**

4. **In Leopard, choose the Ethernet adapter from the list on the left. In Tiger, select the Ethernet adapter from the Show drop-down menu list on the top of the window.**

5. **Select the desired option (Off or choose an IP address method if you want the adapter on, for instance, Using DHCP) from the Configure drop-down menu.**

Using Ubuntu

In Ubuntu, you can easily disable your networking adapters by right-clicking the network icon on the toolbar. When the drop-down menu appears, simply select or deselect the Enable Networking or Enable Wireless options to turn your adapters on or off.

Connecting to Wireless Networks

When connecting to wireless networks, you generally bring up the list of available wireless networks and choose one to connect to. It is as simple as that! But the following sections show you step-by-step how to do it.

Book IV
Chapter 1

Dealing with Your Network Connections

If you don't see your wireless network, you may have the network name (SSID) broadcasting disabled for security reasons. Some vendors of wireless adapters may call this your network's "visibility." If this is the case, you need to manually connect to the network. For help with doing so, see the "Managing Your Wireless Network Connection Preferences" section, later in this chapter.

Connecting by using your manufacturer's utility

Most wireless adapters come with a configuration utility to manage your wireless connections. Here, I refer to this application as your manufacturer's utility. Unless you specify otherwise, this is usually set as your default utility, rather than Windows XP's or Vista's built-in utilities. If you are using Windows 2000, though, the manufacturer's utility is the only wireless configuration utility available. But in Windows XP and Vista, you can revert to using the Windows built-in utilities by referring to the next section, "Switching between the Manufacturer's and Windows Utility." In Mac OS X, you use the built-in AirPort utility to manage your wireless connections.

If your manufacturer's utility is the active wireless utility, you can usually open it using the following methods:

✦ **System tray icon:** You can access your manufacturer's utility from its icon in the system tray (or notification area) in the bottom-right corner of Windows. You can usually double-click or right-click the icon to bring up the utility.

✦ **Start menu:** You can also open your manufacturer's utility through its entry on the Start menu. Simply click Start, search for the manufacturer's name under the programs, and click the icon for the utility.

✦ **Desktop icon:** If your manufacturer's utility installed a desktop icon, you can double-click it to open the utility.

After you bring up your manufacturer's utility, follow these steps to connect to a wireless network:

1. **Select your desired wireless network.**

The networks are identified by the network name (SSID), and possibly include signal strength, security, and channel status. Figure 1-4 shows an example.

You should find yours listed with the network (SSID) that you set for your wireless router. If you haven't changed the default network name, you can refer to your wireless router's documentation for the default value if you don't know it. But most likely, the strongest network is yours.

2. **Click Connect.**

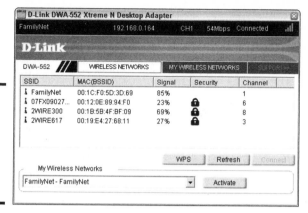

Figure 1-4:
The manu-
facturer's
utility of a
D-Link
wireless
adapter.

3. **Enter the encryption key, if prompted.**

If the network is encrypted with WEP or WPA, you have to enter the key.
If it's your network, you created a key when you set up your wireless
router. Enter the key and click Connect.

That's it — you should be connected now!

Switching between the Manufacturer's and Windows Utility

When you install the software and drivers for your wireless adapter, you usually install a program to manage your wireless connections — which is your
manufacturer's configuration utility. When it is installed, the wireless utilities
of Windows XP or Vista are usually automatically disabled. But you can
revert back to using the built-in utilities of Windows — and vice versa.

In Windows XP, you can manually switch between your manufacturer's utility
and Windows by following these steps:

1. **Double-click your adapter's icon in the system tray.**

If you don't see the icon, refer to the "Using Network Icons to Gain Quick
Access to Network Settings and Options" section earlier in this chapter.

2. **On the Network Connection Status window, click the Properties
button.**

3. **On the Network Connection Properties window, click the Wireless
Networks tab.**

4. **On the Wireless Networks tab, select or deselect the Use Windows to
configure my wireless network settings option.**

**Book IV
Chapter 1**

Dealing with
Your Network
Connections

Connecting to wireless networks using Windows XP

The first thing to do in Windows XP in order to connect to wireless networks is to bring up your available wireless network list. You have many ways you can do this; following are two:

✦ **System tray icon:** The simplest way to view the wireless networks available in your area is by right-clicking the wireless adapter's icon in the system tray, and selecting View Available Wireless Networks.

If you don't see the icon, refer to the "Using Network Icons to Gain Quick Access to Network Settings and Options" section, earlier in this chapter.

✦ **Start menu:** You can also get to the window to view networks from the Start menu. To do so, click Start and then click Connect To (or, if using the Classic Start menu, click Settings and then click Network Connections). Then, right-click the wireless adapter and select View Available Wireless Networks.

When you're viewing the available wireless networks, you can easily connect, as follows:

1. **Select your desired wireless network.**

   As Figure 1-5 shows, the networks are identified by the network name (SSID). Plus for each network the signal strength is shown along with its encryption status.

   You should find yours listed with the network (SSID) that you set for your wireless router. If you haven't changed the default network name, you can refer to your wireless router's documentation for the default value if you don't know it. But most likely the strongest network is yours.

2. **Click Connect.**

3. **Enter the encryption key, if prompted.**

   If the network is encrypted with WEP or WPA, you have to enter the key. If it's your network, you created a key when you set up your wireless router. Enter the key and click Connect.

4. **Click Connect Anyway, if prompted.**

   This dialog box comes up if the network you're trying to connect to isn't encrypted with WEP or WPA.

If you're having problems connecting, see Book V, Chapter 1.

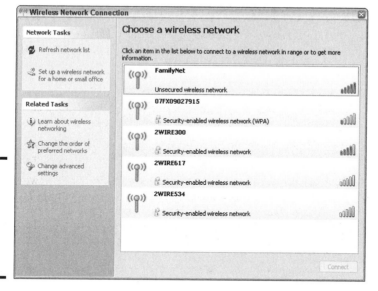

Figure 1-5:
Available
wireless
networks
window in
Windows
XP.

Connecting to wireless networks using Windows Vista

To connect to your network when using Windows Vista, you should first bring up the window that shows the wireless networks available in your area. You can do that in either of the following ways:

✦ **System tray icon:** The easiest way to view the wireless networks available in your area is by clicking the network icon in the system tray and selecting Connect to a Network.

✦ **Start menu:** You can also get to the window to view your available networks from the Start menu by clicking Start and then Connect To.

When you're viewing the available wireless networks, you can easily connect to them as follows:

1. **Select your desired wireless network.**

As Figure 1-6 shows, the networks are identified by the network name (SSID). The signal strength for each network is shown along with its encryption status.

You should find yours listed with the network (SSID) that you set for your wireless router. If you haven't changed the default network name, you can refer to your wireless router's documentation for the default value if you don't know it. But most likely, the strongest network is yours.

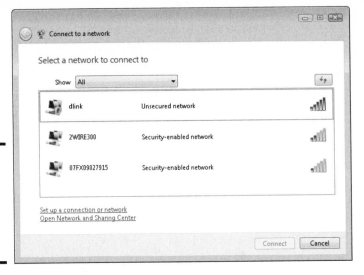

Figure 1-6:
Available
wireless
networks
window in
Windows
Vista.

2. **Click Connect.**

3. **Enter the encryption key, if prompted.**

If the network is encrypted with WEP or WPA, you have to enter the key.
If it's your network, you created a key when you set up your wireless
router. Enter the key and click Connect.

4. **Click Connect Anyway, if prompted.**

If you're prompted that you are connecting to an unsecured network,
click Connect Anyway.

5. **Classify the network type or location.**

The first time that you connect to a network, you must classify its type:
Home, Work, or Public. Figure 1-7 shows you the prompt you receive.

Classifying your network helps to prevent unauthorized access of your
documents when you're on public hotspots and other untrustworthy
networks. However, when you want to share your resources, you should
classify your network as a Home network.

Connecting to wireless networks using Mac OS X Tiger and Leopard

Apple has made it incredibly easy to connect to wireless networks with Mac
OS X Tiger and Leopard. You just have to click the AirPort icon on the menu
bar to view the wireless networks that are available and select one. In Leopard,
encrypted wireless networks have a padlock icon next to their names,
whereas unsecured networks have no icon.

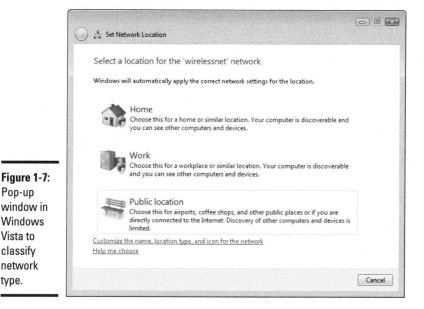

Figure 1-7:
Pop-up
window in
Windows
Vista to
classify
network
type.

When connecting to an encrypted network (such as with WEP or WPA), you're prompted to enter the password or key. If it's your network, you created a key when you set up your wireless router. If you want the network and encryption keys saved so that Mac OS X automatically connects to the network, select the Remember this Network option in Leopard or the Remember Password in My Keychain option in Tiger.

Connecting to wireless networks using Ubuntu

Connecting to a network in Ubuntu requires just two clicks. Simply click the network icon on Ubuntu's toolbar. Then select the network you want to connect to. When connecting to a secured wireless network, you're prompted to enter the encryption key.

Managing Your Wireless Network Connection Preferences

No matter what operating system (Windows XP or Vista or Mac OS X) or manufacturer's configuration utility you're using to manage your wireless adapter and connections, all use some type of preferred network scheme. The purpose of this scheme is primarily to define what wireless networks you are automatically connected to.

Looking through your wireless network preferences and preferred list is rec-ommended if you carry a laptop and use it on multiple wireless networks, you (or someone else) connect to your neighbors' wireless networks, or you try to connect to a network with broadcasting disabled.

The following gives you an idea of how most network configuration utilities work:

✦ When you connect to a wireless network from the list of available networks in Windows XP, that network is automatically added to your preferred list.

✦ You are automatically connected to wireless networks based upon the order of your preferred network list.

✦ When a wireless network is on the preferred list, any encryption keys previously entered (when adding a network manually to the list or when connecting from your list of available networks) are saved.

Accessing network preferences in Windows XP

Here's how to access your wireless network preferences in Windows XP:

1. **Double-click your adapter's icon in the system tray.**

If you don't see the icon, refer to the "Using Network Icons to Gain Quick Access to Network Settings and Options" section earlier in this chapter.

2. **On the Network Connection Status window, click the Properties button.**

3. **On the Network Connection Properties window, click the Wireless Networks tab.**

You should now see the list of your preferred networks. Figure 1-8 shows an example.

You can also access this same spot when viewing your available wireless networks by clicking the Change the Order of Preferred Networks link that appears under the Related Tasks on the left pane.

At this point, you have several things you can do, as the following sections describe.

Add a network to your preferred list

1. **On the Wireless Networks tab of the Network Connection Properties window, click the Add button.**

The Wireless Network Properties dialog box appears.

Figure 1-8:
Wireless
network
preferences.

2. **In the Wireless Network Properties dialog box, enter the network you want to add into the Network Name (SSID) field.**

   If adding your network, this is the name you used for your wireless router.

3. **Specify encryption settings. If the network is not encrypted, set Network Authentication to Open and Data Encryption to Disabled.**

   If the network is encrypted using WEP, set Network Authentication to Open and Data Encryption to WEP, and make sure that the The Key Is Provided for Me Automatically option is not selected. Then type the encryption key into the two Network Key fields.

   If the network is encrypted using WPA, set Network Authentication to WPA or WPA2 (depending on which version the network is using) and Data Encryption to TKIP or AES, and make sure that the The Key Is Provided for Me Automatically option is not selected. Then type the encryption key into the two Network Key fields.

4. **Click the Authentication tab to specify the authentication settings**. You can deselect the Enable IEEE 802.1*x* Authentication for This Network option since 802.1*x* is used on encrypted corporate networks. You don't have to worry about, or change, the other settings.

5. **Click the Connection tab, and select the Connect When This Network is in Range option if you want Windows to automatically connect to the wireless network when it is available.**

6. **Click OK.**

   Now the network is on your preferred list.

If you don't see the WPA encryption option it may be because your wireless adapter doesn't support this newer encryption method or Windows XP is not up-to-date.

Change the order of preferred networks

On the Wireless Networks tab of the Network Connection Properties window, you can select a network from your preferred network list and click the Move up and Move down arrows. Windows XP will try to automatically connect your preferred wireless networks, starting with the first network and going down the list, connecting to the first available network. Of course, whether Windows automatically connects depends upon the Connection settings you specified for each network, but by default it's set to automatically connect.

Remove a network from your preferred list

On the Wireless Networks tab of the Network Connection Properties window, simply select a network and click Remove. Now Windows won't automatically connect to the network, and any saved encryption keys are deleted.

If you just want to prevent Windows from automatically onnecting to a certain network on your preferred list, you can choose the network from the Preferred Networks list, click the Properties button, click the Connection tab, deselect the Connect When This Network is in Range option, and click OK, rather than remove it from the list.

View and edit a preferred network's properties

To view and edit properties, on the Wireless Networks tab of the Network Connection Properties window, you select a preferred network and click the Properties button. You can then change encryption, authentication, and connection settings.

For help, refer to Steps 3 through 6 in the earlier "Add a network to your preferred" section.

Change your preferred network's advanced settings

On the Wireless Networks tab of the Network Connection Properties window, you can click the Advanced button to set the types of networks you want to connect to and if you want to automatically connect to networks not on your Preferred Network list.

It's best to leave the Networks to Access setting as the default, which is Any Available Network. Also, you should leave the Automatically Connect To Non-Preferred Networks option unselected so that Windows doesn't automatically connect to any wireless network it picks up.

Accessing network preferences in Windows Vista

Here's how to access your wireless network preferences in Windows Vista:

1. **Click the network icon in the system tray.**

2. **Click Network and Sharing Center.**

3. **Under Tasks in the left pane, click Manage Wireless Networks.**

   You should now see the list of your preferred networks, as shown in Figure 1-9.

At this point, you have several things you can do, as described in the following sections.

Add a network to your preferred list

To add a network to your preferred list in Windows Vista, follow these steps:

1. **On the Manage Wireless Networks window, click the Add button.**

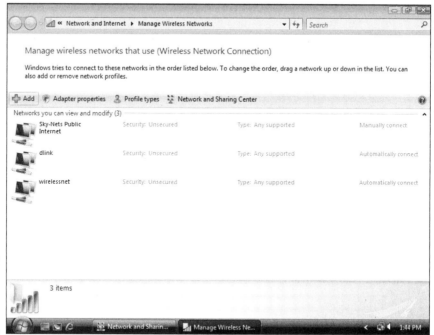

Figure 1-9:
Wireless network preferences.

**Book IV
Chapter 1**

**Dealing with
Your Network
Connections**

2. **On the How Do You Want to Add a Network page of the window that opens, select the first option, Add a Network That Is in Range of This Computer if the wireless network is nearby, or select the second option, Manually Create a Network Profile, if you aren't near the wireless network you're trying to add to the preferred list, in which case you can manually add the network.**

   If you selected the first option, you'll be taken to the Select a Network To Connect To window, just as if you had right-clicked the network icon in the system tray and selected Connect to a Network.

   If you selected the second option, the Enter Information for the Wireless Network You Want to Add window appears.

3. **If you selected the first option in Step 2, choose the network you want to connect to and add to your preferred network list from the list of detected networks, and click the Connect button.**

   If the network is encrypted, you'll see the Type the Network Security Key or Passphrase window, where you must enter the WEP or WPA key/passphrase and click the Connect button. (If it's your network, you created a key when you set up your wireless router.) When you're successfully connected to the network, select the Save This Network option (and the Start this Connection Automatically option if you want Windows to connect to the network whenever you're in range) and click the Close button.

   The network is added to your preferred list, on which you can edit its priority and other preferences. Since you're done, you can skip the rest of the steps, which cover manually adding the network.

4. **If you selected the second option in Step 2, enter the network name (SSID) you want to connect to in the Network Name field.**

   If adding your network, this is the name you used for your wireless router.

5. **Specify the encryption settings.**

   If the network is not encrypted, select No Authentication (Open) from the Security Type drop-down menu list, and skip to the next step. If the network is encrypted, select an encryption method from the Security Type drop-down menu list, and then type in the encryption key/passphrase into the Security Key/Passphrase text field.

   WPA-Personal and WPA2-Personal is the same as WPA-PSK and WPA2-PSK. If you don't see the WPA encryption option, this may mean that your wireless adapter doesn't support this newer encryption method.

6. **Select the Start this Connection Automatically option if you want Windows to connect to the network whenever you're in range.**

7. **If you are adding a nonbroadcasted or hidden wireless network, select the Connect Even if the Network Is Not Broadcasting option.**

   Turning broadcasting off can help secure your wireless network, as discussed in Book III, Chapter 2. By default, wireless routers always come with broadcasting on.

8. **Click Next.**

   Now the network is on your preferred list.

9. **On the Successfully Added window, click Connect To to connect to the newly added network (or another network), click Change Connection Settings to access the connection settings of the newly added network, or close the window by clicking the Close button.**

Change the order of preferred networks

You can select a network from your preferred network list and click the Move up/down buttons.

Windows Vista tries to automatically connect to your preferred wireless networks, starting with the first network and going down the list, connecting to the first available network. Of course, what Vista tries to connect to depends upon the Connection settings you specified for each network.

Remove a network from your preferred list

To remove a network, simply select a network and click Remove. Now Windows won't automatically connect to the network, and any saved encryption keys are deleted.

If you want to prevent Windows from automatically connecting to a certain network on your preferred list, you can edit its connection setting to not automatically connect, rather than remove it from the list.

View and edit a preferred network's properties

To edit a network's properties, right-click a preferred network and select Properties. Then you can change connection and encryption settings.

Accessing network preferences in Mac OS X Tiger

Here's how to access your wireless network preferences in Mac OS X Tiger:

1. **Click the Apple icon on the menu bar.**

2. **Click System Preferences.**

3. **In the System Preferences window, click the Network icon.**

4. **On the top of the Network window, click AirPort on the Show drop-down list.**

   Figure 1-10 shows the AirPort page of the Network window.

5. **Choose the connectivity scheme you prefer from the By Default, Join drop-down list. Select Automatic if you want Mac OS X to remember all the networks you connect to and try to connect to these automatically.**

   (You're notified when a new network is available and given the choice to connect.) Otherwise, select the Preferred Networks option, which lets you add wireless networks to a list on which you can prioritize them in the order you want Mac OS X to connect.

6. **Click the Options button.**

7. **On the pop-up window that appears, choose what Mac OS X should do if no recent or preferred networks are available by selecting an action from the If No Preferred Networks Are Found drop-down list.**

   Selecting Ask Before Joining an Open Network or Keep Looking for Recent Networks is usually a safe choice. For security reasons, I don't recommend automatically joining open networks.

Figure 1-10:
AirPort
wireless
adapter
settings
window in
Mac OS X
Tiger.

8. **Specify what actions you want Mac OS X to require an administrator's password for by selecting or deselecting the checkboxes under the Require Administrator Password To label.**

   Requiring administer passwords is good if you have children who use the computer.

9. **(Optional) Select the Automatically Add New Network to the Preferred Networks List option.**

   If you often connect to other people's networks, you may want to leave this feature off.

10. **(Optional) Select the Disconnect from Wireless Network When I Log Out option.**

    If you often switch between Mac OS X accounts on your computer, you may want to leave this feature off so that you or other users don't have to reconnect to a wireless network that the computer is connected to when logging off to switch accounts.

11. **Select the Enable Interference Robustness option if you suspect that your wireless connection is being interfered with by other wireless networks or radio products (and you use Apple's AirPort Express or Airport Extreme adapter).**

Accessing network preferences in Mac OS X Leopard

Here's how to access your wireless network preferences in Mac OS X Leopard:

1. **Click the AirPort icon on your menu bar.**

   If you don't see the icon, it's probably hidden. You can enable the icon by referring to the "Using Network Icons to Gain Quick Access to Network Settings and Options" section, earlier in this chapter.

2. **On the icon's drop-down list, click Open Network Preferences.**

3. **On the Network window that appears, click AirPort from the list on the left.**

   From this window, you can see the first option involving your wireless connection preferences.

4. **Click the Advanced button.**

   You can view and edit your preferred network list and connectivity settings, which the next set of bullets discusses.

When you're at the AirPort tab in the Network window, you can

+ **Add a network to Your preferred list:** Click the plus sign to add a network to your preferred list. A window pops up in which you input the network name (SSID) you want to connect to into the Network Name field, and select the encryption type from the Security drop-down list and type the encryption key/passphrase. When you're done, click Add to make the addition and return to the AirPort tab of the Network window.

+ **Change the order of preferred networks:** You can simply click and drag your preferred networks into your desired order.

  Mac OS X tries to automatically connect your preferred wireless networks, starting with the first network and going down the list, connecting to the first available network. This also depends on the connection settings you specified for each network.

+ **Remove a network from your preferred list:** Simply select a network and click the minus button. Now Mac OS X won't automatically connect to the network, and any saved encryption keys are deleted.

+ **View and edit a preferred network's properties:** You can select a network from the Preferred Networks list and click the edit (pencil) button. A window pops up, in which you can change the network name (SSID) and security settings.

Accessing network preferences in Ubuntu

Ubuntu doesn't come with an active wireless network management tool that lets you prioritize the network and so forth as you can in Windows and Mac OS X. However, you can install and use a package called WiFi Radar that serves as a network management tool. This package is already included with Ubuntu but has to be installed, and here's how to install it:

1. **On the Ubuntu toolbar, choose System⇨Administration⇨Synaptic Package Manager.**

2. **In the prompt that appears, enter your account password and click OK.**

3. **In the Synaptic Package Manager window, choose Settings⇨Repositories.**

4. **In the Software Sources window that appears, select the Canonical-Supported Open Source Software (Main) option and then click the Close button.**

5. **If prompted with the Repositories Changed dialog box, click the Close button.**

6. **In the Synaptic Package Manager window, click the Reload button.**

7. **Click the Search button, type** wifi-radar **into the Search field, and click Search.**

   The program should search and make an entry for the WiFi Radar package that appears in the list box on the Synaptic Package Manager window.

8. **Right-click :wifi-radar and select Mark for Installation from the menu that appears.**

9. **Click the Apply button, review changes, and click Apply.**

10. **Close Synaptic Package Manager.**

After you have installed WiFi Radar, you can run the following commands from the Terminal, accessible by choosing Applications⇨Accessories:

✦ **Scan and connect to any available profile:** sudo wifi-radar -d

✦ **Bring up WiFi Radar to manage profiles:** sudo wifi-radar

You probably will need to access WiFi Radar from time to time when using the computer. You can access the tool from the Ubuntu toolbar by clicking Applications⇨Internet⇨WiFi Radar.

Checking Network Connection Status

Sometimes you may want to check your network connection status. Maybe the Internet doesn't work and you want to check to see whether you're connecting to the network, or you're using your laptop and keep getting disconnected from the wireless network. Whatever the reason, you can easily check your computer's network status.

Checking connection status in Windows 2000

If the network adapter's icon is in your system tray (taskbar) of Windows 2000, you can simply hover the mouse cursor over it to see the speed (data rate) and activity. You can also double-click the network adapter icon to bring up the Connection Status window.

If you don't see your network adapter's icon, refer to the "Using Network Icons to Gain Quick Access to Network Settings and Options" section, earlier in this chapter.

Double-clicking the network icon, however, offers only one more piece of information: the duration of the connection. To view the IP and Physical Address (MAC) information of your connection in Windows 2000, you have to bring up the Command Prompt (in DOS). To bring up the Command Prompt, follow these steps:

1. **Click the Start button.**

2. **Choose Programs⇨Accessories.**

3. **Click Command Prompt.**

4. **Enter** ipconfig /all **and press Enter.**

You see the overall network status plus the status information for each network adapter.

Checking connection status in Windows XP

You can get a quick idea of your network status by glancing at the icon or icons in the system tray. Network icons have a red *X* through them when you aren't connected, for either a wired (Ethernet) or wireless adapter.

If you don't see the icon for your network connections, refer to the "Using Network Icons to Gain Quick Access to Network Settings and Options" section, earlier in this chapter.

If you are connected and there is activity on the network from your computer, you see some kind of animation; for example, for wireless icons, the three small radio waves light up in green once in a while. You also can hover the mouse cursor over the icon to get a quick idea of the status. If you want more information on the status, just double-click the network icon and the Network Connection Status window appears if you're currently connected to a network.

On the Network Connection Status window, for either a wired or wireless connection, you should see the status (whether connected), duration of your connection to the network, speed (that is, data rate) of your connection, and an activity section showing the amount of data packets that your computer has sent and received.

On the Network Connection Status window, for wireless connections, you also see the network name (SSID) and signal strength of your connection.

On the Network Connection Status window, for either a wired or wireless connection, you can click the Support tab to view IP address information. This is a common place to visit when troubleshooting network issues.

The following bullets describe the items on the Support tab (of the Network Connection Status window):

✦ **Address Type:** Specifies how your IP address came into existence, which can include the following:

- **Assigned by DHCP:** The address was given to your computer from the network (router).

- **Manually Configured:** This means that you assigned a specific IP address to your computer, which is usually not necessary unless you disabled your DHCP server on your router (as some people do as a security measure).

- **Automatic Private Address:** This indicates that you haven't manually assigned an address and your computer can't get one from the network. This is common when connecting with a computer-to-computer (ad hoc network); however, if you're connecting to a regular wireless network, seeing this appear for your Address Type means that you have a problem.

✦ **IP Address:** This is your computer's unique IP address on the network, which can be described as your "ID number" for sending and receiving Internet and network traffic.

✦ **Subnet Mask:** This is a number that identifies the subnet of the network. You shouldn't have to worry about doing anything with this number. (It should probably be 255.255.255.0.)

✦ **Default Gateway:** The IP address of your router.

✦ **Details button:** Clicking this button brings up a small window with a few more pieces of information, including your network adapter's Physical Address (MAC), which can be useful if you set up the MAC address filtering on your router for security purposes.

✦ **Repair button:** If you're having problems with your network connection (getting an automatic private address), you can click this button to try to fix it. Windows will try a few things, including disabling and reenabling the network adapter and requesting another IP address for your computer.

Checking connection status in Windows Vista

The quickest way to get an idea of your network status is by clicking (or hovering the mouse cursor over) the network icon. This brings up a list of all your active network connections. The network name (SSID) and signal strength are shown for your wireless connections.

If you want more information you can click the icon and then click the Network and Sharing Center link. The Network and Sharing Center shows you just about the same information at first glance. To see more in-depth information, click the View Status link for any of the network connections listed in the Network and Sharing Center. Doing so brings up the connection status windows, such as Figure 1-11 shows.

On the Network Connection Status window, for either a wired or wireless connection, you should see the duration of your connection to the network, speed (data rate) of your connection, and an activity section showing the amount of data packets that your computer has sent and received.

On the Network Connection Status window, for wireless connections, you also see the network name (SSID) and signal strength of your connection.

On the Network Connection Status window, for either a wired or wireless connection, you can click the Details button to view detailed IP address information for the connection, which is a common place to visit when troubleshooting network issues.

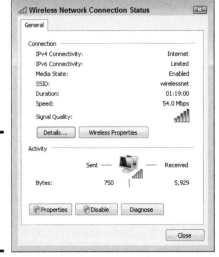

Figure 1-11:
Network
connection
status
window for
a wireless
connection.

Checking connection status in Mac OS X Tiger

Here's how you can view the status of your network adapters and connections in Mac OS X Tiger:

1. **Click the Apple icon on the menu bar.**

2. **Click System Preferences.**

3. In the System Preferences window, click the Network icon.

You should see whether you're connected to a network by looking at the status lights.

4. On the Network window, click the Ethernet adapter from the Show drop-down list to view its status.

On the TCP/IP tab that appears you can see the IP address information of the current wired connection. Also, you can find the Ethernet ID (your adapter's Physical Address (MAC) on the Ethernet tab, which you may need to know for future reference.

5. On the Network window, click AirPort from the Show list to view your wireless connection status.

On the AirPort tab that appears you see the preferred network settings, along with your AirPort ID (your adapter's Physical Address (MAC). To check the IP address information for the wireless connection, click the TCP/IP tab (see Figure 1-12).

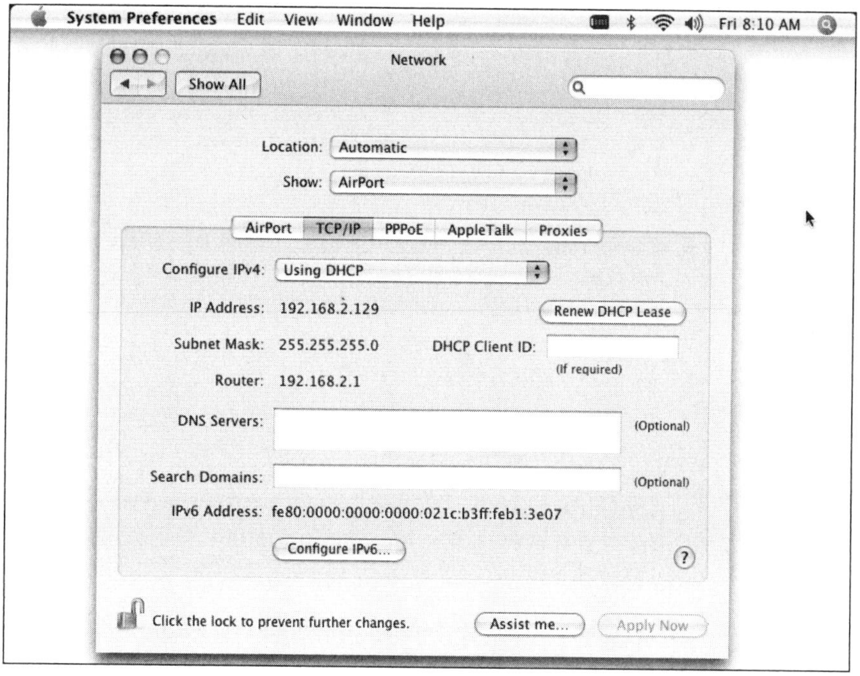

Figure 1-12: AirPort wireless status window in Mac OS X Tiger.

Checking connection status in Mac OS X Tiger and Leopard

In Mac OS X Leopard, you can find the status of your network adapters and connections through the Network Preferences window by following these steps:

1. **Click the AirPort icon on your menu bar.**

   Clicking the AirPort icon shows you whether the AirPort wireless adapter is on or off and whether you're connected to a wireless network, as indicated by a check mark next to the network you're connected to.

   If you don't see the icon because it's hidden or you just don't have an AirPort wireless adapter, you can find out how to enable the icon by referring to the "Using Network Icons to Gain Quick Access to Network Settings and Options" section, earlier in this chapter.

2. **In Leopard, click Open Network Preferences on the icon's drop-down list; in Tiger, click the Apple icon, select System Preferences, and click the Network icon.**

3. **On the Network window that appears, click the Ethernet adapter from the list to view its status.**

   You can see the IP address information of the current wired connection. You can click the Advanced button to view even more details, including the Ethernet ID (your adapter's Physical Address (MAC), that you may need to know for future reference.

4. **Choose the AirPort adapter in Leopard by choosing the adapter from the list on the left; in Tiger, choose it by selecting the adapter from the Show drop-down list on the top of the window.**

   As Figure 1-13 shows, right off the bat, you see whether you're connected to a network.

   If you are connected to a wireless network, you can see your IP address under the status field, and just below that, you can see the Network Name (SSID) of the wireless network. For more details, you can click the Advanced button. This brings up another window to tab through. Some items you see are IP address information, AirPort ID (your adapter's Physical Address (MAC), and preferred network settings.

Mac OS X Tiger and Leopard offers the Network Utility, in which you can view your network status and access miscellaneous network troubleshooting tools. To use this utility, follow these steps:

1. **Click Go on the menu bar.**

2. **Click Utilities.**

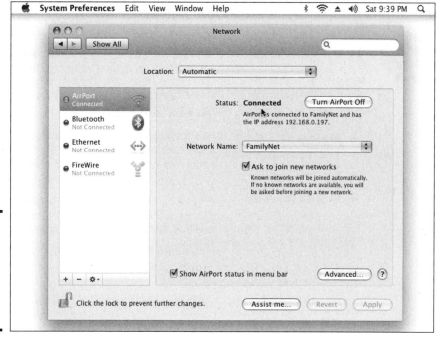

Figure 1-13:
AirPort
wireless
status
window in
Mac OS X
Leopard.

3. Find and double-click the Network Utility icon.

The first tab (Info) lists the status of each of your network adapters. You can choose the desired adapter from the Network Interface list, which shows some of the same information that you can find in the Network Preferences window; however, the Network Interface list includes more items, such as Link Speed (data rate) and data packets sent and received from the adapter.

Checking connection status in Ubuntu

In Ubuntu, you can quickly see your network status by right-clicking the network icon and clicking Connection Information. You see the main connection and IP address details of the network you're currently connected to.

Assigning Static IP Addresses to Your Network Adapters

If you have disabled the DHCP server of your router (for security reasons) or are connecting to another network that requires you to manually set your IP address (maybe at work), you can assign a static IP address to your network adapter. Additionally, you may need to set a static IP address when setting up network accessories.

If you don't know what I'm talking about, you can probably ignore this section!

If you did disable the DHCP server of your home router and are trying to connect with a static IP address, here's an example of the information you input if your router's IP address is 192.168.1.1:

+ **IP address:** 192.168.1.2 (or anything between 192.168.1.2 and 192.168.1.255)
+ **Subnet mask:** 255.255.255.0
+ **Default gateway:** 192.168.1.1

The next sections show you where to input this information, based on the operating system you are using.

If you connect to networks with static and dynamic IP addressing, see the "Using the alternative IP address feature of Windows" sidebar, later in this chapter, to find out how to use Windows's alternative IP address feature.

Assigning a static IP address in Windows 2000

Here's how you can assign a static IP address to your network adapter in Windows 2000:

1. **Choose Start⇨Settings⇨Network and Dial-up Connections.**
2. **On the Network and Dial-up Connections window, right-click the desired network adapter and select Properties.**
3. **Select the Internet Protocol (TCP/IP) entry in the list box and click the Properties button.**
4. **On the Internet Protocol (TCP/IP) Properties window that opens, select the Use the Following IP Address radio button.**
5. **Enter the IP address information for the network into the IP Address, Subnet Mask, and Default Gateway fields.**

Sometimes you have to designate a DNS server in order for the Internet to work on your computer. You can do this by inputting the IP address of your router (which is the Default Gateway) into the Preferred DNS Server field.

6. **Click OK.**

Assigning a static IP address in Windows XP

If you're using Windows XP, here's how you can assign a static IP address:

1. **Double-click your adapter's icon in the system tray.**

If you don't see the icon, refer to the "Using Network Icons to Gain Quick Access to Network Settings and Options" section, earlier in this chapter.

2. **On the Network Connection Status window, click the Properties button.**

3. **On the Network Connection Properties window, select the Internet Protocol (TCP/IP) entry in the list box and click the Properties button.**

You must scroll down the list box to find this item.

4. **On the Internet Protocol (TCP/IP) Properties window that opens, select the Use the Following IP Address radio button.**

5. **Enter the IP address information for the network into the IP Address, Subnet Mask, and Default Gateway fields.**

Sometimes you have to designate a DNS server in order for the Internet to work on your computer. You can do this by inputting the IP address of your router (which is the Default Gateway) into the Preferred DNS Server field.

6. **Click OK.**

Assigning a static IP address in Windows Vista

If you're using Windows Vista, here's how you can give your network adapter a static IP address:

1. **Click the network icon in the system tray.**

2. **Click Network and Sharing Center.**

3. **Under the Tasks area in the left pane, click Manage Network Connections.**

4. **In the Manage Network Connections window, right-click the desired adapter and select Properties.**

If User Account Control is active, click Continue on the prompt.

5. **On the Network Connection Properties window, select the Internet Protocol Version 4 (TCP/IPv4) entry in the list box and click the Properties button.**

6. **On the Internet Protocol Version 4 (TCP/IPv4) Properties window that opens, select the Use the Following IP Address radio button.**

Book IV
Chapter 1

Dealing with
Your Network
Connections

7. **Enter the IP address information for the network into the IP Address, Subnet Mask, and Default Gateway fields.**

Sometimes you have to designate a DNS server in order for the Internet to work on your computer. You can do this by inputting the IP address of your router (which is the Default Gateway) into the Preferred DNS Server field.

8. **Click OK.**

Assigning a static IP address in Mac OS X Tiger and Leopard

Here's how you can manually input an IP address for your network adapters in Mac OS X Tiger and Leopard:

1. **In Mac OS X Leopard, click the AirPort icon on your menu bar and choose Open Network Preferences; in Mac OS X Tiger (and in Leopard if you don't see the AirPort icon), choose Apple⇨System Preferences and click the Network icon.**

2. **To assign a static IP address to your Ethernet adapter (in Tiger), choose the adapter from the Show drop-down list, or (in Leopard) select the adapter from the list of connections on the left and select Manually from the Configure drop-down list.**

   Now enter the IP address information for the network into the IP Address, Subnet Mask, and Router fields. When you're done, click Apply Now or OK to save the settings.

3. **To assign a static IP address to your AirPort wireless adapter (in Tiger), choose the adapter from the Show drop-down list, or (in Leopard) select the adapter from the list of connections on the left, click the Advanced button, and click the TCP/IP tab from the window; or in Tiger, click the TCP/IP tab from the main window.**

   Now select Manually from the Configure drop-down list and enter the IP address information for the network into the IP Address, Subnet Mask, and Router fields. When you're done, click Apply Now or OK to save the settings.

Assigning a static IP address in Ubuntu

Here's how you can set up Ubuntu with a static IP address:

1. **Click the network icon from the Ubuntu toolbar and choose Manual configuration.**

2. **In the prompt that appears, enter your account password and click OK.**

3. **On the Network Settings window, click the desired network adapter from the list box and click the Properties button.**

   This should bring up the adapter's Properties window.

4. **In the Properties window that appears, deselect the Enable Roaming Mode option.**

5. **Select the Static IP Address option from the Configuration drop-down menu list.**

6. **Enter the IP address information for the network into the IP Address, Subnet Mask, and Default Address fields.**

7. **Click OK to apply the changes.**

Enabling DHCP for Your Network Adapters

You may have manually assigned your adapter with an IP address if you disabled your router's DHCP server for security reasons, connected to another network that requires you to manually set your IP address (maybe at work), or had to do so to set up a network device. But now you're trying to connect to a network that has DHCP active.

Using the alternative IP address feature of Windows

Do you use a network with a static IP addressing scheme (such as at work) that requires you to manually configure your adapter with an IP address? Do you also connect to other networks (such your home network) with automatic IP addressing provided by a DHCP server? If this is your situation, you may find yourself frequently having to configure your network adapter's IP address. This makes you a good candidate for the alternative IP address feature found in Windows.

To use this feature, follow the steps in the previous sections to open the Internet Protocol (TCP/IP) Properties dialog box. Then click the Alternative Configuration tab, select the User Configured option, and enter the information for the network you use with static IP addressing. (You can refer to the previous sections for more on what information is needed.) When you're done, click OK to apply the changes.

Now, when you connect to a network, your adapter will first look for an automatic IP address provided by a DHCP server (such as your home network) and if that address is not provided, your adapter will configure itself with the alternative configuration you just set up.

**Book IV
Chapter 1**

**Dealing with
Your Network
Connections**

If you previously assigned a static IP address to a network adapter and you want to connect to a network now that hands out IP addresses, you can revert to using DHCP for your adapter.

If you don't know what I'm talking about, you can probably ignore this section!

Enabling DHCP in Windows 2000

You can enable DHCP for your network adapter in Windows 2000:

1. **Choose Start➪Settings➪Network and Dial-up Connections.**

2. **On the Network and Dial-up Connections window, right-click the desired network adapter and select Properties.**

3. **Select the Internet Protocol (TCP/IP) entry in the list box and click the Properties button.**

4. **On the Internet Protocol (TCP/IP) Properties window that opens, select the Obtain an IP Address Automatically and Obtain DNS Server Address Automatically radio buttons.**

5. **Click OK.**

Enabling DHCP in Windows XP

If you're using Windows XP, here is how you can make your network adapter use DHCP:

1. **Double-click your adapter's icon in the system tray.**

If you don't see the icon, refer to the "Using Network Icons to Gain Quick Access to Network Settings and Options" section, earlier in this chapter.

2. **In the Network Connection Status window, click the Properties button.**

3. **In the Network Connection Properties window, select the Internet Protocol (TCP/IP) entry in the list box and click the Properties button.**

4. **In the Internet Protocol (TCP/IP) Properties window that opens, select the Obtain an IP Address Automatically radio button.**

5. **Click OK.**

Enabling DHCP in Windows Vista

Here's how you can enable DHCP for your network adapter in Windows Vista:

1. **Click the network icon in the system tray.**

2. Click Network and Sharing Center.

3. Under the Tasks area in the left pane, click Manage Network Connections.

4. In the Manage Network Connections window, right-click the desired adapter and select Properties.

   If User Account Control is active, click Continue on the prompt.

5. On the Network Connection Properties window, select the Internet Protocol Version 4 (TCP/IPv4) entry in the list box and click the Properties button.

6. On the Internet Protocol Version 4 (TCP/IPv4) Properties window that opens, select the Obtain an IP Address Automatically radio button.

7. Click OK.

Enabling DHCP in Mac OS X Tiger and Leopard

Here's how you can enable DHCP for your network adapter in Mac OS X Tiger and Leopard:

1. In Mac OS X Leopard, click the AirPort icon on your menu bar and choose Open Network Preferences; in Mac OS X Tiger (and in Leopard, if you don't see the AirPort icon), click the Apple icon, select System Preferences, and click the Network icon.

2. To enable DHCP for your Ethernet adapter, choose the adapter from the Show drop-down menu list (in Tiger) or select the adapter from the list of connections on the left (in Leopard), select Using DHCP from the Configure drop-down list, and click Apply Now or OK to save the settings.

3. To enable DHCP for your AirPort wireless adapter, choose the adapter from the Show drop-down menu list (in Tiger) or select the adapter from the list of connections on the left (in Leopard); then, click the Advanced button and click the TCP/IP tab from the window (or, in Tiger, click the TCP/IP tab from the main window).

   Select Using DHCP from the Configure drop-down list and click Apply Now or OK to save the settings.

Enabling DHCP in Ubuntu

Here's how you can enable DHCP for your network adapter in Ubuntu:

1. Click the network icon from the Ubuntu toolbar and select Manual configuration.

Book IV
Chapter 1

Dealing with
Your Network
Connections

2. In the prompt that appears, enter your account password and click OK.

3. On the Network Settings window, click the desired network adapter from the list box and click the Properties button.

   This should bring up the adapter's Properties window.

4. In the Properties window that appears, select the Enable Roaming Mode option.

5. Click OK to apply the changes.

Chapter 2: Remote Connections

In This Chapter

✔ Setting up and using remote desktop connections

✔ Using VPN clients in Windows, Mac OS X, and Ubuntu to access your files when away

✔ Configuring your firewall and router so that remote connections work

✔ Discovering the remote administration feature of your router

*W*ish you could access your files and applications on your home computers when away on vacation or business trips? Remote desktop and VPN connections let you do just that. Plus, your router lets you manage your network remotely. As you find out in this chapter, you aren't limited to using your home network at home — you can use it anywhere.

In this chapter, you discover how to set up and use remote desktop connections so that you can work on your home computers from anywhere. You also find out how to set up VPN connections (which give you secure access to your files on your home network when you're away.

Control Your PC from Across the Room or Anywhere in the World

It's possible to remotely access your desktop from other computers on your network or via the Internet. You can log in to a computer, view its desktop (see Figure 2-1), and work and play as though you were sitting in front of the computer.

Hosting a Windows Remote Desktop connection

Though most Windows versions include or support the Windows Remote Desktop client application, not all can host the connection. You can only remotely connect to Windows computers that are loaded with Windows XP Professional or Windows Vista Business/Ultimate — with the official Windows tool (that is, Remote Desktop). But you can connect to these computers with virtually any computer using Windows 95 or later and Mac OS X version 10.2.8 or later — or even from supported Pocket PCs and Smartphones.

If you want to remotely connect to other Windows versions, you can use third-party remote desktop solutions, such as the free TightVNC software (www.tightvnc.com).

To use the Windows Remote Desktop, the host computer you are trying to connect to must have a password on its Windows account. If you don't have a password, you can create one by accessing the User Accounts from the Control Panel.

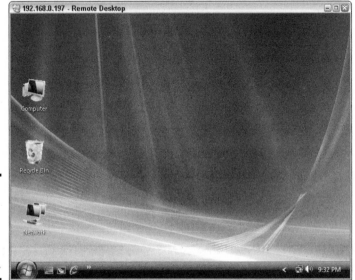

Figure 2-1:
Using the Remote Desktop Connection of Windows.

Enabling the Remote Desktop in Windows XP

Here's how to turn on the Remote Desktop feature in Windows XP Professional so that it can be remotely connected to:

1. **Right-click My Computer and select Properties.**

   This can be on your desktop or Start menu.

2. **Click the Remote tab.**

3. **Select the Remote Desktop option (see Figure 2-2).**

4. **To specify who can remotely connect to the computer, click the Select Remote Users button.**

   This brings up the Remote Desktop Users window, where you can add users to the list. When you're done choosing users, click OK, and you return to the Remote tab of the System Properties window.

Administrator accounts are automatically authorized whether or not they are listed, as long as they are password protected.

5. Click OK.

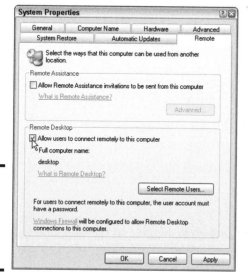

Figure 2-2:
Enabling
Remote
Desktop in
Windows
XP.

Enabling the Remote Desktop in Windows Vista

Here's how you can enable Remote Desktop in Windows Vista
Business/Ultimate:

1. Right-click the Computer icon and choose Properties.

This icon can be on your desktop or Start menu.

2. In the Tasks pane on the left, click the Remote Settings link.

The Remote tab of the System Properties window appears, as shown in
Figure 2-3.

3. Under the Remote Desktop section, select the bottom (more secure) option if you plan on connecting to the computer from another Windows Vista PC on the same network; or, select the middle (less secure) option if you plan on remotely connecting from a computer loaded with XP or an earlier Windows version.

**Book IV
Chapter 2**

**Remote
Connections**

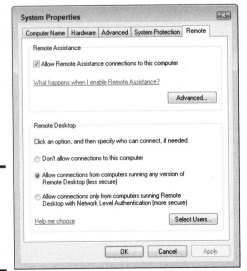

Figure 2-3:
Remote
connection
settings in
Windows
Vista.

4. **To specify who can remotely connect to the computer, click the Select Users button, which brings up the Remote Desktop Users window, where you can add users to the list.**

   When you're done choosing users, click OK, and you return to the Remote tab of the System Properties window.

   Administrator accounts are automatically authorized whether or not they are listed, as long as they are password protected.

5. **Click OK.**

Even though you have enabled the Remote Desktop feature for Windows, your firewall can prevent the connection. So you should check the settings of Windows Firewall in Windows XP and Vista, and of any third-party firewall applications you have installed. You can refer to the "Letting Remote Desktop or VPN Traffic through Your Firewall" section of this chapter for help.

Enabling Screen Sharing in Mac OS X Leopard

The Screen Sharing feature in Mac OS X Leopard is just like the Remote Desktop feature in Windows. Screen Sharing lets you remotely view a computer and work on it as though you were in front of it.

Before Mac OS X Leopard, you could use the software application called Apple Remote Desktop to remotely connect among Mac computers. This software included many other management features, which were useful in the enterprise world but came at a cost. However, in Mac OS X Leopard, you can use a new feature, called Screen Sharing, which is a piped-down version of Apple Remote Desktop. It's free and comes already loaded with Leopard.

TIP

If you want to share your screen in Mac OS X Tiger or earlier, you can use third-party remote desktop solutions, such as the free TightVNC software (www.tightvnc.com).

To open your Mac OS X Leopard computer(s) for remote connections, you can enable the Screen Sharing feature:

1. **Click the Apple icon and then click System Preferences.**

2. **In the System Preferences window, click the Sharing icon.**

3. **Select the Screen Sharing option (see Figure 2-4).**

4. **For the Allow Access For setting, specify whom you want to give access to by either clicking the Allow Users radio button or the Only These Users radio button and clicking the plus (+) button to add users.**

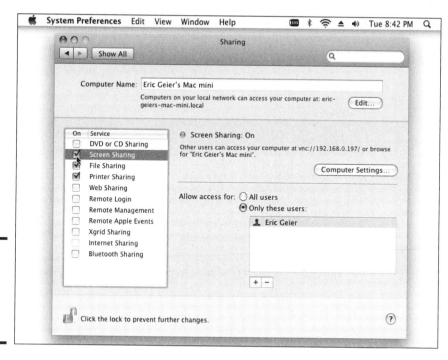

Figure 2-4:
Screen
Sharing
settings in
Mac OS X
Leopard.

**Book IV
Chapter 2**

**Remote
Connections**

5. **To set additional settings, click the Computer Settings button.**

   A pop-up window appears, where you can select the Anyone May Request Permission to Control Screen option to let anyone on your network access this computer and you can select the VNC Viewers May Control Screen With Password option to let people using VNC viewers remotely connect by entering a password into the text field.

   Leaving the Anyone May Request Permission to Control Screen option unselected is usually best. Enabling the VNC Viewers May Control Screen with Password option allows you to remotely connect from computers not using Mac OS X Leopard — such as Windows, Ubuntu, or previous versions of Mac OS X. The remote computer just needs a VNC viewer (such as the free TightVNC software, at www.tightvnc.com) to connect.

6. **When you're done setting the additional settings, click OK and click the Close button to exit the Sharing window.**

Enabling Ubuntu's remote desktop feature

You enable the remote desktop feature in Ubuntu so that you can access the Ubuntu computer from other computers running Ubuntu, or from any other computer by using a VNC type of remote desktop client application (such as the free TightVNC software, available at www.tightvnc.com).

Here's how to enable the remote desktop feature in Ubuntu:

1. **From the Ubuntu toolbar, choose System⇨Preferences ⇨Remote Desktop.**

2. **Select the Allow Other Users to View Your Desktop option, and if you prefer, the Allow Other Users to Control Your Desktop option.**

   Selecting both options lets you or others remotely connect and use the computer just as though you or the other person were in front of the computer (like the Remote Desktop feature in Windows).

3. **If you want Ubuntu to prompt you and make you authorize remote desktop connection requests, select the Ask You for Confirmation option.**

   Enabling this option isn't recommended if you plan to be away from your computer when you remotely connect.

4. **If you want to require users to enter a password to remotely connect, select the Require the User to Enter This Password option and type in a password.**

   For security reasons, enabling this option is recommended.

5. **Click Close when you're done.**

Connecting to a Windows remote desktop

If you are using any edition of Windows XP or Windows Vista, you probably already have the Remote Desktop Connection program installed. But if you're using a previous version of Windows (or Mac OS X), you have to download the Remote Desktop Connection client application. Go to Microsoft's download site at www.microsoft.com/download/, search for "Remote Desktop Client," choose the client for the appropriate operating system, download it, and install it on your desired computers.

Connecting to a Windows remote desktop from Windows

When you are ready to access your host computer from Windows, follow these steps:

1. **Choose Start⇨Programs (or All Programs in Vista)⇨Accessories ⇨ Communications ⇨Remote Desktop Connection.**

Figure 2-5 shows the Remote Desktop Connection application.

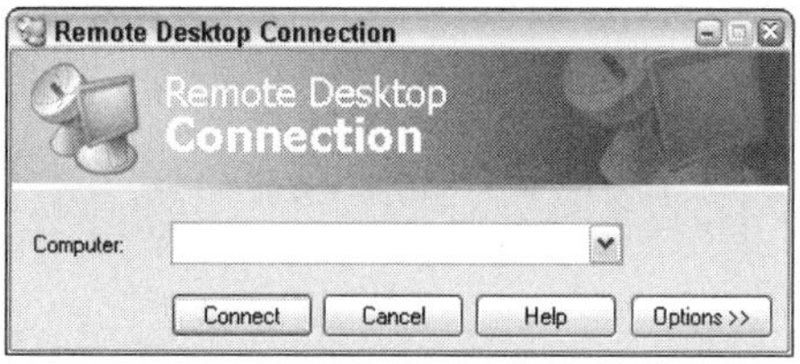

Figure 2-5:
The Remote
Desktop
Connection
application.

2. **In the Computer field, enter the Computer Name or IP address you want to connect to.**

If connecting to a computer on your home network, enter the Computer Name or IP address of the PC you want to connect to. If you need help finding these pieces of information, refer to Book IV, Chapter 3.

If connecting from the Internet away from home, enter your home's *Internet* IP address, or domain name. If you need help figuring out your Internet IP address, refer to Book IV, Chapter 3. You won't have a domain name for your home's Internet connection unless you set one up. Also, even to connect from the Internet, you have to change some settings on your router, which the later section, "Remotely connecting over the Internet," explains.

3. **Choose Connect.**

When prompted, type in the username and password of the Windows account you want to log in as and then click OK.

**Book IV
Chapter 2**

**Remote
Connections**

As if by magic, the desktop of the computer appears. You can work or play just as though you were sitting in front of that computer. People looking at the computer you're remotely connected to won't see what you're doing, and the Windows login screen is displayed on the screen. Someone can, however, disconnect you by entering another account or logging in to your account by entering your password.

As shown in Figure 2-6, Remote Desktop Connection features a toolbar on the top. If you want to enable auto-hide (which hides the toolbar until you put your cursor on the top of the screen), click the pushpin icon on the left of the toolbar. Then you can make the toolbar appear by moving your cursor to the top of the desktop.

If you want to use the computer you're currently on (the one in which you brought up the Remote Desktop program and connected to the remote computer with), you can just minimize Remote Desktop Connection. When you want to disconnect from the remote computer, you can click the X on the toolbar. You can also choose Logoff from the Start menu.

Figure 2-6:
The Remote
Desktop
Connection's
toolbar.

Connecting to a Windows remote desktop from Mac OS X

If you downloaded the Remote Desktop Connection Client for Mac, you can connect to Windows computers from Mac OS X. To do so, follow these steps:

1. **Choose Go⇨Applications.**

2. **Double-click the Remote Desktop Connection icon.**

3. **In the Remote Desktop Connection window that appears, enter the Computer Name or IP address you want to connect to into the Computer field.**

   If connecting to a computer on your home network, enter the Computer Name or IP address of the PC you want to connect to. If you need help finding this information, refer to Book V, Chapter 3.

   If connecting from the Internet away from home, enter your home's *Internet* IP address, or domain name. If you need help figuring out your Internet IP address refer to Book V, Chapter 3. You won't have a domain name for your home's Internet connection unless you set one up. Also, even to connect from the Internet, you have to change some settings on your router, which the later section, "Remotely connecting over the Internet," explains.

Connecting to a Windows remote desktop from Ubuntu

You can connect to Windows computers from a computer using Ubuntu by following these steps:

1. **On the Ubuntu toolbar, choose Applications⇨Internet⇨Terminal Server Client.**

   Figure 2-7 shows an example of the remote desktop program.

2. **Enter the Computer Name or IP address you want to connect to into the Computer field.**

   If connecting to a computer on your home network, enter the Computer Name or IP address of the PC you want to connect to. If you need help finding these pieces of information, refer to Book V, Chapter 3.

   If connecting from the Internet away from home, enter your home's *Internet* IP address, or domain name. If you need help figuring out your Internet IP address, refer to Book V, Chapter 3. You won't have a domain name for your home's Internet connection unless you set one up. Also, even to connect from the Internet, you have to change some settings on your router, which the later section, "Remotely connecting over the Internet," explains.

**Book IV
Chapter 2**

**Remote
Connections**

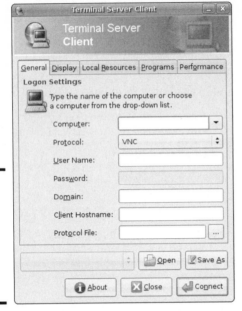

Figure 2-7:
Ubuntu's
remote
desktop
program,
Terminal
Server
Client.

3. **Click Connect.**

4. **When prompted, type in the username and password of the Windows account you want to log in as and then click OK.**

Connecting to a Mac's shared screen

If you're using the Screen Sharing feature of Mac OS X Leopard for the computer you want to connect to, plus you want to remotely connect from another computer loaded with Leopard, this process is very simple:

1. **Open your Web browser.**

2. **Enter** vnc://*IP address***(see Figure 2-8) and click Return.**

   Of course, you need to replace the italicized part of that entry with the actual IP address of the Leopard computer you want to remotely connect to. If you need help finding this piece of information, refer to Book V, Chapter 3.

   If connecting from the Internet away from home, enter your home's *Internet* IP address. If you need help figuring out your Internet IP address, refer to Book V, Chapter 3. To connect from the Internet, you have to change some settings on your router, which the later section, "Remotely connecting over the Internet," explains.

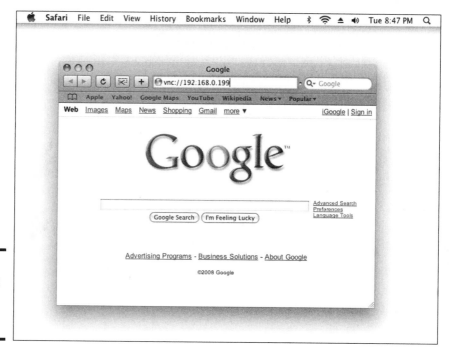

Figure 2-8:
Connecting
to another
Leopard's
screen.

To connect to a computer from any previous version of Mac OS X (or from Windows or Ubuntu), you can use third-party remote desktop solutions, such as the free TightVNC software (www.tightvnc.com).

Connecting to an Ubuntu remote desktop from Ubuntu

To access the desktop of an Ubuntu computer from another Ubuntu computer, you can use the built-in client. Just follow these steps:

1. **On the Ubuntu toolbar, choose Applications⇨Internet⇨Terminal Server Client.**

2. **Enter the Computer Name or IP address you want to connect to into the Computer field.**

If connecting to a computer on your home network, enter the Computer Name or IP address of the PC you want to connect to. If you need help finding these pieces of information, refer to Book V, Chapter 3.

If connecting from the Internet away from home, enter your home's *Internet IP* address, or domain name. If you need help figuring out your Internet IP address, refer to Book V, Chapter 3. You won't have a domain name for your home's Internet connection unless you set one up. Also, even to connect from the Internet, you have to change some settings on your router, which the later section, "Remotely connecting over the Internet," explains.

3. Click Connect.

To connect from a computer with any other operating system (Windows or Mac OS X), you can use a third-party remote desktop solution, such as the free TightVNC software (www.tightvnc.com).

Remotely connecting over the Internet

To connect to your computers from the Internet, you have to set up your router to forward the remote desktop traffic to the particular computer you want to remotely access. As mentioned in the previous sections, when you connect, you enter your home's Internet IP address, or domain name, in the Remote Desktop Connection application. This essentially connects you to your router at home and does nothing unless you have told your router to forward the remote desktop traffic to the computer that has been set up to accept Remote Desktop Connections. This is true for all remote desktop applications, not just the Windows feature.

Using the "Setting Up Your Router for Access through the Internet" section, which nears the end of this chapter, as your guide, you need to forward the ports for the particular remote desktop technology you're using to the computer that's set up to accept/host the connection. Those ports are as follows:

✦ **Windows Remote Desktop Connection:** UDP 3389

✦ **VNC:** TCP 5500, TCP 5800 – 5806, and TCP 5900 – 5906.

✦ **Apple Remote Desktop:** TCP/UDP 3283, TCP 5900, and TCP 5988

Securely Accessing Your Files from Anywhere Over the Internet

Another method to connect to your computers when away is to set up and use a Virtual Private Network (VPN). This lets you securely connect back to your home network and computers over the Internet, from anywhere. With VPNs, you can do the following:

✦ **Access your files:** You can access and open your files on your computers.

✦ **View network cams:** If you have a video camera (or other device) connected to your home network, you can view and access it when away.

✦ **Encrypt your Internet:** Being connected to your VPN server encrypts your Internet traffic on the remote computer, in addition to encrypting the communications between your home network and your remote connection.

To get started with VPN, you first need to figure out which VPN server you want to set up and use. Here are some tips to help you do that:

✦ **VPN server software:** The cheapest way is to use VPN server software, such as the features offered in Windows (discussed in the next section) or a third-party application.

✦ **VPN router:** You can purchase a special router with a built-in VPN server. You may be able to find VPN routers for as low as $70 to $130, such as the Linksys WRV200 and WRV54G.

Setting up a VPN server using Windows XP

To set up the VPN (PPTP) server on Windows XP Professional, you can use the Create a New Connection wizard, as follows:

1. **Click the Start button.**

2. **Click Control Panel.**

If using the Classic Start menu, hover over Settings and then click Control Panel.

3. **Choose the Network and Internet Connections category.**

If using the Classic Control Panel view, ignore this step.

4. **Click the Network Connections icon.**

5. **In the Network Tasks area, click Create a New Connection.**

6. **On the New Connection Wizard that appears, click Next.**

7. **On the Network Connection Type page, select the Set Up an Advanced Connection option and click Next.**

8. **On the Advanced Connection Options page, select the Accept Incoming Connections option and click Next.**

9. **On the Devices for Incoming Connections page, deselect any options you want and click Next.**

10. **On the Incoming Virtual Private Network (VPN) Connection page, select the Allow Virtual Private Connections option and click Next.**

**Book IV
Chapter 2**

**Remote
Connections**

11. On the User Permissions page, select the checkbox next to the name of any user whom you allow to connect to the VPN server and click Next.

12. On the Networking Software page, click Next.

You shouldn't have to make any changes on this screen.

13. On the Completing the New Connection Wizard page, click Finish.

Setting up a VPN server using Windows Vista

Here's how to set up the Windows VPN (PPTP) server in Windows Vista:

1. Click the network icon in the system tray.

2. Select Network and Sharing Center.

3. Under Tasks in the left pane in the Network and Sharing Center, select Manage Network Connections.

4. Press the Alt key on your keyboard to make the toolbar appear.

5. Click File on the toolbar and choose New Incoming Connection.

If UAC is active and you received an alert, click Continue.

6. On the Who May Connect to this Computer page, specify the user(s) who can connect to the VPN server by selecting their checkbox and click Next.

7. On the How Will People Connect page, select the Through the Internet option and click Next.

8. On the Networking Software allows this Computer to Accept Connections from other Kinds of Computers page, click the Allow Access button.

You shouldn't have to make any changes on this screen.

9. On The People You Chose Can Now Connect to this Computer page, click the Close button to exit the wizard.

Now this VPN connection should be listed as an incoming connection under your Network Connections (where you can edit its settings), as Figure 2-9 shows:

Even though you have set up an incoming VPN connection for Windows, your firewall can prevent the connection. So you should check the settings of Windows Firewall in Windows XP and Vista, and any third-party firewall applications you have installed. You can refer to the "Letting Remote Desktop or VPN Traffic through Your Firewall" section, near the end of this chapter, for help.

Figure 2-9:
Your
incoming
VPN
connection
shows up in
the Network
Connections
window.

Telling your router which computer is hosting the VPN

In order for the VPN server to be accessible over the Internet, you must set up your router to forward the VPN traffic to the particular computer you set up the VPN server or incoming connection on. Using the "Setting up Your Router for Access through the Internet" section, which is near the end of this chapter, as your guide, forward the following ports (for both TCP and UDP) to the computer that's set up with the VPN server:

✦ **50**

✦ **51**

✦ **500**

✦ **1723**

Connecting to a VPN from Windows XP

In order to be prepared when you're out and about and need to connect to your VPN server, you can set up a network connection for the VPN server on the computers you'll be connecting from.

**Book IV
Chapter 2**

**Remote
Connections**

Here's how to do this in Windows XP:

1. **Click Start.**

2. **Select Connect To.**

If using the Classic Start menu, click Settings, right-click Network Connections, click Open, and skip to Step 4.

3. **Select Show All Connections.**

The Network Connections windows should appear. You should see an icon for the incoming connection and each of your network adapters.

4. **Under the Network Tasks on the left, select the Create a New Connection link.**

5. **In the New Connection Wizard that appears, click Next.**

6. **On the Network Connection Type page, select Connect to the Network at my Workplace and click Next.**

7. **On the Network Connection page, select Virtual Private Network connection and click Next.**

8. **On the Connection Name page, enter a name for the connection into the Company Name field and click Next.**

9. **On the VPN Server Selection page, enter the Domain or Network Name or IP address of the VPN server into the text box and click Next.**

Enter your home's Internet IP address, or domain name. If you need help figuring out your Internet IP address, refer to Book V, Chapter 3. You won't have a domain name for your home's Internet connection unless you set one up. Also, even to connect from the Internet you have to change some settings on your router. (For help, refer to the previous section, "Telling your router which computer is hosting the VPN.")

10. **Click Finish.**

Connecting to a VPN from Windows Vista

To set up Windows Vista so that you can connect to your VPN server, follow these steps:

1. **Click the network icon in the system tray.**

2. **Select Network and Sharing Center.**

3. **Under Tasks in the left pane in the Network and Sharing Center, select Set Up a Connection or Network.**

4. **In the Set Up a Connection or Network wizard that appears, select Connect to a Workplace and click Next.**

You'll probably have to scroll down to see this option.

5. **On the How Do You Want to Connect page, select Use My Internet Connection (VPN).**

6. **On the Type the Internet Address To Connect To page, enter the Domain or Network Name or IP address of the VPN server into the Internet address field.**

    Enter your home's Internet IP address, or domain name. If you need help figuring out your Internet IP address, refer to Book V, Chapter 3. You won't have a domain name for your home's Internet connection unless you set one up.

7. **On the same page, enter or specify the other items and click Next.**

8. **On the Type Your User Name and Password page, enter the account details of the accounts that you specified could connect to the VPN server when you set it up, and click Connect.**

9. **Click Create.**

10. **Click Close.**

Now this VPN connection should be listed as a VPN connection under your Network Connections, where you can connect (and edit its settings) by following these steps:

1. **Open Network Connections in Windows XP by choosing Start⇨ Connect To⇨Show All Connections. If you're using Windows Vista, click the network icon in the system tray, select Network and Sharing Center, and choose Manage Network Connections.**

2. **Find the icon for the VPN connection, under the Virtual Private Network section.**

    The Network Connections window should appear. You should see an icon for the VPN connection (pointed out in Figure 2-10), and each of your network adapters.

3. **To edit the VPN account settings, right-click the icon and select Properties.**

4. **To connect to the VPN, double-click the icon and in the connection window that pops up, enter the Username and Password of an account that you specified you can connect to when you set up the incoming connection, and click Connect.**

When you're connected, an icon representing the VPN client will appear in the Network Connections window of the Windows computer that's *hosting* the VPN server, as you can see in Figure 2-11.

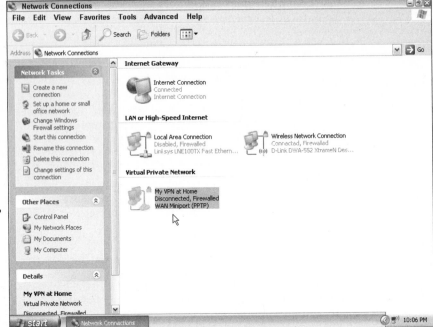

Figure 2-10:
Where your
VPN
connection
is listed
(Windows
XP).

Figure 2-11:
Where you
can see
clients
connected
to the VPN
server.

For the computer that's *connected* to the VPN server — the client — the icon representing the VPN connection will appear active in the Network Connections window of the Windows.

If you're using Windows XP to connect to or host the VPN server, you'll also see another network icon in your system tray that represents the VPN connection.

Connecting to a VPN from Mac OS X

Although Mac OS X doesn't include a VPN server feature, you can connect to Windows (or other) VPN servers using a built-in client application. As with Windows, you must first set up a network connection for the VPN connection before you actually connect. Here's how to do this in Mac OS X Leopard:

1. **Click the Apple icon and then click System Preferences.**

2. **In the System Preferences window that appears, click the Network icon.**

3. **In the Network window, click the plus (+) sign under the list of network connections on the left.**

4. **In the pop-up window that appears, select VPN from the Interface drop-down list.**

5. **Choose the appropriate VPN technology your VPN server uses from the VPN Type drop-down menu list.**

If connecting to a computer using Windows built-in VPN server, select PPTP.

6. **Enter a name for the connection into the Service Name field.**

This can be anything you wish.

7. **Click the Create button.**

This should add an entry to menu in the Network screen and show the configuration screen for the new VPN connection.

8. **On the configuration screen for the new VPN connection, enter the IP address (or domain name) of the VPN server into the Server Address field.**

Enter your home's Internet IP address or domain name. If you need help figuring out your Internet IP address, refer to Book V, Chapter 3. You won't have a domain name for your home's Internet connection unless you set one up.

9. **Enter a username for the VPN server into the Account Name field.**

If you're connecting to a VPN server hosted with a Windows built-in feature, the Account Name will be one of the Windows account usernames that you selected when you set up the server.

10. **Click the Authentication Settings button, enter the password for the VPN account into the Password field (on the drop-down window that appears), and click OK.**

11. **On the configuration screen for the new VPN connection, specify whether you want an icon shown in the menu bar for the VPN connection by selecting or deselecting the Show VPN Status in Menu Bar option.**

   For convenience, you can select the option to show the VPN icon in the menu bar, which lets you quickly connect/disconnect.

12. **When you're done, click Apply.**

If you're using Mac OS X Tiger, here's how to set up a VPN connection:

1. **On the menu bar, choose Go⇨Applications.**

2. **In the Applications window that opens, double-click the Internet Connect icon.**

3. **With the Internet Connect window open, select File on the menu bar and select New VPN Connection.**

4. **In the pop-up window, choose the appropriate VPN technology your VPN server uses by clicking the L2TP over IPSec or PPTP radio button and click Continue.**

   If connecting to a computer using a Windows built-in VPN server, click PPTP.

   After you click Continue, you'll be taken back to the Internet Connect window, opened to the tab where you configure the VPN connection.

5. **On the configuration tab for the new VPN connection, enter the IP address (or domain name) of the VPN server into the Server Address field.**

   Enter your home's Internet IP address, or domain name. If you need help figuring out your Internet IP address, refer to Book V, Chapter 3. You won't have a domain name for your home's Internet connection unless you set one up.

6. **Enter a username for the VPN server into the Account Name field.**

   If connecting to a VPN server hosted with Windows built-in feature, this would be one of the Windows account usernames selected when you set up the server.

7. **Enter the password for the VPN account into the Password field.**

8. **Specify whether you want an icon shown in the menu bar for the VPN connection by selecting or deselecting the Show VPN Status in Menu Bar option.**

   For convenience, you can select the option to show the VPN icon in the menu bar, which lets quickly connect/disconnect.

9. **When you're done, you can exit or connect.**

In Tiger and Leopard, after you've added an entry for your VPN connection, you can connect (or disconnect) to the VPN server by using the icon in the menu bar, if enabled, or via the Network (in Leopard) or Internet Connect (in Tiger) window, as shown in Figure 2-12.

Figure 2-12:
Connecting
or discon-
necting a
VPN using
the icon
in the
menu bar.

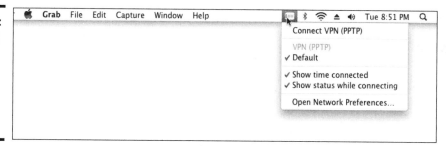

Connecting to a VPN from Ubuntu

Ubuntu doesn't come with a VPN client application by default, but you can install the network-manager-pptp package to connect to Windows-based VPN servers. To do so, follow these steps:

1. **On the Ubuntu toolbar, choose System⇨Administration⇨Synaptic Package Manager.**

2. **In the prompt that appears, enter your account password and click OK.**

3. **In the Synaptic Package Manager window, click Settings from toolbar and choose Repositories.**

4. **In the Software Sources window that appears, select the Community-Maintained Open Source Software (Universe) option and then click the Close button.**

5. **If prompted with the Repositories Changed dialog box, click the Close button.**

6. **In the Synaptic Package Manager window, click the Reload button.**

7. **Click the Search button, type** network-manager-pptp **into the Search field, and click Search.**

   The software should search and make an entry for the network-manager-pptp package and appear in the list box on the Synaptic Package Manager window.

8. **Right-click "network-manager-pptp" and choose Mark for Installation from the menu that appears.**

9. **Click the Apply button, review changes, and click Apply.**

10. **Close Synaptic Package Manager.**

11. **Restart Ubuntu so that the changes can take effect.**

When the network-manager-pptp package is installed, you can configure a VPN connection by following these steps:

1. **Click the network icon on the toolbar.**

2. **Hover over VPN Connections and choose Configure VPN.**

3. **On the VPN Connections window that appears, click the Add button.**

   The Create VPN Connection wizard appears.

4. **On the Create VPN Connection wizard, click Forward.**

5. **On the Create VPN Connection 1 of 2 page, choose the VPN technology that your VPN server uses from the Connect To drop-down menu list, and click Forward.**

   To connect to the Windows VPN server, select the PPTP Tunnel option.

   After you click Forward, a window appears, in which you enter connection information.

6. **On the Create VPN Connection 2 of 2 page, enter a name for the VPN connection into the Connection Name field.**

   Type in whatever your heart desires to identify the VPN connection.

7. **In the Gateway field, enter the IP address (or domain name) of the VPN server.**

   Enter your home's Internet IP address, or domain name. If you need help figuring out your Internet IP address, refer to Book V, Chapter 3. You won't have a domain name for your home's Internet connection unless you set one up.

8. **Click Forward.**

9. **On the Finish Creating VPN Connection page, review your settings and click Apply.**

After you've set everything up, you can easily connect to the VPN server by following these steps:

1. Click the network icon up on the toolbar.

2. Hover your mouse cursor over VPN Connections and select the connection you want to connect to (see Figure 2-13).

3. Enter the username and password and click OK.

If connecting to a Windows VPN server, this would be the username and password of the accounts you choose during the setup of the server.

To disconnect from the VPN connection, you can go back to the menu of the network icon.

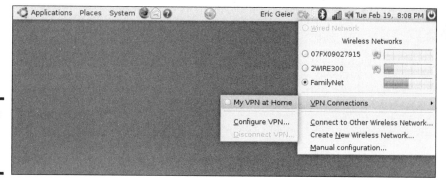

Figure 2-13:
Connecting to a VPN in Ubuntu.

Letting Remote Desktop or VPN Traffic through Your Firewall

For Remote Desktop connections or VPN servers, you must make sure that traffic is authorized to pass through the firewalls that are on the computers that are hosting the service. To allow traffic through the firewall of a host computer, follow these steps first to open the Windows Firewall program:

To open Windows Firewall in Windows XP, follow these steps:

1. Choose Start↪Control Panel.

If using the Classic Start menu, choose Start↪Settings↪Control Panel.

2. In the Control Panel window, select the Network and Internet Connections category.

If using the Classic Control Panel view, ignore this step.

3. Click the Windows Firewall icon.

Here's how to access Windows Firewall in Windows Vista:

1. **Choose Start➪Control Panel.**

If using the Classic Start menu, choose Start➪Settings➪Control Panel.

2. **In the Control Panel window, select the Security category.**

If using the Classic Control Panel view, ignore this step.

3. **Click the Windows Firewall icon.**

4. **In theWindows Firewall window, click the Change Settings link.**

If UAC is active and you received an alert, click Continue.

5. **In the Windows Firewall Settings window that appears, make sure that the Don't Allow Exceptions (for XP) or Block all incoming connections (for Vista) option is not selected.**

Figure 2-14 shows this option in Windows XP.

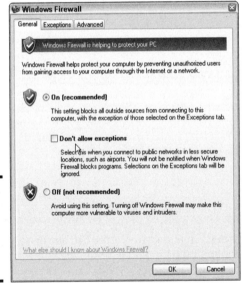

Figure 2-14:
Do not select the Don't Allow Exceptions option.

6. **Click the Exceptions tab.**

7. **Make sure the appropriate options are selected.**

If hosting a Remote Desktop Connection, make sure the Remote Desktop option is selected. If you can't find this option, or you're hosting a VPN server, you'll probably have to manually add the ports. If you have to manually add ports for either service, click the Add Port button.

Following are the ports used for remote desktop connections:

- **Windows Remote Desktop Connection:** UDP 3389

- **VNC:** TCP 5500, TCP 5800 – 5806, and TCP 5900 – 5906.

- **Apple Remote Desktop:** TCP/UDP 3283, TCP 5900, and TCP 5988

Windows VPN server application uses the following ports:

- TCP/UDP 50

- TCP/UDP 51

- TCP 500

- UDP 1723

8. **Click OK.**

In addition to the built-in firewall utilities of Windows, a third-party firewall can prevent you from accessing your computer remotely. If you purchased or downloaded another Internet security suite or firewall solution, you should check it to see whether the Remote Desktop or VPN traffic can go through it. You may need to manually input the port numbers (given in Step 7) that you want to authorize.

Setting up Your Router for Access through the Internet

If you want to use a Remote Desktop or VPN Server via the Internet when you're away from home, you must configure your router to forward the applicable traffic to the computer that's hosting the connection or server. To do so, follow these steps:

1. **Bring up your Web browser (Internet Explorer, Netscape, Firefox, or other).**

2. **Type in the IP address of your router or gateway and press Enter.**

Keep in mind that some manufacturers may use a domain name (http://www.routerlogin.net) that looks like a Web site address, instead of an IP address (192.168.1.1).

If you don't know the IP address or the username or password, refer to Book V, Chapter 3, for help.

3. **When prompted, enter the username and password.**

If you don't know the default username and password, refer to Book V, Chapter 3.

**Book IV
Chapter 2**

**Remote
Connections**

4. **Click the Virtual Server or Port Forwarding tab (or other tab containing port forwarding settings).**

Figure 2-15 shows an example of this type of page.

5. **Enter the port details, for each port you need to forward (discussed in the applicable chapter earlier) by entering information into the appropriate text boxes or selecting options from list boxes.**

For example you may find that you must enter a name, which would be for your reference, so enter what you would like; for example, *remote desktop* or *VPN server*. You may also have to enter the IP address of the computer that's set up to accept the remote desktop connection or set up with the VPN server. This is where the router will forward the applicable traffic to. (If you need help finding your computer's IP address, you can refer to Book V, Chapter 3.) You'll probably have to enter the port(s) of your remote desktop or VPN server application, which were given earlier.

6. **Click the Save or Apply button, on the top or bottom of the page, to save your changes.**

The device may reboot and you may be disconnected for a minute. When you're connected to the network again, the Web-based utility may return to the page that you left off on. Sometimes, though, it goes to a Not Found page.

Figure 2-15:
Port
forwarding
settings of a
wireless
router.

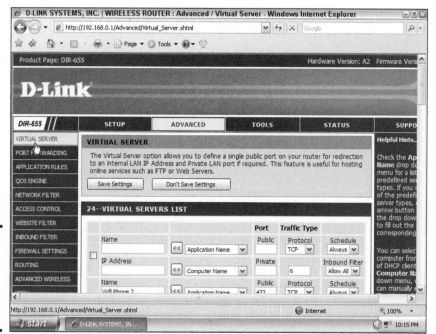

If the Internet connection (where the Remote Desktop Connection or VPN server resides) uses a dynamic IP address (which changes frequently), you can use a service such as Dynamic DNS to obtain a domain name (such as `yourname.getmyip.net`) to use instead of your Internet IP address. This domain name will automatically point to the current IP address of your Internet connection. You can sign up for the service at `www.dyndns.com`. After you get your Dynamic DNS account information, you have to set up the service with your router or gateway. Search your router's configuration screens for the Dynamic DNS settings.

Logging In to Your Router over the Internet

Just about every router for home networks has a remote administration feature that lets you access the Web-based configuration utility of your router via the Internet. This means that you can check the status of your router and change settings when you are away. This feature is useful when, for example, you want to help diagnose network problems for your spouse when you're away. You can even set the remote administration feature up on friends' or family members' routers at their houses so that you can help them if they have problems.

Getting the router ready for remote administration

Here's how to enable the remote administration feature for routers:

1. **Bring up your Web browser (Internet Explorer, Netscape, Firefox, or other).**

2. **Type in the IP address of your router or gateway and press Enter.**

Keep in mind that some manufacturers may use a domain name (`http://www.routerlogin.net`) that looks like a Web site address, instead of an IP address (192.168.1.1).

If you don't know the IP address or the username or password, refer to Book V, Chapter 3, for help.

3. **When prompted, enter the username and password.**

If you don't know the default username and password, refer to Book V, Chapter 3.

4. **Click the Tools or Admin tab (or other tab containing the remote management settings).**

Figure 2-16 shows an example of this type of page.

**Book IV
Chapter 2**

**Remote
Connections**

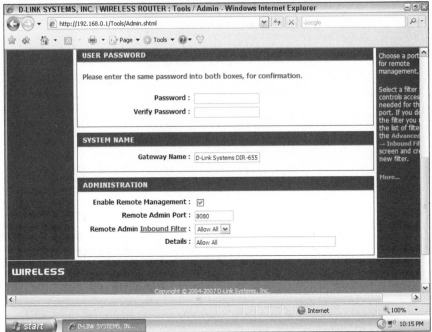

Figure 2-16:
Remote
management
settings of a
wireless
router.

5. **Enable remote access by selecting an option or checkbox.**

6. **If the option exists, specify who (what Internet IP addresses) is allowed to access the router remotely by selecting an option or entering an IP address.**

   This is the IP address of the remote computer, for example, your home's WAN (Internet connection) IP address if that's where you want to remotely connect to the router. (If you need help figuring out the address of an Internet connection, refer to Book V, Chapter 3.) Some devices allow you to open access to any IP address (by inputting an asterisk into the address field), which is useful if you plan to log in from a variety of places.

7. **If the option exists, choose whether you want to enable SSL (HTTPS) for remote access (which encrypts the remote connection, along with the login credentials, when traveling over any networks and the Internet) by selecting an option.**

   If you have this option, use it.

8. **If the option exists, specify the port you want to use for the remote access by entering a port number within the range accepted by the device into the appropriate text box.**

   The port is usually 8080 by default, which is perfectly fine.

9. **Click the Save or Apply button, on the top or bottom of the page, to save your changes.**

   The device may reboot and you may be disconnected for a minute. When you're connected to the network again, the Web-based utility may return to the page that you left off on. Sometimes, though, it goes to a Not Found page.

If the Internet connection (where the router resides) uses a dynamic IP address (which changes frequently), you can use a service such as Dynamic DNS so that you don't always have to check the current IP address.

Logging in to the router

After you set up the remote access feature, you can log in to the Web-based utility by opening your browser and typing the IP address of the Internet connection that's connected to the router you want to access. If you've set up a domain name (by using Dynamic DNS, for example) to point to the IP address, you can enter that instead. At the end of the IP address or domain name, you must enter a colon and the port number that you specified during the setup. Here's an example: 000.000.000.000:8080 (see Figure 2-17).

Figure 2-17: Remotely logging into your router's Web-based configuration utility.

Book IV Chapter 2

Remote Connections

Chapter 3: Allowing Sharing of Files and More

In This Chapter

✔ **Enabling file and printing sharing for Windows and Macintosh**

✔ **Discovering your sharing options in Windows**

✔ **Making Windows and Macs talk**

✔ **Opening the sharing gates of firewalls**

*J*ust think of it: You can sit with your laptop in your living room and fetch a file from the PC in your den, kitchen, or home office without even having to stand up, much less go to another computer. And if you need to print something from that very same laptop but your printer is connected to the PC in your home office, you can just go ahead and send the file to the printer, again without even having to move. How cool is that? Even cooler still is the fact that if one of your computers is a Mac and the rest are Windows PCs (or vice versa), no problem! You can actually exchange files and share resources between your Mac and Windows computers. All this happens through a feature called sharing.

But before you can share folders and printers among the computers on your network, you have to first take your computers to kindergarten and teach them how to share. This chapter tells you how to enable sharing on your operating system, whether Windows, Mac, or Ubuntu (or all), and get your firewall to cooperate in letting shared files and resources pass through it.

Telling Windows It's Okay to Share

In Windows, the File and Printer Sharing feature is what lets you share, view, and access your resources on the network. This feature is enabled by default in Windows; however, before you start trying to share, you may want to double-check that the features are on — and that someone didn't get bored or curious and mess with the settings.

First you must open the Properties window for the network adapter you want to enable sharing for. Here's how to do this in Windows 2000:

1. **Choose Start⇨Settings⇨Network and Dial-up Connections.**

2. In Network and Dial-up Connections, right-click the network adapter that you're using on this computer and select Properties.

If you're using Windows XP, here's how to open the Properties window for a network adapter:

1. Double-click your adapter's icon in the system tray.

2. In the Network Connection Status window, click the Properties tab.

Here's how to open the Properties window for a network adapter in Windows Vista:

1. Click the network icon in the system tray.

2. Select Network and Sharing Center.

3. In the Tasks section on the left, select Manage Network Connections.

4. Right-click the adapter that your computer is using and select Properties.

If User Account Control is active, click Continue on the prompt.

After you have the Network Connection Properties window up for your adapter, here's how you can verify that sharing is enabled:

1. Select the File and Printer Sharing for Microsoft Networks option.

Figure 3-1 shows this option.

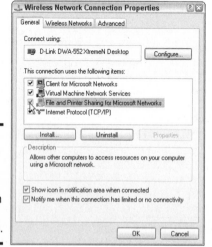

Figure 3-1:
Make sure this item is checked so that you can share files and printers.

If this item isn't listed, you can add it: Click the Install button, select Service, click Add, choose File and Printer Sharing for Microsoft Networks, and click OK.

2. Select the Client for Microsoft Networks option.

If this item isn't listed, you can add it: click the Install button, select Service, click Add, choose File and Printer Sharing for Microsoft Networks, and click OK.

3. Click OK.

In Windows Vista, you have more settings you must enable before sharing is active:

1. Click the network icon in the system tray.

2. Click Network and Sharing Center.

3. Enable Network Discovery and File Sharing by clicking the down arrow to the far right of the items in the Sharing and Discovery section (which expands its settings) and by clicking the Turn On Network Discovery and Turn On File Sharing radio buttons.

These settings are under the Sharing and Discovery section, pointed out in Figure 3-2.

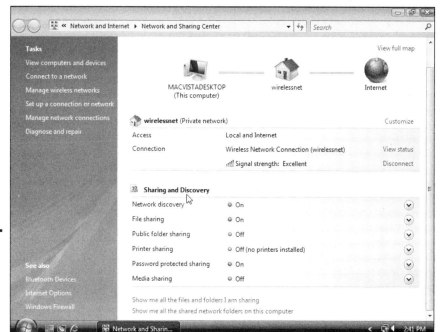

Figure 3-2:
Windows Vista's sharing and discovery settings.

**Book IV
Chapter 3**

Allowing Sharing of Files and More

In Windows Vista, the first time you connect to a network, you must classify its type: Home, Work, or Public. This classification helps prevent unauthorized access of your documents when you're on public hotspots and other untrustworthy networks. However, when you want to share your resources; you should classify your network as a Home network. You can also change your network classification at anytime via the Network and Sharing Center.

In order for Windows XP computers to show up on the new network map feature in Windows Vista, you must install the Link Layer Topology Discovery (LLTD) Responder feature on each of the XP computers. You can download this feature from the Microsoft site by visiting www.microsoft.com/ downloads/, searching for LLTD, and following the directions to download and install it.

Your Sharing Options in Windows

Windows offers two main ways for you to share resources:

+ **Simple File Sharing:** As it sounds, this is a simple way to share. The folders and printers you share are available to anyone on the network.

+ **Controlled access:** This method lets you specify exactly who on your network can access your shared resources and what they can do with them.

The sharing methods vary between the different Windows versions:

+ **Windows 2000:** Supports only controlled access.

+ **Windows XP Home Edition:** Supports only Simple File Sharing.

+ **Windows XP Professional:** Supports Simple File Sharing, which comes enabled by default, but can be disabled to activate controlled access.

+ **Windows Vista:** Supports controlled access (with password protection), which comes enabled by default, but can be disabled to activate Simple File Sharing.

In Windows XP Professional, here's how you can toggle between the Simple File Sharing and controlled access sharing methods:

1. **Choose My Computer⇨Tools⇨Folder Options.**

The Folder Options dialog box opens.

2. **Click the View tab and then deselect or select the Use Simple File Sharing option.**

3. Click OK.

The sharing method you choose is enabled.

In Windows Vista, you can disable the Password Protected Sharing feature that's on by default. To do so, follow these steps:

1. **Click the network icon in the system tray.**

2. **In the menu that pops up, select Network and Sharing Center.**

The Network and Sharing Center opens.

3. **In the Sharing and Discovery section, click the down arrow to the far right of the Password Protected Sharing option, and then click the Turn Off Password Protected Sharing radio button.**

If the option is indeed enabled already, the radio button is labeled On and is filled in with green. If the option is already disabled, the radio button is called Off and is gray.

You can't really force Windows Vista to use just the Simple File Sharing feature, but disabling password protection makes it one step closer to it. Even with password protection off, you can still specify which users can access your resources and what they can do if you want.

Setting Up Sharing for the Mac

Your Mac computers can also share their files and printers on the network. Follow these steps to enable sharing from a Mac OS X Tiger or Leopard computer with other Macs on your network:

1. **Click the Apple icon on the menu bar.**

2. **Choose System Preferences.**

3. **In the System Preferences window, double-click the Sharing icon.**

4. **In the Sharing window, select the checkboxes next to the File Sharing (Personal File Sharing in Tiger) and Printer Sharing options, as shown in Figure 33.**

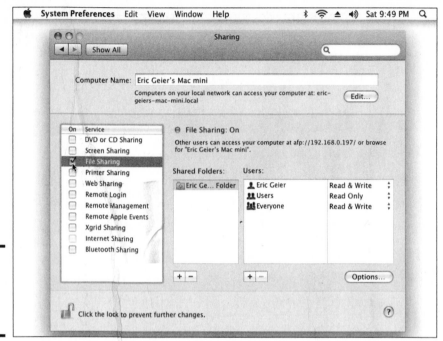

Figure 3-3:
Sharing
enabled in
Mac OS X
Leopard.

Sharing Among Windows and Macs

If you have Mac OS X Tiger or Leopard, you can host shared files and print-ers among Windows PCs on your network. After you make the necessary set-ting changes, people in your home using Windows can access the shared resources of the Mac computer as they normally can through My Network Places or Network. They are prompted for a username and password from one of the Mac accounts you choose to set up with the Windows Sharing feature.

If you intend to view the shared resources of a Mac with Windows 98, make sure that your Windows username matches your Mac OS X account's short name. If needed, you'll need to create a new Windows account that matches.

Here's how to do the magic in Mac OS X Tiger:

1. **Click the Apple icon on the menu bar.**

2. **Choose System Preferences.**

3. **In the System Preferences window, double-click the Sharing icon.**

4. **In the Sharing window, select the checkbox next to the Windows Sharing option.**

5. **Click the Accounts button.**

6. **In the drop-down window that appears, select the checkbox next to the account(s) you want to use to connect to the Mac computer from your Windows computers, enter the password for the account into the dialog box that appears, and click OK.**

   When you've selected the desired accounts, click Done.

If you're using Mac OS X Leopard, here's how to enable Windows computers to access your Mac's shared resources:

1. **Click the Apple icon on the menu bar.**

2. **Select System Preferences.**

3. **In the System Preferences window, double-click the Sharing icon.**

4. **In the Sharing window, select the checkbox next to the File Sharing option.**

5. **Click the Options button.**

6. **In the drop-down window that appears, select the Share Files and Folders Using SMB option, select the checkbox next to the account(s) you want to use to connect to the Mac computer from your Windows computers, enter the password for the account into the dialog box that appears, and click OK.**

   When you've selected the desired accounts, click Done.

The default Workgroup name for Windows networking in Mac OS X is WORK-GROUP. I recommend that all your computers reside in the same workgroup. You can find out how to change your Mac's Workgroup in Book II, Chapter 4.

Putting Ubuntu into the Network Mix

If you use the Linux distribution, Ubuntu, for your operating system, you still can share your files and printers with your Windows PCs and Windows-networking–enabled Macs. People in your home who use Windows can access the shared resources of your Ubuntu computers just as they normally would through My Network Places or Network. However, they will be prompted for a username and password from one of the accounts that you set up for sharing before they can access the computer's shared resources.

To get your Ubuntu computer on the Windows network you need to install the SMB package that enables file and printer sharing with Windows. To do so, follow these steps:

1. **On the Ubuntu toolbar, choose System⇨Administration⇨Shared Folders.**

**Book IV
Chapter 3**

**Allowing Sharing
of Files and More**

2. **On the prompt that appears, select the Install Windows Network Support (SMB) option and click OK.**

   Figure 3-4 shows an example of the prompt. If you don't get the prompt, you may already be set up to share with Windows.

If the SMB package doesn't install and the prompt keeps appearing, you need to install the samba package:

1. **On the Ubuntu toolbar, choose System⇨Administration⇨Synaptic Package Manager.**

2. **In the prompt that appears, enter your account password and click OK.**

3. **In the Synaptic Package Manager window, click Settings from toolbar and choose Repositories.**

4. **In the Software Sources window that appears, select the Canonical-Supported Open Source Software (Main) option and then click the Close button.**

5. **If prompted with the Repositories Changed dialog box, click the Close button.**

6. **In the Synaptic Package Manager window, click the Reload button.**

7. **Click the Search button, type** samba **into the Search field, and click Search.**

   The software should search and make an entry for the samba package in the list box on the Synaptic Package Manager window.

8. **Right-click "samba" and choose Mark for Installation from the menu that appears.**

9. **Click the Apply button, review changes, and click Apply.**

10. **Close Synaptic Package Manager.**

Now you have to create a username for samba:

1. **Click Applications on the Ubuntu toolbar.**

2. **Choose Accessories.**

3. **Open Terminal.**

4. **Type** sudo smbpasswd -a *username*.

    Replace the word *username* with the username of your Ubuntu account, as Figure 3-5 shows.

    You can find out what your username is by typing **whoami** into the Terminal and then pressing Enter.

5. **Enter your Ubuntu account password.**

6. **Enter a password for the SMB account.**

7. **Reenter the password for the SMB account.**

Windows sharing for your Ubuntu computer should now be enabled. You can start sharing files (see the next chapter in this minibook to find out more about sharing files and folders).

The default Workgroup name for Windows networking in Ubuntu is MSHOME. I recommend that all your computers reside in the same Workgroup. You can see how to change Ubuntu's Workgroup in Book II, Chapter 4

Figure 3-5:
Creating an
SMB
password.

Opening the Sharing Gates of the Firewall in Windows XP and Vista

Even though you have enabled sharing for Windows and have set up folders or printers to share, your firewall can prevent the sharing. To check the sharing settings, you must first bring up the Windows Firewall program. Here's how to do it in Windows XP:

1. **Choose Start⇨Control Panel.**

If using the Classic Start menu, choose Start⇨Settings⇨Control Panel.

2. **In the Control Panel window, select the Network and Internet Connections category.**

If using the Classic Control Panel view, ignore this step.

3. **Click the Windows Firewall icon.**

Here's how to access Windows Firewall in Windows Vista:

1. **Choose Start⇨Control Panel.**

If using the Classic Start menu, choose Start⇨Settings⇨Control Panel.

2. **In the Control Panel window, select the Security category.**

If using the Classic Control Panel view, ignore this step.

3. **Click the Windows Firewall icon.**

4. **In the Windows Firewall window, click the Change Settings link.**

If UAC is active and you received an alert, click Continue.

When you have the Windows Firewall window open, make sure that the Don't Allow Exceptions (for XP) or Block All Incoming Connections (for Vista) option is *not* selected, as seen in Figure 3-6.

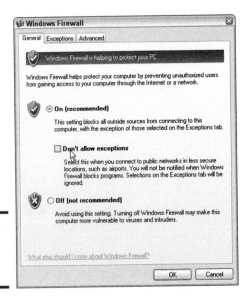

Figure 3-6:
Do not
select this
option.

Then you should click the Exceptions tab, and make sure that the File and Printer Sharing option is selected, as shown in Figure 3-7.

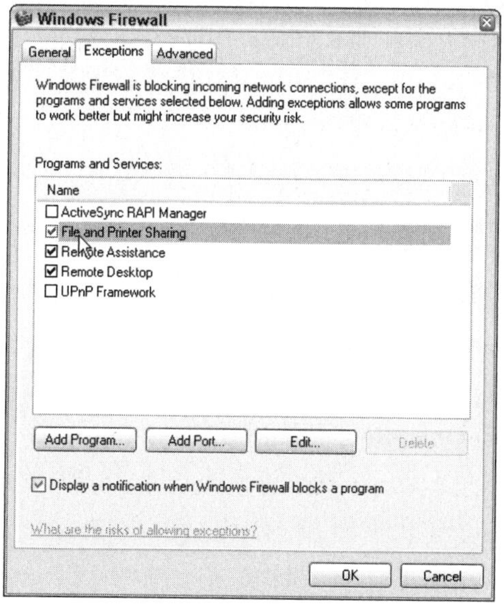

Figure 3-7:
Make sure
to select
this option.

Sharing and the Mac's Firewall

Your Mac is smart — the firewall in Mac OS X Tiger and Leopard automatically adapts to the sharing settings you specify. No configuration of your Mac firewall is needed. Unless you have third-party firewall software installed, you're good to go.

However, if I have piqued your interest in the Mac firewall, you can access its settings with these simple steps:

1. **Click the Apple icon on the menu bar.**

2. **Select System Preferences.**

3. **In Tiger, click the Sharing icon; in Leopard, click the Security icon.**

4. **In the Sharing or Security window that opens, click the Firewall tab.**

Opening Third-Party Firewalls

In addition to the built-in firewall utilities of Windows and Macintosh, a third-party firewall can prevent you from accessing its shared resources from other computers on your network. If you purchased or downloaded another Internet security suite or firewall solution, you should also check it to see whether you have authorized sharing. You should do this for each computer you have hosting files or printers.

When you bring up your firewall program, you may see an option that lets you easily allow or block sharing; if not, you may have to manually enter the ports that are used when sharing. If you need assistance, try searching the Help files of your firewall program.

In case you need to manually input them, here is a list of the ports used for sharing:

✦ **To discover other computers running Windows Vista:**

- UDP 3702
- TCP 5357
- TCP 5358

✦ **To discover other computers running Windows XP and for file and printer sharing for both Windows XP and Vista:**

- UDP 137
- UDP 138
- TCP 139
- TCP 445

✦ **For Windows computers to discover devices on your home network:**

- UDP 1900
- TCP 2869

Chapter 4: Sharing Files: Hosting a Folder Party

In This Chapter

✔ **Sharing folders in Windows 2000, XP, and Vista**

✔ **Using the new Public folder of Windows Vista**

✔ **Sharing in Mac OS X Tiger and Leopard**

✔ **Remembering what you've shared**

The previous chapter of this minibook tells you how to make your operating system and firewall willing to cooperate in sharing your files, folders, and other resources. In this chapter, you find out how to actually start sharing! Whether you're using Windows, Mac, or Ubuntu, in order to share a specific file, you have to share the whole folder that contains that file. When you share a folder, you share all the files and subfolders in it.

In this chapter, I present the basic steps that you need to use to share folders in Windows, on the Mac, and in Ubuntu. Feel free to skip around to whatever sections pertain to the operating system or systems you have.

Sharing a Folder in Windows 2000

Here's how to share a folder in Windows 2000 among the computers on your network:

1. **Right-click the folder you want to share and choose Sharing.**

   The folder can be anywhere — on your Desktop, in My Computer, or in Windows Explorer.

2. **Select the Share This Folder radio button.**

3. **Enter a name for this shared folder into the Share Name field.**

   This is the name of the folder that is displayed when you or others view the shared resources of this computer from the other computers on the network. (The real name of the folder on the computer that shares the folder remains the same.)

4. **Specify the User Limit by selecting either the Maximum Allowed radio button, or selecting the Allow (blank) Users radio button and then entering the desired number of users in the text box (the blank).**

    Leaving the Maximum Allowed option enabled is usually the best option.

5. **Set the permissions for the access of the folder by other computers on the network by clicking the Permissions button, editing the permissions, and clicking OK; or leave permissions at their default levels.**

    By default (when the permission settings aren't changed), users on the network have full control of the files and directories in the folder, which means that everyone on the network can access, edit, and delete files.

6. **Set the caching settings for the folder by clicking the Caching button, editing the settings, and clicking OK; or leave the caching settings at their default levels.**

    Caching lets you specify how the files and programs from this folder are opened from the computers on your network. When a file or program is opened from a computer on the network, by default it isn't cached on the remote computer. This means that the file or program remains on the computer hosting the file, rather than be temporarily downloaded to — or *cached* on — the remote computer.

    Caching lets you disconnect from the network when you have a file or program open from another computer. If you disconnect without having caching active, you'll probably receive errors, and you may lose any changes you made to the file if it's a document such as a Microsoft Word document. If you disconnected, even if caching is enabled, you can't save the file to the computer hosting the file; however, you probably can edit the file while disconnected, and then when reconnected to the network, you can save the file to the host computer.

7. **Click OK.**

    You did it! You should now be able to access the folder from the other computers on your network. See Book IV, Chapter 7 for help on accessing shared folders on your network.

Sharing a Folder in Windows XP

As discussed in the previous chapter of this minibook, you have two methods available for sharing in Windows XP:

✦ **Simple File Sharing:** As its name suggests, this is a simple way to share. The folders and printers you share are available to anyone on the network.

✦ **Controlled access:** This method (a term I'm using here but that isn't an official name) lets you specify exactly who on your network can access your shared resources and what they can do with them.

The sharing methods that are supported vary among the different Windows versions as follows:

✦ **Windows 2000:** Supports only Simple File Sharing.

✦ **Windows XP Home Edition:** Supports only Simple File Sharing.

✦ **Windows XP Professional:** Supports Simple File Sharing, which comes enabled by default but can be disabled to activate controlled access.

✦ **Windows Vista:** Supports controlled access (with password protection), which comes enabled by default but can be disabled to activate Simple File Sharing.

To switch between Simple File Sharing and controlled access, see Book IV, Chapter 3.

If you haven't disabled Simple File Sharing, here's how to share a folder:

1. **Right-click the folder you want to share and choose Sharing and Security.**

2. **Select Share This Folder on the Network, as shown in Figure 4-1.**

3. **Enter a name for this shared folder into the Share Name field.**

This is the name of the folder that is displayed when you or others view the shared resources of this computer from other computers on your network. (The real name of the folder on the computer that shares the folder remains the same.)

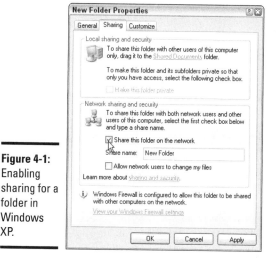

Figure 4-1:
Enabling sharing for a folder in Windows XP.

**Book IV
Chapter 4**

**Sharing Files:
Hosting a
Folder Party**

4. **Specify whether you want users on the network to be able to make changes to your files by selecting (or deselecting) the Allow Network Users to Change My Files option.**

5. **Click OK.**

   You did it! You should now be able to access the folder from the other computers on your network. See Book IV, Chapter 7 for help on accessing shared folders on your network.

If you have disabled Simple File Sharing and are using the controlled access method, here's how you can share a folder:

1. **Right-click the folder you want to share and choose Sharing and Security.**

   The folder's Properties window appears with the Sharing tab opened.

2. **Select the Share This Folder radio button.**

3. **Enter a name for this shared folder into the Share Name field.**

   This is the name of the folder that is displayed when you or others view the shared resources of this computer from other computers on your network. (The real name of the folder on the computer that shares the folder remains the same.)

4. **Specify the User Limit by selecting either the Maximum Allowed radio button or the Allow This Number of Users radio button and entering the desired number of users in the text box.**

   Leaving the Maximum Allowed option enabled is usually the best option.

5. **Set the permissions for the access of the folder by other computers on the network by clicking the Permissions button, editing the permissions, and clicking OK; or leave the permissions at their default levels.**

   By default (when the permission settings aren't changed), users on the network have full control of the files and directories in the folder, which means everyone on the network can access, edit, and delete files.

6. **Set the caching settings for the folder by clicking the Caching button, editing the settings, and clicking OK; or leave the caching settings at their default levels.**

   This lets you specify how the files and programs from this folder are opened from the computers on your network. You have the choice between three different caching settings, as follows:

   • **Automatic Caching of Documents:** When you open a document, such as a Microsoft Word file, from a computer on the network, it's temporarily downloaded — cached — to the remote computer.

This lets you disconnect from the network when you have a document open from another computer. If you disconnect without caching active, you'll probably receive errors, and you may lose any changes you made to the file if it's a document such as a Microsoft Word document. If you disconnected, even if caching is enabled, you can't save the file to the computer hosting the file; however, you can probably edit the file while disconnected, and then when reconnected to the network, you can save the file to the host computer.

- **Automatic Caching of Programs and Documents:** Similar to the previous setting, but offers caching for program applications in addition to documents.

- **Manual Caching of Documents:** Set by default, this setting doesn't automatically cause documents to be cached. When you or someone else opens documents from this folder from other computers on your network, you must manually activate caching.

7. **Click OK.**

You did it! You should now be able to access the folder from the other computers on your network. See Book IV, Chapter 7 for help on accessing shared folders on your network.

Sharing a Folder in Windows Vista

One way to share files among users on your computer and others on the network is to use the Public folder. Simply copy or drag folders or files into the Public folder of your account. Though this way of sharing files can be useful because the folder is already set up to be shared on the network, moving files or folders to this folder can mess up the organization of your files and folders. Therefore, as discussed next, you can still manually share individual folders anywhere on your computer.

In Windows Vista, you can also use the File Sharing Wizard to share specific folders:

1. **Right-click the folder you want to share and choose Share.**

The File Sharing Wizard, shown in Figure 4-2, appears.

The list box with the Name and Permission Level attributes appears, showing those who can access the shared folder. (I call it the Access List here.) The Windows account you're currently logged in to is automatically added to the Access List.

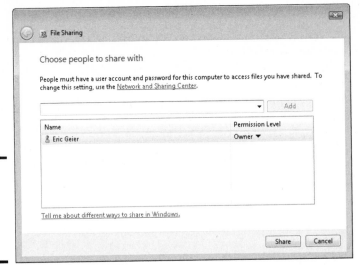

Figure 4-2:
The File
Sharing
Wizard in
Windows
Vista.

2. **Using the drop-down list (just above the Access List and to the left of the Add button), choose whom you want to add to the Access List (or choose the Everyone option to specify sharing settings for all accounts simultaneously) and click Add.**

3. **For each of the accounts in the Access List, choose the Permission Level you desire by clicking its arrow.**

   When a user account is set to the Reader Permission Level, the user can view shared files but not add, alter, or delete them. When an account is a Contributor, the user can view and add shared files but can alter or delete only the files that he or she has contributed to the shared folder. When an account is labeled as a Co-owner, the user can view, add, alter, or delete any shared files in the folder.

4. **Click Share.**

   You did it! You are now able to access the folder from the other computers on your network. See Book IV, Chapter 7 for help on accessing shared folders on your network.

To configure more settings, such as the folder's Share Name, User Limits, and Caching, you can activate the old-style window of a folder's Sharing properties of previous Windows versions, which is similar to using the Control access method of sharing discussed earlier. Here's how to do it:

1. **Choose Start⇨Computer.**

2. **On the toolbar of the Computer window, click Organize and select Folder and Search Options.**

3. **Click the View tab.**

4. **Deselect the Use Sharing Wizard option in the list box labeled Advanced Settings.**

5. **Click OK.**

After you've completed the preceding steps to disable Windows Vista's File Sharing Wizard, here's how to share a folder using the old-style window with more settings:

1. **Right-click the folder you want to share and choose Share.**

2. **Click the Advanced Sharing button.**

If UAC is active and you received an alert, click Continue.

3. **Select the Share this Folder option if the folder isn't already set to be shared.**

4. **Enter a name for this shared folder into the Share Name field.**

This is the name of the folder that is displayed when you or others view the shared resources of this computer from other computers on your network. (The real name of the folder on the computer that shares the folder remains the same.)

5. **In the text field to the right of the Limit the Number of Simultaneous Users To label, specify the desired number of users you want to be able to access the folder at the same time.**

Leaving the default value of 10 is usually fine.

6. **Set the permissions for the access of the folder by other computers on the network by clicking the Permissions button, editing the permissions, and clicking OK; or leave the permissions at their default levels.**

By default (when the permission settings aren't changed), users on the network have full control of the files and directories in the folder, which means that everyone on the network can access, edit, and delete files.

7. **Set the caching settings for the folder by clicking the Caching button, editing the settings, and clicking OK; or leave the caching settings at their default levels.**

This lets you specify how the files and programs from this folder are opened from the computers on your network. As the following bullets discuss, you have the choice between three different caching settings:

- **Only the Files and Programs That Users Specify Will Be Available Offline:** Set by default, this option doesn't automatically cache documents. When you or someone else opens documents from this folder from other computers on your network, caching must be manually activated.

- **All Files and Programs That Users Open From the Share Will Be Automatically Available Offline:** With this option enabled, when you open a document, such as a Microsoft Word file, from a computer on the network, it's temporarily downloaded — or *cached* — to the remote computer.

  This caching lets you disconnect from the network when you have a document open from another computer and still be able to use that document. If you disconnect without having caching active, you'll probably receive errors, and you may lose any changes you made to the file if it's a document such as a Microsoft Word document. If you disconnected, even if caching is enabled, you can't save the file to the computer hosting the file; however, you probably can edit the file while disconnected, and then when reconnected to the network, you can save the file to the host computer.

- **Files or Programs from the Share Will Not Be Available Offline:** This option prevents automatic and manual caching of files and programs.

8. **Click OK.**

Sharing in Mac OS X

In Mac OS X Leopard, you can specify particular folders to share among other Macs and (if Windows Sharing is enabled, as discussed in Book IV Chapter 3) Windows computers:

1. **Click the Apple icon and then click System Preferences.**

2. **In the System Preferences window, click the Sharing icon.**

3. **In the Sharing window that opens, select File Sharing.**

   A list of the folders you've shared appears, as shown in Figure 4-3. Also listed (to the right of each folder name) is the type of permission you've assigned to that folder.

4. **Click the plus sign to add a folder to the shared list.**

5. **Browse to the desired folder, click it, and then click Add.**

   The folder is added to the Shared Folders list box.

6. **You can click each folder in the Shared Folders list to edit its access permissions for each user, which is done by clicking the up and down arrows to the right of each user.**

As does Windows, Mac OS X Leopard lets you easily share folders by right-clicking them:

1. **Right-click the folder you want to share and choose Get Info.**

2. **In the My Folder Info window, select the Shared Folder option (see Figure 4-4).**

3. **To specify sharing permissions, scroll down to the bottom of the folder's Info window, click the padlock icon, enter your account's name and password, and click OK. Then in the Sharing & Permissions section, click the up and down arrows to the right of each user to select a permission level for each user.**

Figure 4-3:
Sharing
settings for
Mac OS X
Leopard.

In Mac OS X Tiger, you can't share specific folders. However, by default, your Public and Sites folder is automatically shared with users on the same computer and with other computers on the network. Therefore, to share files with other computers, you can simply copy or drag folders or files into the Public folder of your account.

**Book IV
Chapter 4**

**Sharing Files:
Hosting a
Folder Party**

All your folders (Desktop, Documents, Music, Pictures, and so on) in your Mac personal folder are shared with Windows users who log into your Mac with your account password. Additionally, in Mac OS X Leopard, the entire system is shared. However, the Windows user is allowed to access only the Public and Sites folder of the personal folder of other accounts on your Mac. If you don't like this, you can create a new account on your Mac that's for connecting from your Windows accounts only.

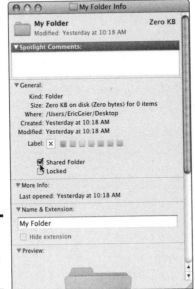

Figure 4-4:
Sharing a
folder in OS
X Leopard.

Sharing Folders in Ubuntu

If you use Ubuntu Linux, here's how you can share folders:

1. **Click System from the Ubuntu toolbar.**

2. **Choose Administration.**

3. **Open Shared Folders.**

4. **Enter your account password.**

5. **Click the Add button.**

    You should see a window similar to Figure 4-5.

6. **Select the folder you want to share from the Path field.**

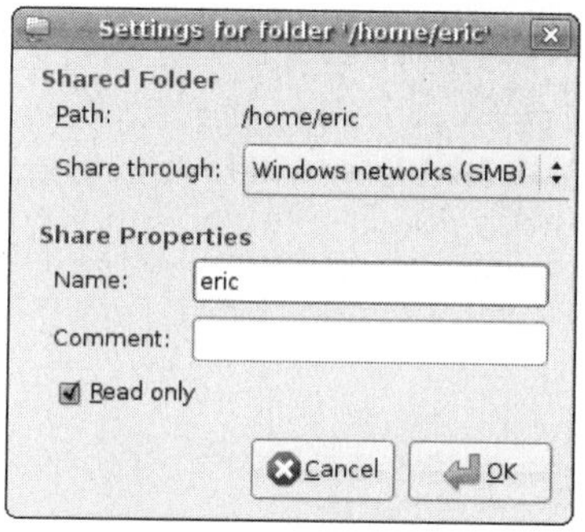

Figure 4-5:
Sharing a
folder in
Ubuntu.

7. **Enter a name for this shared folder into the Share Name field.**

This is the name of the folder that will be displayed when you or others view the shared resources of this computer from other computers on your network. (The real name of the folder on the computer that shares the folder will remain the same.)

8. **Specify the permissions for the folder by deselecting or selecting the Read Only option.**

Deselecting this option lets others have full access to the shared folder.

9. **Click OK.**

Remembering What You've Shared

It's very easy to forget which folders you've shared over time. So it's a good idea to periodically check what folders you've shared, their permission settings, and their contents to make sure that you don't unintentionally share something that's private or sensitive. That way, you can better protect your data and privacy, which is particularly important if you often use untrustworthy networks such as Wi-Fi hotspots.

Using Windows Vista's new shared listings

In contrast to Windows XP, Windows Vista allows you to easily and quickly see all the folders you're sharing. To do so, follow these steps:

1. **Click the network icon in the system tray.**

2. **Click Network and Sharing Center.**

3. **Scroll all the way to the bottom of the Network and Sharing Center.**

4. **Click the links (see Figure 4-6) to view the files and folders you are sharing.**

**Book IV
Chapter 4**

**Sharing Files:
Hosting a
Folder Party**

Viewing the list of shared folders in Windows 2000 and XP

In Windows 2000 and XP, you can view your shared resources via the Computer Management utility:

1. **Click the Start button.**

2. **Click Control Panel.**

If you're using the Classic Start menu in XP or in Windows 2000, hover over Settings and then click Control Panel.

3. **Choose the Performance and Maintenance category.**

If you're using the Classic Control Panel view in XP or in Windows 2000, ignore this step.

4. **Double-click the Administrative Tools icon.**

5. **Double-click Computer Management.**

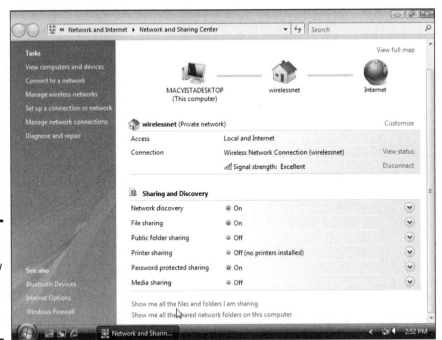

Figure 4-6:
Click these links to view your shared folders in Windows Vista.

6. **Click Shared Folders and then click the Shares folder.**

The list of shared folders appears, as shown in Figure 4-7.

You should see all your PC's shared directories. Keep in mind that by default, Windows adds a few shared directories (such as for remote administration functions, typically used only in enterprise networks); however, these should be protected so that, for example, people on Wi-Fi hotspots or other public networks won't be able to access these shared resources.

To check to see whether a folder has been shared for administration purposes, you can double-click a folder, and an alert will appear, informing you that it has been.

Seeing what you've shared in Mac OS X Leopard

For Mac OS X Leopard, you can easily find the folders you have set up for sharing:

1. **Click the Apple icon on the menu bar.**

2. **Click System Preferences.**

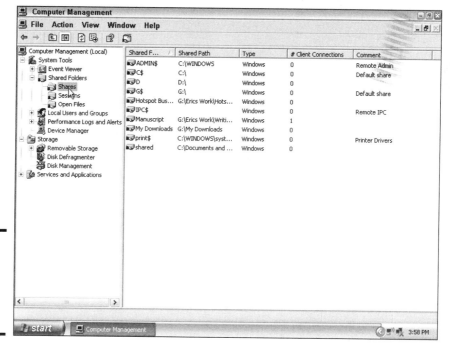

Figure 4-7: The list of shared folders in Windows XP.

3. **Click the Sharing icon.**

4. **Choose File Sharing.**

   You see the folders you've shared and their permissions.

Seeing what you've shared in Ubuntu

In Ubuntu, you can just go to where you share folders to see a list of them:

1. **Click System from the Ubuntu toolbar.**

2. **Choose Administration.**

3. **Open Shared Folders.**

4. **Enter your account password.**

   You can select a shared folder and click the Properties button to make changes to the shared folder settings.

Chapter 5: Sharing a Printer: Spreading the Ink

In This Chapter

✔ Sharing printers attached to computers in Windows 2000, XP, and Vista

✔ Enabling the sharing of printers between different platforms

✔ Freeing your printer from a PC and hooking it directly to the network

✔ Adding printers to your computer that are shared on the network

✔ Adding shared printers from a variety of platforms

✔ Editing the properties and preferences of shared printers

*A*fter you've enabled file and printer sharing for your operating system (Windows, Mac, or Ubuntu) and your firewall, as discussed in Chapter 3 of this minibook, you can start sharing your printers. This chapter shows you how to share a printer on your network, using the following methods:

✦ Use your operating system's sharing functionality to share a printer attached to your computer, which doesn't require any additional features or cost but does require that the host computer (the one with the printer) be turned on.

✦ Share a printer by hooking it directly to your network, using a print server that you must purchase separately. This way, you don't have to have a certain computer on to print.

✦ Hook a network-ready printer directly to your network. This method doesn't require a host computer to be turned on.

After you've set up to share printers on your computers, you can add the printers to the other computers on the network, which this chapter also covers. The printer will then function just the same as though it's directly connected to any of your computer. The same goes for any network-ready printers you have hooked to your network or printers using a print server.

This chapter tells you how to enable printer sharing and make your printers accessible to all the computers on your network.

Sharing Printers

If you want to share a printer that's attached directly to a computer on the network (as opposed to one that's hooked to the network with a print server, or a network-ready printer that is directly connected to the network), you must first go to that computer and share the printer. The following sections help you through setting this feature up in the different operating systems.

Sharing printers in Windows 2000

Here's how to share printers connected to Windows 2000 machines:

1. **Choose Start⇨Settings⇨Printers.**

2. **Right-click the printer you want to share and click Sharing.**

3. **Select the Shared As radio button.**

4. **Enter a name for the shared printer into the Share Name field.**

   You can use any name you want to help identify and distinguish this printer on the network.

5. **Click OK.**

Sharing a printer in Windows XP

If you're using Windows XP, follow these steps to share your attached printers:

1. **Choose Start⇨Printers and Faxes.**

   If you're in Windows Classic view, hover the mouse cursor over Settings first and then click Printers and Faxes.

2. **Right-click the printer you want to share and click Sharing.**

3. **In the window that appears, select Share This Printer, as shown in Figure 5-1.**

4. **In the box next to Share Name, enter a name that you want to use to identify this printer on the network.**

5. **Click OK.**

Sharing a printer in Windows Vista

Follow these steps to share printers attached to computers that use Windows Vista:

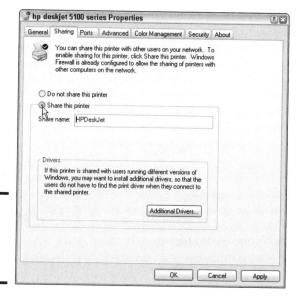

Figure 5-1:
Sharing a
printer in
Windows
XP.

1. **Choose Start➪Control Panel.**

2. **In the Hardware and Sound category, click Printer.**

   If in Classic View, double-click the Printers icon.

3. **Right-click the printer you want to share and on the drop-down menu that appears, choose Sharing.**

4. **In the printer's Properties window that appears, click the Change Sharing Options button.**

   If UAC is active and you receive an alert, click Continue.

5. **Select Share this Printer, as shown in Figure 5-2.**

6. **In the box next to Share Name, enter a name that lets you identify this printer on the network.**

7. **Select the Render Print Jobs on Client Computers if you want the print jobs started from other computers listed in their print queues as well.**

   It's usually best to select this option.

8. **Click OK.**

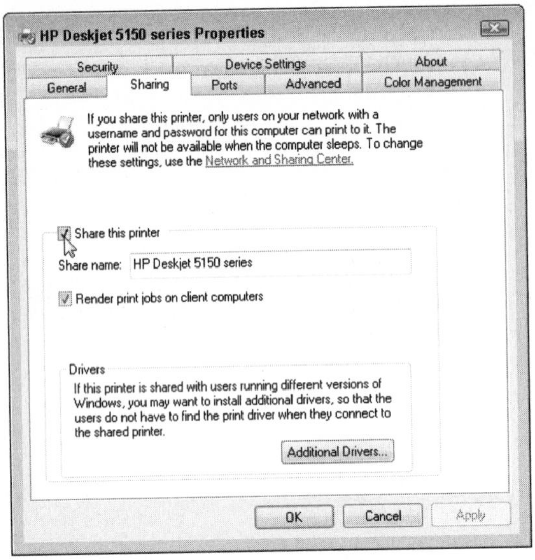

Figure 5-2:
Sharing a
Printer in
Windows
Vista.

Sharing a Printer in Mac OS X

Sharing a printer in Leopard

Here's how to share your printer(s) attached to a computer loaded with Mac OS X Leopard:

1. **Click the Apple icon and then click System Preferences.**

2. **In the System Preferences window that appears, click the Sharing icon.**

3. **In the Sharing window that opens, select the Printer Sharing option on the list that appears in the left pane.**

4. **In the right pane, select the printer(s) you want to share, as shown in Figure 5-3.**

   Now your printer is shared with other Mac OS X computers.

5. **To share the printer with Windows computers, you must enable File Sharing for Windows:**

   a. **Select the File Sharing option from the list on the left.**

   b. **Click the Options button.**

   c. **Select the Share Files and Folders Using SMB option.**

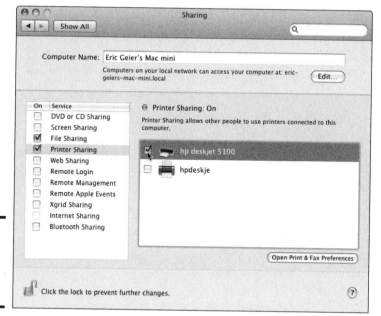

Figure 5-3:
Sharing a
Printer in
Mac OS X
Leopard.

> d. **Choose the account(s) you want to use to connect to the Mac computer from your Windows computer(s), enter the password, and click OK.**
>
> e. **Click Done.**

Sharing a printer in Tiger

To share your printer(s) attached to a Mac OS X Tiger computer, follow these steps:

1. **Click the Apple icon and then click System Preferences.**
2. **In the System Preferences window, click the Print & Fax icon.**
3. **In the Print & Fax window, click the Sharing tab.**
4. **Select the Share These Printers with Other Computers option.**
5. **Select the printers you want to share.**

   Now your printer is shared with other Mac OS X computers.

To share the printer(s) with Windows computers, you must enable File Sharing for Windows, if you haven't already, by following these steps:

1. Click Show All, which appears next to the Back and Forward buttons.

2. In the System Preferences window that appears, click the Sharing icon.

3. In the Sharing window, select the Windows Sharing option.

4. Click the Start button (if you don't see a Stop button).

5. Click the Accounts button.

6. In the pop-up window that appears, choose the account(s) you want to use to connect to the Mac computer from your Windows computer(s), enter the password, and click OK.

7. Click Done.

Sharing a Printer in Ubuntu

You can share printers attached to computers running Ubuntu. To do so, follow these steps:

1. From the Ubuntu toolbar, choose System⇨Administration⇨Printing.

2. Click Server Settings, which appears in the list on the left.

3. Select the Share Published Printers Connected to This System option, which appears under the Basic Server Settings.

4. Click the printer you want to share from the list on left.

5. Click the Policies tab.

6. Verify that the three checkboxes under the State section are selected, as shown in Figure 5-4.

The three boxes are Enabled, Accepting Jobs, and Shared.

7. Click Apply.

Now your printer(s) are shared with other Ubuntu computers.

To share the printer with Windows computers, file and printer sharing for Windows must be enabled. If you haven't already done this and you need help figuring it out, refer to Chapter 3 of this minibook.

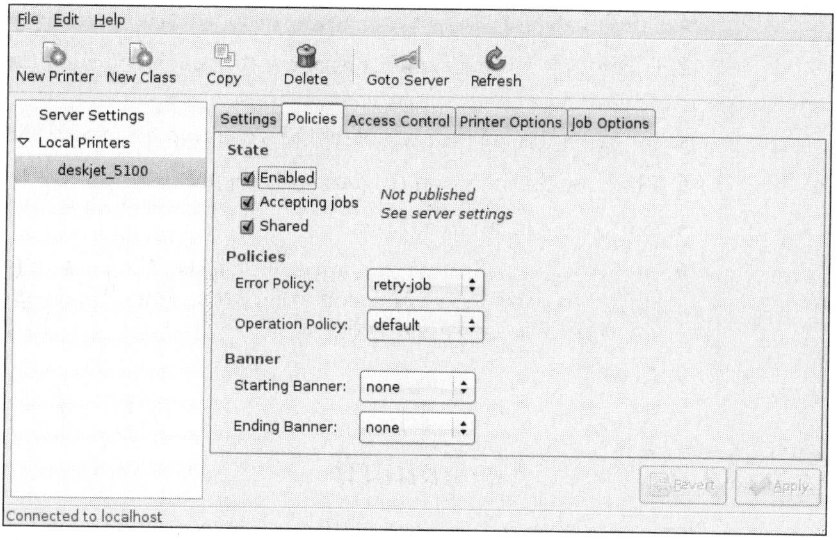

Figure 5-4:
Make sure that the three State options are selected.

Using a Print Server or Network-Ready Printer

Instead of hooking printers directly to your computers to share them with the other computers on your network, you can connect printers directly to your network. This way, you don't have to have a certain computer (the one that has the printer hooked to it) on and booted up to print to that particular printer from the other computers. A device called a *print server* makes this printer-to-network connection possible. A print server can be purchased as a stand-alone device that you put between your printer and network. Additionally, some printers have built-in print servers; these are referred to as *network-ready* printers.

Because the installation and setup of print servers and network-ready printers can vary greatly among different vendors and models, I can't provide the exact steps to get these up and running. I can, however, offer the following tips:

✦ Not all functions on a multifunction printer (for example a scanner, fax, copier, and printer) may function correctly, or at all, when using a print server from a different manufacturer than that of the multifunction printer. Most print server vendors and manufacturers provide a list of the supported printers and their functions in their product details on their Web site or on the box.

**Book IV
Chapter 5**

Sharing a Printer:
Spreading the Ink

✦ Wired print servers and network-ready printers are the easiest to install. Installation usually consists simply of connecting the printer to the server using a USB cable, connecting the server to the network with an Ethernet cable, and powering on.

✦ Wireless print servers and network-ready printers usually require you to first hook up the server to the network with a cable and then configure the wireless settings using the Web-based configuration program that comes with the server.

✦ Whether you're using a wired or wireless server or network-ready printer, you'll probably have to install software or drivers on each PC, using the included CD.

Adding and Using Shared Printers in Windows

After you've set up a printer to be shared on your network (discussed in the previous sections), you can go to each of your computers to add the shared printer to your computers. This way, whenever you want, you can print (to the shared printer) from any of your computers on your network. The following sections show you how to add shared printers in Windows.

Adding shared printers in Windows 2000

If you want to add shared printers to your Windows 2000 machine, follow these steps:

1. **Choose Start⇨Settings⇨Printers.**

2. **Double-click the Add Printer icon.**

3. **On the Add Printer Wizard that appears, click Next.**

4. **On the Local or Network Printer page, choose Network printer and then click Next.**

5. **On the Locate Your Printer page, don't enter anything; just click Next.**

6. **On the Browse For Printer page, double-click the network Workgroups and computers in the Shared Printers list box until you find and select the printer you want to add, and then click Next.**

When clicking the Workgroup names and computer entries in the Shared Printers box, you may have to wait because it takes some time to load. The same is true after you choose the printer and click Next.

After you click Next, Windows tries to find a driver for the shared printer.

7. **If Windows can't locate the correct driver for your printer, choose a driver from the dialog box that appears.**

    For help in locating the driver your printer needs, refer to Step 8 in the "Adding shared printers in Windows XP" section that follows. Then come back here and proceed with the next step.

8. **Choose whether you want this printer to be the default for your computer and click Next.**

    Enabling this option means that when you print from an application, your print job will go to this printer automatically.

9. **Review your settings and click Finish.**

Adding shared printers in Windows XP

Follow these steps to add shared printers to Windows XP:

1. **Choose Start⇨Printers and Faxes.**

    If you're in Windows Classic view, hover the mouse cursor over Settings first and then click Printers and Faxes.

2. **From the task pane on the left, click Add a Printer.**

    If you don't see the task pane, click File from the menu bar.

    The Add Printer Wizard appears.

3. **Click Next.**

4. **Select the A Network Printer, or a Printer Attached to Another Computer option, as shown in Figure 5-5, and click Next.**

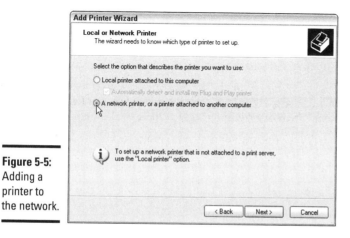

Figure 5-5:
Adding a printer to the network.

5. **Choose Browse for a Printer and click Next.**

   The wizard searches for Workgroups, computers, and printers. Sit back or go grab a cup of coffee; this search may take some time.

6. **On the Browse For Printer page, double-click the network Workgroups and computers in the Shared Printers list box until you find and select the printer you want to add and click Next.**

   When clicking the Workgroup names and computers entries in the Shared Printers box, you may have to wait because it takes some time to load. The same is true after you choose the printer and click Next.

7. **If you receive an alert asking whether you trust the computer hosting the printer, click Yes.**

8. **If the wizard does not find the correct driver, the notice shown in Figure 5-6 appears. Click OK.**

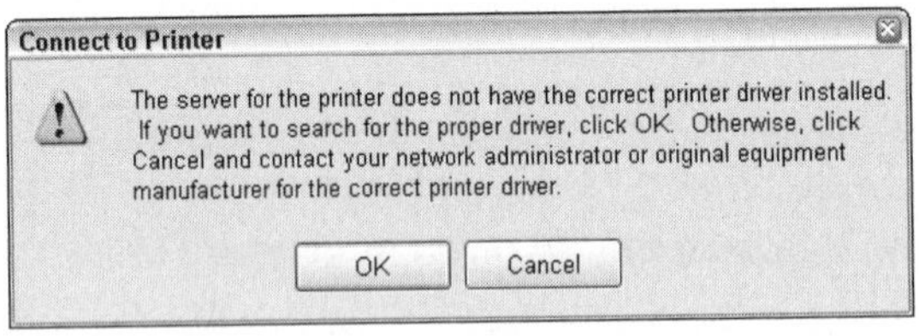

Figure 5-6: The message you see when the wizard does not find a driver.

> **Connect to Printer** ☒
>
> ⚠ The server for the printer does not have the correct printer driver installed. If you want to search for the proper driver, click OK. Otherwise, click Cancel and contact your network administrator or original equipment manufacturer for the correct printer driver.
>
> [OK] [Cancel]

A dialog box appears, listing printers made by many different manufacturers.

Here's how to proceed, based upon the operating system that the shared printer is attached to:

a. **For Windows and Ubuntu:** Select the manufacturer of your printer, try to find the particular model, and then click OK.

   If you can't find your printer in the lists, you can use the drivers on the installation/setup disc that came with your printer, or download them from the manufacturer's Web site. To do this, click the Have Disk button, click Browse, find and select the driver from your installation/setup disc or from where you downloaded the driver from the manufacturer's Web site, and click Open.

   For Windows and Ubuntu, if you don't have any success in locating your printer's drivers, you can try to use the MS Publisher Color Printer driver from the Generic manufacturer list. This should give you basic printing functionality.

b. **For Mac OS X:** Select the Generic manufacturer, find and select MS Publisher Color Printer (a PostScript printer driver that works well with Apple computers), and then click OK.

If you are having problems setting up printers shared from Mac computers, you can use a free software application provided by Apple, called Bonjour. This is downloadable at www.apple.com/bonjour.

9. **Choose whether you want this printer to be the default for your computer and click Next.**

Making this printer the default means that when you print from an application, your print automatically goes to this printer.

10. **Review your settings and click Finish.**

Adding shared printers in Windows Vista

If you're using Windows Vista, here's how to add shared printers to your computer:

1. **Choose Start⇨Control Panel.**

2. **Under the Hardware and Sound category, click Printer.**

If in Classic View, double-click the Printers icon.

3. **Click the Add a Printer button on the menu bar.**

4. **In the Add Printer window, select the Add a Network, Wireless, or Bluetooth Printer option.**

Windows begins searching for printers on your network and displays the screen shown in Figure 5-7 while it searches.

Figure 5-7: Windows searches for the printer your want to add to your network.

When you see the printer you want to add — give it some time — simply choose it and click Next.

If you still don't see the printer after searching is complete, and you are trying to add a printer from a computer using Ubuntu or Mac, try adding it directly from the network, as described in the upcoming "Adding a shared printer directly from the network" section. You should also refer to Step 8 in the steps that appear in the earlier "Adding shared printers in Windows XP" section to pick a driver that will work with Ubuntu or Mac.

5. **If you receive an alert asking whether you trust the computer hosting the printer, click Install Driver on the prompt.**

   If UAC is active, click Continue when prompted.

6. **If Windows notifies you that it can't find the correct driver, click OK.**

   A dialog box appears, listing printers from many different manufacturers.

   Select the manufacturer of your printer, try to find the particular model, and then click OK.

   If you can't find your printer in the lists, you can use the drivers on the installation/setup disc that came with your printer, or download them from the manufacturer's website. To do this, click the Have Disk button, click Browse, find and select the driver from your installation/setup disc or from where you downloaded the driver from the manufacturer's Web site, and click Open.

   If you don't have any success in locating your printer's drivers, you can try to use the MS Publisher Color Printer driver from the Generic manufacturer list. This should give you basic printing functionality.

7. **Choose whether you want this printer to be the default for your computer and click Next.**

   This means that when you print from an application, it will send the output to this printer automatically when using a quick print button and by default when chosen in the printing dialog box.

8. **Click Finish.**

Adding a shared printer directly from the network

You can also add shared printers to your Windows computers when navigating the network in My Network Places (in Windows XP) or Network (in Windows Vista). Simply right-click a printer and choose Connect. Then follow the directions given to you on the screen.

If you are trying to add a shared printer to Windows Vista, but it's attached to a non-Windows computer, you'll probably have to access the computer with the IP address if you don't see it in Network. Type *<IP address>* into the location or Web site field of the Computer, Network, or Internet Explorer window. You need to replace the placeholder "IP address" with the IP address of the non-Windows computer.

Editing shared printer properties and preferences

The shared printers that you add to Windows appear in your Printer and Faxes (just Printer in Vista) window, shown in Figure 5-8. To open the Printer and Faxes window in Windows XP, choose Start➪Printers and Faxes. (If you're in Windows Classic view, hover the mouse cursor over Settings first and then click Printers and Faxes.) To open the Printers window in Windows Vista, choose Start➪Control Panel➪Printer (in the Hardware and Sound category).

Figure 5-8:
Shared printers listed in the Printers and Faxes window in Windows XP.

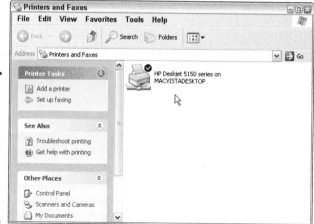

In this window, you can right-click the shared printer and delete the printer from your computer or view and edit its properties and printing preferences. You can also double-click the printer icon to see the status of the printer and what's printing.

Adding Shared Printers in Mac OS X

After you've set up a printer to be shared on your network (discussed earlier in the chapter), you can go to each of your computers to add the shared printer to your computers. This way, whenever you want, you can print to the shared printer from any of your computers on your network. The following sections show you how to add shared printers in Mac OS X Tiger and Leopard.

Adding shared printers in Leopard

Here's how to add shared printers to a computer loaded with Mac OS X Leopard:

1. **Click the Apple icon and then click System Preferences.**

2. **Click Print & Fax.**

3. **Click the plus sign (see Figure 5-9).**

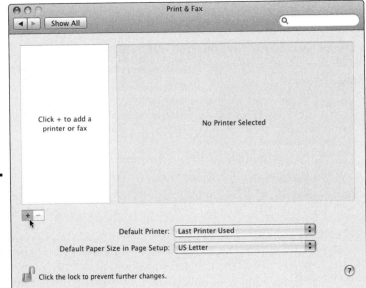

Figure 5-9:
Adding a printer to your computer in Mac OS X Leopard.

4. **Select the printer you want to add.**

The Default tab appears with a list of automatically detected printers.

If you're adding a shared printer attached to a Windows computer, click the Windows tab and navigate to the desired printer by double-clicking Workgroup names and computer icons to locate the printer you're looking for. After you find the printer you're looking for, select it, and when prompted, enter a username and password of the Windows account that is set up for sharing. After entering this information, click Connect. Then select the desired shared printer from the list on the far right. Click the Select a Driver to Use option from the Print Using list.

Next, browse or search for the printer manufacturer and model.

If you can't find your printer in the list, you can use the drivers on the installation/setup disc that came with your printer, or download them from the manufacturer's Web site (that is, if your printer is supported in Mac OS X). To find a driver on the installation disc, insert the disc in the CD drive, click Other from the Print Using list, find and select the driver, and click Open.

If you have no success in locating your printer's driver, you can try to use a driver in the list for a printer whose model number is similar to yours.

5. **Click the Add button.**

Adding a shared printer in Tiger

If you are using a Mac OS X Tiger computer, follow these steps to add a shared printer:

1. **Click the Apple icon and then click System Preferences.**

2. **Click Print & Fax.**

3. **Click the plus sign.**

4. **Select the printer you want to add.**

   The Default Browser tab appears with a list of automatically detected printers.

   If you're adding a shared printer attached to a Windows computer, click the More Printers button, and choose Windows Printing from the first drop-down menu. Navigate to the desired printer by double-clicking Workgroup names and Computers icons to locate the printer you're looking for. After you find the printer you're looking for, select it, and when prompted, enter a username and password of the Windows account that is set up for sharing. After entering this login information, click Connect.

   Now you must choose the printer manufacturer and model from the Printer Model drop-down menu.

   If you can't find your printer in the list, you can use the drivers on the installation/setup disc that came with your printer, or download them from the manufacturer's Web site (that is, if your printer is supported in

Mac OS X.) To find a driver on the installation disc, insert the disc in the CD drive, click Other from the Print Using list, find and select the driver, and click Choose.

If you have no success in locating your printer's drivers, you can try to use a driver already loaded in the list for a printer whose model number is similar to yours.

5. **Click the Add button.**

Shared Printers in Ubuntu

You can also share printers attached to computers running Ubuntu. To do so, follow these steps:

1. **From the Ubuntu toolbar, choose System⇨Administration⇨Printing.**

2. **In the Printing Configuration window that appears, select the Show Printers Shared by Other Systems option, which appears under Basic Server Settings.**

3. **Click the New Printer button on the menu bar.**

To add a shared printer on a Windows computer, select the Windows Printer via SAMBA option. Then click the Browse button, select the printer, and click OK. In the New Printer window, you can check to see whether you can connect to the printer by clicking the Verify button.

4. **Click Forward.**

5. **Select the manufacturer of the printer and click Forward.**

6. **Select the model of the printer and click Forward.**

7. **Enter your desired names and information into the Printer Name, Description, and Location fields, using the recommendations given in the window.**

8. **Click Apply.**

Chapter 6: Other Sharing Options

In This Chapter

✔ Sharing your entire hard drive(s)

✔ Discovering network storage drives and servers

✔ Mapping shared folders or drives for quick and easy access

✔ Creating hidden shares

✔ Setting up access to shared files when offline (disconnected from your network)

*F*olders and printers aren't the only things or ways you can share on your home network, and in this chapter, you find out how to have full access to all your files on your network by sharing the entire hard drive of all your computers. This chapter also describes how you can use network storage drives, which are specifically designed for sharing files on networks. And finally, I tell you how you can manipulate the way in which you share or access shared resources by using hidden sharing, having offline access to shared files, and creating virtual drives mapped to shared folders.

Hosting a Drive to Share Everything

If you find yourself sharing a lot of folders, or you would simply prefer sharing everything, you may want to share an entire drive. You can share internal and external hard drives, flash drives — any drive. Just keep in mind that opening access to entire drives gives access to the important Windows and system files. However, if you keep your network secure — which is mainly a concern for wireless networks — and prevent unauthorized access to your network, sharing a drive shouldn't cause any problems. But you may want to think twice if you have children in the house who might be tempted to mess around with your files.

Sharing a drive in Windows 2000

Here's how to share a drive in Windows 2000 among the computers on your network:

1. **Choose Start⇨My Computer.**

2. **Right-click the drive you want to share and click Sharing.**

3. **Select the Share This Folder radio button.**

   If this option is already selected, it's already shared either by you or another user, or Windows has the drive securely shared for administration purposes. You can, however, still set up the drive to be accessible from your computer by disabling and re-enabling file sharing. To do so, select Do Not Share This Folder and click OK, and then repeat the steps.

4. **Enter a name for this shared drive into the Share Name field.**

   This is the name of the drive that will be displayed when you or others view the shared resources of this computer from the other computers on the network. (The real name of the drive on the computer that shares the drive will remain the same.)

5. **Specify the User Limit by selecting either the Maximum Allowed radio button, or selecting the Allow (blank) Users radio button and enter the desired number of users in the text box (the blank).**

   Leaving the Maximum Allowed option enabled is usually the best option.

6. **Set the permissions for the access of the drive by other computers on the network by clicking the Permissions button, editing the permissions, and clicking OK; or leave the permissions at their default levels.**

   By default (when the permission settings aren't changed), users on the network have full control of the files and directories on the drive, which means that everyone on the network can access, edit, and delete files.

7. **Set the caching settings for the folder by clicking the Caching button, editing the settings, and clicking OK; or leave the caching settings at default levels.**

   Caching lets you specify how the files and programs from this folder are opened from the computers on your network. When a file or program is opened from a computer on the network, by default it isn't cached on the remote computer. This means that the file or program remains on the computer hosting the file, rather than being temporarily downloaded to — or *cached* on — the remote computer.

   Caching lets you disconnect from the network when you have a file or program open from another computer. If you disconnect without having caching active, you'll probably receive errors, and you may lose any changes you made to the file if it's a document such as a Microsoft Word document. If you disconnected, even if caching is enabled, you can't save the file to the computer hosting the file; however you can probably still edit the file while disconnected, and then when reconnected to the network, you can save the file to the host computer.

8. **Click OK.**

You did it! You should now be able to access the drive from the other computers on your network. See Book IV, Chapter 7 for help on accessing shared resources on your network.

Sharing a drive in Windows XP

As discussed in Book IV, Chapter 3, you have two methods to approach sharing in Windows XP: Simple File Sharing and controlled access.

If you haven't disabled Simple File Sharing, here's how to share a drive in Windows XP:

1. **Choose Start⇨My Computer.**

2. **Right-click the drive you want to share and choose Sharing and Security.**

3. **Click the link to confirm to Windows that you understand the risks.**

4. **Select the Share This Folder on the Network option.**

If this option is already selected, the folder is already shared either by you or another user, or Windows has the drive securely shared for administration purposes. You can, however, still set up the drive to be accessible from your computer by disabling and re-enabling file sharing. To do so, choose Do Not Share This Folder and click OK, and then repeat the steps.

5. **Enter a name for this shared drive in the Share Name field.**

This is the name of the drive that will be displayed when you or others view the shared resources of this computer from other computers on your network. (The real name of the drive on the computer that shares the driver will remain the same.)

6. **Specify whether you want users on the network to be able to make changes to your files by selecting or deselecting the Allow Network Users to Change My Files option.**

7. **Click OK.**

You did it! You are now able to access the drive from the other computers on your network. See Book IV, Chapter 7 for help on accessing resources on your network.

If you have disabled Simple File Sharing and are using the controlled access method, here's how you can share a drive in Windows XP:

1. **Choose Start⇨My Computer.**

2. **Right-click the folder you want to share and choose Sharing and Security.**

3. **Select Share This Folder.**

   If this option is already selected, it's already shared either by you or another user, or Windows has the drive securely shared for administration purposes. You can, however, still set up the drive to be accessible from your computer by disabling and re-enabling file sharing. To do so, choose Do Not Share This Folder and click OK, and then repeat the steps.

4. **Enter a name for this shared drive into the Share Name field.**

   This is the name of the drive that will be displayed when you or others view the shared resources of this computer from other computers on your network. (The real name of the drive on the computer that shares the drive will remain the same.)

5. **Specify the User Limit by selecting either the Maximum Allowed radio button or by selecting the Allow This Number of Users radio button and entering the desired number of users in the text box.**

   Leaving the Maximum Allowed option enabled is usually the best option.

6. **Set the permissions for the access of the drive by other computers on the network by clicking the Permissions button, editing the permissions, and clicking OK; or leave the permissions at their default levels.**

   By default (when the permission settings aren't changed), users on the network have full control of the files and directories on the drive, which means that everyone on the network can access, edit, and delete files.

7. **Set the caching settings for the drive by clicking the Caching button, editing the settings, and clicking OK; or leave the caching settings at their default levels.**

   This lets you specify how the files and programs from this drive are opened from the computers on your network. You have the choice between three different caching settings, as follows:

   - **Automatic Caching of Documents:** When opening a document, such as a Microsoft Word file, from a computer on the network, it's temporarily downloaded — cached — to the remote computer.

     This lets you disconnect from the network when you have a document open from another computer. If you disconnect without caching active, you'll probably receive errors and you may lose any changes you made to the file if it's a document such as a Microsoft Word document. If you disconnected, even if caching is enabled, you can't save the file to the computer hosting the file; however, you can probably still edit the file while disconnected, and then when reconnected to the network, you can save the file to the host computer.

- **Automatic Caching of Programs and Documents:** Similar to the previous settings, but offers caching for program applications in addition to documents.

- **Manual Caching of Documents:** Set by default, this setting doesn't automatically cause documents to be cached. When you or someone else opens documents from this folder from other computers on your network, you must manually activate caching.

8. **Click OK.**

   You did it! You should now be able to access the drive from the other computers on your network. See Book IV, Chapter 7 for help on accessing shared folders on your network.

Sharing a drive in Windows Vista

Here's how to share a drive in Windows Vista:

1. **Choose Start⇨My Computer.**

2. **Right-click the drive you want to share and select Share.**

3. **Click the Advanced Sharing button.**

   If UAC is active and you received an alert, click Continue.

4. **Select the Share this Folder option.**

5. **Enter a name for this shared folder in the Share Name field.**

   This is the name of the drive that will be displayed when you or others view the shared resources of this computer from other computers on your network. (The real name of the drive on the computer that shares the drive will remain the same.)

6. **In the text field to the right of the Limit the Number of Simultaneous Users To label, specify the desired number of users you want to be able to access the folder at the same time.**

   Leaving the default value of 10 is usually fine.

7. **Set the permissions for the access of the folder by other computers on the network by clicking the Permissions button, editing the permissions, and clicking OK; or leave the permissions at their default levels.**

   By default (when the permission settings aren't changed), users on the network have full control of the files and directories in the folder, which means that everyone on the network can access, edit, and delete files.

8. **Set the caching settings for the folder by clicking the Caching button, editing the settings, and clicking OK; or leave the caching settings at their default levels.**

This lets you specify how the files and programs from this drive are opened from the computers on your network. As the following bullets discuss, you have the choice between three different caching settings:

- **Only the Files and Programs that Users Specify will Be Available Offline:** Set by default, this option doesn't automatically cache documents. When you or someone else opens up documents from this drive from other computers on your network, caching must be manually activated.

- **All Files and Programs that Users Open from the Share will be Automatically Available Offline:** With this option enabled, when you open a document, such as a Microsoft Word file, from a computer on the network, it's temporarily downloaded — cached — to the remote computer.

  This lets you disconnect from the network when you have a document open from another computer. If you disconnect without caching active, you'll probably receive errors, and you may lose any changes you made to the file if it's a document like a Microsoft Word document. If you disconnected, even if caching is enabled, you can't save the file to the computer hosting the file; however, you can probably still edit the file while disconnected, and then when reconnected to the network, you can save the file to the host computer.

- **Files or programs from the share will not be available offline:** Prevents automatic and manual caching of files and programs.

9. **Click OK.**

Sharing a drive in Mac OS X

In Mac OS X Leopard, you can share drives among other Macs and (if Windows Sharing is enabled, as discussed in Book IV, Chapter 3) Windows computers:

1. **Click the Apple icon and then click System Preferences.**

2. **In the System Preferences window, click the Sharing icon.**

3. **In the Sharing window that opens, choose File Sharing.**

   A list of the folders you've shared appears. Also listed (to the right of each folder name) is the type of permission you've assigned to that folder.

4. **Click the plus sign to add a drive to the shared list.**

5. **Browse to the desired drive, click it, and then click Add.**

6. **Click any folder or drive in the Shared Folders list to edit its access permissions for each user, which you do by clicking the up and down arrows to the right of each user.**

7. **When you're done adding shared folders, you can close the window by clicking the red X in the upper-left corner of the window.**

Sharing a drive in Ubuntu

If you use Ubuntu Linux, here's how you can share drives:

1. **From the Ubuntu toolbar, choose System⇨Administration⇨Shared Folders.**

2. **Enter your account password.**

3. **Click the Add button.**

4. **Select the drive (file system) you want to share from the Path field.**

5. **Enter a name for this shared drive in the Share Name field.**

   This is the name of the drive that will be displayed when you or others view the shared resources of this computer from other computers on your network. (The real name of the drive on the computer that shares the drive will remain the same.)

6. **Specify the permissions for the folder by deselecting or selecting the Read Only option.**

7. **Click OK.**

Network Storage for Sharing and Back-up Flexibility

Another way to share files among the computers on your network is to use a network storage device. When you use such a device, you don't have to enable sharing of drives and folders on your computer. Instead, you can connect a network storage device directly to your network. This method provides some great benefits, as follows:

✦ You gain access to your documents, photos, videos, and other files from all your computers without depending on a certain PC to be powered on and hosting the files.

✦ You have an easier and more convenient way to access your files on the Internet when away from home.

✦ Typically, network storage devices come with a print server, which means that a host PC doesn't have to be running in order to print.

✦ Backup features are usually included, so you can easily protect all your computers from loss of files if you experience system failures or crashes.

The new Windows Home Server platform, available on limited network storage servers, offers even more benefits, including numerous third-party add-ons and enhancements. It also includes a Web address (domain name) so that you can easily access your files on the Internet when away from home.

You have several choices when it comes to network storage devices, with the following being the most popular types:

✦ **Routers with storage support:** These typically are regular wired or wireless routers with USB ports into which you can plug external USB hard drives or flash drives. This type of storage device is a good choice if you're thinking about upgrading your router.

✦ **Network storage adapters:** These are (empty) network storage enclosures that you can slip hard drives into or plug in to external USB drives, thereby linking the storage device to your network. Figure 6-1 shows an example of a network storage adapter.

✦ **Network storage servers:** These are essentially network storage adapters but come already loaded with drives. Also, these servers can include more features and offer better performance and reliability than the other two devices. See Figure 6-2 for an example of a network storage server.

Figure 6-1: Network storage enclosure.

Courtesy of D-Link.

✦ **Do-it-yourself (DIY) server:** If you are a do-it-yourselfer, you can even whip up a storage server yourself. You can use an older PC equipped with wireless or Ethernet connectivity and a hard drive with lots of storage space. Optimizing the operating system and dedicating the PC to serve this sole purpose would be best. This may include reformatting the drive and reinstalling Windows, setting the PC to never sleep (at least during the times you want to access it), and even setting up a software-based *file transfer protocol* (FTP) application and a Web server. Because you won't need these parts anymore, you can even remove the monitor, keyboard, and mouse from the computer after you set everything up. Just set up a Windows Remote Desktop (discussed in Book IV, Chapter 4) so that you can access the server from other computers.

Figure 6-2:
Storage server with Windows Home Server.

Courtesy of HP.

Here are the most important features and characteristics to look for when you're shopping for a network storage device:

✦ **Price:** For most people, this is likely to be one of the top deciding factors, and the price for network storage devices can vary greatly. The Windows Home Servers usually lead the pack in price, costing several hundreds of dollars. On the other hand, network storage adapters, enclosures, and links range from $75 to $100.

✦ **Storage size:** One of the most significant variations among storage network devices is their storage size, which can vary between 500GB and 2TB. (TB stands for terabytes, and one terabyte equals 1,000GB.) To decide on an appropriate size for your needs, check out the capacity and used space on the hard drives of your computers, which you find out by right-clicking the drive in My Computer (or Computer in Vista) and then clicking Properties. The size of the storage device you need also depends on whether you plan to use the network storage just for backing up all your computers or intend to use it to serve files, as well. Keep in mind that full backups take up just as much space on the network storage device as the used space on all your hard drives.

✦ **Network connectivity:** The usual network connectivity interface is Ethernet, which means that you can plug the storage device into your router. Some devices, however, may include wireless connectivity. To ensure the best transfer speeds and performance, you should connect the network storage device directly to your router. Also, you should wire any computers that will be accessing the shared storage to the router with Ethernet cabling. If you really need to go wireless, be sure to get a storage device that uses the best Wi-Fi standard (which is wireless N, discussed in Book I, Chapter 1).

✦ **Backup features:** Most network storage devices have backup functionality; however, vendors take different approaches to backing up your data. So before you buy, be sure to examine the particular backup features provided. If you use a Mac, you may want to have support for the Apple's Time Machine feature.

✦ **Server features:** You should keep your eye out for the types of server features, such as features for printing and using FTP, Web (HTTP), and UPnP AV media server features.

✦ **Operating system support:** Just about every network storage device supports Microsoft Windows; however, if you use Mac or Linux, you should check to be sure that these operating systems are supported.

✦ **Product reviews:** If you search the Web, you can find a bewildering number of network storage devices offered for sale. For help in deciding on one, I encourage you to check out the user ratings and comments and search on product review sites.

Creating Shortcuts with Mapped Drives

If you often access a certain shared folder on the network, you can save time and energy by creating a mapped network drive. This is similar to creating a simple shortcut on your Desktop or somewhere else that opens a shared folder. A network drive is much better than a shortcut, though, as I explain in the following subsection. Mapping a network drive (called *mounting* in Mac and Ubuntu) makes the shortcut look like a hard drive.

Mapping shared drives in Windows

After you've set up a mapped drive and you're in My Computer (or just Computer in Vista) browsing through your files in Windows, you see another drive, shown in Figure 6-3. When you double-click the drive, you'll be taken to the shared folder you specified. Additionally, this drive will be listed in dialog boxes where you select files, making it easier for you to get to the shared folder when opening documents in applications and finding places to download a file.

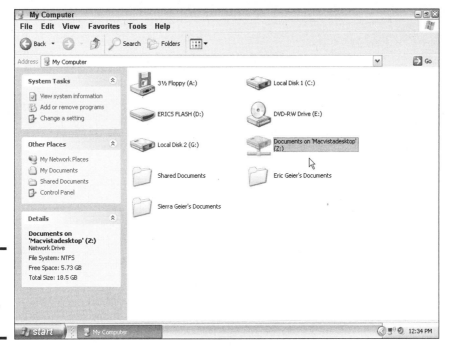

Figure 6-3: Mapped network drive in My Computer.

Here are some tips to keep in mind when you're working with mapped network drives:

✦ **For consistency, you may want to map the same shared folders on each of the computers you use.**

✦ **Use the same drive letters when mapping the same network drives on different computers.**

✦ **If you prefer, you can also map a network drive for an entire shared drive.**

Here's how to map a shared folder as a drive in any Windows version or edition:

1. **Browse to the shared folder you want to map as a drive.**

Refer to the next chapter in this minibook if you need help accessing shared folders.

2. **Right-click the desired shared folder and click Map Network Drive.**

Figure 6-4 shows the window you'll see in Windows XP, which is similar to what you would see in any other Windows version or edition.

Figure 6-4:
The Map
Network
Drive
window in
Windows
XP.

You can also access this Map Network Drive tool from any My Computer (or just Computer in Vista) or Windows Explorer window. Click Tools from the menu bar and select Map Network Drive. In Windows Vista, you find a button for this feature right on the menu bar. When you click it and the Map Network Drive window opens, follow the same process as the following steps describe, except that you have to find and select the shared folder you want to map.

3. **In the Map Network Drive window, click the drop-down list box to choose a letter to represent the mapped network drive.**

4. **Select the Reconnect at Logon option if you want to mapped network drive to remain active after you reboot your computer.**

   If you don't enable this option, the mapped drive won't be active when you start your computer again. Most likely, you want to select this option.

5. **If needed, specify a specific username and password to connect with.**

   You should do this if you've set up special sharing permissions for a particular user account or have to login to access the computer, such as when you're setting up a mapped drive from a Mac or Ubuntu.

   To specify a username and password, click the Different User Name link. In the window that appears, enter the account information requested and click OK.

6. **Click Finish.**

To change the default name of the network map drive, right-click the drive in My Computer (or Computer), choose Rename, type something, and then press Enter.

To remove a mapped network drive from your computer, click My Computer (or just Computer in Vista), right-click the mapped drive, and click Disconnect.

Mounting shared drives in Mac OS X

If you've used the Connect to Server tool in Mac OS X to manually connect to computers on the network, you probably know that this tool temporarily mounts (that is, essentially creates a mapped drive of) the shared folder you want to access. When you restart your computer, poof! The mount is gone. However, it's very easy to set up Mac OS X to always have a shared drive or folder mounted, and you can then access it from the Finder.

Here's how to mount a shared folder or drive in Mac OS X Leopard:

1. **Click the Apple icon and then choose System Preferences.**

2. **Click Accounts.**

3. **Choose the account you want the shared folder(s) or drive(s) mounted on.**

4. **Click the Login Items tab.**

5. **Click the plus sign.**

6. **Browse to and select the shared folder or drive you want to mount and click Add.**

   You can repeat Steps 5 and 6 to add more folders or drives.

To permanently mount a shared folder or drive in Mac OS X Tiger, you first have to create a small AppleScript application. To do so, follow these steps:

1. **Click Go on the menu bar.**

2. **Click Applications.**

3. **Double-click AppleScript.**

4. **Double-click Script Editor.**

5. **Enter the following code (see Figure 6-5 for an example):**

```
tell Application "Finder"
Mount volume "cifs://USER:PASSWORD@COMPUTER NAME/SHARE
    NAME"
end tell
```

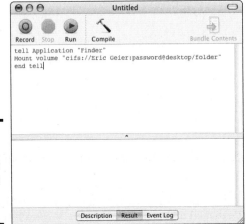

Figure 6-5:
The AppleScript that mounts a shared folder.

Remember to replace all the placeholders in the script (as signified by upper case and italics) with your particular information. The user and password is the Windows, Mac, or Ubuntu account you want to connect with. The Computer Name is the computer's network name you want to connect to, and the Share Name is the folder or drive you want to connect to.

To mount multiple shared resources, simply enter a Mount Volume line for each, in between the `tell` and `end tell` lines in the script.

6. **Choose File⇨ Save.**

7. **On the pop-up window that appears in the Save As text box, enter a name for the script, and in the Where drop-down menu, choose where you want to save the application.**

8. **Click the File Format drop-down menu and choose Application, as shown in Figure 6-6.**

9. **Click Save.**

Figure 6-6:
Selecting to
save the
AppleScript
as an
application.

You can test the script by browsing to it and opening it. It should mount the shared folder or drive.

After you have created the AppleScript application, you can add it to your Login Items so that the shared folder or drive is mounted each time you start your computer. To do so, follow these steps:

1. **Choose System Preferences.**

2. **Click Accounts.**

3. **Choose the account you want the shared folder(s) or drive(s) mounted on.**

4. **Click the Login Items tab.**

5. **Click the plus sign.**

6. **Browse to and select the AppleScript Application you just created and click Add.**

Mounting shared drives in Ubuntu

You can permanently mount shared folders and drives on computers in Ubuntu that have Windows sharing enabled. (See Book IV, Chapter 3 for information about enabling Windows sharing in Ubuntu.) To do so, you use the Connect to Server tool, as follows:

1. **Click Places from the Ubuntu toolbar.**

2. **Choose Connect to Server.**

3. **Select Windows Share for the Service Type.**

4. **Enter the Computer Name or IP address of the computer that has the shared resource in the Server field.**

5. **Enter the shared name of the folder or drive in the Share field.**

6. **Enter a name for the mount in the last field.**

You can choose whatever you want that will help you identify the shared folder or drive.

7. **Click Connect.**

Now you can open the shortcut to the computer. You find the shortcut under the Places menu on the Ubuntu toolbar and on the Desktop.

Creating a Hidden Share

When you create a hidden share in Windows, most computers (besides Ubuntu) won't see the shared folder or drive when browsing through the computers on the network. To enable computers to see the folder or drive, you must manually connect to a hidden share (or you can create a network map drive, as described in the "Mapping shared drives in Windows" section, earlier in this chapter. Creating a hidden share is a good idea when you don't want others on your network — such as the kids — easily noticing (and messing with) shared resources.

Another level of security that results from using the hidden share feature is password protection. Anyone who attempts to manually connect to the hidden share must type in a username and password for an Administrator account on the computer.

Creating hidden shares is very simple. You create the share almost exactly as you do any folder (see Chapter 4 in this minibook) or entire drive (see the "Hosting a Drive to Share Everything" section of this chapter). The difference, though, is that you add a dollar sign ($) to the end of the Share Name, as shown in Figure 6-7.

Figure 6-7:
Creating a hidden share by appending a dollar sign to the Share Name.

To connect to the shared folder or drive from other computers, you connect manually, as described in Chapter 7 of this minibook.

Making Shared Folders Available (Offline) Anytime

If you use Windows 2000, XP Professional, or Vista (Business, Enterprise, or Ultimate), you can use the Offline Files feature to access shared files and folders when they are offline. This means that you can still access files even if the computer that hosts the shared resources is shut down or disconnected from the network, or if you're using a laptop and are away from your home network.

This feature works by copying and synchronizing files between the host computer and the computer that is set up to access the files and folders when they're offline. First, you enable the Offline Files feature for the particular shared file(s) or folder(s) you want anytime access to. The files are immediately copied to your computer, and your computer receives any updates to the original files that happen over time. Then when your host computer is offline, or you take the computer that has the Offline Files away from your home network, you have access to those copies of the original files. When your computer can make a connection with the host computer again, the files will be synchronized.

The following subsections show you how to set up files and folders to be available offline, and the next chapter shows you how to access these offline files and folders.

Similar file-synchronization features are available in Mac OS X but require you to have a .Mac account to use them, which you have to pay for.

Setting up offline access in Windows 2000

In Windows 2000, the Offline Files feature is enabled by default; however, you can review and make any desired changes to the default settings by accessing the Offline Files preferences:

1. **Choose Start⇨My Computer.**

2. **On the Tools menu, choose Folder Options.**

3. **Click the Offline Files tab.**

Now you can set up a shared file or folder for offline access in Windows 2000 by following these steps:

1. **Browse to the computer that has the shared folder or drive you want to make available when offline.**

2. **Right-click the shared folder or drive and choose Make Available Offline.**

   If you want to set up just a single file, open the shared folder that has the file in it, right-click the file, and choose Make Available Offline.

   The Offline Files Wizard appears.

3. **Click Next.**

4. **Choose whether you want to set up automatic synchronization and click Next.**

5. **Specify your alert and shortcut preferences, and click Finish.**

   The Synchronization window appears, showing the progress of the transfer of files from the computer hosting the files. This window disappears when transfer is complete.

6. **Specify whether you want to include subfolders and click OK.**

   If you're enabling offline access for a single file, you can ignore this step.

   The Synchronization window appears, showing the progress of the transfer of files from the computer hosting the files.

The next chapter shows you how to access these offline files and folders.

Enabling offline access in Windows XP

In order to use the Offline Files feature in Windows XP, you must first turn off Fast User Switching. Here's how:

1. Choose Start⇨Control Panel.

If using the Classic Start menu, hover over Settings, and then click Control Panel.

2. Choose the User Accounts category.

If using the Classic Control Panel view, ignore this step.

3. Click the User Accounts icon.

4. Click the Change the Way Users Log On or Off link.

5. Deselect the Use Fast User Switching option. (Figure 6-8 shows this option deselected).

6. Click Apply Options.

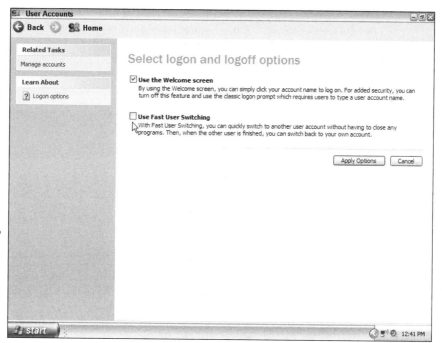

Figure 6-8: Disabling Fast User Switching in Windows XP.

Next, you enable the Offline Files feature for Windows XP:

1. **Choose Start⇨My Computer.**

2. **On the Tools menu, choose Folder Options.**

3. **Click the Offline Files tab.**

4. **Select the Enable Offline Files option, shown in Figure 6-9.**

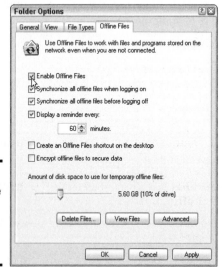

Figure 6-9: Enabling the Offline Files option in Windows XP.

5. **For full synchronization and protection, select all options.**

6. **Click OK.**

Finally, you can set up certain shared files, folders, or drives in Windows XP to be available when offline, as described in the following steps:

1. **Browse to the computer that has the shared folder or drive you want to make available when offline.**

2. **Right-click shared folder or drive and choose Make Available Offline.**

If you want to set up just a single file, open the shared folder that has the file in it, right-click the file, and choose Make Available Offline.

3. **Specify whether you want to include subfolders.**

If you're setting up access to only a single file, you can ignore this step.

The Synchronization window appears, showing the progress of the transfer of files from the computer hosting the files. This window disappears when the transfer is complete.

The next chapter shows you how to access these offline files and folders.

Enabling offline access in Windows Vista

In Windows Vista, the Offline Files feature is enabled by default; however you can review and make any desired changes to the default settings by accessing the Offline Files preferences:

1. **Choose Start➪Control Panel.**

2. **Choose the Network and Internet category.**

If using the Classic Control Panel view, ignore this step.

3. **Click Offline Files.**

Follow these steps to make shared folders in Windows Vista available when offline:

1. **Browse to the computer that has the shared folder or drive you want to make available when offline.**

2. **Right-click the shared folder or drive and choose Always Available Offline, as shown in Figure 6-10.**

If you want to set up access to just a single file, open the shared folder that has the file in it, right-click the file, and choose Make Available Offline.

The Synchronization window appears, showing the progress of the transfer of files from the computer hosting the files.

The next chapter shows you how to access these offline files and folders.

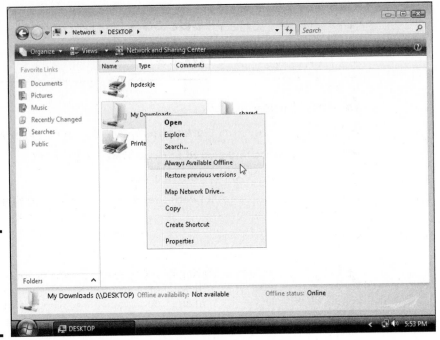

Figure 6-10:
Enabling
offline file
access in
Windows
Vista.

Chapter 7: Accessing Shared Files and Folders

In This Chapter

✔ **Browsing through the Workgroups and computers on your network**

✔ **Accessing and using shared folders, files, and printers**

✔ **Manually accessing shared resources**

✔ **Connecting to shared network files, folders, and offline files between different platforms**

*A*fter you've enabled sharing and identified the folders you want to share, you can access these shared resources on all your computers across your home network. In any operating system, whether Windows, Mac OS X, or Ubuntu, you have two main ways to go about accessing shared resources on your network:

✦ Browse to computers on your home network through a Network or My Network Places window.

✦ Manually access the shared resources of a computer on the network by typing the IP address or network name of the computer.

This chapter tells you how to get to all that good stuff you store and use on all your computers so that you can start reaping the benefits of having a home network.

Browsing to Shared Resources in Windows

Accessing shared resources in Windows is similar across all Windows versions and editions. One exception is the name of the window that you open to view the network and computers. This window is named My Network Places in Windows XP and earlier versions of Windows, but in Vista, it's simply called Network. Some of the navigation techniques and functionality vary among the different Windows versions as well, so the following sections cover how to access shared resources in Windows 2000, XP, and Vista.

Remember, it may take a good amount of time to load when browsing through the Workgroups and computers on your network. If you experience a time lapse, just wait. Clicking other items and getting impatient may make things worse, causing your computer to freeze or the Network or My Network Places to become nonresponsive.

Accessing shared resources in Windows 2000

If you're using Windows 2000, here's how you can access the shared resources on your home network:

1. **Double-click the My Network Places icon on your Desktop.**

The My Network Places window appears.

2. **To view computers in the same Workgroup, double-click the Computers Near Me icon (which will load icons for the computers in the Workgroup) and then double-click a computer's icon to view its shared resources.**

3. **After you're done browsing through computers in the same Workgroup, you can browse through computers in other Workgroups, but you first must return to the main My Network Places window by clicking the back arrow until you reach it.**

4. **To view computers in a different Workgroup on your home network, double-click the Entire Network icon from the main My Network Places window, click the Entire Contents link on the left side of the window, double-click the Microsoft Windows Network icon, double-click a Workgroup icon (which will load icons for the computers in the Workgroup), and then double-click a computer's icon to view its shared resources.**

For each computer icon you access you'll see the shared folders along with a Printer and Scheduled Tasks folder.

Accessing shared resources in Windows XP

Here's how to access and view your shared folders and files in Windows XP:

1. **Choose Start⇨My Network Places.**

The My Network Places window appears, showing you shortcuts to shared folders on your network and any Internet sites or FTP locations that you've added.

If you see the shared folder you want to access from these shortcuts, you can double-click the folder, skip the next step, and proceed as described in Step 3; otherwise, continue with Step 2 if you can't find the shared folder.

If you have many shared folders on your network, it may be harder to find the folder you want from this unorganized list of shortcuts that's shown by default. You can, however, set it to group your shared folders and network places by computer. Simply right-click in the whitespace in the My Network Places window, select Arrange Icons By, and choose Computer.

2. To browse to computers on the network, click the View Workgroup Computers link on the left task pane.

A list of all the computers that Windows detects in your Workgroup appears. To view computers on your home network in different Workgroups, click the Up button on the menu bar, shown in Figure 7-1.

When you double-click the desired Workgroup, you see all the computers (again, the ones that Windows detect) in that workgroup.

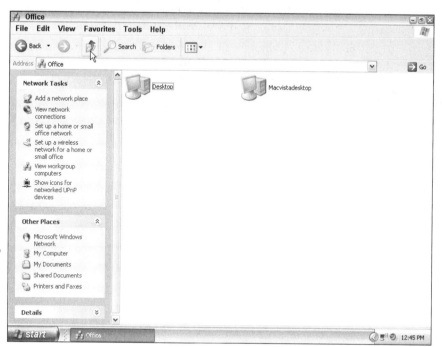

Figure 7-1:
Click the
Up button to
see all the
Workgroups.

**Book IV
Chapter 7**

**Accessing Shared
Files and Folders**

Sometimes it takes some time before computers show up in My Network Places (because of computers having been recently booted up), or sometimes they don't show up at all (because of other quirks), so if you don't see the computer you want, you should try to manually access the computer as discussed later in the "Manually Accessing a Computer's Shared Resources" section. However, if you still can't access a computer, you can try to troubleshoot the problem, as discussed in Book V, Chapter 2.

3. **When you see the computer that has the shared resources you want to access, double-click it.**

   The computer's shared folders and printers, along with a Printer and Scheduled Tasks folder, appear.

Accessing shared resources in Windows Vista

If you're using Windows Vista, here's how you can view and access the shared resources on your network:

1. **Choose Start⇨Network.**

   The Network window appears, showing you the icons for each of the computers and any UPnP devices (such as your router) on your network (that Windows detects).

Sometimes it takes some time before computers show up in My Network Places (because of computers having been recently booted up), or sometimes they don't show up at all (because of other quirks), so if you don't see the computer you want, you should try to manually access the computer as discussed later in the "Manually Accessing a Computer's Shared Resources" section. However, if you still can't access a computer, you can try to troubleshoot the problem, as discussed in Book V, Chapter 2.

If you have multiple Workgroups, you may find it useful to group this list of computers by Workgroups. Simply right-click the whitespace in the Network window, select Group By, and choose Workgroup.

2. **Double-click the computer that has the shared resources you want to access.**

   The computer's shared folders, along with a Printer folder, appear.

Accessing a Mac or Ubuntu computer from Windows

The first time you try to access a Mac OS X or Ubuntu computer from Windows, you'll be prompted to log in before you can access the computer. Enter the username and password of the Mac or Ubuntu account(s) you set up to be used with Windows sharing (discussed in Book IV, Chapter 3). When you do so, the shared resources of the computer appear.

The username and password are saved, and you won't have to log in again unless the Windows sharing preferences on the Mac or Ubuntu computer are changed.

Browsing to Shared Resources in Mac OS X

Follow these steps to access the shared resources of your network in Mac OS X Leopard:

1. **Click Go on the menu bar.**

2. **Choose Network.**

All the shared computers on your home network appear, as shown in Figure 7-2.

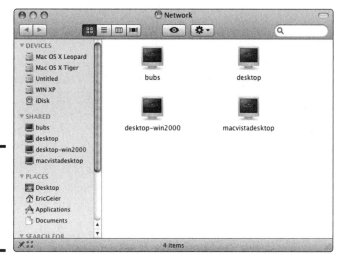

Figure 7-2:
The Network window in Mac OS Leopard.

3. **Double-click the computer that has the shared resources you want to access.**

If you're connecting to a Windows or Ubuntu computer, you'll be prompted to log in before you can access the computer. Enter a username and password of a Windows or Ubuntu account. When you do so, the computer's shared folders appear.

If you use Mac OS X Tiger, here's how to access the shared resources of your network:

1. **Click Go on the menu bar.**

2. **Choose Network.**

Icons representing the Workgroups on your computer appear.

3. **Double-click the Workgroup that has the computer and shared resources you want to access.**

4. **Double-click the desired computer.**

If connecting to a Windows or Ubuntu computer, you'll be prompted to log in before you can access the computer. Enter a username and password of a Windows or Ubuntu account.

You may be able to enter Guest as the login name and leave the password blank.

Browsing to Shared Resources in Ubuntu

Surprise! You can access the shared folders and files on your network from Linux Ubuntu. To do so, follow these steps:

1. **Click Places from the Ubuntu toolbar.**

2. **Click Network.**

The shared computers that are in the same Workgroup appear.

3. **To access computers from other Workgroups, double-click the Windows Network icon and then double-click the desired Workgroup.**

4. **Double-click the computer that has the shared resources you want to access.**

Manually Accessing a Computer's Shared Resources

If you can't find the computer you want from browsing through My Network Places or Network, you may be able to access it using one of the following methods:

✦ Use the Computer Name.

✦ Use the computer's local IP address.

If you need help finding the Computer Name or IP address of a computer, refer to Book V, Chapter 3.

If you are using a Windows computer and trying to access the shared resources of a Windows computer (or a Mac or Ubuntu computer with Windows Sharing enabled), you can enter two backslashes and the

Computer Name or IP address of the computer you want to access in a Web browser or My Computer. Figure 7-3 shows an example.

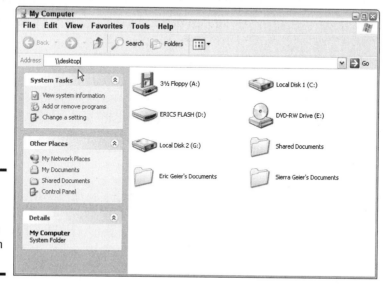

Figure 7-3: Manually accessing a Windows computer in Windows.

If you want to go directly to a shared folder on the network, you can also enter the Share Name of the folder. For example, in Windows, type *computername**foldersharename*.

If you are on a Mac OS X computer and want to access another Mac, you can enter **afp://** and the Computer Name or IP address of the Mac computer. You can enter this into a Web browser or use Connect to Server from the Go menu, shown in Figure 7-4.

Figure 7-4: Manually accessing a Mac computer in Mac OS X.

To go directly to a shared folder, you can type the following into a Web browser or use the Connect to Server from the Go menu: afp:// computername/foldersharename.

If you are on a Mac OS X computer but wanting to access a Windows computer (or Ubuntu computer with Windows Sharing enabled), you can enter **smb://** and the Computer Name or IP address of the computer, shown in Figure 7-5.

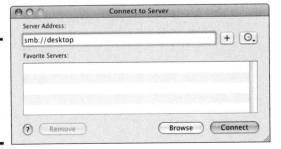

Figure 7-5: Manually accessing a Windows computer in Mac OS X.

To go directly to a shared folder, you can type the following into a Web browser or use the Connect to Server from the Go menu: **smb://** *computername/foldersharename*.

When using Ubuntu, you can manually access Windows computers using the Connect to Server tool. To do so, follow these steps:

1. **Click Places from the Ubuntu toolbar.**

2. **Choose Connect to Server.**

3. **Select Windows Share for the Service Type.**

4. **Enter the Computer Name or IP address of the computer you want to access into the Server field.**

To go directly to a shared folder, type the Share Name of that folder into the Share field.

5. **Click Connect.**

Now you can use the shortcut to the computer. The shortcut appears directly on the Places menu Network and your Desktop.

You can also access a Mac computer from Ubuntu by enabling Windows Sharing in Mac OS X (discussed in Book IV, Chapter 3) and connecting to it just as if it were a Windows computer.

Accessing Hidden Shares

You can access hidden shares just as you would if you were manually accessing any other shared folder on the network, as discussed in the previous section. Just don't forget to append the dollar sign to the end of the Share Name when you enter it in the Address field of the My Computer window. Figure 7-6 shows an example.

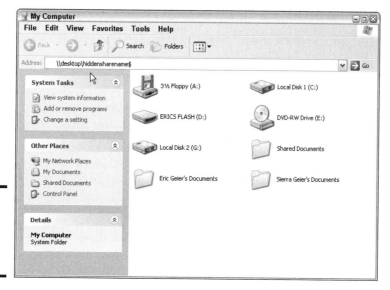

Figure 7-6:
Accessing a hidden share in Windows.

Accessing and Working with Offline Files

One of the biggest things you'll need to know — which isn't that obvious — when working with Offline Files is how to access them when working offline, or away from the shared folder. (The previous chapter in this minibook shows you how to enable the Offline Files feature.) Here are a few ways:

✦ **In My Network Places or Network:** Even though you may not have a connection to the computer hosting the Offline Files, the computer will still be accessible from My Network Places (in Windows 2000 and XP) or Network (in Windows Vista) just like normal. When you open the computer, you'll see the files and folders you set up as Offline Files.

✦ **Desktop shortcut to Offline Files:** If you specified in the Offline Files preferences to create a shortcut to Offline Files on your Desktop, you can just double-click this icon. Then you'll see all the offline files.

**Book IV
Chapter 7**

**Accessing Shared
Files and Folders-**

If you want to access the Offline Files settings, refer to the previous chapter. Windows Vista, however, doesn't offer this shortcut option, but you can create a shortcut: Bring up the Offline Files settings from the Control Panel, click the View your Offline Files button, click on the icon to the left of the address bar, and drag it to the Desktop.

Another task you may want to know is how to manually start the synchronization of your Offline Files. This may be necessary just before the connection between the computers is broken — take your laptop out or shutdown a computer — so you're sure the Offline Files are all up-to-date.

In Windows 2000 and XP, here's how to manually start the synchronization process:

1. **Click Start.**

2. **Choose Programs.**

3. **Choose Accessories.**

4. **Click Synchronize.**

You can also click the Setup button to change the synchronization preferences.

5. **Choose the desired items and click Synchronize.**

The synchronization window appears, showing the progress of the transfer of files from the computer hosting the files.

If you're using Windows Vista, here's how to manually start the synchronization process:

1. **Click Start.**

2. **Choose All Programs.**

3. **Choose Accessories.**

4. **Click Sync Center.**

5. **Choose the desired item and click Sync.**

If you want to synchronize all the items, click Sync All, which is visible when you don't have any items selected.

Moving and Editing Shared Files and Folders among Computers

When you display a computer's shared resources, you can do the following (depending on the permissions you've set for the shared folder):

✦ **Transfer files or folders to the remote computer:** You can copy files or folders by selecting them and dragging them to the computer's Desktop (as shown in Figure 7-7) or other location. You can also move files and folders by selecting them, right-clicking, choosing Cut, and browsing to the new location you want them in. You then choose Paste to deposit them in that location.

Figure 7-7:
Copying
files to a
computer
from a
shared
folder.

✦ **Open and edit files directly over the network:** You can simply double-click files to open them. Anyone who has permission to edit the files can do so and then save the files and exit. Remember that when you save a file, you're saving it over the network to the original computer, so that original computer needs to be on and connected to the network, or your changes may be lost.

✦ **Create shortcuts to the shared folders or files:** To create shortcuts to shared folders or files in Windows, you select the files or folders you want to create shortcuts for, right-click them, drag them to a location on the computer, release the mouse button, and then click Create Shortcuts Here (see Figure 7-8).

✦ **Add a shared printer to your computer:** When viewing the shared resources of computers in Windows, when you see a shared printer among any shared files and folders, you can easily add that shared printer to the computer you're working on. Just right-click the printer icon and click Connect, and then follow the instructions shown on your screen. Adding shared printers to your computers is covered in detail in Book IV, Chapter 5.

If you frequently access shared files and documents, you can create shortcuts with mapped drives, as discussed in the previous chapter.

Book IV
Chapter 7

Accessing Shared
Files and Folders-

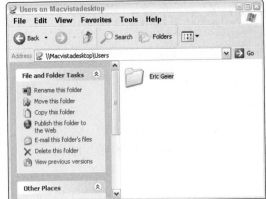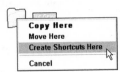

Figure 7-8:
Creating shortcuts on a computer to shared folders or files.

Chapter 8: Serving Files over the Internet

In This Chapter

✓ Getting a domain name on the Internet

✓ Setting up a Web server to host files or Web pages

✓ Setting up an FTP server to host files

✓ Configuring your firewall and router to work with your servers

The ability to share files and folders is not restricted to your home network — you can also share files over the Internet, for you or others to access from all over the world. You can do this by setting up your own Web server, which also lets you host your own Web site. You can also set up an FTP server, thereby giving you or others on the Internet the ability to upload files to and download files from your computer. This chapter takes you through setting up these various types of servers and configuring your home network with the required settings.

Creating Your Own Web Server

You can set up your own Web server to serve files over the Internet or host a Web site. After the setup work is done, you or anyone can access your files or Web pages (that you specify to share) on the Internet. Even if you aren't a tech head, you can do it — with my help.

First, you should understand how people will be able to access your Web server. When you set up a Web server, it becomes accessible to you or others on the Internet by entering the IP address of your Internet connection where you normally enter a Web address in a browser. An example of an IP address is 255.255.255.255. However, for an easier and more appealing address to use, you can get a domain name, which then points to the IP address of your Internet connection or Web server. The next two sections discuss two ways to go about getting a domain name (one for free; the other for a price).

Getting a free Web site address

One way to get a free domain name is to sign up for the Dynamic DNS service from www.dyndns.com. When you do so, you end up with a hostname (domain name) consisting of a prefix of your choice and your desired domain that's available from this service's list. (You have many choices.) For example, you can sign up for a domain name of *yourhostname*.getmyip.com or *yourhostname*.is-a-geek.com (where *yourhostname* is the name you've chosen to identify your domain, and the rest of the address is the domain you've chosen from the list of available domains).

After you've created an account with DynDNS, you can sign up for a hostname by going to your main My Account page and clicking the Add Host Services link, which takes you to the Add New Hostname page (shown in Figure 8-1). On this page, in the Hostname field, enter your desired prefix and select an available domain. You should just leave the Wildcard and Service Type fields alone. For the IP address field, click the Use Auto Detected IP Address link that also includes your Internet IP address.

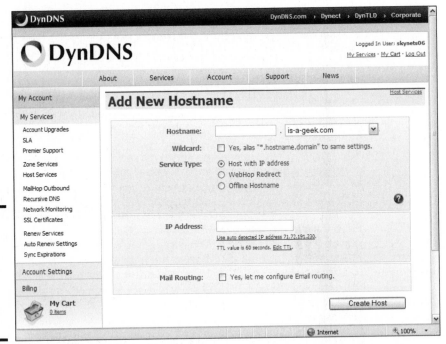

Figure 8-1:
Create a new Dynamic DNS hostname on dyndns.com.

Next, you need to set up your router to work with the Dynamic DNS service. To do so, follow these steps:

1. **Connect to your router and login.**

To make setting changes, you must log in to the Web-based utility:

a. **Open your Web browser (Internet Explorer, Netscape, Firefox, or other).**

b. **Type the IP address of your router and press Enter.**

c. **When prompted, enter your login credentials.**

If you don't know the IP address or the username or password, refer to Book V, Chapter 3 for help. Keep in mind that some manufacturers may use a domain name, which looks like a Web site address, instead of an IP address.

2. **Find the Dynamic DNS settings.**

This is usually in an Advanced or Tools section of the Web-based configuration utility. Figure 8-2 shows an example.

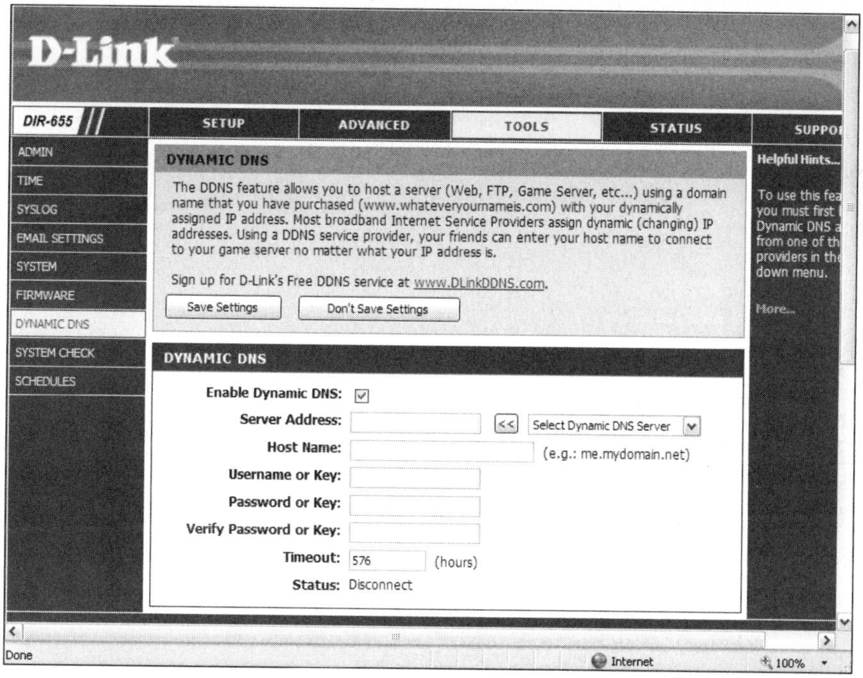

Figure 8-2:
Dynamic
DNS
settings in
a router.

Book IV
Chapter 8

Serving Files over
the Internet

3. **Enter the account details.**

You'll probably find the following settings that you must specify:

- **Server Address:** Enter or select the server for the Dynamic DNS service you signed up for, such as www.dyndns.com.

- **Host Name:** Enter your hostname that you registered, such as *yourhostname*.**getmyip.com**.

- **Username and Password:** Enter the login credentials for your account at the Dynamic DNS service.

4. **Save your changes.**

You need to save and apply the changes by clicking a Save button on the top or bottom of the page.

The device may reboot, and you may be disconnected for a minute. When you're connected to the network again, the Web-based utility may return to the page that you left off on. Sometimes, though, it goes to a Not Found page.

Purchasing your own domain name

If you prefer your very own domain name, for example *yourname*.com, the process is a bit more involved:

1. **Find and purchase an available domain name.**

First, you need to decide where you want to buy your domain name. Here are a few places you may want to check out:

- www.godaddy.com

- smallbusiness.yahoo.com

- www.networksolutions.com

When comparing domain registrars, keep these items in mind:

- **Price:** You'll probably find that you can register dot com domains for around $10 per year.

- **DNS control:** To host your site on your own Web server, you need DNS *(Domain Name System)* control, which is very common among domain registrars. DNS control simply means that you can change the DNS settings (particularly the name servers) for your domain name so that you can point your name to different Web servers.

- **Private registration:** Usually available at a small additional cost, this feature hides your personal contact information from the public on domain listing directories. Hiding your information prevents spammers from getting your contact information from these domain directories, which is a common problem.

- **Domain locking:** Usually provided free, this feature helps prevents unauthorized changes and transfers to your domain name and Web site hosting services.

- **Extras:** Some domain registrars provide many free extras, for example online photo services, e-mail service, and free Web site hosting. These extras may be your deciding factor when picking a domain registrar.

***2.* Get Domain Name Service (DNS) service.**

To point your domain name to your Web server at home, you must set up a DNS service.

You can sign up for free DNS service at www.zoneedit.com. After registering, access your account using the link and login credentials sent to you in an e-mail confirmation message. You should add a zone to your account with the domain name you purchased. See Figure 8-3 for an example.

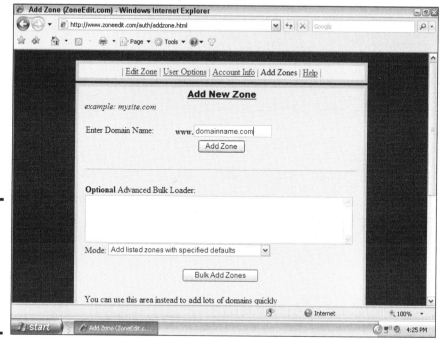

Figure 8-3:
Adding a zone (domain) to an account at zoneedit. com.

You can then access the zone settings by clicking the Edit Zone link on the top of the Web site and selecting your zone. Next, click the IP addresses (A) link from your zone page. Enter the IP address of your Internet (WAN) connection into the Numeric IP field (leaving the Name field blank) and click the Add New IP Address button. Figure 8-4 shows an example of the page where you set up your DNS service to point to your server at your home.

If you need help figuring out your Internet (WAN) IP address, refer to Book V, Chapter 5.

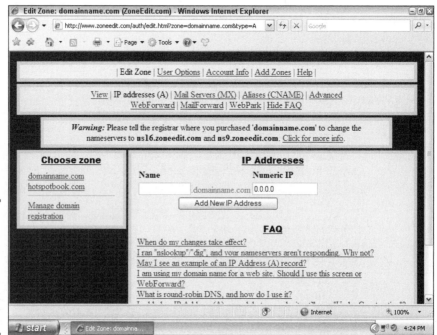

Figure 8-4:
Setting up a domain to point to an IP address (home Internet connection).

Click the first Yes button so that both addresses point to your Web server.

If your Internet connection uses a dynamic IP address — and virtually all home connections do — you now have to set up a Dynamic DNS client on your computer. You do this to automatically update the IP address entered in ZoneEdit when your Internet IP address changes at home so that the domain name will point to your Web server.

If you're using ZoneEdit, you can download a supported Dynamic DNS client from the ZoneEdit Web site at `www.zoneedit.com/doc/dynamic.html`. Look for a client for your particular operating system (Windows, Mac, or other). After you download and install the client, configure it with your ZoneEdit account details.

Now when the IP address for your Internet connection changes, ZoneEdit will be notified, and your domain name will point to your new IP address and Web server.

3. **Change the Nameservers at your domain name registrar.**

   Go to the Web site of the registrar you used to purchase your domain name. Access the settings of the domain name and enter the custom Nameservers available from your DNS service. If using ZoneEdit, these are the addresses given on the main page for your zone, under the Nameservers section.

It can take up to 72 hours for your Web server to be accessible from your domain name after changing the Nameservers.

Setting up a Web server (Apache)

You can probably find a variety of Web servers by searching google.com. But you'll find that one of the most popular Web server applications is Apache HTTP Server — and it's free! For that reason, I use it as an example of setting up a Web server.

Here's how to get started with the Apache HTTP Server:

1. **Obtain the Apache HTTP Server by going to `httpd.apache.org` and downloading the file called Win32 Binary Including OpenSSL.**

2. **Click the `.msi` file you just downloaded and, when it opens, follow the directions given in the Installation Wizard.**

3. **To configure the Web server during the installation, in the Server Information window, enter the hostname you created with the Dynamic DNS service or the domain you purchased for the Network Domain and Server Name.**

   Make sure that you also select the All Users option. Figure 8-5 shows an example of information entered in this window.

Configuring your firewall and router

With your Web server set up, you next need to configure your firewall and router to work with your Web server. To do so, you must first have your firewall set to allow inbound and outbound access for your Web server software, and your router must be told which computer has the Web server. I tell you how to do both those tasks in two later sections in this chapter, "Letting Servers through Your Firewall" and "Letting Server Access through Your Router." Refer to those sections, and then return here and continue with the next subsection.

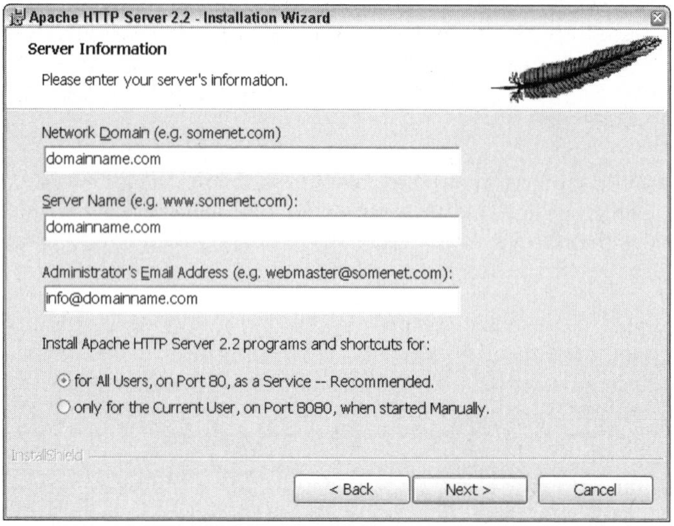

Figure 8-5:
Configuring
the Apache
HTTP
Server.

Testing the Web server

It's time to see whether the Web server works! From your computer, enter your hostname or domain name into your Web browser and press Enter . If your Web server software is loaded with a test or default Web page, that page should appear. Or, if you're using the Apache HTTP Server, you should see the It Works! page appear. If you don't see the default Web page, check the Web server's documentation on troubleshooting the problem.

Using the Web server

After you confirm that your Web server is installed and working, you can move your files and Web pages to the public or root directory folder of your Web server software and delete the default pages and files. Only the files in this folder will be accessible from the Internet. If you are using the Apache HTTP Server, you find this folder at

```
C:\Program Files\Apache Software Foundation\Apache2.2\htdocs
```

Creating Your Own FTP Server

If you want to regularly exchange files with others on the Internet, you may want to set up a File Transfer Protocol (FTP) server. After you have the server software set up on your computer, you can drag or copy files into the server's root folder. Then, using an FTP client application — Windows XP and Vista have one built in — you or others can download these files from the Internet, plus (if you prefer) upload more files and delete files. You can let anyone access the FTP server or set passwords by creating user accounts.

Searching on google.com will reveal countless FTP server applications. To serve as an example here, I use Cerberus FTP Server, which is free for personal use — plus it's user friendly and full featured. Before getting started, here are buzz-terms you should familiarize yourself with:

✦ **Root or home directory:** After you install the FTP server, you'll have a root, or home, directory for it. This is where you put files and folders to be accessible when connecting to the FTP server. This directory is also where files will appear if FTP users on the Internet upload files to your server.

✦ **Start/Stop server:** FTP server programs commonly have a Start and Stop button, which enable you to start and stop the server.

✦ **Users:** When you or someone else wants to access the files on your FTP server (in the root directory), login is required. If anonymous access is enabled on the FTP server, you can usually click an option in the client program to use an anonymous username and password. If you set up specific user accounts in the FTP server, however, you enter the username and password of the account when logging into the FTP server from a client application.

✦ **Secure FTP:** This term means that encryption is used to secure connections between users and the FTP server. This is good if you or someone else plans to access your FTP server from public networks such as Wi-Fi hotspots. If you want to support this feature for your FTP users, you must use a server that supports it. (Cerberus FTP Server does,) Keep in mind that the FTP client application has to support secure FTP as well.

✦ **Messages:** Some FTP server programs let you specify messages to use for certain alerts, such as the Welcome and Goodbye messages that are shown to users when they connect to your server. These messages display in the session log window (see Figure 8-6) when using a traditional FTP client.

**Book IV
Chapter 8**

**Serving Files over
the Internet**

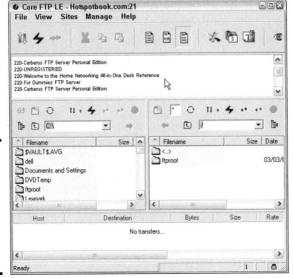

Figure 8-6:
FTP session
log showing
my custom
messages
configured
for my FTP
server.

Setting up the FTP server

To set up an FTP server, you first must download it. If you want to use the same one as in the examples and steps to follow, download Cerberus FTP Server from www.cerberusftp.com. When you have it downloaded, complete the installation and then follow these steps:

1. **In the Getting Started Wizard that appears, select Personal Use — if this application is for your personal use — and click Next.**

2. **On the User Creation screen, specify the initial user details, as shown in Figure 8-7 and described in the following paragraphs, and when you're done with this screen, click Next.**

   An anonymous user account is set by default, which is fine if you want to offer access to anyone who tries to connect. However, upload permission isn't recommended for anonymous logins. You can toggle between allowing upload and download capability by selecting or deselecting the Allow Download and Allow Upload options near the bottom of the User Creation screen in the wizard.

   If you want to create an actual user account, simply deselect the Anonymous option and then type your desired username and password.

   As discussed earlier, the root is the directory on your computer that contains the files served on the FTP server. If you want to choose a different folder, click the button to the right of the root name.

   Specify whether you want to allow this user (or anonymous users) to download and upload.

3. **When you get to the Continue with WAN IP Auto-Detection dialog box, make sure you're connected to the Internet and then click Yes to allow WAN IP auto-detection.**

If the wizard can't detect your Internet IP address, you can manually input it later in the Configuration windows of the main application.

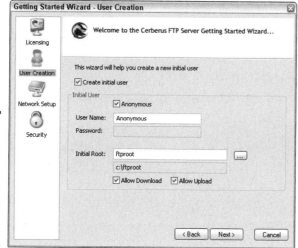

Figure 8-7: Entering initial user details during the installation of Cerberus FTP Server.

4. **On the Network Setup screen, click Next.**

5. **On the Security screen, specify whether you want to enable SSL/TLS (secure FTP) and then click Finish.**

Enabling this feature makes the FTP connection much more secure; however, the FTP client you or others use to connect to your FTP server must support SSL/TLS connections. Not all clients (including the built-in FTP client in Windows) support it.

If you choose to enable it, fill out the information.

Configuring your firewall and router

To configure your firewall and router to work with your FTP server, your firewall must be set to allow inbound and outbound access for your FTP server software, and your router must be told which computer has the server. For help in performing these tasks, refer to the later sections, "Letting Servers through Your Firewall" and "Letting Server Access through Your Router." Then return here and continue with the next section.

Book IV
Chapter 8

Serving Files over
the Internet

Connecting to the FTP server

When you have the FTP server, firewall, and router configured to work with your FTP server, you should test the server. If you are using Windows, you can use the built-in FTP client, as follows:

1. **Open the Add Network Place Wizard:**

   In Windows XP: Choose Start⇨My Network Places. Then click Network Tasks in the left pane and click the Add a Network Place link.

   In Windows Vista: Choose Start⇨Computer. Then right-click in the Computer window and select Add a Network Location.

2. **In the wizard, click Next.**

3. **Select the Choose Another Network Location option and then click Next.**

4. **In the Internet or Network Address text box, type ftp:// and your Internet IP address, as shown Figure 8-8, and then click Next.**

   If you have already set up a hostname or domain name (for a Web server) to point to your Internet IP address, you can enter those names here as well, after the FTP:// part of your entry.

   If you want to access your FTP server from computers on the same network, you can use the local IP address of the computer that's hosting the server.

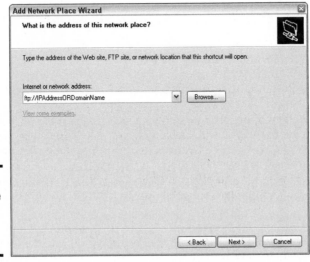

Figure 8-8:
Entering the address of an FTP server.

If you need help figuring out these IP addresses, refer to Book V, Chapter 3.

5. Specify a username to use and click Next.

If you set up anonymous access, you don't have to do anything on this screen. But if you specified a particular user account, deselect the Anonymous option and input the username of the account you created in the FTP server.

6. Enter a name for the shortcut and click Next.

You can enter anything you want to help you distinguish this network shortcut from the others in My Network Places.

7. Click Finish.

If you keep the option selected, the shortcut (for your FTP server) will appear when you click Finish. Otherwise, you can access the shortcut in My Network Places. If you have set up the Network Place to connect to a user account with a password, you'll see the Log On As prompt.

Enter your password, choose whether you want to save the password, and click Log On.

To securely connect to your FTP server using SSL/TLS, you must use a third-party FTP client, as discussed in the next paragraph. Keep in mind, though, even when the SSL/TLS feature is enabled in Cerberus FTP Server, you can choose to connect normally.

You can also use other third-party FTP clients to connect to your FTP server. Here are some Web sites to check out a few possibilities:

+ www.coreftp.com

+ www.smartftp.com

+ www.goftp.com

These FTP client applications usually have a site list that you can add your FTP shortcuts to. All you will probably have to do is input the host address (your Internet IP address or host/domain name) and specify whether you want to log in as Anonymous or input a username and password. You can leave the default port and other settings alone. If you want to connect securely, you'll probably see an SSL option or protocol that you can enable.

Letting Servers through Your Firewall

In order for any server (whether Web, FTP, or other) to work properly, you need to add that server to your firewall's list of authorized programs. After installing and opening the server application, you may be prompted by the

Windows or other firewall program to block or unblock the application. If you choose to unblock it, you're good to go. Additionally, the server application may have added itself to the firewall authorized list; however, you should double-check.

If using Windows Firewall, here's how you can let your server(s) through the firewall:

1. **Open Windows Firewall:**

Here's how you can access the firewall in Windows XP:

a. **Choose Start⇨Control Panel.**

If you're using the Classic Start menu, hover the mouse cursor over Settings and then click Control Panel.

b. **Choose the Network and Internet Connections category.**

If using the Classic Control Panel view, ignore this step.

c. **Click Wireless Firewall.**

Here's how to access the firewall in Windows Vista:

a. **Choose Start⇨Control Panel.**

b. **In the Control Panel, choose the Security category.**

If using the Classic Control Panel view, ignore this step.

c. **Click Wireless Firewall.**

If UAC is active and you received an alert, click OK to continue.

2. **Click the Exceptions tab.**

3. **Click the Add Program button.**

4. **Find and select the server program and click OK.**

If using the Apache HTTP Server, browse to and select the following:

```
C:\Program Files\Apache Software Foundation\
    Apache2.2\bin\httpd.exe
```

If using the Cerberus FTP Server, browse to and select the following:

```
C:\Program Files\Cerberus\Cerberus.exe
```

Letting Server Access through Your Router

To enable people to access the files and Web pages on your Web or FTP server, you must configure your router. You need to tell your router which computer has the server on it. To do so, follow these steps:

1. **Connect to your router and login.**

To make setting changes, you must log in to the Web-based utility:

a. **Open your Web browser (Internet Explorer, Netscape, Firefox, or other).**

b. **Type the IP address of your router and press Enter.**

c. **When prompted, enter your login credentials.**

If you don't know the IP address or the username or password, you can refer to Book V, Chapter 3 for help. Keep in mind that some manufacturers may use a domain name that looks like a Web site address instead of an IP address.

2. **Find the Virtual Server or Port Forwarding settings.**

These settings are usually in an Advanced section of the Web-based configuration utility and may be named Virtual Server or Port Forwarding settings. Figure 8-9 shows an example of Virtual Server settings.

3. **Enter the port details for each port you need to forward.**

You'll probably find that you must specify the following settings:

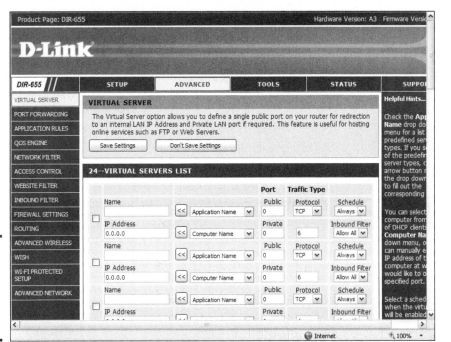

Figure 8-9: Virtual server settings of a wireless router.

Book IV
Chapter 8

Serving Files over the Internet

- **Name:** This is for your reference, so enter what you want, for example, **Web server** or **FTP server**.

- **IP address:** You need to enter the IP address of the computer that's set up with the server. This is the computer that the router will forward the applicable traffic to. If you need help finding your computer's IP address, refer to Book V, Chapter 5.

- **Ports:** You need to enter the server ports of your application. For Web servers, this is usually port 80, and for FTP servers, port 21.

4. **Save your changes.**

   You need to save and apply the changes by clicking a Save button on the top or bottom of the page.

   The device may reboot and you may be disconnected for a minute. When you're connected to the network again, the Web-based utility may return to the page that you left off on. Sometimes, though, it goes to a Page Not Found page instead.

Things to Remember When Serving

Here are a few things you should understand when using servers:

+ **Internet down, server down:** If your Internet connection at home is not working, you or others can't access any servers that are hosted at your home.

+ **Don't let your PC sleep:** If your computer that's hosting the server is sleeping, the servers are inaccessible. So you should look over your Power Options, which are accessible from the Control Panel. You may want to make sure the hard drive and system standby options are set to Never.

+ **Local IP changes:** When you set up your router to forward your server traffic to the computer that has the server on it, all you did was forward the traffic to its IP address. The problem is if you're using DHCP on your network — which is always set by default — the IP addresses of your computers can change once in a while. Therefore, after a while, your router will forward the traffic to another computer (or no computer), and your server will be inaccessible from the Internet.

   Most routers have a static DHCP or DHCP reservation feature that lets you force a particular IP address for computers, while still using DHCP. Another option is to disable DHCP and manually configure each computer/device with a static IP address; doing so, however, takes time and is beyond the scope of this book.

Book V

Network Troubleshooting

The 5th Wave   By Rich Tennant

"Roger! Check the sewing machine's connection to the PC. I'm getting e-mails stitched across my curtains again."

Contents at a Glance

Chapter 1: Dealing with Connection and Performance Problems

In This Chapter

✔ **Troubleshooting and fixing your wired and wireless connections**

✔ **Diagnosing and combating wireless interference**

✔ **Repairing network adapters**

✔ **Fixing Internet problems**

*H*aving problems connecting with your network? Can't get on the Internet? Are you ready to give up and throw the networking gear out the window? Well, before you give up, go through this chapter. It will help you troubleshoot the underlying cause and should assist you in getting your network and Internet back online.

Fixing Wireless Connections

Maybe you can't connect to your wireless network or are intermittently being disconnected from your wireless network. Or your network vanishes from your list of available wireless networks. If any of these situations apply to you, you're at the right spot for getting answers.

If you're using a laptop or mobile device, move closer to the wireless router. This can help determine the underlying cause.

The first step to help troubleshoot the problem is to look over the following common underlying causes and then pick one to try to resolve:

✦ **Adapter problem:** Issues from device or connection settings can be identified by the following, especially if you are using special or proprietary features or technologies (range or speed boosting, MIMO, wireless N, and so on):

- Computer won't connect at all when relatively close to the router, and usually doesn't happen regularly.

- Computer connects with another neighboring network intermittently.

- Data rate never hits expectations, such as getting only 11 Mbps instead of 54 Mbps, or only 54 Mbps instead of something higher.

✦ **Interference:** Being adversely affected by other radio waves, or RF interference, may be identified by the following symptoms, and more so if you are aware that you have common interfering devices around (discussed later):

- Disconnections from the wireless network.

- Disappearance of your wireless network from your list of available networks

✦ **Poor range:** If you experience the following when you're relatively distant from the router, you likely just don't have the wireless coverage you desire, rather than have a real problem:

- Low speed (data rate), when relatively far from router.

- Computer won't connect at all or disconnects, when relatively far from router.

Now you can proceed with the following sections, which help you try to resolve the underlying cause. Start with the one that seems the most likely for your particular situation, and if the problem still persists, proceed with the next likely cause, and so on, until you have success.

Addressing adapter problems

First, look over the specific issues and possible solutions described in this section:

If you keep automatically connecting to neighboring wireless networks

Examine your connectivity and preferred network settings by following these steps:

1. **Check the preferred list.**

Make sure your home network (or the network you want to stay connected to) is on the top of your preferred network list.

2. **Clean the preferred list.**

You may try removing all the other preferred network entries, leaving just your home network.

3. **Check advanced settings.**

In Windows XP's advanced network connectivity settings, make sure you don't have the Automatically Connect to Non-Preferred Networks option selected.

If you need help finding these settings for Windows, Mac, or Ubuntu, refer to Book IV, Chapter 1.

Generally, when your wireless adapter automatically connects to neighboring wireless networks, it's because those networks have a better signal than your home network. This can be due to an interfering device near your wireless router or poor range of your network. So you may want to think about investigating if you have interference problems, discussed in the next section, and possibly expanding your wireless coverage, discussed in the last subsection of this section.

If you can't connect to a wireless N router with an older (wireless B) wireless adapter

Try changing wireless mode from Mixed (wireless N, G, and B) to wireless G and B or wireless G only, as follows:

1. **Log in to your router's Web-based configuration utility.**

   Open your Web browser, type the IP address of your router, and press Enter. If you don't know the IP address, refer to Book V, Chapter 3. Enter your login credentials when prompted. If you don't know the password, refer to Book V, Chapter 3.

2. **Find the wireless mode option in the wireless settings.**

   Wireless settings usually have their own tab or are in the main or general section. However, sometimes the wireless mode option is in the advanced wireless section.

3. **Change the wireless mode and apply the changes.**

   Select an option to eliminate wireless N, usually wireless G and B or wireless G only.

If you aren't getting the high speed (data rates) you were hoping for from your equipment

Remember that to use special features such as speed boosting; your router and all the adapters in the computers must also have the same feature, and generally be the same brand of equipment. This is similar to using different wireless standards/technologies. Even though the wireless b, g, and n standards are interoperable, the speeds and performance vary. For example, if you're using a wireless n router to get the high speeds advertised by the vendor, you must also use wireless N adapters in your computers — at least for the computers you want to have the high speeds. Plus, some routers and adapters may only achieve the highest performance when using the same brand.

Solving other miscellaneous problems

Here are a few tasks you can try to fix general wireless adapter problems:

✦ **Reboot your network.** Unplug the power cords for your Internet modem and router and wait 30 seconds. Then reconnect the power to just the Internet modem, wait 30 seconds, and reconnect the power to your router.

✦ **Reset your wireless adapter.** You start by giving your adapter a fresh start. Disable your problematic wireless adapter, wait a few seconds, and then re-enable it. If you need help, refer to Book IV, Chapter 1.

✦ **Restart your computer.** Next, you should refresh your computer — give it a nice Restart.

✦ **Reinstall your adapter.** If you haven't fixed the problem yet, and you still think you have an isolated problem with your wireless adapter, you may want to reinstall the adapter's driver.

This should fix any quirks of the adapter you may be experiencing. Also, when you reinstall the driver, you should get the latest release, which may fix your problem and other known issues. You should refer to Book II, Chapter 5 for more information on updating your adapter's driver.

If you can't get any of your computers to connect to your router, you may want to try resetting it to factory defaults. See Book V, Chapter 3 for more information.

If you are having problems connecting to a WEP-enabled wireless network in Mac OS X Tiger, try putting a dollar sign in front of the WEP key.

Dealing with interference

Electrical and radio devices that use — or bleed onto — the same frequency band (2.4 GHz) of your wireless network can interfere with it. These devices include the following:

✦ Neighboring wireless networks

✦ Cordless phones

✦ Baby monitors

✦ Wireless speakers and headphones

✦ Kitchen microwaves

If you're using the less popular wireless A equipment, then you're using the 5 GHz frequency band instead. You may experience interference from other similar 5 GHz devices.

As mentioned earlier, being intermittently disconnected from your network and not being able to see your network are signs of interference, especially if you have these common interfering devices around. Plus, two more things can help troubleshoot if interference is your problem:

✦ **Pay attention when the problem occurs.** When you have a problem with connecting to your network, take a quick look around, scratch your head, and see whether someone is using one of the common interfering items, such as those listed in the previous bullets.

✦ **Disable suspect interferers:** Sometimes, interfering devices don't have to be used to cause problems. For example, a 2.4 GHz cordless phone may constantly interfere with your network even when the phone is hung up and charging. So to help find the interfering device, unplug your suspected devices one at a time to see whether the problems go away.

If you know or suspect that interference is your problem, here are several things you can try to fix the problem.

Change your wireless router's channel

The interfering device may affect only a portion of the frequency band of wireless networks, so changing the channel of your wireless network may fix the problem. Here's how you can change the channel of your wireless router:

1. **Log in to your router's Web-based configuration utility.**

Open your Web browser, type the IP address of your router, and press Enter. If you don't know the IP address, refer to Book V, Chapter 3. Enter your login credentials, when prompted. If you don't know the password, again refer to Book V, Chapter 3.

2. **Find the wireless channel setting (see Figure 1-1 for an example).**

You can find this with all the other general wireless settings, which are usually on their own tab or are in the main or general section.

3. **Change the channel and apply the changes.**

Select a different channel, preferably channel 1, 6, or 11; however, you can try the other channels after you try the recommended ones.

Keep trying different channels by repeating the steps until the problem goes away or you have tried all the channels.

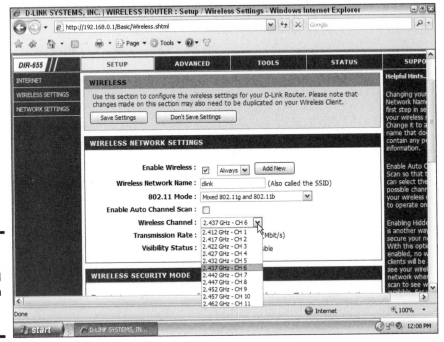

Figure 1-1:
Example of the channel setting for a wireless router.

Move away from suspect interferer

Interfering devices have a greater negative impact on your wireless network when closer to your wireless router and network adapters. Therefore, try separating them to be as far apart as possible, either by moving the interferer or your wireless router and computers.

Get rid of the interferer

Of course, if you've found the interferer and can't stop the interference with your network, you can stop using the interferer. If you're currently using wireless B, G, or N, you can try using wireless A, which usually doesn't have as many interference problems; however, it isn't as popular, so the products will cost more. Also, keep in mind that many Wi-Fi hotspots (and probably most of your friends' networks) don't support wireless A, so if you do want to try wireless A, you should purchase dual-or tri-band wireless adapters (which support wireless A along with wireless G, N, or both) for your computers.

Addressing range issues

If you believe that poor range of your wireless network is the cause of your connectivity problems, you should think about expanding your wireless coverage. However, before spending money, here are two things you can try:

✦ **Reposition your router.** It's best to put your wireless router right in the middle of your desired coverage area. Positioning your router in this spot helps ensure that you have relatively equal coverage in all directions. Figures 1-2 and 1-3 give you examples of the differences between good and bad placements.

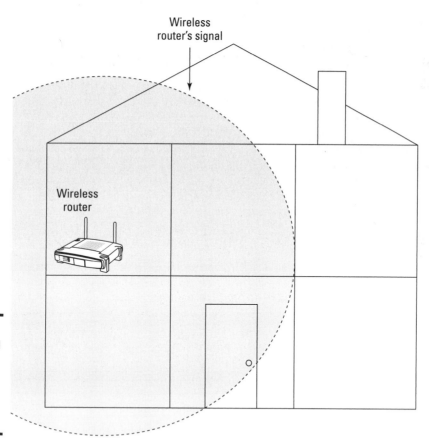

Wireless router's signal

Wireless router

Figure 1-2:
Not so good placement of a wireless router in a home.

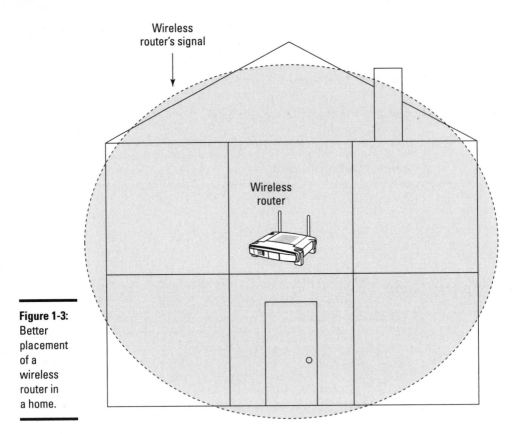

Wireless
router's signal

Wireless
router

Figure 1-3:
Better
placement
of a
wireless
router in
a home.

The locations of cable or phone outlets can impact where you can place your wireless router, but you can try to work around this roadblock. You can think about running a cable or phone line to the optimum spot for your wireless router, or consider installing new outlets.

✦ **Reposition your computer.** You may also think about bringing your computers closer to the wireless router by moving rooms. But even small changes can help, such as bringing your PC tower up off the ground onto a desk so that the antenna has more exposure to the router.

If you're still having connectivity issues, here are several ways you can really increase the range of your wireless network:

✦ **Replace your antennas.** This can be a very easy and cheap way to increase the coverage of your network. If you have just one or two computers out on the fringe of the wireless coverage, you can purchase better antennas for them. If you want more all-around coverage, get a replacement antenna for your wireless router. To get the best results for computers on or outside the coverage fringe, replace both your router and adapter antennas.

+ **Upgrade to wireless N.** This can give you much better range and performance over older wireless standards, such as wireless G or B.

+ **Install a wireless extender/repeater.** This involves purchasing a wireless extender that will act as a repeater for the wireless traffic between your wireless router and distant computers.

+ **Add access points (APs).** This involves purchasing one or more APs (similar to wireless routers) and placing them around your home. This provides the greatest increase in range but generally requires the most time and money.

For more information on all these methods, refer to Book II, Chapter 7.

Reconnecting Wired (Ethernet) Connections

Fixing connectivity issues with wired network connections usually is much easier than it is with wireless connections. Wired connections don't require troubleshooting interference and range issues. You'll usually just find an unplugged cable or hardware quirk that's fixed by restarting your hardware and computer. Here are some things to try:

+ **Check physical connections.** Take a quick look behind your computer to see whether the Ethernet cable somehow popped out of the Ethernet port. Then follow the Ethernet cable all the way to the router or Internet modem to see whether little Billy got hold of the scissors and decided to take a cut at the cable. Finally, check whether the other end of the Ethernet cable is securely plugged into your router or Internet modem.

+ **Reboot your network.** Unplug the power cords for your Internet modem and router and wait 30 seconds. Then reconnect the power to just the Internet modem, wait 30 seconds, and reconnect the power to your router.

+ **Reset your network adapter.** You should give your adapter a fresh start. Disable your problematic network adapter, wait a few seconds, and then re-enable it. If you need help, refer to Book IV, Chapter 1.

+ **Restart your computer.** Refresh your computer — give it a nice Restart.

+ **Reinstall your adapter.** If you haven't fixed the problem yet, and you still think you have an isolated problem with your network adapter, you may want to reinstall the adapter's driver.

This should fix any quirks of the adapter you may be experiencing. Plus, when you reinstall the driver, you should get the latest release, which may fix your problem and other known issues. You should refer to Book II, Chapter 5 for more information on updating your adapter's driver.

If you can't get any of your computers to connect to your router, you may want to try resetting it to factory defaults. See Book V, Chapter 3 for more information.

Fixing Internet and Limited or No Connectivity Issues

Can you connect to your network but can't access the Internet? Are you getting "Limited or No Connectivity" alerts in Windows XP, such as that shown in Figure 1-4? If you answered yes to one of these, read on.

Figure 1-4:
The Limited or No Connectivity alert in Windows XP.

Getting the Limited or No Connectivity alert typically means that your computer is properly connected to your router or Internet modem, but your router or Internet modem is misconfigured or experiencing a quirk.

If you've just installed Service Pack 2 for Windows XP and are receiving the alert, go to `support.microsoft.com/kb/892896`.

Here are several things you can do to try to fix the problem:

✦ **Repair the connection.** You can first run the network repair process in Windows to see whether it fixes your problem. In Windows XP, double-click your adapter's icon in the system tray, click the Support tab, and then click the Repair button.

If you don't see the network icon, refer to Book IV, Chapter 1.

In Windows Vista, right-click the network icon and select Diagnose and Repair.

If you're using Mac OS X Leopard, you can use the Network Diagnostics utility, accessible by choosing the Apple icon⇨System Preferences⇨Network and then clicking the Assist Me button on the bottom of the window.

✦ **Reboot your network.** Unplug the power cords for your Internet modem and router and wait 30 seconds. Then reconnect the power to just the Internet modem, wait 30 seconds, and reconnect the power to your router.

✦ **Restart your computer.** Next, you should refresh your computer — give it a nice Restart.

✦ **Check router DHCP settings.** If you have messed around with your router's settings, you may want to check to see whether you disabled DHCP, which is set by default. To do so, log in to your router's Web-based configuration utility.

Next, open your Web browser and type the IP address of your router and press Enter. If you don't know the IP address, refer to Book V, Chapter 3. Enter your login credentials when prompted. If you don't know the password, refer to Book V, Chapter 3. Next, find the DHCP settings (see Figure 1-5 for an example).

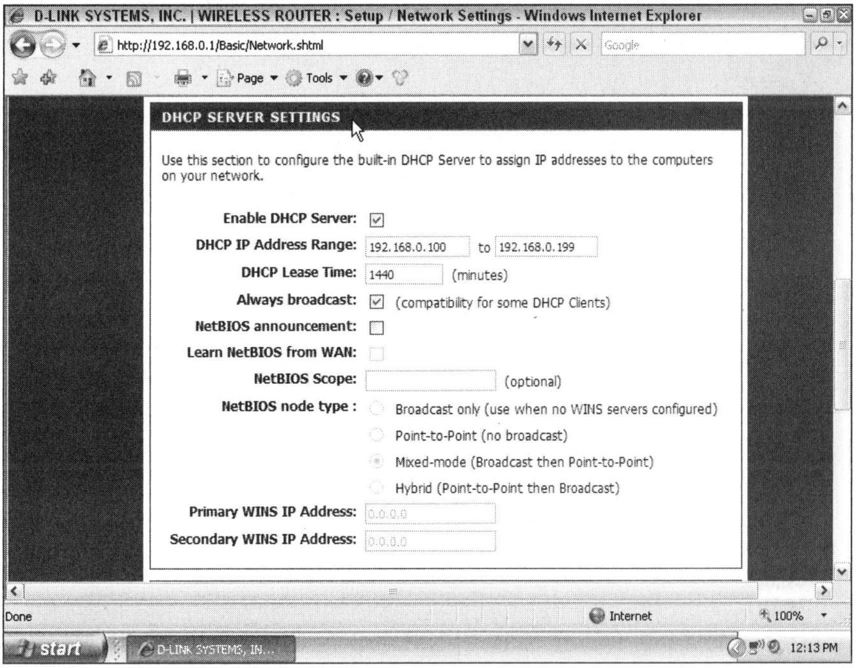

Figure 1-5:
An example of the DHCP settings of a router.

These are probably with the other general network settings, including the IP address setting for the router. Now you can verify whether DHCP is enabled.

✦ **Reset Internet Protocol (TCP/IP).** If you've tried all the other steps and you aren't having problems with all your other computers, the Internet Protocol on your computer may be corrupted. Microsoft offers Guided Help (automatic repair) and instructions on resetting Internet Protocol (TCP/IP) in Windows XP at support.microsoft.com/kb/299357.

If you're using Windows Vista, here's how you can manually reset these services: Click Start and type cmd in Start Search. Then right-click the cmd icon and choose Run as Administrator. If UAC is active and you received an alert, click OK to continue. Next, type netsh winsock reset (see Figure 1-6) and press Enter.

Figure 1-6:
Resetting the winsock service in Windows Vista.

Now, restart your computer and bring up the command prompt again, just as you did in the first two steps. Finally, type **netsh int ip reset** (see Figure 1-7) and press Enter. Restart your computer.

If you aren't getting any alert or error, but simply can't access the Internet, here are several things you can do:

✦ **Make sure you're connected to the network or Internet modem.**

✦ **Check your Internet modem.** You can verify if your Internet connection is down by looking at the status lights on your Internet modem. If it doesn't look as though you're getting an Internet connection, call your Internet service provider (ISP) to see what the problem is.

✦ **Restart your computer.** Rebooting your computer may help fix the problem.

✦ **Reboot your network.** Unplug the power cords for your Internet modem and router and wait 30 seconds. Then reconnect the power to just the Internet modem, wait 30 seconds, and reconnect the power to your router.

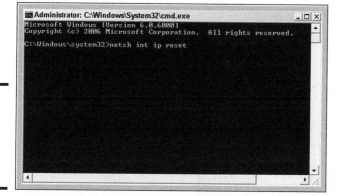

Figure 1-7: Resetting the TCP/IP service in Windows Vista.

✦ **Set static IP address correctly.** If you've manually set a static IP address for your network adapter, try setting the DNS server to your router's IP address, as shown in Figure 1-8.

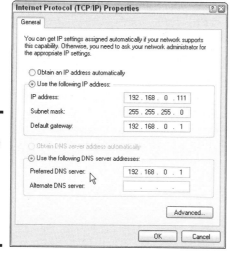

Figure 1-8: Entering the router IP address in the DNS field when setting a static IP.

If you can't get any of your computers to connect to the Internet, you may want to try resetting your adapter to factory defaults. See Book V, Chapter 3 for more information.

Chapter 2: Fixing Sharing Issues

In This Chapter

✔ **Troubleshooting and fixing file sharing problems**

✔ **Restoring shared printers**

✔ **Troubleshooting and fixing sharing issues between Windows, Mac OS X, and Ubuntu**

Are your computers connecting to the network but you can't seem to get them to talk to each other? Are you having problems accessing shared folders and printers? This chapter steps you through some tasks that you can use to try to get your system functioning like a network if you're having such issues.

Troubleshooting and Fixing Sharing Issues

If you don't see your computer(s) in My Network Places or Network, or you can't access shared folders or printers, this chapter may be able to help you. As you'll soon find out, many things can prevent sharing on your network.

If you're having problems with shared printers only, start with the "Getting a Shared Printer Back Online" section, later in this chapter, and then come back here.

The following sections help you to troubleshoot and fix your sharing issues.

Check to see whether computers are connected

You should verify whether the computer you're using and the one you're trying to access the shared resources on are logged into the operating system (Windows, Mac, Ubuntu, or any other) and connected to the same network. Book IV, Chapter 1 shows how to check your network status and connect to networks.

If you have more than two computers and you're trying to access more than one computer's shared resources, the problem is likely with your router. First, try rebooting your network. If you've messed with your router's settings, make sure that you haven't enabled client or AP isolation. The last resort is to reset your router to factory defaults, as discussed in Book V, Chapter 3.

Try to manually access shares

It can take a few minutes for computers to show in My Network Places and Network after you boot up your computer and connect to the network. However, you can use a computer's name or IP address to manually access shared resources, such as shown in Figure 2-1 and discussed in Book IV, Chapter 7.

Manually accessing a computer on the network in a Web browser.

Figure 2-1: Manually accessing a Windows computer in Windows.

If you are having trouble accessing only certain shared folders or printers but can see other shared resources from the same computer, sharing for the problematic folder(s) or printer(s) may have been disabled. Try setting up the folder or printer for sharing again. If you need help with setting up sharing, refer to Book IV, Chapters 4 and 5.

Verify your firewall settings

You should make sure that file and printer sharing is enabled in your operating system's firewall (see Figure 2-2), and in any other third-party firewall program you use, for all computers you're having trouble with.

Third-party firewalls may have a network trust mechanism that requires you to specify that you trust the network before sharing is enabled. You may also have to select an option to enable sharing, or manually input the ports used by sharing.

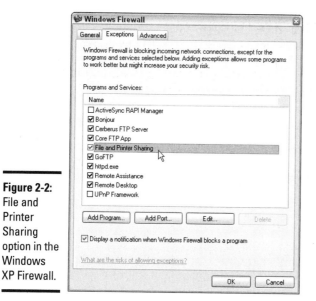

Figure 2-2:
File and
Printer
Sharing
option in the
Windows
XP Firewall.

See Book IV, Chapter 3 for more information on sharing and firewalls.

Check the network location in Windows Vista

The first time you connect to a network in Windows Vista, you must classify
its location or type: Home, Work, or Public. If you choose Public, such as
when connecting to a Wi-Fi hotspot, sharing and other applicable settings
are automatically disabled. Therefore, you should verify that Home or Work
is selected for all the Windows Vista computers that are giving you problems
sharing.

You can, however, change your network classification at any time through
the Network and Sharing Center by following these steps:

1. **Click the network icon in the system tray.**

2. **Click Network and Sharing Center.**

3. **Click the Customize link for the network.**

4. **Click Private and click Next.**

   If UAC is active and you received an alert, click Continue.

5. **Click Close.**

Reset your network adapter

Giving your network adapters a fresh start may fix any quirks that they're experiencing. Disable the network adapters on the computers, wait a few seconds, and then re-enable them. If you need help disabling and enabling your adapter, refer to Book IV, Chapter 1.

Reboot your computers

Rebooting your computers sometimes works like magic to fix any kinks that your network adapters and operating systems are experiencing that prevent sharing. (Rebooting your computer sometimes solves lots of other mysterious problems, too!)

Reboot your network

Unplug the power cords for your Internet modem and router and wait 30 seconds. Then,, reconnect the power to only the Internet modem, wait 30 seconds, and reconnect the power to your router.

Verify that sharing is enabled by your operating system

Make sure that you have properly enabled sharing on your operating system, which is discussed in Book IV, Chapter 3.

Check computer network names and Workgroups

Failing to follow the recommended computer-naming format while in the same Workgroup may interfere with sharing. You should analyze all the computer names and Workgroup designations of all the computers that you are having trouble hosting or accessing sharing resources on. Refer to Book II, Chapter 4 for details on accessing these settings.

Here are a few tips to follow:

+ Assign the same Workgroup name for all your computers.

+ Pick unique computer names for each computer.

+ Don't use computer names longer than 15 characters.

+ Avoid using spaces or any special characters in your computer names.

+ Use all uppercase characters for computer names.

Reinstall your adapter

If you haven't fixed the problem yet, and you still think you have an isolated problem with your network adapter, you may want to reinstall the adapter's driver. Doing so should fix any quirks that the adapter may be experiencing. Also, when you reinstall the driver, you should get the latest release, which may fix your problem and other known issues. Refer to Book II, Chapter 5 for more information on updating your adapter's driver.

Getting a Shared Printer Back Online

Can't see your shared printer in My Network Places or Network? Can't add a shared or network printer to your computer? Can't print to a shared printer? If the answer is yes to any of these questions, you obviously have a shared printer problem. Here are several things you can try to get the shared printer back online:

✦ **Check the printer.** Go to the printer you are trying to access and make sure it's powered on and plugged into the computer, print server, or directly into the network.

✦ **Reboot the printer.** Simply turn the printer off and then on again. This may cure the problem.

✦ **Verify that the printer works on the host computer.** If you are sharing the printer through a computer that's connected to the network rather than through a print server, make sure that the printer is recognized on the host computer and that you can print. If you can't, then the problem is with the printer or host computer. Your problem is not a shared printer issue.

✦ **Verify that the printer is shared.** If you are sharing the printer through a computer that's connected to the network, verify that sharing for the printer isn't disabled in the operating system. For example, in Windows, when you display the printer properties, you should see the Share This Printer radio button marked as shown in Figure 2-3.

If you are using a print server, refer to the product documentation and Help feature for any related software that's installed on your computer for information on how to troubleshoot the problem.

✦ **Perform general sharing troubleshooting.** If you still can't print to shared printers, see the subsections pertaining to general sharing issues in the first section of this chapter.

Accessing Mac and Ubuntu Computers from Windows

Can't access a Mac OS X or Ubuntu computer from Windows — or vice versa? Having trouble transferring files between these different platforms? Here are a few steps and tips that may help.

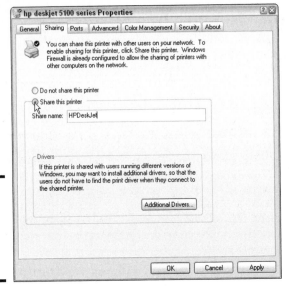

Figure 2-3:
Shared
printer
settings in
Windows
XP.

✦ **Check to see whether Windows sharing is enabled in Mac OS X or Ubuntu.** If you are having problems seeing or accessing Mac OS X or Ubuntu computers from Windows, you should verify Windows sharing is enabled. To see exactly how to do this, go to Book IV, Chapter 3.

To share between Mac OS X and Windows 98 computers, the Windows username must match the account short name in Mac OS X.

✦ **Check share names.** Make sure share names for folders and printers in Windows don't include hyphens or spaces; Mac OS X doesn't like these. In Mac OS X and Ubuntu, don't include any special characters in the share names for shared folders and printers — Windows doesn't like this.

If you're receiving an alert message containing `Error code = -43` in Mac OS X when accessing or copying to or from a Windows shared folder, the share name or file name(s) contains characters that Windows doesn't allow. Remove any special characters from share names and file names.

✦ **Perform general sharing troubleshooting.** If you still haven't resolved the problem, you can try the general sharing troubleshooting techniques discussed in the first section of this chapter.

If you're having problems sharing between Mac OS X and Windows, Apple offers a software program called Bonjour that might help. You can download it for free from Apple's Web site:

`www.apple.com/support/downloads/bonjourforwindows.html`

Chapter 3: Troubleshooting Methods and Tools

In This Chapter

✔ Finding the IP and MAC (physical) addresses of your networking gear

✔ Discovering the Computer Name and Workgroup settings of your computers

✔ Resetting your router to factory default settings

✔ Pinging computers or servers for troubleshooting purposes

This chapter is filled with steps on various troubleshooting tasks that aren't covered in the previous chapters. This chapter can help you identify common "need to know" pieces of information — IP and MAC addresses — of your networking hardware and computers. Additionally, different miscellaneous troubleshooting techniques—pinging and resetting your network gear—are covered.

Discovering IP and MAC Addresses of Devices

Sometimes you may need to find the Internet Protocol (IP) addresses used on your home network and by your Internet connection. You may find this necessary when trying to use remote desktop applications or other servers within your network or back to your network when you're away from home. You also may need to know IP addresses when troubleshooting or setting up the Media Access Control (MAC) address filtering security feature. Whatever the case, the following sections show you a few ways to get this piece of important information.

Locating your Internet (WAN) addresses

If your Internet connection hooks to a router rather than directly to a PC, you have two ways you can go about finding your Internet (WAN) IP address. Read on to find out about those two ways.

Go to whatismyip.com

This is usually the quickest way to figure out what IP address you're using for the Internet connection. Just type this address into a Web browser and your address will appear.

If you don't like the whatismyip.com site, want to just try another, or don't remember it in the future, keep in mind that you can go to Google for these types of sites and search with terms such as *my ip* or *ip address*.

Check your router's Web-based configuration utility

Another way you can always check your Internet IP (and release and renew it for troubleshooting reasons) and MAC address is to bring up the Web-based configuration utility for your router. To do so, follow these steps:

1. Open your Web browser (Internet Explorer, Netscape, Firefox, or other).

2. Type in the IP address of your router and press Enter.

If you don't know the IP address, you can refer to the next section for help. Keep in mind that some manufacturers may use a domain name, instead of an IP address, that looks like a Web site address.

3. Enter your username and password when prompted.

If you don't know the username and password, refer to the "Getting Around Forgotten Usernames and Passwords" section, later in this chapter.

4. Click the Status tab (or other tab containing the Internet (WAN) information, such as that shown in Figure 3-1).

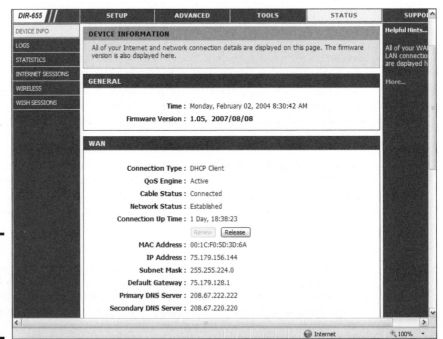

Figure 3-1: Example of the Internet (WAN) status page of a router.

Finding the IP address of your infrastructure device

Sometimes you may need to look up the IP address of your router, access point (AP), or wireless extender — I'll simply refer to these as *infrastructure devices.* This may because you want to log into its Web-based configuration utility. For any reason, you have many ways to check. First, if you haven't changed the IP address of your infrastructure device refer to Table 3-1 for the list of default values for the popular brands.

Table 3-1	Default IP Addresses for Major Networking Brands
Brand	*IP Address*
Linksys	192.168.1.1
D-Link	192.168.0.1
Apple Airport	192.168.1.1 or 192.42.249.13
Netgear	192.168.0.1 or 192.168.1.1
Belkin	192.168.2.1
Buffalo	192.168.11.1
ASUS	192.168.1.1
SMC	192.168.2.1

If your brand isn't listed in the table, you've changed it, or it doesn't work, you can easily check the IP address of your infrastructure device from a computer currently connected to it. The following sections tell you several ways to look for this address.

Check your network connection status

If you are using Windows XP you can double-click on the network icon in the system tray and click the Support tab. You'll see a Default Gateway address — this is the IP address for the infrastructure device you're currently connected to.

If you're using Windows Vista, right-click on the network icon, click Network and Sharing Center, click View Status next to the network connection name, and then click the Details button. The IP address for the infrastructure device you're currently connected is listed for the Default Gateway, for either IPv4 or IPv6.

If you're using Mac OS X Leopard, open Network Preferences. In Leopard you can click the AirPort icon on your menu bar and choose Open Network Preferences. In Tiger (and in Leopard if you don't see the AirPort icon), select System Preferences from the Apple icon and open Network. If connected to a wired network in Leopard, click Ethernet from the menu on the left and refer to the Router field.

If connected to a wireless network in Leopard, click AirPort from the menu on the left, click the Advanced button, click the TCP/IP tab, and refer to the Router field.

If connected to a wired network in Tiger, select the adapter from the Show drop-down list and refer to the Router field. If connected to a wireless network in Tiger, select the adapter from the Show drop-down list, click the TCP/IP tab, and refer to the Router field.

In Ubuntu, right-click on the network icon on the Ubuntu toolbar, click Connection Information, and refer to the Default Route value.

Use the Windows ipconfig tool

If you are using Windows 2000, XP, or Vista you can run the `ipconfig` command to get the IP address information of the infrastructure device you're currently connected to:

1. **Open a Command Prompt.**

This is available on the Accessories section of the Start menu. You can also open the Run prompt, enter *cmd*, and press OK.

2. **Type** ipconfig /all **and press Enter (see Figure 3-2).**

3. **Look under the information for the particular network connection.**

The Default Gateway (see Figure 3-2 for an example) is the IP address for the infrastructure device you're currently connected to.

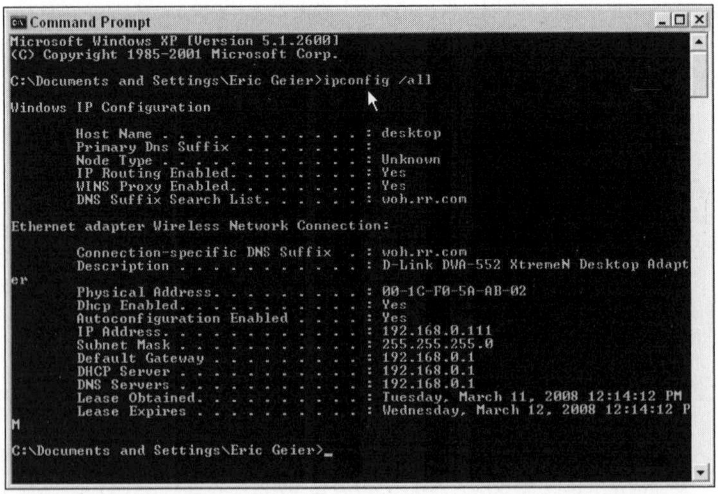

Figure 3-2:
Using the
ipconfig tool
in the
Command
Prompt of
Windows.

```
Command Prompt                                                    _ □ ×
Microsoft Windows XP [Version 5.1.2600]
(C) Copyright 1985-2001 Microsoft Corp.

C:\Documents and Settings\Eric Geier>ipconfig /all

Windows IP Configuration

        Host Name . . . . . . . . . . . . : desktop
        Primary Dns Suffix  . . . . . . . :
        Node Type . . . . . . . . . . . . : Unknown
        IP Routing Enabled. . . . . . . . : Yes
        WINS Proxy Enabled. . . . . . . . : Yes
        DNS Suffix Search List. . . . . . : woh.rr.com

Ethernet adapter Wireless Network Connection:

        Connection-specific DNS Suffix  . : woh.rr.com
        Description . . . . . . . . . . . : D-Link DWA-552 XtremeN Desktop Adapt
er
        Physical Address. . . . . . . . . : 00-1C-F0-5A-AB-02
        Dhcp Enabled. . . . . . . . . . . : Yes
        Autoconfiguration Enabled . . . . : Yes
        IP Address. . . . . . . . . . . . : 192.168.0.111
        Subnet Mask . . . . . . . . . . . : 255.255.255.0
        Default Gateway . . . . . . . . . : 192.168.0.1
        DHCP Server . . . . . . . . . . . : 192.168.0.1
        DNS Servers . . . . . . . . . . . : 192.168.0.1
        Lease Obtained. . . . . . . . . . : Tuesday, March 11, 2008 12:14:12 PM
        Lease Expires . . . . . . . . . . : Wednesday, March 12, 2008 12:14:12 P
M

C:\Documents and Settings\Eric Geier>_
```

Go to My Network Places or Network

If your infrastructure device supports Universal Plug and Play (UPnP), and UPnP is enabled on Windows XP or Vista, you may be able to see an icon for your infrastructure device in My Network Places (XP) or Network (Vista), as shown in Figure 3-3.

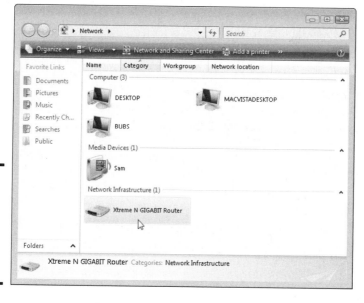

Figure 3-3:
UPnP
devices list
in My
Network
Places or
Network.

Try right-clicking on the icon, clicking Properties, and clicking the Network Device tab. You should see the IP and MAC address of the infrastructure device.

Finding the MAC address of your router, access point, or wireless extender

If you ever need to figure out the MAC address of any of your infrastructure devices — router, AP, or wireless extender — you can find this information on the device's Web-based configuration utility. To do so, follow these steps:

1. **Open your Web browser (Internet Explorer, Netscape, Firefox, or other).**

2. **Type in the IP address of your router and press Enter.**

   If you don't know the IP address, you can refer to the next section for help. Keep in mind that some manufacturers may use a domain name, instead of an IP address, that looks like a Web site address.

3. **Enter your username and password when prompted.**

   If you don't know the username and password, refer to the "Getting Around Forgotten Usernames and Passwords" section, later in this chapter.

4. **Click the Status tab (or other tab containing the LAN or Wireless LAN information) and look for the MAC address there.**

   Some infrastructure components may list both on the Status tab or have a separate tab for each.

Finding the IP or MAC address for your computers and network adapters

Probably the most needed IP or MAC address is that of your computers or network adapters. You need this information for any computers you are setting up with an FTP or Web server or a remote desktop connection, and you also need it if you're setting up MAC address filtering. Following are a few ways to go about getting your computer's or network adapter's IP and MAC addresses.

Look at your network connection status

If you're using Windows XP, double-click the network icon in the system tray and click the Support tab. You should see the IP address for your network adapter. Click the Details button and look for Physical Address, which is the MAC address.

If you're using Windows Vista, right-click the network icon in the system tray and then select Network and Sharing Center. When the Network and Sharing Center appears, click View Status, which appears next to the network connection name. In the Network Connection Status dialog box that appears, click the Details button, and you can find the IP address listed for either IPv4 or IPv6. Also listed is the Physical Address, which is the MAC address.

If you're using Mac OS X Leopard, open Network Preferences. In Leopard you can click the AirPort icon on your menu bar and select Open Network Preferences. In Tiger (and in Leopard if you don't see the AirPort icon), choose System Preferences from the Apple icon and open Network. In Leopard, the IP address will be stated under the Status section of the adapter you're using.

In Tiger it depends upon the network type you're connected to. If connected to a wired network in Tiger, select the adapter from the Show drop-down list and refer to the IP Address field. If connected to a wireless network in Tiger, select the adapter from the Show drop-down list, click the TCP/IP tab, and refer to the IP Address field.

In Ubuntu, right-click the network icon on the Ubuntu toolbar, click Connection Information, and refer to the IP and Hardware Address values.

Use the Windows ipconfig tool

If you're using Windows 2000, XP, or Vista, you can run the `ipconfig` command to get the IP and MAC addresses of your network adapters. To do so, follow these steps:

1. **Choose Start➪All Programs (or just Programs)➪Accessories➪ Command Prompt.**

The Command Prompt window should appear, which has a dark screen.

2. **At the command prompt, type** ipconfig/all **and press Enter (see Figure 3-2 shown earlier).**

The general Windows IP Configuration information and IP information for each network adapter will appear.

3. **Look through the information until you find the listing for the network connection you're looking for.**

You should see the IP Address listed, as well as the Physical Address, which is the MAC address.

Finding the IP or MAC address for media players, VoIP phones, and more

You may need to figure out the IP or MAC address used for devices such as media players and VoIP or Wi-Fi phones connected to your network. The following sections tell you how to find these addresses.

Look in the device's interface

You should always be able to access the network connection status, which includes IP and MAC address information, using the interface for the network device. For instance, if you are trying to get your media player's IP information, bring up the media player screen on your TV and find the network menu.

Go to your router's Web-based configuration utility

Another way you can find the IP and MAC address information for devices on your network is through your router's Web-based configuration utility:

1. **Open your Web browser (Internet Explorer, Netscape, Firefox, and so on).**

2. **Type in the IP address of your router and press Enter.**

If you don't know the IP address, you can refer to the "Finding the IP or MAC address for your computers and network adapters" section, earlier in this chapter, for help in locating it. Keep in mind that some manufacturers may use a domain name, instead of an IP address, that looks like a Web site address.

3. **Enter your login credentials, when prompted.**

If you don't know the username and password, refer to the "Getting Around Forgotten Usernames and Passwords" section in this chapter.

4. **Click the Status tab (or other tab that contains the list of computers, and their IP and MAC addresses, that are connected to the network, as shown in Figure 3-4).**

5. **Identify the device.**

You may be able to distinguish the devices from each other by the amount of devices listed (compared to how many computers you have) and their names.

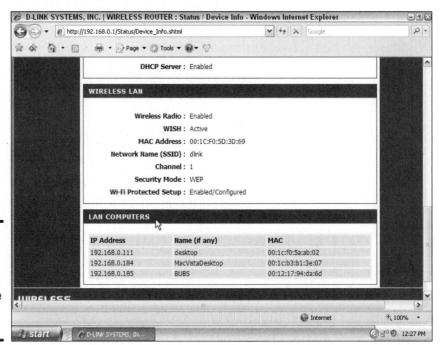

Figure 3-4: Example of a router's status page showing the connected computers.

Discovering whether you have a dynamic or static Internet IP address

Sometimes you may want to check whether your Internet IP address is dynamic (changes) or static (stays the same). For instance, when setting up a server or remote desktop connection to be accessible through the Internet, you can check by logging into your router's Web-based configuration utility:

1. **Open your Web browser (Internet Explorer, Netscape, Firefox, or other).**

2. **Type in the IP address of your router and press Enter.**

   If you don't know the IP address, you can refer to the "Finding the IP or MAC address for your computers and network adapters" section, earlier in this chapter, for help in locating it. Keep in mind that some manufacturers may use a domain name, instead of an IP address, that looks like a Web site address.

3. **Enter your log-in credentials, when prompted.**

   If you don't know the username and password, refer to the "Getting Around Forgotten Usernames and Passwords" section in this chapter.

4. **Click the Status tab (or other tab that contains the Internet or WAN information).**

Getting Around Forgotten Passwords

You are human — you may forget the passwords for your networking equipment, namely your router. Don't worry — you can get around this if you do forget. If you didn't change your router's password (as I recommend that you do), you can look up the default login credentials listed in Table 3-2.

You can also find the default login details for your router in its documentation.

Table 3-2   Default Usernames and Passwords for Major Networking Brands

Brand	Username	Password
Linksys	(blank)	admin
D-Link	admin	(blank)
Apple Airport	(blank) or root	public or password or admin
Netgear	admin	1234 or password
Belkin	(blank)	(blank) or admin
Buffalo	root or admin	(blank) or password
ASUS	admin	admin
SMC	(blank) or admin	smcadmin or barricade

But if you changed the password for your router and you can't seem to break it (and you didn't post it on the bottom of your router, as I recommend), you can use the last resort and reset your router back to factory defaults, discussed in the next section.

Resetting Your Router to Default Settings

Whether you've forgotten your router's default log-in credentials or are having problems with your router, you have two ways to restore your router to factory settings, described shortly.

If you're having problems on your network, make sure that you've tried troubleshooting the issue(s), as I describe in the previous chapters of this minibook, before proceeding.

All your router's settings will be lost. If you've changed settings on your router or have to input details (username, password, static IP address) for your Internet connection, you may want to review the pages of your Web-based configuration utility to write down these details.

Here are the ways to return to your device's factory settings:

+ **Reset the button on your router:** The easiest way to reset your router to defaults is to use the reset button on the back. Sometimes this button may be pretty noticeable; however, sometimes it may just be a tiny hole and it may (or may not) be labeled with the word reset. Use a paper clip or pen tip (depending upon the size of hole/button) to push and hold the button for at least 10 seconds. During or after holding the button, you'll probably see the lights on the router change.

+ **Your router's Web-based configuration utility:** Another way — but not if you don't know the password you created — to reset to factory defaults is via your router's Web-based configuration screen. To do so, open your Web browser and type in the IP address of your router and press Enter to go to your router's Web-based configuration utility. If you don't know the IP address, refer to the first section of this chapter. Enter your log-in credentials, when prompted. If you don't know the password, refer to the "Getting Around Forgotten Passwords" section.

    Next, go to a Tools, System, or Utilities tab of the utility and look for a feature called Restore to Factory Defaults or something similar.

When you've restored factory defaults, remember to make necessary settings changes. For instance, input details for your Internet connection (if needed), change your router's password, and enable security if using a wireless router.

Finding the Wireless Standard (A, B, G, or N) You're Using

When you're troubleshooting issues or you're about to head out on the search for wireless networking gear, you should know the wireless standard of your current equipment. Here are several ways you can check:

+ **On the product:** Check to see if the product has the standard marked on it somewhere.

+ **Product box:** If your product box hasn't yet made it to your local land-fill, or isn't buried under your junk in the garage, you can find the wireless standard listed on it.

+ **Search on Google or some other search engine for the model number:** Even if your product doesn't have the standard listed on itself, it will typically have the model number. Get the model number and enter it into Goolge.com (or your other favorite search engine) and find some specifications on the product.

+ **Your router's Web-based configuration utility:** Log in to the product's Web-based configuration utility and look for the Wireless Mode option (or something similar) in the wireless settings, an example of which is shown in Figure 3-5.

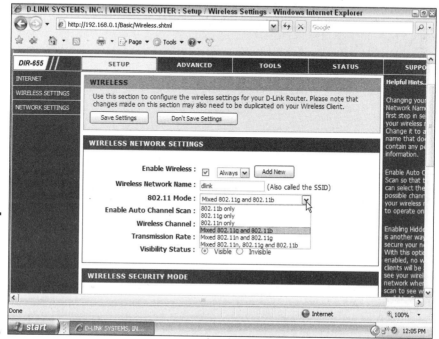

Figure 3-5:
Example of the wireless mode option of a wireless router.

Pinging: Finding the Broken Link

One simple troubleshooting method you may find useful is called pinging. Pinging helps you establish whether your computer can communicate with the Internet or other computers. For instance, say that you can't access the Internet from your Web browser, so you start pinging. First you ping a Web site and get no response. Then you ping a computer on your network and do get a response. You can now assume that your computer isn't the problem, the Internet connection is. On the other hand, if you can't successfully ping a Web site, the problem probably lies with the particular computer.

Pinging is done the same way in all the Windows versions:

1. **Choose Start⇨All Programs (or just Programs)⇨Accessories⇨ Command Prompt.**

    The Command Prompt window opens.

2. **Type** ping **and an IP Address (of a computer or router), a Computer Name (of a computer on the network), or Domain Name (of a Web site) (see Figure 3-6) and then press Enter.**

Figure 3-6:
Pinging in
Windows.

By default, Windows will ping the server or computer. If you receive a `Request timed out` message, this usually means that you can't communicate with the server or computer. If the ping is successful, the replies will be shown, such as seen in Figure 3-6.

To ping in Mac OS X Leopard and Tiger, follow these steps:

1. **Click Go on the menu bar.**

2. **Choose Utilities➪Open Network Utility.**

3. **On the Network Utility window, click the Ping tab.**

4. **Enter an IP Address (of a computer or router), a Computer Name (of a computer on the network), or a Domain Name (of a Web site) (see Figure 3-7) and then click Ping.**

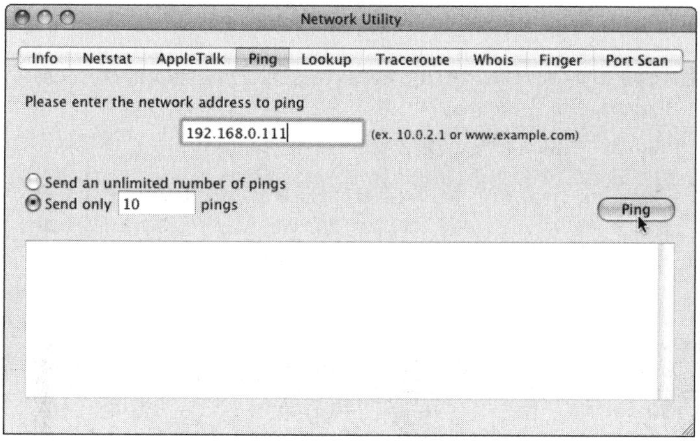

Figure 3-7:
Pinging in
Mac OS X
Leopard and
Tiger.

In Ubuntu, you can ping using these steps:

1. **Click Applications from the Ubuntu toolbar.**

2. **Choose Accessories➪Terminal.**

3. **Type** ping **and an IP Address (of a computer or router), a Computer Name (of a computer on the network), or a Domain Name (of a Web site) and then press Enter (see Figure 3-8).**

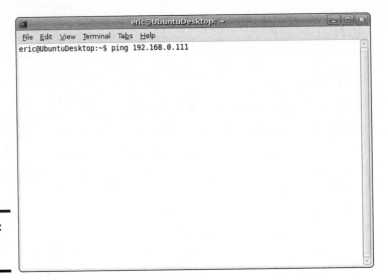

Figure 3-8:
Pinging in
Ubuntu.

By default, Ubuntu keeps pinging the server or computer forever. To stop the pinging, press Ctrl+C on your keyboard. Alternatively, you can specify ahead of time how many pings to perform. For example, if you want to ping five times, enter **ping -c 5** and the address.

Chapter 4: Getting More Help

In This Chapter

✔ Contacting and using manufacturer tech support

✔ Obtaining product documentation

✔ Scouring Google for information, solutions, and fixes

✔ Discovering online publications full of computing and networking
information

✔ Using discussion forums for assistance

*I*f you still don't have your problem solved after using the troubleshooting
techniques and check lists from the previous chapters — or your expertise of home networking gained from reading this book — you might need to
resort to getting outside help. You have many resources out there on the
Web and on the phone, so don't give up. Utilizing sources given in this chapter should help get your problem fixed or your question answered.

Getting Tech Support from the Manufacturer

One option at your disposal is the tech support provided by your networking equipment manufacturers, typically via online chat, e-mail, or over the
phone. The manufacturers' support teams can help with issues directly
caused by their devices, although they usually do not provide much (if any)
support or troubleshooting information for other manufacturers' products
or for multibrand networks. They may walk you through verifying the correct configuration of their products and performing some troubleshooting
tasks.

Networking gear these days usually doesn't come with printed product man-
uals (my guess is to save money and paper) but instead with just a simple
installation guide. The full product manual, though, typically contains tips
on general network configuration and a bit of troubleshooting information,
along with details on the product's features and settings.

You are most likely to obtain your product's documentation in the following
ways:

✦ **On the CD:** If your networking product came with a disc, pop it in and
browse the contents. This is particularly useful if you can't access the
Internet at the time.

✦ **On the Web:** Go to the manufacturer's Web site and find the Downloads or Support section to download the product manual or installation guide. You may find these in the same area of the site that lets you download drivers and firmware.

Table 4-1 lists the contact information of many networking manufacturers.

Table 4-1	Contact Information for Major Networking Brands		
Name	*Web site*	*E-Mail Address/Online Form*	*Phone*
2Wire	2wire.com	support@2wire.com	877-347-8680
Actiontec Electronics	actiontec.com	support@actiontec.com	888-436-0657
Apple	apple.com	support@apple.com	800-275-2273
ASUS	asus.com	vip.asus.com/eservice/ techserv.aspx	812-282-2787
Belkin	belkin.com	support@belkin.com	800-2BELKIN
Buffalo	buffalotech.com	support@buffalotech.com	866-752-6210
Creative Labs	creative.com	us.creative.com/support/ contact/emailform.asp	405-742-6655
D-Link	dlink.com	support@dlink.com	877-453-5465
Dynex	dynexproducts.com	dynexproducts.com/ EmailForm.aspx	800-305-2204
Gigafast	gigafast.com	techsupp@gigafast.com	888-433-6788
Linksys	linksys.com	support@linksys.com	800-326-7114
Motorola	broadband.motorola.com	support@motorola.com	877-466-8646
Netgear	netgear.com	support@netgear.com	888-638-4327
Netopia	netopia.com	ask_netopia@netopia.com	510-597-5400
SMC	smc.com	support@smc.com	800-762-4968
TiVo	tivo.com	http://customersupport.tivo. com/contactsupport.aspx	877-367-8486
TRENDnet	trendnet.com	support@trendnet.com	866-845-3673
ZyXel	zyxel.com	support@zyxel.com	800-255-4101

If you can't find the brand you're using in the table (in which case, I would be surprised), a quick search on google.com of the brand name should take you to the Web site you need. On the site, you can also find the other contact information.

Doing Some Google-ing

A great way to find out more about your networking problems (and hopefully solutions) is to spend some time searching on `google.com` — or your own favorite search engine. Picking the right keywords is the key to having a successful search. You should include the following pieces of information in your search phrases:

✦ **Symptoms:** Include the symptoms you're experiencing, such as:

- Computer doesn't connect

- Computer frequently disconnects (intermittent signal)

- Data rate is low (or slow)

- Signal is low

- Can't get on Internet (or Internet doesn't work)

✦ **Error message:** If you're receiving a specific error message or number, include it in the search phrase.

✦ **Technology terms:** It may help to include the name of the technology you're using or that's giving you the problem, such as wireless N or G, Speedbooster, or Ethernet.

Another search engine that you're bound to find useful, other than the regular ones that search the entire world, is Microsoft's Help and Support site at `support.microsoft.com`. This site offers you straightforward solutions to many networking issues relating to Windows.

You can spend hours searching, trying different keywords, and paging through the results — so keep track of the time. If you can't find any helpful Web pages fairly quickly (say, within 15 minutes), you may want to move on to another method, such as posting on discussion forums.

Referencing Online Publications

The World Wide Web can provide you with a barrage of articles, columns, tutorials, how-tos, and reviews. These writings can help troubleshoot your network, let you know how to build it better, and open your mind to new networking features.

The following Web sites are great places to find these types of writings:

✦ `homenethelp.com`

✦ `wi-fiplanet.com`

- ✦ compnetworking.about.com

- ✦ pcmag.com

- ✦ microsoft.com/WindowsXP/using/networking

- ✦ smallnetbuilder.com

- ✦ PRACTICALLYNETWORKED.com

You might even find me (Eric Geier) contributing to these types of sites. My Web site (egeier.com) lists the sites to which I contribute.

Asking for Help from Peers Online: Hitting the Forums

You may find that some online publications (such as those listed in the previous section) have a discussion forum for readers to ask questions about problems, or you may find Web sites dedicated to just forums. Either way, discussion forums can be a great way to get feedback or solutions to your experiences and problems you have faced or are currently facing. You'll probably find many experts, self-proclaimed computer geeks, and average Joes willing to help you out.

Here are some sites on which you can probably find help:

- ✦ forums.wi-fiplanet.com

- ✦ networking-forum.com

- ✦ techguy.org

- ✦ forums.speedguide.net

- ✦ computing.net/forums

- ✦ forums.practicallynetworked.com

If you're new to using discussion forums, listen up. Generally, you must create an account (such as by clicking a link named Register) to post questions or respond to postings. Discussion forums are usually divided among topic categories and sometimes even subcategories. Starting a new discussion (such as one about your problem) is called creating a new "thread." Threads contain all the postings for a particular discussion. And beware: You don't want to barge into a thread devoted to another topic and drop your problem into it. That's a definite no-no. (This is just a quick overview of the basic interworkings of discussion forums — so consider yourself officially briefed but not thoroughly informed.)

When using discussion forums, keep the following in mind — you'll have a much better forum experience:

+ **Search before posting:** Before posting a question or problem, search the forum for any previous discussions on the same issue. It's great if your issue can be answered without posting a new thread. If this is the case, add your input or thanks to the existing thread.

+ **Look for "sticky" postings:** Most forum moderators will create sticky threads or postings that appear on the top of the thread listings of discussion categories. These sticky postings usually contain information, such as frequently asked questions, for your review before posting any questions.

+ **Look for rules:** Though frequently generic, most forums have rules posted that you should follow when using the discussion forum. You may want to review them before using the forum to make sure that you don't violate any rules or cross any lines.

+ **Post your solution:** After you figure out what fixed your problem, post your solution on your forum thread. You do this to help any other people who are experiencing the same problem.

+ **Use e-mail notification:** Most forums use an e-mail notification feature that sends you an e-mail when another forum member posts a reply to your thread. Additionally, some forums allow you to subscribe to other threads. This feature is very useful because it means that you don't have to keep checking the Web site for replies.

+ **Provide input and help:** If you turn to discussion forums for help, you should also try to contribute — that is, answer or give feedback on any postings on topics that you're knowledgeable about.

+ **Beware of hardheads:** You may find that some members or moderators of forums may be a bit sarcastic, bigheaded, and every so often just plain rude. Just remember to stay civil and be thankful for any help or advice you receive.

These tips apply to discussion forums of any type, not just those concerned with computer-related topics.

When you're posting a question about a problem you're having with your network, include as much relevant information as possible. That way, the other forum members, moderators, and experts who read your question have sufficient information in order to come up with a possible solution (or more questions for you to answer as they help you troubleshoot the issue).

Along with describing your exact problem or issue, you may want to ask yourself, and answer in your post, several questions, such as the following:

+ What's your level of expertise in networking? Newbie? Moderate?

+ When did the problem start?

+ Is the problem with all your computers?

+ What's the specific error message or number you are being prompted with?

+ What operating system(s) (Windows, Mac, or other) are you using?

+ How's your network setup? Are all your computers using the same wireless standard? How many computers are wired directly to your router?

+ What have you already tried to do to fix the problem?

Thinking about these questions may even help you troubleshot your problem before you post or before you receive a reply.

Book VI

Networking Gadgets

Courtesy of Nikon.

A Wi-Fi—enabled digital camera is just one of many cool networking gadgets coming onto the scene. Read all about 'em in this part.

Contents at a Glance

Chapter 1: Voice and Video

In This Chapter

✓ Discovering the cost savings and benefits of digital phone solutions.

✓ Grasping the basics of setting up and using VoIP and Wi-Fi phone solutions

✓ Looking into using network video cameras for surveillance and Webcams

✓ Discovering Internet video conferencing solutions

Your home network can work with more than just your PCs and laptops; it can provide a backbone to the Internet for some neat voice and video gadgets, such as

✦ Digital (VoIP or Wi-Fi) phones

✦ Surveillance or Webcam cameras

✦ Video conferencing systems

Give them a try, and you'll probably find that these types of applications save you some dough on long distance conversations — and bring you much closer to family or friends when using videophones or conferencing systems. In this chapter, I explore the voice and video applications of your home network.

Wi-Fi and VoIP Phones: Skype, Vonage, iPhone, and More

Using digital phone systems has some great benefits:

✦ You and your family and friends can save money on local, long-distance, and international calls — and possibly talk totally free.

✦ Save on your mobile minutes and Internet access fees, when using dual-line cell phones.

✦ Receive a signal from your Wi-Fi phone where your cell phone does not.

✦ Access your account information, settings, and voice mail online.

You have two main digital phone options to choose from:

✦ **Wi-Fi phones:** Using Wi-Fi phones could be comparable to using cellular phones; however, instead of wirelessly connecting to cell towers, Wi-Fi phones connect to Wi-Fi wireless networks to use the Internet connection to access a digital phone service provider. For instance, a Wi-Fi phone could connect to your wireless router at home, a public Wi-Fi hotspot, or municipal Wi-Fi networks provided in a city. Wi-Fi signals don't fill the air as cell signals do, so the locations where you can use Wi-Fi phones are very limited — though just being able to use the phone at home may be enough.

✦ **VoIP (Voice over IP) phones:** This type of phone is very similar to Wi-Fi phones, except VoIP phones don't use Wi-Fi. Instead of wirelessly connecting to an Internet connection, VoIP phones are wired directly to an Internet connection (or PC connected to the Internet) so that the phone can communicate with a digital phone provider. You can use either VoIP phones or VoIP phone adapters that let you plug in traditional (corded or cordless) phones.

Your digital voice options

Though only two main digital phone systems exist (Wi-Fi and VoIP), you have many components to choose from that are related to your digital phone experience, which are discussed in the following sections.

Phone adapters: Simple and easy

A VoIP phone adapter (see Figure 1-1) — essentially a converter — provides a link between your wireless or wired router (your Internet connection) and your traditional phones.

Figure 1-1:
An example
of a VoIP
phone
adapter.

Courtesy of D-Link Systems, Inc.

Figure 1-2 shows an example of the placement of a VoIP phone adapter on a typical home network.

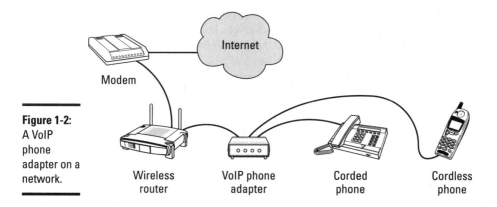

Figure 1-2:
A VoIP phone adapter on a network.

Internet

Modem

Wireless router

VoIP phone adapter

Corded phone

Cordless phone

**Book VI
Chapter 1**

Voice and Video

This is a similar type of device that your local cable company or other digital phone service provider will install if you go that route.

VoIP routers: Space savers

A VoIP router (see Figure 1-3) is a converged router and VoIP phone adapter.

Figure 1-3:
Example of a VoIP router.

Courtesy of Linksys.

As shown in Figure 1-4, a VoIP router eliminates the need for a separate VoIP phone adapter and replaces any existing router you have currently set up. You can plug traditional phones directly into a VoIP router.

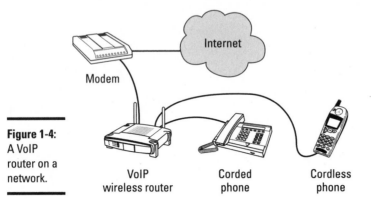

Figure 1-4: A VoIP router on a network.

Dual-line home phones: Supporting traditional and digital

Dual-line home phones (see Figure 1-5) support both traditional and VoIP calls.

Figure 1-5: An example of a dual-line home phone.

Courtesy of Consumer Network Solutions.

Figure 1-6 shows how this system is set up. You connect your traditional telephone line and your Internet connection (from your wireless or wired router) into the dual-line adapter.

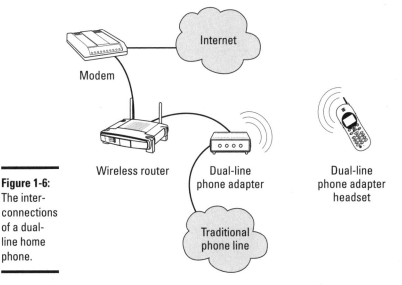

Book VI
Chapter 1

Voice and Video

Figure 1-6:
The inter-
connections
of a dual-
line home
phone.

These dual-line systems typically come with just one phone (or headset), but are usually expandable to as many as four phones.

Dual-line cell phones: For people on the go

Dual-line cell phones (see Figure 1-7) allow you to choose between using the cellular system or a nearby Wi-Fi wireless network to make and receive calls. This gives you a way to save those valuable minutes through your cellular service. Plus you can use the phone through a Wi-Fi Internet connection when you don't have a good cellular signal (or one at all); which can be beneficial even in your home.

This capability is depicted in Figure 1-8.

Some cell phones, for example the iPhone (see Figure 1-9), have Wi-Fi capability but don't support calls over Wi-Fi. Instead, the Wi-Fi capability provides an Internet connection for Web browsing and Internet applications. Although most cell phones can use some type of Internet through the cellular system, cellular companies don't charge when using Wi-Fi connections. Additionally, a Wi-Fi connection can provide much faster speeds than the Internet through the cellular system.

Figure 1-7:
An example
of a dual-
line cell
phone.

Courtesy of D-Link Systems, Inc.

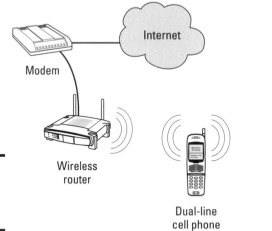

Internet

Modem

Wireless
router

Dual-line
cell phone

Cell tower

Figure 1-8:
Using a
dual-line
cell phone.

Figure 1-9:
The iPhone.

Courtesy of Apple.

Wi-Fi phones: A total wireless option

Wi-Fi phones (see Figure 1-10) connect only to Wi-Fi wireless networks, such as your router at home, public Wi-Fi hotspots, or municipal Wi-Fi networks.

Figure 1-10:
A Wi-Fi
phone.

Courtesy of NETGEAR.

Figure 1-11 shows an example of the simple setup behind Wi-Fi phones.

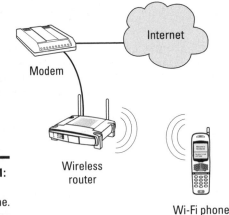

Figure 1-11:
Using a
Wi-Fi phone.

Modem

Internet

Wireless
router

Wi-Fi phone

Choosing a digital phone solution

Here are some things to keep in mind when picking out a digital phone solution:

✦ **What service they use:** You should remember most digital phone solutions only support a single service provider — pick your phone (and service) wisely. The following are some popular digital phone service providers:

- **Skype:** Skype offers totally free calls to and from any location in the world between Skype users over the Internet. To make calls to real phone numbers or for others to call you from a real number, you must pay for premium service, but it is really cheap — around only $5 per month.

- **Vonage:** Unlike Skype, this service is more oriented for a landline (real phone service) replacement. Service costs more than Skype but may include more traditional features such as caller ID and 911 support, which Skype does not offer.

- **Cable companies:** Your local TV cable company probably offers digital phone service. If you go with digital phone service with a cable company, they most likely take care of everything: supplying the equipment (a VoIP phone), installing it, and configuring it.

✦ **Price:** Of course, price is one of your considerations when shopping for anything. As you'll discover, VoIP phone adapters are usually the cheapest route — around $50. But a converged device might be the way to go if you're planning to make another related purchase soon. For example, if you want to upgrade your wireless router (maybe from wireless g to n), a VoIP router may be the same or lower cost compared to purchasing both items separately. Likewise, if you need a new traditional home phone or cell phone, you could think about buying one with Wi-Fi/VoIP capability.

✦ **Amount of travel:** If you're a frequent traveler, a dual-line (Wi-Fi capable) cell phone or Wi-Fi phone may be the way to go. This way, you can still benefit from your digital phone purchase when away from home. Lugging around and setting up the other hardware options usually isn't practical.

✦ **Landline replacement:** If you're looking to replace your traditional home phone and service, you may find luck in a VoIP router or phone adapters. These pieces of equipment provide a more practical and reliable digital phone solution.

✦ **Reviews:** Reading editorial and consumer reviews on different types of VoIP equipment and particular products can give you some great advice before deciding on which items you would like purchase.

✦ **Emergency call capability:** It's very important to understand a digital phone solution's emergency call capabilities — this should be your top deciding factor if you're replacing your traditional home phone service. Many digital phone systems and service providers support 911 calls that route to local authorities, but check to make sure. For mobile systems such as cell and Wi-Fi phones, look for a feature called E911.

Setting up your digital phone solution

The first thing you should do is sign up with a digital phone service provider. After you have an account, you can do the physical installation and configuration of your equipment, which I discuss in the following sections.

Phone adapters

Connecting and setting up a VoIP phone adapter usually consists of the following steps:

1. **Connect your phone(s).**

Plug the telephone wire from a traditional (corded or cordless) telephone to one of the phone ports on the back of the phone adapter.

2. **Connect the Ethernet cable to your router.**

Plug one end of an Ethernet cable (probably included with your phone adapter) to the Ethernet port of your phone adapter, and plug the other end into an Ethernet port of your router.

3. **Power it on.**

Plug the power adapter into an electrical outlet and connect to your phone adapter.

VoIP routers

Setting up a VoIP router is more complex than the other options because it includes a wireless router in addition to a phone adapter, and a VoIP router may not be configured with your digital phone service provider's information. You should find that setting up a VoIP router is similar to setting up a regular wireless router, but with a few more settings to worry about.

Here are the basic steps to set up and configure a VoIP router:

1. **Unplug and remove any existing router.**

2. **Connect a phone.**

Plug the telephone wire from a traditional (corded or cordless) phone into one of the phone ports on the back of your VoIP router.

3. **Connect the Internet.**

Plug one end of an Ethernet cable (probably included with your router) to the Ethernet port of your Internet modem, and plug the other end into the WAN or Internet Ethernet port of your router.

4. **Power it on.**

Plug the power adapter into an electrical outlet and connect it to your VoIP router.

5. **Connect to the router.**

In order to configure the VoIP router, you must connect a computer to the router. You can connect wirelessly or connect an Ethernet cable to one of the Ethernet ports on the VoIP router and the other end to your computer's Ethernet port.

6. **Access the Web-based configuration utility:**

a. Open your Web browser (such as Internet Explorer, Netscape, Firefox, and so on).

b. Type the IP address of your VoIP router in the Address box and press Enter.

c. When prompted, enter your login credentials in the dialog box that appears.

If you don't know the IP address or the username or password, refer to Book V, Chapter 5 for help. Keep in mind that some manufacturers may use a domain name, instead of an IP address, that looks like a Web site address.

7. Configure the router and wireless settings.

Before concerning yourself with the VoIP features and settings, you need to configure the router's basic and security settings, including

- Configuring your Internet connection, if needed
- Changing your network name (SSID)
- Enabling (WPA or WEP) encryption
- Changing the default login password

You can refer to Book II, Chapter 3 for information on how to set these items.

8. Configure the VoIP service settings.

Refer to your router's and digital phone service provider's documentation and instructions.

After you've followed these steps, you should be able to make and receive calls, just like normal, from the phone(s) that are plugged into the VoIP router.

Dual-line home phone

Here are the typical steps to set up and configure a dual-line home phone:

1. Connect the Internet.

Plug one end of an Ethernet cable (probably included with your phone) to the Ethernet port of your Internet modem, and plug the other end into the Internet Ethernet port of your phone adapter.

2. Connect the phone line.

Plug one end of a regular telephone cord (probably included with your phone) into the phone input port of your Internet modem, and plug the other end into the WAN or Internet Ethernet port of your phone adapter.

3. Power it on.

Plug the power adapter into an electrical outlet and connect to your phone adapter.

Now you should be able to receive calls like normal from your digital and traditional phone carriers, while being able to choose the carrier for your outgoing calls on the phone before you dial.

Dual-line cell and Wi-Fi phones

Because Wi-Fi phones and dual-line cell phones aren't a piece of equipment that you install on your network, there isn't much setup involved. But here are the typical steps to get it working — which are usually straightforward when you are working with the device:

1. **Turn on your phone.**

2. **Connect to a wireless network.**

3. **Sign in to the digital phone service.**

Tips on using VoIP and Wi-Fi phones

The following bullets give you some tips to make your VoIP and Wi-Fi phone experiences even better:

✦ **Limit Internet activity:** To help ensure good quality calls on a VoIP or Wi-Fi phone, try to limit your network or Internet activity while using it — remember it's also using your Internet connection. Downloading or transferring files from the Internet or between computers on your network and watching online videos use a great deal of bandwidth and may cause poor quality or dropped calls.

✦ **Lower quality setting:** For VoIP solutions, if you frequently experience dropped calls, lowering your service's codec (quality) setting may help. Sacrificing a bit of call quality may be better than having calls dropped all together.

✦ **Using Wi-Fi phones at hotspots:** If you have a Wi-Fi phone and plan to travel, you can plan ahead and check the Wi-Fi hotspot availability of the areas you plan to visit. Book VII, Chapter 1 gives you many ways to find hotspots. You should keep in mind, though, that you might not be able to use your Wi-Fi phone at every Wi-Fi hotspot. You may run into problems with hotspots that require you to log in or accept terms and/or payment before using the Internet. But you may be able to load account information of your Wi-Fi hotspot memberships into your Wi-Fi phone, which may let you use your phone at the location.

Video Cameras: For Surveillance

Network video cameras (see Figure 1-12 for an example) can be used for on-location or remote surveillance and Webcam applications for your small business or home. These video cameras can be connected to your wired or wireless network rather than having to run A/V or coaxial cable. Many consumer- and enterprise-level network video camera solutions are available, with varying video quality, prices, and features.

Figure 1-12:
A network
video
camera.

Courtesy of Linksys.

Here are some features and tips to keep in mind when shopping for your
video cam solution:

✦ **Video quality:** The video quality between cameras can vary. You can look
for the resolution. You may also research low-light or infrared (IR) features that provide quality video in low-light or total darkness situations.

✦ **Wireless security:** You should check to see whether the video camera
supports the encryption method (WPA, WPA2, and so on) used on your
wireless network. The new methods may not be supported by all the
video cameras.

✦ **Remote control:** Some video cameras let you remotely control the cam
from a local PC or online with tilt, pan, and zoom functions.

✦ **Software:** You may want to compare the software utilities (if any)
included with particular cameras, specifically for features that enable
video viewing, archiving, and uploading.

✦ **Enclosures:** If you are planning for an outdoor placement of your video
camera, you should check to see whether a compatible enclosure exists.

✦ **Reviews:** You may want to check the Internet for any product reviews
and user/consumer ratings before going with a particular cam.

A great way to take a sneak peak at the features and user friendliness offered by particular video cameras is to download and review the documentation provided by the manufacturers.

Video Conferencing: Face-to-Face Over the Web

Network video conferencing systems, usually called *videophones,* can bring video to your mundane phone meetings or conversations. This is very useful and a huge cost-saver in business when face-to-face meetings are usually preferred. These systems are also great for families and couples. Instead of just speaking to your loved one, you can both see each other — whether you're across town or on the other side of the world.

You can pick between two main video conferencing solutions:

✦ **Stand-alone videophone:** These systems are basically about the same size and look like a TV cable box but with a camera lens protruding from the front. See Figure 1-13 for an example.

Figure 1-13:
A stand-alone videophone system.

Courtesy of D-Link Systems, Inc.

You place the stand-alone videophone on top of a TV and connect to the Internet wirelessly or via an Ethernet connection to transmit and receive the video feed. Additionally, you connect a regular phone to the videophone box so you can dial and receive calls to other videophones.

✦ **Videophone with built-in screen:** As Figure 1-14 shows, these are actual telephones with built-in screens.

Figure 1-14: A videophone with a built-in screen.

Courtesy of D-Link Systems, Inc.

You would connect a phone line to the videophone so you can still make traditional calls. You would connect an Ethernet cable to the phone so you can make and receive video calls to other videophones.

You may also find consumer-oriented videophone products, such as the digital photo/video frame shown in Figure 1-15. However, these consumer-level videophones may only support communications over traditional phone lines instead of high-speed Internet connections, which affects the video quality.

Choosing your video conferencing system

Here are some features and tips to look for when shopping for your video cam solution:

✦ **Video quality:** The video quality between conferencing systems can vary. You can look for the resolution or the frames per second for comparison reasons.

✦ **Remote control:** Some video conferencing solutions come with remote controls.

Figure 1-15:
A digital
photo/video
frame.

Courtesy of D-Link Systems, Inc.

✦ **Wired versus wireless:** You have the option of purchasing a wired or wireless video conferencing camera. Of course, wireless systems enable you to move the system around your office or home more easily, but they have some downsides, too: Wireless systems cost more, you may experience interference, and they can use up your wireless bandwidth — meaning that your other wireless applications may run a bit slower.

✦ **Wireless security:** You should check to see whether the system supports the encryption method used on your wireless network. The new methods may not be supported by all systems.

✦ **Reviews:** You may want to check the Internet for any product reviews and user/consumer ratings and comments before going with a particular system.

✦ **Price:** You may be able to find consumer-level solutions for $100 or less, but higher quality systems cost around $150 for wired systems and $250 for wireless systems. Videophones with built-in screens run about $350.

A great way to take a sneak peak at the features and user friendliness offered by particular video cameras is to download and review the documentation provided by the manufacturers.

Setting up your video conferencing system

The installation of stand-alone videophones usually consist of the following:

1. **Connect TV.**

Plug one end of a set of A/V or RCA cables (probably included with your videophone) to your TV or VCR, and the other end into the video out connections on your videophone.

2. **Connect the Internet.**

Plug one end of an Ethernet cable (probably included with your videophone) to an Ethernet port on your router, and plug the other end into the Ethernet port of your videophone.

3. **Attach the antenna.**

If you have a wireless videophone system, screw on the included antenna.

4. **Connect a phone.**

Plug the telephone wire from a traditional (corded or cordless) phone into one of the phone ports on the back of your VoIP router.

5. **Power it on.**

Plug the power adapter into an electrical outlet and connect to your videophone.

To install a videophone with built-in screen, you usually have to do the following general steps:

1. **Connect to the Internet.**

Plug one end of an Ethernet cable (probably included with your videophone) to an Ethernet port on your router, and plug the other end into the Internet Ethernet port of your videophone.

2. **Connect the phone line.**

Plug one end of a traditional phone wire into a wall jack, and plug the other end into the phone port of your videophone.

3. **Power it on.**

Plug the power adapter into an electrical outlet and connect to your videophone.

Chapter 2: Family Entertainment

In This Chapter

✔ **Checking out the wireless capabilities of digital cameras**

✔ **Discovering the media display possibilities of media players and digital picture frames**

✔ **Getting a handle on the ins and outs of TiVo's networking features**

✔ **Exploring the gaming realm of networking**

*H*aving a home network lets you enjoy much more than just Internet and file sharing or wireless access for your notebook computers. Your home network can also provide connectivity for the growing number of electronics and gadgets available these days with wired or wireless networking capabilities. The following are just a few examples:

✦ Digital cameras

✦ Digital picture frames

✦ TiVo DVRs

✦ Gaming systems

You've spent time and money in setting up your home network; now you should think outside of the box. It's time to see what networking can bring to your family room!

Sending and Sharing Photos with Digital Cameras

Using a Wi-Fi–enabled digital camera means you don't have to mess with those sync cables or cradles to transfer your photos to your computer anymore. A digital camera with Wi-Fi capability streamlines your camera-to-PC transfer process. Figure 2-1 and the following bullets give you several examples of what you may be able do with a Wi-Fi–enabled digital camera:

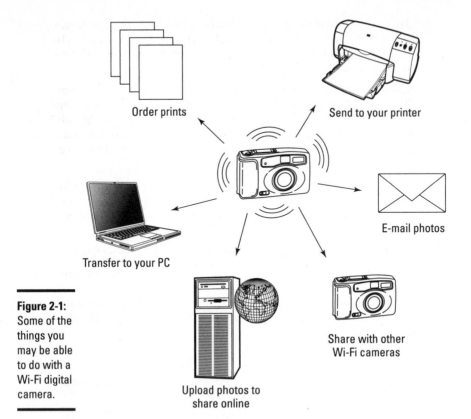

Order prints

Send to your printer

Transfer to your PC

E-mail photos

Upload photos to share online

Share with other Wi-Fi cameras

Figure 2-1:
Some of the things you may be able to do with a Wi-Fi digital camera.

✦ **Transfer:** The photos from your camera are automatically transferred to a specified location on your PC when you're in range of your wireless home network or with a touch of a button. Just imagine the convenience when you're on vacation. You don't have to unpack the transfer cable (if you remembered it), plug it in, access your photo software, start the transfer, wait around until it's done, and pack your cable up again. With a Wi-Fi–enabled camera, you just have to open your laptop, turn on your camera, freshen up or channel flip while the transfer takes place, come back and close your laptop, and shut off your camera. In some cases, the camera may even automatically shut off.

✦ **Share online:** From your wireless home network or a Wi-Fi hotspot — when you're out in town or on vacation — you can upload pictures to your favorite photo Web sites for all your family and friends to check out. Supported sites may include Shutterfly, Facebook, Picasa Web Albums, Flickr, or TypePad.

✦ **Share with other cameras:** Wi-Fi capable digital cameras may even allow you to share your photos with other cameras so that you can share photos as you take them.

✦ **Order prints:** You can send your photos to online photo stores, such as Kodak (`www.kodak.com`) and Wal-Mart (`www.walmart.com`), to be printed and shipped to your home or for pickup at a local store — all ordered from your digital camera.

✦ **Send to your printer:** You can send your favorite photos to your computer's printer over your wireless network or to your special digital photo printer that's also equipped with Wi-Fi. Picture the possibilities. While you're eating cake at your daughter's birthday party, you can be printing out your favorite shots — from the kitchen table — to give grandma on her way out the door.

✦ **E-mail:** Wi-Fi–enabled digital cameras may even support e-mailing your photos when connected to your wireless home network or Wi-Fi hotspot — offering another way to share your beloved snapshots.

Options to make your digital camera wireless

You can choose from the following to make your digital camera wireless:

✦ **Integrated Wi-Fi:** When browsing the Web or the shelves, you may find a few digital cameras with integrated Wi-Fi — for example, the one pictured in Figure 2-2.

**Book VI
Chapter 2**

Family
Entertainment

Figure 2-2:
A digital
camera with
integrated
Wi-Fi.

Courtesy of Nikon.

This is a great way to go wireless with your photos when you're looking for a new digital camera; you don't have to mess with a separate Wi-Fi card that you can lose or break.

✦ **Wi-Fi capable:** Instead of building Wi-Fi into the camera, some manufacturers produce cameras to support Wi-Fi by offering a separate wireless card, usually a Secure Digital (SD) card that just slides into the slot of your camera. If you already have a digital camera, check with the manufacturer to see whether it has a compatible Wi-Fi card. If you are shopping for a new camera, keep your eyes open for one that's Wi-Fi capable/supported.

✦ **Universal Wi-Fi cards:** You can also consider getting a universal Wi-Fi card, such as the one shown in Figure 2-3, for around $100. These Wi-Fi cards are perfect if your camera doesn't have integrated Wi-Fi or a compatible card from the manufacturer. You may find that these can work with just about any digital camera.

Figure 2-3:
An example of a universal SD Wi-Fi and storage card.

Courtesy of Eye-Fi.

As is true of the manufacturer's cards, these universal cards usually also include memory for photo storage, which can make the purchase even wiser if the card includes more memory than your existing card(s). The universality means you can pop it into just about any other digital camera you own — you can also let family and friends take it on outings so they can quickly share their photos with you.

✦ **Bluetooth:** You may come across some digital cameras that also support Bluetooth. Although Bluetooth is a wireless technology, you usually can't connect to the Internet via Bluetooth, so your options are limited. You can usually use Bluetooth to just print wirelessly to special photo printers, which must also have Bluetooth. Nevertheless, you may want to investigate any Bluetooth cards produced by your camera manufacturer.

Selecting your digital camera wireless solution

When it comes time to do your shopping, keep these thoughts in mind:

✦ **Wireless and Internet features:** The main difference you'll likely see between wireless SD cards and Wi-Fi cameras are the types of features they support. One option may support print ordering from Kodak, whereas another may support Wal-Mart's photo center, or none; one may support uploading to Web sites, whereas another may just support wireless transfers to your computer. To help you decide, examine the details to see exactly what features, Web sites, and functionality are supported.

✦ **Card interface:** Most digital cameras have an SD slot, so most wireless cards for cameras are SD cards; however, you may also see some with USB interfaces. If you're looking into a wireless card that's not made or recommended by your camera manufacturer, you may want to double-check to be sure both items are compatible.

✦ **Wireless technology:** If you are looking at Wi-Fi cards or Wi-Fi cameras, you should check which standard is used. Faster standards, such as wireless g or n, provide much faster transfer speeds than older standards, such as wireless B.

✦ **Memory:** You should compare the amount of memory (for example, 1GB or 2GB) included on the wireless cards.

✦ **Don't forget other features:** The wireless features can definitely be useful, but don't focus on them exclusively and forget about the photo and camera features — these may impact your photos forever.

✦ **Price:** You should be able to find digital camera Wi-Fi cards for around $100 and Bluetooth cards for around $50.

✦ **Reviews:** You may want to check the Internet for any product reviews and user ratings before going with a particular digital camera or Wi-Fi card.

Network Media Players: Stream Media to Your TV

Do you have any video, music, or photos on your computers? If you do, you may want to think about getting a hardware accessory called a media player for your network. This gadget lets you stream and display these items and online media on your TV; see Figure 2-4 for a visual.

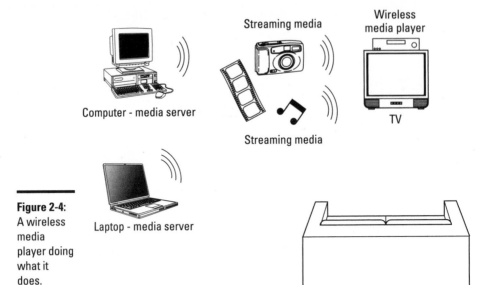

Computer - media server

Streaming media

Wireless media player

TV

Streaming media

Streaming media

Figure 2-4: A wireless media player doing what it does.

Laptop - media server

TIP

Instead of everyone having to crowd around the PC to see the latest photos, you can just flip on the media player so that everyone can see them from the comfort of the family room couch. Or you can play music from your collection on your PC through your TV or surround system when entertaining, or when you're scrubbing those dishes or dusting the house.

Media players can also open the door to a whole new family entertainment option with online services such as Intel Viiv (`www.intel.com/viiv`)and Active-TV (`www.amd.com/us-en/Processors/ComputingSolutions/ 0,,30_288_14819,00.html`). These services give you access to Internet-driven content, including the following:

✦ On-demand music and music videos

✦ Information services

✦ Sports and TV shows

✦ Full-length movies

✦ Personal Video Recording (PVR)

Figure 2-5 shows an example of a media player.

Book VI
Chapter 2

Family
Entertainment

Figure 2-5:
A wireless
media
player.

Courtesy of D-Link Systems, Inc.

Choosing your media player

When shifting through the shelves or browsing the Web for a media player,
keep the following in mind:

✦ **Different names:** You may see these devices named as media center
extenders and digital entertainers, in addition to media players. You may
also see music players (also named *music bridges*), which of course support only audio formats such as MP3s and WMAs.

✦ **Wireless technology:** If you are thinking about getting a wireless media
player, you should compare the supported wireless technologies, such
as wireless g or n. These are discussed in Book I, Chapter 1.

✦ **Wireless security:** You should check whether the media player supports
the encryption method (WPA, WPA2, and so on) used on your wireless
network. The new methods may not be supported by all the media
players.

✦ **Supported operating systems:** Make sure you check which operating
systems are supported by the media player. Some may support only
Windows Vista, whereas others may support computers loaded with any
Windows versions.

✦ **Extra features:** Discover and compare any extra features, such as

• **Remote PC desktop:** This lets you view and control your PC's
Desktop and applications such as e-mail applications or Web
browsers.

• **Personal video recording (PVR):** Some media players may support
PVR functions with the help of a TV tuner card installed in your PC,
allowing you to schedule recordings and to pause and rewind live TV
from your living room.

✦ **Online media services:** Look for any online services, such as Intel Viiv and Active-TV. These online functions usually vary from media player to media player.

✦ **Supported file formats:** Though most media players support the popular file formats you likely have on your PCs, you should compare for any special file formats and versions. You can expect to see formats such as the following:

- `.MP3`, `.WAV`, `.AIFF`, and `.WMA` (audio)

- `.JPEG`, `.BMP`, `.PNG`, `.TIF`, and `.GIF` (pictures)

- `.MPG`, `.AVI`, and `XviD` (video)

✦ **HD support:** You'll see some media players that support HD. Keep this in mind when picking one out. If you have an HD TV (or you plan to in the near future), you may want to get a media player that supports HD so that you can show your photos and videos with the high-quality display.

✦ **DVD player included:** Various networking manufacturers even produce media player-DVD combo devices. This is a great way to conserve space on your entertainment shelves, plus reduce the number of remotes flying around — or getting lost.

✦ **USB/card reader support:** You may come across media players with USB or card reader ports. These let you plug in and access any media on removable drives such as USB flash drives and SD, MS, xD, and MMC cards. You don't even have to transfer your photos to your PC to view them on your TV; just take the card out of your camera and plug it into your media player.

✦ **Reviews:** You may want to check the Internet for any product reviews and user/consumer ratings before going with a particular media player.

Setting up your media player

Figure 2-6 and the following bullets show the basic steps of setting up a media player.

1. **Install server software.**

If your media player requires you to install server software on your computer(s), install it now.

2. **Connect the TV.**

Plug one end of a set of A/V or RCA cables (probably included with your media player) to your TV or VCR, and the other end into the video out connections of your media player. If your TV and media player support it, you can connect s-video, digital, or HD cables instead.

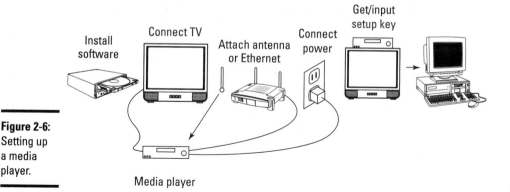

Figure 2-6:
Setting up
a media
player.

Install
software

Connect TV

Attach antenna
or Ethernet

Connect
power

Get/input
setup key

Media player

3. Connect the Ethernet cable or attach the antenna.

If you have a wireless media player and want to wirelessly connect to
your computer(s), screw on the included antenna. If you are going to use
a wired connection, attach the Ethernet cable (run from your router) to
the port on the media player.

4. Power it on.

Plug the power adapter into an electrical outlet and connect to your
media player.

5. Get the setup key.

If your media player (usually one designed just for Windows Vista) displays a setup key when you boot it up, write it down. Then insert the CD
that came with the media player into your computer and run the setup.
You should be asked for the setup key during this process.

Tips on using media players

Here are a few tips on using media players:

✦ **Computers must be set up:** Typically, you must install server software
or configure a setup key on all the computers you want to access with
your media player.

✦ **Computers must be on:** The computers you want to access with the
media player must be on and running.

✦ **You should update firmware:** Just as with your other networking
devices (routers, adapters, and so on), you should keep your media
player up-to-date. This involves periodically checking for new firmware
releases and updating them when necessary. These firmware updates
may include new features and functions, media or network related, in
addition to fixes.

TiVo Networking: Stream Media to Your TV and More

TiVo offers not only TV guide and DVR (Digital Video Recorder) solutions to complement your basic or digital cable service but also some neat online and networking features. This sets TiVo apart from other digital cable box services you may be able to get from your local cable provider. Additionally, you may see better overall features and functionalities from TiVo service.

Basic TiVo service

Basic TiVo service, not considering online or networking features, provides the following two items:

+ **On-screen TV guide:** TiVo provides an easy-to-use TV guide similar to what you may obtain from your local cable provider's digital cable service and box. This lets you check for shows and movies currently playing and coming up. This guide appears directly on your TV screen (see Figure 2-7) with a touch of a button.

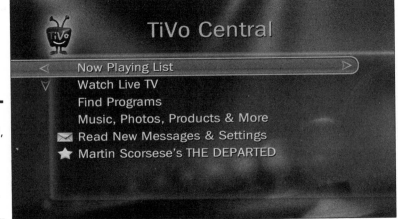

Figure 2-7: TiVo Central, the main menu to access the TiVo features.

In addition to browsing the guide, you can search by show or movie title, actor, and type.

+ **DVR capabilities:** You can schedule recordings of your shows and movies, to be stored directly on your TiVo box (see Figure 2-8).

Similar to the DVR service that your local cable provider may offer, TiVo lets you schedule to record random shows and movies or select an entire series.

Figure 2-8:
A TiVo box.

TiVo service doesn't provide any real cable or programming services — these must be purchased separately through your local cable or satellite provider (for instance, Time Warner, Comcast, or Dish Network).

TiVo service costs anywhere from $10 to 15 per month and a one-time fee of $100 to $400 for each TiVo box.

Figure 2-9 shows an example of how you may set up TiVo in your home for the basic TiVo features.

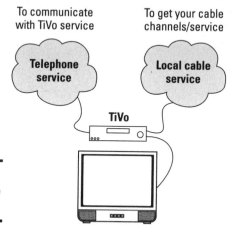

To communicate
with TiVo service

To get your cable
channels/service

**Telephone
service**

**Local cable
service**

TiVo

Figure 2-9:
A basic TiVo
box setup.

You must connect a phone line to the TiVo box so that the TV guide can be updated. Your cable line must also be connected to the box.

TiVo's online and networking features

The following are online and networking features and services you can enjoy with TiVo:

✦ **Online music services:** Services such as Music Choice, Rhapsody Music, and Podcaster (see Figure 2-10) on TiVo let you search, view, and play music videos, songs, and podcasts.

Figure 2-10:
TiVo's
Podcaster
screen.

✦ **Local information:** On-demand access to local information and services lets you do things such as check the weather (see Figure 2-11) or order movie tickets — all from your TiVo remote, from the comfort of your couch.

✦ **Multi-room viewing:** You can access shows and movies recorded on any of your TiVo boxes from all your boxes. Unlike DVR service that your local cable provider may offer, you can record a show in the living room and play it back on your bedroom TV — or vice versa.

✦ **Media sharing:** Services such as Photobucket on TiVo (see Figure 2-12) let you share and view your digital photos from your TV.

✦ **TiVoToGo:** You can transfer any shows and movies recorded on your TiVo boxes to a supported device so that you can enjoy them on a plane, in the car, or anywhere.

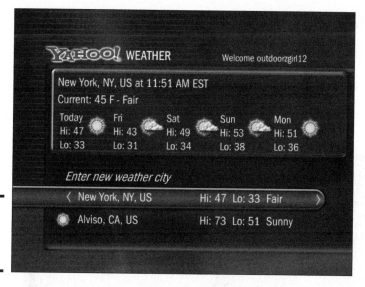

Figure 2-11:
Yahoo!
Weather
on TiVo.

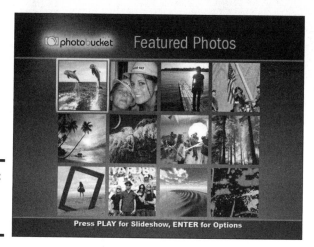

Figure 2-12:
Photo-
bucket on
TiVo.

+ **Online scheduling:** This gives you the option of scheduling your recordings on the Internet from anywhere in the world. For instance, if you
forget to set up your TiVo to record a show before you leave on a trip,
simply log in to the TiVo Web site (www.tivo.com), schedule the
recording, and have it on your TiVo when you get home.

The online and networking features come into play when you connect your
TiVo box to the Internet, either via an Ethernet cable or a Wi-Fi (wireless)

network, such as the one shown in Figure 2-13. Your box can then communicate with the TiVo service through the Internet, eliminating the need for a connection to your phone line.

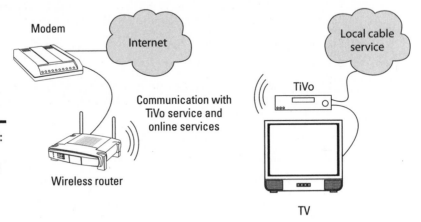

Figure 2-13: Online and networking TiVo box setup with Wi-Fi.

Modem

Internet

Local cable service

Communication with TiVo service and online services

TiVo

Wireless router

TV

Setting up TiVo on your network

To get your TiVo(s) setup to work with your home network, follow these steps:

1. **Connect to your network.**

You can either run an Ethernet cable from a router to your TiVo, or purchase and plug in a USB wireless adapter (see Figure 2-14) for your TiVo so that you can wirelessly connect to your wireless router.

Figure 2-14: TiVo's USB wireless adapter.

For a list of supported wireless adapters, go to www.tivo.com/network.

2. Configure your TiVo box settings online.

To identify your TiVo boxes more easily when using the networking features, you should name them. To do so, follow these steps:

a. Go to www.tivo.com/manage.

b. Log in to Manage My Account.

Use the username and password you created when you registered to use TiVo Manage My Account. If you haven't yet registered, you can do so from this Web page.

c. Choose DVR Preferences on the left menu.

Don't forget to specify the sharing settings of your TiVo boxes.

3. Download and install TiVo Desktop on your computer(s).

You can download the free TiVo Desktop application at

www.tivo.com/desktop

Download and install the software on each computer that you want to work with TiVo.

4. Configure your Media Access Key(s).

You need to enter your Media Access Key on your computer(s) after installing TiVo Desktop. This secures your TiVo recordings from being played or transferred outside of your home.

You can view the Media Access Keys from your TiVo boxes:

a. Go to TiVo Central.

b. Select Messages & Settings.

c. Select Account & System Information.

d. Select Media Access Key.

You can also find your Media Access Key(s) by logging into your account online at www.tivo.com/manage.

5. Enable home network applications:

You can enable the home network applications from your TiVo boxes:

a. Go to TiVo Central and scroll down.

b. Select Enable Home Network Applications.

c. Press THUMBS UP three times, and press ENTER.

Now you can access these applications and features from TiVo Central.

Book VI
Chapter 2

Family
Entertainment

Using the networking features of TiVo

After you have set up your TiVo boxes with your network, you can start enjoying the new features and functionality, which the following sections discuss.

Transferring shows or movies to your computer

You can use the TiVoToGo software loaded on your computer(s) to transfer shows or movies from your TiVo boxes to your PC or laptop:

1. **Open TiVo Desktop from your computer.**

2. **Click the Pick Recordings to Transfer button.**

After a moment, you should see the Now Playing List for your TiVo.

If you have multiple TiVo boxes connected to your home network, you can view a selected Now Playing List by selecting it from the drop-down list.

3. **Select the shows or movies to transfer.**

Check the box next to the title of the shows or movies you want to transfer; Figure 2-15 shows an example.

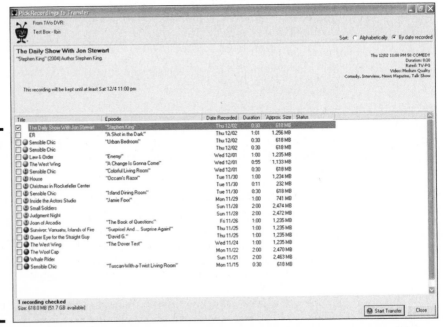

Figure 2-15: Selecting TV shows and movies to transfer to your mobile devices with the TiVoToGo software utility.

You can set up the software to automatically transfer programs that are parts of a series. Simply select the program and click the Auto-Transfer this Series button.

4. **Click the Start Transfer button.**

Watching your shows or movies on your computer

The programs you transfer to your computer appear in the Now Playing List of TiVo Desktop. You can begin watching your transferred programs on your computer even before the transfer is complete. Just select a program from the Now Playing List, click Play in TiVo Desktop, and your default media player (for example, Windows Media Player) launches and begins playing the program.

Book VI
Chapter 2

Family
Entertainment

Transferring or viewing shows or movies between TiVo boxes

If you have multiple TiVo boxes connected to your home network, you can easily transfer or watch shows or movies between them. For instance, if a show is recorded in the living room, you can play it back on your bedroom TV — or vice versa. Here's how to do it:

1. **Go to the TiVo box that you want to view the program on.**

2. **Select the source TiVo box.**

   Bring up the Now Playing List, highlight the TiVo box that has the programming you want to watch, and press SELECT to see its Now Playing List.

3. **Select the program to watch.**

   Select the program you want to watch, press SELECT, and choose Watch on this TV. The program now exists on both TiVo boxes.

You can still watch shows or movies still on and not completely recorded from other TiVo boxes. Simply pause the program on the original TiVo box that recorded it, and then go back through these steps and choose the Watch from the paused location option that appears.

Converting shows or movies for portable media players

After you have your shows or movies transferred from your TiVo DVR box(s) to TiVo Desktop Plus on your computer, you can transfer them to portable devices. First, though, you have to convert them to a format supported by the portable device, if it's not a Windows-compatible device. No conversion is necessary if you are transferring to a Windows-compatible device.

To convert your TiVo recordings, you must first purchase and upgrade to TiVo Desktop Plus. You can upgrade by visiting www.tivo.com/mytivo/domore/tivotogo/.

If required, here's how you convert your shows or movies to a supported format for your non-Windows–compatible device:

1. **Select the program to transfer.**

   Select a movie or show in the Now Playing List of TiVo Desktop Plus.

2. **Convert the program.**

   Right-click the movie or show and select Convert for, and then select your portable device. The converted recordings automatically appear in the My TiVo Recordings for Portables folder of your My Documents folder.

Transferring shows or movies to your portable media player

To transfer movies to your portable media player, you can simply drag and drop them:

1. **Find the files.**

   On your computer, browse to the folder where your TiVo or converted recorded files are located:

   - **Converted recordings:** In the My TiVo Recordings for Portables folder of your My Documents folder.
   - **TiVo recordings:** In Windows Media Player's media library.

2. **Access your portable media player.**

   Open a new window to browse to your portable media player's contents.

3. **Drag and drop.**

   You can copy the files by clicking and dragging them to the window of your portable media player's contents.

Transferring video from your computer to your TiVo box

You can transfer a variety of video files — footage from your digital camcorder or downloaded clips from the Internet — from your computer to your TiVo box.

The following are the supported video formats:

- ✦ Windows Media Video (.WMV)
- ✦ QuickTime Movie (.MOV)
- ✦ MPEG-4/H.264 (.MP4, .M4V, .MP4V)

✦ MPEG-2 (.MPG, .MPEG, .MPE, .MP2, .MP2V, .MPV2)

✦ DivX or XviD (.AVI, .DIVX, encoded with the DivX codec, version 4 or higher, or with the XviD codec. No other video formats are supported within .AVI files.)

You can't transfer videos protected with DRM (Digital Rights Management) or another copy protection method to your TiVo. TiVo doesn't support these features.

Here's how to transfer video files to your TiVo box:

1. **Place video in the My TiVo Recordings folder.**

Put the video files in the My TiVo Recordings folder that's located in the My Documents folder of your computer. You can do this in a variety of ways. For example, open windows for both the folder of the video files and the destination folder so that you can drag and drop or copy the video files and paste them into the destination folder.

2. **Select the source computer from your TiVo box.**

Select your computer from the Now Playing List of your TiVo box — it's marked with the computer icon.

3. **Select the program to transfer/watch.**

Select the program you want to transfer/watch, press SELECT, and choose Watch on this TV. The program begins transferring to your TiVo box and now exists on both your TiVo box and your computer.

Publishing music and photos on your computer

Unlike video from your computer, music and photos aren't transferred and stored on your TiVo boxes. When you play music or view photos from your computers on your TiVo, the files are only streamed, not stored, to the TiVo box. But these files on your computers aren't automatically set up for streaming, so you must publish them — or in other words, give TiVo Desktop the permission to share them with your TiVo boxes.

TiVo boxes support the .MP3 file format for music and audio and the following playlist formats:

✦ .M3U (Winamp Playlist file)

✦ .PLS (Generic Playlist File)

✦ .ASX (Advanced Stream Redirector File)

✦ .B4S (Winamp 3+ Playlist)

TiVo boxes support the following photo file formats:

✦ .BMP (Windows Graphics File)

✦ .TIFF (Tagged Image Format File)

✦ .DIB (Device-Independent Bitmap Graphic)

✦ .GIF (Graphic Interchange Format)

✦ .JPG (Joint Photographic Experts Group)

✦ .PNG (Portable Network Graphics)

Publishing these media files involves the following steps:

1. **Open TiVo Desktop from your computer.**

2. **Click the Publish Media icon.**

3. **Select whether to publish music or photos.**

   Click the Music or Photos tab, and then click the Add Music or Add Photos button.

4. **Publish the files.**

   Go to the folder containing the files you want to publish. To publish a whole folder of files, select the folder and click the Add button. To publish individual files, select them from the list on the right, and then click the Add button.

Playing music from your computer on your TiVo box

After publishing music on your computer, you can listen to it on your TiVo boxes:

1. **Go to TiVo Central.**

2. **Select Music, Photos, Products & More.**

3. **Select a music file or playlist and press PLAY.**

Viewing photos from your computer on your TiVo box

After publishing photos on your computer, you can view them on your TiVo Series2 boxes:

1. **Go to TiVo Central.**

2. **Select Music, Photos, Products & More.**

3. **Choose a photo selection.**

   For each computer, you'll see a photo selection named by your user and computer name (for instance, Madison's Photos on the Family PC).

Creating your own TiVo channel to share your home movies

If you enjoy making home movies of your kids, vacations, and hobbies, you can now share the footage with family and friends across the country on their TV. Home Movie Sharing gives you a private channel for family and friends to see your photos and videos with their TiVo box.

TiVo has teamed up with One True Media, an online service that helps people create video montages or home movies. It is the fastest way of uploading your film content and turning it into polished pieces of art done Hollywood-style. Sign up today at onetruemedia.com/tivo, or go to TiVo Central and select Music, Photos, Products, & More, and then Home Movies by One True Media.

Using the online scheduling feature

Browse TV listings and schedule recordings on your home DVR using TiVo Central Online. To start searching, sign in at tivo.com/tco.

Use the Search TV box at the top of the page to look for program titles, actor names, director names, or keywords. You can narrow your search to specific categories using the drop-down menu.

Digital Picture Frames: Showcasing Your Photos

You can showcase your favorite photos from your computers or media cards on digital picture frames (see Figure 2-16) — now Bill Gates isn't the only one with this high-tech gadget in his home.

Although the features and functionalities of these digital picture frames vary greatly, along with simple digital photo display, you may also be able to

✦ Play MP3s with built-in speakers

✦ Connect to your home network with Wi-Fi

✦ Perform simple photo editing with built-in capabilities

✦ Automatically receive and display pictures from your (or others') online galleries

Consider the following items when scouring local or online stores for a digital picture frame:

✦ **Price:** Certainly price is one of the biggest considerations. You can probably find a good digital picture frame for anywhere from $70 to 250. Prices typically increase with larger frame sizes.

Figure 2-16:
Example of
a digital
picture
frame.

Courtesy of CEIVA Logic, Inc.

✦ **Size:** You may find photo display sizes between $5\frac{1}{2}$ to 10 inches. Think about what size is best for you.

✦ **Interfaces:** Discover and compare the media interfaces — for instance, USB, SD or other memory cards, and Wi-Fi.

✦ **Internal memory:** Some digital picture frames contain internal memory to store your photos; compare the amount of memory offered on different models when shopping.

Playing Online with Wireless Gaming Routers and Adapters

Hooking up your or your child's gaming systems (Xbox, PlayStation, and so on) to your home network (see Figure 2-17) can offer some great benefits:

✦ Opens the door to online play among gamers worldwide

✦ Offers much faster speeds than using a phone connection

✦ Enables you to play head-to-head with other gamers in your home

✦ Lets you move the game console around using wireless gaming adapters

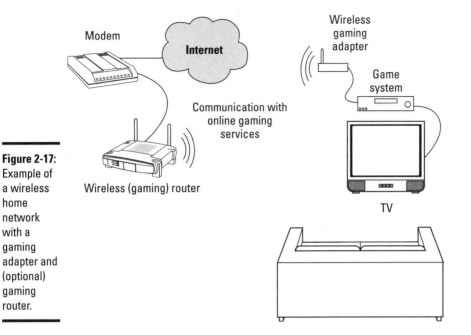

Figure 2-17:
Example of
a wireless
home
network
with a
gaming
adapter and
(optional)
gaming
router.

Some networking manufacturers produce special wireless routers and
adapters designed for online gaming, depicted in Figure 2-18. These gaming
devices operate and act almost identically to their traditional networking
counterparts, but they sometimes include features and enhancements to
provide a better gaming experience than is possible with regular networking
equipment, including

✦ Higher-performance CPUs

✦ Gaming platforms and intelligence to better support high-demand
applications

✦ Pre-configured ports and settings for games and applications

✦ High-gain antennas for better wireless coverage and performance

These gaming devices also may provide better performance with other multimedia network applications, such as

✦ Media players

✦ Digital cameras

✦ Video cameras

✦ Video and audio (VoIP) streaming

Your network gaming options

You have two options when it comes to specialized network equipment for gaming:

✦ **Wireless gaming adapter:** This gives your game system(s) a Wi-Fi wireless connection to a regular or gaming wireless router or access point. A wireless gaming adapter (see Figure 2-18) works with Ethernet-ready game consoles and is essentially a wired-to-wireless bridge.

Figure 2-18:
A wireless gaming adapter.

Courtesy of Linksys

You may see this type of functionality in other wireless devices and as stand-alone bridge products, with virtually no difference between them and those devices specifically sold as gaming adapters. This means that you can hook just about any other Ethernet-ready product or device (such as a media player, video camera, or computer) to it to make it wireless.

✦ **Wireless gaming router:** Gaming routers (see Figure 2-19) support computers and other wireless or wired devices just as regular wireless routers do but can provide a better overall experience when used for online or peer-to-peer gaming.

Figure 2-19:
A wireless
gaming
router.

Courtesy of D-Link Systems, Inc.

As far as networking equipment for gamers, a gaming router is where the beauty lies. The gaming router provides the intelligence and special features that can be used in conjunction with a game console, wired or wirelessly connected. If you are a serious online gamer and want the best of the best, a gaming router may be for you. One feature that stands out is that it automatically gives the gaming traffic priority over other, less-sensitive data transfers such as file transferring and downloading files from the Internet.

Choosing your network gaming devices

Here are a few things to keep in mind when shopping for gaming devices for your home network:

✦ **Wireless technology:** Consider the wireless technology of any gaming adapters or routers. Faster standards such as wireless n provide much faster transfer speeds than older standards, such as wireless g or b. Also keep in mind that your wireless router and adapter must have the higher standard. For instance, if you have only a wireless g router, but you buy a wireless n gaming adapter, your adapter operates only as wireless g, unless you upgrade your router to wireless n.

✦ **Auto-connect feature:** This feature is very convenient, so keep an eye out for it in the gaming adapters you come across. Instead of your having to manually set up the connection between your gaming console and network, this feature does it automatically.

✦ **Gaming features and enhancements:** Gaming adapters typically don't include — and don't need to include — any special gaming features and enhancements; however, gaming routers do. So carefully compare the specifications of gaming routers to see how many and what types of gaming features are included.

Setting up your gaming devices

If you choose to use a wireless gaming adapter, you set it up by connecting one end of an Ethernet cable (probably included with your gaming adapter) to the Ethernet port of your game console, and the other end to the port of your gaming adapter. Then, plug the power adapter into an electrical outlet and connect to your gaming adapter.

Next, do one of the following (depending on your system):

✦ If your gaming adapter has an auto-connect button, press it. It should automatically connect to your wireless network.

✦ If your adapter doesn't have an auto-connect button, but you're using one that's the same brand as your wireless router, configuration might not be necessary.

✦ If you're using an Xbox, its network configuration utility may be adequate. Just bring up the Network Configuration menu on the Xbox after you've hooked up the gaming adapter.

If you aren't using an adapter of the same brand as your router, you probably need to configure it with the adapter's Web-based configuration utility via a computer. To do so, follow these steps:

1. **Connect the Ethernet cable to your computer.**

If necessary, unplug the Ethernet cable from the game console. You want to connect one end of the Ethernet cable to the gaming adapter, and the other end to the Ethernet port of your computer.

2. **Verify that you have an IP address.**

If your computer doesn't receive an IP address and doesn't indicate that it's connected after the gaming adapter is hooked to your computer, you need to manually assign one:

Look in the installation guide or manual of your gaming adapter to figure out the default IP address and subnet mask (most likely 255.255.255.0). These are the two pieces of information you need to configure your computer with a correct static IP address.

After you know the default IP settings, configure your computer with an address in the same range.

For instance, if the IP address is 192.168.0.210, you could use 192.168.0.211 or 192.168.0.212; or if the default is 192.168.0.30, you could use 192.168.0.31 or even 192.168.0.166.

If you need help with configuring static addresses, refer to Book IV, Chapter 1.

3. **Bring up your Web browser (such as Internet Explorer, Netscape, or Firefox).**

4. **Type in the IP address of your gaming adapter and press Enter.**

   If you don't know the IP address or the username or password, refer to Book V, Chapter 5 for help. Keep in mind that some manufacturers may use a domain name, which looks like a Web site address, instead of an IP address.

5. **When prompted, enter the login credentials provided in your product documentation.**

Chapter 3: Traveling Gadgets

*N*etworking doesn't have to take a break when you go on vacations or work trips — networking gadgets abound for your travel needs. If you can't live without having wireless for your laptop, you can pack a compact travel router just in case you stay somewhere without Wi-Fi. If you want to watch your favorite shows or movies, you can set them up on your TV or DVR and home network before you leave, and then you have your home entertainment anywhere you go. You can even watch your recorded stuff using your DVR anywhere, as long as you have an Internet connection. No more changing everyone's plans just for your viewing pleasure or freaking out if your hotel doesn't have the right channel! And to make sure that you can easily find a Wi-Fi hotspot that enables you to connect to your home entertainment center or do other things online, you can slip a Wi-Fi finder into your pocket. In this chapter, I give you a laundry list of handy networking gadgets that can make your life on the road easier, more fun, and more productive.

Travel Routers: Taking Wireless with You

Some wireless networking manufacturers produce travel or pocket routers/access points (APs), which are compact versions of the regular devices, seen in Figure 3-1.

These devices are made for you to create a wireless network when you're away from home. For example, during business trips or vacations, you can plug a travel wireless router into the Internet connection of the hotel (or your relative's home), depicted in Figure 3-2, so that you can reap benefits such as

✦ Being free of wires with a wireless connection.

✦ Encrypting and securing your wireless communications, which is not the case when you use public wireless networks (Wi-Fi hotspots).

Figure 3-1:
An example
of a travel
router.

Courtesy of Linksys

✦ Sharing files among your friends or family connected to your travel router, which usually isn't possible or secure to do on public wireless networks (Wi-Fi hotspots).

✦ Playing multiplayer games with friends or family over the network.

✦ Saving money by sharing a fee-based connection. For example, you might have to pay for a hotel's wired Internet connection. Instead of just plugging one laptop into the Internet port, plug in a travel router to give access to your family, friends, or colleagues.

If your travel router comes with a USB power cable, as most do, you don't have to plug it into an electrical outlet. You can just use the USB port on your laptop to power the router — magic, huh? This gives you the opportunity to create your own wireless network just about anywhere. For instance, you can even set up the travel router in the car when traveling so that you can share files or play games with people in the car. You can even do the same with people in a trailing or leading car if the two vehicles stay close. You might also find a travel router convenient to use in public areas, such as airports, libraries, or schools, that offer a wired Internet connection.

Shopping for a travel router

Here are several things to look for when choosing a travel router:

✦ **Multiple personalities:** Some travel routers include multiple modes, such as Router, AP, and Client modes, which can offer additional features and functionality that may come in handy.

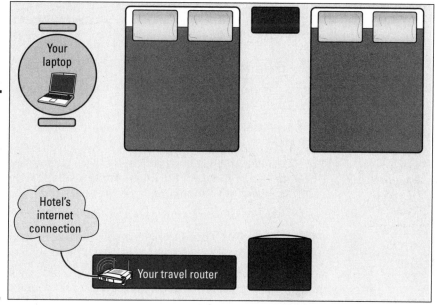

Figure 3-2:
Depiction of using a travel router in a hotel room to create your own wireless network with an Internet connection.

✦ **USB power cable:** You may want to be on the lookout for travel routers that include a USB power cable, in addition to a regular power adapter that plugs into an electrical outlet. Powering from your laptop's USB port lets you set up the travel router just about anywhere — this can be especially useful when traveling to countries that have different types of outlets.

✦ **Wireless security:** You should check whether the travel router supports your desired encryption method. The new methods, such as WPA or WPA2, may not be supported by all travel routers.

✦ **Carrying case:** Most travel routers come with a nifty carrying case to pack the router and all accessories in.

✦ **Reviews:** You may want to check the Internet for any product reviews and user/consumer ratings and comments before going with a particular router.

Setting up your travel router

Setting up your travel router consists of the following steps:

1. **Connect the travel router to the Internet connection.**

Plug one end of an Ethernet cable (probably included with your router) to the Internet connection, and plug the other end into the WAN or Internet port of your router.

2. Power up the travel router.

Plug the power adapter into an electrical outlet (or USB port, if it's a USB power cable) and connect it to your travel router.

3. Perform the initial configuration.

After you get your travel router out of the box, you should do some initial configurations:

a. Connect to the router.

In order to configure the travel router, you must connect a computer to the router. You can connect wirelessly or connect one end of an Ethernet cable to one of the Ethernet ports on the travel router and the other end to your computer's Ethernet port.

b. Access the Web-based configuration utility:

Bring up your Web browser (Internet Explorer, Netscape, Firefox, and so on), type the IP address of your travel router in the address box, and press Enter. When prompted, enter your login credentials.

If you don't know the IP address or the username or password, refer to Book V, Chapter 3 for help. Keep in mind that some manufacturers may use a domain name, which looks like a Web site address, instead of an IP address.

c. Configure the router and wireless settings.

After you're logged into the configuration utility, you need to find and configure the router's wireless and security settings:

- Change your network name (SSID) and channel.
- Enable (WPA or WEP) encryption.
- Change the default login password.

Refer to Book II, Chapter 3 for information on how to set these items.

Now your travel router is ready to take along on trips and outings. To get it working, just follow the first two steps of the preceding list and you'll have wireless access.

Taking Home Entertainment Anywhere with Sling Media

Sling Media has a product line that enables you to access your home entertainment center from anywhere in the world via the Internet, letting you

✦ **Watch your TV programming**

✦ **Access and watch recorded shows and movies from your DVR**

✦ **Access and play your DVD player or other media devices**

Just think, no more missing that favorite show or movie because the hotel doesn't receive the channel. Just hook up to the hotel's Internet service and watch it on your laptop! Plus, you won't have to wait until you get home to get caught up on all the shows your DVR recorded. It's like bringing your home entertainment center with you wherever you go.

How Sling Media works

Sling Media produces a product called a Slingbox that you connect to a source (cable or satellite box, TV cable, DVD player, and so on) and the Internet, as shown in Figure 3-3.

**Book VI
Chapter 3**

Traveling Gadgets

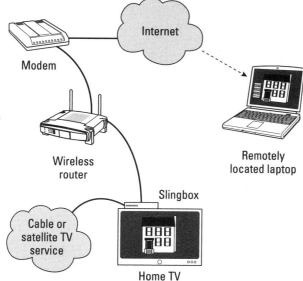

Figure 3-3:
Depiction of using Sling Media to remotely access and watch your home entertainment center.

Then when you travel or you're away from home, you can use the SlingPlayer software to access your home entertainment center from devices such as

✦ **Laptops** (see Figure 3-4)

✦ **Cell phones** (see Figure 3-5)

✦ **PDAs**

Figure 3-4:
SlingPlayer
on a laptop.

Figure 3-5:
SlingPlayer
on a Palm
Treo cell
phone.

Your Slingbox options

The Slingbox (see Figure 3-6) is the heart of this Sling Media technology. You can pick from a few different Slingboxes:

Figure 3-6:
The Slingbox that you connect to your cable or audio/video source at home.

✦ **Slingbox AV:** Supports one input device, using its set of composite audio/video or S-video inputs.

✦ **Slingbox SOLO:** Supports one input device (HD-compatible), using its set of composite or component audio/video inputs, or S-video inputs. Also included are outputs for all the inputs, so you can pass-through the audio/video to another device — you won't have to unhook and rehook your connections each time you want to view your audio/video from the Internet.

✦ **Slingbox PRO:** Supports up to four input devices, using its set of composite audio/video inputs, S-video and left/right audio inputs, or the HD port — each input also comes with an output, such as the Slingbox SOLO. This box also comes with a built-in cable tuner, so someone can watch TV at home while you're watching a different channel from the Internet.

You should figure out how you're going to connect the Slingbox to your Internet — depending upon your setup, this may require more time and money than you originally thought. Here are several routes that you can take:

✦ **A direct connection to your router:** You can connect an Ethernet cable to one of the ports on your wired or wireless router, such as Figure 3-7 shows. This is best if your Slingbox, source, and router are closely located to each other.

✦ **Use a wireless adapter/bridge:** You can purchase a wireless adapter/bridge, usually called a *gaming adapter* for consumer-level products. You just plug it into the Internet port of the Slingbox, and the wireless adapter wirelessly connects to your wireless router, as shown in Figure 3-8.

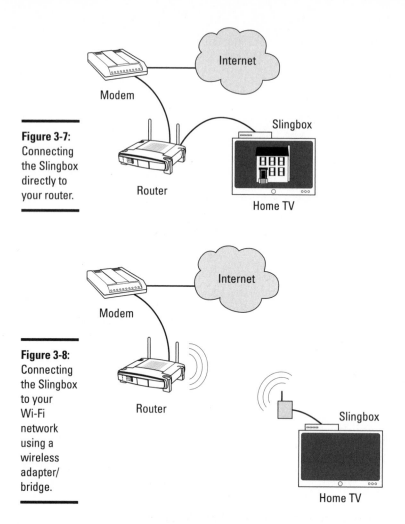

Figure 3-7:
Connecting
the Slingbox
directly to
your router.

Figure 3-8:
Connecting
the Slingbox
to your
Wi-Fi
network
using a
wireless
adapter/
bridge.

✦ **Use power-line (HomePlug) adapters:** You can purchase a set of power-line (HomePlug) adapters to use your electrical system as a courier for your Internet/network connection. Figure 3-9 shows an example.

One adapter plugs into an electrical outlet near your wired or wireless router or Internet modem, and an Ethernet cable is connected between the power-line adapter and your router or modem. The other power-line adapter plugs into an electrical outlet near your Slingbox, and an Ethernet cable is connected between the power-line adapter and the Slingbox.

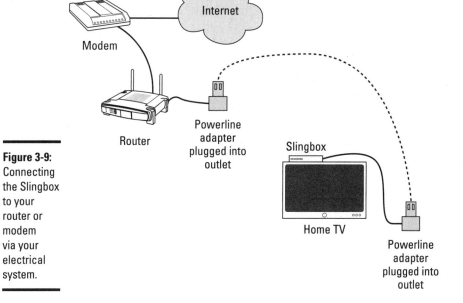

Figure 3-9:
Connecting
the Slingbox
to your
router or
modem
via your
electrical
system.

Setting up your Sling Media system

When you're ready, you can set up your Sling Media system by following
these steps:

1. **Connect the cable and/or A/V source(s).**

   Using the supplied TV cable, s-video and/or composite A/V cables, connect the source (cable box, TV cable, DVD player, and so on) to your
   Slingbox.

2. **Connect and place the remote control IR cable.**

   If your Slingbox came with a remote control IR cable, connect it to the IR
   plug on the back of the Slingbox. Then place the IR cable heads on the
   top and bottom of your source (cable or satellite box, DVD player, and
   so on) so that they point to its remote control IR sensor (usually a small
   black or dark green window on the front).

   The cable heads send IR signals just as your remote would, originating
   from the Slingbox by your command when you are using the SlingPlayer.
   Therefore, you have full control of the source device remotely.

3. **Connect to your home network Internet.**

   Plug one end of an Ethernet cable into the Internet port on the back of
   the Slingbox, and the other end into the Internet connection device

you're using — for example, your router, a wireless adapter/bridge, or a power-line (HomePlug) adapter. These methods are discussed in the previous section.

4. Plug in the power.

Plug the power adapter into an electrical outlet and connect to your Slingbox.

5. Write down information about the source device.

To properly configure the SlingPlayer's remote control, you need to know the following information about the source device when doing the installation:

- Device type
- Brand
- Model
- Connection method

6. Install SlingPlayer.

Using the supplied CD-ROM disc, install the SlingPlayer software on the computers or mobile devices you plan to use when away from home.

If you've misplaced the disc, you can download the SlingPlayer at

```
http://downloads.slingplayer.com
```

For the mobile device versions of the SlingPlayer, go to

```
http://www.slingmedia.com/slingplayermobile
```

For the Macintosh version of the SlingPlayer, go to

```
http://downloads.slingmedia.com/go/desktop-us
```

When you're away (or at home), you can access your Slingbox and home entertainment center by following these simple steps:

1. Power on your mobile device.

Turn on your laptop, PDA, or phone that's loaded with the SlingPlayer software.

2. Connect to the Internet.

Connect to the Internet, either via an Ethernet, Wi-Fi, or cellular connection.

3. Open SlingPlayer.

Wi-Fi Hotspot Finders

If you find yourself frequently wondering whether a Wi-Fi network is nearby when you're traveling or out and about, a Wi-Fi finder may be just what you need. With one touch, you can see what networks are nearby. No more opening and booting up your laptop just to check for wireless networks. You can just glance at your Wi-Fi finder; see Figure 3-10 for an example of one.

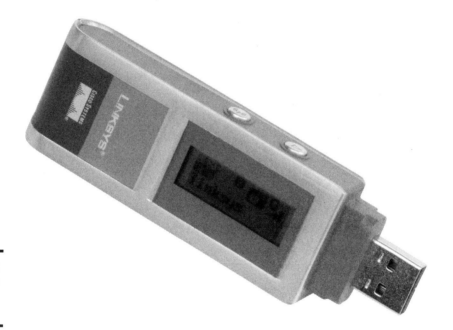

Figure 3-10:
An example
of a Wi-Fi
finder.

Wi-Fi finders let you know when wireless networks are nearby, and most will display all their pertinent information, such as

✦ **Signal strength**
✦ **Network name**
✦ **Security status**

This is typically enough information to determine if a public hotspot is around — rather than just private networks belonging to businesses and residents.

Consider these things when shopping around for a Wi-Fi finder:

✦ **Display:** Be conscious of the display: Does it show text or just LED lights to show signal strength? An LCD screen with text can show much more information about the detected wireless networks.

✦ **Durability:** Try to gauge the durability of the device by examining it and reading any comments made by users.

✦ **Wireless technologies:** Most Wi-Fi finders support the popular wireless technologies, such as b/g/n; however, if you use wireless a, you need to consider this when searching for a Wi-Fi finder because not all finders support it.

✦ **Size:** Think about the size of Wi-Fi finders you come by. Most are small and compact, but some may be too bulky to carry comfortably in your pocket.

✦ **Combination devices:** You may want to consider a combination device, such as a USB wireless adapter with a built-in Wi-Fi finder. This is good if you also need to buy a wireless adapter (to upgrade to a newer wireless standard or to get wireless capability for the first time).

✦ **Product reviews:** You should prowl the Internet for any product reviews or user feedback.

Chapter 4: Bluetooth Devices

In This Chapter

✔ **Discovering what you can do with the Bluetooth wireless technology**

✔ **Checking out which gadgets have Bluetooth**

✔ **Figuring out how to equip your device with Bluetooth**

✔ **Synchronizing your cell phone or PDA with your PC**

The Bluetooth wireless technology brings more than just wireless headsets to your cell phone — it can bring audio and data streaming and synchronization to many devices you use every day, including

✦ Car navigation systems

✦ Car speakers

✦ Home audio systems

✦ Printers

✦ PDAs

✦ Media players

✦ Mobile phones

This chapter shows you how to get Bluetooth connectivity for your electronic devices and what you can do with them after they have it.

How You Can Use Bluetooth

Bluetooth is a short-range wireless technology used to transfer and stream data to and from portable devices. Whether at the desk in your home or work office, or in your car on vacations or around town, Bluetooth offers countless benefits for a variety of applications and devices such as PDAs, mobile phones, or laptops. The following sections give you insight into Bluetooth uses and applications that can become a part of your everyday life.

Synching data and taking your peripherals wireless to the office

Bluetooth can offer data synchronization and wireless capabilities to devices such as

✦ **PDAs/mobile phones:** You can synchronize your calendar, appointments, contacts, phone images, and more between your computer and PDA or mobile phone.

✦ **Wireless input devices:** You can use a Bluetooth mouse, keyboard, or input tablet to connect to your computer wirelessly. Eliminating the wires and cords is great in the office or when traveling — wireless input devices take up less space and reduce clutter.

✦ **Printers:** A Bluetooth-enabled printer enables you to print from your computer, PDA, or mobile phone — without being wired to the printer.

✦ **Headset:** Bluetooth headsets aren't limited to use with your mobile phone. You may find it useful to have a headset wirelessly connected to your PC or laptop, especially if you use Skype or another Internet phone.

Streaming music and other data in your car

You can stream audio and other data to your car's stereo and computer systems by using the following Bluetooth-capable devices:

✦ **Mobile phones:** You may be able to do things such as access your mobile phone's contacts from your car's navigation display and make hands-free phone calls. You also may be able to wirelessly connect to your car's powerful, outside mounted, cellular antenna for better reception.

✦ **GPS systems:** You may be able to do things such as update your GPS and map information through the Internet connection of a mobile phone that's connected to the GPS system with Bluetooth.

✦ **iPods and other media players:** Using a Bluetooth adapter with your iPod or other media player, or a Bluetooth phone, you can stream music to your car's stereo system.

The exact functionality and features you have available depend upon your particular Bluetooth device and the capabilities of your car's Bluetooth and navigation system.

Going wireless with your cell phone accessories and transfers

Your cell phone data transfers to other devices and your use of phone accessories are made easier and quicker with Bluetooth. For example, here is a list of devices and what you can do with them:

✦ **Printers:** You can send photos from your mobile phone to your Bluetooth-enabled printer.

✦ **Headsets and headphones:** Bluetooth headsets aren't limited to use during calls on your mobile phone. If your phone supports MP3s, you can also listen to your favorite songs with your wireless Bluetooth headset or head phones.

✦ **Computers:** You can synchronize your calendar, appointments, contacts, phone images, and more between your computer and mobile phone.

✦ **Cars:** A Bluetooth-enabled navigation or GPS system in your car may be able to communicate with your Bluetooth mobile phone.

Saving time and hassle with your digital photos

Bluetooth-enabled digital cameras can open up the possibility to seamless communication with the following Bluetooth-capable devices:

✦ **Printers:** A Bluetooth-enabled digital camera lets you print to your Bluetooth-enabled compact photo or regular printers — straight from your camera, before you even transfer your photos to your computer.

✦ **Mobile devices:** You may be able to send photos from your digital camera directly to another Bluetooth-enabled camera, mobile phone, or computer.

✦ **TVs:** If your TV has Bluetooth capability, you can send your photos directly to your TV so that everyone can view them without having to wait for you to transfer the photos and create a slide show on CD or DVD.

✦ **Digital picture frames:** If you have a Bluetooth-capable digital picture frame or photo viewer, you can send and share photos easily with your Bluetooth-enabled camera.

Streaming and transferring music and audio easily

Bluetooth can enable the possibility of easy music and audio streaming and transferring to devices such as

✦ **Headphones and speakers:** You may find that you can listen to music from a variety of sources with a set of Bluetooth wireless headphones or speakers.

✦ **Computers:** You may also be able to listen to music and audio from your computer on Bluetooth-enabled speakers placed around the room or Bluetooth wireless headphones.

✦ **Mobile devices:** Using a Bluetooth adapter with your iPod or other media player, or a Bluetooth phone or PDA, you can stream music to a set of Bluetooth headphones.

✦ **Home entertainment:** You may also be able to create a wireless surround-sound system. The music and audio from your computer or TV entertainment center can be sent to your Bluetooth-enabled speakers placed around the room — no more tripping on speaker wires.

✦ **Cars:** A Bluetooth-enabled iPod or other media player lets you stream music and audio to your car's Bluetooth-enabled stereo system, letting you throw out those old scratched CDs that hold much less music.

The exact functionality and features you'll have available depend upon the capability of particular Bluetooth devices.

Getting Bluetooth Connectivity

Enough with the examples of what you can do with Bluetooth. In this section, I get into making these Bluetooth applications work. First, you must have Bluetooth in the devices that communicate with each other. In some types of devices and products, Bluetooth is already integrated; in other cases, you may have to purchase a separate Bluetooth adapter.

You should remember that manufacturers may not produce all their products to be Bluetooth-integrated or compatible with Bluetooth adapters. Additionally, the features and functionality of Bluetooth-enabled devices vary. For instance, one Bluetooth mobile phone may stream all music and audio to Bluetooth headsets, whereas another may stream the audio only from calls.

Devices loaded with Bluetooth

The following are devices that may have Bluetooth already integrated within them:

✦ Cell phones

✦ PDAs

✦ MP3 and other portable media players

✦ Digital cameras

✦ Car navigation (GPS) systems

✦ Headphones and headsets

✦ TVs

✦ Speakers

✦ Digital picture frames

It's always good to double-check to see whether your gadgets already have Bluetooth before searching for a compatible adapter.

Adapters to make your device Bluetooth-enabled

For devices that don't have Bluetooth in them, you can use Bluetooth adapters, such as the following:

✦ **USB Bluetooth adapters:** These give your desktop or laptop computer — and almost any other device with a USB port — Bluetooth connectivity. See Figure 4-1 for an example.

Figure 4-1: A USB Bluetooth adapter.

Courtesy of D-Link Systems, Inc.

✦ **Digital camera Bluetooth adapters:** These give your digital camera the capability to communicate with other Bluetooth devices. For instance, you may be able to wirelessly print to standard or compact photo printers or transfer files to your computer or other cameras.

Bluetooth adapters for digital cameras may come in the form of an SD card or USB adapter.

Make sure you examine the supported features and functions when searching for a Bluetooth adapter for your digital camera. In addition to checking with the manufacturer of your camera, you can search for universal adapters that support your camera.

✦ **PDA Bluetooth adapters:** These adapters put the power of Bluetooth in your PDA so that you can transfer files and synchronize your contacts, appointments, e-mail, and more without being tied to a cable or cradle. These adapters may come in the form of a Compact Flash or SD card.

✦ **Printer Bluetooth adapters:** These let you wirelessly print from other Bluetooth devices, such as your PDA, phone, or digital camera.

✦ **Bluetooth car kits:** These kits let you listen to music from Bluetooth devices and calls with Bluetooth phones through your car's speaker system. You can probably find a system offered by your cell phone vendor, car radio manufacturer, or by searching the Web.

Shopping for Bluetooth devices and adapters

Here are a few tips that can help you when searching for that perfect Bluetooth solution:

✦ **Check the Bluetooth Web site:** Rummaging through the Bluetooth Web site (www.Bluetooth.com), especially the Product Zone, can help.

✦ **Bluetooth version:** Keep an eye out for the Bluetooth versions supported by devices and adapters you come across. The newer versions can offer better security, increased battery life, and more.

✦ **Combination devices:** If you look hard enough, you may even find combination Wi-Fi/Bluetooth adapters and devices.

✦ **Multi-use adapters:** You should consider the possibility of using Bluetooth adapters for multiple devices. For example, a single USB Bluetooth adapter may work with your digital camera, computer, and mobile phone. This may help reduce the amount of adapters you need to purchase.

Synchronizing Your Cell Phone or PDA with Your PC

In this section, I cover how to synchronize or transfer data between your cell phone or PDA and your computer using Bluetooth. However, you need to refer to product documentation for help on using Bluetooth with other specific devices or other noncomputer communication applications, such as computer peripherals, media players, your car, or home entertainment center.

The first thing you should do is set up your USB Bluetooth adapter for your computer. Setting up a USB Bluetooth adapter typically involves the following steps:

1. **Install the driver/software.**

Your Bluetooth adapter should have come with an installation CD so that you can load its driver and install any software. Insert your CD and complete the installation.

2. **Plug it in.**

Simply plug your USB Bluetooth adapter into one of your computer's USB ports.

3. **Set up the client software.**

Now you can install and use any software that came with your Bluetooth-enabled device(s).

If you're using a Microsoft-based PDA, use ActiveSync (if your computer has Windows XP or earlier) or Windows Mobile Device Center (if your computer has Windows Vista). If you're using a Palm PDA/mobile phone, you should use the Palm Desktop software.

You can download ActiveSync for free at

```
www.microsoft.com/windowsmobile/activesync/
```

Windows Mobile Device Center is installed on Windows Vista by default and available on the Start menu by choosing All Programs➪ Accessories➪Sync Center.

If you're using a cell phone, you'll probably have to use that company's software. However, you may be able to get some type of functionality through Windows by adding a Bluetooth device and setting it up through the Bluetooth utility in the Control Panel.

Chapter 5: Network Magic: Ways to Manage Your Home Network

In This Chapter

☛ Discovering the flavors of Network Magic

☛ Installing and setting up Network Magic on your computers

☛ Getting the grand tour of Network Magic

☛ Taking a look at the add-ons for more functionality

*I*f you have several computers on your home network with various operating systems — maybe Windows XP or Vista, the old Win 98, or even a mixture of Macintosh and PCs — Network Magic can help by streamlining everything involving your network. This includes management and access of shared folders, easy Web sharing, and troubleshooting help. But even if you don't have a mixture of operating systems, Network Magic still has benefits over using your operating system's built-in, or vendor, network configuration utilities. Network Magic's user-friendly platform and shortcuts can help improve your networking experience. In this chapter, I take you on the tour of Network Magic and show you how it can reduce the time you spend configuring your network.

Seeing What's So Magical about Network Magic

Network Magic can streamline your networking configurations and tasks. It offers support for both PC and Mac computers — you can easily share files and printers between these different platforms. Network Magic gives you more features and functionality than what you receive from the built-in networking tools of the Windows and Mac operating systems, such as the following:

✦ Network health and security alerts

✦ File and printer sharing among Macs and PCs

✦ Easy configuration of your wireless network's security

✦ Same user interface for any operating system

✦ Remote access to files and online sharing

Network Magic comes in a few different flavors:

+ **Free trial:** Offers all the features of the Pro version for a short amount of time, usually seven days. After the time is up, you can still use the limited version, offering basic networking configuration, network history, a record of the activity on your network, and health and security alert features that detect issues and help you resolve them.

+ **Essentials:** Offers advanced features and functionality, such as remote access, network reports, and online backup are left out of this version. However, this version offers many more features than the free version (after the trial period has expired), such as Easy File Sharing, Automatic Printer Sharing, and Wireless and Broadband Protection.

+ **Pro:** Offers advanced features, such as Remote Access to Files, Network Reports, and Network-Attached Storage (NAS) device support. Plus, this version includes licensing and support for more computers — up to eight instead of three provided by Essentials.

For a quick comparison of Network Magic's two for-pay flavors, see Table 5-1.

Table 5-1	Comparing Different Network Magic Versions	
Feature	*Essentials*	*Pro*
Easy to Use		
Wizards guide you through networking	x	x
Centralized dashboard	x	x
Connect Devices and Share Folders and Printers		
Add a Device Wizard	x	x
Easy file sharing	x	x
Automatic printer sharing	x	x
Wireless Connection Manager	x	x
Network-Attached Storage (NAS) device support		x
Centralized shared file directory	x	x
Remote access to files		x
Network Protection		
Wireless and broadband protection	x	x
PC Shield	x	x
Maintain and Repair Network		
Visual Network Map	x	x
Internet connection repair	x	x

Feature	Essentials	Pro
Network reports		x
Internet speed test		x
Network history	x	x
Network health and security alerts	x	x
Network Magic Advisor	x	x
Online File Backup		
Six months free from Carbonite		x
Licensing and Support		
Licensing and support: Number of computers	Up to three PCs	Up to eight PCs
Free technical support	x	x
Priority premium support phone line	x	x
Mac Integration		
	Network Magic for Mac Add-on: Must be purchased separately	Network Magic for Mac Add-on: Must be purchased separately

Here are some of the great features and functions of Network Magic:

✦ **Easy to use:** Network Magic is very helpful and user-friendly:

   • *Wizards guide you through networking:* When using the network or sharing troubleshooting wizards, and throughout other spots in Network Magic, appropriate networking concepts are explained in an easy to understand manner.

   • *Centralized dashboard:* From any main screen in Network Magic, you can access buttons that take you to the different screens. You can also see the status area that lets you know whether you're connected to your network and of any network health or security alerts.

✦ **Easy to connect devices and share folders and printers:** Many features are included to help you connect devices and computers and share between them:

   • *Add a Device Wizard:* This wizard helps you through the process of adding a new device to your network.

   • *Easy file sharing:* Network Magic lets you easily select folders from your computers to be shared among all the users on the network. Additionally, accessing these shared folders is also very easy.

- *Automatic printer sharing:* Printers connected to the computers on your network are automatically shared. Of course, if you want, you can disable sharing of any printer.

- *Wireless Connection Manager:* Shows a list of nearby wireless networks, your favorite list, and lets you connect and disconnect from networks. This is similar to the wireless utilities of Windows XP and Vista.

- *Network-Attached Storage (NAS) device support:* Any folders shared on network storage devices, such as Microsoft's Home Server, are displayed in Network Magic's Shared Folder section.

- *Centralized shared file directory:* The Shared Folders page of Network Magic lists all the shared folders in your network, sorted by each computer.

- *Remote access to files:* Lets you set up remote access to files from anywhere in the world. Simply point to your Net2Go Web site that you set up, from any computer connected to the Internet, and you have access to the folders you specified. (Net2Go is a feature in Network Magic Pro that lets you create a personal Web site where you can share files with anyone who has access to the Internet.) You can specify to share folders publicly so that anyone can access them, or you can set them as private so that a password must be entered for access.

✦ **Improved network protection:** Network Magic helps protect your home network and computers:

- *Wireless and broadband protection:* Helps you protect your computers on your network, including easy changes of your wireless router's security settings right from Network Magic.

- *PC Shield:* If you connect to other networks, for instance with your laptop to a public Wi-Fi hotspot, PC Shield protects your computer and files.

✦ **Easier to maintain and repair network:** Network Magic includes the following features to help you manage your home network:

- *Visual Network Map:* Gives you a visual diagram of your network. The Internet, router, and all your computers and devices have their own icons. By clicking an item, you have quick access to its available tasks, details, and alerts.

- *Internet Connection Repair:* ICR first tries to automatically fix your Internet connection problem and then, if needed, helps you troubleshoot for the problem, telling you what to do.

- *Network reports:* A daily report on the network activity, including usage graphs, a list of software applications used on your computers, and the Web sites visited. You can either access the latest report manually in Network Magic, or have it e-mailed to you each day.

- *Internet speed test:* Lets you run a test to see the download and upload maximum speeds of your Internet connection and computer-to-computer traffic on your local network.

- *Network history:* Logs the activity that has taken place on your network: for instance, computers and devices connecting and disconnecting, including possible intruders.

- *Network Health and Security Alerts:* Lets you know when you should address a detected problem, such as not having a security method implemented on your wireless network or a computer that is not running the latest Windows updates.

- *Network Magic Advisor:* Provides useful information on networking, including recommended accessories for your particular setup.

✦ **Online file backup:** When you purchase Network Magic Pro, you get the following offer:

- *Six months free from Carbonite:* Carbonite's software continually backs up all your files to their secured online storage, so if you accidentally delete something, or your entire computer crashes, all you have to do is go to the Carbonite Web site to restore your files. To find out more, visit www.carbonite.com.

✦ **Mac integration:** You can make use of both PC and Mac computers on your network with the following:

- *Network Magic for Mac Add-on:* This is the Macintosh version of Network Magic that must be purchased separately. Purchasing and installing this on your Mac computers lets you share files and printers among both your Macs and PCs.

Getting Started with Network Magic

The first thing you should do is install Network Magic. For best results, you should install the software on all the computers that use your network. You have a few ways of going about doing this.

One way is to install it from your router's setup disc. If your router includes Network Magic (the seven-day trial), which is usually indicated on the router's box, you can install it from the setup disc of your router, as follows:

1. **Insert your router's setup CD in your computer.**

2. **Find Network Magic.**

   If it's loaded on the disc, you can usually find it under the Extras or Tools.

3. **Click Network Magic.**

4. **Click Install and follow the instructions.**

You can always easily download the most current version of Network Magic from the Web site. To do so, follow these steps:

1. **Open your Web browser and go to** www.networkmagic.com/download.

2. **Click Start Download Now.**

3. **In the dialog box that appears, click either Run or Save.**

In the File Download prompt, click either Run to start the download and install Network Magic immediately, or Save to save the install file to your computer and then run it after it downloads.

If you choose to save the file, specify where to save it on your computer, and then click Run when the file has finished downloading.

4. **Follow the instructions.**

You can also purchase Network Magic from a local or online store. Just insert the Network Magic CD in the computer, click Install Network Magic, and follow the instructions.

After you have Network Magic installed on all your desired computers, you should perform some initial configurations by following these steps:

1. **Open Network Magic.**

From any of your computers that are on the network and have Network Magic installed, open the Network Magic software. You can find the icon on your Desktop or Start menu.

2. **Enter your router login information.**

In order for Network Magic to properly work with your router, you need to enter your username and password of your router into Network Magic. Here's how:

a. **Click the Network Map button.**

b. **Click the icon for your wireless router.**

This icon is probably located just to the right of the Internet icon.

c. **Click Change Access to Router Settings, as Figure 5-1 shows.**

As shown in Figure 5-1, it's on the Tasks tab listed on the right of the screen.

d. **Enter the username and password.**

In the window that pops up, enter the username and password that you use to log in to your router's Web-based configuration utility, and click OK.

e. **When you're done, click OK to close the window.**

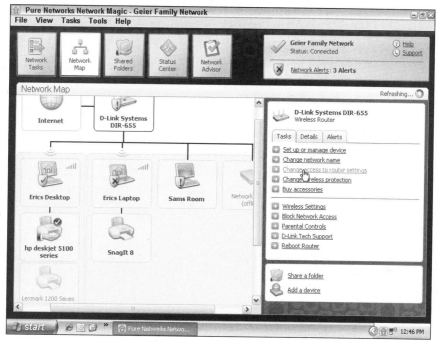

Book VI
Chapter 5

Network Magic:
Ways to Manage
Your Home Network

Figure 5-1:
Opening up
the window
to input your
router's
login
information.

3. **Give your network a name.**

You can assign a name to your network, which is used for just Network Magic's purposes. This doesn't change your wireless network name (SSID) that's configured in your wireless router; it just changes the name that's displayed throughout the Network Magic software. Here's how to configure your network name for Network Magic:

a. **Click the Network Map button.**

b. **Click the icon for your wireless router.**

This is probably located just to the right of the Internet icon.

c. **Click Change Network Name, shown in Figure 5-2.**

As shown in Figure 5-2, it's on the Tasks tab, at the right of the screen.

d. **Enter your desired name.**

In the window that pops up, enter your desired name and click OK.

4. **View and deal with any alerts.**

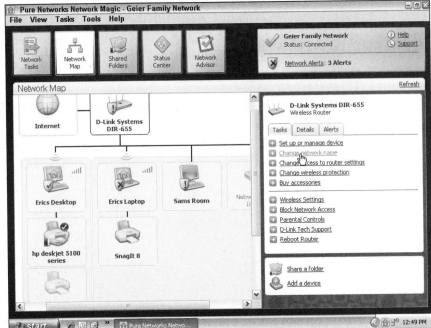

Figure 5-2:
Opening the window to change your network name for Network Magic.

Network Magic detects problems or issues with your network, alerts you of them, and gives recommendations on how to resolve them. Before you go any further and use your network, you should resolve any alerts:

a. **Click the Network Alerts link shown in Figure 5-3.**

A window should pop up and show any active alerts, usually indicated by a small icon of an exclamation point or cross with red text, highlighted with yellow.

b. **Fix each alert.**

Click each item's Fix This Alert link for more information and resolve the issue.

5. **Check your wireless protection methods.**

Network Magic offers a very easy way to configure a few different wireless security methods, such as encryption, hidden network, and MAC address filtering. If Network Magic supports your router for this feature, you should think about enabling these security methods, if you haven't already.

Enabling the hidden network and MAC address filtering features is typically seen as optional, but encrypting your wireless network is very important and necessary to protect your files and privacy.

Book VI
Chapter 5

Network Magic:
Ways to Manage
Your Home Network

Figure 5-3:
Getting
more
information
on current
alerts.

Here's how to access Network Magic's wireless configuration settings:

a. **Click the Network Tasks button.**

b. **Click Change Wireless Protection.**

Look under the Protect category.

c. **Review each protection method.**

The Wireless Protection window should pop up. Click each tab to see status, more information, and how to enable each protection method.

Even if your router isn't supported with Network Magic's easy wireless configuration feature, you can access your router's Web-based configuration utility from Network Magic:

a. **Click the Network Map button.**

b. **Click the icon for your wireless router.**

This is probably located just to the right of the Internet icon.

c. **Click Set Up or Manage Device.**

Look under the Tasks, listed on the right of the screen, for your router.

6. **Start sharing your folders and printers.**

After you have set up Network Magic, you can go ahead and start sharing folders and printers among the network. Here's how:

a. **Click the Shared Folders button.**

b. **Click Share a Folder.**

Look under the Tasks tab, located on the right side of the page.

c. **Select a folder to share.**

In the Share a Folder dialog box, navigate to the folder you want to share and select it.

d. **Decide whether you want to share the folder on the Web.**

If you want the folder to be accessible to anyone with an Internet connection, click Share It on the Web with Net2Go. Net2Go is a feature in Network Magic Pro that lets you create a personal Web site where you can share files with anyone who has access to the Internet.

If you do want to set up a Net2Go Web site and want to make the shared files available on that site, specify whether a password is required for viewing your shared files. This password is required only when using Net2Go to access the files. For complete details about the Net2Go feature, open the Network Magic Help and open the Share on the Web with Net2Go topic.

e. **Click Share.**

The folder appears on the Shared Folders page as "shared." When other users on your network open the Network Magic Shared Folders page on their computer, they see this folder and everything in it. They can open and copy files in the shared folder.

When sharing files, security is even more important than usual. Be sure to enable the Network Magic security features to protect your shared information. To find out more about Network Magic security features, open the Network Magic Help and open the Protect Your Network topic.

When you install Network Magic, it automatically detects printers attached to any of the computers in your network. It then adds the printer(s) to the Network Map. If you add a printer later, Network Magic detects that as well and updates the Network Map.

Network Magic automatically shares printers connected to computers in your network. For example, if you have a computer in your office with a printer connected to it, a computer in the family room, and a wireless laptop, the computers without a printer can print to the printer in the office. For complete details about printer sharing, open the Network Magic Help and open the Share Printers topic.

Using and Unleashing the Magic

It's time! Time to check out the Network Magic software and its magical features, that is. Don't worry; you don't have to be a magician. If you already have Network Magic installed on your computer, you can follow along on your screen while reading through the following sections.

Tour of the software

Network Magic is laid out very simply. Big buttons to access all the screens are always on the top. To the right of the buttons, you see a status area that lets you know if you're connected to your network and displays any network health or security alerts. Without further ado, in the next sections, I go through each screen or page of the software.

Network Tasks

Network Tasks is the main screen of Network Magic, shown in Figure 5-4.

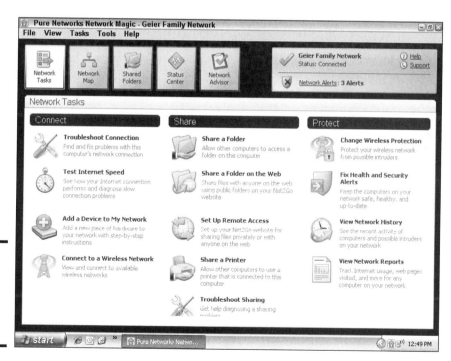

Figure 5-4:
Network
Tasks
screen in
Network
Magic.

This screen contains shortcuts to the tasks you use most often. This includes connecting to your wireless network, fixing connectivity, performance, or network problems, sharing folders or printers, and accessing network history and reports.

You have access to these tasks under the Connect section:

✦ **Troubleshoot Connection:** When you're having a problem with your network or Internet connection, click this button. It tries to automatically detect and fix the problem. If it's not successful, it may ask you to check various things to troubleshoot the problem.

✦ **Test Internet Speed:** If your Web browsing, downloading, or network transfers seem slower than usual — or if you're just curious — you can check your Internet and local network download and upload speeds.

✦ **Add a Device to My Network:** If you need help setting up a new device on your network, this helps you through the process.

✦ **Connect to a Wireless Network:** This brings up the list of nearby wireless networks (Figure 5-5 shows an example), from which you can select the one you want to connect to. If you've been using the Windows XP or Vista wireless utility, this interface will seem familiar.

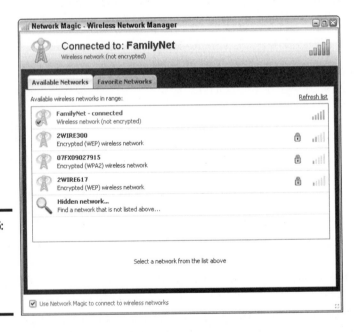

Figure 5-5: Network Magic's Wireless Network Manager.

The Share section offers the following tasks:

✦ **Share a Folder:** Here you can select folders on your computer that you want to share with all the other computers on your network.

✦ **Share a Folder on the Web:** You can set up folders to share on the Web with the free service provided by Net2Go. A Web site is automatically created (for example, `yourname.net2go.com`) to enable you or others to access your shared folders from your home or around the world. Folders you mark as public are accessible on your Web site to anyone, but folders you mark as private are only accessible by entering a password.

✦ **Set Up Remote Access:** From here, you can set up your Net2Go account and Web site so that you can share folders on the Web. After remote access is set up, this link changes to View Remote Access Web Site. This link brings up your Net2Go account settings, including your Web site's title, welcome message, and upload settings. Plus, you can access your Net2Go Web site from here.

✦ **Share a Printer:** You can easily select printers on your computer to share or to stop sharing. Sharing a printer lets anyone on your network print to your printer.

✦ **Troubleshoot Sharing:** If you are having problems accessing shared folders or printers, this feature helps you troubleshoot the problem.

The Protect section contains the following tasks:

✦ **Change Wireless Protection:** This brings up the Wireless Protection window, where you can change three main security features of your wireless network:

  • *Network Lock:* When enabled, your wireless network utilizes a feature of your router usually known as MAC address filtering. This prevents any other computers besides yours from connecting to your wireless network.

  • *Network Name Visibility:* Enabling this feature hides your SSID (network name), so that the average computer user doesn't even know your wireless network exists.

  • *Encryption:* Although Network Magic doesn't automatically configure encryption, it does give you step-by-step instructions on how to do so.

✦ **Fix Health and Security Alerts:** This link brings up a window with more details on any active alerts with links to find out more.

✦ **View Network History:** This brings up a window that shows the activity that has taken place on your network. Figure 5-6 shows an example.

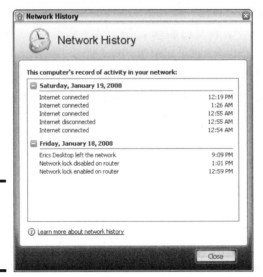

Figure 5-6:
Network
Magic's
Network
History.

✦ **View Network Reports:** Here you can choose which computers you would like network reports created for each day. These reports can be automatically e-mailed to you. Figure 5-7 shows an example of a network report.

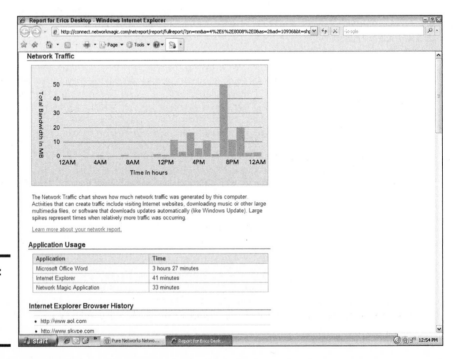

Figure 5-7:
Network
Magic's
Network
Report.

Network Map

When you click the Network Map button, you see a page similar to Figure 5-8.

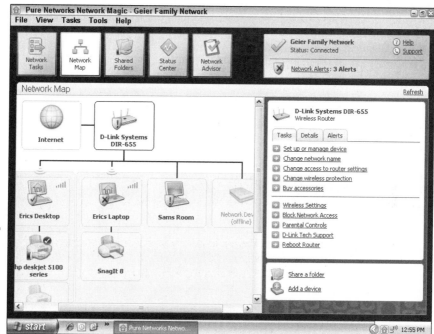

Figure 5-8:
The
Network
Map screen
in Network
Magic.

Here you can see a map of your network, including your Internet connection and router, and your computers and the devices attached to them. You can select any device from the Network Map and see its available tasks, details, and alerts.

Shared Folders

The Shared Folders screen (see Figure 5-9) shows you all the shared folders on your network.

From here, you can open shared items and view and edit their sharing settings.

Status Center

The Status Center (see Figure 5-10) displays the status, information, and alerts for all your Internet, network, and security settings.

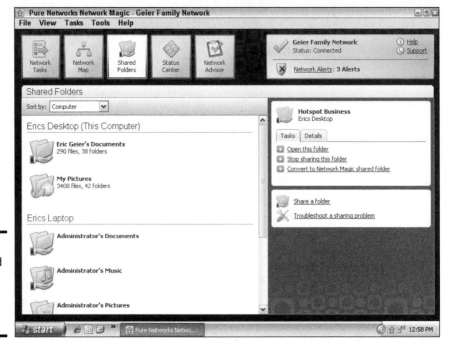

Figure 5-9:
The Shared
Folders
screen in
Network
Magic.

Figure 5-10:
The Status
Center
screen in
Network
Magic.

When you want to know where your network stands and whether there are any problems, you can go to this page.

Network Advisor

The Network Advisor provides useful information about home networking. Here you can find hardware accessories that are recommended for your network, and you may find popular news and help information.

Taking advantage of add-ons

You can get even more features in Network Magic with add-ons such as

✦ **Forwarded Ports:** Provides an easy way to manage port mappings on your router. Just like with the wireless protection settings, you don't have to mess with your router's Web-based configuration utility. Instead, Network Magic makes the changes for you.

✦ **PhotoCast:** This application lets you subscribe to photos from a friend's Net2Go Web site. The desired Net2Go addresses are inputted into PhotoCast so that the photos are automatically updated and shown in real-time. If your friends don't use Net2Go, you can tell them about PhotoCast so that they can see your photos.

✦ **Speed Meter Pro:** This shows you real-time graphs and history of your network and Internet download/upload activity. This lets you check whether your son is downloading a lot of stuff, for example, or what your max upload or download rate is over a period of time.

✦ **Folder Hit Counter:** This lets you see how popular your Net2Go folders are by keeping a running tally of how many times they are visited.

To browse through the other available add-ons, you can access the Network Magic Lab Web site from Network Magic's toolbar by choosing Tools⇨ Add-ons⇨Download Add-ons.

Book VI
Chapter 5

Network Magic: Ways to Manage Your Home Network

Book VII

Wi-Fi Hotspots

The 5th Wave   By Rich Tennant

"Ironically, he went out there looking for a 'hot spot.'"

Contents at a Glance

Chapter 1: Wi-Fi Hotspots, Hot Zones, and Cities

In This Chapter

✔ Untangling the public Wi-Fi types — Wi-Fi hotspots, hot zones, and muni wireless networks

✔ Equipping yourself to search for public wireless Internet

✔ Connecting to public Wi-Fi networks

✔ Securing your Wi-Fi communications

✔ Getting past the e-mail block on Wi-Fi hotspots

*Y*our home network is not the only place where you can access the Internet. These days, you have a dazzling array of places to choose from — hundreds of thousands of Wi-Fi hotspots, hot zones, and municipal networks — to connect to the Internet with your laptop and other mobile devices. These Wi-Fi locations throughout the world can serve as an extension of your home network, connecting you to the digital world when you're away from home.

In this chapter, you discover exactly what types of public networks are out there, how to find and connect to them, and how to stay secure.

Understanding Wi-Fi Hotspots and Hot Zones

Wi-Fi hotspots are locations or areas with wireless Internet access that is *intended for public use,* usually within a single building. In a hotspot or hot zone, Internet access may be provided either for free or for a fee. You can find Wi-Fi hotspots at just about any location where you might pop open your laptop or pull out your PDA, VoIP phone, or other mobile device that makes use of the Internet, including:

✦ Hotels, motels, timeshares, and vacation homes

✦ Airplanes and cruise ships

✦ Cafés, coffee shops, and restaurants

✦ Bookstores and libraries

✦ Airports and train and bus stations

✦ Shopping centers and shipping and mailing stores

When wireless Internet access covers larger areas, such as a few city blocks or a collection of buildings, it's referred to as a *Wi-Fi hot zone*. This type of network, such as what you find on a college or company campus, can support access for hundreds or thousands of users.

Even larger Wi-Fi networks exist that offer wireless Internet access to hundreds of thousands of users (or even more than a million). These networks are called municipal (*muni* for short) or Metro-scale networks, and in the past several years, cities and counties (and even some small countries!) have set up wireless networks to support the Internet needs of their residents, businesses, travelers, and government departments.

Though all the public Wi-Fi location types are discussed in this chapter, in many areas you'll see that the text refers only to hotspots, but in many cases this applies to all public network types, Wi-Fi hot zones, and municipal wireless networks as well. The way you go about finding the different types of Wi-Fi locations varies, but the way you connect with, use, and secure each type is pretty much the same across the board.

Finding Wi-Fi Hotspots

These days, most major brands or chains of hotels, restaurants, and stores offer some type of wireless Internet access. Even some mom-and-pop stores are getting techy and setting up hotspots. When it comes to figuring out whether a certain place offers wireless Internet or searching for locations, you have many available options and techniques.

Keep your eye out for signs

When you're out and about, the best thing to do when trying to find a Wi-Fi hotspot is just open your eyes. Most places that offer this access let you know with signage. You may find a decal, for example (see Figure 1-1) on the doors or windows of the location.

You may also see signs or tent cards displayed within the establishment. These signs may say something like "Wi-Fi Hotspot," "Wi-Fi Here," or "Wireless Internet."

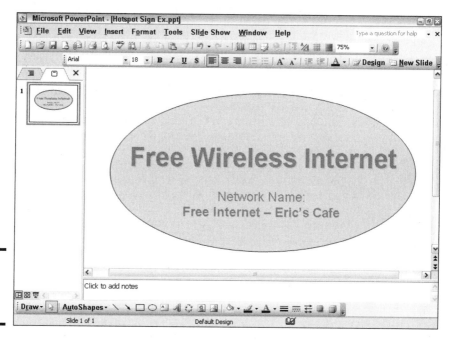

Figure 1-1:
Example of
a "Wi-Fi
here" sign.

Check online from your home computer or while on the go

If you need to plan where you can get Internet access before you leave home, or if you can't find a hotspot location on foot, you can always turn to the computer and search the following:

✦ **Online directories:** When you have access to the Internet, you can check online directories of hotspots on Web sites, such as

```
www.jiwire.com

www.wi-fihotspotlist.com

www.wifinder.com

www.hotspot-locations.com
```

✦ **Downloadable directories:** If you plan on using Wi-Fi hotspots often, you might want to download hotspot directories to your computer. That way, if you get nervous because you can't find a hotspot when you're out in the world, away from your usual Internet access, you can just pop open your laptop to find the nearest hotspot location. Check out the following Web sites (or hotspot directories) that offer downloadable software directories:

```
www.jiwire.com

www.boingo.com

http://hotspot.t-mobile.com
```

✦ **Mapping software and Web sites:** Another way to find Wi-Fi hotspots is through mapping software and Web sites, such as Yahoo Maps (`http://maps.yahoo.com`) and Google Maps (`http://maps.google.com`). Though this type of software shouldn't be your only source, you can usually use the search function of mapping applications (just search using the keyword "hotspot") to find hotspots near the location you're zoomed in on. This is a great (and timesaving) way to take a quick look for hotspots when getting maps or directions.

Check your network list

When trying to locate a hotspot, you can always just turn on your laptop or mobile device and see what nearby wireless networks show up on your list of available networks (which you find by accessing your network icon). Look for unsecured or unencrypted networks. Keep in mind, though, that you might see some private networks left unsecured, which you should leave alone because connecting to them is illegal. Sometimes it's difficult to differentiate these from networks intended as public hotspots; however, here are a few tips that can help you verify them:

✦ **Look:** Check for signs in the establishment.

✦ **Ask:** Ask the staff or property owners whether wireless Internet access is available there.

✦ **Assume:** If neither of the preceding suggestions works out, you're probably safe in assuming that a wireless network named after an establishment or company that is left unsecured is a public hotspot.

Use Wi-Fi finders

If you regularly use Wi-Fi hotspots, a Wi-Fi finder (Figure 1-2 shows an example) might be something you can really use. You can carry the gum-pack–sized device around in your pocket. When you want to check what wireless networks are around, you can pull out the device and see information about nearby networks on the small LCD screen. You see information on each network, such as signal strength, network name, and security status. This is usually enough information to differentiate a hotspot from a public network.

You can even get combination devices, such as USB wireless adapters with built-in Wi-Fi finders. See Book VI, Chapter 3 for more information.

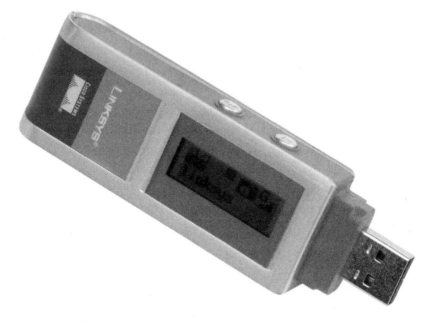

Figure 1-2:
Use a Wi-Fi
finder to
locate
nearby
wireless
networks.

Courtesy of Cisco Systems, Inc.

Sign up for reliable access

If you are a frequent traveler or hotspot user and are willing to pay for access, you should look into signing up with a Wi-Fi hotspot provider. Having this resource gives you better chances of finding reliable hotspots throughout the United States and abroad. As you may have found out already, finding free hotspots isn't always easy and can be frustrating.

Rather than pay per hotspot session or per day, you can get monthly subscriptions for as low as $20 per month that you can use with more than 100,000 locations. Plus, you won't have to search for free hotspots anymore. Before you leave home, you can see exactly where wireless networks exist in the areas you're traveling through and around your destination.

Two popular hotspot providers are Boingo (www.boingo.com) and T-Mobile (http://hotspot.t-mobile.com).

Finding Municipal Networks

You can use the same searching techniques for municipal Wi-Fi networks as those for traditional Wi-Fi hotspots (discussed in the previous section), plus the techniques described next.

Local media outlets

Check the Web sites of local newspapers and news stations and search the news or IT (Information Technology) section of the city or county Web site.

Online news sites

Browse through online Web sites that cover municipal Wi-Fi topics, such as the following:

✦ www.muniwireless.com: In particular, the list of U.S. cities and counties available in the resources section

✦ www.wifinetnews.com: In particular, the Metro-Scale Networks category

Connecting to Wi-Fi Hotspots

Using Wi-Fi hotspots is similar to using your wireless network at home; however, you should understand a few important differences, discussed throughout this section.

When you find a Wi-Fi hotspot, connecting is similar to what you do with your home network. Here are the basic steps:

1. **Connect to the Network.**

Choose the network name from your list of available wireless networks and click Connect or OK. For step-by-step directions, refer to Book IV, Chapter 1.

2. **Open your Web browser.**

If your regular home page shows up, you're probably done and can start using the Internet as you want. However, most hotspots have a splash or portal page, which automatically comes up instead of your home page; this feature is called *captive portal*. Figure 1-3 shows an example.

3. **Accept terms, make payment, or both.**

If a splash screen does appear, it usually displays the terms of service or rules of using the hotspot, or maybe shows just a portal page with advertisements. After reviewing the page, you should know whether you can access the Internet for free or have to pay for it first. Follow the directions given and, if necessary, accept the terms and make payment to proceed.

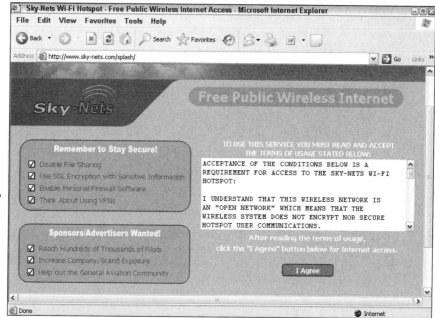

Figure 1-3:
A hotspot
splash page
opens
instead of
your home
page.

Securing Your Hotspot Connections

Using a Wi-Fi hotspot poses risks similar to using your wireless home network without encryption, as discussed in Book III, Chapter 2. Wi-Fi eavesdroppers can capture the Web sites you visit and the login information you
use for unsecured (non-SSL) Web sites and services (including POP3 e-mail
accounts). Furthermore, any files or folders you have shared may be accessible to the other hotspot users.

What's an "SSL" Web site, you're wondering? SSL stands for *Secure Socket
Layer* (also sometimes seen as *Secure Sockets Layer*), which is an encryption
standard for securing Web pages.

Securing your real-time traffic

Real-time traffic consists of the Web sites you visit, login information, and
any other content or data transferred to and from your computer and the
public network. To secure your real-time traffic, you should follow a few
safety measures:

Use a virtual private network (VPN) connection

A virtual private network, or VPN, is a technique to securely connect remote computers. A VPN network can consist of computers around the world, connected via the Internet, with all the traffic being encrypted and extremely secure from one computer to another. VPNs traditionally are used within businesses to allow employees to access their work files when away from the office.

You can also use VPN technology to secure your hotspot traffic. This method can provide even better encryption and security than what you get on your wireless home network using WPA or WEP. Here are a few ways to use VPNs to make your hotspot connections secure:

Use a company-provided VPN

If your work involves regular computer usage, you should inquire with your boss or the company IT or tech team about any available VPN access and the procedures and rules related to its use. Even though you may not always want to access your work files, you can connect to and use the VPN connection to secure your real-time traffic from people at the hotspot locations.

Use hosted hotspot access or software

You may want to consider using hosted hotspot security solutions that make use of VPN or SSL technology, such as the following:

+ **AnchorFree Hotspot Shield** (www.anchorfree.com/hotspot-shield/): Free

+ **JiWire Hotspot Helper** (www.jiwire.com/hotspot-helper.htm): Free trial, then around $25 per year

+ **WiTopia's personalVPN** (www.witopia.net): Around $40 per year

What to do if you don't use a VPN connection

If you don't use a VPN (or SSL) connection to encrypt all your real-time traffic while you're on a hotspot, you should at least follow a few minimal security measures, as follows:

+ **Secure any services used:** Make sure any Internet services you use, such as POP3 e-mail and FTP for file transfers, are secured. Some e-mail hosts provide SSL encryption for e-mail accounts, which you have to set up in your e-mail client. If not, most e-mail providers do offer secure access to accounts through a Web site.

✦ **Use SSL (or HTTPS) Web sites:** Don't log in to accounts or services that require you to use a username and password, unless they're secured with SSL (see earlier in this section for an explanation of SSL) and use an HTTPS address (note the *S* at the end of *HTTP*) — for example, `https://www.website.com`. Most Web browsers also display a padlock icon when a Web site is using SSL. Figure 1-4 shows an example of the padlock in Internet Explorer 7. Previous versions of Internet Explorer and other Web browsers, however, display their padlocks in the lower-right corner of the browser window.

This technology encrypts the communications between your computer and the particular Web site. You can still visit unsecured (or non-SSL) Web sites; however, when you do so, all the Web page's contents can be captured and viewed by others. This should be fine when you're visiting nonsensitive Web sites.

Padlock icon

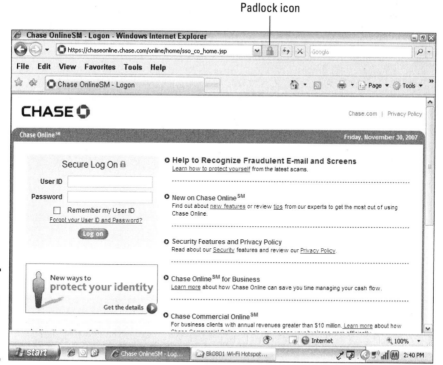

Figure 1-4: SSL padlock indicator in Internet Explorer 7.

Book VII Chapter 1

Wi-Fi Hotspots, Hot Zones, and Cities

Protecting your computer

Depending upon the equipment used at particular hotspot locations, connecting to a hotspot can open your computer to being accessible to other hotspot users. For example, if you have set up folders to be shared, some hotspot solutions out there may not block user-to-user communication, making your shared files accessible to other hotspot users, just as they are for your home network. Regardless of the hotspot solution you use, you can safeguard your computer and personal documents in the following ways:

✦ **Disable sharing:** Before connecting to a Wi-Fi hotspot, you should disable the sharing of any files, folders, and services that you may not want others to view, use, or edit. Refer to Book IV, Chapter 3 for step-by-step directions on checking for and disabling shared resources. Turning off sharing while you're away from home and then reactivating it for your home network is easy, after you get the hang of it, so I urge you to get in the habit of doing it. It's an important aspect of safeguarding your computer.

✦ **Use personal firewall software:** When connecting to hotspots — and even your home network — you should use personal firewall software. This software helps protect you from Internet intruders and hackers. Windows XP and Vista have built-in firewall utilities, accessible via the Control Panel. Or, if you prefer, you can use a third-party firewall application, such as ZoneAlarm (www.zonealarm.com) or whatever is included with your antivirus software. (You *do* keep a regularly updated antivirus application running, right?)

✦ **Keep your OS up-to-date:** Make sure that your operating system (Windows, Mac, or any other) is up-to-date at all times so that you're receiving patches for security holes and fixes for known issues. See Book II, Chapter 5 for information on how to update your operating system.

Watching out for fake hotspots

A technique used by some techy criminals is to set up a fake hotspot — sometimes referred to as an "evil-twin hotspot" — copying the look and feel of a real hotspot, and maybe even a specific hotspot provider's brand. The intention is for people to connect to the hotspot and make a payment so that the criminals can capture the users' credit card and personal information. This is known as a "man-in-the-middle" attack.

You may find spotting these fakes difficult, but you do have several ways to check the legitimacy of a hotspot, as follows:

✦ **Make sure that payment pages are secure:** If the hotspot requires payment, the pages where you make payment and log in should be protected with SSL encryption; otherwise, you may be on a fake hotspot. A properly secured Web page should use an HTTPS address (the *S* at the end signifies that it's a secure site), and a padlock icon should be displayed in your Web browser. For examples, see Figure 1-4, shown previously.

✦ **Check the SSL certificate:** If the hotspot does require payment and its payment and login pages are secured with SSL, look at the SSL certificate details. You may find some clues as to the legitimacy of the hotspot. If the certificate contains any errors or problems, you shouldn't use the hotspot. In Internet Explorer, you can check the SSL certificate details by double-clicking the padlock icon that appears on the right of the Address bar or in the lower-right corner of the browser.

✦ **Check for signage:** If you are suspicious of a hotspot, you can check for signs or with the staff at the location to see whether the establishment even has a hotspot.

Sending E-Mail on Hotspots

If you use POP3 e-mail accounts, you may find that some Wi-Fi hotspots — and even some ISPs, such as your home Internet connection — block the outgoing port(s) so that you can't send any e-mail through your POP3 e-mail server. This is a security measure put in place by the hotspot owner so that the owner's Internet connections aren't used to send spam messages. You have a few ways to get around this security feature:

✦ **Use Web-based e-mail:** Use a different account that's Web-based, or find out whether your POP3 account provider offers Web-based access (that's secured by SSL, of course).

✦ **Use a redirector:** You can use an SMTP port relay or redirector, such as the one offered by the JiWire Hotspot Helper (`www.jiwire.com/hotspot-helper.htm`).

✦ **Try another port:** You may have success with other outgoing e-mail ports, such as 2525 or 587, in place of the usual port 25. For help on making these changes, you can refer to the documentation and Help files of your e-mail client application or your POP3 account provider.

Chapter 2: Making Your Location a Wi-Fi Hotspot

In This Chapter

✔ Discovering what it takes to be a Wi-Fi hotspot owner

✔ Deciding whether to provide free or fee-based wireless Internet access

✔ Choosing a Wi-Fi hotspot solution

✔ Setting up and configuring your hotspot: Things to remember

✔ Promoting your Wi-Fi hotspot to attract more visitors and customers

*I*n addition to having a home network, you might benefit from setting up a Wi-Fi hotspot of your own — especially if you own a store or small business. Even if you don't, think about any friends or family members who do — you might discover you have the passion to help them bring wireless Internet to their location.

The following businesses and locations can serve as great Wi-Fi hotspot locations:

✦ Hotels, motels, bed-and-breakfast establishments, and vacation homes

✦ Cafés, coffee shops, and restaurants

✦ Bookstores and libraries

✦ Shopping centers and shipment stores

✦ Any establishment in a high tourist, travel, student, or business area

In this chapter, you find out what's involved in offering wireless Internet to the public. You also discover various types of hotspot solutions and how to set up a hotspot.

Weighing the Benefits and Costs of Having a Wi-Fi Hotspot

Before diving deeply into the hotspot world, you need to understand the benefits and costs of setting up and hosting a Wi-Fi hotspot. Though the benefits usually outweigh the costs, you should know what you're getting into. The next sections tell you a bit about what's good and what's not so good about hosting a hotspot.

The benefits

Following are some of the main points in favor of hosting a hotspot:

✦ **Attracts more visitors:** Being on the hotspot map — that is, being listed in online hotspot directories and having signs posted — can attract new visitors to your location.

✦ **Pleases your current visitors:** Perhaps you've had visitors inquiring about wireless Internet. Well, make them happy! You'll also be pleasing all the other visitors who haven't asked but wished your location offered this.

✦ **Creates a possible new revenue stream:** If your business is in a high-traffic area for hotspot users (such as a bookstore, hotel, or tourist or traveler location) and you choose a fee-based solution, this venture may be a profitable one that can bring in extra revenue.

✦ **Allows integration with your private network:** Some hotspot solutions even have support for integrating a private network with the hotspot (using the same Internet connection), so your communications are secure. Having a separate connection for your private communications is more practical than using the public wireless connection if you plan to use the wireless Internet regularly for the business. Without a separate, encrypted wireless connection, you can't share files between your business computers, and your communications can be intercepted.

For a general overview of Wi-Fi hotspots, take a look at Chapter 1 of this minibook.

What'll it cost you?

Of course, setting up and hosting a Wi-Fi hotspot has its disadvantages as well. Be sure to consider the following costs carefully:

✦ **Your time:** Remember that you'll have to invest a good deal of time in picking a solution, setting it up, and supporting it. You may find that the time you invest is more costly than the price of the equipment.

✦ **Money for hotspot equipment:** The cost of hotspot solutions varies greatly and can be anywhere from $40 to $800 or more. Normally, packages you purchase to offer free hotspot access are on the lower end of this range and for-fee services range at the higher end. Additionally, solutions that require more in-depth setup are cheaper compared to out-of-the-box hotspot equipment for hotspot gateways, which I discuss later in this chapter in the "Choosing Your Hotspot Hardware" section.

✦ **Money for business-class Internet connection:** You'll probably have to set up a business-class Internet connection (DSL or cable), which usually costs $60 or more per month. An Internet service provider (ISP) usually doesn't allow customers of the lower-cost connections (which are intended for residences) to share access or provide it to others. You should check with your ISP to make sure.

Understanding What Makes Your Location a Wi-Fi Hotspot

Wi-Fi hotspots generally are very similar to your home network. Many hotspots consist of a single hotspot gateway that is just like a wireless router used in homes, but with some extra features. Some of the extra features and functionalities that hotspots and gateways include are the following:

✦ **Open (unsecured) access:** Wi-Fi hotspots are meant to be open to the public, so hotspots are left unencrypted. You can find out more about the risks of using these unsecured public networks in the first chapter of this minibook.

✦ **Advertised access:** Hotspots are advertised by signs at the locations and in hotspot directories, whereas the existence of home networks should be kept private.

✦ **Captive portal:** On some hotspots, after you connect to the Internet and open your Web browser, your regular home page appears and can start using the Internet as desired. However, many hotspots use a captive portal feature, which causes a splash, or portal, page to appear when you open your Web browser. This splash page doesn't let you move on until you accept the terms of the service or make payment (or both). Figure 2-1 shows an example of a hotspot splash page.

✦ **Account control:** Some hotspots require user accounts, meaning that users must log in before they can get Internet access. These accounts can exist whether or not users are charged an access fee.

✦ **Content filtering:** Most hotspots filter or block certain traffic, such as access to adult Web sites and even outgoing e-mail through a POP3 e-mail account (to prevent spammers from sending messages). These content filtering features can make your hotspot much safer for the users, the other visitors in your location, and your business.

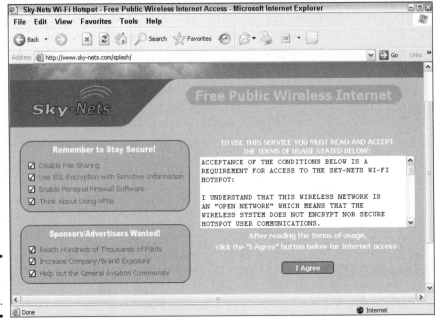

Figure 2-1:
A hotspot
splash page.

Deciding Whether to Charge a Fee

Here are several things for you to consider when making the decision on whether to give away free access or to charge people for using your hotspot:

✦ **Check out the competition.** Find out what your nearby competitors are doing. If the ones with hotspots provide free access, it's probably best to do the same. If they charge for access, you can try that with your hotspot to see how much money you make. On the other hand, providing access for free when your competitors are charging can draw more business to your location.

✦ **Fee-based solutions cost more.** For-fee hotspot solutions usually cost more and require more time to set up because of the complexity of the system and third-party services required in order to accept payments.

✦ **Free is usually the way to go.** Going with a free hotspot is usually the best way to go unless you're in a high-traffic location for hotspot users, such as a bookstore, hotel, or a location with a high number of tourists or travelers. (People using and carrying laptops are good signs.) If this description doesn't fit your location, providing free access is probably the best bet.

✦ **Beware of freeloaders.** When giving free access, you open your hotspot to Wi-Fi freeloaders. Your intent in setting up free Internet access is to give your visitors and customers a service. However, neighbors might regularly use the wireless Internet, slowing everyone's connection speeds in addition to getting a free service without being a "paid customer."

Choosing Your Hotspot Hardware

Browsing the Web — using google.com, for example @md can reveal countless hotspot hardware options and packages, either for self-installation and support or through a service provider. When sifting through your options, consider the following:

✦ **Whether to offer the service to your visitors for free or for a fee:** Discussed in the preceding section.

✦ **Price (including any monthly or yearly fees):** This can range from purchasing a hotspot gateway for $300 to $600 dollars with no strings attached to hotspot packages and services requiring a setup fee and an ongoing monthly fee.

✦ **Additional hardware or software requirements:** Make sure you understand whether you must use additional hardware (such as a computer that you must dedicate to the setup) or software with the hotspot setups you find.

✦ **Time involved for setup:** Whether you set up and install the hotspot yourself or go through a service provider, you need to understand how much time it will take to get the hotspot working and to support it.

✦ **Type and availability of support:** When sifting through your options, compare the type (telephone, e-mail, on-site) and availability (24 hours a day, seven days a week versus business days only) of support from the hotspot equipment or service provider.

You have many different ways to create a hotspot, each with its advantages and disadvantages. For example, simply installing a wireless router such as what you have at home is cheap, but doesn't offer the hotspot features discussed earlier. Alternatively, you can load special software on your home wireless router to offer the hotspot features; however, this approach requires much more time. Another way to go is to buy a piece of hardware (a hotspot gateway) specifically designed to offer public Internet; this approach, however, can cost several hundreds of dollars. Yet another way to go is through a service provider that supplies a package of preconfigured hardware and ongoing support, but that option also involves an ongoing fee.

**Book VII
Chapter 2**

**Making Your
Location a Wi-Fi
Hotspot**

Following are ways you can offer public wireless Internet:

✦ **Using a simple wireless router:** You can simply use a wireless router just like you would use at home (but without any security or encryption enabled) to give away free access. You don't get the traditional hotspot features, such as captive portal or user accounts, so you can't display any usage terms or collect payments. This solution, though, is cheap and requires minimal investment of your time.

✦ **Taking advantage of the AnchorFree Hotspot Network:** AnchorFree is the world's largest free hotspot network. It offers free hotspot equipment and marketing materials (decals and signs) to location owners throughout the United States. The cost of the equipment is offset by advertising revenue generated from the hotspots. This solution provides everything you need to offer free wireless Internet, is the cheapest, and doesn't require much time to set up. For more information, go to www.anchorfree.com.

✦ **Using hotspot gateways:** These devices are similar to wireless routers; however, they have been specifically designed for public hotspot solutions.

Some gateways can handle user account, captive portal, and payment features without additional hardware or services; however, some require external servers (or hosted services) at an additional cost. Most hotspot gateways have compatible ticket printers. This lets you easily hand out passwords for the hotspot. For example, say that you want to give Internet access only to paying customers. You can restrict hotspot access to people with a password. When you want to give out access to the hotspot, click a button on the ticket printer to print a password, and give it to the customer to input into the hotspot login page. Some hotspot gateways may also have private ports so that you can easily integrate a private network securely. Following are examples of hotspot gateways:

- *SMC's EliteConnect Wireless Hotspot Gateway (SMCWHSG44-G):* www.smc.com

- *ValuePoint's Wireless Controller 3000 (WC-3000):* www.valuepointnet.com

- *Versa's 802.11b/g Multifunction Hot Spot Subscriber/Gateway (VX-HG11G):* www.versatek.us

- *ZyXEL's 802.11g Wireless Hot Spot Gateway (G-4100):* www.zyxel.com

- *Nomadix's Wireless Gateway (AG 2100):* www.nomadix.com

✦ **Open source (free) solutions:** These solutions typically offer free software or firmware replacements for you to use with your own simple wireless router. Features such as captive portal and user account control, among others, are usually provided. This is a great way to set up a hotspot while keeping the cost down; be aware, however, that the setup and configuration require some patience and learning.

Here are a few open source, firmware-based hotspot options you can look into:

- *ZoneCD* (`www.publicip.net`): Available for free hotspots only.

- *Less Networks* (`www.lessnetworks.com`): Also available for free hotspots only.

- *DD-WRT* (`www.dd-wrt.com`): Includes hotspot solutions for both types of hotspots: those offered to visitors for free and those that charge a fee for access.

✦ **Hosted services:** These types of solutions usually offer a hotspot management system that let you log in to a Web site to manage the settings and user accounts of your hotspot(s). You configure your supported hotspot gateway (which includes using cheap wireless routers with firmware upgrades, mentioned in the preceding bullet) with the server information of the hosted service you choose. Then your hotspot gateway will be managed through the service and gain all the features offered by the service. This type of solution can also be cost effective, but usually requires a monthly or one-time fee. It offers very good features, including usage reports, ability to manage multiple locations, and payment collection. Here are a few companies you may want to check into that offer hosted hotspot services:

- Sputnik (`www.sputnik.com`)

- WirelessOrbit (`wirelessorbit.com`)

- WHOTSPOT (`www.whotspot.com`)

✦ **Turnkey solution providers:** These companies offer prepackaged hotspot kits and customized hotspot installations. These solutions are relatively high priced (costing at least a few hundred dollars) and are best for high-traffic, fee-based hotspot locations that will definitely draw users. One advantage of going with one of these companies is that some operate under larger hotspot providers (such as Boingo Wireless). Being listed in their database can help draw even more people to your hotspot location. Here are a few turnkey solution providers:

- SurfAndSip (`www.surfandsip.com`)

- NetNearU (`www.nnu.com`)

- Cafe.com (`www.cafe.com`)

- FatPort (`www.fatport.com`)

Configuring Your Hotspot

If you have chosen a solution specifically designed for hotspots, you likely have instructions to follow that will help you install and configure your hotspot. Otherwise, if you are "winging it"— by, for example, using a simple wireless router, as discussed in the previous section — you won't have any direction on what to do. But help is here! Just plug in your wireless router and make sure you follow the configuration tips given in this section, and you should be fine. Additionally, these tips can also help you if you're implementing real hotspot solutions.

Going through the important settings

First, you should ensure that the important settings on your router or hotspot gateway are good to go. The following subsections take you through these steps. But first, you must connect and log in to your router:

1. **Bring up your Web browser (Internet Explorer, Netscape, Firefox, or other).**

2. **Type the IP address of your router or gateway and press Enter.**

   Keep in mind that some manufacturers may use a domain name (such as `http://www.routerlogin.net`) that looks like a Web site address instead of an IP address (192.168.1.1).

   If you don't know the IP address or the username or password, refer to Book V, Chapter 3 for help.

3. **When prompted, enter the username and password.**

   If you don't know the default username and password, refer to Book V, Chapter 3.

Change your network name (SSID)

In order for your visitors and customers to identify your hotspot network, you need to change your router's network name (SSID). To do so, follow these steps:

1. **Click the Wireless tab (or other, similarly named tab containing the basic wireless settings).**

   Some newer wireless products may offer wizards to help with wireless configuration; however, you should still be able to manually configure the wireless settings, which is needed to perform these steps.

2. **Enter your own name in the Network Name (or SSID) field, as shown in Figure 2-2.**

Figure 2-2:
Entering the network name of a hotspot.

SSID stands for *service set identifier,* and you can change this identifier to anything you want. You should use your business or organization name so that hotspot users can readily associate that network with your business. If your hotspot is free, you might want to mention that in the network name as well. Also keep the following in mind:

- You can use any of the characters on your keyboard, but be aware that the network name will be case sensitive (so be sure to use capital and lowercase letters exactly as you want them to appear) and must not exceed 32 characters.

- Include information so that users can easily identify the location (such as your business name) and that the network is intended for the public — meaning that you might want to include the word "hotspot" or "public" in your network name.

- If you aren't charging for access, you may want to include the word "free."

3. **Click the Save or Apply button, on the top or bottom of the page, to save your new network name.**

   The device may reboot, and you may be disconnected for a minute. If you were connected wirelessly (rather than by an Ethernet cable), you'll have to reconnect with the new network name. You can probably just choose the new network name from your available wireless network list, which is accessible from your network icon on the main task or menu bar.

When you're connected to the network again, the Web-based utility may return to the page that you left off on. Sometimes, though, a Not Found page appears instead. If this happens, you need to access the router's admin utility again, flip back to the "Going through the important settings" section, and then continue with the next subsection.

Verify that security and encryption are turned off

You need to make sure that you *do not* use any encryption methods on your router or hotspot gateway. Using encryption, such as WPA or WEP, prevents your visitors from connecting to the hotspot because they have to have the encryption key in order to connect.

Though you might think using encryption and giving the key to your visitors can help secure the hotspot connections, keep in mind that it doesn't do much when the key is public, and eavesdroppers can get it to "unlock" the network traffic.

Here's how to check your security settings:

1. **Click the Wireless tab (or tab relating to the basic wireless settings).**

2. **Click the Wireless Security tab if the encryption settings aren't included with the basic wireless settings.**

Figure 2-3 shows an example.

Some newer wireless products may offer wizards to help with security and wireless configuration; however, you should be able to manually configure wireless security settings, which is needed to perform these steps.

3. **Choose None or Disabled for the Security (Encryption) Mode option.**

You turn off encryption because you're setting up a public network.

4. **Click all the other tabs that deal with security, filtering, or blocking, and choose Disable or Off, or remove any entries.**

To hunt all these settings down, you'll have to look through each main section, including the Advanced section. Some of these security features may offer a Disabled or Off option; however, some may not, in which case just make sure that no entries or items are listed or applied to the feature.

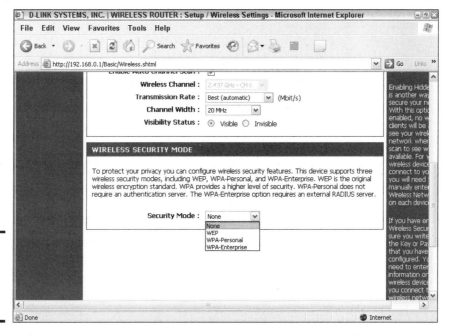

Figure 2-3:
Encryption
settings on
a wireless
router.

5. **Click the Save or Apply button, on the top or bottom of the page, if
you made any changes to settings...**

The device may reboot, and you may be disconnected for a minute.
When you're connected to the network again, the Web-based utility may
return to the page that you left off on. Sometimes, though, it errors out
and goes to a Not Found page. If this is the case, when you know you're
reconnected, follow the directions in Step 1 again to log back in and then
come back here.

Change the default login password

If you haven't already done so, you need to change the password of your
router or gateway to something other than the default. It's easy to find these
default passwords. If not changed, someone can log in to your router or
gateway and cause problems.

Here's how to change your password:

1. **Click the System Settings, Maintenance, Administration, or Tools tab
that contains the advanced router settings...**

2. **Click the Management or Administration subtab if the password settings aren't included with the advanced router settings.**

3. Enter a new password in the appropriate fields (and if available, a new username as well).

Some wireless products may allow you to specify a user account (that can't make any changes) in addition to the necessary administration account (that has full privileges). This is useful if you have employees who need to be able to check the status of the router.

4. Click the Save or Apply button, on the top or bottom of the page, to save your new password.

The device may reboot, and you may be disconnected for a minute. When you're connected to the network again, the Web-based utility may return to the page that you left off on. Sometimes, though, it errors out and goes to a Not Found page. If this is the case, when you know you're reconnected, follow the directions in Step 1 again to log back in and then come back here.

Block or filter services/ports

You can use filtering methods to control the type of traffic that passes through your wireless router or gateway. If possible, just to be on the safe side, you can block all ports and services except a few that enable very basic Internet use:

1. Click the Advanced, Content Filtering, or Access Restrictions tab that contains the router's advanced or port/services filtering settings.

2. Click each of the subtabs and configure the settings as desired.

The exact filtering features and functionality vary between manufacturers and models; however, try to see whether you can edit a list of *approved ports* (Figure 2-4 shows an example) rather than make a long list of ports to block.

If you can, allow only the following ports:

- 80 for web browsing (HTTP)
- 443 for secure web browsing (HTTPS)
- 110 for e-mail retrieval (POP3)

If that isn't possible, however, you should make sure you at least block port 25. This prevents the sending of POP3 e-mail to help prevent spam from originating at your hotspot.

3. Click the Save or Apply button on the top or bottom of the page.

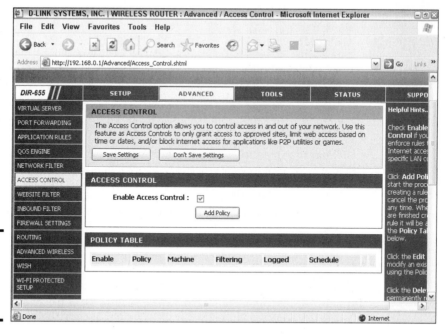

Figure 2-4:
Filtering
settings on
a wireless
router.

Book VII
Chapter 2

Making Your
Location a Wi-Fi
Hotspot

The device may reboot, and you may be disconnected for a minute. When you're connected to the network again, the Web-based utility may return to the page that you left off on. Sometimes, though, it errors out and goes to a Not Found page. If this is the case, when you know you're reconnected, follow the directions in Step 1 again to log back in and then come back here.

Verifying that your advanced settings are set for hotspot use

Although most the advanced settings of Wi-Fi routers and hotspot gateways are usually configured appropriately by default, you should verify to make sure. To do so, follow the steps given in the following subsections.

However, first you need to connect to your router or hotspot gateway and log in:

1. **Bring up your Web browser (Internet Explorer, Netscape, Firefox, or other).**

2. **Type the IP address of your router or gateway and press Enter.**

Keep in mind that some manufacturers may use a domain name (such as `http://www.routerlogin.net`) that looks like a Web site address instead of an IP address (192.168.1.1).

If you don't know the IP address or the username or password, refer to Book V, Chapter 3 for help.

3. When prompted, enter the username and password.

If you don't know the default username and password, refer to Book V, Chapter 3.

Verify that wireless mode is mixed

You should use mixed mode (for example, b/g or b/g/n), so that you're supporting all the hotspot users you can. Here's how to check this:

1. **Click the Wireless or Advanced Wireless tab, whichever contains the wireless mode settings (which may alternatively be labeled as 802.11g only or 802.11 mode).**

Figure 2-5 shows an example.

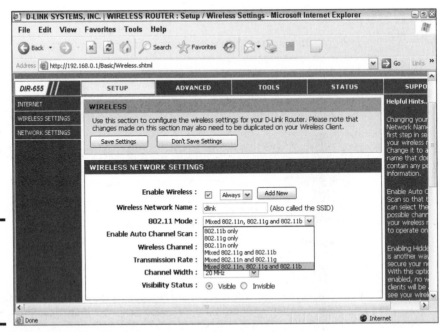

Figure 2-5: Wireless mode setting of a wireless router.

2. **Choose the option from the Wireless Mode field that supports as many standards or modes as possible.**

The device may reboot, and you may be disconnected for a minute. When you're connected to the network again, the Web-based utility may return to the page that you left off on. Sometimes, though, it errors out and goes to a Not Found page. If this is the case, when you know you're reconnected, follow the directions in Step 1 again to log back in and then come back here.

Turn AP isolation on

This should be enabled so that hotspot users can't communicate with each other on the network and access others' shared files. This feature is beneficial to users who forget to disable file sharing on their computers while using the hotspot.

You can enable this feature by following these steps:

1. **Click the Advanced Wireless tab (or similarly named tab that contains the AP or Client isolation or WLAN Partition settings).**

Figure 2-6 shows an example.

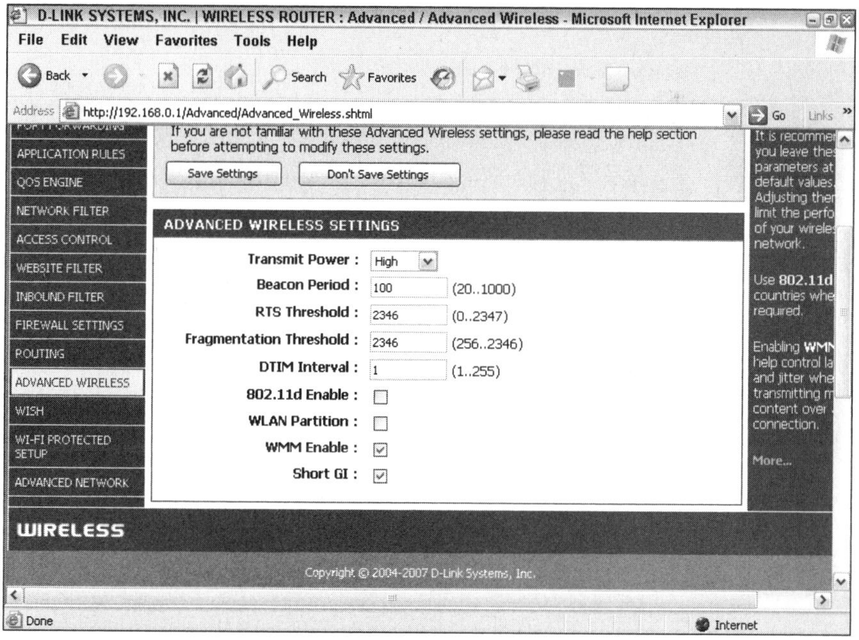

Figure 2-6:
AP isolation
setting of a
wireless
router.

2. **Select Enabled for the AP or Client isolation or WLAN Partition feature.**

3. **Click the Save or Apply button on the top or bottom of the page, if you made any setting changes.**

   The device may reboot, and you may be disconnected for a minute. When you're connected to the network again, the Web-based utility may return to the page that you left off on. Sometimes, though, it errors out and goes to a Not Found page. If this is the case, when you know you're reconnected, follow the directions in Step 1 again to log back in and then come back here.

Verify that VPN pass-through is enabled

Some wireless routers and hotspot gateways have a VPN pass-through setting. When enabled, hotspot users can use their VPN client applications to connect to VPN connections. Users might do this so that their hotspot traffic is encrypted and/or so that they can access files from home or work. Additionally, some Wi-Fi hotspot security techniques use VPN technology.

Some devices have the VPN ports opened by default, and the pass-through settings are not visible; however, you should check whether your router has the setting by following these steps:

1. **Click the Security or Firewall tab, whichever contains the VPN settings.**

   Figure 2-7 shows an example.

   If you can't find the settings, you can assume that the router has the VPN ports automatically opened.

2. **Select Enable for all the VPN Pass-through options (IPSec, PPTP, and L2TP).**

3. **Click the Save or Apply button on the top or bottom of the page, if you made any setting changes.**

   The device may reboot, and you may be disconnected for a minute. When you're connected to the network again, the Web-based utility may return to the page that you left off on. Sometimes, though, it errors out and goes to a Not Found page. If this is the case, when you know you're reconnected, follow the directions in Step 1 again to log back in and then come back here.

Verify that network name (SSID) broadcasting is on

To make sure that your hotspot comes up on users' available wireless network list, make sure the SSID of your router or gateway is being broadcasted:

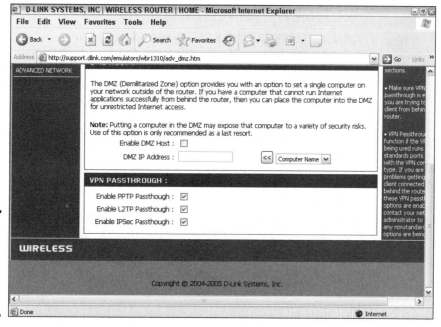

Figure 2-7:
VPN pass-
through
settings of a
wireless
router.

1. **Click the Advanced Wireless (or just Wireless) tab that contains the wireless broadcast settings (which may alternatively be labeled as Hidden Wireless or Visibility Status).**

Some newer wireless products may offer wizards to help with wireless configuration; however, you still may be able to manually configure the wireless settings, which is needed to perform these steps.

2. **Using radio buttons or a drop-down menu, choose the option from the Broadcast (or Hidden Wireless or Visibility Status) field to make your network name visible or broadcasted.**

3. **Click the Save or Apply button on the top or bottom of the page, if you made any setting changes.**

The device may reboot, and you may be disconnected for a minute. When you're connected to the network again, the Web-based utility may return to the page that you left off on. Sometimes, though, it errors out and goes to a Not Found page. If this is the case, when you know you're reconnected, follow the directions in Step 1 again to log back in and then come back here.

Setting up time restrictions and remote access (optional)

Although doing so is not required, you may want to configure two more settings as follows:

✦ **Access (time) restrictions:** You can disable Internet access during desired times. For example, you can prevent people from using the hotspot during the time (hours or days) your business or public location is closed.

✦ **Remote Web access:** This setting lets you access the Web-based configuration utility of your router or gateway from computers not directly connected to the router or gateway. Enabling this feature means that you can check the status and change settings when you are away from the hotspot over the Internet. This can come in handy when problems arise with the hotspot and others at the location don't know what to do; you can simply log into the hotspot from home (or any computer connected to the Internet).

First, you must connect and login to your router, as follows:

1. **Bring up your Web browser (Internet Explorer, Netscape, Firefox, or other).**

2. **Type the IP address of your router or gateway and press Enter.**

   Keep in mind that some manufacturers may use a domain name (`http://www.routerlogin.net`) that looks like a Web site address instead of an IP address (192.168.1.1).

   If you don't know the IP address or the username or password, refer to Book V, Chapter 3 for help.

3. **When prompted, enter the username and password.**

   If you don't know the default username and password, refer to Book V, Chapter 3.

Define your Internet access schedule

Here's how you can configure access or time restrictions for your hotspot:

1. **Click the tab that contains the Internet schedule settings (Content filtering, Access Control, or Access Restrictions).**

   Figure 2-8 shows an example.

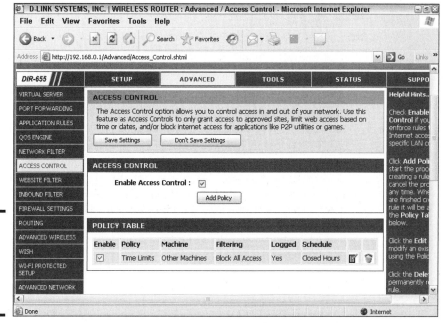

Figure 2-8:
Time
restriction
settings of
a wireless
router.

2. **Using the particular method (usually either by creating a policy with a wizard or selecting checkboxes), specify the times and days you don't want to offer Internet access for your hotspot.**

   If needed, use the Help functions of your Web-based utility to learn more.

3. **Click the Save or Apply button on the top or bottom of the page, to save your changes.**

   The device may reboot, and you may be disconnected for a minute. When you're connected to the network again, the Web-based utility may return to the page that you left off on. Sometimes, though, it errors out and goes to a Not Found page. If this is the case, when you know you're reconnected, follow the directions in Step 1 again to log back in and then come back here.

Set up remote Web access

Here's how you can set up remote Web access to your router or gateway:

1. **Click the tab that contains the remote management settings (usually in a Tools or Admin tab).**

2. **Select the checkbox or select Enabled from a drop-down menu for the Remote Management feature.**

3. **(Optional) Enter the IP address of the Internet connection from which you plan to remotely access the hotspot configuration utility (such as your home's Internet connection) into the appropriate IP address field.**

   If you need help figuring out the address of an Internet connection, refer to Book V, Chapter 3. Some devices allow you to specify multiple addresses or open up access to any IP address (sometimes by using an asterisk), which is useful if you plan to log in from a variety of places.

   If the Internet connection for your hotspot or the remote connection uses a dynamic IP address (which changes frequently), you can use a service such as Dynamic DNS to obtain a domain name (such as yourname. getmyip.net) to use instead of your Internet IP address. This domain name will automatically point to the current IP address of your Internet connection.

   You can sign up for the service at www.dyndns.com. After you get your Dynamic DNS account information, you have to set up the service with your router or gateway.

4. **(Optional) Mark the checkboxes or select from a drop-down menu the type of access (regular HTTP or the encrypted HTTPS) you want enabled.**

   This will be available only on select devices that are capable of using SSL (HTTPS) for remote access, in which case the remote connection, along with the login credentials, are encrypted when traveling over any networks and the Internet. If you have this option, use it.

5. **(Optional) Enter the port number that you want to use for the remote connection into the appropriate port field.**

   Most devices have this setting, usually 8080 by default.

6. **Click the Save or Apply button on the top or bottom of the page, to save your changes.**

   The device may reboot, and you may be disconnected for a minute. When you're connected to the network again, the Web-based utility may return to the page that you left off on. Sometimes, though, it goes to a Not Found page. If this is the case, when you know you're reconnected, follow the directions in Step 1 to log back in and then come back here.

Now you can log in to the device's configuration screen by typing the WAN/Internet IP address (domain name, if using Dynamic DNS) of the hotspot's Internet connection, and the port number you specified during the setup (preceded by a colon), into a Web browser; for example: 000.000.000.000:8080.

Getting Signage: Pull In the Public

After you have set up your hotspot, let your visitors and passing pedestrians know by sticking some decals and signs around your establishment.

How do you go about getting this signage? Here are a few ways:

✦ **Register as a Wi-Fi Zone:** When you register your hotspot location(s) under the Wi-Fi ZONE program (developed by the Wi-Fi Alliance), you're given the rights to use its Wi-Fi ZONE logo (shown in Figure 2-9). This logo can help catch the eye of regular Wi-Fi hotspot-ers. You can print this logo by itself and use it for your signage, or include it with a larger sign that you create on your own, as discussed in the next bullet.

You must meet only one main requirement in order to register in the program: You have to use WI-FI CERTIFIED equipment for the hotspot. This shouldn't be a problem because all Wi-Fi equipment available for purchase almost always has this certification.

After you've registered and received approval, you can start using the logo on signs or decals you create and print.

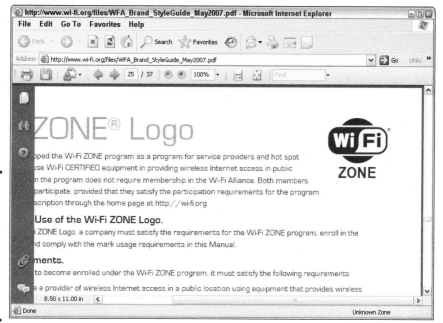

Figure 2-9:
You can print the Wi-Fi ZONE logo on signs and decals to put around your store.

✦ **Make your own:** You can make your own signage using your simple home computer and printer. Though it may take some time and effort to create professional-looking signs, this is still a great way to save some money. You can use Microsoft PowerPoint or Word (or some other program) to make them appealing and then print them on regular or colored paper. You can also browse your local office supply store for different printable media types that you can use at home, such as window decals, stickers, and magnets.

Here are a few phrases you can use for the text of your signage:

- FREE Wireless Internet

- Wireless Internet Available

- Free Wi-Fi

- Wi-Fi Here

- Wi-Fi Hotspot Here

If you signed up on the Wi-Fi ZONE program (discussed in the preceding bullet), you can even include the popular Wi-Fi ZONE logo on your sign.

You might also think about including the network name (or SSID, explained previously in this chapter) of your hotspot so that users will know exactly what network you're talking about when they view their list and see all available neighboring networks.

If you want to make your sign fancy, check out the font and other effects and clip art of the creative software you're using.

Figure 2-10 shows an example of a sign created fwith Microsoft PowerPoint.

✦ **Buy some:** If you feel that your signage doesn't look professional enough, or you want to quickly get professional decals and stickers (which is hard to do yourself), think about purchasing signage.

Listing Your Hotspot in Directories to Attract Hotspot Searchers

After setting up your Wi-Fi hotspot, you should submit your location to online hotspot directories. This way, when people search for hotspot locations (see Figure 2-11) around your area, your location will pop up and you may get a new visitor or customer! In case you're wondering, listings on these directories are always free.

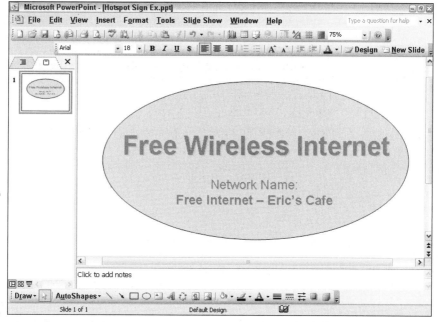

**Book VII
Chapter 2**

Making Your
Location a Wi-Fi
Hotspot

Figure 2-10:
A home-made hotspot sign can easily suit the purpose.

Hotspot directories usually require you to submit the following information:

✦ Location address

✦ Business/location name

✦ Network name (SSID)

✦ Hotspot type (free or for a fee)

✦ Wireless type (A, B, G, or N, as of this writing)

✦ Location owner contact information (to verify the listing)

When you have a half an hour or so of free time, you can start submitting away. Following is a list of directories to get you started:

✦ Wi-Fi ZONE (`wi-fi.jiwire.com`)

✦ JiWire (`www.jiwire.com`)

✦ AnchorFree (`www.anchorfree.com`)

✦ Wi-FiHotSpotList.com (`www.wi-fihotspotlist.com`)

✦ Wi-Fi-FreeSpot Directory (`www.wififreespot.com`)

✦ Wi-Fi 411 (www.wifi411.com)

✦ The Hotspot Haven (www.hotspothaven.com)

✦ WiFinder (www.wifinder.com)

✦ Hotspot Locations (www.hotspot-locations.com)

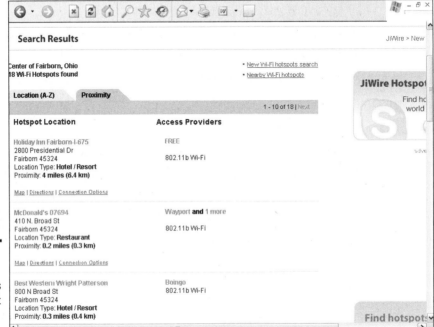

Figure 2-11: Searching for locations on a hotspot directory.

Chapter 3: Using FON to Share or Get Wireless Internet Access

In This Chapter

✔ Discovering FON and the power of sharing

✔ Sorting out the differences between the two profile or account types

✔ Deciding on your hardware options

✔ Setting up and configuring a FON Spot

The big idea behind FON — a Wi-Fi sharing community based upon a concept known as social Wi-Fi networking — is to make free Internet access more available in public around the world. The FON community's method to spread the Internet is to get people like you in homes and small businesses to share your Internet, creating a global hotspot network. In return, you receive free wireless Internet access at other FON Spots throughout the world. But even if you choose not to share, you can still get limited free access to all the FON Spots.

As it has grown, FON has developed many tradition-breaking relationships, including ones with Internet service providers (ISPs) that would normally oppose organizations that promote sharing Internet connections. This is because the ISPs don't want to lose you as a customer and start using a shared connection, which would cut into their revenue. This is just one example of how FON is trying to make Internet access free and universal. Skype and Google are also on the same page, investing millions into the company. In this chapter, you discover how FON works, get to know the FON community's unique terminology, and find out how to set up your own FON Spot.

Discovering FON

Joining the FON community allows you, more or less, to make your location (home or business) a Wi-Fi hotspot (see the caveat in the next paragraph). Your wireless network is advertised for public use, both to users nearby who are searching for wireless connections and to anyone who searches on the FON Web site for FON Spots in your area.

However, FON Spots differ from traditional Wi-Fi hotspots in that FON Spots are usually located within homes. Therefore, the majority of FON locations may be off the beaten path and hard to pinpoint, thereby making them somewhat impractical as Wi-Fi hotspots. Keep this in mind before joining and setting up a FON Spot.

After you set up a FON Spot, and if you are actively sharing your wireless Internet (FON calls you a *Foneros*), you have unlimited free access to any other FON Spots throughout the world. However, if you've signed up on FON's Web site but aren't sharing your Wi-Fi Internet (FON calls you an *Alien*), you are allowed free limited access for only 15 minutes and are forced to view an advertisement per FON Spot, or you can pay for 24 hours of access by purchasing FON Passes.

Overall, the only way to get the free unlimited access to FON Spots is to share your Internet at home or other location with other FON users. Remember, this is the same for everyone else, including those who connect to your FON Spot.

Understanding FON Profile Types

After you've set up the sharing of your wireless Internet, you can pick between the two different FON profiles:

+ **Bills:** Having a Bills profile enables you to make money. You receive 50 percent of the revenue from FON Passes purchased and advertisements viewed by Aliens (people who don't share their wireless Internet) at your FON Spot. Any earnings can be sent to your PayPal account.

+ **Linus:** Selecting this profile simply means that you opt out of the revenue-sharing program. Meanwhile, the user experiences of the people connecting to your FON Spot is the same as if you were a *Bill*.

Again, take a step back. Before you get all hyped up about making money from your FON Spot, understand that you need users on your FON Spot to make any money. You may never get even one user connecting to your service, or you might get one every hour. As in real estate, it all boils down to location, location, location. If your FON Spot is in a high-traffic or dense area full of people with computers, you're in luck. You won't even have to worry about the users slowing down your Internet connection. Later, when you configure your FON Spot settings, you can specify how much bandwidth (or available speed) of your Internet connection you want to offer to others.

Choosing among Hardware Options to Make Your Location a FON Spot

To make your location a FON Spot, you can either purchase a FON router from the FON Web site or load the free FON firmware (a file that acts as the router's brain) on a router of your own that you've verified as being supported by FON. If you purchase a router from FON, you may lay down $40 or $50, which gets you a preconfigured and branded FON wireless router called *La Fonera* or *La Fonera+,* which is shown in Figure 3-1.

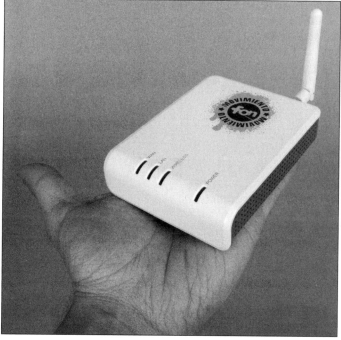

Figure 3-1:
The
La Fonera+
edition of
FON's
wireless
router.

Courtesy of FON.

**Book VII
Chapter 3**

Using FON to Share
or Get Wireless
Internet Access

Despite the expense, purchasing this router rather than loading firmware on your own router for free has some benefits, including the following:

✦ Installation and setup are easier.

✦ Support is provided by FON in the form of installation and user guides, as well as firmware updates.

✦ You have a separate, private wireless network (with the network name of MyPlace) that's secured and encrypted using the WPA-PSK encryption standard. This private network comes in addition to the public FON access, so you can still securely use your Internet connection and private network.

The alternative to buying a router from the FON Web site is to use a FON-supported one (a list of them appears later in this chapter, in the "Preparing Your Own Wireless Router" section) that you already have lying around. (See Figure 3-2 for an example.) In that case, you can upload the FON firmware to it to make your router FON-capable.

Figure 3-2:
Router
supported
by FON.

Courtesy of Linksys, a division of Cisco Systems, Inc.

However, this method usually doesn't support multiple SSIDs, which means that you won't have an automatically created private network. Therefore, I recommend this method only if you plan to dedicate your Internet connection to public access.

There is, however, a workaround that you can use to obtain a private, secured wireless network (or SSID) in addition to the FON access that's open for the public, even if you're using your own router. That workaround involves using the DD-WRT firmware replacement instead of the FON firmware. For further details, visit the DD-WRT Web site:

www.dd-wrt.com/wiki/index.php/fon_hotspot

Refer to Book II, Chapter 4 for help on installing and setting up DD-WRT.

Untangling the FON terms

FON is fond of using terminology that can be quite confusing to newbies, and you need to be familiar with these terms when setting up your FON Spot and even when browsing through the FON Web site. This sidebar presents a brief review of Fon terms:

- **Aliens:** People who join but do not share wireless Internet.

- **Foneros:** People who join and share wireless Internet are called Foneros. Foneros are divided into two categories, Linus and Bills, explained next.

- **Linus:** People who simply share their wireless Internet without monetary compensation.

- **Bills:** People who receive a share of the revenues from Aliens who use their FON Spot.

FON currently produces and sells the following hardware for Foneros:

- **La Fonera:** The first wireless router that was produced to be FON-ready, thereby providing a much easier and better experience than using your own router.

- **La Fonera+:** An improved version of the La Fonera wireless router produced by FON.

- **La Fontenna:** A high-gain directional antenna that you can use with your La Fonera or other router possessing the proper (reverse SMA) antenna connector.

This replacement (or after-market) antenna gives your FON Spot a much longer range. You can point a La Fontenna toward the area you want to cover and give people who are usually out of range the ability to connect to your FON Spot.

Joining FON: To Use or to Share

The first step to using FON, whether you intend to share your Wi-Fi or just use existing FON Spots, is to join by creating a user account. To do so, follow these steps:

1. **Open your Web browser and go to www.fon.com.**

2. **Click Join FON.**

If you don't see a Join FON button, look for a Register link below the e-mail and password fields. Figure 3-3 shows a page similar to the one you should see.

3. **Fill out the form and click the Submit button.**

4. **Verify your e-mail address.**

Complete the joining process by checking your e-mail Inbox for a verification message that you receive from FON and then clicking the link provided in that message.

Figure 3-3:
Example of
FON user
form.

Now you're a FON member (an Alien) and you can continue with the next section to find out how to turn a router into a FON Spot. Or you can purchase an official router from FON (in which case, you can skip to the "Configuring Your FON Spot" section).

Preparing Your Own Wireless Router

As mentioned previously, you can choose to use your own wireless router rather than purchase an official FON router. If you decide to go this way, you need to prepare by doing the following:

1. Get a supported router and the FON firmware (the software that you need for the router).

2. Flash, or upload, the FON firmware to your router.

The following sections tell you what you need to do to accomplish these steps.

Obtaining a FON-supported router and the FON firmware

Obviously, you can't do much without a router, so your first step is to round up a supported wireless router (that is, a router that the FON service will work on). Here are brands and model numbers of the FON-supported routers:

- ✦ Linksys WRT-54G/GL
- ✦ Linksys WRT-54GS (versions 1-4)
- ✦ Buffalo WZR-RS-G54
- ✦ Buffalo WHR-G54S
- ✦ Buffalo HP-G54

You can find an updated list of supported routers by viewing the firmware versions available for download on the FON Web site (go to `www.fon.com/download`). You'll find the list of routers by clicking the Other FON Routers link.

When you know that you have a compatible router, you need to download the firmware file, based on the particular router you're using, from the same section (the download section) of the FON Web site. Use the same link (Other FON routers) to view the list of firmware files and choose the one you need for your router.

To make the firmware file easier to access, when you transfer it to your router later, save the firmware file to your account's root directory (for example, `C:\Documents and Settings\Eric Geier\`.)

Flashing your router with the FON firmware

Flashing your router with the FON firmware replaces your router's "brain," converting your mundane router into a FON Spot router. The FON firmware changes how your router works and what its configuration screens look like. You have two ways to get this firmware on your router:

- ✦ **Use a Web-based utility:** You can upload the FON firmware to the router using the firmware upgrade feature on its Web interface. This method is easier than the next and is supported by most routers except Buffalo devices.

- ✦ **Use Trivial File Transfer Protocol (TFTP):** A simple file transfer method using a command-line interface. This method is required for Buffalo devices.

As with any firmware replacement, it's very important to follow all the directions and precautions because one mistake could ruin your router and make it useless (commonly called *bricking* a router).

To flash your router by using the Web-based utility, you can follow the steps in Book II, Chapter 5. However, the following steps show you how to flash your router using the TFTP method in Windows.

First, you must disable any active security software applications on your computer to make sure that they don't prevent the firmware transfer. Here's how to disable the Windows XP Firewall protection:

1. **Click Start.**

2. **Click Control Panel.**

    If using the Classic Start menu, click Settings first.

3. **Click the Network and Internet Connection category.**

    If you're in Classic view, skip this step.

4. **Open Windows Firewall.**

5. **Select the Off option and click OK.**

If you're using Windows Vista, here's how to disable Windows Firewall:

1. **Click Start.**

2. **Click Control Panel.**

    If using the Classic Start menu, click Settings first.

3. **Click the Security category.**

    If you're in Classic view, skip this step.

4. **Click the Turn Windows Firewall On or Off link.**

5. **Click Continue on the UAC prompt.**

6. **Select Off and click OK.**

After you're done with the firmware transfer, repeat these steps but select the On option in the Windows Firewall window.

You also need to disable any third-party firewall and security software that's running. You may be able to do this by clicking or right-clicking its system tray icon (in the lower-right corner of Windows) and selecting an option to disable or turn off the protection. If you don't see an option, open the application's main window and look for where you can disable the protection. Sometimes you may be able to temporarily deactivate the protection rather than turn it completely off.

Now you can connect the router to your computer by plugging one end of an Ethernet cable to one of the ports on the back of the router, and connecting the other end to the Ethernet port of your computer (the port that matches the connection on the cable). You also need to plug the router's power cord into the back of the router and the other end into an electrical outlet.

In order for the transfer to work, you must assign a static IP address to your computer (as opposed to getting an IP address automatically, which is the usual case), within the range of the IP address of your router. The following steps show you how to do this when your computer is connected to the router.

First, you must check the network connection status on your computer to find the IP address of your router (so that you come up with an address with the same range):

1. **In Windows XP, double-click the network icon in the lower-right corner of the screen. In Windows Vista, right-click the network icon and select Network and Sharing Center, and then, under the network adapter connected to the router, click the View Status link.**

You should now see the Network Connection Status window.

If you need help finding your network connection status (specifically, your router's IP address) in other operating systems (Mac OS X or Ubuntu) refer to Book IV, Chapter 1.

2. **In Windows XP, click the Support tab. In Windows Vista, click the Details button and then refer to the Default Gateway (IPv4 Default Gateway in Vista) value, which is your router's IP address.**

An example of a router (or Default Gateway) IP address is 192.168.11.1 or 192.168.1.1.

3. **Write down an IP address (which you'll input into your computer later) within the range of your router.**

You should choose an address with all matching sets of numbers besides the last set. The last number set of the address must be a number higher than the number in the router address, but a number at or lower than 254.

For example, if your router IP address is 192.168.11.1, any number between 192.168.11.2 and 192.168.11.254 is fine.

If your router IP address is 192.168.1.1, any number between 192.168.1.2 and 192.168.1.254 will work.

After you've figured out a static IP address to use (by following the preceding steps), you must configure your computer's network adapter by following these steps:

1. **In Windows XP, double-click the network icon in the lower-right corner of the screen and click the Properties button. In Windows Vista, right-click the network icon, select Network and Sharing Center, click the View Status link under the network adapter connected to the router, and click the Properties button. (If User Account Control is active, click Continue on the prompt.)**

You should see the Connection Properties window for the network adapter the router is connected to.

For help on configuring a static address in other operating systems (Mac OS X or Ubuntu), refer to Book IV, Chapter 1.

2. **In Windows XP, select Internet Protocol (TCP/IP) and click the Properties button. In Windows Vista, select Internet Protocol Version 4 (TCP/IPv4) and click the Properties button.**

   You may have to scroll down the list box to find this item.

   You should now see the Internet Protocol Properties window.

3. **Select the Use the Following IP Address option (see Figure 3-4).**

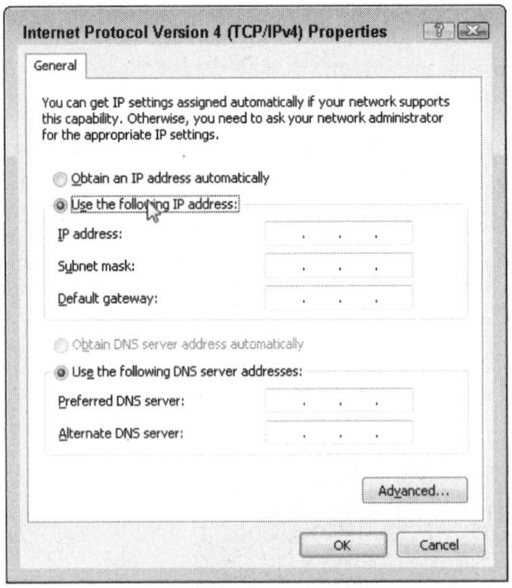

Figure 3-4:
Configuring
a static IP
address in
Windows
Vista.

4. **Enter the static IP address you came up with earlier into the IP Address field.**

5. **Enter 255.255.255.0 into the Subnet Mask field and click OK.**

   You would normally enter a default gateway and DNS address when configuring a static IP address; however, leave these fields blank so that the transfer will work properly.

Now that you have prepared your computer for the transfer, you can continue with these steps:

1. **Open a Command Prompt window by choosing Start➪All Programs➪ Accessories➪Command Prompt.**

To see the Accessories folder on the Start menu in Windows Vista, you may have to scroll down using the scroll bar on the Start menu.

The Command Prompt window has a black background, and the default path of your Windows account is shown.

2. **In the Command Prompt window, navigate to the directory to which you saved the firmware file (using the commands given in the following paragraphs), if needed.**

If you followed the Tip given earlier when you downloaded the firmware file to your computer from the FON Web site, you should already be in the correct directory, and you can skip to the next step.

If the firmware file is located in a different directory from the one that the Command Prompt window opened into, you can use the following commands to navigate to the correct directory:

- Type **cd..** and press Enter to move a directory back. For example, if you are in C:\Documents and Settings\Username, this command moves you to the Documents and Settings directory.

- To go to a subdirectory of the current directory, type **cd** followed by the desired directory name, as shown in Figure 3-5. (The command used there is cd desktop.)

Figure 3-5:
Changing directories in the Command Prompt window.

3. **Type the following command in the Command Prompt window, filling in the italicized parts with the appropriate information (and don't press Enter yet):**

```
tftp -i [your router's IP address] PUT [the filename of firmware file]
```

See Figure 3-6 for an example.

Figure 3-6:
Typing the
TFTP
transfer
command.

4. **Unplug the power cord from the back of the router, make sure you have the Command Prompt window open on your computer screen, plug the power cord back into the router, and when you see on the computer that you're connecting to the router, press Enter to run the command you entered.**

   This step starts the transfer. As directed in the step, it's important that you start the transfer just after the router boots and your computer connects. If the command isn't sent at just the right time, the transfer won't work. It will time out (you see a `Timeout occurred` message), and you can try again. You may have to try many times before you are successful. If you have to try again, you can save some time by holding down the right-arrow key on your keyboard to make the command appear again.

   When the transfer is successful, you get a `Transfer successful` message with the amount of time the transfer took and the number of bytes transferred. The router should reboot into the FON firmware, and you should see a FON network name broadcasted when you view your available wireless networks.

5. **Unplug the router from your computer.**

   Now that you've transferred the FON firmware to the router, you don't need to have the router connected by cable to your computer.

Next, change your computer's IP address settings back to being able to receive an address automatically. Do so by following these steps:

1. **In Windows XP, double-click the network icon in the lower-right corner of the screen and click the Properties button. In Windows Vista, right-click the network icon, select Network and Sharing Center, click the View Status link under the network adapter connected to the router, and click the Properties button. (If User Account Control is active, click Continue on the prompt.)**

You should see the Connection Properties window for the network adapter that the router is connected to.

For help on configuring network adapters to use DHCP and to obtain an IP address automatically in other operating systems (Mac OS X or Ubuntu), refer to Book IV, Chapter 1.

2. **In Windows XP, select Internet Protocol (TCP/IP) and click the Properties button. In Windows Vista, select Internet Protocol Version 4 (TCP/IPv4) and click the Properties button.**

   You may have to scroll down the list box to find this item. After clicking the Properties button, you should see the Internet Protocol Properties window.

3. **Select the Obtain an IP Address Automatically option.**

Configuring Your FON Spot

Whether you've purchased an official FON router or you're using your own wireless router, the process of setting up and configuring your FON Spot with your Internet connection details and FON Spot user account is the same — just follow these steps:

1. **Plug an Ethernet cable into the Internet/WAN port of the FON router and the other end into the Ethernet port of your Internet modem.**

2. **Wirelessly connect to your FON Spot.**

   When viewing your available wireless network list, you should see a network name beginning with *FON_*. This is the network name (SSID) for the public to use to connect to your FON Spot.

   If you are using an official FON router, you should also see a network named My Place, which is your separate, private, secured connection to the Internet through the FON router. Your unique, preconfigured encryption key for the private network should have been included with your FON router, or on the router itself. If you are using your own router, you probably will see only the public network.

   If you're using your own router, you can connect to the public network. If using the La Fonera+, you should connect to the private network. If you're using the original La Fonera, connect to the public network.

   You can connect (see Figure 3-7) to either network as you would on any other network. If you need help, refer to Book IV, Chapter 1.

Figure 3-7:
Connecting
to a
wireless
network in
Windows
Vista.

3. **Configure your Internet connection, if needed.**

You may have to configure the router with your Internet connection
information. This is required if your Internet connection uses anything
other than DHCP, through which you get your Internet IP address automatically. For example, you must configure your Internet connection
settings in the FON router if you have a DSL connection that requires
login information or if you have a static IP address. To do this, enter the
IP address (192.168.10.1) of your FON Spot router into your Web
browser. Log in with the default username and password (which is
admin), find the Internet Connection settings, configure as needed, and
save the settings.

4. **Open your Web browser and enter one of the following URLs, as
appropriate, to open the FON registration page:**

If you're connected to your private network (My Place), go to
`http://registerlafonera.fon.com`. If you're connected to the
public network, you should log in to the portal page (such as the one
shown in Figure 3-8) that should automatically appear when you open
your Web browser. (If it doesn't load automatically, go to `http://
wifi.fon.com`.) You should see an alert and be taken to the FON Spot
registration page after you log in.

5. **Fill out and submit the registration form.**

You should specify your location, desired FON Spot profile — Linus or
Bill — (see the "Understanding FON Profile Types" sidebar, earlier in this
chapter, for more information), and any other settings. Completing the
registration should activate more settings in your user account.

Figure 3-8:
The FON
Spot portal.

6. **When you're signed into your account on FON's Web site, click the Configure your FON Router link and configure the settings that appear on the following pages:**

**Book VII
Chapter 3**

Using FON to Share or Get Wireless Internet Access

- **Locate your FON Router:** If you haven't done so already, enter the location information of your FON Spot, including placing the indicator of the map on your location so that others can see where your FON Spot is located on the map. Simply click and hold the indicator, drag to your location, and let go.

- **Settings:** Here you can limit the amount of bandwidth (that is, amount of Internet speed) you would like to share with the users that connect to your FON Spot. Essentially, this means that you can limit the downloading speeds of public users who connect to your FON Spot. If bandwidth were unlimited, a user might download large files, making a considerable negative impact on your Internet speeds. To change the amount of bandwidth available to your FON Spot users, click and drag the indicator on the slide bar to your desired settings.

  The Public Signal settings allow you to indicate the extension (what comes after "FON_") of your public network name. It's best to use a name that lets the public know where the FON Spot is located — by including, for example, the name of the business, your street, or a close intersection.

  So, for instance, if your business is called *Eric's Café,* your network name (or SSID) for the public FON access might be FON_Erics Cafe.

Here you can also specify a new password for your router so that the default password (which is widely known) isn't active.

- **Friends and Family:** Here you can create accounts for your friends and family (or even yourself) that provide unlimited guest access to your FON Spot.

7. **Pull the power cord from the back of your FON router and then plug it back in to reboot your router.**

   This forces your router to update with the new settings you just configured. If this isn't done, it will take some time before the new settings are sent from the FON Web Site to your router.

Personalizing Your FON Spot

Personalizing your FON Spot portal page that appears in the user's Web browser lets you add a personal touch and informs the public about you or your location. If you choose, you can personalize your FON Spot's portal page by clicking the Personalize Your FON Spot link in your USER zone. From that page, you can configure the following settings:

- ✦ **Web site with unlimited access:** You can specify any Web site that you would like to place a link of on your FON Spot's portal page. Unlimited access is given to users of this Web site without their having to log in. Using this feature is a great way to promote your personal or business Web site.

- ✦ **Welcome text:** You can include a message that's displayed on the portal. You may use it to welcome users or describe your location or attractions. You can also leave it blank, if you prefer.

- ✦ **YouTube URL:** This setting allows you to choose a video from YouTube (http://youtube.com) to be shown on your portal page. You might enjoy sharing the latest funny clip you've come across or even link to your own video.

- ✦ **Flickr Album URL and Flickr Photo URL:** Flickr is a popular online photo management and sharing Web site. You can input the address of a Flickr album or single photo to be displayed on the portal page. You can browse through and add other people's photos and images found on the Flickr Web site (www.flickr.com), or you can link to your own photos that appear on your Flickr account.

Figure 3-9 shows these elements on the portal page.

**Book VII
Chapter 3**

**Using FON to Share
or Get Wireless
Internet Access**

Figure 3-9:
Customizable
elements on
the FON
Spot portal.

Tips on Being a FON Spot

Being a part of the FON network doesn't make you immune from the issues inherent in using or hosting unsecured public networks, so make sure that you properly secure your private networks and connections to your public FON network. You can review Chapter 1 of this minibook, as well as the "Configuring Your FON Spot" section, earlier in this chapter, for ideas. Most issues and situations are similar to those that arise with traditional Wi-Fi hotspots.

For more help on using, setting up, or hosting a FON Spot, here are a few places you can lean on:

✦ **The FON question and answer database:** www.fon.com/help

✦ **FON discussion forum:** www.fon.com/external/boards

✦ **FON technical support (via e-mail):** support@fon.com

Index

F

BUSINESS, CAREERS & PERSONAL FINANCE

Accounting For Dummies, 4th Edition*
978-0-470-24600-9

Bookkeeping Workbook For Dummies†
978-0-470-16983-4

Commodities For Dummies
978-0-470-04928-0

Doing Business in China For Dummies
978-0-470-04929-7

E-Mail Marketing For Dummies
978-0-470-19087-6

Job Interviews For Dummies, 3rd Edition*†
978-0-470-17748-8

Personal Finance Workbook For Dummies*†
978-0-470-09933-9

Real Estate License Exams For Dummies
978-0-7645-7623-2

Six Sigma For Dummies
978-0-7645-6798-8

Small Business Kit For Dummies, 2nd Edition*†
978-0-7645-5984-6

Telephone Sales For Dummies
978-0-470-16836-3

BUSINESS PRODUCTIVITY & MICROSOFT OFFICE

Access 2007 For Dummies
978-0-470-03649-5

Excel 2007 For Dummies
978-0-470-03737-9

Office 2007 For Dummies
978-0-470-00923-9

Outlook 2007 For Dummies
978-0-470-03830-7

PowerPoint 2007 For Dummies
978-0-470-04059-1

Project 2007 For Dummies
978-0-470-03651-8

QuickBooks 2008 For Dummies
978-0-470-18470-7

Quicken 2008 For Dummies
978-0-470-17473-9

Salesforce.com For Dummies, 2nd Edition
978-0-470-04893-1

Word 2007 For Dummies
978-0-470-03658-7

EDUCATION, HISTORY, REFERENCE & TEST PREPARATION

African American History For Dummies
978-0-7645-5469-8

Algebra For Dummies
978-0-7645-5325-7

Algebra Workbook For Dummies
978-0-7645-8467-1

Art History For Dummies
978-0-470-09910-0

ASVAB For Dummies, 2nd Edition
978-0-470-10671-6

British Military History For Dummies
978-0-470-03213-8

Calculus For Dummies
978-0-7645-2498-1

Canadian History For Dummies, 2nd Edition
978-0-470-83656-9

Geometry Workbook For Dummies
978-0-471-79940-5

The SAT I For Dummies, 6th Edition
978-0-7645-7193-0

Series 7 Exam For Dummies
978-0-470-09932-2

World History For Dummies
978-0-7645-5242-7

FOOD, HOME, GARDEN, HOBBIES & HOME

Bridge For Dummies, 2nd Edition
978-0-471-92426-5

Coin Collecting For Dummies, 2nd Edition
978-0-470-22275-1

Cooking Basics For Dummies, 3rd Edition
978-0-7645-7206-7

Drawing For Dummies
978-0-7645-5476-6

Etiquette For Dummies, 2nd Edition
978-0-470-10672-3

Gardening Basics For Dummies*†
978-0-470-03749-2

Knitting Patterns For Dummies
978-0-470-04556-5

Living Gluten-Free For Dummies†
978-0-471-77383-2

Painting Do-It-Yourself For Dummies
978-0-470-17533-0

HEALTH, SELF HELP, PARENTING & PETS

Anger Management For Dummies
978-0-470-03715-7

Anxiety & Depression Workbook For Dummies
978-0-7645-9793-0

Dieting For Dummies, 2nd Edition
978-0-7645-4149-0

Dog Training For Dummies, 2nd Edition
978-0-7645-8418-3

Horseback Riding For Dummies
978-0-470-09719-9

Infertility For Dummies†
978-0-470-11518-3

Meditation For Dummies with CD-ROM, 2nd Edition
978-0-471-77774-8

Post-Traumatic Stress Disorder For Dummies
978-0-470-04922-8

Puppies For Dummies, 2nd Edition
978-0-470-03717-1

Thyroid For Dummies, 2nd Edition†
978-0-471-78755-6

Type 1 Diabetes For Dummies*†
978-0-470-17811-9

***** Separate Canadian edition also available

† Separate U.K. edition also available

Available wherever books are sold. For more information or to order direct: U.S. customers visit www.dummies.com or call 1-877-762-2974.
U.K. customers visit www.wileyeurope.com or call (0)1243 843291. Canadian customers visit www.wiley.ca or call 1-800-567-4797.

INTERNET & DIGITAL MEDIA

AdWords For Dummies
978-0-470-15252-2

Blogging For Dummies, 2nd Edition
978-0-470-23017-6

**Digital Photography All-in-One
Desk Reference For Dummies, 3rd Edition**
978-0-470-03743-0

Digital Photography For Dummies, 5th Edition
978-0-7645-9802-9

**Digital SLR Cameras & Photography
For Dummies, 2nd Edition**
978-0-470-14927-0

**eBay Business All-in-One Desk Reference
For Dummies**
978-0-7645-8438-1

eBay For Dummies, 5th Edition*
978-0-470-04529-9

eBay Listings That Sell For Dummies
978-0-471-78912-3

Facebook For Dummies
978-0-470-26273-3

The Internet For Dummies, 11th Edition
978-0-470-12174-0

Investing Online For Dummies, 5th Edition
978-0-7645-8456-5

iPod & iTunes For Dummies, 5th Edition
978-0-470-17474-6

MySpace For Dummies
978-0-470-09529-4

Podcasting For Dummies
978-0-471-74898-4

**Search Engine Optimization
For Dummies, 2nd Edition**
978-0-471-97998-2

Second Life For Dummies
978-0-470-18025-9

**Starting an eBay Business For Dummies,
3rd Edition†**
978-0-470-14924-9

GRAPHICS, DESIGN & WEB DEVELOPMENT

**Adobe Creative Suite 3 Design Premium
All-in-One Desk Reference For Dummies**
978-0-470-11724-8

**Adobe Web Suite CS3 All-in-One Desk
Reference For Dummies**
978-0-470-12099-6

AutoCAD 2008 For Dummies
978-0-470-11650-0

**Building a Web Site For Dummies,
3rd Edition**
978-0-470-14928-7

**Creating Web Pages All-in-One Desk
Reference For Dummies, 3rd Edition**
978-0-470-09629-1

**Creating Web Pages For Dummies,
8th Edition**
978-0-470-08030-6

Dreamweaver CS3 For Dummies
978-0-470-11490-2

Flash CS3 For Dummies
978-0-470-12100-9

Google SketchUp For Dummies
978-0-470-13744-4

InDesign CS3 For Dummies
978-0-470-11865-8

**Photoshop CS3 All-in-One
Desk Reference For Dummies**
978-0-470-11195-6

Photoshop CS3 For Dummies
978-0-470-11193-2

Photoshop Elements 5 For Dummies
978-0-470-09810-3

SolidWorks For Dummies
978-0-7645-9555-4

Visio 2007 For Dummies
978-0-470-08983-5

Web Design For Dummies, 2nd Edition
978-0-471-78117-2

Web Sites Do-It-Yourself For Dummies
978-0-470-16903-2

Web Stores Do-It-Yourself For Dummies
978-0-470-17443-2

LANGUAGES, RELIGION & SPIRITUALITY

Arabic For Dummies
978-0-471-77270-5

Chinese For Dummies, Audio Set
978-0-470-12766-7

French For Dummies
978-0-7645-5193-2

German For Dummies
978-0-7645-5195-6

Hebrew For Dummies
978-0-7645-5489-6

Ingles Para Dummies
978-0-7645-5427-8

Italian For Dummies, Audio Set
978-0-470-09586-7

Italian Verbs For Dummies
978-0-471-77389-4

Japanese For Dummies
978-0-7645-5429-2

Latin For Dummies
978-0-7645-5431-5

Portuguese For Dummies
978-0-471-78738-9

Russian For Dummies
978-0-471-78001-4

Spanish Phrases For Dummies
978-0-7645-7204-3

Spanish For Dummies
978-0-7645-5194-9

Spanish For Dummies, Audio Set
978-0-470-09585-0

The Bible For Dummies
978-0-7645-5296-0

Catholicism For Dummies
978-0-7645-5391-2

The Historical Jesus For Dummies
978-0-470-16785-4

Islam For Dummies
978-0-7645-5503-9

**Spirituality For Dummies,
2nd Edition**
978-0-470-19142-2

NETWORKING AND PROGRAMMING

ASP.NET 3.5 For Dummies
978-0-470-19592-5

C# 2008 For Dummies
978-0-470-19109-5

Hacking For Dummies, 2nd Edition
978-0-470-05235-8

Home Networking For Dummies, 4th Edition
978-0-470-11806-1

Java For Dummies, 4th Edition
978-0-470-08716-9

**Microsoft® SQL Server™ 2008 All-in-One
Desk Reference For Dummies**
978-0-470-17954-3

**Networking All-in-One Desk Reference
For Dummies, 2nd Edition**
978-0-7645-9939-2

**Networking For Dummies,
8th Edition**
978-0-470-05620-2

SharePoint 2007 For Dummies
978-0-470-09941-4

**Wireless Home Networking
For Dummies, 2nd Edition**
978-0-471-74940-0